TIBERIUS THE POLITICIAN

Tiberius has always been one of the most enigmatic of the Roman emperors. At the same time, his career is uniquely important for the understanding of the Empire's development on the foundations laid by Augustus.

Barbara Levick offers a comprehensive and engaging portrait of the life and times of Tiberius, including an exploration of his ancestry and his education, an analysis of his provincial and foreign policy and an examination of his notorious final years and his posthumous reputation.

This new edition of *Tiberius the Politician* contains a new preface and a supplementary bibliography.

Barbara Levick was until recently a Fellow and Tutor in Literae Humaniores at St Hilda's College, Oxford. She is the author of *Claudius* (1990) and *Vespasian* (1999).

TIBERIUS THE POLITICIAN

BARBARA LEVICK

London and New York

First published 1976 by Thames and Hudson Ltd
Reprinted 1986 by Croom Helm Ltd

Revised edition published 1999
by Routledge
11 New Fetter Lane, London EC4P 4EE

Simultaneously published in the USA and Canada
by Routledge
29 West 35th Street, New York, NY 10001

Routledge is an imprint of the Taylor & Francis Group

© 1976 Barbara Levick
Preface and supplementary bibliography © 1999 Barbara Levick

The right of Barbara Levick to be identified as the Author of this
Work has been asserted by her in accordance with the Copyright,
Designs and Patents Act 1988

Typeset by RefineCatch Limited, Bungay, Suffolk
Printed and bound in Great Britain by
TJ International Ltd, Padstow, Cornwall

British Library Cataloguing in Publication Data
A catalogue record for this book is available from the British Library

Library of Congress Cataloguing in Publication Data
A catalogue record for this book has been requested

ISBN 0-415-21753-9

To the Memory
of my Father and Mother

CONTENTS

PREFACE   ix

PREFACE TO THE 1999 EDITION   xi

I   ANCESTRY AND EDUCATION   11

II   FIRST YEARS IN POLITICS:
       TIBERIUS IN THE SERVICE OF THE PRINCEPS   19

III   EMINENCE AND ECLIPSE   31

IV   REHABILITATION:
       THE FINAL STRUGGLE FOR THE SUCCESSION   47

V   THE 'ACCESSION' OF TIBERIUS   68

VI   THE POLICY OF THE PRINCEPS   82

VII   POLICY IN PRACTICE:
       THE SENATE AND ITS MEMBERS   92

VIII   *EQUITES* AND *PLEBS*   116

IX   PROVINCIAL AND FOREIGN POLICY   125

X   THE DYNASTIC CATASTROPHE   148

XI   TIBERIUS AND THE LAW:
       THE DEVELOPMENT OF *MAIESTAS*   180

XII   LAST YEARS AND POSTHUMOUS REPUTATION   201

LIST OF ABBREVIATIONS   226

NOTES   228

SELECT BIBLIOGRAPHY   295

MAPS:

1   ITALY IN THE TIME OF TIBERIUS   303

2   THE EASTERN ROMAN EMPIRE   304–5

3   THE WESTERN ROMAN EMPIRE   306

STEMMATA:

A THE CONNEXIONS OF TIBERIUS   307

B THE FAMILY OF AUGUSTUS   308

C THE DESCENDANTS OF SCRIBONIA   309

D *STEMMA* OF SEJANUS (CONJECTURAL)   310

INDEX   311

PREFACE

To my friends and colleagues, some of whom have lived with Tiberius for five years, I owe great debts. Those that are specific can be acknowledged in the notes; others are more general: patience in listening to what I had to say; generosity in lending me books; active help in improving preliminary or final drafts. Each person to whom I owe a debt of this kind will know what he has done, and how grateful I am; here I can only give a list of names: Miss P. R. Ellis, Mr and Mrs S. Gordon, Mr A. S. Hall, Mrs A. Howarth, Miss D. C. Innes, Miss D. Nash, Mr J. Nicols, Miss E. M. Smith, Professor J. M. C. Toynbee, Mr M. Vickers, Dr K. V. Wilkes, Mr and Mrs H. Wolfram.

I am conscious of working from a sketch of Tiberius that was drawn for me by Mr C. E. Stevens when I was an undergraduate and which has been in my mind since, although it has been a good deal altered in the course of time. Another powerful influence on this book, as it must be on any study of Roman politics written since 1939, has been Sir Ronald Syme's *The Roman Revolution*. I make no attempt to reconcile the differences between Stevens's outlook and that of Syme; they represent a genuine conflict between two factors in Tiberius' political life which he had to resolve.

When Stanley Baldwin said that what took him into politics was 'the ideal of service', he was claiming a motive that a Roman audience would not have found plausible. Roman politicians sought power, position, and prestige. Each man worked ultimately for himself, and it is not surprising that the structure of Roman politics remains a matter of dispute. The 'parties' that were discerned in the nineteenth century dissolved under scrutiny and less formal associations, based on family groupings, were marked out in their place. The concept of the 'family faction' has not escaped criticism, on the grounds that the structure it imposes is still too rigid: political alliances at Rome, far from lasting a generation or more, were *ad hoc* affairs surviving no more than a single election campaign. Telling in detail, these criticisms do not destroy the whole prosopographical method. The ties posited are natural and durable ones, and they can be seen enduring.

Yet self- and even family interest are not all. What of the Roman constitution, its customs and legal principles, the *res publica, mos*, and *ius* ever present in the mouth of Cicero and in the pages of historians and moralists? Was there no respect for these in the scramble for the top? In the first century BC that issue became the dominating one in Roman politics: was the Republic to survive in the form which it had assumed in the Hannibalic War, government in the hands of the senatorial oligarchy that Sulla restored to power in 81; or was one man, by mobilizing counter-forces, the people and the army, to take control? Cato, Brutus, and Cicero all fought for the old constitution and died for it.

Another thread that tied Republic to Principate was the form of the constitution. Every politician still had to discover how to operate the machinery of Republican politics, making his way through patronage and friendship, forming groups of his own to reach high office and maintain his eminence. And the more eminent he became the more acutely would press on him the dual problem: the senator's place under the Principate, the Princeps' place in *res publica*.

These are the themes that I have examined in this book. For the skill and patient care of my publishers at all stages of its preparation I should like to express my warmest thanks.

B. M. L.

March 1976

PREFACE TO THE 1999 EDITION

Since this book was published, work relevant to its subject has continued in three main forms (the Supplementary Bibliography is divided accordingly). First, there have been additional books and articles directly on Tiberius and members of his family. They include the studies of D. C. A. Shotter and N. Kokkinos, and A. Massie's fiction. R. Syme continued until the end writing illuminatingly on Tiberian themes. Relevant work on the imperial family covers the *domus* and Augustus' plans for the succession; they have received their share of attention, with opinions of all shades in evidence and little unanimity.

Most impact, however, has been made by epigraphic finds in Spain and elsewhere. The *Tabula Siarensis*, constitutes the first part of the text of which the *Tabula Hebana* had already provided a version of the later sections: honour to the deceased Germanicus (the original publication has been followed by many indispensable contributions in *ZfPE* from W. A. Lebek), including an account of his activities which gives a more serious picture of the threat to Roman power in the North-West than was entertained previously: there were Germans in Gaul in 13 to be expelled by Germanicus, and order to be restored. This confirms the implications of the stone commemorating Fabricius Tuscus (*EJ²* 368). Further revelations as to Germanicus' position (he was formally subordinated to Tiberius Caesar) are made in the even more sensational *Senatus Consultum de Cn. Pisone patre*, a record of the senate's findings, dated 10 December AD 20, in the case of Cn. Piso, with his wife, son, and aides as accessories, accused of murdering Germanicus, diminishing the majesty of the Roman People, and extortion. The document was splendidly published with German translation and commentary by W. Eck and others in 1996; M. T. Griffin has provided an illuminating review, including an English translation. The late date of the verdict appears to contradict the chronology of the trial implied in Tacitus; not everyone is convinced that it provides an immediate record of verdicts and sentences; it could be a later summary. The *SC* seems to contradict Tacitus in another important detail: the confiscation of Piso's estate in Illyricum, given him by Augustus, on the pretext that his servants were troubling local provincials, antedates the confiscation of C. Silius' property by four years, the first occasion, says Tacitus, *Annals* IV, 20, 2, on which such a thing happened. But it strikingly confirms Tacitus' picture of a bootlicking senate, which should never have been doubted when we already had the language of Velleius Paterculus. His work (II, 130, 5) and the *SC*, separated by a decade, strike similar attitudes towards Livia's position in the state; and her intervention in this trial looks as effective in the *SC* as it does in Tacitus – though differently seen. Altogether the *SC* gives a powerful presentation of the imperial *domus* and its public and quasi-religious status, backing up the work of R. A. Bauman on *Impietas in Principem*. The language of the *SC* and of Velleius (II, 124, 1) coincide also in referring to the imperial position as a *statio*, post; the use of this word in an official document may seem to confirm the suggestion made in this book that it was included in the senatorial *relatio* that welcomed the accession of Tiberius to sole power.

As to social history, considerable light has been thrown on the shadier activities of the upper class and how they were discouraged by the *SC* from Larinum of AD 19 which, like the contemporary documents from Spain, affects interpretation of the literary evidence for the legislation. The existence of these documents (many comparable must have failed to survive) reveals concern outside Rome to keep abreast of, and conform with, the thinking of the rulers. (This topic and that of the *domus* is dealt with in forthcoming works of G. D. Rowe.)

The third path on which advances have been made since the book was completed is historiographical. There have been editions of Tacitus and valuable 'conventional' studies, but his work and, to a lesser extent, that of other historians has been re-examined with the help of fresh techniques, and new interpretations advanced, some convincing, others less so. This was to be expected: the reduction of history to a fabric, almost a fabrication, created by historians who are also great writers has particularly stimulated scholars in the last quarter of this century. Such enquiries, stressing the rôle of the artist, necessarily affect attempts to interpret the regime itself.

Influential and disturbing analyses have been performed by A. J. Woodman, who has considered, among other matters, the aim that has generally been ascribed to Tacitus in writing *Annales*, and, even more significantly, Tiberius' accession: he claims that Tiberius was genuinely refusing to accept the place that was being offered to him, and that on this occasion Tacitus does not accuse him of hypocrisy. Discussion has also focused on the question of the characters of secondary figures such as Germanicus, and on the alleged immutability of character in ancient historians, and its application to interpretations of Tiberius' life and reign.

One welcome development on the literary side has been the increasing interest in writers who have received less than their share of attention, notably Velleius Paterculus and Valerius Maximus. Syme despised Velleius, but his value, and that of the equally conformist Maximus, lies precisely in their conscious echoing of official lines taken in the documents, and the contrast that that provides with later writers, especially Tacitus.

SUPPLEMENTARY BIBLIOGRAPHY

(★ indicates works with particularly useful bibliographies)

1. Tiberius' life, reign, and contemporaries

Brunt, P. A., 'The Role of the Senate in the Augustan Régime', *CQ*, 34, 1984, 423–44.

'Lex de Imperio Vespasiani', *JRS*, 67, 1977, 95–116.

Corbier, M., 'Male Power and Legitimacy through Women: the Domus Augusta under the Julio-Claudians', in R. Hawley and B. Levick, edd., *Women in Antiquity, New Assessments*, London and New York, 1995, 178–93.

★Kokkinos, N., *Antonia Augusta: Portrait of a Great Roman Lady*, London and New York, 1992.

Levick, B. M., 'A Cry from the Heart from Tiberius Caesar?', *Hist.*, 22, 1978, 95–101.

Massie, A., *Tiberius: the Memoirs of the Emperor*, Sevenoaks, 1992.

Purcell, N., 'Livia and the Womanhood of Rome', *PCPS*, 32, 1986, 78–105.

Rodewald, C., *Money in the Age of Tiberius*, Manchester, 1976.

Sage, M. M., 'Tacitus and the Accession of Tiberius', *Ancient Society*, 13/14, 1982/3, 293–321.

Shotter, D. C. A., *Tiberius Caesar*, London and New York, 1992.

Solin, H., 'Germanicus in Patrai', *ZfPE*, 41, 1991, 207 f.

Syme, R., 'Diet on Capri', *Ath.*, 77, 1989, 261–72 = *Rom. Pap.*, 6, Oxford, 1991, 409–20.

The Augustan Aristocracy, Oxford, 1986.

2. Documents

Cooley, A., 'The Moralizing Message of the *Senatus Consultum de Cn. Pisone patre*', *G and R*, 45, 1998, 199–212.

Eck, W., Caballos, A., and Fernández, F., *Das Senatus Consultum de Cn. Pisone patre, Vestigia*, 48, Munich, 1996.

González, J., '*Tabula Siarensis*, Fortunales et Municipia civium Romanorum', *ZfPE*, 55, 1984, 55–100.

González, J. and Arce, J., *Estudios sobre la Tabula Siarensis, Anejos de Arch. esp. de Arqueología*, 9, Madrid, 1988.

Griffin, M. T., 'The Senate's Story' (review of Eck *et al.* 1996), *JRS*, 87, 1997, 249–63.

*Lebek, W., 'Welttrauer um Germanicus: das neugefundene Originaldokument u. die Darstellung des Tacitus', *Ant. u. Abendland*, 36, 1990, 93–102.

'Standeswürde u. Berufverbot unter Tiberius: das *SC* der Tabula Larinas', *ZfPE*, 81, 1990, 37–96.

Levick, B. M., 'The *Senatus Consultum* from Larinum', *JRS*, 73, 1983, 97–115.

*McGinn, T., 'The *SC* from Larinum and the Repression of Adultery at Rome', *ZfPE*, 93, 1992, 273–95.

Millar, F. G. B., 'Imperial Ideology in the *Tabula Siarensis*', in González and Arce 1988, 11–19.

Richardson, J. S., 'The Rogatio Valeria Aurelia: Form and Content', in González and Arce 1988, 35–41.

'The Senate, the Courts and the *SC de Cn. Pisone patre*', *CQ*, 47, 1997, 110–18.

3. Literary works

Baar, M., *Das Bild des Kaisers Tiberius bei Tacitus, Sueton u. Cassius Dio, Beitr. z. Altertumskunde*, 7, Stuttgart, 1990.

*Benario, H. W., 'Six Years of Tacitean Studies: an Analytical Bibliography on the "Annales" (1981–1986)', *Aufstieg und Niedergang der römischen Welt*, 2, 33, 2, 1990, 1467–98.

Gill, C., 'The Question of Character-Development: Plutarch and Tacitus', *CQ*, 33, 1983, 469–87.

Ginsburg, J., *Tradition and Theme in the Annals of Tacitus*, Salem, 1981.

Goodyear, F. A., *The Annals of Tacitus*, 2 vols. (Books 1 and 2), Cambridge, 1972, 1981.

Griffin, M. T., 'Tacitus, Tiberius and the Principate', in L. Malkin and Z. W. Rubensohn, edd., *Leaders and Masses in the Roman World*, Leiden, 1995, 33–57.

Herbert-Brown, G., *Ovid and the Fasti: an Historical Study*, Oxford, 1994.

Keitel, E., 'Tacitus on the Deaths of Tiberius and Claudius', *Herm.*, 109, 1981, 206–14.

Kuntze, C., *Zur Darstellung des Kaisers Tiberius und seiner Zeit bei Velleius Paterculus, Europ. Hochschulschr.*, 3, 247, Frankfurt, 1985.

Luce, T. J., 'Tacitus' Conception of Historical Change', in I. S. Moxon, J. D. Smart, and A. J. Woodman, edd., *Past Perspectives: Studies in Greek and Roman Historical Writing*, Cambridge, 1986, 143–58.

'Tacitus on "History's Highest Function": *praecipuum munus annalium* (Ann. III, 65)', *Aufstieg und Niedergang der römischen Welt*, 2, 33, 4, 1991, 2904–27.

Luce, T. J. and Woodman, A. J., *Tacitus and the Tacitean Tradition*, Princeton, 1993.

Martin, R. H., *Tacitus*, London, 1981.

'Structure and Interpretation in the "Annals" of Tacitus', *Aufstieg und Niedergang der römischen Welt*, 2, 33, 2, 1990, 1500–81.

Martin, R. H. and Woodman, A. J., *Tacitus Annals Book IV*, Cambridge, 1989.

*Mellor, R., *Tacitus*, New York and London, 1993.

Miller, N. P., 'Tacitus' Narrative Technique', *G and R*, 25, 1978, 13–22.

Pelling, C. B. R., 'Tacitus and Germanicus', in Luce and Woodman 1993, 59–85.

Sage, M. M., 'Tacitus' Historical Works: a Survey and Appraisal', *Aufstieg und Niedergang der römischen Welt*, 2, 33, 2, 1990, 851–1030, 1629–47.

*Shotter, D. C. A., 'Tacitus and Tiberius', *Ancient Society*, 19, 1988, 225–36. *Annales Book IV. English and Latin*, Warminster, 1989.

Sinclair, P., *Tacitus the Sententious Historian*, University Park, Pa, 1995.

*Suerbaum, W., 'Zweiundvierzig Jahre Tacitus-Forschung: systematische Gesamtbibliographie zu Tacitus' Annalen (1939–1980)', *Aufstieg und Niedergang der römischen Welt*, 2, 33, 2, 1990, 1032–76.

Syme, R., *History in Ovid*, Oxford, 1978.

'Tacitus: Some Sources of his Information', *JRS*, 72, 1982, 68–82 = *Rom. Pap.*, 4, Oxford, 1988, 199–222.

'The Year 33 in Tacitus and Dio', *Ath.*, 61, 1983, 3–23 = *Rom. Pap.*, 4, Oxford, 1988, 223–44.

Vielberg, M., 'Ingenium und Mores: Beobachtungen zur historischen Begriffsbildung in Tac. *Ann.* VI, 51, 3', *Mnem.*, 49, 1996, 452–6.

Wille, G., *Der Aufbau der Werke des Tacitus*, Amsterdam, 1983.

Woodman, A. J., *Velleius Paterculus: the Tiberian Narrative*, Cambridge, 1977.

'Self-imitation and the Substance of History: Tacitus, *Annals* I, 61–5 and *Histories* 2.70, 5.14–15', in D. West and A. J. Woodman, edd., *Creative Imitation and Latin Literature*, Cambridge, 1979, 143–55, 231–5.

'A death in the First Act (*Annals* I, 6)', *Papers of the Leeds International Latin Seminar*, 8, 1985, 257–74 = *Tacitus Reviewed*, 23–39.

'History and Alternative Histories: Tacitus'. in A. J. Woodman, *Rhetoric in Classical Historiography: Four Studies*, London and Sydney, 1988, 160–96 = *Tacitus Reviewed*, 104–41.

'Tacitus' Obituary of Tiberius', *CQ*, 39, 1989, 197–205 = *Tacitus Reviewed*, 155–67.

'*Praecipuum munus annalium*: the Construction, Convention, and Context of Tacitus, *Annals* III, 65, 1', *MH*, 52, 1995, 111–26 = *Tacitus Reviewed*, 86–103.
* *Tacitus Reviewed*, Oxford, 1998.
Woodman, A. J. and Martin, R. H., *The Annals of Tacitus. Book III*, Cambridge, 1996.
Wuilleumier, P., *Tacite: Annales Livres I–III*, ed. 2, Paris, 1978.

CHAPTER I

ANCESTRY AND EDUCATION

Tiberius Caesar publicly expressed the hope that he would be judged worthy of his ancestors. Like his nephew Claudius, he was versed in the history of the aristocracy, and of his own family in particular, and it would be interesting to know if he had in mind a particular branch, or particular individuals.[1] The models they offered were diverse enough, although by blood he was a Claudian on both sides. Tiberius' parents were Ti. Claudius Nero and Livia Drusilla, daughter of a Claudius Pulcher who, having been adopted by M. Livius Drusus, the tribune of 91 B C, introduced a third line into Tiberius' ancestry.[2]

The *stemma* of the patrician Claudii sprang from Appius or Attus Claudius (Attius Clausus in Livy), an early immigrant from Regillum in the Sabine country.[3] It claimed its first consulship for 493 B C, and by the end of the Republic boasted twenty-eight consulships, five dictatorships, seven censorships, six triumphs, and two ovations (Suetonius' count). The political outlook of a family prominent for nearly half a millennium has not surprisingly been a matter of controversy since ancient times: ultra-patrician on one view, the Claudii emerge as champions of the people, the urban *plebs*, on the other.[4] Annalists and publicists of the late Republic worked up the family traditions and information provided by the *Fasti*, or lists of magistrates, into accounts that reflect their own preoccupations and prejudices.[5] They offered Suetonius a rich harvest of anecdotes illustrating eccentricity, ambition, and self-confidence (the notorious Claudian *adrogantia*) and Tacitus a facile explanation of some aspects of the conduct and manner of Tiberius.[6]

The first outstanding figure in the family was Ap. Claudius the Decemvir, who in 450 B C helped to draw up Rome's first written code of law, the Twelve Tables, and who was alleged to be bent on making his office a permanency. Even more famous than the Decemvir was Ap. Claudius Caecus, the censor of *c.* 312 B C. It was to the two sons of the censor, Claudius 'the Fair' and Claudius 'the Brave' (the name is Sabine), that the Pulchri and the Nerones traced their ancestry.

The Pulchri were the senior line, and it continued to produce outstanding individuals until it perished in the principate of Tiberius. By way of example, men from three successive generations of the branch may be shown in the forefront of politics acting in a variety of interests

besides their own. Ap. Claudius Pulcher, the consul of 143 B C, cemented
a friendship with the Sempronii by marrying his daughter to a member
of that family – Ti. Gracchus. Appius himself became a staunch supporter of Gracchus' policy of settling the landless on the public domains,
and until his death he was a member of Gracchus' land commission.
His son, after losing his army to Cinna in 87, was outlawed and returned
to hold the consulship in 79 as a pillar of the Sullan restoration. He
served the annalists as a model for his arrogant namesake, the consul
of 471.[7] In the next generation P. Clodius showed himself a genuine
champion of the *plebs*, author in 58 B C of a proposal to distribute grain
to the people free of charge, and of another to restore the political
clubs that had been dissolved. With their help he became the master of
crushingly powerful gangs which he used alike against his personal
enemy Cicero and the dynast Pompey.[8]

To this family belonged by birth the father of Livia. The forwardness
of its female members was a theme to the taste of Suetonius, bringing
to mind the domineering character of the Princeps' mother; but
Cicero had tried to shame the most famous (or rather notorious) of
them all, Clodia, by adducing the distinction of her female forbears,[9]
and this alone is proof of the survival of a favourable tradition about the
Claudii and their women. Claudius Pulcher's adoption made him M.
Livius Drusus Claudianus, and through his daughter he was to transmit
the *cognomen* (surname) Drusus to the imperial family. Adoption
was an important feature of Roman political life. It gave a man the
next best thing to a son of his own body, who would take the name of
his father and inherit not only his property but his dependants.[10]
Pulcher might have been expected on his adoption to take on a distinctive political colouring. M. Livius Drusus, tribune in 122 B C, had
been one of the most effective opponents of C. Gracchus, bearing the
title '*patronus senatus*'. Thirty-one years later his son, another M. Livius
Drusus, took the tribunate, again in the interests of senatorial government. His object was, by satisfying the wants of each class and pressure
group, to recover control of the law courts for the Senate and to re-
establish the crumbling position of the nobility, more especially of the
Metellan group, of which he was a leading member. Opposition was
too strong, and Drusus was assassinated while still a sacrosanct tribune.
He died a martyr to his cause, asking characteristically when Rome
would see his like again.[11] Not, it seemed at first, in the person of his
adopted son. Claudianus had his way to make; by 70 B C Metellan
ascendancy was a thing of the past, and it was not as clear to everyone
else as it was to Cicero that the Republic had died when the First

Triumvirate came into being. In 59 BC Claudianus was supporting Pompey, Caesar, and Crassus, and could hope that they would grant him the embassy to Alexandria that they were unwilling to allow P. Clodius. By the spring of the same year, at latest, he was married. The bride, a daughter of M. Alfidius, a councillor of Fundi, was an aristocrat in her home town, but of consequence at Rome only for her dowry. Claudianus was praetor or *iudex quaestionis* (president of a court) in 50 BC, and we may well believe that his rise was financed partly from his father-in-law's purse. To Alfidia in return Claudianus gave the *entrée* to high society. It was a common arrangement, and hostile politicians were fond of reminding men of their municipal mothers.

After the assassination of the Dictator, Julius Caesar, Claudianus returned to the principles of his adoptive family. Proscribed at the end of 43 BC, he followed the Liberators to the East and killed himself at Philippi, a fact which Tiberius' panegyrist, Velleius Paterculus, is at pains to transmit.[12]

Claudianus' son-in-law, Ti. Claudius Nero, did not share his glory. Nor could he boast any distinction in his immediate ancestry. The Nerones had never equalled their cousins the Pulchri. When the time came for Horace to celebrate the achievements of Tiberius and his kin, all he could cite from the past was C. Nero, great-grandson of the censor, who in 210 BC, after the defeat and death of the Scipios in Spain, took over their armies and who three years later revenged them and dealt a severe blow to Hannibal by destroying Hasdrubal on the Metaurus.[13] But C. Nero's success was not enough to keep the family in the front rank. The last consul it produced in the Republic was his cousin, in 202 BC, whom Scipio Africanus blamed for a dilatoriness and greed that delayed the final victory over Hannibal in Africa. Later members of the branch are too obscure to reveal much of their political allegiances; we cannot even trace the *stemma* with certainty. Towards the end of the Republic it seems that hope of advancement ranged them behind the dynasts. A Ti. Nero was serving in 67 BC as legate of Pompey in the war against the pirates; his speech in the Senate four years later against the summary execution of the associates of Catiline may have been made with an eye on Pompey.[14] His relationship to Ti. Nero, father of the future Princeps, is uncertain; probably they were father and son.

Tiberius' father made his first appearance in 54 BC, seeking a conventional *début* on the political stage. He competed against C. Memmius and the brother of Mark Antony for the right to impeach A. Gabinius for extortion, with Cicero's approval.[15] Four years later Nero

was competing for something else: the hand of Cicero's daughter; but
he and his suit, though well received by Cicero, then absent from Rome
in his Eastern governorship, came too late. Tullia had been disposed of
elsewhere by her mother. Would Cicero have been more chagrined
if he had thought that he was losing the chance of becoming the grandfather of Rome's second Princeps?[16] But Nero did not remain on the
straight course that Cicero might have prophesied for him. In 48 BC
we find him, on the same side as many to whom the dominant oligarchy held out small hope of advancement, acting as quaestor to the
successful rebel Julius Caesar and in command of his fleet at Alexandria.
He was rewarded for his services by admission to a priesthood, the
pontificate, in 46, and by a chance of further work: the foundation of
Caesarian colonies in Narbonese Gaul. Yet only two years later, after
the assassination of Caesar, he was proposing that the killers should be
rewarded.[17] Like many of his followers, Nero may have been disil-
lusioned by the Dictator's failure to 'restore the Republic'. But
Republicanism in 43–42 showed itself a losing cause. Nero attached
himself to Mark Antony, who seemed to some to be less of a menace
than the young Octavian. He was elected to the praetorship in 43, and at
the end of his year refused to lay down the rods of office. Octavian was
confiscating land in Italy for Caesarian veterans, the victors of Philippi,
and Nero committed himself to the attempt made by Antony's brother
Lucius, his wife Fulvia, dissident Republicans, and landowners to raise
Italy against him. Perusia, the insurgent stronghold, fell to Octavian
and Nero made his way to Praeneste and Campania, where he tried to
provoke another rising. When that failed he took his wife and infant
son Tiberius to join Pompey's son Sextus in Sicily. There the cause of
the Republic was still being maintained. But the dynastic combinations
of these years were not stable; Octavian, who had to confront the
returning Antony, moved closer to Sex. Pompeius; and Nero and his
family were sent on their travels again, to Antony in the East. It was
only in the spring of 39 BC, when the treaty struck at Puteoli by the
Triumvirs and Sex. Pompey guaranteed their impunity, that they could
return to Italy.[18]

The marriage of Nero and Livia had taken place between 46 or
45 BC, when the bride reached marriageable age, and the first months
of 42 (Tiberius was born on 16 November 42[19]). The engagement may
have been of long standing but the political thinking of the two
Claudians had most in common in the years between 49 and 44; they
may have come to differ in their attitude to Antony. If political considerations cemented the marriage, it was Octavian's passion for Livia

alone that brought it to an end. Some months after their return to
Italy Nero divorced his wife, so that she might marry the Triumvir.
He even presided over the wedding feast on 17 January 38 BC, when
she was six months pregnant with his second son Drusus. Wags quoted
a verse on the luck of a couple whose children were brought to birth
after only three months' gestation; to end the scandal Octavian sent
both children back to their father. Nero's complaisance would be in-
credible, if it had not had a political motive. To marry Livia, Octavian
too had to be divorced – from the formidable Scribonia, whose
brother was the father-in-law of Sex. Pompey. It had been a political
match, made in 40 after the break with L. Antonius and Fulvia. By
destroying it Octavian's passion for Livia would help to loosen his
alliance with Pompey. Nero, as an old ally of Antony, would not be
loth to make a sacrifice in that cause; he himself, after all, had been
repudiated by Pompey when an alliance with Octavian had been on the
cards.[20]

The surrender of his wife brought Nero no advancement that we
know of. The consulship eluded him, generous though the Triumvirs
were to their partisans; nor did he follow Antony to the East. When
he died he consigned his sons to the tutorship of Octavian, and the
elder, now nine years old, delivered the funeral oration. The composition of that speech can have been no easy task for Tiberius' mentors,
in 33 or 32 BC, when war between Octavian and Antony was imminent; the naval achievements of Nero and his forbears and his foundation of colonies were safer topics than his political career.[21] Indeed, this
was one field in which the Nerones outshone the notoriously un-
military Pulchri, whose creation of the Roman navy had not been
followed by much success in its use. Tiberius, his brother, and his
nephew all sought and won distinction as soldiers; and all made free
use of their fleets to achieve it. Here the heritage of the young Tiberius
was ancient and unambiguous. In politics he would take in divergent
traditions: on his mother's side, the brilliant Pulchri and their ruthless
exploitation of patronage for the benefit of the house; from his father's
career, flexibility and ambition, tempered by principle; and, by adoption of his maternal grandfather, the unyielding conservatism of the
Livii Drusi, priggish, ostentatious, and magnificent, that had finally
claimed the allegiance of Claudianus at Philippi.

Tiberius' education may have begun, as that of all Roman children
should, at his mother's knee.[22] But in his case this stage must have
ended earlier than usual, at the age of three, soon after the divorce of
his parents. His primary education (reading and writing in Greek and

Latin, and numbers) had not lasted much more than two years when he delivered his father's funeral oration. Henceforward he probably studied alongside M. Claudius Marcellus, Octavian's nephew, who was only six months older than himself, at home in private rather than in a school.[23] When he reached the age of eleven or twelve, Tiberius passed into the care of the *grammatici* (grammarians) to study the classics of literature – just too early to benefit from the reforms of Q. Caecilius Epirota, who introduced Virgil and other contemporary Roman poets into the curriculum.[24] His diet in Latin would have been highly moral in tone and mainly poetic in form: Livius Andronicus, Ennius, the comic poets, the moral distichs of Cato, and, even at this stage, probably Cicero. From this part of his education Tiberius acquired a distinctive taste in Latin literature that may be illustrated from his vocabulary and choice of quotations[25] – and a liking for literary quizzes. Late in life he would invite *grammatici* to dinner and (turning the tables on the schoolmasters) tease them with questions culled from his daily reading.[26] Tiberius' interest in literature was not simply that of a reader and critic. Even in verse he could compose (Latin and Greek): he wrote an elegy on the death of L. Caesar, presumably in AD 2 or 3; and his Greek models reveal a preference for the learned and elaborate; that is, for the Alexandrian.[27]

The distinction between the provender offered by *grammaticus* and *rhetor* (teacher of oratory) was not sharp, but it was usually after taking the toga of manhood at fourteen that a boy embarked on the last stage of his education, that mastery of the art of oratory that was essential equipment for the lawyer or politician. In Tiberius' case that would have been in 27 BC: he took the toga on 24 April.[28] Besides rhetoric, Tiberius studied philosophy, alongside his cousin Marcellus, with the Academic Nestor, and perhaps with the Peripatetic Athenaeus as well. To judge by his later expertise, law and history were also included in his diet.[29] That he should get the best was only to be expected. He was a precocious boy; and Augustus had high hopes of Marcellus and a respect for education that reminds us of the incompleteness of his own.[30] But Tiberius' civil education was interrupted by public duties; there was no time for leisurely study at Athens or any of the other centres of learning favoured by Romans. But when he went East in 20 BC he took with him a 'studious company' of literary men: historians and poets. This literary retinue was the precursor of others, of which the last, assembled on the island of Capri, consisted not of ambitious young amateurs, Italian and perhaps Gallic, but of Greek professionals.[31] On his return from Armenia, Tiberius took time off for a course of study on Rhodes. Those few weeks were not enough: fifteen years later it could be claimed that Tiberius was retiring there to continue his studies; and in fact his interest in rhetoric and philosophy was still passionate. The attraction of Rhodes in 20 lay in the presence of Theodore of Gadara, one of the leading rhetoricians of the day; Tiberius had already been his pupil at Rome, and became an avowed member of his school. Theodore attached importance to the oratory of politics, but did not consider clearness and brevity always advisable, a fact which may throw light on a dominant feature of Tiberius' own style.[32] In Latin, Tiberius had as his teacher M. Valerius Messalla Corvinus, consul in 31 BC and presumably Tiberius' master during his apprenticeship as a public speaker after he took the toga of manhood. Corvinus was an exponent of a plain, unadorned style. With plainness and purism should go clarity. Not so with Tiberius; his utterances display a conservative, even archaic vocabulary; many of his expressions have a common history: the comic poets, colloquial speech, and late prose; and he became a byword for obscurity. His intelligence was not at fault, nor his education; one might point rather to his character, to the ingrained hesitancy of a man who has grown up in a stepfather's household; to his political situation, to the dilemma of a man who as Princeps must not say too much and who as a senator is bound to speak; to his literary taste, a delight in understatement and irony (dissimulatio). His enemies, however, invoked the calculated dishonesty of a crafty tyrant.[33]

However austere in his Latinity (as Princeps Tiberius excised intrusive Greek expressions from official papers), he was a philhellene, ready when on Rhodes to hobnob with Greek intellectuals and even, when he became a private individual, to adopt their dress. Some of the leading men of the Principate, those closest to Tiberius, L. Piso the pontifex, L. Seius Strabo, L. Aelius Sejanus, L. Seius Tubero, are prominent as the patrons of Greek philosophers and literary men. Even on Rhodes, however, Tiberius did not take up gymnastic exercises, though he was ready to stroll in the gymnasium. That part of Greek education had never achieved respectability at Rome. Instead, he indulged in the riding and target practice that formed the chief physical exercises of noble Roman youths; and he sent teams to compete in the chariot races at Olympia and Thespiae.[34] These self-imposed limits, and his invocation of his official powers (imperium) against a pert antagonist, show that Tiberius' affability was a conscious act of condescension, likely to be reversed if his superiority were threatened. He remained a Roman throughout, but one who believed that he could assimilate

Greek culture without endangering those qualities of character that were prized at Rome: a sense of duty, a sense of purpose, and a sense of one's own worth. Intellectual and aesthetic interests (Tiberius was a collector of sculpture and painting[35]) were kept apart from moral principles, which were antique, Roman, and thoroughly conventional.

How far Tiberius' strong sense of duty was grounded in a theoretical basis of Greek philosophy is not clear. The only master under whom he is known to have studied was an Academic; but Roman amateurs picked out and made use of whatever suited them from the systems that were on offer, Academic, Stoic, or Epicurean. Throughout his life, Tiberius' behaviour could be interpreted as that of a man acting and reacting without conscious appeal to a philosophical system. At moments of stress or grief his utterances were simple and couched in practical terms that would have been familiar at Rome before she was touched by philosophy. His behaviour after the deaths of his brother and sons could have been modelled on patterns held up by the philosophers (his fortitude was such that it roused criticism and even suspicion); but the philosophers themselves were taking their examples from the early history of Rome, and that was accessible to the humblest teacher and the most superficial student. Nevertheless, Tiberius' conduct and sentiments and in particular his marked sense of propriety (everything had its place and its function) suggest the Stoic. When he went abroad to study it was to Panaetius' native island and the place in which Posidonius had set up his school (if he did not inherit it from Panaetius).[36]

It was before the end of his second stay on Rhodes that Tiberius developed another interest, and one which was entirely consistent with determinist Stoicism. He became intimate with the celebrated savant Thrasyllus of Alexandria, to whom by AD 4, perhaps by 1 BC, he had given the Roman citizenship. Astrology was becoming all the rage, not least among those who moved in high society and had the highest hopes of advancement. Tiberius became an adept. If astrology was not part of his Stoic's intellectual furniture, Tiberius' interest may be explained in another way: by a failure to find adequate consolation in philosophy at a time of humiliation and fear. At any rate he kept Thrasyllus with him; after his experiences on Rhodes he could not do without the confidence that he gained from knowledge of his destiny.[37]

CHAPTER II

FIRST YEARS IN POLITICS: TIBERIUS IN THE SERVICE OF THE PRINCEPS

We first meet Tiberius as a babe in arms – and as a political refugee; and Tacitus' portrait shows him a political personality to the end of his days.[1] There were early bids for his allegiance. After the family's return to Italy Tiberius became the heir of a man (evidently childless) called M. Gallius; along with the property he was to accept the name of his benefactor, leaving his brother Drusus to preserve that of the Nerones. The Gallii may be found serving both Caesar and Antony; and Q. Gallius, praetor in 43 BC, was alleged to have plotted against the life of Octavian, was deprived of his magistracy, and perished mysteriously at sea.[2] These men seem to have followed a political course similar to that of Ti. Nero; and we may assume that they were his political associates as well as his personal friends. Tiberius was allowed to accept Gallius' property – but neglected to assume his name.

Ti. Nero died in 33 or 32 BC without receiving further political advancement; latterly his Antonian connexions could have done him no good. Octavian brought his stepson closer to himself, and not only as his ward. His leading ally, M. Vipsanius Agrippa, was married to the daughter of Cicero's friend and correspondent, the *eques* ('knight') Atticus. Their child was hardly a year old when she was betrothed to Tiberius. Both sides gained: the young Tiberius drew nearer the centre of political power, and Agrippa could promise himself grandchildren who would be members of the Claudian *gens* ('clan'), no small attraction for a *novus homo* (a man new to senatorial rank).[3]

The closeness of Tiberius' connexion with the dynasty was demonstrated in 29 BC, not only when he led the troop of senior boys at the *Lusus Troiae*, but when Octavian celebrated his triumph for the victory of Actium. As one of Octavian's young male relatives, Tiberius accompanied the chariot, riding the trace-horse on the left. The more honourable position naturally was reserved for the only son of Octavian's full sister, M. Claudius Marcellus; so it was to be for the rest of Marcellus' life.[4] Nearly two years later, on 24 April, Tiberius was taken into the Forum by his guardian (now known by the style of Caesar

Augustus) to have his names inscribed on the list of citizens and to lay
down his childhood dress and take up the garb of manhood, the *toga
virilis*.[5] Towards the middle of the year Augustus left Rome, first for
Gaul, then for Spain, where he was to embark on his two campaigns
against the Cantabri, in 26–25. Marcellus and Tiberius accompanied
Augustus to Spain or followed him there; the campaigns became a
means of introducing them to military life and, what was more important, to the soldiers; and games were held in the camp in their names
as a means to that end.[6]

It was probably in the spring of 25 BC that Marcellus and Tiberius
returned to Rome, Marcellus to marry Augustus' daughter Julia. It
seemed that, failing a son of his own, Augustus was going to bring
forward Marcellus as the future head of the dynasty.[7] Sure enough, in
24 the former junior officer (Marcellus and Tiberius would have held
the rank of *tribunus militum*) received extraordinary privileges. Although
he had held no previous magistracy, the Senate gave him permission to
stand for the aedileship of 23, and for the consulship ten years before
the legal age; and he was to rank as an ex-praetor; for Tiberius Augustus asked only the quaestorship and a five years' remission when he
stood for praetorship and consulship.[8]

We hear nothing of Marcellus' attainments; but Tiberius made the
normal *début* of a Roman politician at an exceptionally early age and
already had notable performances to his credit. He had spoken before
Augustus, probably in 26 BC while they were still in Spain, in defence
of a client king, Archelaus of Cappadocia (this certainly with success),
for the people of Tralles in Asia (25), and perhaps for the Thessalians
(25); and when he returned to Rome he intervened in the Senate on
behalf of two Asian towns and the island of Chios, which had been
devastated in the earthquake of 27 BC. It was not only his talent that
had attracted these clients, nor his position at court, which was inferior
to his cousin's; Tiberius' father already had close relations with the
people of Nysa, near Tralles, that made it natural for the Trallians to
look to Nero's son for help: and it is possible that Archelaus too was
bound to Nero by the ties of clientship.[9]

Normally a magistrate's sphere of duty was assigned to him by lot.
That was not the case with Tiberius. His functions were allocated to
him by special request of Augustus: Tiberius was to be responsible for
the movement of corn up the Tiber to Rome, perhaps as *quaestor
Ostiensis*, a magistrate whose duties were notoriously more exacting
than honorific, perhaps with the much greater prestige of a quaestor
to the consul.[10] There was already a corn shortage; that was the occasion

for the commission. But for all Tiberius' efforts and the administrative experience that he had gained as *tribunus militum* in Spain, the shortage persisted or recurred, and in the following year Augustus himself at public insistence had to cope with it.[11]

But it was as a politician rather than as an administrator that Tiberius was to be put to the test, in 23 BC. As prosecuting counsel in a trial for high treason he played his full part in mounting the counter-attack against opponents of the Augustan principate and in ensuring its survival; and it is worth examining in some detail the issues that were at stake in that year.

In 28-27 Augustus had handed the *respublica* over to Senate and people, restoring its ancient form.[12] No matter that he received in return ten-year control of a vast area, Gaul, Spain, and Syria – and the armies it contained; that only guaranteed the free working of the constitution.[13] What did matter was that Augustus went beyond his constitutional rights in the period 27-24. He had no title to decide questions of peace and war;[14] but he ordered (his own word) an expedition against Ethiopia, and another against Arabia (neither very successful); and an invasion of Britain was mooted.[15] Again, when Tralles had been devastated by the earthquake of 27 and appealed to Augustus for help, so massive was the aid he sent that it amounted to a virtual refounding of the city. Augustus was in Spain at the time; there is no sign that he consulted the Senate before he intervened in a province which was not under his direct control.[16] Tiberius had defended Trallians and Thessalians in Augustus' court; he went on to speak on behalf of Laodicea, Thyatira, and Chios before the Senate; caution had perhaps set in. If so, it was too late. Plans were in hand to expose constitutional improprieties to the publicity of a trial in the courts, and so to end them. Ostensibly the defendant was Marcus Primus, just back from his governorship of Macedonia (25-24).[17] The unknown prosecutor charged him with making war on a friendly tribe, the Thracian Odrysae. His only defence was superior orders—from Augustus. So the prosecution displayed Augustus not merely intervening in other men's provinces which, as consul, he might do at a pinch, but on his own initiative and unknown to the Senate ordering a proconsul to make war. Primus, as might be expected, secured the services of a distinguished advocate, Licinius Murena, elected consul for 23 BC and, as the brother-in-law of Maecenas, a man close to the Princeps.[18] Murena's duty to his client was clear: if Primus' defence of superior orders was not to collapse, Augustus would have to appear as witness and admit giving them; and he and his supporters would have to weather the ensuing storm as best they could. Augustus evidently refused to be called, or threatened that if he were he would deny having issued any such orders; so Murena lost his witness and the prosecution had no need to give Augustus the chance of lying in court: the public would draw the correct conclusion from his absence. The trial proceeded without Augustus. But not for long. Unsummoned, the Princeps made an appearance and swore he had given no orders. Murena knew what the result would be for his client. He challenged Augustus: what was he doing there? Who had called him? 'The good of the state', was Augustus' reply: a claim that the stability of the new regime was worth more than the career of an individual. Augustus' denial made conviction inevitable; even so, there were not a few votes for acquittal.

Murena had chosen Primus against Augustus. Whether he followed one act of disloyalty with another or whether Augustus considered the first too grievous for Murena to survive it, we do not know. The Princeps was informed of a plot against his life, its leaders the counsel for Primus and Fannius Caepio, a man already known for his Republicanism.[19]

Rumour had it that Murena was warned of his danger by his sister, the wife of Maecenas, and that this caused an estrangement between Maecenas and Augustus.[20] That may be so, but Murena's flight gave weight to the charge brought against him. For the conspirators did not stand their trial. They intended to go into exile, and absented themselves from the *nominis delatio* (the formal lodging of the charge) so that the case went by default.[21] They had not allowed for Augustus' vindictiveness: they were sought out and Fannius Caepio and Murena were killed.[22]

The trial went on. Once again Augustus had looked for reliable counsel—and this time chose his stepson. A bold prosecution often opened a young man's career; but Tiberius in 23 BC was not a beginner. He had several oratorical successes to his credit and was unlikely to add to his reputation by prosecuting a man who was dead before the trial opened. Not altogether honourably, Tiberius put party loyalty first; whether he did so with conviction we do not know.[23] Any sympathy that he felt for the Republican Fannius might be destroyed in the exhilaration of oratory successfully deployed for a kinsman and backer. But Tiberius' oratory did not quite overwhelm his audience. Once again there was a considerable number of votes for acquittal, and the philosopher, Athenaeus of Seleucia-on-Calycadnus, who had accompanied Murena on his flight, was found not guilty and allowed to go home.[24]

The trial of Primus and the discovery of the conspiracy made
Augustus' constitutional position untenable. He had been set at logger-
heads with the Senate. In the high summer of 23, he resigned the consulship, taking instead the powers of the office that had once been held
by the Gracchi, Saturninus, and Clodius: those of the tribunate. Not
only did Augustus receive the *tribunicia potestas*: he kept most of the
provinces that had been assigned him in 27; and in addition his *imperium* (in this case authority in the provinces) was defined as *maius*
(greater) than that of the other proconsuls.[25] Agrippa too was accorded
imperium in the East and a wide-ranging mission there.[26] He went off
in haste – but travelled no farther than Lesbos, an island well situated
for a commander who might wish to take over the legions of Syria or
the Balkans.[27] If anything happened to Augustus the dissidents would
have Agrippa to reckon with.

Paradoxically, the 'settlement' of 23 BC was just as much a restoration of the Republic as that of 28–27; not, it is true, of that harmonious
Republic of the early and mid-second century, but of the Republic of
the seventies, sixties, and fifties BC, when generals bid for their great
commands, but the Senate still had the spirit to resist them. The rift
that opened up in 23 BC gave the Republicans their chance at Rome.
Murena's place was taken up by Cn. Calpurnius Piso, who had steadfastly refused to stand for the office before (or who had known he
could not win it); that of Augustus was taken by L. Sestius, a man who
cherished portraits of Brutus in his house.[28] Augustus soon left Rome,
abandoning the capital to the control of consuls and Senate. His
absence lasted until 19 BC, broken only by a short visit ,when senatorial
authority proved inadequate. The grain shortage grew worse, and the
people so discontented that they threatened to burn the Curia over the
Senate's head and demanded the Dictatorship for Augustus. That was
at the beginning of 22.[29] Two campaigns for the consulate (those for
21 and 19) ended in chaos; the people insisted on offering the office
to Augustus.[30] By 19 the wave of Republicanism had spent itself. The
Senate gave way to those who preferred order to freedom. All the
powers that Augustus had lost with the consulship were restored to
him. He was not to take the office itself but to hold *imperium* equivalent
to that of the consuls, divorced from the magistracy. Nobody would
be kept out of office; for him there would be no retiring at the end of
the year, no need for annual election.[31]

The part that Tiberius had played in the crisis of 23 BC had won him
no credit, except with the Princeps. By the end of that year it was
his misfortune to be one of the few members of the innermost circle

still left in Rome; Marcellus had died in the autumn, it was said from
the same malady that had nearly carried off Augustus at the height of
the political crisis;[32] Augustus was in Campania, eventually to leave for
Sicily and the East, Agrippa on Lesbos; Maecenas presumably was at
Rome, but unlike Tiberius he did not have to sit in the Senate. We
can imagine that Tiberius' duties as quaestor kept him fully occupied
and often detained him at the port. But Suetonius brackets Tiberius'
administration of the corn supply with another task, that of inspecting
the Italian *ergastula* in which agricultural slaves were kept. In them were
detained, or lurked, free men kidnapped on the public highway or
deserters avoiding military service. Tiberius' job was to liberate the
free men and to render deserters up to the army. No doubt his duties
extended into 22 and kept him away from city and Senate.[33]

The death of Marcellus had left a gap that was to be filled partly by
Tiberius' future father-in-law, Agrippa, and partly by Tiberius him-
self. The suspicion that Augustus was planning in some way to make
Marcellus his political heir had contributed to his unpopularity in sena-
torial circles. But it was only between the years 22 and 18 BC that
Augustus developed his first serious plans for the succession. In 21
Agrippa married Marcellus' widow; in 18 he was associated with the
Princeps in the second grant of a five-year term of *tribunicia potestas*.[34]
With the reconciliation of Senate and Princeps and the grant of consular
power, the radical and demagogic connotations of the *tribunicia potestas*
could be allowed to recede and it could be exploited in a different way:
held by the two leading men in the state (Agrippa acquired an ever-
widening competence and by 13 BC he was substantially equal in power
to Augustus), and only by them, it came to betoken their unique position: '*summi fastigii vocabulum*'.[35] For Tiberius there were tasks that were
not only responsible but honourable, tasks which his cousin might
once have expected to fulfil. Some of the embarrassments of 23–22
were wiped away in 20, when Tiberius was called to the East to undertake his first military command.

In the early years of Augustus' principate there had been uneasy
peace between Rome and Parthia.[36] Neither the Parthian invasion of
the eastern provinces in 40 BC nor Antony's answering expedition of
four years later had been successful or prestigious for its sponsors.
Many old scores remained to be settled, the most famous being the
defeat of Crassus in 53. Roman standards lost by Crassus, Decidius
Saxa, and Antony, and a dwindling number of Roman captives, remained in Parthian hands. By 30 BC Phraates IV was once more on the
throne of Parthia and the pretender he had defeated, Tiridates, was

enjoying political asylum in Syria. The Romans also held the brothers
of Artaxes, who occupied Armenia Major under Parthian protection.
To the west, Augustus established on the throne of Armenia Minor a
bitter enemy of the Parthians, the Mede Artavasdes, who could be
relied upon to defend his kingdom (and so the provinces of Asia
Minor) to the death; in the south-west Rome's interests were secured
by the client kings of Cappadocia and Commagene. These arrangements, supported by the garrison of Syria (three or four legions),
seemed to provide a solution satisfactory for the moment. When Parthian ambassadors approached Augustus in 30–29 they were not unfavourably received. But a permanent solution had to be reached.
Parthia posed no serious military threat to the Roman Empire, but she
had the unpopularity of Roman rule in the eastern provinces on her
side. It was particularly acute after Actium, when the Greeks realized
that they had backed their third losing horse (Pompey and the Liberators were followed by Antony) in twenty years. Then there was
Armenia Major, which Antony had invaded in 34 BC and kept as a
province for two years. When the Romans were driven out, Artaxes
massacred all the businessmen who had stayed behind. Augustus inherited a claim to Armenia Major; geographically and ethnically it
was much closer to Parthia, but politically the Romans could count on
support from disaffected factions within the country. Roman public
opinion demanded action against Parthia to restore Roman prestige and
perhaps dominion over Armenia Major as well.

In 26–25 Tiridates made from Syria another attempt on the throne
of Parthia. He failed and once more took refuge with the Romans,
this time bringing with him Phraates, the son of the Parthian king, and
so adding to Rome's bargaining counters. The date of the Parthian
embassy that now approached Augustus is uncertain: 24 or 23. Augustus' reply was to refuse the surrender of Tiridates, though he promised
not to aid him in any further attempts on the throne; he also gave up
young Phraates, perhaps in return for a promise that the standards and
prisoners of war would be handed back. By the beginning of the winter
of 21–20 Augustus in his tour of inspection had reached Samos. The
Parthians showed no sign of fulfilling their side of any bargain, and
a request came from the Armenian dissidents that Rome should replace
Artaxes with his younger brother Tigranes, who was a hostage at
Rome. Augustus, not currently preoccupied by Spanish unrest or the
political crisis at Rome, decided to exert pressure on Parthia for the
return of the standards and to depose Artaxes. That was Tiberius'
task.

Invested no doubt with the title *legatus Augusti pro praetore* (legate of
Augustus with praetorian rank), Tiberius would have crossed from
Brundisium to Dyrrachium; assembled an army of at least two legions,
probably more, from the Illyrian and Macedonian forces; and marched
east along the Via Egnatia.[37] From the eastern end of that route Tiberius'
quickest way was through Bithynia to Ancyra and Cappadocia, where
he would be met by its client king, Archelaus, a man probably bound
to Tiberius by hereditary connexions, certainly by the obligations of a
client to his advocate: Archelaus' reliability as a mentor was assured.
Augustus preceded or accompanied Tiberius in Anatolia; his journey
of inspection took him through Asia, Bithynia, and Syria, and he
arrived on the frontier in time to receive the standards on 12 May
20 BC.[38] The weakness of Parthia gave the pro-Roman party in
Armenia courage and they themselves killed Artaxes before Tiberius
arrived with the new king. It was a walkover, and Tiberius had only
to crown the new monarch, establishing the doctrine that Rome,
without converting Armenia into a province, claimed to exercise
effective suzerainty over it.[39]

The doctrine proved to be an unsatisfactory compromise, and the
success on which Tiberius prided himself so much was (as a hostile
source picked up by Dio points out[40]) cheaply won. But the apparently
successful solution of the Parthian and Armenian problems was a theme
to which Augustan propaganda returned again and again.[41] Important
as this psychological victory was for the Roman people, it was of
equally great significance for Augustus himself: success abroad won
back ground lost in the domestic catastrophe of 23. It put Augustus in
a position to read his peers a lecture against expansionism; and when he
returned to Rome in 19 magistrates and Senate prepared to come out
to greet him.[42]

Tiberius shared the glory. It was recognized by the award of a
praetor's insignia (the office itself he was yet to hold), and sacrifices
were offered.[43] As he sailed into the mouth of the Tiber on his return
he knew he was marked out as a rising soldier and as one of the most
important props of the regime. But it was on the outward journey
that there occurred the first supernatural manifestation to be associated
with Tiberius since his birth. As he approached the colony of Philippi
a noise was heard coming from the field on which Antony had defeated the forces of the Liberators, and altars once consecrated by the
victorious legions, which had settled veterans in the colony, burst spon-
taneously into flame. It is not to be wondered at that fire sprang up
on Antonian altars when the son of Ti. Nero approached.[44] There was

more in this than nostalgia; men had their future needs to consider, and Tiberius had already shown what his patronage could achieve. Even if the scope of his mission was not as wide as Velleius would have us believe, he was able to revive and create connexions with men important in the East.[45]

The next few months are likely to have been happy ones. It was probably in 20 or 19 BC that Tiberius celebrated his marriage to Agrippa's daughter, Vipsania, she now being of marriageable age; and in 19 his younger brother was advanced in the same way as he had been himself: Nero Drusus was to hold the quaestorship in 18, at the age of nineteen, and to be eligible for praetorship and consulship five years before the normal age.[46]

About the two years that followed nothing can be said with certainty. Tiberius' services as an advocate may have been in demand again, new contacts imposing new claims on him. Some have thought that the governorship of Gallia Comata mentioned by Suetonius belongs, not to 16–15, but to 19–18. That would help to fill a puzzling gap, but there is no proof.[47]

The year 16 saw Tiberius praetor. He cannot have held any but the most honourable post in this college, that of urban praetor; by now he had a sound knowledge of the law, and his interest in it was life-long. But he was not to serve his term out peaceably in Rome. The Germans were infiltrating over the Rhine into Gaul all through this decade. In 17 the governor, M. Lollius, lost an eagle in a defeat at the hands of the Sugambri and their allies.[48] In spite of the publicity it received, the defeat was a minor one, soon retrieved. But there was a consequential decline in the morale of the province and the Gauls were not to be trusted. Complicated perhaps by upheavals in Britain, the situation in Gaul demanded the presence of Augustus himself, and he took Tiberius with him. Young Nero Drusus was left to perform the praetor's functions.[49] Tiberius spent about a year blocking raids from the German tribes and in the more difficult diplomatic task of assuaging the quarrels of leading Gallic nobles. Probably he had been intended for the province after his praetorship; but now his predecessor, M. Lollius, was dismissed unexpectedly and prematurely. Lollius became his enemy for life.[50]

The next two years, 15 and 14, gave Tiberius still more military experience, gained alongside his brother. Together they conquered the Alpine tribes of Raetia and Vindelicia. Rome was haunted by fear of invasion from beyond the Alps. At the beginning of the fourth century BC Gauls had captured the city and destroyed it; the Cimbri and Teutones had made their first appearance in 113 and Rome had not been relieved of the menace until Marius finally defeated them in 100. There could be no security until the Alps were Roman. One minor nuisance, caused by the Salassi, was removed when they were crushed in 25 BC. In their valley the colony of Augusta Praetoria was founded, flanking the much older colony of Eporedia on the north-west, as Augusta Taurinorum (27 BC?) flanked it on the south. With Parthian affairs settled and Spain temporarily pacified, Augustus could carry out his plans in the north: he would win control of the Alpine passes, then push the frontier away from Italy, completing the subjugation of the Balkans and at least keeping the German tribes on the farther banks of the Rhine and the Danube. The operations, first of Nero Drusus alone, then of both brothers, following up those undertaken in 17–16 by P. Silius Nerva, secured the Alps.[51]

But there was a corollary to the policy: the removal of the re-entrant angle between the sources of the Rhine and the Danube and the shortening of the frontier through the permanent occupation of Germany between the Rhine and the Elbe.[52] It was a fearsome task, but the rewards were great (and the momentous consequences for Germany and the future of Europe easily imagined). In 12 BC Augustus began operations. The incursions of the Germans were making the Gallic tribes restive, the more so because of the census that Nero Drusus had conducted among them in 13 and which had been sabotaged so effectively that it had to be repeated. The Germans swept over the Rhine in 12 BC; Nero Drusus repulsed them and opened the drive into Germany. In the same year began the construction near Lugdunum of the great altar dedicated to Rome and Augustus; it was to serve as a focus for the loyalty of the Gallic chiefs, providing a substitute for Druidical ritual and a distraction from German intrigue.[53] In that year alone Nero Drusus tackled four of the most formidable tribes, Usipetes, Frisii, Bructeri, and Chauci. His task, the wearing down of the Germans, was hardly interrupted by his praetorship. That came in 11 BC, one year later than it should have been; probably Nero Drusus had been kept in Gaul by the unrest.[54] Augustus was fortunate in his stepsons. He might have been reluctant to undertake the conquest of Germany, if not of the Alps, if these men, reliable as well as competent, had not been available. Their roles were important, their distinction increasing.[55] But what was their place in the hierarchy of the ruling faction?

The answer is likely to be that it was ambiguous, and that Tiberius and Nero Drusus did not know how high they were likely to rise.

We have seen Agrippa reaching the position of near equality with
Augustus: tribunician power at home, *maius imperium* in the provinces;
and by his marriage to Vipsania Tiberius had been brought very close
to Agrippa. But Agrippa's own marriage to Augustus' daughter Julia
was proving fertile. One son, Gaius, was born in 20 BC, a second,
Lucius, in 17. Augustus adopted both children simultaneously; they
became his sons, and took the names Gaius and Lucius (Iulius) Caesar,
officially shedding the plebeian and obscure 'Vipsanius', which M.
Agrippa himself had quietly let drop, in favour of a *nomen* and *cognomen* once borne by the Dictator, then by his son.[56] Clearly they too
were intended to wield the power held in one form or another by their
parent and grandparent by adoption. Transmission was the problem.
With the death of the Princeps there would expire the *imperia* and
potestates accorded to him. There could be a gap, in which anything
might happen: a quick military coup, a long-drawn-out struggle. By
18 BC Augustus had his solution ready:[57] a system of overlap, two men
with powers identical, or so nearly identical as to make no difference.
If one died, the other would be left, unassailable. Below that a second
pair, to be brought forward through the same steps and stages to positions from which they too, when the time came and the surviving
senior partner died, could not be dislodged (proconsular *imperium
maius* was enough). If death took from both generations, once more
creating the possibility of a hiatus in power, there was still another
resource: the survivors themselves would become partners, the
younger receiving not only the *imperium* but also the near equality
implied by a grant of *tribunicia potestas*. Parity of esteem, of course,
could never be achieved; that depended on family, age, personality,
and achievements; but it was never the aim of the scheme to achieve
perfect equality in prestige and influence as well as in official power;
the object was rather to ensure that certain persons were brought to
unassailable positions of power into which others might be co-opted.
The unity of such a group and its immediate circle was assured, for they
would all be members by blood or marriage of the same family. It
was the apotheosis of the family faction and it was developed at a time
when Augustus had regained the upper hand: in the teens dynastic
schemes were by no means out of place. The year 17 BC saw a new age
ushered in by celebration of the Secular Games. The Principate was
truly established, and the dynastic blueprint that it employed was to be
followed again and again in the Julio-Claudian era; by Augustus, by
Tiberius, and by Claudius.
    In the dynastic plan of the teens it is clear that the leading pair were

Augustus and Agrippa, and that Gaius and Lucius were ultimately to take their place. But there was doubt. Agrippa and Augustus were of an age (both born in 63 BC);[58] was either of them likely to survive long enough to see the boys invested with proconsular *imperium*? One at least would have to survive into his sixties, and Augustus' health was weak. It might become necessary, if one of the holders of tribunician power died, to introduce a third pair from an intermediate generation to secure the succession.[59] But for the moment there was no need for additional honours for Tiberius and Nero Drusus. When Tiberius came into office as *consul ordinarius* on 1 January 13 BC it was with another patrician, P. Quinctilius Varus, who, like Tiberius, was son-in-law to Agrippa. Upon them devolved the duty of introducing the legislation that made Agrippa virtually Augustus' equal in power.[60] Again, young Gaius, now six or seven years old, attended the games that Tiberius gave during his consulship. The public roared with delight to see him in the theatre, and Tiberius dutifully brought him up to the front of the box, giving him a place next to Augustus – to the disapproval of the circumspect Princeps.[61]

The year 13, then, saw Tiberius, at twenty-eight years of age, reach the pinnacle of a normal career: he had gone higher than any of his ancestors for two hundred years, winning glory to recall that of the victor of the Metaurus. There were more victories to look forward to, perhaps a triumph and a second consulship. The same year gave him a son, born on 7 October.[62] To look for more would be to count on the speedy death of his stepfather or father-in-law. No honourable man would consciously be guilty of that.

CHAPTER III

EMINENCE AND ECLIPSE

Legislation and publicity in Agrippa's favour proved in vain. He was in Campania after a short autumn foray in the Balkans, when he died in mid-March 12 B C.[1] From the military point of view alone the death of Augustus' greatest marshal was momentous. Who would fill that place? There was need of Nero Drusus in Gaul, and indeed it was in the same year that the offensive on Germany was launched. Tiberius was the obvious choice for Agrippa's place in the Balkans, and they were to be his field of operations as Augustus' legate for the whole or part of the next four seasons, beginning with a 'bellum Pannonicum' against the Dalmatae and Breuci, between Sirmium and Siscia.[2] Tiberius was assuming the mantle that had been worn by the greatest general of his age.

There was more than that; and no wonder that on his way to the Balkans Tiberius sought out the Gallic oracle of the three-headed Geryon near Patavium, the oracle that had given advance notice of Caesar's victory at Pharsalus – and was given a most favourable sign: he was told to throw golden dice into the fountain of Aponus and scored the highest possible number; the dice were still being pointed out under the water in Suetonius' day.[3] When Agrippa died, his wife was pregnant again, with the child who was to be known as Agrippa Postumus. The law prescribed a period of ten months or a year before a widow remarried, to avoid confusion of paternity in the offspring (besides, she had to mourn). Tiberius divorced his wife and married Julia after the due interval.[4] This marriage was one of the first signs of Tiberius' rise to supremacy, a part cause of his eclipse, and a source of misunderstanding of his position during the next decade both in ancient and in modern times. The death of Agrippa, says Dio, made Augustus, reluctant though he was, advance Tiberius. The view has been developed by modern scholars.[5] Tiberius was to be a kind of 'regent' for Gaius and Lucius, evidently to retire gracefully from power as soon as they came of age – or to do away with them like a wicked uncle. But it will not do to import notions proper to established monarchies into the early years of the Principate. *Imperium* was conferred for use, not show, and it could be used to secure an indefinite number of renewals; nor was there any global, monarchical power which could temporarily be conferred on a 'guardian'. If Tiberius was advanced to a position of unassailable power, the step was virtually irrevocable and the power would last, if he chose, for the rest of his life. But it is for another reason that Dio's conception will not do. It takes no account of Nero Drusus. His career was running parallel with that of Tiberius: they won the same military honours in the years after Agrippa's death, and Drusus duly came to his consulship five years before the normal age. In Augustus' will he was co-heir with Gaius and Lucius Caesar; he was one of the two props and stays of Augustus; and he was going to be a great *princeps*. When he died in 9 BC his funeral was modelled on the same pattern as Agrippa's; a pattern which in turn was to be followed at Augustus' own funeral in AD 14.[6] In the years 12–9 BC Augustus intended that on his death affairs were to come into the hands of Tiberius and Nero Drusus and that they were to remain there for the term of their natural lives.

Augustus did not take the step without serious reflection. He thought of bestowing his daughter on at least one person of equestrian rank and so removing her altogether from the political board.[7] At a pinch he could continue with the original plan of advancing his grandsons, and gambling on his own survival. He had good political reasons for hesitating about the Claudian brothers. The antecedents of Tiberius and Drusus did not make them natural supporters of a disguised monarchy, and more than ten years had passed since Tiberius delivered his youthful attack on Fannius Caepio, the would-be assassin of the people's champion. Clear evidence now emerges. Nero Drusus wrote Tiberius a letter in which he proposed that they should force Augustus to restore the Republic. Tiberius, in Suetonius' language, 'betrayed' it to Augustus.[8] The letter must belong to the years between the deaths of Agrippa and Nero Drusus, when the brothers commanded the armies of Germany and the Balkans, most probably to 10 BC. In that year Tiberius travelled to Gaul with Augustus, perhaps to attend the dedication of the altar at Lugdunum to Rome and the Princeps, while Drusus was campaigning in Germany; a revolt in Illyricum forced him to return to his province, but at the end of the year the three men journeyed to Rome together, Tiberius to ride into the city in the lesser triumph, the ovation, Nero Drusus to take up his consulship. On that journey they may have thrashed out the problems that the letter, perhaps shown to Augustus in Gaul, had raised.[9]

Suetonius regards the 'betrayal' of the letter as the first manifestation of Tiberius' hostility towards his kin. But Tiberius loved his brother. When he heard that Nero Drusus was near death in Germany he made a record-breaking ride of two hundred miles in twenty-four

hours to reach his side, and he went before the body on foot all the
way to Rome.[10] None the less, the two were very unlike each other:
Tiberius proud, slow to speak, often brief and ironical when he did,
disdaining to court popularity however much he might want it; Nero
Drusus affable, open and friendly, combining the display of impeccable principles with ,intense personal ambition. Men thought that
Augustus must be his father – yet they also thought that Augustus
might have been responsible for his death.[11] What would Nero Drusus
mean by the restoration of the Republic? Many had been dissatisfied
with the settlement of 28–27; even more with that of 19, to judge by
the disturbances and conspiracies that had followed it.[12] The workings
of the free Republic were distorted by the powers and influence of
Augustus. On a simple view, the Republic would be restored only
when those powers and that influence were swept away. What was
required was a total resignation of all powers (they were due for renewal in 8 BC[13]) after the manner of Sulla, who had set the Senate in
the saddle and stepped aside. On the face of it a noble scheme: if
Augustus gave up his *imperium*, the commands of the legates would
likewise lapse. Nero Drusus, however, was safely designated consul for
9 BC, and proconsular command would follow – no inconsiderable
command either, if the Senate knew what gratitude was. But Tiberius,
even in youth, probably was not possessed of Nero Drusus' unclouded
idealism. Sulla's Republic did not survive ten years in its pristine form;
and the Second Triumvirate came into being less than two years after
the death of Caesar the Dictator: Tiberius believed as fervently as his
brother in the Republic; without it, ambition and office were meaning-
less. But in the conditions created in the post-Gracchan period it needed
to be defended; and that should be the function of the Princeps. He
should keep the armies that had been the downfall of the Republic,
and which had now been entrusted to him, out of unscrupulous hands,
using them in the interests of the state and as directed by the Senate.[14]
To be sure, this *tutor reipublicae* (guardian of the state) would be a politician, but only one among many, a senator among senators. Essentially the idea was Cicero's. He had hoped to coax Pompey into the
role, even Caesar, and finally the young Octavian (cast for a short run).
Augustus' original claim in 28–27 was that he was fulfilling it. It will
be from that period, perhaps from the autobiography that Augustus
composed at the end of his wars in Spain, that there comes the story
of the dreams of Q. Catulus. That true-blue optimate and supporter
of senatorial policies had been warned by Jupiter that Octavius was to
be brought up 'ad tutelam rei publicae'.[15]

Nero Drusus' views were common knowledge, and a source of his popularity. It was known that he intended to restore 'pristinum rei publicae statum' as soon as he could.[16] By revealing Nero Drusus' proposal for immediate action, Tiberius might hope at once to modify the autocratic tendencies of the Princeps, and to disarm a revolutionary move that might lead to civil war, chaos, and despotism.

Augustus may already have been forced to pay lip-service to the views of his stepsons. In 11 BC the Senate and people, not for the first time, contributed sums of money for statues of Augustus; he diverted it: Salus Publica, Concordia, and Pax took Augustus' place. The refusal itself was something that Dio found worth mentioning; but all these personifications were dear to Cicero, two of them being invoked in his attack, made in the Senate, on the radical bill of Rullus.[17] Concordia in particular we shall meet again. In the year of Nero Drusus' consulship, 9 BC, Augustus brought new measures into force which were designed to strengthen the Senate in its deliberations. Two regular meetings were to be held every month, on days that were cleared of legal and other business. Attendance was still compulsory and fines for non-attendance were increased. If the quorum now fixed was not reached, decisions were to be recorded as informal rather than formal decrees of the Senate – auctoritates senatus rather than as senatus consulta. The right of praetors to bring business before the Senate was reiterated.[18] This was a gesture. So was Augustus' reluctance (noted at this same time by Dio) to appear in court without informing the Senate of his intentions. What prompted this announcement we do not know, but it shows a renewed political delicacy.

Nero Drusus was probably not convinced. Passion for glory combined with scepticism to suggest another test. He intended to win the spolia opima (spoils of honour), a distinction accorded only to those generals who had killed the enemy leader in single combat. M. Licinius Crassus, consul in 30 BC and grandson of the Triumvir, had fulfilled that condition fighting against the Bastarnae in 29; but he had not been allowed the prize. Augustus had found documentary proof that the last man to win the honour had been fighting as consul, and so under his own auspices. That vitiated Crassus' claim, preventing him from outshining the triumphant Princeps. Now a consul was to put Augustus to the test.[19] So far, Tiberius and Nero Drusus had not been allowed even a triumph, and that undervaluing of their achievements (in their own eyes, at least) may have been an additional spur to Nero Drusus.

The refusal of triumphs and of the title imperator to Tiberius and Nero Drusus has been another obstacle in the way of historians who

have sought to place them in Augustus' dynastic schemes. But theirs
were not the first triumphs to be refused in recent years. None of the
three voted to Agrippa by the Senate had been celebrated. Agrippa's
modesty (or disdain) made it difficult for lesser men to make a claim;
perhaps that was the intention. There had been triumphs in plenty in
the Triumviral era and in the first years of the Principate; but the last
had taken place in 19 BC, a year in which Agrippa had refused; and
that had been awarded to L. Cornelius Balbus of Gades, a man who
could not by any stretch of the imagination be seen as a threat to the
Princeps. Senators cannot have been pleased. Now, when informed in
dispatches that the soldiers had acclaimed Tiberius and Nero Drusus in
the field, they gladly took the hint, in hopes of triumphs for their
peers – but the Princeps forbade his stepsons to accept salutation or
triumph, perhaps on the grounds that, as his legates, they held no
independent *imperium*. It was to be clear who was master of the
soldiers. In 12 BC Tiberius and in 11 Nero Drusus were allowed the
insignia of a triumph; these were to be the limit for the ordinary
senator's ambition, and it may be no coincidence that in about 11 BC
they were awarded to and accepted by Tiberius' friend L. Piso the
pontifex, consul of 15, for successes in Thrace. In 10 BC Tiberius was
deemed to have earned the right to the lesser triumph, the ovation, in
which the general rode into the city on horseback rather than in a
chariot; and in the following year Nero Drusus won the same prize.[20]
It was not until 7 BC that Tiberius was finally allowed the highest
honours, the principle now established that only members of the
imperial family were eligible for the award of triumphs proper; and
it was for services in Germany, not the Balkans.[21] For Nero Drusus
had been less lucky. The nearest he came to his celebrating his ovation
was in his funeral procession. Still pursuing the *spolia opima*, he was
fatally injured while riding, in the late summer or autumn of 9 BC.[22]
    The political consequences were momentous. Within four years
two men of high importance had been removed from the scene. It
was not only for themselves and for their services that Augustus
mourned them. They were links in a dynastic chain, now broken,
both Augustus and Tiberius lacking the partners who gave the chain
its strength. It had to be repaired by the forging of a new partnership,
that of Augustus and Tiberius; that is to say, by the advancement of
Tiberius to near equality with the Princeps.[23] The next consular
elections, those of 8 BC, saw Tiberius returned for a second time. This
consulship marks the beginning of a new stage in his career; when
he laid it down he was to take up powers that were new to him:

tribunicia potestas and *proconsulare imperium maius* over the eastern provinces.[24] None could fail to see that such grants of power were intended to perpetuate the Principate to the advantage of Tiberius. But it was never easy to refuse a request of the Princeps, especially on a matter of supreme importance. The dynastic nature of the grants was never made explicit enough to trouble cowardly consciences. The burden of office was always invoked, and it was genuine enough. Augustus complained of it in private correspondence; the Princeps was not shielded from his tasks by an army of secretaries or a well-trained civil service.[25] In this case reference would be made to Eastern affairs, as it must have been in 23 BC. Relations with Parthia were deteriorating, and needed an experienced man on the spot; and Tiberius knew the terrain.

The narrative of Dio shows that these requests by Augustus were not actually made until 6 BC; Tiberius' first five-year period of tribunician power no doubt began at the end of June, on the same day that Augustus entered upon his eighteenth year of tenure.[26] The consulship of 7 admittedly delayed Tiberius' advancement to the all-important power; but it had another function besides that of giving the new co-regent a flying start and conferring on him the *auctoritas*, the prestige and influence, of a man who has been twice consul. It gave belated respectability to an action of Augustus that had been taken in haste and anger: in 7–6 the move from consulship to tribunician power was institutionalized, even ritualized; and the development of formality and convention in the advancement of members of the imperial house was something to be encouraged, giving as it did an appearance of conservatism to the encroachments of the dynasty.

Tiberius entered his second consulship at Rome, as etiquette demanded, but outside the Pomerium, for he was about to celebrate his triumph. He did not spend the whole year at Rome; his presence was required on the northern frontier, which a new commander would soon take over; but he stayed long enough to make his political cast of thought perfectly clear. On the first day of the year the consul summoned the Senate to the Curia Octavia, and announced that he was taking upon himself the restoration of the temple of Concord; it would be paid for in the conventional manner from the spoils of the German wars and re-dedicated in the name of his brother Nero Drusus and himself.[27] Some held that the temple had been founded in the fourth century by the conservative politician and conqueror of Veii, M. Furius Camillus, in the aftermath of the disturbances caused by the Licino-Sextian Laws; certainly a temple had been erected on the site in 121 BC by L. Opimius, the man responsible for the deaths of Gaius Gracchus and his supporters. The temple was often used for meetings of the Senate, notably on the occasion on which Cicero had exposed the designs of the Catilinarian conspirators. The building, like the Bastille, had strong associations, and in undertaking to restore it Tiberius was taking on himself the mantle of two famous champions of government by the senatorial oligarchy.[28]

As Tiberius moved from one distinction to another in his public life, his private life (if we can keep the two apart) grew wretched. At first his marriage had been a success; and sentiment over his regret for Vipsania is out of place. He was a free agent, acting as thousands of Romans had acted before him: for political reasons. Julia went to northern Italy to be near her husband when he campaigned in the Balkans, and it was at Aquileia that she gave birth to their son, probably in 10 B C; but he died. In 9 Julia was still, publicly at least, on good terms with Tiberius. When he celebrated his ovation, she joined Livia in entertaining the wives of senators to a banquet; but she is not mentioned as playing any part in the triumphal festivities of 7.[29] It is no coincidence that the decline in relations belongs to the very years of Tiberius' rise to power. Julia was more than a witty woman of fashion. She sought political power as the daughter, wife, and mother of *principes*; as she said herself, she never forgot that she was Caesar's daughter.[30] Vipsania had been a child when she married Tiberius: Julia was twice a widow, and only two or three years his junior. But for a man of Tiberius' austere stamp there was no room for women in politics; that came to be a sensitive point, as men said that he owed his position to his mother's marriage. Once Julia had established this disagreeable fact about her husband, she found other cause for complaint: he was not her equal, for his ancestors, though blue-blooded, were obscure and second-rate.[31] Alarm as well as contempt took hold of her. She and Tiberius had no living child, but Tiberius had a son of his own, young Drusus. If Tiberius were left in control of affairs by Augustus, he might give way to the temptation to advance his own son at the expense of hers. Julia had friends who shared her fears and her distaste for the regime that Tiberius seemed likely to introduce. Two efforts were made to prevent the consummation of Augustus' plans. In 6 B C the people (not unprompted, as we shall see) elected Gaius Caesar to a consulship.[32] He was nearly, if not quite, fourteen years old, but had not yet taken the toga of manhood and in Roman eyes was still a child. No request had been made by Augustus for his early advancement; and there is no evidence that Augustus knew what was going on. Certainly Gaius

was not an 'official' candidate at the election, but that in itself was no
bar to his being successfully elected.[33] The election may have been
preceded by a demonstration in the theatre led by Lucius, Gaius'
eleven-year-old brother. We have already noticed Gaius' popularity
with the urban *plebs*. It had been enhanced by Augustus' featuring of
both boys on the coinage; and when he took Gaius to Gaul with him
in 8 BC, the event was given due prominence on coins struck for the
Rhine armies.[34] The elevation of Tiberius to a position of co-regency
met no recognition of this kind at all, but that may have been at
Tiberius' wish rather than at Augustus': the first portrait of a living
man to appear on the Roman coinage had been that of Julius Caesar.
It was an aspect of the Principate – the cult of the personality – for
which Tiberius had little use.[35]

Augustus himself was a candidate for the consulship of 5 BC – it was
the year in which he was to conduct Gaius into the Forum and see
him put on adult dress – and he was probably present at the election,
awaiting the results with pretended anxiety. Now he found the people
insisting on making the boy his colleague. It was not only the consulship they had in mind; and they went on insisting even after he remon-
strated with them. He had prayed that it might never be necessary for
a man less than twenty years of age to become consul, as had once
happened in his own case. That was a reference to the dreadful year
of 43 BC, in which Octavian had marched on Rome after the death of
the consuls and taken the office for himself; and the immediate sequel
had been the Triumvirate and proscriptions. One ought not to hold
the office until one was able to avoid error oneself (a knock at Gaius,
if he had intrigued for his election) and resist popular clamour (another
knock, if he had not). The outcome was a compromise: Gaius' consulship was deferred until his twentieth year, and as soon as he assumed
the garb of manhood he was to join the Senate in its deliberations and
in social events; he was to take the title *princeps iuventutis*, becoming
the leading member of the equestrian order.[36]

Tiberius was in Rome for investment with his new powers. The
election made him burn. It was not so much that Gaius was to hold the
consulship in AD 1; that was probably not far off what Augustus had
intended in any case; Marcellus would have been only twenty-two or
twenty-three when he entered on his consulship; but the attempted
election of Gaius to a consulship of 5 BC constituted a massive vote of
no confidence in himself as a politician and as a stepfather. It may be
that the episode of the election by itself was enough to put the idea
of retirement into his head. But there was also a letter of complaint

against Tiberius (we do not know its date), sent by Julia to her father, though composed for her by one of her friends.[37] Moreover, Augustus had compromised, giving way to some extent to the demonstrators. Gaius' consulship had not been vetoed, merely postponed. Did Augustus himself trust Tiberius' integrity? The stepson might wonder. There were other considerations. Tiberius would become sole Princeps because of the accident of his brother's death – and ultimately because of his mother's second marriage. Even if he were capable of realizing it without Nero Drusus' support, would his conception of the Principate, by perpetual work and diplomacy, watching of himself and others, survive him? It seemed unlikely, if Gaius and Lucius were to be brought up to rule as of right or by favour of the people.

It is improbable that Augustus began by taking Tiberius' request to retire seriously. The noisy irruption into politics of two boys was no cause for the eclipse of a man of proved achievement who had just been invested with powers that took him far beyond any rival. Only after Tiberius had gone without food for four days was Augustus convinced. He announced the proposed retirement in the Senate, complaining bitterly about it as an act of desertion. A pretext had to be offered. Tiberius was worn out and overwhelmed by the honours conferred on him. He needed rest, and wished to resume his studies on the island of Rhodes. But Dio also reports that before he left Tiberius opened and read his will in the presence of Augustus and Livia. This was a way of demonstrating his integrity. A will institutes heirs: that of Tiberius named Gaius and Lucius, *primo gradu* (in the first instance) alongside Tiberius' son Drusus, or even taking the greater portion.

Only a few friends saw Tiberius off. He gave them a hasty kiss and went on board at Ostia. His retinue was not large: only one senator, a few *equites*, and the lictors and *viators* who attended holders of *imperium* and tribunes of the *plebs*. Tiberius travelled quietly, like a private individual. He was still off Campania when the ship was intercepted. Bad news of Augustus: the Princeps was dangerously ill. It was his last throw. Tiberius hesitated awhile, but the winds were favourable and he did not want to seem to be lingering.

The voyage gave time for second thoughts. Tiberius had allowed himself to be manoeuvred into destroying his own political position. He too had made his last throw, and lost. There was nothing now he could do, short of armed rebellion, to force Augustus to withdraw the concession made to Gaius, and he had shown by asking leave to retire that he did not intend to go to extremes. It was too late now to make that use of his powers. Once his greatest asset, they were now useless to him, potentially even a source of danger. The two men were in a position that allowed no movement: Tiberius could not return without recognizing the role the people had in the creation of *principes*, and Augustus could not withdraw the consulship that was the cause of the dispute without damaging his own authority and the future of Gaius. It was Tiberius' fault. He had made a political blunder of the first magnitude, ruinous to himself, his plans, and his dependants, and in committing it he had put himself in the wrong. No wonder that Livia too, as well as Augustus, had tried to dissuade him from it.[38] Righteous indignation was going to have to spread a long way. Tiberius gave vent to it. He put in at Paros and there saw a statue of Hestia, the Greek equivalent of Vesta, goddess of the hearth. The Parians did not want to sell, but Tiberius uncharacteristically forced them (he was not going to be thwarted in his gesture). The statue was despatched to Rome, to stand in the temple of Concord. It was a token of his wife's victory – she as well as Livia could be associated with the goddess – and Vesta had another connotation as well: she was the deity to whom Roman magistrates sacrificed when they took up office – and when they laid it down.[39]

Pride and pique had ruined the dynastic scheme that Augustus had been building up since 12 BC, even since 18. As the Princeps entered his fifty-eighth year he found himself in exactly the same case over the succession as he had been at the end of March six years before, except that a man with *imperium maius* and *tribunicia potestas* was sitting uselessly and resentfully in island seclusion, a man well known to the armies of the Balkans and the Rhine, and in whose favour there might be a declaration when the Princeps died. There was one course open to Augustus: to advance the careers of Gaius and Lucius as much as he could and pray for his own survival until they had the power to look after themselves. He did survive to see Gaius take up, in 1 BC, the *imperium* in the East that the expiry of Tiberius' grant laid open to him.[40] When Gaius became consul in AD 1 he was abroad, exercising that *imperium* (protocol went by the board). As he passed his sixty-third year Augustus wrote Gaius a letter in which he expressed his overwhelming relief and thankfulness and looked forward to seeing the two boys gradually taking over his own position.[41] For Lucius was not to be passed over. In 2 BC, after the three-year interval that their ages made appropriate, he too was conducted into the Forum by Augustus, now consul for the thirteenth time, and promised command of the armies of the Spanish provinces (to match the command

of Gaius in the East; Germany was too important to be entrusted
to so inexperienced a commander), and a consulship in five years'
time.[42]

Augustus did nothing about the group that had engineered Gaius'
election and brought about the retirement of Tiberius. For the moment
their interests were his own. Retaliation on behalf of his stepson would
not have brought him back – if so unstable a character was worth
recall. Then, the year before Gaius took up his *imperium*, a scandal of
high candlepower led to the disgrace and exile of Julia and the death
or banishment of men alleged to have been her lovers.[43]

The ringleader was Iullus Antonius, the younger son of Mark
Antony and Fulvia, who had been educated at Rome by Augustus'
sister Octavia. He had married her daughter, the elder Marcella, and
held the consulship in 10 BC and subsequently the proconsulship of
Asia. Parentage and close association with the imperial family made
his intrigue with Julia evidence of ambition as much as licentiousness;
Iullus was allowed to commit suicide.[44] There is nothing new in the
suggestion that the plan of Julia and her supporters was to replace
her husband Tiberius with a new consort – Antonius. They did not
believe, or so they claimed, that Gaius and Lucius could hold their
own without the backing of an older man who could command
loyalty in his own right. If that is a correct interpretation, time was
running out for them in 2 BC. Soon there would be no excuse for
putting forward a replacement for Tiberius. Augustus would hold
that Gaius and Lucius could stand on their own feet. Increased pressure from Julia's friends was only to be expected in the year before
Gaius' admission to proconsular *imperium*. One of them was tribune
of the *plebs* in that year and could not be prosecuted until he had come
to the end of his term. This unnamed tribune may have been, but
probably was not, that Sempronius Gracchus who composed Julia's
letter to Augustus and who now was exiled to Cercina.[45] Another
sympathizer was the consul of 9 BC, Quinctius Crispinus Sulpicianus.[46]
Then there was an Appius Claudius, great-nephew of P. Clodius and
Fulvia, cousin to their child Claudia; and a Scipio, grandson of
Octavian's former wife Scribonia, the mother of Julia.[47] With her
we come to the centre. Scribonia accompanied her daughter into exile,
guaranteeing that adultery was not the sole cause of Julia's downfall,
and remained with her until her death. Nobody could accuse Scribonia
of lightness, in any sense of the word.[48] Julia's party was a clique of
aristocratic intellectuals;[49] but it has too the air of a family faction,
centred on Scribonia and recalling the rapprochement of 40 BC between

the parties of Antony and of Sex. Pompeius that was finally destroyed when Octavian divorced Scribonia to marry Livia. Julia complained that Tiberius was not her equal, and here is another clue. The 'adulterers' bear the names of families that were not merely blue-blooded, but powerful in the late Republican and Triumviral eras. Were these families, the kin of Octavian's first betrothed, Claudia, and of his first wife, to be outdone by obscure Nerones? There is a hint too of demagogy. One of the offences of the group was to decorate with garlands a statue of Marsyas that stood in the Roman Forum. It was not merely a symbol of Bacchic license but, with the fig tree that overhung it, was regarded as the symbol of a free city. One of the conspirators was a Sempronius Gracchus, one a tribune; and it was precisely in the year 2 B C that tribunician agitation broke out in Rome.[50] The details are missing, but the tribunes were sent to Augustus about certain reforms and he came to consult with the people about their demands. In a word: Julia and her friends stood for an alliance of palace and people. It makes a contrast to the austere and oligarchic programme of Tiberius.

A man who stands for the rule of an élite and the reduction of the people to a position of respectful docility cannot in the nature of things expect to command mass support; but Tiberius had a following outside the ranks of his legions: relatives, men who shared his views, those who enjoyed his patronage or hoped to benefit from it in the future. It is time to look at men who may have regretted his departure in 6 B C, and who may have tried to dissuade him from it, if they were in Rome.

Tiberius' influence on the consular *Fasti* of A D 5 onwards is generally acknowledged. If the view taken here of his position before 6 B C is correct, one might expect to find some trace of it soon after Agrippa's death. Indeed, Tiberius was not without influence before that, unless it was by coincidence that one of the consuls he declared elected in 13 B C was the able upstart P. Sulpicius Quirinius, always a friend to Tiberius.[51] In 6 itself there was a hitch in the conduct of the elections, when votes were cast for Gaius; if Augustus was not already on the spot, the consul in charge stopped proceedings long enough for him to hurry down and remonstrate. He was probably C. Antistius Vetus, son of a Republican of the same name.[52] His predecessor, Tiberius' coeval and colleague in 7 B C, was a loyal subject to the end of his days: he was Cn. Calpurnius Piso, son of that Piso who had taken up the challenge presented by Augustus in 23.[53] The consuls of 8 and 3 B C, C. Marcius Censorinus and M. Valerius Messalla Messallinus, might also be classed as well disposed, at least to judge by the way they are handled by Tiberius' panegyrist Velleius Paterculus.[54] Censorinus' colleague, C. Asinius Gallus, is more difficult to assess. He had married Tiberius' ex-wife, and relations were said to be bedevilled by that fact, but as the stepfather of Tiberius' son Drusus and the father of Drusus' numerous half-brothers, he would have an interest in the advancement of Tiberius and his son.[55] One of the suffects of 5 BC, C. Sulpicius Galba, was a hunchback (there was nothing wrong with his intelligence), and he was the subject of a jibe of Tiberius' deadly enemy, M. Lollius. Galba's son rose high through the influence of his patron, Livia.[56] Galba was followed as Princeps in AD 69 by Otho, grandson of another of Livia's protégés. M. Salvius Otho entered the Senate with her help and the coins he struck as *monetalis* (it was surprising that a new man should be honoured with the post of moneyer) display a Victory which probably alludes to Tiberius' triumph of 7. His son Lucius was a great favourite with Tiberius; in fact there was a resemblance between them which caused some gossip.[57] In 2 BC the command of the Praetorian Guard was entrusted to two men, perhaps to strengthen the Princeps' hand against the pressure exerted on him by Julia and her friends, or in the aftermath of the scandal.[58] One of the new prefects was Salvius Aper, but relationship with the Salvii Othones is not established. The other was Ostorius Scapula, the owner of slaves who passed into the hands of Livia and her son; he went on to the Prefecture of Egypt during the second ascendancy of Tiberius.[59] So much for domestic posts. Tiberius was to be superseded in the north when he took up his eastern command. L. Domitius Ahenobarbus and C. Sentius Saturninus are both written well of by Velleius. Domitius served on the Danube during Tiberius' absence; Saturninus, after his governorship of Syria, probably moved to Germany and Gaul (6–1 BC). A possible second term in the same office was not interrupted by Tiberius' return to power. Two of Saturninus' sons held consulships in AD 4.[60] In Syria Saturninus was succeeded by P. Quinctilius Varus, a patrician of undistinguished antecedents (though his father, like Tiberius' grandfather, had committed suicide after Philippi); Varus was Tiberius' colleague in the consulship of 13 and likewise a son-in-law of Agrippa. He was to hold another great command during the second ascendancy of Tiberius, fatal to himself and damaging to the state; but there was no mistaking the favour he enjoyed while he lived.[61] Sulpicius Quirinius, consul in 12, is found in the East as governor of Galatia soon after 6 BC. Had he been destined to go as Tiberius' comrade in arms, or was he sent as a partial substitute?[62] In

Asia for the year 6–5 we find Asinius Gallus; in Egypt C. Turranius, who was later to be put in charge of the corn supply and to remain in post throughout Tiberius' principate.[63]

Caution must be exercised. Many of these men were of noble birth or outstanding merit; they would have won distinction without support from Tiberius. But the one senator who accompanied Tiberius to Rhodes evidently had nothing to keep him in Rome. His name, Lucilius Longus, is not a famous one. But a Lucilius impersonated Brutus after the battle of Philippi and was taken prisoner in his stead; nor did he desert Antony in 31 BC. If Tiberius' friend was the son of this man, their choice of leaders and of causes is an interesting one: Brutus, Antonius, Tiberius.[64]

The adherents of Tiberius, as far as we can make them out, display no homogeneity. He was intimate with aristocrats and men who were the first in their families to enter the Senate, as befitted any politician of sense. The preponderance of military men, as of 'Republican' antecedents, is notable. Tiberius may have found many friends amongst the military. He had spent years on campaign and 'Biberius Caldius Mero' had learned young to drink with the best.[65] It was another contrast with Julia's city clique.

When he retired, Tiberius' powers had five years to run. He might return. Roman governors and other officials travelling to and fro on business in the East thought it worth while to call and pay their respects. In 2 BC came news of his wife's disgrace. A moment of rejoicing, of belief that he would be vindicated (there was a small crop of dedications that can be dated to the years 2–1), was followed by misgivings.[66] The charges brought against Julia had nothing to do with her intrigues against Tiberius, and they left the arrangements made in 6–5 quite undisturbed: the onward march of Gaius and Lucius was unaffected – and the tie that bound Tiberius to the imperial family and strengthened his claim to the succession was severed. Augustus sent Julia notice of divorce in her husband's name.[67] Not surprisingly Tiberius wrote again and again begging for mercy to be shown the errant wife; with her gone, his fate might soon rest in the hands of the two boys. His pleas were disregarded, and in the following year, when his powers had expired, Gaius appeared in the East, after introducing himself to the armies in the Balkans that his stepfather knew so well,[68] and took over the *imperium* that Tiberius had lost and to which he was now, ironically, to be subject. When Gaius arrived on Samos, or Chios according to one version,[69] Tiberius paid him a visit; but he was frigidly received. Tiberius realized that he was in danger. Time and

again he asked permission to return, explaining that he had withdrawn
to avoid competing with Gaius and Lucius. It was a disingenuous plea
to come from a man who had been second in the state, but it could be
offered to the public as an explanation in 1 BC. Augustus refused.
Tiberius was still too great to be allowed to come back into circulation;
besides, there was much to forgive: the anxiety of the last five years,
and the scandal of 2, which would not have blown up if Tiberius had
stayed at his post. Hence the savage tone of the reply: Tiberius had been
eager enough to desert his family and friends; now he had better forget
them. Only Livia's intervention secured him the title of legate, a cover
for virtual exile. Even now, officials were still paying their respects
when they put in at Rhodes. To avoid their well-meant, dangerous
homage, Tiberius moved into the interior. A rumour became current
that centurions who had received their commission from Tiberius were
returning from furlough bearing treasonable messages (eloquent testimony to the following he was believed to have in the armies, and far
more convincing than the raptures of Velleius). Tiberius repeatedly
begged for an observer of any rank to be stationed with him. At length
he was driven to abandoning his riding and drill, in case they gave
substance to the idea that he was planning a coup; he even laid aside
Roman dress and took (it is hardly to be believed) to the Greek cloak
and slippers. He had ceased to be Roman. To the ends of the Empire,
it was clear that Tiberius was finished. The people of Nemausus in
Gaul had divided loyalties. Tiberius' father had been active in the
Rhône valley, settling Caesar's veterans and founding colonies.
Tiberius himself may have paid special attention to the town during
his governorship; certainly it received its walls and gates from Augustus
in 16 BC. Nemausus had busts and statues of Tiberius. But Agrippa
had also been a benefactor, starting the building now known as the
Maison Carrée, and Gaius was a patron.[70] Nemausus made its loyalties
clear. Tiberius' portraits were thrown down. In the East, in the retinue
of Gaius, detestation of the recluse reached greater heights. His head
was offered to his stepson. Gaius did not accept. The moment of
extreme danger passed.
    The leading member of the entourage, and an enemy of Tiberius,
was M. Lollius. In AD 2 the Parthians revealed that Lollius was in the
pay of certain client kings. Whether that was true or not, Gaius
quarrelled with him. A few days later Lollius died, by suicide or natural
causes.[71] He was replaced by Sulpicius Quirinius, whose advice to
Gaius on the subject of his stepfather was different from Lollius'. In a
few months, after two years of ceaseless anxiety, Tiberius was allowed

to return to Rome; Augustus made it clear that it was expressly by permission of Gaius.

This return from Rhodes was quite unlike the first, twenty-two years before. Then Tiberius stood at the beginning of a brilliant career, which had now been brought to a humiliating end. He was a man retired into private life who was unlikely to hold office ever again – even if he were lucky enough to survive Augustus. His conduct was correspondingly meek, but we need not doubt that a lesson had been learned. The occasion of Tiberius' return was probably the coming to manhood of his son Drusus. The ceremony over, he moved out of the limelight again. He gave up his former house, which had once belonged to Pompey and then to Mark Antony, and was unsuitable for him as much for its associations as for its conspicuous siting in the Carinae, on the western slope of the Esquiline Hill, and took up residence in a house in the Gardens of Maecenas, farther away from the centre of the city, to the north-east.[72] Tiberius had not long been back in Rome when news came from Massilia that Lucius Caesar had died there on 20 August, on his way to Spain.[73] Tiberius had no public part to play in the funeral, but advertised his proper grief by composing a poem, 'A Lament on the Death of Lucius'. Augustus was shaken, but not shattered; it was said that he bore his relatives' deaths with greater fortitude than their errors. It was as well: in AD 4 news long feared came from the East: Gaius had succumbed on 21 February to a wound received at the siege of an Armenian town.[74] Augustus was alone.

CHAPTER IV

REHABILITATION: THE FINAL
STRUGGLE FOR THE SUCCESSION

Augustus had reacted with decision in 2 B C, but with relative mildness.
Only one man is known to have died, and the exile that the other culprits suffered might be modified or cancelled. Nor were their relatives
penalized. A Sempronius Gracchus is found in the entourage of L.
Caesar, and T. Quinctius Crispinus Valerianus was not prevented by
his brothers' misdemeanours from reaching a suffect consulship in
A D 2. Only a few politicians can have committed themselves to Iullus
Antonius and the quick but uncertain profits that his manoeuvres might
win; more were content to build their hopes on future favours from
the rising *principes inventutis*. Augustus needed their support if Gaius
and Lucius were to come peacefully into their political inheritance.

Experienced politicians and débutants alike followed the young men.
We have seen Quirinius serving Gaius even as he laid up credit with
Tiberius. Velleius Paterculus and L. Aelius Sejanus, officers at the beginning of their careers, would have been pleased to go East.[1] A fair
prospect opened up before those who were fortunate enough to be connected by marriage with the *principes*. Gaius married within the dynasty,
the sister of Germanicus; Lucius was betrothed to Aemilia Lepida,
sister of the consul of A D 11. Their sister Julia the younger went to a
member of the same *gens*, L. Aemilius Paullus, whose father had been
consul in 34 and censor in 22 B C. He duly reached the consulship
(*ordinarius*, holding office from 1 January) in 1 B C, as the colleague of his
brother-in-law.[2]

When Lucius died in A D 2, a tremor of alarm must have passed
through the circle. The fortunes of the family and its supporters now
depended on the life of Gaius alone, unless Augustus chose to find him
a new partner. That way lay greater security and a possible danger.
Tiberius' elegy on the death of Lucius showed him in conciliatory and
disarming mood. Or was he angling for a renewal of former powers?
Velleius hints that an offer was made and declined, but in language that
is misleadingly ambiguous. Pride and principle would be against
acceptance; but it is not easy to believe that after his years of anxiety on
Rhodes, Tiberius would have refused powers that might preserve his
life after Augustus was gone. The possibility of rehabilitation must have

been canvassed at the time, for it was countered by a move that bears
the hall-mark of Tiberius' opponents: popular agitation for the recall
of the elder Julia reached such intensity that Augustus had to face the
people in a *contio* (public meeting), and wished on them daughters and
wives (a touch made for Tiberius' benefit) of her sort; he would bring
her back when fire mixed with water. But the populace brought their
torches and threw them into the Tiber, and eventually in AD 3 Gaius'
mother returned, not indeed to Rome but to Rhegium, where some of
the restrictions on her daily life were relaxed.[3]

Much more acceptable to Gaius and his followers than the rehabilitation of Tiberius would have been the advancement of the youngest
child of M. Agrippa. Born probably in the second half of 12 BC,
Agrippa Postumus would be fourteen in AD 3 and might expect to
take the toga of manhood towards the end of the year or at the
beginning of the next. He did not do so, nor was the delay due to
Gaius' death and the mourning that followed: Gaius died on 21 February
AD 4, but the news did not become known at Pisae in Italy until 2 April,
and by that time Agrippa should have taken the toga.[4] Moreover, when
Gaius and Lucius reached manhood they were brought into the Forum
by Augustus, who took the consulships of 5 and 2 BC for that purpose.
Augustus was not elected to the consulship of AD 4. Evidently by midway
through 3 he had decided to advance Gaius to partnership with himself
rather than find a substitute for Lucius. In that case the anxieties of Julia,
her husband Paullus, and Agrippa would be intensified, and rightly
so: the plan was to meet with no success.

In the autumn of 3 news reached Rome that Gaius had been wounded
in the siege of Artagira in Armenia on 9 September.[5] Gaius' own behaviour after that mishap is hard to explain, so hard that two sources
claim that his mind was affected: he requested leave to retire into private
life somewhere in Syria. Augustus communicated his wish to the Senate
but asked him at least to return to Italy; after that he could do as he
wished. The testimony of Velleius, who was in the entourage, cannot
be ignored, though it must be handled with care. And Velleius says
paradoxically enough that Gaius was brought to his despondent frame
of mind by intercourse with men whose 'toadyism' (*assentatio*) made
his failings worse. Augustus, then, was trying to get Gaius to return to
Rome after the fall of Artagira; perhaps he saw the success as a suitable
occasion for the conferment of tribunician power, a ceremony that
always took place at Rome. No one was in a better position than the
'toadies' to see how serious Gaius' condition was; they may well have
preferred an alternative policy: that of advancing Agrippa Postumus

(it is clear from Velleius' attitude that their candidate was not Tiberius). But their plans seem to have succeeded too well: Gaius intended to resign his powers and remain in Syria as a private individual. Eventually he agreed to return – but not to receive the tribunician power. At the beginning of AD 4 he began the journey home, and the question of his future was finally resolved with his death at the Lycian port of Limyra.

Augustus, now in his sixty-sixth year, had to find a new dynastic scheme. The clamour of advice that had been growing ever since the previous autumn must have reached its climax in the three months that followed the news of Gaius' death. On the one hand the merits of Rome's most distinguished (or at least most experienced) living general, whose talents had gone to waste for a decade, would be urged by his mother, his friends, and those who had no taste for the popular dynasticism of the last few years; on the other, there was a youth rising fifteen whose sister and brother-in-law would support his claim to the position that Gaius and Lucius had vacated.

The pressure exerted on Augustus may be gauged from the dispositions he made on 26 June. Augustus adopted both Tiberius and Agrippa Postumus. Tiberius obtained a renewed grant of tribunician power and a command in Germany, occasioned by trouble in that area. The extent of his *imperium*, the grant of tribunician power for ten rather than the hitherto normal five years, and the fact that, according to Velleius, he spoke against the grant in private and in the Senate, are eloquent testimony to the strength of Tiberius' position in AD 4.[6] Augustus and his peers had to argue their case – and in so doing they thoroughly and publicly committed themselves to it. There was to be no second journey into exile. Justifying his action, as he was legally required to do, at a public meeting, Augustus could claim that he was adopting the Claudian for the benefit of the state: the adoption of a consular of forty-five, in addition to a grandson, was an anomaly in family law. As children of Augustus, Tiberius and Agrippa Postumus were to be equal, but the normal forms of advancement were violated; one of the two adopted children was in the same position as Gaius and Lucius had been between 17 and 6 BC; the other in a position much closer to that of their father Agrippa between 18 and 13: as holder of the *tribunicia potestas*, Tiberius was co-regent as well as heir. Nobody could expect him to accept mere equality with the younger brother of the boys who had secured his political downfall in 6 BC. Worse, from the point of view of Agrippa's friends, Tiberius had a son of his own, whose future had already been a source of discord. This time his father made sure that he was included in the dynastic scheme. On the adoption of Tiberius, this boy became

Augustus' grandson and would expect to have his share of imperial power when the time came. So too would the son of Tiberius' brother Nero Drusus, whom Tiberius adopted just before his own adoption.[7] That gave Augustus a second grandson, a partner for young Drusus Caesar, strengthening the Claudian element still further. There was little comfort for the friends of the dead Gaius and Lucius Caesar in all this. Now only Agrippa Postumus stood between the offspring of Livia and complete supremacy. But Augustus tried to mitigate their fears. Germanicus Caesar was married, probably in the following year, to Agrippina, the second daughter of Julia the elder and M. Agrippa, and his young brother Claudius was betrothed to the daughter of L. Paullus and the younger Julia, Aemilia Lepida.[8] Not that that would be much consolation to Julia. Her son, also L. Paullus, would be outside the innermost circle of the dynasts, and her husband, recently colleague in the consulship with his young brother-in-law, the senior of Augustus' heirs, now found himself politically dependent on a boy whose whole future, if Augustus should die, lay in doubt.

Whether the alliance of Germanicus and Agrippina did anything to cement the two sides of the family together may be doubted. Tacitus' comments on the relations between Tiberius and his adopted son, and the incontestably bad relations that developed after Germanicus' death between the Princeps and Agrippina, should not mislead us. The earliest date at which any rivalry is hinted at is AD 14, when soldiers on the Rhine, perhaps not with very serious intent, or only to embarrass their commander, mooted a declaration for Germanicus; and Tacitus stresses his perfect loyalty on that occasion. He lost no time in swearing in provincials and legionaries to his father. To be sure his dynastic claim to power rested partly on his relationship to Augustus, partly on his marriage to Augustus' granddaughter. By blood he was not close: as Octavia's grandson (no connexion, be it noted, of Scribonia) he was Augustus' great-nephew; but he was also a grandson by adoption – and by the same token a son of Tiberius. His father and uncle had been devoted to each other and to some extent at least had shared political opinions which Germanicus too was thought to hold. Germanicus' relations with Drusus Caesar, his brother by adoption, remained untroubled to the end of his life. And during the crisis of the Pannonian revolt, in AD 6–8, when Agrippa's disgrace made it impossible to send him to Pannonia with reinforcements, Germanicus went instead. A distinction was being drawn between the two young men, not necessarily because Germanicus was three or four years older than Agrippa, or more able, but because he could be trusted. Blood, political views, and self-interest should have kept Germanicus by the side of his adopted father.[9]

The position of Agrippina was more ambiguous. The suspicion that grew up between her and Tiberius in later years may have had its roots in Tiberius' adoption and the disgrace of her brother and sister and so, ultimately, in the downfall of her mother, the elder Julia. On the other hand it may have arisen only after Germanicus' death, when she thought that her own children's prospects were in danger; it might have been only then that she began to see the fate of her kinsfolk as the result of Tiberius' scheming. Certainly her ambition for herself, her husband, and her children would not in the years 4–8 have seen its easiest fulfilment in improving the position of Agrippa Postumus, still less that of L. Paullus; it was through the line of Tiberius, whether by blood or by adoption, that the power was to pass; and it is not hard to believe that the marriages of Julia the younger and Agrippina may have destroyed rather than enhanced their natural sisterly affection.[10]

If the settlement made in A D 4 was a compromise, it was one heavily weighted in favour of Tiberius, and the fears of his opponents were soon justified. At best they would have to make room for his supporters in the senior magistracies; at the worst they might lose their own positions of influence, even their seats in the Senate. A purge came in 4, only months after the adoptions, and, says Dio, it was made possible by that move. It was combined with grants of money to deserving men who could not maintain themselves in the House. All the Augustan purges came at the end of a struggle for power, or with a change of personnel at the tip of the pyramid of power. None was really successful; on this last occasion too, not many men could be brought to remove themselves 'voluntarily' from the roll; they hung on in hope.[11]

A complementary measure followed in A D 5, a law brought in by the consuls, both well disposed towards Tiberius. The *lex Valeria Cornelia* created ten new centuries of voters, five each named after Gaius and Lucius Caesar (an ironical touch) to act as *centuriae praerogativae*, centuries which voted first and had their results declared, so giving a strong lead to the rest of the centuries in the election of consuls and praetors in the *comitia*. The new centuries consisted of senators and leading knights. Ten years before, the *comitia centuriata* (centuriate assembly) had helped to blight Tiberius' career by offering the consulship prematurely to Gaius Caesar. The new arrangement increased the influence of the highest classes on the outcome of consular and praetorian elections, thus partly neutralizing the popularity that the family and friends of Julia the elder enjoyed amongst the rank and file.[12] The *lex* did not put an end to electoral disturbances; on the contrary, in AD 7 they were so bitter that Augustus had to appoint the magistrates himself. But it may be seen as the precursor of the measure adopted in AD 14 – the first undertaking of Tiberius' principate. That reserved the election of magistrates to the Senate, leaving the popular assemblies (*tributa* as well as *centuriata*) no option but to ratify the Senate's choice. [13] Their special position under the new scheme would have flattered members of the Senate, and even more those *equites* who were associated with them. The same year saw another privilege conferred on the equestrian order: they were provided with separate seats in the circus, again alongside those of the senators. Senate and *equites* were to be united behind the Princeps and his dynasty in a latter-day *concordia ordinum*, the harmony between the two upper classes of Roman society that Cicero had advocated. From that *concordia* the *plebs* and the irresponsible politicians who appealed to it were to be excluded, and by it they were to be made harmless.

The effectiveness of the new measure is hard to gauge. Syme examined the *Fasti* of Augustus' last decade and found them replete with the partisans of Tiberius. Not that his friends are absent even before AD 4: his friendship was far from being the only relevant factor. In AD 4 itself we find the friendly Sex. Aelius Catus and C. Sentius Saturninus as *consules ordinarii*, with Cn. Sentius Saturninus as suffect. [14] But there were certainly men in office after that year who would not have reached the consulship if they had not been kin to Tiberius, shared his views, served him, or impressed him with their military ability in Germany or the Balkans. The number and success of men who seem to have had little in their favour beyond a connexion with Tiberius illustrate the extent and the effectiveness of his patronage.

M. Furius Camillus represented a patrician family not recently prominent (like of that of Tiberius himself). He was descended from the Dictator who allegedly had built the first temple of Concord. Camillus gave his son to L. Arruntius, consul in AD 6, and betrothed his daughter Livia Medullina to the young Claudius (she died on the wedding day). [15] His colleague in the consulship of two years later was Sex. Nonius Quinctilianus, by birth the son of P. Quinctilius Varus, consul in 13 BC, another relatively obscure patrician, but connected by marriage with Tiberius. In AD 6, L. Nonius Asprenas had been suffect; and four years later a cousin, P. Dolabella, who was to be given full credit by Velleius for the quiet conduct of his legions at the transfer of power in AD 14, was *ordinarius*. Varus himself governed Gaul for two years with Nonius as his legate before his destruction in 9. [16] L. Volusius Saturninus,

consul in 12 BC and governor of Syria in AD 4–5, was kin to Tiberius
and (by marriage) to the Quinctilii and Nonii, while Asprenas was a
connexion of a trusted friend and boon companion of Tiberius, L. Piso
the pontifex, consul in 15 BC and appointed Prefect of the city in the
year before Augustus' death, perhaps in anticipation of disturbances
that that event might cause.[17] M. Plautius Silvanus, though not related to
Tiberius, may have claimed descent from the Plautius who in 312 BC
had collaborated with Appius Claudius the censor. And any rate he was
said to owe his success (he was consul in 2 BC) to Livia, and towards the
end of the principate of Augustus his daughter became the first girl to
achieve marriage to Claudius. Silvanus, after his proconsulship of Asia,
was governor of Galatia and in AD 7 brought reinforcements to Tiberius
in the Balkans.[18] Neither were the Cornelii Lentuli related to Tiberius,
but they were by no means ill-disposed, and they figure prominently
amongst the magistrates and pro-magistrates of the decade: Ser. Maluginensis was consul in AD 10, Cn. the augur fought the Daci, and
two Lentuli, Lucius, the consul of 3 BC, who may have offered his
daughter in marriage to Volusius Saturninus (consul in AD 3), and
Cossus, the consul of 1 BC, perhaps were successive governors of
Africa (4–6).[19]

Military merit naturally commended itself to Tiberius. His renewed
command allowed him to do it justice. The Aelii Lamiae were not a
family of long standing in the Senate. L. Lamia, consul in AD 3, is well
spoken of by Velleius Paterculus, and is found in Africa in AD 14, having
previously served under Tiberius in Illyricum.[20] One of the most
notable friends of Tiberius, the military man P. Sulpicius Quirinius, was
rewarded for his success and perhaps for his fidelity with the governorship of Syria in AD 6.[21] Other new men from the municipalities were
C. Visellius Varro, suffect in AD 12, and L. Apronius, suffect four years
earlier – the latter achieved links with M. Silvanus and Lentulus Gaetulicus. He was one of the men who served in Illyricum, as did Vibius
Postumus of Larinum, suffect in AD 5, brother of Habitus, suffect in
AD 8.[22] M. Papius Mutilus the Samnite combined a long pedigree with
novitas, being the first of his family to enter the Senate; he was suffect in
9, and demonstrated his loyalty to Tiberius seven years later by attacking
the memory of a traitor.[23] Two consular governors of 14 seem to be of
municipal descent: certainly C. Poppaeus Sabinus, consul in 9, who came
from Interamnia Praetuttianorum, and was the legate of Moesia long
prorogued by Tiberius;[24] and probably Q. Iunius Blaesus serving in Pannonia, uncle of L. Aelius Sejanus, who by AD 14 had long since lived
down his association with Gaius Caesar and was *magna auctoritate* (had

great influence) with Tiberius, and was appointed colleague to his father L. Seius Strabo in the prefecture of the Guard; Sejanus was to ally himself, if he had not already done so, with the Cornelii Lentuli.[25] One more vital post should be mentioned at this point: the prefecture of the corn supply, in which C. Turranius was to give satisfaction for many years; as we have already seen, he had experience in Egypt dating from the period of Tiberius' first ascendancy. Tiberius rated loyalty very high.[26] That perhaps was the only quality that won his consulship for the suffect of AD 7, Lucilius Longus; but, having spent seven years on Rhodes with Tiberius, he must have been well endowed with it. We have already noticed his political affiliations. Other politicians who emerge now may have shared them. The suffect consul of 11 was a L. Cassius Longinus, and a rhetorical exercise preserved by Dio and Seneca represents the Republican Cn. Cornelius Cinna Magnus as planning the assassination of Augustus and saved by Tiberius' mother.[27] Magnus, as consul in 5, saw to the passage of the *lex Valeria Cornelia*. His colleague was L. Valerius Potiti f. Messalla Volesus. The most distinguished member of that family was M. Messalla Corvinus the orator, Tiberius' instructor in Latin prose, whose reputation for integrity and independence was perhaps greater than he deserved. His children were noted for their loyalty to Tiberius.[28]

As the sons of the men who had been Tiberius' friends in the earlier period of ascendancy pressed on to the consulships and commands that were their due (their parents sometimes surviving in posts of honour), and new men won their way to the top by distinguished service under Tiberius' command, the numbers of the other side will have been decreasing monthly. Their centre was a small family clique, very similar to the clique that had formed round the elder Julia. The similarity was not coincidental: the second was a continuation of the first. That emerges clearly if the connexions of the persons who were involved in the downfall of the younger Julia are examined. Both groups had the same object: the political demise of Tiberius, or at least the advancement of candidates of Scribonia's blood who would be strong enough to maintain their interests against his. In the first case the candidates were Gaius and Lucius, in the second Agrippa Postumus, perhaps with L. Paullus as a running mate. Agrippa and Julia of course were the children of the exiled Julia and grandchildren of Scribonia, and if those two ladies did not play an active part in the events of this decade it was only because they were both still in exile at Rhegium. Paullus' mother was a Cornelia of the Scipios, a daughter of Scribonia by one of her earlier marriages. Paullus was thus his wife's half cousin, and first cousin to one of the

lovers of the elder Julia, Scipio. The marriage could have been celebrated in about 7 or 6 B C, or a year or two later, when Julia's stepfather
was out of the way.[29]
   Julia the younger was convicted of adultery; but we know the
name of only one lover: D. Iunius Silanus. Lepidi and Silani are found in
high positions during the two decades that passed between the departure of Tiberius for Rhodes and his accession to the Principate. Q.
Caecilius Metellus Creticus Silanus held his consulship for the whole of
A D 7; C. Silanus was consul in 10; M. Lepidus, the brother of L. Paullus,
in 6; and M'. Lepidus, his second cousin, in 11. Manius' sister was first
betrothed to L. Caesar, then married to Sulpicius Quirinius. When Julia
and her husband fell, the engagement of their daughter, another
Aemilia Lepida, to Claudius was broken off, and she had to be found a
different husband. He was a Silanus, M. Torquatus, who was to be
consul in A D 19.[30] Connexions between the Lepidi and the Silani went
back to the Triumviral age and beyond. Servilia, mother by D. Iunius
Brutus of M. Brutus the Liberator, married for the second time D.
Silanus, consul, in 62 B C, and became the mother of daughters. One,
Iunia Tertulla, was the wife of Cassius the Liberator (as well as being
Cato's granddaughter) and she survived until A D 22, causing comment
by her will: she omitted to mention the Princeps. Her elder sister was
married to Lepidus the Triumvir. Other connexions of the Silani are
equally significant: they were with the Sempronii (Gracchi?) and the
Quinctii (Crispini?): M. Silanus, consul in 25 B C, was the son of a
Sempronia and the husband of a Crispina. Members of both families
were punished with the elder Julia. So was an Ap. Claudius; and his
sister or cousin Appia Claudia married C. Silanus and became the
mother of Decimus, the *adulter* of the younger Julia.[31]
   An exemplary warning against reckless prosopographical speculation
is afforded by the conduct of M. Lepidus, consul of A D 6. As brother of
L. Paullus, he might have been expected to be at the heart of the group.
In fact he was one of Tiberius' most respected friends – and is one of the
few Roman politicians whose reputation has been assailed neither by
ancient nor by modern historians.[32] He fought alongside Tiberius in the
Pannonian revolt after his consulship and was entrusted with the supreme
command in A D 8 while Tiberius journeyed to Rome. There could be
no greater display of confidence. It was repeated six years later. In
A D 14 Lepidus is found in charge of Tarraconensis and its three legions.
In the reign of Tiberius he betrothed his daughter to Drusus Caesar,
son of Germanicus, and his influence protected the faithless widow
as long as he survived. Principle again, or speculation about the out-

come, may have divided the *gens Iunia*. One of the brothers of the *adulter*, Gaius, became consul in AD 10, the other, Marcus, in 15, with Drusus Caesar as his colleague. Marcus continued to enjoy the esteem of Tiberius, and it was his influence that made it possible for the offender to return to Rome in 20. Moreover, the consul of 7, Q. Creticus Silanus, was legate of Syria when Augustus died, a position he would not have held if he could not be trusted.[33]

Julia and her friends seemed likely to make some progress in 5, when Agrippa finally took the toga of manhood (perhaps at the Liberalia on 16 March). But Augustus did not allow him any of the privileges that his brothers had had: no consulship after a five-year interval, no leadership of the youth, no attendance at meetings of the Senate. Fifteen years later, when he was introducing Germanicus' elder son to the Senate, Tiberius requested for him the privilege that he himself had been accorded in 24 BC: that of holding magistracies five years before the normal age.[34] That would have had an inherent propriety in Tiberius' eyes, and it is unlikely that he would willingly have agreed to anything better for Agrippa; the precedents were both disagreeable and disreputable. It may have been controversy over just that point that delayed Agrippa's assumption of adult dress, and after Tiberius' departure for an autumn campaign in 4, the controversy would have raged all the more. The military situation, though it was less critical than Velleius would have us believe, and the need to win back his place with the armies drew Tiberius away from Rome, but anxiety over the political situation in the city brought him back again almost every winter. Devotion to Augustus is what Velleius calls it; Dio is cruder, but nearer the mark: he was afraid that Augustus might prefer someone to himself.[35] Augustus of course had made his choice; but so he had in 6 BC, and he had shown himself infirm against the manoeuvres of his daughter and friends.

Whatever else was against him, nature now began to play Agrippa's game. In AD 5, according to Dio, there was a solar eclipse (28 March), earthquakes, a seven-day flood, and famine. Nothing could be better calculated to make the populace amenable to the agitation of discontented politicians. It was probably at the end of that campaigning season that Augustus was harassed by another problem: noisy demands for discharge and bounty from the soldiers, who perhaps saw that their opportunities might disappear with the next campaign. The following year was to see the great attack on Maroboduus of the Marcomanni, which was to establish Roman rule within Bohemia and consolidate the conquest of Germany. Again luck was on the side of the malcontents. Before Tiberius was five days' march into enemy territory, he was called back by the news that Pannonia and Dalmatia were in revolt. Augustus made no attempt to hide the seriousness of the situation: he told the Senate bluntly that in ten days the enemy could be within sight of Rome. For three seasons (6–8) the Pannonians occupied Tiberius' attentions; the Dalmatians held out until 9. The sacrifices and privations the war imposed, and Tiberius' circumspection in his dealings with the enemy, added to the effects of inclement weather throughout Italy and destructive fires and floods in Rome, created just the psychological conditions to delight an opposition. The new regime was failing at home and abroad.[36]

The first clear signs of trouble belong to the autumn or winter of AD 5. Velleius tells us that Agrippa began to reveal his true nature about two years before the critical battle against the rebels that was fought in the Volcaean marshes; that came at the end of the campaigning season of 7.[37] Doubtless what Agrippa revealed was a strong desire for speedy advancement. As yet consulship, proconsular *imperium*, and tribunician power were below the horizon. The agitation came to a crisis in the following year. Some change in the status of Agrippa took place in AD 6, recorded on a fragment of the *Fasti Ostienses*.[38] There is no evidence that it was for the better, the grant of a priesthood, for example. More probably the calendar records the first stage of Agrippa's disgrace, which Suetonius clearly states came in two parts, *abdicatio* (the severing of ties with the Julian family) and relegation to Surrentum, and, not much later, permanent exile under guard on Planasia, the island near Corsica, sanctioned by a *senatus consultum*; Dio adds that his property was confiscated.[39] Perhaps we can date the abdication more closely.

Towards the end of the year, reinforcements had to be sent to Pannonia, scraped together from freedmen and the theatrical claques. Velleius Paterculus conducted some of these levies into the field; he was quaestor designate at the time, having returned to Rome to embark on his political career earlier in the year. But civil duties went by the board in the crisis. The useful officer Velleius was exempted from the functions of the quaestorship and stayed to fight in Pannonia.[40] Near the beginning of AD 7, Germanicus followed him, taking further reinforcements; like Velleius, Germanicus remained in the field, beginning operations in the spring of 7. This in spite of holding a domestic magistracy, the quaestorship. Germanicus, says Dio, was a substitute for Agrippa. Evidently there had been a question of sending the latter to the war, perhaps as *tribunus militum*, or of offering him a quaestorship, but disgrace supervened. The abdication belongs to the autumn of the year 6.[41]

What had happened to bring about even the first stage of Agrippa's fall must have been grave. Abdication was the enforced emancipation of a son from his father's authority. Agrippa lost his rights to the property of Augustus after his death, and could be passed over in his will without voiding it; that is to say, in legal terminology he was no longer *suus*. As an *adoptatus abdicatus* (an adopted son who had suffered enforced emancipation), Agrippa was in a worse position than most boys who suffered this extreme penalty (and they cannot have been many): it reduced him to the status of an emancipated member of the *gens Vipsania*; in other words, he lost his all-important adoptive name of Agrippa Iulius Caesar.[42] This and the other consequences that flowed from abdication entailed his exclusion from the political inheritance of Augustus. Political advancement now was out of the question, unless Augustus relented and brought him back into the family. Again we see Augustus dealing with political blunders as if they were moral delicts. The pretext for the abdication was Agrippa's beastly nature, the *ferocia* (intractability) that was the normal justification of the penalty. Modern scholars, taken in as the Roman public was intended to be, have debated the nature of his disease, with schizophrenia winning distinguished support.[43] It was all a blind.

The agitation that Augustus checked by this drastic method should be discernible in the sources. Sure enough, Dio has a quite detailed account of a political scandal of the year 6, to which he attaches the name of one P. Rufus, and a 'conspiracy' of L. Paullus and Plautius Rufus is vouched for by Suetonius.[44]

Now the masses, distressed by the famine and the tax [it had been imposed to support the new military treasury] and the losses sustained in the fire, were ill at ease, and they not only openly discussed numerous plans for a revolution, but also posted at night even more numerous bulletins. Word was given out that all this had been planned and managed by one Publius Rufus, but suspicion was directed to others; for as Rufus could neither have devised nor accomplished any of these things, it was believed that others, making use of his name, were planning a revolution. Therefore an investigation of the affair was voted for and rewards for information were announced. Information began to be offered, and this also contributed to the commotion in the city. This lasted until the scarcity of grain was at an end and gladiatorial games in honour of Drusus were given by Germanicus Caesar and Ti. Claudius Nero, his sons. For this mark of honour to the memory of Drusus comforted the people, and also the dedication by Tiberius of the temple of Castor and Pollux, upon which he inscribed not only his own name . . . but also that of Drusus.

Dio does not say explicitly what the placards contained, but it is clear from the context: complaints about the war, the fire, floods, famine, and tax. 'Revolution' was in the air, but it is unlikely that Augustus himself was to go – only the men who now stood closest to him, primarily Tiberius. The Senate, under its pro-Tiberian consuls, was willing enough to do its duty and look for the real culprits; but Dio does not tell us who they turned out to be. Perhaps they were not exposed until the following year, which Dio treats very sketchily as far as home affairs are concerned. It is not hard to guess who they were: L. Paullus and his wife. The death of Paullus, and the possible relegation of Julia, followed by the repudiation of their daughter by Claudius and his betrothal to a girl whose father would be grateful for the connexion (L. Furius Camillus, the consul of AD 8) may be assigned to the last months of AD 6 or the early months of 7. Dio says that the agitation lasted until the games were held in Drusus' memory; probably on his birthday, and that seems to have been in March.[45] It will have been at the same time that the opening up of the seas after the winter made it possible for fresh supplies of corn to be brought in for the hungry populace.

This phase of the struggle for Agrippa's future ended in defeat for his relatives and friends, and had already brought disgrace on him as Augustus sought to check the agitation by removing Agrippa from the political arena altogether. Augustus failed there, and he failed when he executed L. Paullus or forced him to die. The survivors were undaunted and the intrigues went on. But there was a change. As the situation worsened for them, Agrippa's friends became more desperate and their methods deteriorated. Legitimate political techniques (however they had been handled by Augustus, that was what they were down to the agitation of Plautius Rufus) were displaced by conspiracy, libel, and high treason. As support in higher places fell away, men of a lower social position came to the fore as partisans of Agrippa, and in the end little was left of the group but members of the family and their dependents.

Agrippa, besides being confined to Surrentum and losing his membership of the Julian *gens*, had also lost to his adoptive father a considerable fortune inherited from M. Agrippa. Now, returned to the Vipsanii, he could use this fact against Augustus. Dio reports Agrippa's

complaints that Augustus had embezzled the money that should have
come to him from his father. Perhaps this was the content of the savage
attack on Augustus that was published by one Iunius Novatus in
Agrippa's name.[46]

It may have been at this stage that D. Iunius Silanus (a patron of
Novatus?) saw the opportunity for self-advancement. Julia was now
a widow. If her brother were rehabilitated (and there had been re-
versals of fortune in the house stranger than that), the position of her
consort could still be a fine one. What weapons the group thought
they had is hard to see, but some hopes they must have had, for we
are told that neither Agrippa's conduct nor that of his sister improved
after their disgrace. One of the signs of Agrippa's 'madness' that Dio
reports was that he spent his time fishing and took to calling himself
Neptune. This perhaps was an ironical reference to the victories of his
father M. Agrippa at sea (and we may remember that Sex. Pompeius
had also regarded himself as a protégé of that deity).[47] It was only
natural for Agrippa, deprived of his Julian paternity, to turn to his
natural father and see what could be made of him. Velleius places one
stage of Agrippa's disgrace towards the end of AD 7; that would be
the removal to Planasia. We can deduce agitation for his recall from
Surrentum, and reflect that one effective means of bringing about his
return would be to elect him to a magistracy – the consulship. That
technique had been used before with some success. It may have been
tried again in 7, which happens to be a year in which the elections
were so contentious that Augustus had to appoint all the magistrates
himself.[48] The consuls he lighted on were M. Furius Camillus and
Sex. Nonius Quinctilianus. As for the guard now imposed on Agrippa,
we can surmise that here had been unauthorized trips from Surrentum;
fishing trips, no doubt. But what did Agrippa hope to catch? His pas-
time may have taken him across the Bay of Naples to Misenum, precisely to the naval base that his natural father had founded.

Agrippa's removal to Planasia took place in 7, but that was not the
year of the younger Julia's final relegation. The sources imply the
year 8, as they imply it for Ovid's exile.[49] That Ovid was involved
in the punishment of Julia has usually been accepted, even when their
activities have not been seen from a political point of view (Julia has
often appeared as a nymphomaniac whom Ovid's teaching enabled
to outstrip her over-sexed mother). Ovid hints darkly that he could
have avoided his downfall if he had not associated with persons in high
places. The immorality charge which was brought against him was,
as usual, a smokescreen. The *Ars Amatoria* had been published nine

years when Augustus woke up to the threat it posed. That is why Ovid himself makes so much of the charge; it was the weak part of Augustus' case.[50] But there was an *error*, and a *culpa* too, a mistake, even misconduct; Ovid had seen something of which he failed to realize the true significance, and which he failed to report when he did. Ovid, we may believe, was privy to Julia's plans, whatever they were. Agrippa's advancement was the main plank in her policy. That now seemed impossible, legally at least. Julia could give up or turn to illegality, the removal of Agrippa from his island by trickery or force. Two such attempts are attested: one made by Agrippa's slave Clemens in AD 14, frustrated because Agrippa was killed before he could be rescued; and another, earlier, by L. Audasius, a person of ill repute who was on trial for forgery, and by Asinius Epicadus, descendant of a Balkan prisoner of war.[51] The date of that attempt is not known, and there is something wrong with Suetonius' account of it; he says that they intended to take Augustus' daughter Julia from her island as well as Agrippa, and rush them to the armies. But by the time Agrippa was sent to Planasia, Julia the elder had long been back on the mainland. Possibly Suetonius means Julia the younger, whose ultimate place of exile was the island of Trimerum off Apulia, but the omission of her mother from the plot is surprising: Julia the elder had more of the blood of Augustus in her than her children did. If Suetonius had simply forgotten that Julia had returned to the mainland, the attempt of Asinius and Epicadus may have been engineered by her daughter in AD 8.

To be effective in politics, a woman needed a husband, brother, or son to act for her. So the elder Julia had discovered, and so her daughter and granddaughter, the two Agrippinas, were to find. D. Silanus may have been the political ally and spokesman of the younger Julia, lover too, and perhaps even husband. One source says that they were married; and that marriage may have been the act that Ovid witnessed, without (so he claimed) realizing its significance. Silanus was denied the Princeps' friendship and knew that he had to leave Rome; Julia went off to her island, and the child she bore was not raised.[52] Ovid, like Silanus, avoided trial, but his destination was indicated to him: Tomis on the Black Sea outskirts of the Roman world. The allies of Agrippa were to be well apart. Doubtless it was his secure confinement, and Tiberius' successes in Pannonia, that made it possible for Augustus to be so mild.

The Pannonian insurgents surrendered on the Bathinus in AD 8, and probably when Tiberius entered Rome in the winter[53] a solemn ceremonial was devised. After mounting a tribunal in the packed Saepta in the Campus Martius and greeting Senate and people, he was conducted round the temples and up on to the Capitol, where he took his seat with Augustus between the consuls. In the summer of the following year came news that the Dalmatians had succumbed, and it was greeted with the award of a triumph. Titles commensurate with the services he had given were offered: Pannonicus, Invictus, Pius. They were not accepted; not because they were too great for the man they were designed to honour, but because Augustus knew that it could not be long before Tiberius bore a *cognomen* greater than any of these – his own.[54]

The triumph was put off by Tiberius himself. Almost as soon as Germanicus announced the end of the struggle in Dalmatia in Rome news came of the destruction in Germany of Varus and his three legions. The material loss was grave enough. It also meant the end of Augustus' plan to extend the frontier to the Elbe; and the blow to Roman pride and prestige was even more serious. In the last months of AD 9 the newly victorious Tiberius was needed on the Rhine as much to restore the broken reputation of Rome's generals as to re-organize the shaken survivors and to punish the rebels. These tasks were to last him through 10 and 11, culminating in the defiant celebration of Augustus' birthday, 23 September 11, in enemy territory.[55]

The winter of 9–10 had also seen Tiberius at Rome, and if he did not on this occasion also (or for the first time) make his solemn entry into the Saepta, he took the opportunity of dedicating the temple of Concord, on 16 January.[56] The cost of restoring the temple had been met from the spoils of the German wars, in which Nero Drusus had played his part as well as Tiberius, and the temple was dedicated in the name of both brothers. It was a symbol of the harmony in which they had lived, and the dedication was perhaps meant also to symbolize the end of the factional strife that had raged for the last two decades: Concord and conciliation were to prevail. If so, it was to prove a delusive hope.

To be sure, the way seemed clear. Tiberius' ostentatious display at the side of Augustus, and the acceleration of the careers of Germanicus and Drusus, announced in AD 9 on the occasion of the victory in Dalmatia,[57] must also be brought into connexion with the destruction of Agrippa's faction and his ambitions. As we have seen, Germanicus became quaestor in December of AD 6, perhaps taking the place of the abdicated Agrippa Postumus. He was twenty-one, and holding office exceptionally early, though not as early as his father and uncle had held it; nor was his adoptive brother Drusus Caesar given any extra-. ordinary advancement at this time.[58] The *ad hoc* arrangements of A D 6 were not regularized until after the victories in Pannonia and Dalmatia had been won. Then advancement for both Tiberius' sons became extraordinarily rapid, and they even omitted the praetorship altogether. Germanicus was given the *ornamenta triumphalia* and *praetoria*, the insignia of a triumphing general and of a man who had attained the praetorship, with the special privilege of giving his vote immediately after the ex-consuls. His consulate itself he held in A D 12, at the age of twenty-six. Drusus Caesar meanwhile was admitted at once to membership of the Senate and given the privilege of voting ahead of the ex-praetors as soon as he should become quaestor. Election to that office came in the following year (no doubt the news of the victories arrived after the elections of A D 9 had taken place); his consulship came in 15, three years after that of Germanicus, and also at the age of twenty-six. The collapse of the faction of Julia and Agrippa had finally made it possible to give the sons of Tiberius unusual, and equivalent, privileges. Tiberius' own proconsular *imperium* was still limited, probably to the Gauls or to provinces which he had occasion to enter. It was not until at the eventual celebration of the triumph, on 23 October A D 12, that all territorial limitation was removed.[59] A consular law of 13 made Tiberius' powers equal to those of Augustus, and provided that they should conduct a census together, using their consular *imperium*.[60] From now on Tiberius would always sit at Augustus' side between the consuls. But he never cared for consular *imperium*. When it came to summoning the Senate after Augustus' death Tiberius made a point of exercising his tribunician power, which had been renewed in 13.[61] The consular *imperium* had been granted to Augustus at a moment of defeat for the Senate, and its exercise inevitably infringed the prerogatives of the consuls proper.[62]

Gold coins struck at Lugdunum in the last year of Augustus' life display the Princeps' head on the obverse with the legend CAESAR AVGVSTVS DIVI F(ilius) PATER PATRIAE and Tiberius' on the reverse with TI. CAESAR AVG(usti) F(ilius) TR(ibunicia) POT(estate) XV. They recall the silver issued at Rome near the end of M. Agrippa's career, more than a quarter of a century before: Augustus' head on the obverse, with CAESAR AVGVSTVS, and Agrippa's on the reverse, wearing his naval crown, with the name of the moneyer.[63] It was only in 10 that Tiberius' portrait began to appear on coins at all and that he succumbed to the temptation which had overcome Caesar first of all the dynasts.[64] Now for the second time Augustus had succeeded in bringing his plans for the succession to full fruition; a colleague had reached the plenitude of power, and should survive to carry on the administration when the first Princeps died. In formal terms, the new arrangements left nothing to be desired. But legality was not all that mattered. The prospect of any succession at all created discontent among diehard senators, while the prospect of Tiberius' succession in particular made survivors of Julia's circle fear that their own ambitions would remain unsatisfied. That they could command strong support amongst the people had been shown on more than one occasion. As he lay dying Augustus expected news of rioting; Tiberius did not believe that the funeral would go quietly and felt unable to deprive Rome of a military commander by dispatching the Prefect of the Praetorian Guard, Seius Strabo, to help quell the mutiny in Pannonia that broke out after Augustus' death, in spite of the appointment in AD 13 of L. Piso the pontifex to the prefecture of the city.[65]

Nor was Augustus completely happy in his own mind. A doubt still lingered about Agrippa Postumus. In the last spring of his life, when it would be reasonable to believe him too feeble for the journey, the Princeps voyaged to Planasia to see his grandson.[66] The only man of standing to accompany him was Paullus Fabius Maximus. Tacitus' story has it that the meeting brought about tears and mutual protestations of affection, and that Fabius reported them to his wife Marcia, and she to Livia, who had known nothing of the journey, still less of an outcome so unfavourable to her son. When Fabius died not long afterwards, and just before Augustus, Marcia was heard to reproach herself at her husband's funeral for being the unwitting cause of his death. Dio's version even has Livia making away with Augustus to avoid the consequences of the visit. This last story is too functional to be accepted in its entirety: it shows Augustus and Agrippa reconciled, and the reconciliation brought to nothing by Livia. It is unlikely in the first place that Livia would have been unaware of her ailing husband's absence, or where he was. Nor can the reconciliation be accepted. Augustus made no alteration to the will, sealed on 3 April AD 13,[67] which contained no mention of the abdicated son: since cruel fortune (it was a conventional phrase) had torn his sons Gaius and Lucius from him, Tiberius was instituted heir to two-thirds of the estate, Livia to one-third. The details about the alleged suicide of Fabius and murder of Augustus were built on the coincidence of their deaths and added by way of ornament and corroboration. Are we to dismiss the whole story of the trip as Scribonian fiction? That too is unlikely. The Princeps was a public figure. The testimony of only a

few courtiers would be sufficient to refute a story of a round trip of
320 miles by sea from Ostia. Augustus made the journey, perhaps at
the instance of Fabius,[68] and a painful decision; we can accept the
story up to and including the tearful scene with Agrippa. But even as
he wept, Augustus was steeling himself to leave his grandson on
Planasia.

Perhaps he had to give an even harsher order. The 'first crime of the
new principate', as Tacitus calls the execution of Agrippa on his
island, took place almost at the same time as the death of Augustus in
August AD 14. When a centurion announced to him that 'his orders had
been carried out', Tiberius denied having given any such orders, and
asserted that those responsible would be called to account in the Senate.
But Tiberius did not speak on the subject in the House; he merely
issued a statement that his father had given orders that Agrippa was not
to survive him.[69]

That version did not win acceptance in ancient times. Livia is suggested as the main actor by Suetonius, while Tacitus and Dio put the
blame squarely on the shoulders of Tiberius. Tiberius of course
benefited; and, as Tacitus points out, Augustus had never before proceeded to the execution of a member of his own family. Modern
writers are divided. Augustus' confidential agent, the knight C. Sallustius Crispus, sent papers ('codicillos' in Tacitus) to the tribune on
Planasia, and with Livia is alleged to have dissuaded Tiberius from
having the matter out in the Senate. This has suggested, in ironical
fulfilment of Sallustius' fear of becoming a scapegoat, that he acted
on his own initiative, presumably forging the name of Tiberius on the
fatal document.[70] Yet, unlike some agents of the will of Elizabeth I,
he remained in favour, and what he personally had to gain by hasten-
ing the execution is not clear. Without his complicity there was little
that Livia could do, and nothing but malicious tittle-tattle, of the kind
that made her responsible for the death of the husband who died in
her arms, connects her with the execution. Tiberius too must be
acquitted. If he gave the order it was incredibly careless to have its
accomplishment reported to him before witnesses. We should accept
his account, regarding the *codicilli* either as the actual writ of execution,
which Augustus had left in charge of Crispus or, more probably, as
the paper which took news of Augustus' death to Planasia and brought
automatically into effect the instructions that Augustus (tempering
expediency with as much mercy as he could afford) had already sent
to the island, or left there in the spring.

Augustus' ruthless precautions were not unjustified. As soon as his death became known, a slave who had once belonged to Agrippa (who would have passed to Augustus when Agrippa was abdicated and his property confiscated) made for Planasia with the idea of conveying the prisoner to the German armies. But he travelled on a merchantman and arrived after the execution had taken place.[71] If this last scheme for a coup in Agrippa's favour is borne in mind, Augustus' instructions to the guard on Planasia, especially if they were issued not long before his death, become easier to understand and to forgive. Tacitus and Suetonius write as if Clemens acted on his own initiative. As we shall see, that is not likely; he probably had patrons in high places. When, two years later, the next plan that Clemens formed came to fruition, and he and his accomplices were ripe for arrest, it was the Augustan Walsingham, Sallustius Crispus, whose diligence made it possible to take them into custody. He may have investigated the earlier plot, and reported it to the Princeps. Knowing that the news of his death might trigger off an attempt to rescue Agrippa, Augustus signed a provisional death warrant, to be brought into effect if there were any indication of such an attempt. The alternative, as we shall see, was to arrest, perhaps without proof, a man of family and distinction, whose trial would cause scandal, disturbing the transfer of power that all knew to be imminent.[72]

The struggle between Tiberius and the descendants of Scribonia has not taken more space than its vital importance demands. In its first phase it blighted ten years of Tiberius' life, removing him from politics and war and the opportunities of enhancing his own reputation and influence. It troubled the years of his second ascendancy, undermining the basis of his power at home while he was kept abroad by two successive military crises, and damaging his reputation with the public even as his opponents were worsted. The danger itself was to last into his reign, and the ill-repute that the downfall and death of Agrippa earned him multiplied as other aspirants to power from the descent of Augustus and Scribonia came to grief. Worst of all, the history of the age came to be written largely in their favour (in spite of the disappointment of Gaius Caligula's four-year reign) and not without reference to the memoirs of one of their posterity, Agrippina the younger.[73]

It is impossible now to discern the part played by Tiberius himself in the defeat of his opponents in the period before he came to sole power. Self-defeating pride is manifest in 6 BC, giving place to abnegation (but that could hide the bitterest of resentments). When he came to power again Tiberius insisted, justifiably, on reinstatement to his previous position; but he may also have insisted on slow advancement for Agrippa Postumus, fanning the suspicions that had caused the crisis of 6 BC. He was away from Rome for long periods between 4 and 12, and it was hard, but not impossible, for him to give powerful advice as the political crises arose.[74] But although his role during these years may have been a darker one than that which he had played before the Rhodian exile (and it would not be surprising if his attitude had hardened), no evidence at hand can convict him of disreputable conduct.

CHAPTER V

THE 'ACCESSION' OF TIBERIUS

With the celebration of the triumph, the extension of Tiberius' *imperium* to equality with that of Augustus, and the sealing of the will, the formal preparations for Tiberius' takeover were complete; and the partnership of the two *principes* was shown in action when they used their consular powers to carry out a census together. The ceremonies were completed in May AD 14. Augustus still had a few months to live. Some of his precious days were spent on the arduous trip to Planasia, but high summer found him in Campania. He spent four days holidaying on Capri, then crossed to the mainland to attend a quinquennial gymnastic festival that was being held at Neapolis in his honour (1 August). Tiberius was with him, but there was work to be done in Illyricum and one reason for leaving Capri had been Augustus' desire to accompany Tiberius for part of the way (thereby perhaps silencing rumours about the possible rehabilitation of Agrippa Postumus and showing that there was no rift between himself and his heir). Augustus was already ill with an intestinal complaint, but he reached Beneventum with Tiberius and there they parted. It is not certain whether Tiberius saw Augustus alive again or not; accounts differ.[1] But although Velleius' tale of Augustus rallying at the sight of Tiberius and surviving long enough to give him the charisma of his blessing is suspiciously uplifting, it is categorical; and while Velleius might rhapsodize over the details of the scene, he would hardly have invented it altogether. He has the agreement of Suetonius, who gives the two men a whole day together and Augustus a tart comment on his heir after he had left the bedside: 'Poor Roman people, to be ground in such relentless jaws.' This part of the story, and the version of the 'superior' writers mentioned by Dio who held that Augustus was dead before Tiberius could return from Illyricum, and that Livia concealed his death until her son was on the spot and at the centre of power, emanated ultimately from later sources that were out to show Tiberius as an heir unwelcome or even supposititious.

The time of death was given out, probably after a few hours' delay, as 6 p.m., 19 August. Tiberius cannot have slept that night. There was much to be done: messages to be sent to Rome, to all the armies and the provinces of the Empire, to friends and supporters; and the pomp of the funeral to set in motion. The ceremonies had been planned

long before by Augustus himself, with the solicitude that the great
sometimes have for their last appearance on the stage. Sulla certainly
had displayed it, and his funeral, with that of Caesar, was what Augustus had studied; there had already been two runs through – the funerals
of Agrippa and Drusus. It was not mere vanity. The more honour
shown to a dead statesman, the better for his political heirs. Caesar's
funeral had ended in confusion; Sulla's was the real model, and since
Sulla, too, had died away from Rome (at Cumae), it gave scope for
additional ceremony. Sulla's funeral proper had been preceded by a
stately procession through Italy; so too the funeral of Drusus and presumably that of Agrippa. This time, however, it was to be not soldiers
but civilians who supported the bier: the magistrates of the *coloniae* and
municipia, the country towns, that lay between Nola and Rome were
to take their turn in the relay, moving at night and laying up the
coffin by day in the town hall of each city, or in its principal temple.
Tiberius assigned himself an arduous part, but one less arduous, and
less harrowing, than the similar role that he had sustained in 9 BC:
he was to march behind the coffin all the way. An edict announcing
this was published at Rome, excusing the fact that Tiberius could not
leave his father and, in virtue of the tribunician power (for Tiberius
did not wish to infringe or diminish the prerogatives of the consuls),
summoning the Senate to meet on the day after the body arrived at
Rome. Here again the dead Princeps was to claim all attention; there
was only one item on the agenda: the detailed arrangements for his
funeral.[2]

The chronology of the eight weeks or so that followed Augustus'
death is of vital importance as the framework within which Tiberius'
confirmation in power must be placed. Several dates besides 17 September, the day of Augustus' official consecration, have been suggested
by writers ancient and modern for Tiberius' acceptance of the Principate, some so late (13 October) as to require explanation in terms of
delay caused by the mutinies that broke out amongst the Pannonian
and Rhine legions, others so early (3 September) as to verge on the
indecent.[3]

A rapid chronology may be rejected at once. The date of the arrival
of Augustus' body in Rome, and so of the first meeting of the Senate,
can be calculated with confidence. It was 4 September, too late for the
discussion about the future of the *respublica* at the second meeting to
have taken place before the date implied by Tacitus – 17 September. The
cortège passed through the *coloniae* and *municipia* of Suessula, Calatia,
Capua, Casilinum, Urbana, Sinuessa, Minturnae, Formiae, Fundi, Tar-

racina, Tres Tabernae (not a chartered town, but a necessary resting
place), Aricia, and Bovillae. At that *municipium* Roman knights were
to take up the burden and convey the coffin into Rome. However
well planned the arrangements were, the cortège can hardly have set
off less than twenty-four hours after the Princeps' death. Even if the
body were going in a closed coffin (and Dio tells us that at the funeral
proper only an effigy was visible), it was probably partially embalmed
before it left Nola. Suessula would be reached on the morning of
21 August, and so on, until the procession entered Bovillae on the
morning of 2 September.[4] Tiberius now probably went ahead into
Rome; the body was conveyed into the city on the night of 2–3 September, perhaps early in the morning of the 3rd. On the following
day, 4 September, the Senate duly met for the sole purpose of hearing
the will read and discussing arrangements for the remaining and central
ceremonies: lying in state, cremation, insertion of the bones into the
mausoleum long prepared for them. It fell to Tiberius to deliver a
preliminary oration. He was unable to perform it, broke down, and
handed over his text to his son Drusus Caesar. Public displays of grief
were not in Tiberius' style. He must have been worn out physically
by the dash from Illyricum and the long, slow march from Nola,
mentally by the strain that the political situation imposed upon him;
now in the Senate he must be aware, perhaps for the first time, that
from second place he had moved into first, and that he was on his
own.

Later parallels suggest[5] that there were four clear days between the
entry into Rome and the cremation. Augustus' funeral should have
taken place on 8 September. As Augustus' son, Tiberius continued to
play a leading part in the imposing ritual; it fell to him to deliver a
laudation from the Julian rostra, while Drusus Caesar, the grandson
who was present at Rome, spoke from another platform. As the pyre
blazed on the Campus Martius, an eagle was released from it and
soared upwards, demonstrating that the late Princeps had become one
of the immortals. His bones, however, had to be extracted from the
pyre, gathered together, and wept over. Livia, now in her early
seventies, watched over them for five days, attended by Roman
knights. With their insertion into the mausoleum the *iustitium* (period
of mourning) imposed by the Senate came to an end, and business
could be resumed again. It was now 14 September, and the Senate
met again on the 17th. Its first duty was to declare the late Princeps
a god; its next to discuss matters of state, for the first time since
Augustus died, and in the presence of his successor.

The lapse of nearly a month between the death of Augustus and this debate accords well with the impression given by the ancient sources that Tiberius was dilatory in accepting his new position. It fits, but it is not enough to account for that impression, which Tacitus, Dio, and Suetonius reinforce by describing the awkward exchanges between the members of the Senate and the apparently reluctant Princeps. The unhurried gravity of the proceedings between 19 August and 17 September may be borne in mind, but the debate still remains to be interpreted. The ancient writers were not backward in offering their own explanations. For Tacitus, caution and cunning were behind the Princeps' hesitation: Tiberius wanted to force the Senate into committing itself to him, and to appear as their freely chosen candidate. The version of Dio and Suetonius has won less approval. For them, Tiberius' chief motive was fear, whether of armies in revolt alone or of conspiracy at home as well. For when the armies of Pannonia and the Rhine heard the news of Augustus' death, unrest began. In Pannonia three legions under the command of Q. Iunius Blaesus broke out into revolt, and on the Rhine four, stationed in summer quarters amongst the Ubii under A. Caecina Severus. Their real and declared objects were to increase pay and bounties, improve their conditions, and shorten the length of their service, but on the Rhine there was an idea of declaring in favour of the commander-in-chief, Germanicus.[6] That idea did not get far, but in the view of Dio and Suetonius, Tiberius was afraid to take power until he knew the outcome of these mutinies. It must be said at once that the picture was never a convincing one. Tiberius' only chance of power, even of life, if he was in danger, lay in speed and decisiveness. Refusal of empire would never have saved him. Experience should have told him that: even as an exile on Rhodes, with the succession assured to Gaius Caesar, he had been thought too dangerous to live. Besides, Tiberius was a soldier; he knew that he should seize the initiative and deal any opposition a swift and crushing blow before it grew too strong. Perhaps we are to conclude from this that Tiberius was unaware that the Rhine and Pannonian legions were in revolt until after the debate of 17 September, and that his reaction was swift: the immediate dispatch of his son Drusus Caesar to Pannonia with L. Aelius Sejanus, a detachment of the Praetorian Guard and cavalry, and some leading men to keep him company. But that will not do. For one thing Tiberius seems to have continued to bandy words with the Senate about his constitutional position after 17 September, and after the news of the mutinies had become known.[7] The claim of Suetonius and Dio, that Tiberius accepted the Principate only after the danger had passed, implies that he went on hesitating until after they were over – and so it becomes a matter of some importance to discover how long they continued. Besides, Drusus' massive escort, which included at least one senior consular, cannot have taken only nine days to travel the 467 Roman miles that separated Rome from the legions near Emona in Pannonia, even if the party could have been got together in time to leave Rome on the morning after the debate. For Drusus arrived at the legionary camp on 26 September and with the help of an eclipse of the moon that took place that very night terrorized the mutineers into surrender. The party left Rome before the debate, and if Tacitus really means us to believe that Drusus attended it, he must have sped after the party once the debate was adjourned and overtaken them at a rendezvous near the legionary camp.[8] Tiberius certainly knew of the Pannonian mutiny before the debate, probably before the cremation, and possibly before he ever reached Rome with the cortège.

News of Augustus' death should have arrived at Rome (147 Roman miles distant from Nola) by the evening of 20 August. From there it will have travelled to the provincial governors with all the speed of bad news, and if the courier kept up a rate of 150 Roman miles a day, Q. Iunius Blaesus will have been informed by midday on 25 August. A *iustitium* ensued, and it was this enforced idleness that gave the men time to think about their grievances. The weakness of any chronology is that we can only guess about the length of time that it took for the mutinies to develop. But in Pannonia it cannot have taken long; Dio says that the soldiers mutinied as soon as they heard the news. If we allow three days for trouble to start and to become so serious that it had to be reported at Rome, the first news of it will have arrived in the city after midday on 2 September. Tiberius by now was resting at Bovillae, only eleven Roman miles away. By nightfall he knew what had happened. This first message was not the last, nor was it the worst. We do not know which of them prompted Tiberius to send Drusus Caesar and the Praetorians. Perhaps even the first, if it was carried by the *tribunus militum* Blaesus' son, a cousin of the new Princeps' friend Aelius Sejanus. The messenger was not to know that his departure was the signal for a remission in the mutiny. After a night of reflection Tiberius could have given the Praetorians the order to march in Rome on 3 September.

As we have seen, Drusus Caesar may not have left with the troops; he had his functions to perform in the Senate on the 4th and at the cremation on the 8th, and he may even have been present in the

Senate on the 17th. Hence a double need for the presence in Pannonia of the Praetorian commander with his troops. But the prefect L. Seius Strabo was not sent. He too was needed at Rome at this juncture. Instead his son was associated with him in the prefecture (it could be done by the stroke of a pen, unlike a grant of proconsular *imperium*) and dispatched at the head of the troops. Drusus Caesar, like his distinguished senatorial companions, had no official standing; but his presence would recall the legions to their loyalties by bringing to mind their old commander, now the new Princeps.

On the morning after the eclipse, Drusus Caesar harangued the troops and a further delegation was sent to Tiberius with the requests of the soldiers, this time a party of three of which young Blaesus was one. Their return could be expected in nineteen days at the earliest (even that would not allow Tiberius time to consult the Senate) and Drusus did not wait for it. After seeing the ringleaders summarily punished he stayed only until the legions dispersed to their winter quarters (a period of torrential rain had added to their guilt and fear). It took some little while. The ninth legion was the last to go, and not without hesitation. Drusus could not have left for Rome before the beginning of October.

Much more serious, because more widespread and longer lasting, were the mutinies on the Rhine. Tacitus tells us that they broke out at about the same time as the Pannonian disturbances, but they may have been a few more days getting under way. Not only do the sources take the Pannonian mutiny first (that may be because it ended more quickly) but we hear of no outstanding ringleaders on the Rhine; the movement seems to have been a more general one and may have taken longer to gather momentum. In any case the news of Augustus' death cannot have reached the summer camp of the Lower Rhine legions in the territory of the Ubii until about 27 August: it had about a thousand Roman miles to travel. News of the outbreaks would be correspondingly slow to reach Rome. Not only that: Germanicus was not even with his army when the mutiny began. He was amongst the Sequani and Belgae, administering the oath of loyalty to the new Princeps, and would have returned to camp before dispatching the news to Rome. Tacitus himself hints that nothing was known of the outbreaks on the Rhine until measures had been taken to deal with the Pannonian mutiny and until after at least one debate on the succession.[9] Germanicus quieted the first outbreaks by making concessions and was able to set out for the armies of the Upper Rhine to exact the oath of loyalty to Tiberius; the soldiers at Moguntiacum gave him pause, but those of Vindonissa were quiet enough. By late September Germanicus was back in camp amongst the Ubii, and it was there that a delegation from the Roman Senate found him. These men, led by L. Plancus, the consul of AD 13, were the distinguished senators who had been instructed on 17 September to convey to Germanicus not only the condolences of the Senate on the death of his grandfather, but also the more agreeable news that it had voted him the proconsular *imperium*. The despatch of the embassy is strong evidence that Rome knew nothing of the Rhine mutiny on 17 September. It would be strange to send these men on an errand which was, after all, not vital, to a general known to be dealing with a dangerous mob of mutineers.

The delegation from the Senate were not acting as couriers, and they were carrying good but not urgent news. No pace more rapid than fifty Roman miles a day could be expected of them, and they can hardly have arrived in Germanicus' camp before 7 October. When they did come it was the immediate signal for a further outbreak, which raged on into the night of their arrival. On the following day Germanicus hurried them to safety and (after long deliberation) showed his men what he thought of them by sending his wife away as well. Agrippina could have made her ostentatious and effective exit from the camp as early as 9 October. If we are to believe Tacitus, chagrin at the sight of the general's wife being sent to bear her child amongst a foreign tribe swept the legionaries into remorse and fury against their leaders in revolt. In the summer camp the mutiny could have been over by 11 October. Sixty miles down river there was still unrest at Vetera, the winter quarters into which two of the mutinous legions had been taken by Caecina. Germanicus assembled his forces (about 12–14 October?) and sent a message to the beleaguered legate to say that he was on his way. It could have arrived the same evening (15th?); and the loyalists at Vetera would have acted at once against the mutineers, if only to secure their own safety when Germanicus arrived. But Germanicus probably lingered a day or two, to allow time for his message to take effect. If he and his forces set out down the Rhine on the 17th, they would have arrived at Vetera on the 19th. They found the carnage over. There was nothing for Germanicus to do but weep over the unburied corpses and order their cremation. A short campaign in Germany followed, to wipe away the memory of the mutiny and the bloody retribution that followed it.

If Suetonius and Dio are right in making the end of the mutinies coincide with Tiberius' accession to power, that event should be put in mid-October. Josephus in one place even gives us a firm date, 13 October,[10] that is very near to the second regular Senate meeting of the month, on the Ides (15th): but if anything did happen in the Senate on the Ides of October to justify Josephus' view that Tiberius then assumed the Principate, it cannot have happened *because* the mutinies were over. The slaughter at Vetera came too late to be known at Rome on the Ides, still less on the 13th. The end of the mutinies may have *coincided* with Tiberius' assumption of power, but it did not make it possible. The mutinies, as we already suspected, were not the cause of Tiberius' hesitation.

The true explanation must be sought elsewhere, and it will not be found unless we are willing first to face the question, what essential powers remained to be conferred in August A D 14, to make Tiberius Princeps. The answer is none, for the very reason that Augustus had spent some years ensuring that there should be none and at last had been able to complete plans in favour of a man who, unlike M. Agrippa, survived him. In August 14, Tiberius was in his sixteenth year of tribunician power; he was *collega imperii*, Augustus' colleague, in the full sense: his *imperium* over the provinces was equal to that of Augustus and greater than that of the proconsuls; his *imperium*, like that of Augustus, extended into Rome, where it was equal to that of the consuls; these were the essentials. As for *auctoritas*, prestige and influence, he was already a Iulius Caesar, the senatorial decree of 17 September was to make him *Divi filius*, son of the deified Princeps, and the will imposed the title Augustus.[11] True he was not Pontifex Maximus (that did not come until 10 March A D 15[12]), nor had he been voted the title *pater patriae*, but neither of these positions had been accorded Augustus until well on in his principate and neither was of the essence of power. Hence perverse or despairing views: Tiberius' powers lapsed on Augustus' death, required redefinition, or were surrendered on 17 September.[13] There is no evidence for any of these suggestions, and the first two involve constitutional anomalies. More plausibly some modern scholars have taken their picture from Tacitus, lightening or removing the tint of hypocrisy, and have evolved theories of the type propounded by E. Hohl: Tiberius was seeking, or was trying to extort, the moral sanction of the Senate for his regime; he wanted to know, or he wanted it to seem, that he enjoyed their support.[14] Or (with Béranger) formality had already taken over. A decent papal reluctance was required of the Princeps, and it was all a matter of etiquette.[15] None of these views is really satisfactory. As Tacitus saw, for a man genuinely uncertain whether or not to accede to empire, Tiberius had loaded the dice rather heavily, while in the role of hypocrite he is too reckless: a day should have been enough for the whole farce. Yet it went on, causing bewilderment and irritation, so that the subordinate players began to forget, or to lose patience with, their roles. 'Let him get on with it,' cried one, 'or leave it alone.'[16] But this exclamation gives the game away: it reveals that it was up to Tiberius whether he 'got on with it' or not. By asking what Tiberius was 'hesitating' to do, when his *dies imperii*, the day of his accession, was, or when he took over the Principate, we have been begging the very question we are asking by defining it as a question of a certain kind. For Tiberius was not hesitating to do anything, however later historians saw his behaviour; he was seeking to define the meaning of his powers. It was not only the possession of *imperium* that mattered, but what one did with it. Hence the declarations of intent made by later Principes such as Nero who, in his own accession speech, promised to use his powers not to dominate but to guard the state.[17] This is not the first time that a solution in terms of reinterpretation and redefinition has been offered. G. Kampff holds that Tiberius planned to relieve the Princeps of the bulk of his executive and administrative work, leaving his actual supremacy unaffected – and guaranteed for life.[18] Such a scheme would have been unthinkable for the Principate at this early stage of its development. The comments that Tiberius made in the course of the debate about the crushing burdens imposed on the Princeps (like the dilatoriness that overcame him later in his principate) favour Kampff's view, but they must be explained in another way: up to that time Tiberius had never shown himself a man to neglect his work. If in September AD 14 he said that the weight of empire was too great for any one man (except the divine Augustus) to bear, it was not so much because he consciously shrank from those burdens, as burdens, but because he sought a way of redefining the Principate without denigrating his predecessor. We have already seen that a politician very close to the imperial family had occasion just at the time of the accession to deliver a warning against destroying the essence of the Principate by referring everything to the Senate.[19] What we have in the 'succession' debate is not a refusal of fresh powers, not an abortive or staged attempt to resign established powers only recently renewed or conferred, but Tiberius' attempt to deny the implication that such powers necessarily made a man Princeps in the sense that they imposed on him responsibility for guiding the Empire and shaping policy; it is a rejection of the 'regendi cuncta onus'[20] and a request for help from the numerous distinguished men in the state. They should not refer everything to one

man, but take responsibility themselves. That is the theme of the
speech reported by Tacitus. Naturally it was marred by obscurity,
which Tacitus has darkened still further through his own failure to
understand its import. For clarity would have exposed not only
Tiberius' own political convictions (no harm in that) but thereby his
high-minded view, so galling to his defeated political opponents, that
the principate of the deified Augustus had been subtle tyranny, and
his own intention, even more galling, to change it and play a lesser
part in government. The point had to be disguised as a discourse
on the magnitude of the Empire and his own inadequacy (probably
genuinely felt, and perhaps real). Bolstering his case, he brought out
the *libellus* (memorandum) that Augustus himself had drawn up on
the subject of the Empire. He would do his part, whatever it was that
was entrusted to him by the Senate.[21] Not all the senators even understood what Tiberius meant; some thought it was all show; others,
who knew the man, did not care for what he was proposing, or thought
it impracticable. The realistic and ambitious C. Asinius Gallus was one
of these.[22] What Tiberius wanted was impossible because power was
indivisible. Once gathered into one pair of hands it could not be re-
distributed throughout the body politic; the sway of the Princeps extended far beyond his legal prerogatives and it was useless to pretend
that it did not. What part, he accordingly demanded, did Tiberius
wish to take? Tiberius was taken aback. If he understood Gallus' purpose, which was to force him to admit that responsibility for decision-
making rested with the Princeps, distaste for his position prevented
him from accepting the implication; but he may have missed Gallus'
irony and thought that he really was being invited to choose some
sphere or department of government in which he should be supreme –
a complete distortion of his proposal. Hence his reply, a comment on
the impropriety of refusing the whole and accepting a part (the choice
of a part implying supremacy over the whole). Gallus had to go on,
and spell out what he meant: 'the body politic of the state was a single
entity, and must be ruled by one man's will'. The same idea was put
more bluntly by a man less subtle than Gallus but equally anxious to
preserve the prerogatives of a dynasty with which he to was connected through intermarriage with the family of Agrippa: Q. Haterius.[23]
'How long, Caesar, will you allow the Republic to remain without
a head?' he asked, and felt the lash of the Princeps' tongue. It was the
first time that Tiberius found himself betraying his own principles:
the senator Haterius was choosing to be subservient; the senator
Tiberius tried to force him to be free. The passage of arms left him

only one course, and one means of directing men like Haterius into
a sense of their responsibilities as senators: he apologized for his sharp-
ness; he had been speaking to a senator with a senator's freedom. Then,
turning to the House as a whole, he gave a clear statement of his position:
it was his view (which they were not hearing for the first time) that a
right-minded, serviceable Princeps, whom they had invested with vast
and unrestricted powers, ought to be the servant of the Senate, often of
the whole citizen body, and even sometimes of individual members of
it. He had no regrets at having expressed this view, because he had always
found them right-minded and well-disposed masters.

If we adopt this view of the debate it comes as no surprise that
Tacitus' account of Tiberius' eventual 'acceptance of the Principate' –
a fuller and more ambitious account than that of Suetonius and Dio –
is couched in negative terms. 'Worn out by the general clamour and
the remonstrances of individuals, he gave way gradually, not to the
point of admitting that he was taking up the *imperium*, but so that he
ceased to be importuned and to refuse.'[24] The debate petered out, and
Tiberius stopped protesting that he was not going to be Princeps as
Augustus had been, that he was not stepping into Augustus' shoes. He
had failed to get the senators to acknowledge that the burden of government lay ultimately on them and so he seemed tacitly to accept the
responsibility that they had fallen on their knees to avoid.

On the view put forward here, there was no act on the part of the
Senate that could make Tiberius Princeps. Whether, in Velleius' terms,
he became '*eminens princeps*' or remained '*aequalis civis*'[25] would be determined by his own behaviour and that of the Senate; at the end of
the debate he must have had to content himself with a private resolve
to educate his peers into their responsibilities. But a difficulty arises.
There was a resolution before the Senate at its meeting of 17 September, a *relatio consulum* (motion introduced by the consuls) which
Tiberius might have vetoed, but did not; he was thanked for his forbearance by Mam. Aemilius Scaurus.[26] What can have been the content
of the motion before the Senate?

The clue is given by Velleius Paterculus. In his account, which is
in full accord with the view taken here, what Senate and people were
struggling for was that Tiberius should succeed to his father's post:
'*stationi paternae succederet*'. The word *statio* we have met before in
Augustus' letter to Gaius Caesar: he and Lucius were then to be successors to the *statio*, the post occupied by their adoptive father. The
word was current in the political vocabulary of the time,[27] and the
Senate, turning from the melancholy grandeur of the ceremony of

deifying a dead Princeps and looking for words calculated to please his survivor, will have expressed its pleasure at the prospect of Tiberius' taking up the *statio* of his father; and probably, too, it declared its hope that he would occupy it for many years to come: '*versae inde ad Tiberium preces*'.

The motion was complimentary and formal, and should have passed without division or debate. If that was its nature, the wording may not have been known to Tiberius beforehand, indeed it can hardly have been known to him if it was to perform its complimentary function; it would be its promulgation in the Senate that caused the sudden dispute. For the sensitive Tiberius ('*suspicax animus*' is Tacitus' phrase) the words '*paterna statio*' would be a stumbling block in themselves, with their implication that he was to take over the position of Augustus unaltered and play an identical role in the state. Nor is it difficult to think of words that may have featured in the resolution and which, because more specific, would be even more offensive.[28] A word of *auctoritas* (influence) in the *relatio*, or the suggestion that he might *gubernare* (govern) – a word used of Augustus by Vitruvius in his preface – would certainly have been taken amiss. Tacitus' language suggests that it was lost sight of in the debate, which is not surprising if it was a compliment which had failed to please. The agenda that Tacitus gives for the day of the debate is impossibly long, and it is quite clear that some of the events he describes, notably the praetorian elections and arrangements for the *ludi Augustales*, the games given in Augustus' memory, belong to later sessions. Pursuing events in the Senate, perhaps with the aid of its minutes, Tacitus has telescoped them.[29] It is more than probable, when we consider the late accession dates implied by Suetonius, Dio, Josephus, and Egyptian documents,[30] that discussion continued at the next regular meeting of the Senate, or *senatus legitimus* (careerists thinking that they would build up credit by continuing the pressure, anxious partisans fearing loss of control by the dynasty), on 1 October and even later, on 15 October.

On this view, the problem of Tiberius' *dies imperii* and the date he 'took over' the Principate dissolves. He had no *dies imperii*, except in the sense that Augustus' death left him alone in a position of overwhelming strength, guaranteed by his official powers, *imperium* and *potestas*, and confirmed by his personal relationship to the dead Princeps. Historians writing a century or more later naturally thought in terms of a *dies imperii*. It was legitimate for their own time, when the Principate was entrenched and measurable *lacunae* between the reign of an emperor and his successor could be tolerated. Looking for a decisive point in AD 14 that they could regard as the start of the reign, some found it in the day Augustus died, some in the day on which, they believed, Tiberius' protestations ended and he accepted responsibility for guiding the state. The near synchronism of that occasion with the end of the mutinies gave some historians the explanation of Tiberius' extraordinary conduct. If they had paid attention to Tiberius' slow march to Rome behind the coffin, they would not have believed that he was in fear of the armies; if they had asked themselves what powers he lacked in AD 14 they would not have thought that he was 'hesitating' to take any action whatsoever; and they would have seen that in putting forward their *relatio* the consuls were performing an action that was both unnecessary and distasteful to the new Princeps. The desire to do something when there was nothing to be done led the consuls to take a false step; but it is a desire that can easily be understood in formal and in political terms. Under the leadership of the consuls Sex. Pompeius and Sex. Appuleius and of the equestrian prefects L. Strabo and C. Turranius, senators and knights alike had already shown anxiety to demonstrate their loyalty by taking an oath to the absent Tiberius almost immediately after Augustus' death. We cannot be sure, but both the mass oath-taking and the motion that came before the House on 17 September may have been prompted by nervous fear of the discontent and unrest that are implicit in Velleius' dramatic account of the transfer of power and are strongly suggested by certain actions of the new Princeps.[31]

If the problem of Tiberius' 'hesitation to accept the Principate' can be dissolved, that does not deprive the events of autumn, AD 14, of their significance both in the history of the Principate and in the principate of Tiberius himself. Augustus, in 27, 23, and 19 BC, had acquired with the consent of the Senate unique powers that made it natural for him gradually to be recognized as a Princeps superior to other *principes viri*, leading men in the state. Tiberius in AD 14 was in possession of almost identical powers and soon after Augustus' death was forced tacitly to acknowledge that they made him too Princeps; by AD 21 he was openly and explicitly recognizing his position and the obligations it imposed on him to take a lead and set a tone.[32] So it was natural for Gaius Caligula to become Princeps when the Senate, following the cogent example of the Praetorian Guard, recognized him as such and conferred on him the powers held by Augustus and Tiberius; grant of powers and accession to the Principate coincide for the first time: it is the beginning of the *dies imperii*. Claudius, like Vespasian after him, became Princeps in spite of the Senate, extorting recognition and a grant of powers: Vespasian made the situation explicit by backdating his *tribunicia potestas* and his *dies imperii* nearly six months to the date of his proclamation by the army in Egypt. Principate was almost emancipated from *imperia* and *potestates*. It is ironical that it fell to a man of Tiberius' convictions to open the way to legitimizing and institutionalizing the new monarchy, even more ironical that in doing so he was bowing to the wishes of the Senate.

To Tiberius himself the debate revealed difficulties which he would have to face throughout his principate. First, it exposed the difficulty of convincing men that it was possible (and that he desired) to hold the powers that Augustus had held without exercising them in such a way as to seize the political initiative. Second, it presented him with the problem of altering the system that had been developed by the man to whose efforts he owed his own supremacy, and whose consecration had just made him *Divi filius*. Third, it showed him that his own political principles must prevent him from forcing senators to play a part they were unwilling or frightened to play. He knew too, that they were not all as well disposed towards him as he had said, and that he had worse things to fear than embarrassing attempts to enhance his powers. All in all, it was not a bright outlook.

CHAPTER VI

THE POLICY OF THE PRINCEPS

It would be misguided to expect marked changes in the government of Rome, Italy, and the Empire to become discernible with the accession of the new ruler. The deification of Augustus gave Tiberius immense political advantages;[1] like Octavian himself when Julius Caesar was consecrated in 42 BC, he became *Divi filius*, the son of a divinity. Forty years later again, in AD 54, young Nero's advisers procured the deification of Claudius – and wrote their protégé an accession speech in which he renounced the most objectionable features of Claudius' reign: it was perfectly understood that the new Princeps, for his own sake, had to sanction his adoptive father's deification. But the apotheosis of Augustus was different: the genuine and long-recognized merits of the old ruler were as much a consideration as the needs of the new. That fact imposed restrictions on the political and administrative activities of the man who had presided over the Senate's consecration of Augustus. The Senate swore allegiance to Augustus' acts (one member who failed to do so lost his seat), and the obligation rested most heavily of all on Augustus' heir.[2] Repeatedly Tiberius declared his intention of maintaining one or other Augustan precedent or institution. It was a principle with him – no doubt one that was sometimes convenient to cite.[3] The coinage proclaimed the same message, by continuing Augustan types or by issuing gold coins with reverses that bore Augustus' portrait and the legend DIVOS AVGVST(us) DIVI F(ilius) and copper displaying his radiate head within the majestic legend DIVVS AVGVSTVS PATER.[4]

We need not doubt that Tiberius' devotion was genuine. Augustus was a great man; and if Tiberius was a Stoic, there was room in his philosophy for the new cult.[5] Besides, there was a personal debt of gratitude, and affection despite political differences.[6] Tiberius owed Augustus forty years of political and military advancement, to the Principate itself. It is not surprising to find him paying public tribute in his speeches and constructing a temple and other monuments in Augustus' honour and in honour of the whole Julian house; more significant is the fact that twelve years after he came to power he can be found sacrificing to Augustus apparently in private.[7]

The restrictions imposed on Tiberius by Augustan precedent may not have been as serious as they seem at first glance. True, there were

not only the acts of the Princeps to consider but the political testament
in which Augustus bequeathed his survivors specific and detailed advice.
Yet, of the policies it advocated, one, the restriction of the Empire
within its existing limits, seems to have been in accord with Tiberius'
own inclinations, and another, the plan to transfer elections to the
Senate, was certainly to his advantage.[8] Moreover, Tiberius had been
in the innermost circle of power, on and off, for a quarter of a century.
His influence on Augustus' actions could be detected not long after M.
Agrippa's death; since AD 4 his influence had been paramount and
hardly challengeable. It might be asked what part he played in drawing
up the political testament. Not only that: there are vicissitudes of
Augustan policy even before 12 BC to remember. There were few
touches of the tiller that some Augustan precedent, or utterance at
least, would not justify.

Outside the influence of Augustus himself there are other factors
that must be taken into account if we are to appreciate the continuity between the two principates; one is the weakness of individuals,
however powerful and heroic, in the face of the tides of history – and
the pressures exercised on them by their contemporaries. Then, Roman
indifference to extensive plans and programmes; the rising politician
was pragmatic, adaptable, even opportunist. But that tendency should
not be exaggerated. Too much adaptability became *levitas*, irresponsi-
bility; *constantia*, steadiness, was a quality generally admired, and certainly admired by Tiberius. He had had time to develop considered
views on men and affairs, or at any rate principles of conduct, and there
is the evidence of his own utterances as to what they were. Tiberius'
speeches and letters to the Senate show that he had a clear idea of his
own and their roles in government and politics. It is noteworthy how
much of his discourse takes the form of definitions and rulings on the
functions and duties of Senate, magistrates, and Princeps. The loftier
the role, the heavier the obligations it imposed. Tiberius had the interest
in the perfect fulfilment of a given part that was the mark of a Stoic,
though it was not exclusive to that sect.[9]

Since he came to political maturity, at the time of his first consulship, Tiberius had been known to stand for something in Roman
politics. There is no need to cite evidence already brought forward, or
the asseverations of September and October AD 14, to show that the
main plank in his platform was the supremacy of the Senate in government. Those asseverations were repeated in later years, and the sources
are at one in giving Tiberius the credit for substantiating them, for a
time at least. Yet he went down into history as a tyrant, and even

modern apologists have detected in his principate a centralizing tendency that was by no means to the advantage of the Senate, and which was to be carried further by his nephew Claudius. Tiberius owes his reputation for hypocrisy to this fact among others. But before we trace the working out of Tiberius' policies, the validity and coherence of his views themselves, as far as they can be ascertained, are worth examining a little more closely.

Our sources are disparate. Coin types and legends are not always to be interpreted or even dated with certainty. Nor is it clear how far the Princeps himself was involved in choosing them, even if it were universally accepted that they represent an attempt to bring round a populace (or a section of it) to one or other view of its ruler and his policies. There is a safer hypothesis: the coins show the Princeps as he wished, or those close to him thought he wished, to be seen; possibly as he wished to be.[10] They display principles, adumbrate plans, and recall achievements. Inscriptions erected by well-meaning but not always well-informed individuals and corporate bodies take us further from the centre of power into circles where a word rich in historical meaning becomes a parroted slogan. More hope lies in literature, in the writings of Velleius Paterculus and Valerius Maximus, men acutely sensitive to the mind of the Princeps, and in those of later historians, both for the utterances of Tiberius himself which they report, and for the echoes or mockeries of official claims embedded in their works.

No one word will cover all this ground, least of all the word 'virtues'. That is not because virtues can be exhibited in private as well as in public life, and lack political content. At Rome not party programmes but the personal merits of politicians (as well as their birth) were of prime importance, and the history of the last century of the Republic was interpreted in moral terms.[11] The Romans were very ready to recruit moral and emotive words into the service of politics. But the virtues of one man, even if he is an autocrat, which precisely was what Tiberius declined to be, do not guarantee the felicity of an empire; the word 'virtues' leaves out too much (*concordia*, for example) and assumes too much, namely that preaching entails practice. 'Principles' is better, but once again there is an assumption of sincerity and no place for *concordia*; besides, principles must be formulated and arranged in a hierarchy of status. Our subject is less well defined: it is stated or implied on Tiberian coinage and inscriptions, and in language used by or about the Princeps.

For all that, it will be convenient to divide discussion of these concepts into two parts, passing from Tiberius' attitude to the political exigencies of his day to qualities which he claimed to deploy in face of them.

Tiberius prided himself on his insight; his posture was that of a realist, even a pessimist, without illusions about human destiny, human nature, and politics.[12] It was in his harsh view of human nature that Tiberius' veneration for the law had its roots. If the laws could be enforced they had a part to play in keeping men and institutions to their proper functions; those that could not were worse than useless. In times of peace and order the impersonal authority of the law defined and restrained the ambitions and powers of individuals, even those of the Princeps himself. It was only where the law did not lay down guidelines that Tiberius allowed that the expansive *imperium* and *potestas* of the magistrates might have some play.[13]

That did not mean the abdication of an individual's responsibility. The Senate's position in the constitution had crumbled in the last century B C before the onslaughts of ambitious magistrates and private individuals; finally law itself had given the latest and most ruthless of them, Octavian, an entrenched and invulnerable position within the constitution. Tiberius, unlike his brother Nero Drusus, realized that overwhelming military power and executive authority had to be conferred on a man who would use it for the protection of the Senate in its functions. Nor did he fail to recognize that such a man must enjoy immeasurable influence outside the sphere of his authority proper. It was for this man to rise to heights which lesser men could not reach;[14] one of those heights was the voluntary restriction of his own *imperium* and *potestas* to the smallest possible area and the circumscription of his own *auctoritas*; as concomitants, the discouragement of servility, flattery, and the 'cult of personality'; and the curbing of personal servants, their numbers and power. In the last analysis, responsibility rested on an individual, the Princeps, with support from the constitution that was quite inadequate.[15] In the present case the Princeps was a man who may indeed have mistrusted himself, but who had accumulated reasons for mistrusting the ambitions of his family and peers. Tiberius' view of the future of Rome cannot have been optimistic.

His duties lay in the present, and Tiberius made it plain to those whose opinion mattered to him what he hoped to achieve. He made no attempt to appeal to the masses through the media of coins and inscriptions (one notable exception to that rule will be considered later). Not surprisingly: they would not have liked what he had to tell them. It was an omission that must have contributed to his reputation for *adrogantia*. But despite the well-known austerity of his coinage the types and legends that were chosen are of some significance, and illustrate his 'optimate' policy. Plainest of all in its implications is his continued interest in Concordia, a deity whose hey-day was commonly held to have coincided with that of the Senate in the second century BC. To the restoration of her temple he had vowed the spoils of Germany in his second consulship, and dedicated it on 16 January AD 10, with that day celebrated as a holiday in consequence. Whether Concordia herself figures on the early coinage of Tiberius or not is problematical; if she does she is not named; but there is no doubt that the temple represented on sesterces of AD 35–37 is hers. Concordia was offered public dedications in AD 16 after the conspiracy of Libo Drusus had been crushed, and others from the hands of private individuals, senators and *equites*, perhaps on the same occasion, perhaps later in the principate, when Sejanus' time was running out.[16] The appearance of the temple on coins may celebrate the twenty-fifth anniversary of its dedication; the offerings of AD 16 were only to be expected at a time when the harmony in the state that was guaranteed by the supremacy of Tiberius and the Senate was shown to have been in danger.

Concordia is not an isolated theme. *Salus* is a political idea that comes, as we might infer from the statues set up side by side in 11 BC, from exactly the same conservative and senatorial political stable: when Marius put down Appuleius Saturninus he showed himself *'salutaris civis'*. In the conventional medical terms a healthy state of the body politic (*salus*) is produced when all its parts are functioning together in harmony (*concordia*). Augustus on his deathbed knew whom to summon if he was to leave all *salva*, safe and sound, behind him; SALVS AVGVSTA is proclaimed on the coinage of AD 22–23; Salus Perpetua Augusta figures on an inscription set up at Interamna in AD 32, after the fall of Sejanus; and Tiberius liked to think of himself as *'bonus salutarisque princeps'*.[17] The equivalent abroad of domestic *concordia* was *pax*, likewise honoured in 11 BC and manifestly an objective cherished by Tiberius, though it is not proclaimed on the official coinage. Uninterrupted tranquillity emerges, not surprisingly, as a dominant ideal of the conservative Princeps; indeed, it was a firm hope precisely of *salus*, *quies*, *pax*, and *tranquillitas* that shone forth (in Velleius' view) as soon as Tiberius was adopted in AD 4.[18] What we have seen of the opposition to his rise shows that he would not attain it easily; indeed, the fragility of the Tiberian calm is exposed by the very themes used to advance it: to proclaim *concordia* was to acknowledge that opposition existed.

Confronted by other men's failings and his own unpopularity, a man who knew his responsibilities might naturally take comfort in his own virtue and its defiant display. (*Noblesse oblige*, but it has its consolations.) That Tiberius was a self-conscious cultivator of his own *virtutes* (merits) is suggested by more than one phrase of Tacitus, as well as by his confessed willingness to ignore hatred, as long as he had respect. The Princeps cared for his reputation, but he was willing to bear present odium if it would enhance his later fame. The noble posture was an open invitation to his detractors to accuse him of hypocrisy and vice.[19]

But Tiberius' *virtutes* were not mere hot-house plants. Allusion to them in public implies their serviceability to the state. First amongst them comes the startling *clementia*, startling because the opening chapters of Seneca's essay on the subject display it as the virtue of an autocrat, not of a man who aspired to be *aequalis civis*, a citizen on equal terms with his fellows, and first because of the four cardinal virtues of the Stoics that had been attributed to Augustus on the shield set up in the Senate-house in 27 BC, the *Clupeus Virtutis*, this is the one that received most attention in Tiberius' principate.[20] *Iustitia* we shall examine below; but both *pietas* and *virtus* might well be claimed as Tiberian virtues, the latter for the Princeps' prowess in war, the former for his devotion to Augustus' example and memory. Indeed, even during Augustus' lifetime there had been a proposal that his adopted son should take the name Pius. It had been rejected, because he intended Tiberius to bear his own more distinctive *cognomen*.[21] *Pietas* has its place on the coinage of AD 22–23; but whatever his admirers claimed for him, Tiberius may have been conscious that his title had been weakened by his conduct in 6 BC and would be diminished further by the changes he was introducing into the Principate.[22] As for *virtus*, Tiberius' claims were indeed great, but they were not again to be reinforced by personal appearance on the field; like *pietas*, *virtus*, though it was not exclusively a military quality and might still have scope in the whole field of government, made promises that could not wholly be fulfilled; besides, its Marian associations might make it unacceptable to Tiberius.[23] The prominence of *clementia* (with *moderatio*) on the reverses of coins (*dupondii*) variously dated to AD 22–23 and AD 34–37, and the dedication of an *Ara Clementiae* by the Senate in AD 28, have prompted more than one explanation.[24] The reverses are dedicated to *clementia* or *moderatio* and each type displays a shield containing a bust. That image recalls the shield presented to Augustus, and it was suggested long ago that in 21 Tiberius too may have been offered an honour in this form. The year 21 was one that saw only one conviction for treason, and in which Tiberius upbraided the Senate for its precipitate execution of Clutorius Priscus; in A D 28, by contrast, the downfall of Agrippina and Nero Caesar had begun, and it was the misgivings of the Senate that caused *clementia* to be invoked.[25] R. S. Rogers demurred; he held that Tiberian *clementia* has a wider reference. *Clementia* towards external enemies had already been shown at the triumph of 12: the Pannonian leader Bato, instead of being strangled in the Tullianum, had been established in a comfortable exile at Ravenna. As commander-in-chief Tiberius had occasion to extend mercy to Rome's enemies abroad as well as to criminals at home. But of the plentiful instances of the Princeps' clemency towards foreign opponents that Rogers cited few were exercised directly by Tiberius,[26] and such acts were not likely to awake much admiration in the minds of those for whose use the coinage was struck. *Clementia* belongs at home and, as the context of the references to it makes clear, it was exercised on political offenders. The diligence of Rogers himself uncovered nearly two score examples of such domestic *clementia*, some too trivial to be thought of as the basis of Tiberius' claim to the virtue, others more significant. *Clementia* was what Tiberius had begged for his wife Julia in 2 B C, what he extended to those who opposed his rise to power, even (so he claimed) to the conspirator of A D 16, Libo Drusus. He continued to offer it to lesser political offenders; but there could be nothing more instructive than the Senate's erection of an altar of *clementia* in the year that the younger Julia died on her island. That Agrippina's fall was imminent must have been suspected; the altar served the double purpose, commemorative and hortatory, for it was known that the idea that he practised *clementia* was one that appealed to the Princeps. Five years after Julia's death Tiberius reported that of Agrippina to the Senate, and grimly congratulated himself on his forbearance towards her: he could have had her executed, and her body thrown on the Gemonian steps.[27] Hence an attractive explanation for the *dupondii* with the *clementia* legend. H. Gesche, advocating a late date for the *dupondii* on numismatic grounds, connects them with the golden offering made to Jupiter in A D 33 in recognition of Tiberius' *clementia* towards Agrippina, and with the amnesty granted to her followers and those of Sejanus. Alternatively, we might think of the aftermath of the conviction of Libo Drusus in A D 16. In any case, Tiberian *clementia*, like Tiberian *concordia*, was in origin Tiberius' response, from a position of strength, to defeated and convicted rivals. It is an invitation to forgive and forget. It is no coincidence that Nero offered *clementia* after he killed his mother, and that it was proclaimed on the coins of the victorious Vitellius ten years later.[29]

Moderatio, which was coupled with *clementia* on the 'shield' reverses, was a constant theme, harped on by Tiberius' admirers, guyed by his detractors. Ubiquitous because its field is so much wider than that of *clementia*, *moderatio* (or words related to it) was used to refer to Tiberius' attitude towards his powers and to the manner in which he exercised them, to the tone of his first edict, for example, and to his undertaking to commend no more than four candidates for the praetorship; or to his refusal of further powers (that of nominating twelve praetors every year) and honours (a temple in Spain in A D 25, triumphs) and to his reluctance to allow what he thought were excessive attentions to his relatives, during their lifetime and at their funerals.[29] In short, as Rogers has indicated, the display of *moderatio* was the mark of a mind that was consistently *civilis* (unassuming). This was the cardinal virtue that made Tiberius fear the excesses of *auctoritas*, that lay behind his respect for the law; that consisted partly in the exercise of *clementia*;[30] and that guaranteed the Senate its supremacy in government.

In private life, too, it was a virtue that Tiberius held in high esteem. In A D 22 his speech discouraging the Senate from introducing or reinforcing rules against luxury, which would have laid many of its members open to prosecution and disgrace through the attentions of informers, won him, says Tacitus, a reputation for *moderatio*. In the course of the speech Tiberius looked back to the time when individuals exercised self-restraint ('*sibi quisque moderabatur*').[31]

With *iustitia*, whose bust is represented on the coinage, we turn to another of those Stoic virtues that had been credited to Caesar and Augustus (a respect for rights and property); but C. H. V. Sutherland may be right in attributing to the Tiberian concept a much more closely political interpretation.[32] Inscriptions honour Tiberius as '*iustissimus princeps*', and that may very well represent an ideal of his. Certainly he professed the wish to be judge and senator, rather than Princeps, and sought a reputation for knowledge of the law, both religious and secular. His knowledge he displayed on more than one occasion in the Senate, and he extended it by consorting with at least one distinguished jurisconsult, Labeo's heir as leader of what was to become the Proculian school, M. Cocceius Nerva, who was a member of the entourage on Capri.[33]

Iustitia carries us on to Tiberius' claim to merit as the highest authority in the whole Roman world. The last three themes we have to review are *liberalitas*, *providentia*, and *constantia*. The first finds no mention on coins or inscriptions; perhaps the Princeps thought it an unheroic quality, or one to be taken for granted in a man of his financial resources, or too despotic in its associations.[34] Yet one utterance recorded by Tacitus makes it clear that he was well aware that openhandedness was incumbent upon him. Nor does the historian deny Tiberius' tacit claim. It was not only towards the *plebs* that Tiberius displayed generosity (those benefactions will be mentioned in their place). In AD 15 a senator whose house had been damaged by the construction of a highway demanded compensation from the Treasury. When the officials in charge refused it, Tiberius made a grant from his own purse. The Princeps likewise used his money in the cause nearest his heart by maintaining the fortunes of decent but impoverished members of the nobility. Even the son of Cn. Piso, who lay under a charge of *maiestas* (treason), was received in AD 20 with a generosity that Tacitus says was usual in the Princeps' dealings with young men of his class.[35]

Next, *providentia*. Tiberius was notoriously canny – slow in coming to decisions, acute in taking them at last. There is no doubt that he made a virtue of this and prided himself on his sound judgment, especially in military matters; that much escaped him when he reported to the Senate on the suppression of the Gallic revolt in AD 21.[36] Tiberius' skill in dealing with enemies without had its domestic counterpart, as Rogers pointed out. An inscription of AD 32, set up at Interamna, was dedicated to 'Salus perpetua Augusta, Libertas Publica, the Genius of the Municipality, and the Providentia of Tiberius'; the same quality was commemorated by the governor of Crete, P. Viriasius Naso.[37] The ability to forestall conspiracy is a virtue with a darker side, for which ancient writers give Tiberius full credit.[38] But that is a caricature of *providentia*. The quality has also been connected, rightly, with the securing of the succession; but even that is not wide enough. *Providentia* should be the concern and the capacity to plan ahead that ensure that benevolence is effective. *Providentia* makes it easier to carry out the promises implicit in the other virtues that Tiberius claimed. In particular, he wished to be remembered as a man *providus* of the Senate's interests. That wish was expressed in AD 25; two years earlier he had expatiated on his care for the provisioning of Rome and Italy.[39] In the view of Strabo and Josephus, Tiberius' *providentia* embraced the welfare of provincial peoples as well; and Tacitus' use of the verb *'providere'* in connexion with his care for the provinces may echo, consciously or unconsciously, an official speech or document.[40]

In the same noble speech of AD 25 in which he made known to the Senate how he wished to be remembered, and immediately after putting his claim to be thought *providus* on their behalf, Tiberius expressed the hope that he be found *constans* in danger and fearless of causing offence when the public good demanded it. He had displayed *constantia*, an upper-class and Stoic virtue, in war, not by showing severity to his own troops, a context in which *constantia* is often found, and one alien to Tiberius, but against the enemy.[41] Now he claimed it for his civil life. His reference to unpopularity is significant; in serving the Senate above all other sectors of Roman society Tiberius knew that he was pleasing only a very small minority class, and not the whole of that. He had learned the lesson early, in 6 BC; at that time it could have been held that he had been wanting in *constantia*, and it may be no coincidence that this reference to it of AD 25 came only a year or so before his final departure from Rome. In moments of acute danger, in war or conspiracy, Tiberius did not lose his nerve; but the *constantia* of the long haul was not a virtue to which he has any real claim.

The political and moral themes that were brought to the fore during the principate of Tiberius offer illumination in more than one way. They reveal the preoccupations of the Princeps; and two of them, *concordia* and *clementia*, betray by his insistence on them his awareness of hostility and discord. Another, and fundamental, contradiction in the public image of the Princeps has already been noted in connexion with *clementia*. In advocating *concordia*, practising *liberalitas*, and displaying *providentia*, Tiberius was arrogating no higher place than any great Republican politician might have expected. In claiming to exercise *iustitia*, *clementia*, and *moderatio* – the last his cardinal virtue – he was acknowledging himself the possessor of monarchical powers;[42] for Julius Caesar had displayed, not only the notorious *clementia*, but *moderatio* as well. True, Valerius Maximus could cite good Republican models for these virtues, but he finds most of his worthies in positions of extraordinary power or influence: P. Valerius Poplicola, taking on, as consul, the power of the kings and voluntarily sharing the rods of office with a colleague; Furius Camillus hesitating to take over his command before completing the formalities of his investiture with the dictatorship; Marcius Rutilus Censorinus and L. Quinctius Cincinnatus declining to be continued in their magistracies; Q. Fabius Maximus begging the people to allow his family a rest from office; Q. Scaevola refusing to destroy an accused man with his sole evidence; M. Bibulus, as governor of Syria, returning to Cleopatra the murderers of his sons with the comment that it was not for him but for the Senate to pass sentence on them.[43] If these and other specimens of moderation could serve as blueprints for acts of Tiberius, so much greater the scope and magnitude of his powers.

CHAPTER VII

POLICY IN PRACTICE:
THE SENATE AND ITS MEMBERS

We pass from the principles that underlay Tiberius' administration and from the slogans that gave some of them expression to their working out in practice – no easy thing to trace. Our fullest and most reliable source, the *Annals*, breaks off in AD 29, to resume after the fall of Sejanus. We have other factors to remember. One is the possibility of changes of source which could mislead by shifting the emphasis of extant narratives. Another is the fact that novelty wears off. Tiberius' first actions as Princeps were the object of close study; repeated or become habitual, they passed unnoticed. As he made his inevitable mistakes, these would attract attention, while his successes would be received with boredom or cynicism.

If the Senate was to play the role that Tiberius envisaged for it, if its *maiestas*, its greatness and dignity, was to be enhanced, he had to ensure that its agenda encompassed everything that it might legitimately hold to be its business, and the Senate itself must debate each item for all it was worth. The first task was the easier and there was one step that could be taken immediately. Augustus had set up a formal *consilium*, a group of advisers, to prepare business for the Senate.[1] From AD 13 it consisted of a committee of twenty senators, membership rotating annually, with the consuls, consuls designate, Tiberius and his sons, and other members co-opted *ad hoc*. The views of this body must always have weighed heavily with the rest of the Senate, and its members came to full sessions committed in some degree to the decisions it had reached, whatever they had thought of the proposals in the first instance. Even before AD 13, when its resolutions were accorded the status of *senatus consulta*, its existence diminished the authority of the full House. Not surprisingly, Tiberius abolished this committee under the new regime; in its latest form the only justification for it had been the infirmity of the Princeps. Tiberius eschewed all but a *consilium* of the old, Republican type, which a magistrate gathered round himself to advise him in the execution of his duties and which Augustus himself had also had. Tiberius' *consilium*, which he maintained until his retirement to Capri, had peculiar features. It consisted not only of his trusted friends, but of twenty leading men, probably chosen for him by the Senate. The figure gave the *consilium* a superficial resemblance (perhaps intentional) to the Augustan committee, but its functions were not probouleutic: the twenty members were permanent representatives of the Senate on a body which advised Tiberius on his administrative duties, and their presence enhanced the power and prestige of the Senate. After the Augustan committee was abolished the business that came before the Senate was probably less well prepared and its meetings in consequence longer and less orderly. The Princeps might be defeated, or baffled by unexpected twists in the debate. These were consequences which Tiberius must have foreseen and been prepared to accept; a man easily thrown off his guard and slow to think on his feet would not give up the advantages of the Augustan committee without considera-tion. For all the inconvenience it entailed, it was a simple and mechani-cal matter to discharge the first of Tiberius' obligations towards the Senate. For a substantial part of his principate he kept the agenda papers full: in AD 23 'everything was still being dealt with by the senate, all public affairs and the most important private matters as well'.[2]

The second task was more problematical. Repeatedly we read of the Princeps communicating with the House, orally or by letter, to draw attention to matters that needed it, whether by introducing the subject himself, as must have been the case when privileges and powers of the imperial family were in question, or by suggesting to the Senate before the debate or in the course of it how a problem should be handled.[3] Wherever these interventions came it would be a naïve man who would fail to recognize the effect they must have on the course of the debate.[4] Tiberius was not naïve; he must have realized that each suggestion he made, each lecture delivered on the duties of senators, diminished the authority of the House. It was this that made him sometimes express his views in the form of a statement of what his views would have been, if he had been giving them. Tiberius must have seen himself as an educator; he must have believed that, with training and instruction, a revitalized body would become capable of conducting business efficiently and authoritatively on its own.[5] It is ironical, perhaps, that the most wide-ranging debate of Tiberius' principate – for, whatever the terms of the motion, it became a debate on the constitution – had come at the beginning, in Septem-ber 14. The low level of that debate may have prevented Tacitus from noticing its remarkable nature; but to the new Princeps it must have demonstrated the need for his scheme; and it is the progress of that scheme in detail that is the theme of this chapter.

But Tacitus and Suetonius mention private as well as public affairs. The Senate was to concern itself not only with its own place in the constitution, but with the status and privileges of its members. It was to the Senate that Aurelius Pius appealed in AD 15 when his house was damaged by public works; and the ex-praetor Cn. Corbulo in AD 21 when L. Sulla, a younger man but of nobler birth, refused to give him place at a gladiatorial show.[6] Even after their deaths the honours of senators were the concern of the House, as they had been under the Republic. The Senate was responsible for organizing the obsequies of Augustus, and it gave permission for more than one state funeral in the course of Tiberius' principate, the qualifications for this distinction being (beside consular rank) kinship or close friendship with the Princeps.[7]

'Private affairs' are taken to refer to trials of individuals in the Senate; but that body controlled its members in other ways than by imposing *infamia* (official disgrace) and other penalties on them, important though that was. Some measure of the Senate's authority is given by the case of D. Silanus, who had voluntarily gone into exile in AD 8 when Augustus renounced his friendship. Using his brother Marcus as an intermediary, he begged Senate as well as Princeps for grace. He was successful and returned to the city; not, however, to hold office.[8] Some men, forced to relinquish their seats through poverty that was no fault of their own, the Senate might help by subsidizing them from the state treasury. That at any rate was what Tiberius told them in AD 15 when they applied to him after hearing of one case he had helped. They did not all put their claims with discretion. M. Hortalus, a descendant of Cicero's great rival in oratory, Q. Hortensius, used the senator's licence to depart from the subject under discussion to make a premeditated and insolent plea. His four sons were posted at the door of the House, so that he could show how many children he had raised – purely because Augustus had so advised and because his ancestors deserved posterity. Now he begged Tiberius for a subsidy – or support for a grant from the Aerarium. The Senate was inclined to favour the appeal – or so we are told. Tiberius denounced it, but ended by giving each boy 200,000 sesterces from his own purse; according to Tacitus he was forced to give way to the feeling of the House; it may be that he wanted to make it clear that the Senate's time should be devoted to matters of state, not to the interests of individuals.[9] Tiberius' outburst seems to have deterred the Senate from showing indiscriminate generosity towards its impoverished members. Only the following year certain senators were permitted or required to resign their seats, apparently by *senatus consultum* and on the Princeps' suggestion.[10] Coming so soon after the conspiracy of Libo Drusus this move might be seen as an attack on Tiberius' political opponents. But it was on a very small scale (only five men are named); and although one of the victims, Appius Appianus, may have been the nephew of one of the elder Julia's lovers, another, Marius Nepos, had already benefited from Tiberius' generosity; and yet a third, Q. Vitellius, belonged to a family that was otherwise in high favour with the Princeps and his adoptive son Germanicus.[11] Tiberius did without the systematic purges of the Senate that Augustus had four times attempted, most recently in AD 4. That may be because he disapproved of them; but it is more likely that he realized that they caused more odium than they were worth. Extravagant living was what led to the impoverishment and enforced retirement of the five senators in AD 17, as well as to the downfall of Libo Drusus, and his condemnation was followed at the very next session of the Senate by a debate on the subject. A *senatus consultum* was the result: food might not be served on dishes of solid gold, and males were forbidden silk. Severer measures were discouraged by Tiberius, not only in 16 but also in 22, when the matter was raised again by the aediles. The thing was too widespread to control – and the odium of making the attempt would fall, not on the aediles, but on the Princeps. Here the preoccupations of Senate and Princeps diverged: traditional fear of luxury and of a decline in moral standards were their concern in public, even if what they privately shuddered at was the expense of keeping up with the more dashing members of society. For Tiberius, who may have seen through the moralizing, this was small beer compared with his task of keeping Rome and Italy in their position of political supremacy in the face of declining productivity and the flight of precious metals outside the Empire. Shocking though the neglect of his predecessor's legislation was, Tiberius did nothing to enforce it, showing that he disagreed with Augustus' methods, if not his aims. Instead, an appeal to the Senate's self-respect; what measures Tiberius did take in this field were concerned with public more than private extravagance.[12]

But the first act of the new Princeps was to carry out a proposal recommended by Augustus in his political testament: the transfer of elections from people to Senate. Amongst other things it was a plain intimation that Tiberius intended the Senate to be master in its own house. The procedure of election by *comitia centuriata* and *tributa* was preserved entire; the Senate simply voted beforehand on the candidates and produced a list no more numerous than the number of places available. The people in effect lost all say in the election of magistrates. Tiberius went further. At the first elections to take place under the new dispensation, those for the praetorship, he announced that he would not support more than four candidates – one-third of the places available. Naturally these were sure of election, and Tiberius' undertaking shows that Augustus had not always, or ever, restricted himself to that proportion. The formal process of election in the Senate would be preceded by canvassing and bargaining between the intending candidates, as it had been on the Campus Martius; these negotiations could be carried out more conveniently when the electorate was small and its preferences predictable. Nevertheless, elections for magistracies up to and including the praetorship were normally contested, and sometimes stormy.[13]

The Senate as a body was at liberty to regulate its own procedures on all matters, though it was bound by tradition. So in elections. One of the praetors of 17 died in office, and a suffect had to be elected. The *lex Papia Poppaea* of A D 9 gave preference to candidates with the greatest number of children; but Germanicus and Drusus Caesars pressed for their kinsman, D. Haterius Agrippa, and the law was set aside – though not at once, nor by an overwhelming majority. That the struggle was as real as if it had taken place when the law still counted gave Tacitus a melancholy pleasure.[14]

The new scheme cannot escape criticism. Like the purge of A D 4, the alterations that had been made to the structure of the *comitia centuriata* in A D 5 had as one purpose the curbing of Tiberius' political opponents; the change made in 14 carried those alterations to their logical conclusion by allowing the people no voice in elections at all. And by putting elections into the hands of a limited group, his peers voting openly,[15] Tiberius was increasing the power in his own, and not only because these men would not jeopardize their own futures by voting for men of whom he did not approve. Under the old system, all the influence that the Princeps had enjoyed, great though it was, had been unofficial; he relied on *auctoritas* and largesse, just like any other politician. Now, for the first time, the Princeps seems to have acquired an official role in the electoral process: that of receiving the names of candidates and of reading out the list of candidates in the Senate when it was complete. It sounds innocuous, but there was an obvious opportunity to deter unwelcome candidatures. This may be what lies behind the criticism that Tacitus makes of Tiberius' handling of consular elections.[16] The supreme magistracy was the key to high command abroad, and only four places were available each year, the two consuls *ordinarii* regularly giving way to two suffects for the second half of the year. In Tacitus' day the whole procedure had become formalized; and he was bewildered by the diversity of practice that he found when he examined Tiberius' election speeches. When the Princeps commented on candidates – and that was not always – he was very guarded, and named no names. What Tacitus found most often was that Tiberius simply reported that there were only two candidates for the two *ordinarius* places, and that accordingly he had handed on their names to the consuls who would preside over their formal election in the *comitia centuriata*. There would be no contest in the Senate – unless other candidates declared themselves. Tacitus pronounced this offer empty – or actually deceitful; he must have believed that all the other possible candidates had been privately warned off. But there is another explanation still possible at this stage of the Principate: the horse-trading that went on behind the scenes had been so effective as to destroy open competition. Even in the following principate, when Gaius Caligula tried to restore genuine elections on the Campus Martius, he gave up the experiment because the deals that candidates did before the elections made them a sham.[17]

The Princeps, then, even Tiberius with his powers enhanced by the new form of elections, played a more complex and less decisive part in the disposal of magistracies than might be supposed. But it would be safe to say, with Dio,[18] that nothing was done of which he disapproved, and reasonable to ask in what ways the influence of Tiberius can be detected on the consular *Fasti*. Theories based the proportion of *nobiles* and *novi homines* (men descended from consuls and those who were the first of their families to enter the Senate) appearing on the *Fasti* at various periods of his principate (Tiberius favoured *nobiles*; Tiberius favoured *novi homines*) conflict and are valueless.[19] We must be more cautious. Tacitus mostly approved of the men who reached the consulship in the first seven years of the regime: Tiberius valued illustrious birth, military talent, and the arts of peace.[20] That was conventional, and we cannot generalize from a remark in support of a particular candidate for the praetorship disadvantaged by a low origin: 'Curtius Rufus is his own ancestor.'[21] We have already seen what qualified a man for Tiberius' support in the last years of Augustus' principate; there is no reason to believe that he changed his views when he came to sole power: membership of a consular family would normally take a man to the top; failing that, a long patrician pedigree commended itself; military talent could make up for *novitas*, the want of senatorial forbears; and loyalty created a strong claim.

So much for the highest rungs. There was also the problem of how many *novi homines* should be admitted at all, and from what areas. Indifference to the make-up of the House might betray indifference to its functions and prestige; equally, the Princeps who enrolled large numbers of new men might be interested more in their loyalty than in their merits. As we have seen, Tiberius never undertook a systematic revision of the senatorial roll, but all the evidence shows him concerned with the standing of the whole order as well as individual members. He would not admit men indiscriminately. Indeed, it is usually assumed that he was as sparing in his admission of new men to the Senate as he was in admitting peregrines to the citizenship.[22] And we have the authoritative statement of his nephew Claudius that Tiberius looked no farther than Augustus for new senators, that is, not beyond the confines of Italy.[23] That Claudius was right is suggested by the origins of the military men whom we saw advancing during the last decade of Augustus' principate. But Italy by now had come to include Cisalpine Gaul; and the same period, or the early years of Tiberius' regime, brought in men from Hasta, Brixia, Concordia, Pola, and probably from Atria.[24]

It would be rash to attribute the success of these men to the influence of Tiberius simply because it coincided with his elevation; but when we are dealing with small numbers of exceptional persons, it is natural to believe that there was a personal tie. No more than Augustus did Tiberius offend public opinion by adlecting new men into the Senate at a given rank; they had to secure election to the quaestorship like the members of families already senatorial. They needed encouragement, perhaps even permission, to stand,[25] and support if they were to make their way – the support that we find Tiberius giving to Velleius Paterculus in AD 14.[26] Sex. Palpellius Hister of Pola, suffect consul in 43, certainly was known to the Princeps: he had been assigned to Tiberius by Augustus as a member of his suite before he embarked on his senatorial career, probably at the time of the Pannonian revolt (he would have known the terrain).[27] The father of Pompeius Macer, praetor in AD 15, was an intimate friend of Tiberius.[28] Pompeius, coming from Mytilene, was the first known senator from the eastern part of the Empire, and one of the very few provincials admitted to the Senate by Augustus. His antecedents explain the distinction. His father had served Augustus as procurator of Asia; his grandfather had been Pompey's secretary and biographer; in addition he had wealth and the esteem of his fellow countrymen. Augustus may have admitted two more provincials: Aelius Marullinus of Italica (his origins were ultimately Italian); and Sex. Curvius Silvinus, who perhaps came from Nemausus.[29] But Marullinus may be Triumviral, Silvinus Tiberian. Certainly Tiberius looked beyond even the outermost bounds of Italy, for all that Claudius said. From Corduba in Spain came Iunius Gallio and his kinsman by adoption the philosopher L. Seneca; from Barcino L. Pedanius Secundus; from Saguntum Hispanus Pompeius Marcellus Umbonius Silo. Narbonensis was not far behind. Forum Iulii contributed L. Iulius Graecinus, the father of Agricola, and perhaps his close relative M. Graecinus; Vienna (Vienne) the two brothers Valerius Asiaticus; Nemausus Cn. Domitius Afer, who had connexions with Silvinus and his family; and it may be from an unknown town of Narbonensis that Togonius Gallus emerged. Most remarkable of all, very late in the reign a man from Attaleia on the south coast of Asia Minor, M. Calpurnius Rufus, embarked on a senatorial career, rising to govern his own province as an ex-praetor under Claudius.[30] These provincials seem to have been trickling into the Senate steadily throughout Tiberius' principate. D. Valerius Asiaticus held his first consulship as suffect in 35; he can hardly have been quaestor later than 22. Four years after Asiaticus, Domitius Afer held the *fasces*; but he had been praetor probably in 25 and must have been admitted very early in Tiberius' principate. Pedanius Secundus was not consul until 43; L. Graecinus died as an ex-praetor in 40. These two men would have been a few years senior to L. Seneca, who did not attain his suffect consulship until 56, after a switchback career; they must have held their first magistracy towards the end of the principate.

Tiberius showed himself more enterprising than might have been expected, more so than Augustus had been. Some of his men did well: six consulars among eleven provincial *novi homines* is a high success rate. As for quality, the Graecini and Asiatici seem to have been admirable men; but the brilliant satirical talents of Afer were smirched by the way he used them, and Tiberius himself twitted Togonius Gallus and lambasted Iunius Gallio for their ridiculous adulation. Gallio lost his seat; so did Umbonius Silo, in the principate of Claudius.[31] Tiberius would have been better pleased if he had been able to watch Seneca's career in its final phase. In him ambition took a noble form, and he tried for eight years to manoeuvre the young Nero into accepting for his principate something like the blueprint that Tiberius had drawn up.

It was a cardinal feature of that plan that magistrates high and low should be accorded the prestige and authority proper to their dealings with the Princeps, each other, and the Senate. In AD 14 Tiberius acted through the consuls and studiously avoided devaluing their office by using his own consular *imperium*. He followed this up with sustained courtesy towards the magistrates.[32] The first show of freedom that Tacitus records belonged to the following year and took the form of a dispute between a praetor and a tribune over the treatment of actors: were they or were they not liable to a flogging if they caused disturbances among their audiences? The praetor supported order and severity, the tribune, naturally, vetoed the proposal to flog favourites of the people.[33] A trivial incident, but quarrels between tribunes and other magistrates had made up much of the fabric of Republican political life. At a later point in the *Annals* Tacitus tells of similar wrangles between praetor and tribune, tribune and quaestor.[34] These took place in the early part of Nero's principate, and once again he comments that vestiges of the old freedom still survived. It seems that if the supremacy of the Senate as a body was the centre-piece of Tiberius' policy, individual magistracies were not to become mere rubber stamps. But if we look a little further into the dispute of 15 we see that there was some doubt of the efficacy of the tribune's veto, which might not have stood if it had not been supported by a decision of Augustus; and the Senate devised other means of restraining the power of theatricals. The Neronian incident ended in the powers of tribunes being restricted; both in AD 14 and in AD 56 the political climate was unfavourable to tribunician activity.

In AD 21 the Senate debated whether pro-magistrates should be forbidden to take their wives abroad on tours of duty. There was a vehement protest, and a few words from Drusus Caesar in praise of his own wife settled the question; but a scandal that broke three years later prompted Cotta Messallinus to initiate a *senatus consultum* that laid responsibility for a wife's misdemeanours fairly and squarely on the shoulders of her husband.[35]

That the Senate should be in control of magistrates is in full accord with Tiberius' scheme of government. If the Princeps were the servant of the Senate so must the lesser authorities be. The Senate was to be master in its own house; how much further did its authority reach?

Financial policy should be in the hands of the Senate; that was received doctrine in the second century BC.[36] Practice fell out of step with theory as the resources of the Aerarium became inadequate to meet the needs of government. The wars of conquest conducted by Sulla, Pompey, and Caesar in the late Republic enriched those generals as well as the Aerarium, and the wealth of Augustus exceeded that of the state. By subsidizing the Aerarium from his private funds Augustus established an unofficial control over its expenditure; and he was only nominally responsible for the huge sums allocated to him for the management of the provinces under his charge, for he never gave them up and so never had to render account of the sums in the imperial Fiscus.[37]

Towards the end of his principate, in AD 5-6, Augustus had dealt another blow to the authority of the Senate in financial matters. He forced it to create a new treasury, the Aerarium Militare, with the sole function of ensuring the adequate payment and settlement of the soldiers. It was an important step towards solving a serious problem of long standing, but it was extremely unpopular. For one thing, although the treasury was subsidized at first by donations from Augustus, made from his own property and that of Tiberius and Agrippa Postumus, new taxes were levied to keep it supplied.[38] Besides, the setting aside of funds for a stipulated purpose reduced the Senate's room for manoeuvre in financial matters generally.

Tiberius begins with a very fair record; he used his own fortune to help deserving senators – and that only when the Senate had considered their case;[39] and he resisted the temptation to put pressure on the officials in charge of the Aerarium when their views conflicted with his own.[40] How long this attention to the proprieties lasted we cannot be sure. After the earthquake of 17 Tiberius promised his own help to the ruined cities of Asia, and remitted for five years what they were due to pay Aerarium or Fiscus.[41] Tacitus is using the word 'Fiscus' here to refer to the Princeps' private property in Asia: well and good; but he had no authority to remit what was due to the hard-pressed Aerarium. Yet there is no cause for alarm; a similar measure after the earthquake that destroyed Cibyra in Asia and Aegium in Achaea was carried by *senatus consultum* on his proposal.[42]

Well-founded disquiet sets in when we reach the twenties. In 24 C. Silius anticipated conviction for *maiestas* (treason) by committing suicide; in spite of the normal rule that suicide saved property, that part of his which was calculated to form part of a gift from Augustus was confiscated to the Fiscus. In 32 the property of Sejanus was diverted from the Aerarium to the Fiscus; and in the following year the silver and gold mines belonging to a Spaniard who had suffered execution were 'set aside for Tiberius, although they had been confiscated to the state'.[43] This is ambiguous, but the most probable interpretation is again that the mines were to be exploited for the benefit of the public funds under the control of the Princeps, not for his private enrichment. All the same, the Senate was losing effective control over the sums involved in all three cases.

The explanation (not an excuse) is financial stringency, and specifically shortage of currency. More will have to be said of this later, but the cost of running the imperial provinces and the armies they contained cannot have failed to consume the revenue they brought in; and it was precisely in 33 that Tiberius relieved the indebtedness of the landed gentry by making a loan of a hundred million sesterces. The political rights of the Senate were beginning to take second place to wider economic needs. Nor could they claim consideration. The events of 33 showed both the resources of the Aerarium and the resolution of the Senate inadequate to take measures to deal with the crisis.[44]

The management of religion was an integral part of Roman statecraft; and it is in keeping with the regime in its early stages that we find the Senate, naturally under the learned guidance of the Pontifex Maximus, head of the state religion, playing the prominent part traditionally assigned to it. In 19 the Senate at Tiberius' instigation supervised the choice of a new Vestal Virgin, here taking over a function once exercised by the people. Three years later it heard Servius Maluginensis, the Flamen Dialis, appealing for permission to draw lots for a province and absent himself from Rome; other experts spoke, but that high authority the Pontifex Maximus reserved his decision, which was eventually given as an appendix to another debate on a point of religion. Maluginensis did not long survive the rejection of his plea, and in 24 it fell to the Senate, again at Tiberius' instance, to promote legislation designed to relax the rules that made it so difficult to find a successor. Probably they, or the college of Pontifices, played a part in the eventual selection of Maluginensis' son: the election of priests as well as magistrates had been withdrawn from the people in AD 14. As late as AD 32 we find the Senate deliberating whether an oracle was or was not fit to be included in the canon of the Sibylline Books; but on that occasion there was a difference: Tiberius intervened by letter and made heavy-handed use of his priestly office. Like his predecessor, Tiberius was anxious to prevent the circulation of unauthorized and perhaps seditious prophecy.[45] His action was the more embarrassing for the Senate in that it had already passed a decree admitting the oracle.

In 24 Tiberius asked the Senate indifferently for *lex* or *senatus consultum*, nicely illustrating the fact that early in the Principate the Senate became a source of law. Normal Republican procedure had been to bring legislation before the Senate for approval before it was voted on by the people in the *comitia*: the authoritative *senatus consultum* becoming the binding *lex*. It was the champion of the people Ti. Gracchus who finally established the practice of taking measures to the people without senatorial backing. Under the Principate it became a matter of indifference which machinery was employed. Augustus continued to enact *leges*, either acting through the consuls or bringing them forward himself as *leges Iuliae*. Yet there was none to challenge mere *senatus consulta* if they had his backing; it was a *senatus consultum* (*Calvisianum*)[46] which in 4 BC set up a new, shortened procedure for extortion trials; and it was probably by *senatus consultum* that in AD 14 the people were deprived of their electoral rights. That the consummation of this process should belong to the principate of Tiberius is in full accord with our view of his regime. *Leges* are not unknown, but the certain instances belong to the early years, AD 19 and 24, and none is attested after 28.[47]

In the early Principate senatorial legislation usually took the indirect form of advice to the magistrate on the interpretation of existing law. Under Tiberius there were several discussions in the House which resulted, not to be sure in the repeal of a law or in its amendment, but at any rate in its clarification. We have already seen the Senate in 24 bringing the misbehaviour of a governor's wife within the scope of the *lex Iulia Repetundarum*; but the earliest of these discussions had come in AD 20. The *lex Papia Poppaea* was an enactment only eleven years old, designed with the full approval of Augustus to encourage marriage and the rearing of children by limiting the rights of testators and heirs who were unmarried or childless. The law was being evaded, and that gave informers their chance. The status of senators and knights was threatened if their property was lost to them; and a feeling of insecurity was spreading beyond Rome and even Italy. Tiberius appointed a committee of fifteen senators (ten of them with experience as consuls or praetors); they were not to modify the law (though that may have been the intention of the man who raised the question), but to define its scope.[48]

Widespread though the evil was, it was no doubt the peril of senators that most moved the House. We have already noticed the open self-interest that actuated members. Certainly it was the plight of an individual that prompted the first discussion of the *lex Iulia Maiestatis* and its functioning. C. Cestius complains in 21 that he was being threatened and abused by a woman against whom he could take no action, because she clutched a portrait of the Princeps which it would be *lèse majesté* to violate. There was a chorus of sympathy, and Drusus

Caesar, the presiding consul, threw the woman into prison as a deterrent.[49] It may not be fortuitous that in the following year the Senate was invited to regulate the asylum rights of cities in the eastern half of the Empire, where temples were crammed with delinquent slaves, debtors, and criminals. The Senate, its work cut out, delegated the task to the consuls.[50]

The year AD 21 did not see the last debate on *maiestas*. Three years later an ex-praetor, Caecilius Cornutus, was falsely accused. Unable to bear the anxiety, he killed himself before a verdict was reached. After the collapse of the whole prosecution, it was mooted that accusers should lose their statutory rewards when the accused committed suicide before conviction. The proposal was rejected. Tiberius spoke against it, on the grounds that it would subvert the law.[51] His action may be seen in a sinister light, for two reasons. First, he was seen to be encouraging delation; more serious was the fact of his intervention on the present occasion. We have seen Tiberius playing the part of a senator before. Anxious perhaps that the Senate should not allow sympathy for Cornutus to run away with it, he spoke with decisive authority, depriving the Senate on this important occasion of the opportunity of making up its own mind. The arguments he used were not so recondite that they could not have been discovered and uttered by a private citizen.

Self-interest, or concern for the interests of fellow senators, marks the House's last and most interesting attempt to modify the law in Tiberius' reign. Again it was prompted by the activities of *delatores* (accusers). This time they were attacking men who enriched themselves by usury, violating the law of Julius Caesar which seems to have regulated the proportion of a man's capital that might be lent out at interest – or must be invested in Italian land. So many cases were being brought that the praetor in charge of the court referred the matter to the Senate. Most of its members were implicated, and the House requested an amnesty from the Princeps. Eighteen months were allowed; then they must comply with the law. The calling in of debts all at once led to a shortage of currency, and the Senate's precautions (that only two-thirds of the capital should be repaid immediately, and invested in Italian land) were inadequate: the creditors were not content with less than full payment, and compulsory transactions in land only depressed its price; debtors who were being pressed for cash could not sell. Expelled from their properties, they were losing rank as well as their fortune. It was Tiberius who had to come to the rescue, with three-year interest-free loans to the tune of a hundred million sesterces against the security of double the value in land. As for the regulations of Julius Caesar, which the Senate had re-enacted, Tacitus tells us that they were soon being evaded again.[52] It is sometimes said that Tiberius created a new High Court from the Senate.[53] If that were true it would give strong support to the view of his policies taken here: courts staffed by senators were the rule down to the tribunate of C. Gracchus in 123 BC and for a decade after the dictatorship of Sulla. But Tiberius cannot be given the credit for this innovation; it was of Augustus' devising and came probably not many years after he had almost failed to secure the conviction of M. Primus, Fannius Caepio, and Varro Murena. Trials held in the Senate would have the same advantage for the Princeps as elections held there; but the ostensible function of the court would be to take 'political' cases. At any rate a committee of the Senate had been taking extortion cases since 4 BC; and Ovid was aware that he might have been exiled by a decree of the Senate. Extortion, adultery, and above all treason were its sphere and, in an exceptional case in Tiberius' principate, murder.[54] The ostensible function of the court being entirely in the spirit of Tiberius' principate, he did nothing to detract from its powers but, when he sat with it, merely tried to ensure that it did what he thought to be justice. In this he was not successful; and it is ironical that it was in his principate that the senatorial court became notorious for its handling of treason cases – so much so that the topic demands a chapter to itself.

In any constitutional theory of the Principate that had regard for the past, the Senate was entitled to a say in the running of affairs in Rome and Italy and in the public provinces, without let or hindrance from the consular *imperium* of the Princeps.[55] In 15, the same year as the debate on the disturbances caused by theatrical performers and their *aficionados*, the Tiber flooded and caused havoc, as it had done so many times before. The matter went to the Senate, and Asinius Gallus proposed consulting the Sibylline Books – not a very helpful suggestion, however carefully purged the oracles had been. No doubt Gallus' proposal was sarcastic, and prompted by his earlier experiences with the Tiber and its banks. As consul in 8 BC he had established its boundaries (that too after discussion in the Senate); in the following year, also *ex senatus consulto*, Augustus himself had taken on the task. Tiberius apparently did not contemplate that course; but he rejected Gallus' advice; L. Arruntius and C. Ateius Capito were entrusted with the task of finding a remedy, and, if Dio is to be believed, it was as a result of this inundation that Tiberius set up a permanent senatorial board of five *Curatores Alvei Tiberis*. Certainly Tiberius found it natural to work through senatorial boards; in 16 another was appointed to restore and transcribe public records.[56]

The care of public buildings in Rome and Italy was also taken to be the Senate's concern, and it was to them that M. Lepidus applied when he planned to restore the Basilica Aemilia in 22, the last time that a private person undertook a task that demanded greater means than most men could command and conferred greater prestige than it was safe for them to win. Tiberius himself paid for the restoration of the theatre of Pompey, on the ground that no member of the family could incur such expense; he did not change its name.[57] But the Senate was interested in the moral as well as the material welfare of the people of Rome. In AD 19 it passed severe decrees against prostitution and forbade even the granddaughters of knights from joining the profession. Devotees of Isis, Jews, and Jewish proselytes fared worse after scandals involving two gullible ladies of good birth. Four thousand Jews were transported to Sardinia to fight the brigands there and the rest banished from Italy unless they gave up their faith.[58]

The expulsions of 19 and 24 (actors were the victims) show the Senate exercising its traditional authority in Italy. So did the outcome of the Tiber flood enquiry. Arruntius and Capito discovered a remedy: diverting tributary waters upstream from Rome. But that would affect the amenities and prosperity of certain Italian towns: Florentia, Reate, and Umbrian Interamna. They brought their protests to the Senate – and won their case. Nothing was done. But the Senate did not fail to take cognizance of the catastrophe at Fidena in 27. A jerry-built amphitheatre crammed with Romans in search of amusement collapsed and cost the lives of (it was said) fifty thousand persons. The Senate banished the man responsible for putting on the show and decreed that nobody possessed of less than the equestrian census of 400,000 sesterces might exhibit gladiatorial games, and that the ground on which it was proposed to construct an amphitheatre should be tested for solidity.[59] Equally edifying is our picture of the Senate's dealings with the provinces, an '*imago antiquitatis*'; and Tacitus enthuses over the spectacle of the Senate investigating, with freedom to confirm or emend, the privileges that its ancestors had granted.[60] The question was one of asylum rights, and the embassies came from the provinces of Asia, Cyprus, and Crete. Nero, in the accession speech that Seneca wrote for him, restricted the Senate's autonomous jurisdiction to the 'public' provinces – those governed by proconsuls appointed by lot rather than by legates nominated by the Princeps. The

same restriction seems at first sight to apply in the principate of
Tiberius. The cities to be restored after the earthquake of 17, under the
supervision of an inspector of praetorian rank chosen by the Senate, were
all in the senatorial province of Asia; and while senatorial Achaea and
Macedonia appealed to the Senate in 15 against the tax burdens they had
to bear, it is not clear who heard the complaints of Syria and Judaea
two years later, although they were made known to the House.[61]
But it is worth drawing attention to the contrast between Tiberius'
handling of the stricken cities and Augustus' behaviour after the earthquake of 27 BC. The first Princeps, approached in Spain by a delegation from Tralles, rebuilt the city, probably without consulting the
Senate; and he may have sent an *eques*, Vedius Pollio, to supervise
the operation.[62] The role of the Senate in relieving the sufferings of
Asia, as well as in bringing delinquent administrators to justice, was
acknowledged when the cities of the province asked permission to
erect a temple to Tiberius, Livia, and the Senate; Tiberius said later
that he had been willing to accept the honour because the Senate had
been included in it, and it was the Senate that decided which city was
to have the distinction of housing the cult: Smyrna.[63]
    Another temple was involved in a request from the people of
Segesta in Sicily: it was on Mount Eryx, and dedicated to Venus. In
25 they asked for it to be restored; but Tiberius undertook to pay for
the work himself; after all, it was his ancestress (by adoption) who was
the object of the cult. There came at the same time two other cases for
decision: a dispute between Sparta and Messene over possession of
another temple, that of Diana Limnatis, in which the Senate gave
judgment for the Messenians; and the fate of the inheritance left by an
exile to his adopted city of Massilia (the bequest was allowed).[64]
    One of the incidents just mentioned concerned a province which
in AD 15 had been transferred from jurisdiction of proconsuls to that
of legates of Augustus. Commentators agree that the Senate's handling
of the case of Sparta and Messene represents a special concession made
by Tiberius. Sparta was a free city, no part of the province, but that
was not true of Aegium, one of the cities which in 23 were relieved
of their tribute obligations for three years.[65] The suspicion arises that
Tiberius was ready to acknowledge the senatorial interest, not only
in the provinces governed by proconsuls, but in those under legates;
a more liberal and more logical attitude than that propounded by Nero
in his speech.
    Another striking instance of senatorial involvement in an imperial
province is to be found. When Tiberius opened the trial of Cn. Piso

in AD 20 he spoke of him as a man who had been assigned to Syria as aide to Germanicus '*auctore senatu*' – at the instance of the Senate. However tendentious this sentence (Tiberius was trying to secure Piso a fair trial), and however little real choice the Senate had in the appointment of Germanicus' mentor, Piso's name had been the one that they advanced.[66]

More striking still is Drusus Caesar's promise in AD 14 that the claims of the Pannonian mutineers would be referred to the Senate. The mutineers themselves were quick to point out that the Senate was consulted only when the advantages of the military were in question; they never heard anything about battles or punishments. We do not hear the outcome of Drusus' promise, except that Tiberius certainly reported his and Germanicus' activities to the Senate, which presumably approved the increases. When they were rescinded Tiberius issued an edict – whether in consequence of a senatorial decision is not stated. Suetonius' claim that Tiberius consulted the Senate about levying troops and discharging them is a generalization that may be based on one incident only.[67]

Not even lip-service was paid later, when Iunius Gallio proposed that discharged members of the Praetorian Guard might sit with the knights in their fourteen reserved rows of seats in the theatre. Tiberius wrote a scathing reply to Gallio. What had he to do with soldiers? Their prizes and their instructions should come from the *imperator* and from nobody else. Perhaps Gallio had thought of something that the deified Augustus had overlooked; or was he trying to stir up trouble?[68] The Senate took the hint, deprived Gallio of his seat and then banished him from Italy. Tiberius' irritation with a gross flatterer is understandable; but the attack is an unmistakable sign of the change that had come over Tiberius since his early days as Princeps.

The truth was that the running of the army was too important and too delicate a matter to be left to the Senate, and the complexity of relations between Senate and Princeps is nowhere better illustrated than in Africa, a 'public' province but now the only one containing an army (one legion, fighting under the auspices of the Princeps). In general Tiberius seems to have behaved with propriety towards the province. Even so, it was he who in 21, when serious trouble broke out, informed the Senate, at the same time reminding the House of its responsibilities. It would have to appoint a governor fit for the job of quelling rebellion in desert terrain. The Senate did not rise to the occasion. Instead of allowing only the names of tried soldiers to go forward for sortition, it left the choice to the Princeps. Tiberius would not take on the entire responsibility for selecting the governor. He sent the Senate the names of two men: M. Lepidus and Q. Blaesus. Lepidus immediately withdrew, according to Tacitus because he feared the jealousy of Sejanus' uncle. Lepidus was not a coward, and he was a friend of Tiberius. His excuses (ill-health, young children, a marriageable daughter) could have been genuine. That does not exculpate the Senate.[69]

The incident reveals complexities in an apparently straightforward process: the appointment of provincial governors. The Augustan system had established the Princeps himself as governor of a number of provinces for a fixed term of years (renewable); he chose his own legates, and his choice was ratified by the Senate. For the two plum 'senatorial' provinces of Asia and Africa the two senior consulars (they had to be of at least five years' standing) who were free and willing drew lots; for the remaining 'senatorial' provinces men of praetorian rank. The Senate had to decide, first of all, whether to appoint at all, or whether to prorogue the man already in office. That might depend on the calibre of the latter, as on that of his possible successors. On that matter there might be debate, in which the Princeps could participate.[70] Again, the candidates had to put themselves forward and be accepted as such. P. Dolabella in AD 22 wanted Tiberius to undertake to scrutinize the character of potential candidates, a responsibility which the Princeps declined, with an appeal to the remedial power of *lex* and to mutability of character. Nevertheless, in 36 we find C. Galba committing suicide because a letter from Tiberius had forbidden him to put himself forward for the lucrative consular provinces. It looks as if the Princeps felt less scruple in intervening as time went on, at least in particular cases.[71]

In a different sense Tiberius himself confessed to intervening, when in 33 he complained of the reluctance of consulars to serve. He was speaking of imperial provinces; whether he had been brought to pray men to serve as proconsuls is not revealed. As early as AD 15 he had introduced a regulation which laid it down that lingering proconsuls should be off by 1 June; but it was in imperial provinces that he had to take the extreme step of allowing eminent men to hold office without discharging their duties in person.[72]

Once in his province, how free was the governor from imperial interference? It would be vain to accumulate random examples from all over the Empire, incidents drawn from other principates, when they cannot be compared, in numbers or in kind. But it is worth while drawing a contrast and considering one province in detail. Tiberius acknowledged the principle that a proconsul was supreme in his province and exempt from interference by unauthorized persons, even if they were employees of the Princeps. In AD 23 he protested vehemently that his procurator Lucilius Capito had no right to take over the functions of the proconsul, or to commandeer his troops. Capito was tried by the Senate and exiled. He cannot have been the only procurator to encroach on the functions of his governor, but his fate may have discouraged others for a while. Very different was the attitude of Claudius thirty years later. Far from trying to repress such encroachments, he had them legalized, enhancing the powers of *procuratores* by *senatus consultum*.[73]

Next, the province. Africa's military importance made it the supreme test. We have already noticed the propriety of Tiberius' conduct towards the Senate on the subject of this province, propriety only mildly tempered by military necessity. The same factors may be observed at work in his dealings with its governors,[74] whose name and style continued to appear on the coinage (this was a privilege that they did not keep under Tiberius' successor). Between the years 20 and 24 the governor could command the services of *legio IX Hispana*, besides those of the legion regularly stationed in the province, *III Augusta*; how he deployed them was for him to decide; and if he needed to supplement them by levying fresh troops, he was evidently free to do so – with the Senate's permission. The governor was permitted to make his own awards for bravery – but one was rebuked for the inadequacy of his – and required to report his successes to the Senate.[75] In other conflicts Tiberius showed himself willing to trust the judgment of men on the spot (in the Balkans he had suffered from Augustus' interference); as it was in Gaul in AD 21 and in the Orient in 34–37,[76] so too in the rebellion of Tacfarinas. For Velleius the struggle was won under Tiberius' auspices and by his instructions (*consilia*); the first claim was indubitable, the second probably true as far as overall policy was concerned; Africa, like the Orient, was too distant for detailed instructions to be issued at every juncture. The only instructions from Princeps to proconsul that we know of are those given to Q. Blaesus after the rebel had sent his insolent embassy to Tiberius demanding a home for his men. Blaesus was to grant an amnesty to the rest, and secure the person of Tacfarinas by whatever means he could.[77] There is nothing original in this policy, successful though it was, and it may have been urged on the proconsul only as part of the speech in which Tiberius whipped up the Senate's indignation. P. Dolabella, Blaesus' successor, did not have the *legio IX Hispana*. Tiberius ordered it back to Pannonia after Blaesus' victory; nor did Dolabella dare to detain it (so Tacitus): he was more afraid of Tiberius and his orders than of the dangers of fighting without the extra legion. If that was a blunder on Tiberius' part it was committed on the advice of his man on the spot.[76]

Nor is there much evidence for consistent intervention in routine matters.[79] We can hold that L. Lamia mentioned orders from the Princeps on a road-building inscription because such orders were exceptional; in that case all the other public works attested for the years 14–37 were executed on the sole initiative of governors.[80] There is something inherently implausible in that picture; it is hard to believe that Tiberius was not informed beforehand at least when large-scale works were proposed; and if he were informed, he could suggest modifications. Road works in particular would be a matter of interest to a military man and it comes as no surprise that in his old province of Illyricum the governor P. Dolabella was particularly active. The grammar of the inscriptions differs in Illyricum; Tiberius himself is credited with the roads that Dolabella, his legate, constructed.[81] But perhaps the difference between the two provinces lay less in their constitutional status than in the fact that Tiberius was thoroughly and recently familiar with Illyricum, while he had never set foot in Africa.

Cities which, like Sparta, were free were technically outside the Empire. That was what brought them within the Senate's sphere of competence, foreign affairs. That sphere naturally included kings dependent upon Rome for their position and kept in it for their usefulness. Suetonius specifically says that the Senate was regularly consulted on the subject.[82] Archelaus of Cappadocia was accused before it in AD 17, but acquitted. Again a contrast between the conduct of Augustus and that of Tiberius: one cause of the second trial was said to be Tiberius' resentment at the way Archelaus had treated him when he was on Rhodes. Archelaus owed Tiberius a debt of gratitude for a defence made on his behalf at an earlier hearing. That had been in 27 BC, and the case had been taken by Augustus, then consul, but not before the Senate.[83]

In the following year, AD 18, Maroboduus, whose power had been (so Tiberius said) more of a threat to Rome than that of Pyrrhus or Antiochus III, lost his kingdom in the Bohemian tableland and took refuge south of the Danube. Tiberius' speech was made in the Senate, where the fate of the old chieftain was debated.[84] The fate of another enemy was discussed there in AD 19. A Chattan chieftain had offered to poison Arminius, Rome's great opponent in Germany, whose power and ambition would have been enhanced by the departure of

Maroboduus.[85] Like the previous debate, this one gave Tiberius and the Senate an opportunity to strike a high and generous note. Once again Pyrrhus was invoked. The Senate had disdained to use treachery against him; they would do no worse now. Perhaps the Senate was only brought in to make this propaganda point. But the same period (AD 18) saw another prince on trial in the House: Rhescuporis of Thrace, accused of murder by the widow of his victim Cotys. The Senate sent him into exile and divided the kingdom between his son and those of his victim.[86] Clients could be rewarded as well as punished. When the war with Tacfarinas was finally over, the Senate sent one of its members to Ptolemy of Mauretania. The envoy took with him an embroidered robe of honour, in acknowledgement of services rendered. It was an antique custom; earlier recipients had been Porsena, Massinissa, and Ariovistus.[87]

What all this activity adds up to is hard to say. There was a formal element in the Tiberian policy: important matters were on the agenda; how effectively they were dealt with is another question. And however effective and strong-minded the Senate was, there were limits beyond which it could not go. Tiberius set those limits, but he set them wide, wider than they had been since 43 BC and wider than they were ever to be again, except for a brief interregnum in 41. A few bold spirits, some inspired by malice, dared explore the terrain open to them as far as its limits. Others made a play of it: Valerius Messalla Messallinus is an example, affecting freedom of speech even as he proposed that the oath of allegiance to Tiberius should be repeated yearly.[88]

If the Senate could not venture to broach certain subjects, there were others of which it was not even informed. No debate followed the death of Agrippa Postumus; and the pretender Clemens was quietly executed in the palace. True, he was technically the property of the Princeps, but the matter was one of public concern. We have already seen in the first case that Tiberius' silence may have had no sinister motive; and the backers of Clemens, if allowed to go unmolested, would do less harm than they might as dead or exiled martyrs.[89]

The Senate was not perfectly informed on provincial matters either. They did not hear about the revolt in Gaul until it had been put down, so Tacitus and Velleius report. And Tiberius allegedly hid the losses suffered by L. Apronius in 28 at the hands of the Frisii to avoid having to appoint a commander to deal with them.[90] But these were matters for the executive. The Senate's function was to formulate policy, and there was no question in any of these cases of a change; Tiberius was acting within his competence as a holder of *imperium*.

Much more significant is Tacitus' silence on the outbreak of trouble with Parthia in 35. There were embassies, policy to be formulated, a commander to be appointed. We hear of it in some detail in the pages of Tacitus. Not a word of the Senate.[91]

This is too striking not to indicate a change in Tiberius' attitude, the abandonment of efforts that he had found exhausting and not always worth while. The change will not have come about all at once; turning points can be indicated. There was a change in the tone of the Princeps' recorded dealings with the Senate after 28. His impatient reaction in 32 to Gallio's proposal and to the Senate's acceptance of the Sibylline corpus is far removed from the didactic and ironical, but full and courteous, lectures of the early years. The last serious policy debate reported in our sources came at the time of the financial crisis of AD 33, and a sorry showing the Senate made. There is very little after AD 28, and we cannot attribute this to loss of interest in Tacitus' part or to a change in the sources he was using. It has been thought that until AD 31 he made nearly exclusive use of the *History* of Aufidius Bassus, whose work was then taken up by the elder Pliny. But Tacitus claimed to consult, not only all the available literary authorities but the archives of the Senate as well. Quite apart from the fact that he lets fall clues inadvertently (for example, the fact that the Senate played some part in the appointment of Cn. Piso), Tacitus was keenly interested in our topic, was conscious of the change (for he says that until AD 23 the Senate was handling all business), and was ready to offer a reason for it.[92] His comment on the hushing up of the Roman losses of 28 is that the Senate had other things to think about: the dynastic struggle at home. Exactly the same was true of Tiberius, as Velleius discloses.[93]

This remark of Tacitus points clearly to one cause of trouble. The Senate, functioning as a court, was being exploited by rival factions; its members became committed by their votes to one group or another and through hatred or terror were incapable of operating as a serious deliberative body. In this process we may legitimately regard the fall of Sejanus in October 31 as a decisive point both for the sharp about-turn of thought that it entailed for the Senate as a body and for the calamities that followed.

Even before this process reached its climax other factors must have begun to take effect. One such factor was certainly the final departure of the Princeps from Rome in 26. When he was in the city Tiberius was an assiduous attender, and his presence and interest would keep up the standard of debate.[94] A false step could be retrieved, if the Princeps' displeasure appeared at once; in his absence irreparable blunders such as Gallio's might be perpetrated. Right from the start the Senate was uncertain how much business it could transact during the absence of the Princeps. Cn. Piso's view in AD 16 had been that business should not be put off: it would bring credit on the state that senators and *equites* could perform their functions in his absence; Asinius Gallus countered with the opinion that it was only when business was conducted under the Princeps' eyes that the dignity of the Roman people was adequately maintained. That dignity was the ostensible criterion; in effect the issue was the Senate's freedom of debate and the powers of the Princeps, championed as usual by the ambitious Gallus. The senators took the point, and his view won the day, establishing a pernicious precedent.[95] It was during a temporary absence of 21–22 that the question of extravagance came up for the second time, to be referred to Tiberius at once without discussion. Moreover, the process of decision-making was perceptibly slowed down by the absence of the Princeps on an island three miles off a headland that was itself a hundred miles from Rome. It made it less worth while for him to consult the Senate, especially on matters that required dispatch, and less pointful for them to take pains over the formation of opinion. The centre of government was no longer at Rome, and the Senate's position was weakened in consequence.

But the failure of Tiberius' senatorial policy had been clear to him before he left for Campania and Capri in 26; indeed his departure may be attributed partly to its failure, perhaps to a misguided idea that his absence would encourage the Senate to debate more freely: in 33 he was still insisting that meetings should not be skimped.[96] We have seen that Tiberius inherited a political paradox from his predecessor, and that he tried to deal with it by educating his masters into independence. His failure to do so was due to faults on both sides. His own was inconsistency. Sometimes he would sit silent, as he did at the altercation between Cn. Piso and Asinius Gallus; sometimes he would speak in the middle of the debate, sometimes last; sometimes he would write advice to the consuls, or make use of his tribunician veto; he might remain poker-faced for a while – and then break out into anger. He was a human being and needed rules and precedents to guide him; none adequately limited the Princeps in his dealings with the Senate. The senators did not know where they were.[97] The Senate has received its full share of the blame – as if it was a unified body, not a group of individuals with the interests of individuals. A few men understood and respected the Princeps' policy; others were well-disposed, yet thought him misguided. But even at the beginning of his principate Tiberius was far from enjoying the esteem of the whole body. The House contained men who had backed his rivals and who hated and feared him in consequence. If they had courage they showed their hatred; if not, they followed the example of careerists who voted to please. But the Senate, after all, ought to have been more than a group of individuals. It had privileges and responsibilities. To be sure, throughout this chapter its interest in its privileges has been to the fore. Hardly ever did the Senate dare to oppose a Princeps. One such notable occasion, perhaps the last, was in AD 48, when Claudius proposed to grant permission to stand for senatorial magistracies to the chieftains of Gaul. The Senate was less vociferous about its responsibilities. The Princeps, whose own motto might have been 'noblesse oblige', found that there was nothing to be done with these men. They would listen to lectures on their duties as senators and magistrates and go their own way. 'Ready for slavery' was Tiberius' verdict, a habitual one according to Tacitus.[98] He records it under AD 22; but we can trace a change in the Princeps' thinking before that date. At the time of his accession to sole power he had disclaimed any desire to be a *princeps*; by 21 he was excusing himself from dealing with the Gallic revolt in person and from sending Drusus Caesar by saying that it was unfitting for the Princeps to leave the capital; and in the following year he spoke openly and realistically about his higher obligations as Princeps. It was a recognition of defeat. That five more years elapsed before he signalized it by retreating, seven before he railed at the Senate for allowing a single senator to bring his '*imperatoria maiestas*', his dignity as Princeps, into public ridicule, does him some credit.[99]

CHAPTER VIII

EQUITES AND PLEBS

It is only because Tiberius' overriding policy of favouring the Senate needed separate treatment that the equestrian order finds itself ranged here alongside the common people. Otherwise for the supporter of *concordia ordinum*, harmony between the classes of Roman society, they were not natural bedfellows. The propertied and responsible classes, senators and knights, were to be united in Tiberius' support. To that end, knights as well as senators were assigned to the ten centuries of C. and L. Caesar under the *lex Valeria Cornelia* of AD 5 and to the five of Germanicus and five of Drusus Caesar that were created by *senatus consultum* after the deaths of those *principes*; to that end, knights, also in AD 5, were allocated special seats in the circus alongside those of the senators.[1] Nor, as we have seen, did Tiberius show any reluctance to admit municipal members of the equestrian order to the Senate. Not surprisingly: like many of his peers, he had equestrian antecedents: his grandmother Alfidia and his first mother-in-law Caecilia could claim no higher rank. And finally Tiberius, like most senators, had friends in that order as well as in the Senate; for seventeen years one of his most intimate and influential friends, L. Aelius Sejanus, was an *eques*; a fact that must have given satisfaction to the whole order.[2]

The dignity of that order Tiberius showed himself as anxious to preserve as Augustus had been. A *senatus consultum* of 23 defended the prestige of the *equites* and united the order by allowing the gold ring that distinguished it only to the freeborn sons of freeborn men with freeborn grandfathers on their father's side, provided that they also possessed the equestrian census and were entitled to sit in the fourteen rows of the theatre under the *lex Iulia*. There had been encroachments by men of servile origin, and those were to be brought to an end. In the following year the *lex Visellia* made freedmen who passed themselves off as freeborn men liable to prosecution; one offence specifically mentioned was that of attempting to become a member of a municipal council. The law was not entirely negative: on the old principle that a man who served Rome deserved advancement in status it allowed six years' service in the Vigiles to qualify Junian Latins for full citizenship; but the main purpose of both *senatus consultum* and *lex* was to preserve social distinctions and the privileges and dignity of the upper classes.³ Misconduct by members of the equestrian as well as the senatorial order was sharply checked: women who registered as prostitutes in order to escape from the penalties of adultery, young men who voluntarily degraded themselves in rank so as to appear in the arena or on the stage, all were liable to exile.⁴

On the other hand, the old-fashioned Princeps was acutely aware of the differences in standing between senators and *equites* of high standing and did not mind pointing it out, even to Sejanus himself – if we accept as genuine the letter of 25 in which Tacitus has him making the point.⁵ The Princeps' preoccupation with place and function operated against the order as well as for them. On at least one famous occasion, two years earlier, Tiberius showed his reluctance to allow any equestrian official in his employ to encroach on the privileges and powers of a proconsul. Later in his principate, to be sure, there may have been a change. For one thing, an equestrian procurator of Jamnia, Herennius Capito, is found sending soldiers to exact repayment of a debt from Herod Agrippa of Judaea; but unlike Lucilius Capito he was not thereby usurping rights that properly belonged to a senatorial governor. It would never have occurred to Tiberius to replace a defunct proconsul of Asia, even temporarily, with the procurator of the province, as Domitian did.⁶ In this respect the preserves of the *equites* were less carefully guarded than those of the Senate: we find a freedman, Hiberus, in the normally equestrian post of Prefect of Egypt for a few months in A D 32; and if he had not died in the office he might have gone on holding it. Tiberius is admitted by Tacitus to have exercised strict control over his (relatively few) freedmen, at least until A D 23. The appointment of Hiberus suggests that their influence may have increased as time went on, perhaps because the Princeps became increasingly isolated from all but his immediate household after his departure for Capri. All the same, the months that followed the fall of Sejanus may be seen as a period of crisis; and Tiberius may naturally have been willing to take extraordinary measures to ensure the security of Egypt. But Hiberus is not the only evidence for an increase in the influence of the freedmen. The New Year letter that Tiberius wrote to the Senate in January 28 accused Titius Sabinus, a Roman knight, of offering bribes to his freedmen; and Agrippa of Judaea thought the same enterprise worth his money. When L. Fulcinius Trio was forced to suicide in A D 35 it was Tiberius' chief freedmen he attacked in his will alongside the Praetorian Prefect Macro.⁷

Between Tiberius, the defender of established privilege, and the unprivileged members of society cordiality was not to be expected. Velleius' picture of the rejoicings that attended his return from Rhodes and his adoption, of the popular demand that he should be given the Pannonian command in AD 6, is overdrawn, and significant for that reason; it should be set against the lampoons quoted by Suetonius, of which the second couplet denies Tiberius the rank of *eques*, for want of the property qualification. That is a reference to his adoption by Augustus and its consequences, and the couplet probably belongs precisely to the year that, according to Velleius, saw him return to such rejoicing.[8] The lampoons never stopped from that time; Tiberius had renounced any attempt to win the favour of the people when he entered upon his second consulship with the promise to restore the temple of Concord, and his political opponents repeatedly took advantage of that fact. We have already noticed the city populace demonstrating or threatening to demonstrate in favour of his rivals. Twice, in 6 BC and AD 3, they won their point. They had genuine grievances: hunger, high rents, flooding, fires; and it is probable that in 2 BC and virtually certain that in AD 6 they were encouraged to voice them by those rivals; Tiberius in 6 BC and again in AD 6 was a man in power – a convenient scapegoat for their discontents if Augustus himself was not to be touched. Games celebrated in honour of the dead Nero Drusus in the spring of AD 7 helped to distract them from their anger; on 10 August of the same year an altar to the beneficent deities and providers of corn Ceres Mater and Ops Augusta was dedicated in fulfilment of a vow; and Nero Drusus was commemorated again in the dedication of the temples of Castor and Concord, for which Tiberius paid from his German spoils.[9] But this was not the end of such episodes. The trouble that Augustus expected in AD 14 did not materialize; but in AD 16 the false Agrippa Postumus attracted a huge crowd of supporters in his march on Ostia and Rome; and thirteen years later, when Agrippina and her elder son were attacked in the Senate, the demonstrators outside were persistent and noisy. They were not, it must be admitted, openly hostile to the Princeps; Sejanus rather was their target; and that suggests perhaps that they were under discipline. In 31 Tiberius was given a clear intimation of the preferences of the people when he conferred priesthoods on Gaius Caligula and on Sejanus and his son; and in October, when he staged his coup against Sejanus, Tiberius considered that his only way of securing the populace for his cause was to release his grandson Drusus Caesar from confinement and put him at their head.[10] For Sejanus had been at pains to occupy the place that Tiberius had left empty by courting the *plebs*. He made some headway: the construction of granaries is recorded, and in 22 strenuous efforts to save the theatre of Pompey from destruction by fire and to prevent the fire from spreading (fire was an ever-present terror to the poorer classes of Rome). Sejanus brought his campaign to a spectacular end by having his election to the consulship confirmed on the Aventine Hill. The Aventine had strong associations with the *plebs*: it was there that they had withdrawn in ancient times under patrician oppression and that the plebeian cults of Diana, of Liber and Ceres, the deities of wine and grain, were established, there that Gaius Gracchus had made his last stand in 121 BC. If Juvenal is to be believed, what won Sejanus friends in the urban *plebs* was as much his political success as his ideological pretensions. That is a cynical view; the *plebs* felt genuine affection for the families of Julia the elder and Germanicus, and compared with that any impression made by Sejanus was superficial and did not survive his disgrace by a minute.[11]

It is to the period immediately after the fall of Sejanus that there belongs one piece of evidence that seems to show Tiberius aware of Sejanus' efforts and ready to cajole as well as to intimidate the people.[12] The inscription reads:

> [At n]unc quoniam r[upit pacem (?)]
> [a]nnorum lx Seiani sc[elerata]
> [inc]itatio et improbae comitiae
> [ill]ae fuerunt in Aventino ubi
> [Sei]anus cos. factus est et ego
> [de]bilis inutilis baculi comes
> [u]t supplex fierem, omni nunc <vi(?)>
> [v]os rogo boni contr-
> [ibu]les si semper apparui
> [vo]bis bonus et utilis tri-
> [bul]is si numquam offic-
> [ium deser(?)]ui nec rei [. . .
> —]m coi[—
> —] rif[—:

But now, since the criminal incitement (or perhaps '[*flag*]*itatio*', 'demand') of Sejanus has destroyed the peace of sixty years (?), and that irregular electoral assembly has taken place on the Aventine at which Sejanus was elected consul and I, the feeble companion of an unserviceable staff, was brought to become a suppliant, I ask you with all my might (?), my worthy fellow-tribesmen, if I have always

seemed to you to be a worthy and serviceable member of our tribe,
if I have never deserted my duty nor . . .[13]

The document is extraordinary and in many respects inexplicable;
that alone is enough to guarantee its authenticity. The prime question
it raises is that of the identity of the speaker. The syntax is anomalous
(I have taken '*fierem*' to depend on a '*factus sum*' to be inferred from
'*factus est*') and the grammar worse: '*improbae comitiae*' is a gross
solecism on the part of the man who drafted the appeal or on that of
the lapicide. There is no difficulty with the sense of the phrase. The
comitia centuriata should meet as *iusta comitia* (a duly appointed assembly of the people) on the Campus Martius (not on the Aventine)
and continued to do so even after AD 14 when it merely ratified the
Senate's choice of candidates for consulship and praetorship. The
author of the document knows what he is talking about and has even
the rare word '*contribulis*' at his disposal. He is a person of consequence,
who expects to be known to his fellow tribesmen; and he became a
'*supplex*' at the election of Sejanus, a word used in electoral contexts
of the candidates who sought office. It is natural to think of Tiberius,
who took office at the same election as Sejanus, who was in his seventies
at the time, and who might describe himself literally as the 'feeble
companion of a staff' and metaphorically as 'the companion of a useless
(or harmful) staff' (that is to say, of Sejanus; the word '*inutilis*' was often
applied to persons); who certainly considered himself a slave to his
duty, and who was notoriously given to obscure and convoluted language. The '*improbae comitiae*' remain an obstacle to holding Tiberius
to be the author of the inscription; he was unclear but pedantically
correct in his speech. It is best perhaps to think of an error made by a
hasty stone-cutter, who seems to have made at least one other mistake.
Tiberius, if it is he, is asking a favour of his fellow tribesmen after the
fall of Sejanus. We cannot tell what it is; perhaps no more than an
appeal for order in the aftermath of the disturbances; at any rate the
tone is thoroughly conciliatory.[14]

All the evidence we have considered so far is from Rome and the
neighbourhood. But there was enthusiasm for the false Agrippa in
Italy too, and in AD 33 for a false Drusus Caesar who appeared in the
eastern provinces.[15] Whether Tiberius' concern for the quietude of the
Italian cities was more than a normal dislike for inter-factional strife
and proletarian disturbances is uncertain; the cities had sufficient causes
for such disturbances and there is no need to postulate dynastic politics
as an issue. When Tiberius died the people demanded his corpse as a

lay figure for the spring festival at Atella, but by 37 his unpopularity was very widespread and its original causes seemed remote, if they were not altogether forgotten.[16]

For Tiberius' unpopularity Z. Yavetz has held Tiberius himself largely to blame. Yavetz has allowed the pre-existing unpopularity of the Princeps to slip out of sight; but there is no doubt that Tiberius' principles and pride (*adrogantia*) exacerbated it.[17] We have already seen that he made little or no attempt to present a winning side of himself to the masses of Rome; his very first act as Princeps was effectively to deprive the people of their rights as electors. Yet he was conscious – bitterly conscious – of his unpopularity. By A D 14 it had been made too clear too often to be missed. By A D 23 the cohorts of the Praetorian Guard, which had been dispersed about Rome and Italy, were assembled in one permanent camp just outside the city, and it is a plausible guess that they were concentrated there because it was in Rome that disturbances were most feared, though Sejanus' pretext was military discipline.[18] During Tiberius' principate the populace perforce remained quiet for the most part, making its feelings plain only at times of the greatest strain – that is to say, when corn was short. But Tiberius had his means of sounding public opinion, as Tacitus indicates.[19] It made no difference. Consciousness of unpopularity will have made it even more difficult for Tiberius to pay court to the people.

The underlying tone, then, was hostile. The Princeps had also to deal with day to day fluctuations of public opinion. Nobody knew better than Tiberius what the populace could achieve if it put its mind to it. That knowledge cannot have failed to have its effect on the most tenaciously held of principles. Early in his principate Tiberius, who had a passion for Lysippus' statue the *Apoxyomenos*, had it removed from in front of the Baths of Agrippa and taken to his own bedroom, replacing it with another work. Eventually he gave way to the public outcry in the theatre (the usual place for public demonstrations) and had it put back.[20] Tiberius did not merely react to disorder with speed and decision; he sensibly made every effort to satisfy the reasonable wants of the people. He was conscientious in maintaining grain supplies in face of widespread and persistent shortages, transport difficulties, and perhaps losses due to the rebellion in Africa (17–24). He brought them in, as he himself claimed, from more provinces than Augustus had exploited and on one occasion (in A D 19) subsidized the price; justifiably he resented being accused of negligence.[21] He distributed tips to the people (on appropriate occasions: three is the number that Velleius astutely conceals) on the same scale as Augustus; he was slow in dis-

tributing the largesse that Augustus had left his people, and one anecdote has him savagely making away with a man who criticized him
for his tardiness; but Augustus had allowed a year for the payment of
some legacies, and he may have been a little shorter of cash than he
realized.[22] Real need made Tiberius quicker to act. He made earnest,
if not at first successful, efforts to check the Tiber floods; his generosity
and concern after the fires at Rome in AD 16, 27, and 36 were above
reproach and even won him some short-lived popularity.[23] To attribute
these efforts to prudence does not do Tiberius justice: we must allow
for his sense of duty and his awareness of the responsibilities his position
imposed. A sense of duty as well as prudence is evident in Tacitus'
version of the pronouncement he made during the senatorial debate
on extravagance and luxury in AD 22. That his conduct after the fires
was due to regard for his own repute ('gloria') is hinted by Tacitus;
common humanity may have been a factor, though we should not
make too much of Velleius' stories of the consideration he showed to
his soldiers on campaign: a valuable asset was not to be wasted or mis-
handled; and the interest in the sick that he displayed on the island of
Rhodes may have been scientific rather than humanitarian.[24]

Tiberius did what he thought was his duty. Corn and, to a lesser
extent, *congiaria* (tips) came into that category. Dutifulness was not
enough. His tone was paternalistic. When the commons complained
of the inadequacy of the corn supplies they received a sharp rebuke,
and that was not the only time. Gladiatorial and theatrical performances
and the circus he hated, and attended them only for a short time,
perhaps until he found that the spectators were using them as occasions for bringing pressure to bear on him, not only to put back their
favourite statues, but to emancipate their favourite actors. These shows
he did not regard as obligatory, whatever Augustus' practice had been,
and they were curtailed and a limit set to the number of gladiatorial
contests to be given at any one festival. The people continued to make
use of what opportunities they had left: in AD 32 they were still able
to make a vociferous demonstration in the theatre for several days on
end (it was over a grain shortage). Nor had Tiberius ventured to make
the transition to austerity too sudden; in AD 15 actors' pay was cut,
and unruly members of the profession guaranteed exemption from
corporal punishment only because they could produce a ruling of
Augustus to that effect. Eight years later the Princeps returned to the
attack, drawing the attention of the Senate to the outrageous, seditious,
and licentious behaviour of actors. The old Atellan farce, which was
so much to the trivial taste of the common people, had become so

powerful an influence for mischief that it must be restrained by the Senate. The House obliged by expelling the actors, or some of them, from Italy; and the resentment that that action caused survived until Tiberius died; at any rate, Caligula at once restored the exiles. In AD 27 the people flocked to the fatal amphitheatre at Fidena precisely because there was nothing on at Rome, and Seneca presents us with a gladiator, Triumphus, lamenting the state of the times under Tiberius: 'How fair an age has passed away!'[25]

Nor did the Princeps embark on any fresh large-scale building programme. The few new public buildings he is known to have constructed, even that purely utilitarian project, the barracks for the Praetorians on the Viminal, were put in hand near the beginning of his principate, like those he repaired (except for the rebuilding after the fires); and three of them might have been calculated, were in fact calculated, to remind the *plebs* of the genial and generous Princeps they had lost. An arch for the return of the standards captured in Germany, a temple of Fors Fortuna (a deity with plebeian associations), a temple of the Gens Iulia and a statue of Augustus at Bovillae, all were dedicated in AD 16; a number of temples that Augustus had begun to repair were completed by Tiberius and dedicated in AD 17; the temple of the deified Augustus, to which Tiberius was committed from the moment of consecration, if not the restored *scaena* (stage) of Pompey's theatre, was completed probably by AD 34, but both remained undedicated in the Princeps' absence. Dio gives an impression of substantial building operations undertaken at the beginning of the principate but not exploited by the Princeps to his own glory; Velleius exploits them, but does not go into detail, and this is significant.[26] We may conclude that even in the eyes of an admiring contemporary the programme was relatively modest, especially compared with the achievements of which Augustus could boast (he restored no fewer than eighty-two buildings), and that Tiberius made no capital out of it. He had less faith than most Romans in monuments built of stone as a means of preserving a man's memory;[27] the economical Princeps thought he had more cogent reasons – the very success of Augustus, shortage of cash – for refraining. But the policy was unfortunate even from the economic point of view. Imperial investment in building would have stimulated the economy; certainly it would have provided employment for a number of artisans in the city. But it was the apparent meanness and lack of ambition of the new regime – a dispiriting contrast with the exhilarating grandeur of the Augustan programme – that is our concern as affecting the morale of the populace.

For a man sensitive about his reputation with posterity Tiberius
was remarkably careless of contemporary and lower-class public
opinion, no doubt because history was not written by members of the
urban *plebs*. But their reactions were duly recorded and one thing that
was noted was the contrast between the impression made by Tiberius'
arrogance and by the affability of Germanicus and Agrippina, who
enjoyed and probably courted the favour of the populace. In AD 19
the arrogance was seen to be sinister as well as irritating. Germanicus
died in the East, it was said of poison administered by Tiberius' friend
Cn. Piso; and Tiberius checked the spontaneous mourning of the
people with one of his brusque *communiqués*. When the ashes arrived
in Rome neither he nor Livia attended their interment; and the
common people had no time for the aristocratic and Stoic restraint
that Tiberius habitually showed in face of grief. Besides, he tried to
secure the man charged with the murder a fair trial.[28] When, ten years
later, Germanicus' widow and eldest son fell into disgrace, suspicion
would become certainty. And it was only natural to return the hatred
of a man who had shown his feelings by absenting himself from the
city, issuing instructions that his peace was not to be disturbed, and
finally shutting himself up on an island for purposes clearly divined by
his friends the Atellan *farceurs*: 'Up the island roes the tongue of an
old goat goes.'[29] Upon Germanicus' son, Gaius Caligula, focused hopes
of release from a dreary and in the end, for a limited circle, terrifying
regime; upon the boy's grandfather focused hatred for maintaining it
and for making away with Gaius' father, mother, and brothers.[30]
Gaius Caligula inherited all their popularity; but it was not Gaius'
popularity that prompted the demand 'Tiberius to the Tiber'; his claim
to power rested partly on his kinship with Tiberius and on his recognition in Tiberius' will, and that should have imposed caution on the
people. By making a display of his aristocratic independence and his
senatorial principles, by neglecting public opinion, and by allowing
dynastic faction free play, Tiberius added in no small measure to the
discontent that, through no fault of his own, his original advancement
had roused. In a sense Tiberius had the last word with the *plebs*. The
Senate annulled his will, but Gaius Caligula undertook to pay the
legacies. Each member of the Praetorian Guard received 1,000 sesterces,
of the Urban Cohorts half as much, of the Vigiles and the legions
300 sesterces; the city populace received 45 million sesterces. Tiberius
had arrived at those sums by consulting the will of Augustus; having
calculated his duty down the last *as*, he stuck to it to the end.[31]

CHAPTER IX

PROVINCIAL AND FOREIGN POLICY

Augustus' overall control of the provinces was made explicit in 23 BC when he received *proconsulare imperium maius*. Yet a governor might still see himself as king for a year, and it was in a royal deed that L. Volesus Messalla, proconsul of Asia, exulted as he stalked past the bodies of the men he had condemned. This man held office in the last years of Augustus, but it is usually maintained that there was a marked improvement in the standard of provincial government under the Principate: the Princeps chose many governors himself, supervised them, and made the prosecution of malefactors easier, both by promoting legislation (the *senatus consultum Calvisianum* of 4 BC offered provincials a new and speedier method of redressing non-capital wrongs) and by making himself accessible to delegations of Rome's subjects; from his point of view the support of the provincials, or at least of the influential classes among them, was important as a counterpoise to possible senatorial discontent, as it already had been to dynasts of the late Republic, to Marius, Pompey, and Caesar.[1]

The principate of Tiberius has been singled out for special praise. Not only did it see the system in full working order, but Tiberius made two innovations of his own. First, the long tenure enjoyed by some governors, not only legates in the 'imperial' provinces, but proconsuls. C. Poppaeus Sabinus, legate of Moesia for twenty-four years until his death at the end of AD 35, with Achaea and Macedonia added in AD 15, is a striking example of the first category; P. Petronius, proconsul of Asia perhaps from AD 29 to 35, of the second.[2] These men had more time to learn their jobs, it is claimed, than the normal proconsul, with his single year in office, and even than the legate, with three. Second, and even more remarkable, two men governed in absence. Neither L. Aelius Lamia, legate of Syria from *c*. AD 21 to 32, nor L. Arruntius, legate of Tarraconensis from AD 23 at least until 33, ever went out to his province. Hence the view that Tiberius was planning a centralized administration, a kind of ministry that would govern the provinces from Rome, keeping the man in charge of each under the eye of the Princeps.[3]

More recently, and notably by Brunt, Alföldy, and Orth, provincial government under the Principate, and in particular the administration of Tiberius, have been seen in a less rosy light. The Princeps was concerned more with exploiting the provinces than with advancing their economic and social life and their status. Pontius Pilate was one of the men that Tiberius kept in office for years (in that case nine); there was no shortage of prosecutions for maladministration during his principate, and we have three serious uprisings to account for (the long-lasting rebellion of Tacfarinas in Africa, the revolt of Florus and Sacrovir in Gaul in 21, and that of the Frisii in 28). In Judaea later the complaint was heard that the Princeps in Rome was too far away to know everything that went on; under Tiberius two governors of first-class provinces were at the same distance or not much less.[4] The whole topic of Tiberius' provincial administration needs to be reconsidered in the light of these recent criticisms.

If Tiberius failed it was not for want of personal experience, in this as in other areas of his life. He had seen service abroad from his earliest years, and his training for empire equalled that of Augustus, Vespasian, and Trajan. At sixteen he was fighting in Spain; at twenty-two leading an army through the Balkans and Anatolia into Armenia, and, according to Velleius, giving proof of all his merits by the way, no doubt by making himself affable to men who mattered in the provinces and by promising future services. He had been active in the defence and pacification of Gallia Comata and in the conquest of the Alps, Illyricum, and Germany, and he would have launched the civil administration of those regions, if he did not actually supervise its working. On the island of Rhodes he had seen life in the Roman Empire as private individual as well as army commander and he had taken some part in the life of its people in the gymnasium and schools.[5]

Experience was nothing without reflection. Tiberius had views. He kept his public and his private life in separate compartments. The magistrates of Rhodes approached him as Princeps with a request not completed in due form with prayers for his welfare; they were not spared the trouble of coming to Rome to correct their mistake; and they had feared worse. In A D 22 a dispute over control of a temple was brought to the Senate by Messene and Sparta, which was under Tiberius' patronage; the Messenians won.[6] The aloof impartiality, the harshness to friends, were studied, part of his awareness that more was expected of a Princeps than of men in lower positions.

The same idea played its part in Tiberius' failure to visit any part of the Empire after he came to power. He had spent twenty-eight years or seasons abroad before A D 14. After his accession he never left central Italy. It was a source of grievance in that year that an experienced general, in health and only fifty-six years old, could not or would not approach the mutinous legions of Pannonia and the Rhine. At that

moment Tiberius, as we have seen, may have had closer fears; but
according to Tacitus he was trying to show impartiality towards the
two armies and to hold his own majesty in reserve. Yet public opinion,
or his own anxieties, an idea of using that *maiestas* to intimidate the
mutinous soldiers on the spot or (in 23) to spur on recruiting officers in
the performance of their duty, forced him to prepare for a journey that
would never be made, in AD 14 or any other year. His dilatory behaviour, which earned him the nickname 'Callipides' (after a Greek
runner who made no progress), was contrasted unfavourably with the
energy of Augustus; but the truth was that Augustus' last visit to Gaul
had been undertaken when he was a year younger than Tiberius was in
AD 14. After 8 BC he too was never to leave Italy again. Tiberius, then,
was adopting the same policy that Augustus had pursued for the last
twenty-two years of his principate. Like Augustus, Tiberius could rely,
at least for the first nine years, on members of the dynasty. By the end of
that time, what may have begun as practice had become confirmed
principle, a principle that meant that the Princeps never saw the provinces.[7]

Tiberius' campaigns in Germany and Illyricum from AD 4 onwards
betray no reluctance to delegate responsibility to subordinates, but it
would be wrong to believe that he later stayed in Italy because of a
delicate sensibility towards the feelings of provincial governors or even
towards those of his sons. Germanicus received *imperium proconsulare* in
Germany in AD 14; that did not prevent Tiberius exerting strong pressure on him when he thought that the campaigns ought to be brought
to an end; he made Cn. Piso governor of Syria in AD 17 to restrain the
activities of Germanicus; and the latter's unauthorized entry into Egypt
provoked a sharp and public reaction.[8] Tiberius could intervene at a
distance. Other determining factors can be made out. The Empire was a
monster. Tiberius' very grasp of *minutiae*, the care with which his
campaigns were prepared, may have warned him that he could not
involve himself in the affairs of one province without neglecting the
rest; his province was the world, and a man with an eye for detail but
little creative imagination (his taste in literature reveals these qualities of
mind) had to school himself to see the whole. And finally his appeals to
the majesty of the Principate veiled an abhorrence of solicitation and
flattery that grew less easy to hide as time went on.[9]

Yet it is this man who is credited with two remarkable innovations in
Roman provincial administration – not that the ancient writers saw
much policy in them, or anything creditable. For the prorogation of
governors, Tacitus repeats the reasons he found in the works of his pre-

decessors: a dislike of taking fresh decisions, and an innate conservatism;
the wish to allow as few as men as possible to enjoy authority; a preference for mediocrity. Neither of these last two explanations is credible,
certainly no more credible than Dio's allegation that the depleted Senate
of Tiberius' last years could not provide sufficient numbers of officials
(that at least turns out to be a distortion of the truth). A famous *mot* of
Tiberius compares governors in their provinces with gorged flies on a
sore: it was better to leave them than to drive them off to make way for
fresh ones. If Tiberius said this, it was as a bitter and impatient joke, made
perhaps in reply to criticism, and it is not to be taken as revealing his
true views. In AD 33 Tiberius was heard complaining of the unwillingness of good men to take up provincial commands.[10] Far from preferring
mediocrities, Tiberius wanted to give posts to men of merit; those he
secured he continued in office and did not supersede them with men
less able. That was the theory. Tiberius' dislike of taking decisions[11]
reinforced it, but made the practice less admirable than the theory, for
the incompetent or dishonest were also continued, remaining immune
to prosecution as long as they held their posts. It should cause no surprise
that competent governors were hard to find. Even under the Republic
it was not every senator who jumped at the chance of governing a
province: Cicero was one of those who avoided the experience as long
as he could. Now the political rewards, if not the financial, were mea-
surably less great; some men's ambitions were satisfied by the ennobling
consulship; and the capital had obvious attractions, especially perhaps
when compared with the chilly northern provinces. Tiberius' remedy
aggravated the disease: once his tendency to prorogue was recognized,
men may have been even more seriously deterred from putting themselves forward. It could mean a sentence to a climate not much better
than that of Ovid's Tomis and for a period almost as indefinite.

It is in the same quarter that we must seek an explanation of governorships held in absence. This too Tacitus attributes to Tiberius' inability
to take decisions. Overtly sinister explanations are given by Suetonius
and Dio and by Tacitus elsewhere. Lamia and Arruntius were detained
through the influence of Sejanus, or by the Princeps' own fears. Dio,
however, also reports that governorships in absence were claimed to be
given *honoris causa*. Lamia and Arruntius were men high in Tiberius'
esteem for their trustworthiness and talent. He continued to benefit
from their presence while they held senior office; and they added to
their prestige amidst the comforts of the metropolis. Only for the
provincials were the advantages uncertain. It was probably a deputy of
Arruntius (his name was L. Piso) who was assassinated in Tarraconensis

in AD 25 for his excessive zeal in collecting tribute; Lamia's legate in
Syria was there long enough to 'make it his own' – whatever that
implies.[12]

The governorships in absence reveal Tiberius' fundamental attitude
towards the provincials as clearly as his cleaving to Rome and Italy and
his announcement in AD 23 that he would have to go into the provinces
to *conscript* new recruits for the army because there was an inadequate
supply of *volunteers* from Italy, and those unsuitable.[13] It is illustrated
with succinct clarity by another *mot*, his admonition to the Prefect of
Egypt, Aemilius Rectus: 'I want my sheep shorn, not flayed.' A longer
exposition of his views, reported by Tacitus, is consistent with the
apothegm whether that is genuine or not. The senatorial debate on
luxury in 22 provoked the Princeps to complain of Roman dependence
on supplies from abroad: they had no other means of meeting the needs
of masters and slaves and of making up for the deficiencies of Italian
arable land than by importing from the provinces; and securing these
supplies was the responsibility of the Princeps. We have already noticed
the pressure he was under from the *plebs* to ensure its grain allowance.
His very position forced the Princeps to take up the attitude of a Gaius
Gracchus towards the provinces: they must be exploited – and efficiently
– for the benefit of the people of Rome. For Tiberius Rome and Italy
were the political *caput rerum*, the centre.[14] The provincials had a lowlier
position in this scheme of things. How lowly is shown not only by his
choice of metaphor (they were 'sheep') but by his irritation when he
heard in 19 that Germanicus, who liked to be as an equal among equals,
had curried favour with the people of Alexandria by appearing among
them in Greek dress; and that his body had been stripped and exposed to
the gaze of foreigners at Antioch in an attempt to convince them that
he had been murdered.[15] Even when Roman dignity and the interests
of Rome and Italy were not directly concerned, the same dour realism
prevailed. In AD 15 the provinces of Achaea and Macedonia begged for
relief from their financial burdens. The Senate decided that they would
find it less expensive to be governed by imperial legates than by proconsuls, and decreed their transfer to Tiberius' administration.[16] That
decision will have been welcome. Proconsuls governed in style; the
status and the retinue of the legates were more modest. But what the
inhabitants of the two provinces felt about being united under one
governor, and that the legate of Moesia, is not known. The economies
were made with little regard for their self-esteem.

But economy was not the only consideration. The change made explicit the fact that the centre of gravity in the Balkan peninsula had

altered. As Roman power extended itself towards the Danube during
the principate of Augustus the proconsul of Macedonia had often been
called upon to fight, as he had under the Republic; finally the newly
conquered area had required an administrator of its own, the governor
of Moesia, who emerges in AD 4, in command of the force that had once
been the proconsul's.[17] The existence of this new province diminished
the importance of Macedonia and Achaea; they were the least of the
charges that Poppaeus Sabinus had on him. The unsettled areas of the
Balkans lay elsewhere. Pannonia and Dalmatia had been re-pacified
only in AD 9, and the tribes of Thrace were often to cause trouble during
the principate of Tiberius. There was a strong case for a unified command in the unsettled peninsula (Tiberius had been on his way to
Illyricum in AD 14 when the news of Augustus' final illness reached him)
and in AD 17 hegemony over the whole area, Illyricum, Pannonia,
Raetia, and Noricum, was conferred on Drusus Caesar, with proconsular *imperium*. Tacitus claims that the purpose of the command was to
give Drusus military experience and Tiberius increased security. Coming
as the command did three years after Germanicus' grant of *imperium
proconsulare*, it may have had those purposes as well, but Drusus was not
idle and he had won his ovation by 20. Not only did inland tribes have
to be settled; there were pirates to be suppressed. Those who forced
Cyzicus to block the channels that ran through her isthmus were partly
checked by Drusus' procurator, and he was honoured for it by the city
of Ilium.[18] But the immediate occasion for his appointment was an
appeal from the Suebi against the Cherusci, who now had no Roman
expedition to face and could turn their attention to their southern
neighbours, the Suebian Marcomanni under Maroboduus. The appeal
was rejected, naturally enough now that Roman policy was to allow
the Germans to destroy each other; but Drusus was sent to make sure
that Roman territory remained untroubled and he was perfectly successful. An old enemy, the Goth Catualda, was let loose on the weakened
Maroboduus, whom Tiberius considered as dangerous to Rome as
Pyrrhus or Antiochus III, and he had to throw himself on the mercy of
the Princeps.[19] In the same area we find the legate in Upper Illyricum,
P. Dolabella, constructing roads to run from the cities of the coast,
Salonae and Iader, to the borders to the province. They were to cut
through the central mountain ranges and make the tribes there accessible to coercion and civilization. Tiberius was the most successful
soldier of his age; it was only natural that he should pay careful attention to the defence and pacification of the Empire, especially of this
region which lay so close to its heart – ten days' march from Rome, as

Augustus let out in a moment of panic. The *termini* of the radial roads were connected by routes constructed along the Danube and by the river itself and its fleet. [20]

Even late in the principate of Tiberius, when the interest and energy of the ageing ruler flagged in his seclusion, considerable road works were put in hand in Hispania Tarraconensis, notably in that north-west corner of the province which had proved so intractable to Roman rule and which, as it happened, had been the scene of Tiberius' earliest military operations. Perhaps they should all be attributed to the initiative of the unknown legate. [21]

Africa, too, was of particular concern: according to Josephus it supplied two-thirds of Rome's grain supply. [22] There, some weeks after Tiberius' accession, the proconsul L. Nonius Asprenas was building a road from the legionary camp at Ammaedara to Capsa and Tacape on the coast. In the proconsulate that followed, that of L. Aelius Lamia in A D 15-16, another road was constructed on Tiberius' orders to open up the route inland from Lepcis Magna. [23] These two roads gave speedy access to tribes of the interior, respectively the Musulamii and the Garamantes; the camp at Ammaedara dominated the south-east of Musulamian territory, and the road cut that tribe off from their natural allies, the Cinithii and Garamantes. As the soldiers advanced they would survey and mark off the new territory. There is no evidence that this activity was an immediate prelude to confiscation for land-grabbing immigrants, but the nomads may have seen it in that light, and in any case it hampered their seasonal migrations. By 17 the Musulamii under Tacfarinas were in revolt, and they were to take seven years to defeat. [24]

One modern writer has claimed that Tiberius was responsible for the outbreak in the first place. Tacitus describes the Musulamii as having no part in city life; later he emphasizes Tiberius' vexation at having the rebel write to him as an equal to demand a settled home and land for his people. From this we are to conclude that the rebellion was caused by the exclusion of the Musulamii from urbanization and prolonged by imperial pique. [25] This view is not just. There is no evidence that the Musulamii were ready and eager for city life at the beginning of the outbreak in A D 17, none that there was any urbanization in their area from which they were being excluded. Tacfarinas' later demands for a 'sedes' and 'concessio agrorum', if they are not demands for a return to the old conditions of free migration, were made as a second best. If the advance of a settled life of agriculture made nomadism impossible, the rebels at least insisted on a guaranteed stake in that life. Besides, Tiberius inherited his troubles from his predecessor, as he had inherited the plan to construct the road from Tacape.[26] The rebellion of Tacfarinas is an episode in a continuing process of pacification. When L. Calpurnius Fabatus became Prefect of the seventh cohort of Lusitanians and of the six Gaetulian tribes in Numidia is uncertain; this post may have been created in the aftermath of Tacfarinas' rebellion or in that of a disturbance which broke out twenty years later, to be put down by the future Princeps Galba (he won the *ornamenta triumphalia*). Meanwhile, the limitation of land continued: it is attested in the third year of C. Vibius Marsus' governorship (29–30). Eventually some Musulamian land was hived off to form the territory of the Flavian colony of Madauros, which became imperial or private property. The final hemming in and pacification of the Musulamii did not take place until Trajan's reign. It was hastened by the restrictions placed on the formerly nomadic tribes and by the growth of townships round the forts that Rome used to police the area.[27]

The importance of Tacfarinas' rebellion is not to be exaggerated. Tacitus had his own reasons for magnifying it. It was only one episode in a long process and it constituted no threat to the unity of the Empire. Tiberius depicted the rebel in one of the historical analogies which he used to bring home his assessment of a situation to the Senate, as a deserter from the army, a brigand, of less account than Spartacus, whose depredations were not to be tolerated in an empire at the height of its power and untroubled by other dangers. All the same, Tacfarinas' tactics were hard to counter, his allies were to be found at either end of the province, he could range widely and threaten places as far apart as Lepcis Magna and the district of Cirta. The Roman victory was hard won and Tiberius is to be faulted only for his erroneous judgment of the position at the end of Blaesus' governorship and for his failure to set the record straight by acknowledging the achievement of Dolabella.

The revolt that broke out in Gaul in AD 21 has been assigned a number of causes.[28] Tacitus mentions indebtedness, continual demands for taxes, and the rapacity of governors. The movement began amongst the Andecavi and Turoni, but the important and traditionally loyal tribe of the Aedui was involved, and so were the Treviri to the north. The leaders were two members of the Gallic upper class, the Treviran Julius Florus and the Aeduan Julius Sacrovir. One important factor in the outbreak was the ending of the boom that had taken place in Gaul since the conquest of Caesar. In the reign of Augustus towns had been built or developed, with expensive walls and gates; roads had been constructed, and if the Gauls had thrown themselves with enthusiasm into the business of making money (they were soon to eclipse Italy in the

wine and pottery industries), they had also felt it incumbent upon them-
selves to spend it on the amenities that made Roman life worth living.
Help had come from Augustus: he paid for the walls and gates of
Nemausus and other towns. The roads were built by the state but the
Gauls knew when they paid their taxes that their contribution to the
imperial finances was no mean one.[29]
   The booty of Egypt lubricated the Roman economy for twenty years.
After about 10 BC there are signs of a shortage of cash, aggravated in
Italy because silver was exported to pay for Oriental luxuries, spices and
silk. This economic fact, as well as dislike of the pressure to keep up with
their peers, which could lead individuals into debt and criminal conspiracy, may lie behind the moral arguments against the wearing of silk
by men and the use of gold at table which were heard in the Senate near
the beginning of Tiberius' principate and again in 22.[30] Certainly shortage
of currency was a factor in the financial crisis of AD 33; it was alleviated
for the benefit of the landowning class by disbursements made by the
Princeps. Donations of silver and gold, offered by certain senators and
equites in AD 16 or 31, may have been intended as token sacrifices to the
welfare of the commonwealth.[31] Tiberius' own way of life was frugal;
that habit he carried over into his housekeeping for the state, combining
personal liberality with care for the contents of the state treasury,
Aerarium and Fiscus alike. It was a natural policy to adopt, especially
when money began to be difficult to come by, but it might have been
more advantageous to the Roman economy if Tiberius had hoarded
less; the extravagant expenditure of Gaius Caligula gave it more of a
stimulus.[32] Even more disquieting is the possibility that shortage of
bullion led Tiberius to take an interest in other men's money and property, even to the point of having charges brought against them so that
he might confiscate their wealth or its source (mines). The first time
that Tacitus notices the phenomenon is in AD 24, on the conviction of
C. Silius; then came the property of Sejanus, transferred to the Fiscus at
the beginning of 32, and the gold and copper mines of Sex. Marius, the
richest man in Spain, sequestrated for the Princeps in 33, which happens
to be the year of the financial crisis. The charge cannot be substantiated,
and it is probably coloured by the rapacity of Domitian;[33] but the heavy
cost of running the armed 'imperial' provinces made it natural, when a
man's property was confiscated, for that property to be transferred
from the Aerarium, which was supported by the revenues of Narbonensian Gaul and Asia, to the Fiscus, which was at the disposal of the Princeps.
   That Gaul in particular was victim of Tiberius' demands is a charge

brought against the Princeps by Grenier. According to Suetonius, Tiberius withdrew immunities that his predecessors had allowed. Now the Aedui, a community that possessed a treaty with Rome, were immune from taxation. Grenier suggested that the Aedui reacted by revolting.[34] That explanation will not do for the Treveri, the Andecavi, and the Turoni. Besides, Tacitus speaks of '*continuatio tributorum*', the unremitting demand for taxes, as one of the causes. That does not sound like a burden newly imposed (indeed, the latest census had been completed by Germanicus in AD 16) and Tacitus' summary of the principate down to 23 particularly makes the point that Tiberius was careful not to disturb the provinces by imposing new burdens on them, a remark that would be difficult to make if one of the only serious revolts that took place during that period had been provoked precisely by the imposition of new taxes. (It was *horses* and auxiliary troops that the Gauls had to provide.) Suetonius does not even name the Gauls, and the losses he mentions may refer to other cities; Cyzicus was deprived of its freedom in 25 for a riot in which Roman citizens died.[35] It is safest to think of economic stringency as the main cause of the revolt, with the least astute of the Gauls going to the wall because they could not meet obligations incurred in a period of euphoria and expansion; remorseless taxation, not merely a special tribute continued after the ending of the expedition into Germany, was a secondary cause.

Scholars have adduced other factors, for some of which Tiberius must be held responsible, if they are right. Certainly he was responsible for withdrawing Germanicus from Gaul and Germany (Aquitania, Belgica, and Lugdunensis now came under three separate governors for the purposes of civil administration), and for the absence during the five years before the revolt of all members of the imperial family. Personal attention was something that the Gauls had become used to, and which they may have demanded. The realistic Tiberius was not prepared to gratify them. The effect of this on Gallic morale cannot be measured; perhaps it was not considerable, but one of the grievances was the brutality and arrogance of the officials in charge of the provinces; Germanicus' successors did not give satisfaction. As for the suppression of Druidism, which Pliny credits to Tiberius, the date of the *senatus consultum* is unknown; it may have come after the revolt and it cannot safely be brought in as a contributory cause.[36] If Tiberius is to be blamed, then, it is for husbanding rather than disbursing his resources of gold and silver, for maintaining taxation at unacceptable levels, and for failing to pander to Gallic self-esteem. The revolt was soon ended, in spite of the quarrels of the two commanders on the Rhine, who should have united in suppressing it; the Senate heard of the outbreak and its suppression at the same time.

Prevention, however, was better than cure, and Tacitus gives his subject full credit not only for avoiding the imposition of new burdens, but for ensuring that old ones were not aggravated by plundering and brutality on the part of governors.[37] This verdict summarizes the views of Tiberius' near-contemporaries. It comes in general terms, but it deserves attention. The point about Tiberius' control of his governors is of particular interest. Whether a large number of cases of *res repetundae* is to be taken as evidence of care or of negligence on the part of a Princeps it is useless to speculate; there are too many variables involved, the evidence is scrappy and diverse in quantity and quality as the sources change. One would expect relatively few prosecutions in Tiberius' time if only because of his prorogations, yet Brunt reports eleven such cases from the years 14–37 and only two from the principate of Augustus.[38] Certainly, Tiberius was not inclined to shelter offending officials even when he had appointed them himself. The trial in 23 of Lucilius Capito, procurator of Asia, attests that. In the previous year Tiberius had shown notable severity towards C. Silanus, proconsul of Asia, who was convicted of extortion aggravated by violence. The disproportion must be due to disparity in the sources for the two principates; and it is likely that the provincial organizations that undertook the prosecutions of delinquent governors were not equipped to do so under Augustus: the first attested example is precisely that of C. Silanus.[39]

It was the punishment of these officials, as well as the help given the province after an earthquake, that led the inhabitants of Asia to seek permission to erect a temple to Tiberius, Livia, and the Senate; yet the conduct of Capito in usurping the functions of the governor and exercising jurisdiction outside the imperial estates that were his province was repeated by his successors and eventually became accepted as the norm. Equestrian officials and legates, as appointees of the Princeps, were formidable to senatorial officials and to their subjects. Nevertheless, what led Capito astray may have been not common greed or arrogance, but misplaced zeal for his exacting master.[40]

It is not only Capito's behaviour that can be interpreted in this way. There are three other instances to be considered, from far-flung corners of the Empire. In Hispania Tarraconensis we have seen L. Piso assassinated in AD 25 by one of the Termestini;[41] although the culprit dashed out his own brains before the truth could be tortured out of him it was believed that the whole tribe was implicated. Piso had been exacting taxes with more zeal than the high-spirited Spaniards could stomach.

Three years later came the revolt of the Frisii in Germany.[42] They lived north of the mouth of the Rhine, barbarians of small means, and Tiberius' brother had imposed tribute of ox-hides on them, without specifying size or quality. That was not done until Olennius, the ex-centurion who was in charge of them, demanded buffalo-hides. In Tacitus' touching account it was only when they had sold cattle, lands, and families that the Frisii killed the soldiers who came to collect the tax; Olennius fled to a Roman fort. L. Apronius, now governor of Lower Germany, launched an attack on the Frisii, but met with a serious reverse, losing more than 1,300 men and making no attempt at retaliation. Tacitus gives Tiberius the credit of suppressing the news of the losses in order to avoid having to appoint a commander to avenge them. Apronius kept his post – and the opinion of his troops. His blunder was not serious enough, in Tiberius' mind, to outweigh past services and perhaps present political considerations. The Frisii were still unpacified in AD 47, when Cn. Domitius Corbulo undertook to settle them.

Lastly, the conduct of Pontius Pilate, Prefect of Judaea from AD 27 to 36.[43] One night early in his administration Pilate brought military standards into Jerusalem. They bore the image of Tiberius on them, and their introduction infringed Jewish law. The result was a riot. The city mob, joined by people from the country, made for Pilate at Caesarea, and eventually induced him to remove the standards. That was not the end of the trouble that he caused. He began to use the sacred treasure known as the Corbonas on an aqueduct. When he came to Jerusalem he was mobbed, and a number of Jews were clubbed down or trampled underfoot in the ensuing panic. The last incident came very near the end of his term of office. He insisted on setting up gilded shields in Herod's palace in the Holy City. One thing Pilate had learnt: they bore no image, but but only an inscription that stated the name of the dedicator and that of the person in whose honour the dedication was made. Distinguished Jews begged him to remove them, but he refused. The Jews wrote to Tiberius and he instructed Pilate to set them up in the temple of Augustus at Caesarea.

Pilate's behaviour has led scholars to believe that he was a conscious anti-Semite, acting in concert with Sejanus – for it was after the fall of the Prefect that he was recalled. Certainly Tiberius is given a good press by the contemporary Jewish writer Philo, while Sejanus is seen as bent on destroying the whole race. But Philo's account is suspect. His *Legatio* is an invective against Gaius Caligula, whose conduct has to be contrasted unfavourably with that of Tiberius; and if the Jews suffered under that Princeps (the Jews and their proselytes, with the followers of Isis, were expelled from Italy in A D 19 and four thousand deported to Sardinia to fight bandits) it was only because he was under the influence of Sejanus.[44] There is no reason to believe in a connexion between Pilate and Sejanus, and it is unlikely that the governor deliberately stirred up trouble amongst his subjects, even if he could rely on the support of the Praefectus Praetorio to get him out of the trouble that would surely follow. For as Tacitus and other authors repeatedly emphasize, tranquillity was a prime consideration in Tiberius' provincial government.[45]

There is another explanation of Pilate's conduct: stupid officiousness and, especially when the fall of the Prefect brought on a period of fear and uncertainty, a desire to demonstrate loyalty to the Princeps at all costs. It is in accord with this suggestion that the inscription found at Caesarea shows, not only that the official title of the governor in Tiberius' time was Praefectus, but that Pilate had constructed a building known as the Tiberieum.[46]

Tranquillity was what Tiberius wanted – for its own sake and because it favoured the efficient exploitation of the provinces. It was a safe theme for the admiring historian Velleius, because he achieved it, the disturbances in Africa, Gaul, and Germany serving only to emphasize the profound peace that reigned elsewhere. The transfer of *legio IX Hispana* to Africa was the only movement of the legions that Tiberius found necessary to make during his principate; only four years later he was able to return it to Pannonia. The principate has no spectacular successes to display (Tiberius took the title *imperator* only once after his accession, and there was one triumph to match and one ovation, those of Germanicus and Drusus, with seven known grants of triumphal insignia, ten fewer than Augustus made in not many years more[47]); but that is an index of Tiberius' success. The Principes who came after were to go far beyond Tiberius' modest goal of maintaining peace. There is no sign that he understood as well as his predecessor Augustus the nascent political importance of the provinces. Rome and Italy were the centre of his world and he did not pretend otherwise. In that he was true to his conservative persuasion; for the provincials had been, and were again to be, from the reign of Claudius onwards, a counter-weight to opposition from the Senate. True, Tiberius permitted the entry of some few provincials to that body. Their selection from far-flung parts of the Empire proves that there was nothing systematic in it. More significant would have been extensive grants of citizenship, compensating in some measure for the hard-headed fiscal exploitation of the provinces. We have no reliable figures, but the evidence of inscriptions has been gathered,[48] and it shows men called Ti. Iulius as comparatively rare; fewer than one hundred are known compared with the several thousand C. Iulii whose rights go back to Caesar or Augustus (or are due to Gaius Caligula). They are remarkably rare in the Spanish and Gallic provinces and in Africa; it is as if Tiberius considered that the grants had gone far enough in these provinces, highly Romanized though some of them were. There are more in Upper Germany and they are commoner still in the Danubian provinces, Raetia, Noricum, Pannonia, and Moesia; they are found among the civilians in the first three provinces as well as among former members of the auxiliary forces. The very few Ti. Iulii of Eastern origin belong mostly to ruling circles of the cities of Asia. Perhaps it would not be too sweeping to say, on the basis of the figures we have, that what influenced Tiberius was the ancient criterion of service to Rome in the armed forces, perhaps with hereditary connexions with the Princeps' family operating in the East.

This was not the only sphere in which Tiberius showed little inclination to court the provincials; his attitude was markedly passive. Principes carried on their administration by responding to the pleas and petitions of their subjects; it was the only way for them to cope with the immense labours it involved – Tiberius once ironically made a speaker alter to 'onerous' a reference to his tasks as 'sacred' – and Tiberius did so with a deliberation that suited his policies and character. As time went on, according to Suetonius, his interest and his energy declined; and after his retirement to Capri, he became less accessible to petition; he would keep embassies waiting and so put off contact and decision-making.[49] These wasteful postponements were a fault in Tiberius' later administration. Individuals and whole communities were left uncertain of their status, rights, and obligations. The Anauni and other Alpine tribes 'attributed' for administrative purposes to the city of Tridentum were usurping the privileges of Roman citizenship. That their status remained so long unregulated was blamed on his persistent absence from public life ('pertinaci absentia') by his nephew Claudius.[50] The temperaments of the two men were poles apart – or Claudius' secluded upbringbringing gave him an insatiable thirst for administration that had been quenched in Tiberius long before he came to the Principate.

Correspondingly meagre is Tiberius' record as a builder of cities and founder of colonies. Tiberias on the Sea of Galilee was the creation of Herod Antipas, and Tiberia in Thrace was probably Philippopolis renamed by the grateful client Rhoemetalces; as for Phrygian Tiberiopolis and Pappa Tiberiopolis in Pisidia, their names suggest that they acquired city status and institutions during Tiberius' principate and that they commemorated the change by taking the name of the Princeps;[51] Velleius Paterculus informs his readers of the senatorial view of colonies abroad, which run from Gaius Gracchus through Appuleius Saturninus and Caesar to Augustus. In any case, the objective need for them (strategy and the settlement of the swollen Triumviral legions) had been satisfied by Augustus. The only attested Tiberian colony is Emona in Dalmatia. Others claimed for him there and in Pannonia may belong to the last years of Augustus. But if they do they are themselves exceptional: no Augustan colony has been proved founded later than 15 BC. Tiberius, then, here as in other spheres, was continuing the policies of Augustus' later years.[52]

How popular Tiberius was with his subjects in the provinces we cannot tell, but the conclusions we have reached so far do not suggest that he would be held in high regard. He made no detectable effort to encourage the imperial cult, by AD 14 a conventional weapon in the imperial armoury. The very conventionality of it displeased the realist who, asked to give his own name to the month of his birth, wanted to know what would happen if there were thirteen Caesars. On the other hand, the position that the deified Augustus had held gave dignity to the man who held it after him, personally unworthy though he might feel himself to be and fully conscious of his own mortality (Augustus had half believed in his superhuman nature and the power of his eye; after all he had not owed everything to his predecessor and his name, as Tiberius might feel he did[53]). Augustus glorified the functions of the Princeps; did those functions now glorify his successor? The conflict explains Tiberius' attitude to cult offered him publicly and privately, which he expounded in 25, declining a petition from the province of Baetica that it be permitted to erect a temple to himself and his mother. Where there was a precedent and an occasion, or when it was politically expedient, as had been the case in Asia two years earlier, he accepted. In Baetica none of these conditions was satisfied: there was no precedent in this western province, and no occasion; and the Senate was not to be included in the cult.[54] Nor did Tiberius welcome city or private cult, unless some definite benefit had been conferred (it went on all the same[55]). Not all cases were clear-cut, and indecision or unwillingness to offend well-wishers, rather than calculated ambiguity, is to be detected in Tiberius' reply, probably of the summer of AD 15, to the letter of the ephors and city of Gytheum in Laconia; without giving an outright refusal he expressed himself content with 'more moderate' honours than the divine Augustus was to receive, honours 'suited to a human being'. The proposal had included the erection of statues of Augustus,

Tiberius, and Livia, and six days of festivities devoted also to Germanicus, Drusus Caesar, and Quinctius Flamininus.[56] Not long before this,
Granius Marcellus, proconsul of Bithynia, was beheading another statue
of Augustus and providing the trunk with a new portrait bust.[57] Other
governors must have given a similar lead (not necessarily so parsimonius
a one) to their subjects, if they needed it. A decade earlier, when Tiberius
had been restored to favour in AD 4, the people of Aezani in Phrygia
sent envoys to him at other end of the Empire at Bononia on the
Channel coast and secured promises of his good offices in return.[58] They
will not have been the only people to make that long-term investment.
Once a man became entrenched in power such offerings were made in a
spirit more of duty than of hope; they came to be expected by the ruler
(the same was true of the Principate as a whole). W. Orth has warned
against estimating the popularity of a Princeps by counting the number
of statues and dedicatory inscriptions set up to him. Tiberius knew as
much, but in his time the cult was young enough for his want of interest
in it to cause misgivings.[59]

But Tiberius knew what was expected of a Princeps, as he had known
what was due from a patron. He met all his obligations with considered
generosity, examining all the privileges (*beneficia*) that Augustus had
conferred, and confirming some of them. In return for his good offices
he did not refuse the temple offered him by the cities of Asia after the
earthquake of AD 23 and the convictions of Silanus and Capito – not
the only time that Tiberius made contributions of his own and had taxes
remitted after a natural disaster – just as he had accepted cult at Nysa,
even as a private individual.[60]

As a benefactor Tiberius expected *fides* (loyalty), as it had been shown
him at Nysa in his darkest days. His memory was tenacious of good and
(notoriously) of bad.[61] Nemausus is not known to have suffered from
its action in throwing down his statues while Nysa was maintaining its
devotion, but the sources suggest that King Archelaus of Cappadocia
was to have lost his throne for his undutifulness at that same time. Before
the new principate was two years old he had to face charges at Rome,
but he died before the case was over and it is not clear how it would
have ended; Archelaus had been in danger more than once before. This
time the accusation may have been that he helped a relative, Artaxes
III or Zeno, on to the throne of Armenia without consulting Rome,
reason enough for his deposition, even if Tiberius kept silent about a
private grudge.[62] The incident displays one facet of Roman rule. The
cohesion and stability of the Empire depended not only on the formal
relations of rulers and ruled, on *imperium* and the army, but on personal

ties between a mighty politician and his dependants. Here was a limited place for the intervention of the women of the imperial court: it was said to be a letter from Livia that brought Archelaus to Rome. These ladies might be responsible for the education of hopeful young dynasts destined for client kingdoms, as Antonia was for that of the children of Cotys. Ties formed in this way could be useful to them in later life. Agrippa I was brought up with Drusus Caesar and his mother was a close friend of Antonia. That friendship stood him in good stead when he came to Rome to seek his fortune in the last years of Tiberius. She loaned him money, and when he was accused (rightly) of wishing Gaius Caligula a speedy accession to the Principate, she persuaded Tiberius to hear the accusation and mitigated Agrippa's privations in prison.[63]

Q. Veranius organized the new province of Cappadocia for Germanicus in 17 at the beginning of his mission to the East. It was not the only territory to be brought under direct Roman control at this time. Antiochus III of Commagene died in the same year, and his kingdom was incorporated into the Empire by another legate, Q. Servaeus; yet the principality of the Amanus may have been allowed to continue under a relative of the late ruler, Philopater, who had also died in 17, and Archelaus' son kept dominions in Cilicia Tracheia and eastern Lycaonia. More than the express wishes of a section of the population of Commagene, the upper class, determined Roman policy. The areas taken over were profitable. Cappadocia yielded revenues that made it possible for Tiberius to halve the unpopular one per cent sales tax that had been imposed after Actium; there were also extensive royal lands that went to the state and silver mines that were to feed the mint at Mazaca, which perhaps now took the name Caesarea. Tiberius did not assign Cappadocia a consular or praetorian governor or any troops, although it was a backward land still organized on tribal rather than on urban lines. It was assigned to an equestrian prefect.[64] That shows Tiberius at once underestimating the importance of the area (under Vespasian it was to receive a consular governor and legions, but by then there was a Parthian nominee on the throne of Armenia) and treating it as an exploitable source of revenue. But Tiberius had strategic considerations in mind. Both Cappadocia and Commagene lay on the Euphrates, already recognized in the island encounter between Gaius Caesar and the Parthian monarch as the boundary between the two empires. Tiberius was continuing the policy begun by Augustus of hardening the frontier by taking direct control of the former client kingdoms that bordered it. It was Vespasian who completed the process.[65]

As a rule Tiberius was reluctant to annex new territory simply to round off the Empire. The tetrarchy of Herod the Great's son Philip, consisting in Gaulanitis and Trachonitis, was only a partial exception. When the ruler died in AD 34 his patient and conscientious regime had lasted thirty-seven years; the area, mountainous and once unruly, might be thought ripe for plucking. Tiberius did not quite make up his mind. He transferred the administration of the two districts to the governor of Syria, but without allowing their revenues to flow into the provincial chest. If he chose, Gaulanitis and Trachonitis could be set going again as separate administrative units. But he died without making a permanent decision. Gaius handed the tetrarchy over to Agrippa I, Claudius to Agrippa II, and he had to cope with a rebellion in Gaulanitis; Tiberius may have been right to hesitate.[66]

Elsewhere too Tiberius' resistance to the idea of annexation is patent. In Thrace in AD 19 Rhescuporis, who held the western and rougher part of the kingdom, killed his nephew Cotys with the idea of taking over his half as well.[67] L. Pomponius Flaccus was instructed to lure Rhescuporis to Rome to stand trial (like another Jugurtha – but before the Senate). There he was accused by the dead man's widow and was exiled to Alexandria (he did not long survive). His son, Rhoemetalces II, succeeded to the western kingdom; he had no part in his father's treachery. But Cotys' children were too young to be entrusted with the eastern realm; they were to be educated at Rome in the house of Antonia, and the kingdom governed by a Roman administrator, Trebellenus Rufus. When Trebellenus left Thrace Cotys' heir was still not installed; he had to wait until AD 38; it may be that Tiberius was contemplating the annexation that Claudius was to carry out; if so, he took no further steps towards it. The western kingdom continued troubled and troublesome. In 21 Rhoemetalces was being besieged in Philippopolis by the Coelaletae, Odrysae, and Dii; four years later his levies caused another uprising and he had to be rescued by Poppaeus Sabinus, whose success was important enough to earn him the insignia of a triumph. It is no surprise that Tiberius left the western kingdom untouched; Rhoemetalces was performing, though with moderate success, exactly the duties that Strabo considered to be those of the client king on the spot. The wisdom in Tiberius' policy was made clear in AD 46, when Claudius annexed Thrace and had to fight for it; and the new province, though small in area, proved too difficult for a procuratorial governor to manage; Trajan handed it over to an imperial legate.[68]

Britain was another realm that might have been taken over by Tiberius but was left for Claudius' attention.[69] The policy here was explicit and taken over from Augustus: Strabo, writing soon after Augustus' death, explains that British rulers had secured the friendship of Augustus, making the island virtually Roman, and that there was no need to incur the cost of garrisoning it when the profits from import and export dues were so high. However, the balance of power that Augustus had attempted to establish was destroyed as Cunobelin, king of the Catuvellauni, continued to expand his kingdom and the Atrebates lost ground to his brother Epaticcus. Tiberius did nothing to help the victims, and Verica, king of the Atrebates, finally fled to Claudius in AD 42 or 43.

But the 'consilium coercendi intra terminos imperii' was a general doctrine inherited from Augustus and publicly proclaimed in the documents bequeathed to the state by the late Princeps.[70] Tiberius' adherence to it is shown elsewhere by his avoidance of unnecessary adventures in areas where Rome's established interests were not threatened – he allowed only one such expedition, that of L. Vitellius to punish the Arab vassal Aretas of Petra for an attack on Herod the Tetrarch[71] – but nowhere more clearly than in Germany; for it was in 27 BC that Augustus had last seriously contemplated the invasion of Britain, while he had been committed to subjugating Germany between the Rhine and the Elbe until AD 9. After that date Tiberius' campaigns were punitive demonstrations designed to restore Roman morale (the birthday of Augustus was celebrated in AD 11 in free German territory) and intimidate the victors – if possible into submission. The campaigns of Germanicus were intended by Tiberius to have the same effect. Tiberius' change of heart, after he fought so many years for the conquest, may have caused him doubts as well as regrets. They would have been dissipated when he assumed sole control.[72] The ambitious dash of the elder Drusus was consciously copied by his son Germanicus, and now Tiberius could see it from Augustus' point of view. Risky when the Romans were on the offensive, it was reckless and selfish when the official policy was to repay the Germans for a defeat already inflicted. In a short autumn campaign in AD 14, which had the secondary object of restoring the morale of the mutinous legions, and which was much in the style of Tiberius' own recent piecemeal campaigns, Germanicus marched up the Lippe against the Marsi. The following year saw him exploiting his independent imperium to the full and achieving some spectacular effects. Besides making an attack on the Chatti, he rescued the pro-Roman chieftain Segestes and his reluctant daughter from Arminius, the hero of the German victory over Varus – thus enabling that leader to rally the tribe behind himself. For all this Tiberius proposed that Germanicus should assume the title imperator. The general went on to organize an advance

on the Ems and an attack on the Cherusci by sea and land, and succeeded
in finding and burying the dead from the Varian disaster, though he did
not come upon the elusive Arminius, who so harassed the troops with
A. Caecina on their return march as to spread the belief on the Rhine
that they had been destroyed and that the Germans were coming; only
the determination of Agrippina prevented the cutting down of the
bridge over the Rhine; Germanicus' stormy return by sea was equally
dangerous and very costly in men and materials. Tiberius, alarmed,
thought to bring Germanicus back by having a triumph decreed to him –
even though the state of war subsisted – and the insignia of a triumph to
three of his lieutenants. In vain: combined operations on a larger scale
were planned for the following year, which proved to be Germanicus'
last in his command. The fleet sailed by way of Holland to the mouth
of the Ems and thence to the Weser, which the Romans crossed. Two
battles were fought against Arminius, both successful; but neither
Idistaviso nor the second engagement brought down the leader; only
the Angrivarii were reduced to submission. The weather again proved
disastrous to the returning legions, and restored German morale, but
Germanicus renewed the attack on the Chatti and Marsi before the
campaigning season came to an end and his report promised to complete the conquest in one more year; he had already set up a trophy
commemorating the reduction of the tribes between the Rhine and
the Elbe and it is true that he had established or re-established some
forts beyond the Rhine. But Tiberius added to the inducements to
return: he offered a second consulship, and Germanicus did not have
to make good his word. The Princeps' letters were laudatory, diplomatic, and patient; and the triumphal citation as generous as the
wording of the trophy: 'over the Cherusci, the Chatti, the Angrivarii, and the other tribes up to the Elbe'. The triumphal arch dedicated
at the end of the previous year to celebrate the recovery of the standards
lost with Varus put the achievement of Germanicus on the same level
as that of Augustus and Tiberius in the East in 20 BC – and made it as
definitive; an era was at an end.[73]

The letters of Tiberius spoke of the value of diplomacy in dealing
with the Germans. He had achieved more by that means, he said, than
ever by fighting (not that the two were incompatible, and their ends
were identical).[74] Henceforward in the north diplomacy was to dominate, reinforced by a careful watch on the tribes on the other side of the
Rhine. Tiberius set the tribes, and their leaders within them, one against
the other and put into power chieftains such as the Quadian Vannius who
were well disposed.[75] Vannius took over some of the subjects of Maro-

boduus and his conqueror Catualda in 19, while Maroboduus himself was kept in reserve at Ravenna, Catualda at Forum Iulii, in case the Suebi made trouble. It was the same policy that Augustus had used against the Parthians: blackmail. Tiberius had asked Germanicus to allow Drusus Caesar his share of glory, and Tiberius' policy was immaculately executed by Drusus – from the Balkans. After AD 16 the Rhine frontier disappears from view in Tacitus' account of Tiberius' principate, eclipsed by events in the Balkans and the East: Tiberius deserves credit for anticipating developments that were to become clear only after the fall of the Julio-Claudian dynasty; it was not between the Rhine and the Danube that any large new province was eventually to be created, but north of the Danube, Trajan's Dacia. Meanwhile, along the Rhine and Danube, the construction of permanent military bases in the principate of Tiberius marked out the present limits of Roman ambition: Argentoratum (Strasbourg), Vindonissa, Carnuntum, and Aquincum.[76]

The school in which Tiberius had first learned diplomacy was in the East. Here in 20 BC under Augustus' guidance he had put a king on the throne of Armenia, and discovered that diplomacy, backed up by a credible threat from the Roman army, was a sure means of keeping peace on terms that were satisfactory to Rome.[77] So it had been in 2 BC, at the time of the mission of Gaius Caesar. When Gaius appeared, the upstart king of Parthia, Phraataces, who had probably abetted the seizure of Armenia by the anti-Roman candidate Tigranes III, opened negotiations. The agreement concluded at the meeting recognized Tigranes' claim under Roman suzerainty, but he did not long survive, and Gaius had to invade Armenia to establish his successor, Ariobarzanes of Media. Augustus' luck was out: Ariobarzanes died, and his son Artavasdes was murdered. By about AD 6 Augustus was supporting a grandson of Herod and Archelaus as Tigranes IV; him the Parthians deposed and by the end of the principate the Armenian throne was vacant and Roman influence in Armenia at a nadir. In Parthia Phraataces was in turn deposed by a king (Orodes) whose cruelty was the pretext for an embassy of Parthians to ask Rome to allow the hostage Vonones, the eldest son of Phraates IV, to claim the throne. They approached Augustus in Rome and were referred to Tiberius in Germany.[78] Vonones proved degenerate; he had forgotten Parthian ways in a long sojourn at Rome. For the last two years of Augustus' principate the king of Parthia was Artabanus, an Arsacid on his mother's side; Vonones was reduced to seeking a kingdom in Armenia. There he proved equally unacceptable to Rome and to Parthia, and Q. Creticus Silanus, the governor of Syria, took him into custody, leaving the throne of Armenia unoccupied.[79] Germanicus' mission in the East was concerned not only with incorporating other vacant client kingdoms into the Empire and with the complaints of the provincials (Jews and Syrians both claimed to be over-burdened; perhaps they were emboldened to make representations by the success that the pleas of Achaea and Macedonia had met), but with bringing back to normal Rome's relations with Parthia and establishing on the throne of Armenia a king acceptable to Rome, to Parthia, and even to the Armenians.[80] He entered Armenia, like Tiberius nearly four decades before him, and crowned Zeno of Pontus as King Artaxes. To this scheme the Parthian monarch offered no opposition; he had no wish to see his defeated rival established in Armenia. On the contrary, he sent envoys with a request for a renewal of the old pledges of friendship, for the removal of Vonones to a safe distance, and for a second meeting on the Euphrates. Vonones was removed and met a violent death soon after; only the meeting on the Euphrates did not take place: Rome was now in a stronger position than she had been eighteen years before. It was her candidate and not the Parthian's who was on the throne of Armenia, and there was no need to acknowledge Parthian equality. Tiberius' choice too was astute or fortunate. Artaxes' tastes were those of the Armenians: riding and hunting. He ruled for seventeen years and died in AD 34 still king of Armenia.[81] By then Artabanus was confirmed in his tenure of power and began not only to demand the treasures that Vonones had left in Syria and Cilicia but to lay claim to all the territories that had belonged to the Seleucid and Persian empires. Tiberius responded in a familiar way by dispatching a pretender to the throne of Artabanus: Phraates, youngest of the sons of Phraates IV. He was unlucky. The man was not equal to the anxiety and labour of his task. He died before he could make any impression on Artabanus. Tiberius replaced him with a man from the next generation, Tiridates, and, taking seriously the threat of Artabanus to invade Syria, put that province and Eastern affairs generally under the control of L. Vitellius, the consul of 34. Nor did Tiberius neglect Roman interests in Armenia. He produced another Roman nominee, Mithridates, who invaded the country with Iberian allies. Artabanus found that he could not dislodge the pretender; he made two attempts, one in person, and their failure helped Vitellius in undermining his position at home to such a degree that he had to flee to Hyrcania. Now Vitellius took the offensive into Parthian territory, having Tiridates escorted down the Euphrates to Ctesiphon, where he was crowned. Tiberius had no intention of backing up the luckless king. He was on his own,

and when Artabanus returned in force it was with him that Vitellius
opened negotiations. Tiberius had shown him that his own security
depended on leaving the Roman nominee safely on the throne of
Armenia, and it was on that understanding that for a second time
Roman and Parthian met in mid-Euphrates, so according Roman
recognition to Artabanus, who sent his son Darius to Rome as hostage.
There was little damage to Roman prestige here, for Vitellius was not
a member of the Roman imperial house. These negotiations came at the
very end of Tiberius' principate, so near his death that they could be
ascribed to the reign of Gaius.[82] But Tiberius deserves the credit. True,
all the negotiations had secured was that Armenia should be in the
hands of the Roman nominee; not a yard of new territory came under
Roman control as a result. Their importance lay in the effect they had
on public opinion in the East. Rome's authority had been decisively
asserted, and the stability of her political system demonstrated by contrast with the violent swings of fortune to which Parthian monarchs
were subject. If Rome had disaffected subjects in the East, it was no
use for them to look to Parthia for help; and her friends rejoiced in her
triumph.[83] On occasion to the end of his life Tiberius put to good use
the skills he had learned in his earliest youth.

CHAPTER X

THE DYNASTIC CATASTROPHE

One of Tiberius' first acts when the death of Augustus left him alone in power was to ask the Senate for a grant of proconsular *imperium* for his adopted son Germanicus, who had been supervising the chastisement of the German tribes as Augustus' legate.[1] It was appropriate that this advancement to independent *imperium* should come when the dynasty had been weakened by the death of the man from whom the subordinate command had stemmed; but what Tiberius' request also secured to Germanicus was an immediate grant of a power that he was eventually to share with his adoptive brother. In Tacitus' view there were many who wondered in AD 14 whether Germanicus would be content to wait. If there were such rumours their propagators, and those soldiers of Germanicus who offered to march for the Principate, and really meant their offer, were misinformed. There is no evidence that Germanicus contemplated making a premature and hazardous bid for supremacy when his future position was guaranteed by ancestry, adoption, experience, and powers. All the evidence attests the propriety of Germanicus' attitude towards his adoptive father, from his first appearance in the Balkan campaigns to the end of his life. Nor does Tacitus omit to inform his readers of the impartiality with which Tiberius treated his sons.[2] His testimony is borne out to the full by what we know of the positions held by Germanicus and Drusus during the first four years of the regime. The three years that separated the two young men were matched by the three years that separated their first consulships of AD 12 and 15 respectively, and by the three years that separated the grants of proconsular *imperium* made to them: Drusus' Balkan command dates to AD 17.[3] In the following year, after celebrating his triumph over Germany, the elder brother entered as Tiberius' colleague upon his second consulship, which was to be, like Tiberius' second consulship of 7 BC, the prelude to an Eastern command, and although Drusus' second consulship of AD 21, also as Tiberius' colleague, came two years after his brother's death, it is hard to believe that it was not already in prospect in 18.

Tiberius' impartiality was matched by the good relations that Tacitus says prevailed between the two brothers.[4] Drusus shed tears over his brother's death and treated the suspected murderer with reserve at the public audience he gave him when approached by him in the Balkans.

That could be the judicious conduct of a politician.[5] But the brothers were united to each other and to Tiberius by common descent and by rivalry from another quarter that had threatened them in the decade before Augustus' death and now reared up again with a new head. On 13 September 16, M. Scribonius Libo Drusus, praetor in that year or in 15 and brother of the consul *ordinarius*, was brought to trial by four senators and by other persons on a charge of plotting against the lives of Tiberius, Germanicus, Drusus, and other *principes civitatis*, leading men in the state.[6] The evidence brought forward, as preserved to us by Tacitus, consisted of papers showing amongst other things that Libo had consulted astrologers as to whether he would have sufficient money to pave the Via Appia as far as Brundisium with coin; and the names of members of the imperial family and of senators on a list in his own handwriting, with sinister marks set against them. Libo had been able to find nobody to act as his counsel, and that night, after making an appeal to the Princeps through P. Sulpicius Quirinius and receiving the reply that he should approach the Senate, he committed suicide. The trial continued and Libo was convicted.

Tacitus and Seneca depict a pitiable young man, vapid and extravagant.[7] But the fact that Libo was in debt would not have deterred him from embarking on a scheme to raise himself to the heights; stupidity certainly would have been no barrier, and his trust in astrologers was shared by men of intellect and intelligence. In the aftermath the Senate took account of both dangers: astrologers were expelled from Italy and two of them executed, and at the very next session measures were taken against extravagance: solid gold vessels might not be used at table, men were prohibited garments made of silk; severer measures still were mooted, but failed to find favour.[8]

The affair was taken seriously by Tiberius and by men who favoured his regime. That is shown by the fact that Libo found no advocate, by the aggravated penalties imposed and the generous awards to the accusers, and by the extravagance of the thanksgivings and offerings (to Jupiter, Mars, and the highly significant Concord) that followed the trial; the day of Libo's death was even declared a day of public rejoicing.[9] Tacitus exposes the names of the men responsible for these proposals and (he claims) the early growth of servility: M. Cotta Messallinus, praetor designate and consul in 20; Cn. Lentulus, consul in 14 BC; L. Pomponius Flaccus, consul designate; probably L. Plancus, consul in AD 13; C. Asinius Gallus, consul in 8 BC; M. Papius Mutilus, suffect in AD 9; L. Apronius, suffect in AD 8.[10] The first three were personal friends of Tiberius – for Lentulus at least he had a high regard; the last two were municipal men who owed their advancement to him; one was a connexion and wholly committed to the dynasty. This was not servility but the rallying of senatorial opinion behind Tiberius and his regime by sympathetic (or interested) men of rank – *principes civitatis*.

The danger had lain in Libo's high connexions.[11] There was a link with the family of Livia (the surname Drusus was now forbidden the Scribonii), but Pompey the Great was a direct ancestor, as well as L. Scribonius Libo, whose daughter Scribonia was thus Libo's great-aunt. Probably she was amongst the 'leading women' who had canvassed the houses of the nobility on Libo's behalf at the opening stages of his trial;[12] certainly she was with him at the last, urging him not to do Tiberius' work for him by committing suicide; just as, nearly twenty years before, she had gone with her daughter, the elder Julia, into exile, remaining with her until her death in AD 14.[13] Any plan to destroy Tiberius and his children (Germanicus was no kin to her) would win her backing; Scribonia could have been in the scheme right from its beginning.

That went back some way. The account of Tacitus implies that Tiberius was well aware that something was afoot when he advanced Libo to his praetorship;[14] that is, if he held that office in 15, immediately after Tiberius' accession to the Principate. Suetonius says outright[15] that the conspiracy of Libo was one of the reasons (the other being the mutinies in Pannonia and on the Rhine) for Tiberius' 'hesitation' on that occasion. That idea we need not accept, but it gives a clue to the nature and ramifications of Libo's plan.

It might be said that Libo's high birth alone was enough to bring him down; that the 'plot' was a frame-up by Tiberius devised to rid him of a potential rival; or that, at best, the foolish speculations of the victim allowed the Princeps to destroy him. Yet Suetonius, puerile as are the anecdotes he cites, had it that Tiberius genuinely believed in a plot to assassinate him; and Seneca, who was a very young man at the time of the trial, described Libo as aiming higher than anyone could reach at that epoch – or Libo at any epoch. How he expected to achieve his aim is a problem, until we recall that the conspiracy of Libo was not the only threat to his position that Tiberius had to face in AD 16: there was also the insurrection of Clemens; and the two episodes, though not directly associated with each other in the ancient sources, were convincingly connected by Rogers.[16] Clemens makes his first appearance in an unsuccessful attempt to rescue Agrippa Postumus from Planasia in August 14.[17] The story that he made up for his failure by snatching away the urn containing Postumus' ashes is hard to believe; what would he or his backers have wanted with them? They would not prove Agrippa dead, nor would their loss prevent the authorities producing other ashes as Agrippa's. The only motive can have been devotion to the memory of Agrippa, to secure the ashes fitting burial. Clemens' attempt, if it is to be accepted as genuine, was probably sponsored by a relative of Agrippa; perhaps a woman, one of the Julias or Scribonia herself. The whole story might be dismissed if it were not for the fact that Agrippa was executed; it may indeed have grown out of that fact, but there is a nucleus of material besides which cannot be ignored: the precautions taken by Augustus, Livia, and Tiberius to ensure that Tiberius' accession to supreme power came about quietly,[18] the execution of Sempronius Gracchus on Cercina, and the suicide of Julia the elder.[19]

Clemens made his way to Cosa in Etruria, lay low there until his beard had grown, enhancing his resemblance to Agrippa, then allowed himself to be glimpsed from time to time in the country towns of Italy. Gathering support as he went, he came to Ostia and proceeded to Rome with a large band of followers. There C. Sallustius Crispus' agents quietly arrested him and took him to the Palatium, where he was questioned and executed.

The activities of Clemens stretch from Augustus' death to some time in 16; those of Libo also, except that the terminal date is secure (13 September). With Tiberius and his natural heirs out of the way, a man of Libo's pedigree could consider himself a strong claimant for power, especially if he were allied with one who would attract some of the popular support that the family of Agrippa Postumus all enjoyed. Popular demonstrations, a march on the Senate-house, forcing members to confer the necessary powers on Libo and 'Agrippa', had a good chance of success (the pretender could be made away with when the crisis was over). What of the armies? Germanicus, idol of the Rhine legions, would have perished with his father when he returned from Germany at the end of 16.[20] Behind him he left C. Silius in charge of the Upper Rhine army; in Spain M. Lepidus was probably still in command; certainly P. Dolabella was governing Dalmatia and Q. Creticus Silanus Syria.[21] All these men were loyal supporters of Tiberius or friends of Germanicus; but with Tiberius and his sons gone, they might be persuaded to give up that allegiance. Only two were of the standing to put up any claim of their own; and Lepidus, loyal though he was to Tiberius, was full brother to that Paullus who had lost his life in AD 7 and so second cousin to Libo, while Creticus

Silanus, who was consul in that year, was a Junius by birth, of the same generation as C. Silanus, consul in 10, and his brother, D. Silanus, now in exile for adultery with Julia the younger. These families had been divided in their allegiance for many years, and may have split more over the chances of success of the dynast they backed than on principle. And in 16 Libo could make himself out the champion of Julia the younger, 'Agrippa Postumus', and all their supporters.

It is possible that Libo's supporters did some work with the armies. The mutinies that broke out in 14 cannot be connected with the movement that backed Agrippa Postumus, though Clemens' plan was said to be to rush him to the Rhine legions. Like the armies in Pannonia in AD 6, they had been reinforced, in AD 9, with low-class recruits from the city, some of them ex-members of the theatrical claques, not likely to take to army life in any event but some of them perhaps once the hired supporters of the Julias and Agrippa Postumus.[22] But when the offer to march on Rome was made in AD 14, it was made to Germanicus. Since then, Clemens and others may have been at work. Between 14 and 16, says Dio, he went to Gaul; whether to Cisalpine Gaul or to Comata, where the legions were, Dio does not tell; and Tacitus says nothing of it.[23] Dio has another item: a centurion brought into the Senate to testify in the year 16.[24] He wanted to give his evidence in Greek, but Tiberius would not permit him. The trial of Libo is the only case known to have been taken in the Senate in that year,[25] and the centurion, who must have come from a legion that recruited in the Eastern provinces, was probably serving in the Balkan garrison, which had been reinforced in 6–7 by two legions brought from Syria;[26] it is possible that he offered evidence of attempts on the loyalty of those legions.

It was not only amongst the populace, or even in the army, that 'Agrippa' had his support. According to Tacitus a number of courtiers, *equites*, and senators had furnished money and advice. No enquiry was made, no attempt to expose links between the two movements. With 'Agrippa' – and Libo – gone, the danger was past. Bygones could be bygones; Libo had anticipated Tiberius' *clementia*; but there were others who might feel its sting, and have to accept the *concordia* that was all that their defeat left them.[27] Its celebration on the Capitol was appropriate indeed if Libo's was a popular movement that had been repressed.

The genuine and remarkable concord between Germanicus and Drusus will have been cemented by the episode. Whether their good relations would have survived the strain of the joint administration that

Tiberius had in mind is another matter. Public opinion had its doubts.[28] Even in the lifetime of Germanicus there were signs of rivalry between the wives of the brothers. Agrippina, the granddaughter of Augustus and daughter of Marcus Agrippa, might sit by while her siblings were disgraced and destroyed; but she was fierce for her own claims which, with that ancestry, were high, and for the claims of her numerous children.[29] The wife of Drusus, Livia Julia, or Livilla, was a great-niece of Augustus and had once been married to Gaius Caesar; but her beauty in womanhood was not matched by fecundity; at Augustus' death she had only one surviving child, and that a girl.[30] There was much in the position of Agrippina between 14 and 19 that might anger Livilla, still more in the position of Livilla after the death of Germanicus to make his widow jealous and even fearful for her children, for all the apparent benevolence of Drusus.[31] It would not be surprising if these women saw the power structure of the Principate in nakedly monarchical terms. Their sex forced them to operate behind the scenes, within the confines of the court, using allies and agents that were sometimes senators, more often, since the growth of women's influence meant a corresponding decline in the power of the Senate, knights, freedmen, or slaves. So in the Republic Servilia, mother of M. Brutus, had worked, then Scribonia and Livia, and the two Julias. Tiberius had benefited from his mother's help (and so had other politicians), but perhaps for that reason and because men said that he owed his position to her marriage and her influence over her husband, he showed himself strongly opposed to petticoat government, of which he had had cruel experience in the first decade BC, still more to the open encroachment of women upon the honours and prerogatives of men. It is not surprising that the appellation 'Iuliae filius' offered to Tiberius in AD 14 was refused; it may have been meant to hurt; but other honours paid to Livia during her lifetime and after her death were severely curtailed, or allowed to lapse. That attitude on the part of Tiberius was taken by the public as evidence of a quarrel with his mother; it may be that she would have felt justified in complaining of ingratitude, he of interference. But whatever political activity went on behind the scenes, the 'Ulysses in petticoats' always preserved a decorous front: she was certainly chaste, and her wifely virtues were well publicized.[32]

In the younger generation Tiberius found a woman who, though as chaste as Livia, was certainly no less ambitious, and far less discreet in the way she used her position in the dynasty: Agrippina's interference with the legions in AD 15, when rumour came of a disaster to the expedition in Germany, was heroic – and unprecedented. Not only did she distribute food and bandages to the returning troops, she had taken on the role of general, forbidding the bridge over the Rhine to be broken down, and stood at the bridgehead to greet the men as they came over. This woman was unlikely to be on terms with the conservative and conventional Tiberius, even when their political interests coincided.[33]

In 17 Germanicus set out on his mission to the East, accompanied by Agrippina, who was now pregnant with their ninth and last child. It could be said that the purpose of the mission demanded that Germanicus should have *imperium maius*, and this he was given, on the same terms as Agrippa in 13 BC, Tiberius in 6, and Gaius in 1. The grant's precedents were more important than any use Germanicus was to make of it: when Tiberius gave up his Eastern command in 6, the East had to wait until Gaius was old enough to take it: domestic politics, not provincial or foreign considerations, were paramount.[34] Tiberius did not trust the judgment of his adopted son. They had not agreed on the need for further campaigns in Germany, and it had taken the offer of a triumph, a second consulship, and perhaps the Eastern command, as well as a plea that Drusus should be given a chance to shine, to bring the reluctant hero home. Tiberius removed Germanicus' friend Q. Creticus Silanus from the governorship of Syria, which he had held for three years, and replaced him with a man known to Tiberius all his adult life, his colleague in his second consulship of 7 BC. Cn. Piso's political views were close to those of the Princeps, and he did not hesitate to air them; his abilities may have been mediocre, and his temper ungovernable, but that fact was outweighed by his closeness to Tiberius and by his seniority.[35] There is no need to doubt that he was sent to Syria to head Germanicus off from adventures that would not profit the Empire, or even that he had written instructions to that effect. The young Germanicus had five years before him in the East, and vast powers. He wished to see the lands that were under his sway and which once had been under that of Alexander and that of his grandfather Antony; he wished also to be seen by his subjects and to enjoy the popularity that comes from power and significant ancestry tempered by graciousness. The Athenians had been courted on the journey out, to the disgust of the unsentimental Piso; Egypt could not be omitted from the itinerary of Antonius' grandson, and Germanicus, entering the country in 19, enhanced his popularity by acts of genuine and useful benevolence.[36] But, unlike Gaius Caesar, who may have visited Egypt in connexion with his Arabian expedition, he had no business there.[37] Tiberius evidently had said nothing about a visit, and it caused him embarrassment. No member of the imperial family except Gaius had set foot in Egypt since Octavian's triumphant entry in 30 BC, and the neglect may have been deliberate: Egypt had been stripped of her independence and Italy freed of the fear of a rival for which even her own rulers might abandon her; now the grandson of Antony was courting the Alexandrians, flattering their vanity by appearing amongst them in Greek dress (Tiberius, who must have heard of it from his Prefect of Egypt, C. Galerius, or who had informants in the entourage, alluded to that) and reminding them, perhaps unwittingly, of the great days of Cleopatra and the Triumvirate. Then Germanicus was a senator, and senators, as Tiberius remarked,[38] were strictly forbidden to enter Egypt without the Princeps' permission. It was not that Germanicus had set a dangerous precedent for his peers; he had given them grounds for complaint.

When Germanicus returned to Syria he probably heard some of this from Piso. It was not the only issue: Piso had already failed to send troops to Armenia when Germanicus ordered them, and there had been a banquet given by the king of the Nabataeans at which the gold crowns presented to Germanicus and Agrippina had been the subject of pointed comment from Piso: there was, or should be, a difference between the sons of Parthian kings and of Roman *principes*. (Piso threw aside the lighter crown that he had received.) Then there was the affair of Vonones, who had failed successively as pretender to the thrones of Parthia and of Armenia, and who had been received into Roman protection in Syria by Creticus Silanus.[39] At the request of the incumbent king of Parthia, Germanicus had moved Vonones away from the border, where he was able to stir trouble up amongst the chieftains on the Parthian side. It was a deliberate affront to Piso, and designed to show how little influence he had: for Vonones had won Piso's patronage. While Germanicus was in Egypt Vonones attempted to escape, but was recaptured and killed. For his part Piso took advantage of Germanicus' absence to cancel or reverse all the orders that Germanicus had given the military and civil authorities. Relations deteriorated so far that Piso decided to leave the province. But Germanicus fell ill, and he stayed on until objects designed to bring about the young *princeps'* death by magic were found in his bedroom. Germanicus then formally renounced his friendship with Piso; most of Tacitus' sources claimed that he ordered him out of the province. Piso did not return until he heard on the island of Cos of his superior's death on 10 October,[40] and then he planned to re-enter Syria, which had been taken over by the legate Cn. Sentius Saturninus, by force. But, bottled up in a Cilician fortress, he had to surrender, return to Rome, and face charges of murder, treason, and extortion.

The trial presented Tiberius with a situation of extreme delicacy. The populace of Italy and Rome had already been roused to paroxysms of grief by Agrippina's arrival with the ashes of Germanicus and by the gloomy pomp of her progress from Brundisium towards the capital.[41] It took a familiar form: the urn on the shoulders of officers of the Praetorian Guard, standards before it unadorned, and official rods and axes reversed, the magistrates of the towns of Calabria, Apulia, and Campania doing their part, the people in mourning, the knights in their ceremonial dress as they burned piles of clothes and spices when the procession passed. Drusus Caesar met it at Tarracina, with Claudius and the children of Germanicus who had not gone abroad with him. It was not enough. Tiberius and Livia kept indoors, so did Antonia, the dead man's mother; and although the ceremony of interment was not a funeral proper, as the body had been burnt at Antioch, their absence was noticed and resented, and a comparison drawn between the obsequies of Germanicus and those of his father Nero Drusus – a false analogy, for Drusus' body had been cremated at Rome, like those of Sulla, Agrippa, and Augustus; the interment of Germanicus was better paralleled by those of C. and L. Caesar. The honours decreed when the news of his death arrived were not less than theirs; they were to be exceeded by those accorded Drusus Caesar in 23 (adulation is inflationary, and Germanicus had never held the tribunician power).[42] At the end of March or the beginning of April Tiberius issued an edict, enjoining firmness and reminding the people of their normal pursuits – and pleasures.

The arrival of Cn. Piso will have aroused as much interest as the forthcoming Megalensian games. He showed self-assurance, and his son had been kindly received by Tiberius. The populace grew more angry still.[43] Tiberius refused to take the case himself,[44] but presided over the Senate when it was heard, and very properly instructed the House to hear the case with impartiality, granting vengeance to the parents and children of Germanicus; private quarrels the Princeps would follow up as a private individual, not in his official capacity; the charges of soliciting the troops and of attempting to re-enter the province by force had also to be considered, and the possibility that the accusers (P. Vitellius, Q. Veranius, and Q. Servaeus, all legates of Germanicus, and L. Fulcinius Trio) had exaggerated them; they had already gone too far when they exposed the body to show signs of poisoning. The case still had to be decided, and neither the standing of Germanicus nor the grief of his relatives should affect the issue.

But the Senate was implacable; and the people, unable to get hold of the man, began to drag his statues towards the Gemonian stairs; they were rescued on Tiberius' orders. During the recess Piso's wife Plancina, a friend of Livia, began to prepare for her own escape. She foresaw the outcome, and so did Piso. He was dead before the Senate sat again, leaving behind a document addressed to Tiberius. It contained accusations of conspiracy, directed presumably against Germanicus' legates, protestations of loyalty to Tiberius and his mother, and pleas for his sons. This letter Tiberius had read out in the Senate and interceded, not only for M. Piso but (on behalf of Livia) for his mother Plancina as well, to the indignation of the Senate. Her sons, in spite of Tiberius' urging, failed to speak for her (they probably thought that they were already compromised), but after two more days Livia's pleas were found to be effective: Plancina was acquitted.

That acquittal was a blow to Agrippina. When Tiberius mitigated the sentence on M. Piso and conceded him his father's property she may have seen it in the same light. The Princeps was hostile to her fatherless house, and that of her rival Livilla had just been increased by the birth of twins, which had elated Tiberius so much that he was moved to claim in the House that never before in the history of Rome had twins been born to a man in so high a station as Drusus Caesar; and the event was commemorated on a remarkable coin reverse.[45] It was not only the counterpoint of celebration against mourning that will have grieved Agrippina. The birth of the twins Germanicus and Tiberius could in her eyes give Drusus a motive for displacing her own boys.

There was no justification for such a belief. It was precisely in AD 20 that her elder son, Nero Caesar, was brought into the Forum to take the garb of manhood (the people received a tip to mark the occasion), introduced into the Senate-house by Tiberius and Drusus Caesar, and promised the quaestorship five years before the normal age.[46] That advancement was something of which Tiberius could approve, since it was what he himself had received, and it is unlikely that even Agrippina could have expected more. Not only were the precedents for speedier advancement discouraging in their outcome or constitutionally irregular (Marcellus and Gaius Caesar), they had been superseded by more recent precedents, those of Germanicus and Drusus Caesar themselves.[47] The same year saw the two branches of Tiberius' family linked by marriage: the older of the two heirs, Nero, wed

Julia, the daughter of Drusus Caesar.[48] Further reassurance for Agrippina came in 23, when the same formal introduction to public life was accorded Nero's younger brother, Drusus.[49] The boy's uncle of the same name had by then been some months in possession of the tribunician power, and so virtually partner of the Princeps. Treating the death of Nero Drusus in 9 BC and his own elevation to a second consulship in 7 as a precedent, and yet maintaining the same interval of three years between Germanicus' and Drusus' first and second tenure of the office, Tiberius made Drusus Caesar consul for the second time in AD 21, and had him invested with the tribunician power in the spring of the following year.[50]

How Drusus Caesar would have turned out as sole Princeps after the death of his father is an unanswerable question. Compared with Germanicus, Drusus seems to have been a late starter with the army. The trip to Pannonia in AD 14 is the first attested service abroad, and that was made without any grant of official powers. Dio expressly denies him any part in the suppressing of the Pannonian revolt, to which even Agrippa Postumus was to have been sent. Ill-health may have been the cause, although nothing is heard of that until AD 21.[51] In AD 14 Drusus acted with decisive brutality, and when appointed to high command three years later – 'to accustom himself to a soldier's life', says Tacitus – he showed himself capable; an ovation earned under Tiberius' auspices was truly earned.[52] On the civil side there is no sign of a cultivated talent, and Drusus enjoyed nothing like the popularity of Germanicus.[53] (Not that that is a guarantee of future merit: Caligula inherited all his father's favour.) But there were failings of character: a taste for wine, which Drusus shared with his father; a taste for theatrical and gladiatorial shows, which he did not, but which endeared him to the Roman populace; and an inclination to violence that Tiberius in his own case limited to words.[54] But there is no reason to believe that Agrippina was unlucky in her brother-in-law. On the contrary, it was not long after his death, on 14 September 23,[55] that she came to realize that she had a real enemy to face.

It was once an axiom of the history of Tiberius' principate that L. Aelius Sejanus aimed at succeeding his master; more recently he has been seen as a mere minister, a Thomas Cromwell who rose too high for his master's peace of mind – or for that of his master's close associates.[56] The older view presents formidable difficulties. The house of the Caesars was well stocked in AD 14, even in AD 23; but there was another obstacle that Sejanus could never move: his original station in life.[57] Sejanus stemmed from Volsinii; he was the son of Seius

Strabo, the equestrian Prefect of the Guard at the end of Augustus' life, and he had been adopted, probably by Aelius Gallus, another distinguished *eques*, Prefect of Egypt. The paternity was eclipsed by Sejanus' mother's lineage, which gave him consular brothers and a consular uncle and cousins. Nevertheless, Sejanus was an *eques* and held an equestrian post, that of Prefect of the Guard. Velleius is painfully aware of these facts, and dwells on others that he intends to make them less glaring: the rise to eminence of such *novi homines*, the first men in their family to embark on the senatorial career, as Coruncanius, Marius, Cicero, and M. Agrippa. It is a measure of Sejanus' problem, if he aimed so high, that the first *eques* to become Emperor was Macrinus in 217, another Praetorian Prefect. Vespasian, who came to power in 69, was certainly a *novus homo*, but had been a senator since the time of Tiberius. Yet already in 12 B C it had been only the chances of mortality that had carried off the *novus homo* Agrippa and left Augustus as Princeps. For all his obscure origin, a soldier of renown in possession of *imperium maius* and *tribunicia potestas* could not have been removed from supreme power. Tiberius himself was a patrician of ancient lineage; but his immediate forbears were not distinguished, and he was not by birth a Julius. Drusus Caesar united the houses of the Nerones and the Vipsanii, and his mother's mother was not a Marcella but the daughter of Cicero's equestrian friend Atticus.[58]

Sejanus is first heard of in connexion with C. Caesar; probably he accompanied the young commander to the East in 1 BC as a member of his staff, perhaps *tribunus militum*, at the beginning of his career.[59] When Gaius died, Sejanus may have continued his military service in Germany or Pannonia, perhaps under the rehabilitated Tiberius. He was already influential with him by AD 14 and in the face of the unrest that was expected it was natural to associate him with his father in the Prefecture to act as intermediary when Drusus went without official powers to their beleaguered kinsman, Q. Blaesus. It was not long before Sejanus' father was sent to Egypt, leaving him alone in the command that he was to hold for the rest of his life.[60]

By 23 Sejanus had increased his powers as Prefect by concentrating the troops in barracks on the Viminal just outside the city walls.[61] There were other signs of growing influence and prestige; one is a quarrel with Drusus, who 'could not bear a rival' and knocked this one down, perhaps in about AD 20.[62] The story may be coloured by later events and rumours, but the details are circumstantial. Nothing suggests that Drusus resented Sejanus' presence on his expedition to Pannonia in AD 14; and it may have been a clash between theatrical *claqueurs* and the Praetorian Guard in 15 that began the quarrel. But in 20 Tiberius seems to have spoken of Sejanus in the Senate (so the evidence is good) in terms applicable to the man whom he saw as his partner in power. That would be legitimate cause for resentment in the heir whose destiny was precisely that position.[63] Tiberius requested that the Senate should confer the *ornamenta praetoria*, the insignia of a praetor, on Sejanus, a grant which did him honour (it was the first time they had gone to a man outside the Senate) but brought him no more power than before.[64] More gratifying was the marriage connexion that Sejanus contracted in that year: Sejanus' daughter was to be betrothed to a son of Claudius.[65] Claudius was discounted in the plans for the succession and was playing no part in public life, but Sejanus' grandchildren would be direct descendants of the elder Drusus and of Mark Antony, collateral descendants of Augustus himself. There may be more than that. The death of a political heir is a signal for intrigue. So it had been in 9 BC with the death of Nero Drusus, an event paralleled in Tiberius' reign by that of Germanicus. Tiberius intended to raise his son to parity with himself, following the plan that Augustus adopted in 9; but plans could be upset, as the earlier series of events had shown.

Claudius resented his exclusion from political life: twice he asked Tiberius for a public career, twice he was refused. We do not know when; but it was in the year 20 that Claudius came into prominence. Naturally he was allowed to proceed to Tarracina to meet Agrippina with the ashes of Germanicus and to take part in the interment. But when his name was excluded from the list of those to be thanked for their services in revenging the young *princeps'* death, L. Asprenas rose and asked the consul if the omission had been deliberate.[66] Claudius had friends in the Senate and amongst the *equites*; one of the most powerful would be his new connexion Sejanus. By birth Claudius' claims to advancement were strong, and Sejanus may have thought of urging them on Tiberius, or even have done so and failed. Drusus Caesar would not thank him for that.

The prosecution of Clutorius Priscus in 21 for writing and reciting a poem lamenting (and therefore presupposing) the death òf Drusus Caesar may give another indication of the disturbed state of politics in the two years immediately after the death of Germanicus. The case[67] is usually considered as an example of folly on the part of the poet, cruelty on that of Drusus Caesar, servility on that of the Senate, and as a legal monstrosity. From the political angle it can be taken as an attack on some friends of Germanicus, the Vitellii. The poem set up a situation in which, with Drusus gone, nothing would stand in the way of Germanicus' children. It was read in the salon of P. Petronius, suffect in AD 19, and only his mother-in-law Vitellia persisted in her denial that she had heard the verses; she realized the purpose of the attack. The consul designate proposed the extreme penalty: he was D. Haterius Agrippa, son of a notorious orator whose wife may have been a daughter of M. Agrippa and Marcella; the consul designate shared a distinguished grandfather with Drusus Caesar.[68] P. Petronius was on intimate terms with Claudius, who as Princeps raised L. Vitellius to his second and third consulships and a censorship with himself as colleague; and the circle of the Petronii and Vitellii included members of the gens Plautia, with which Claudius was connected by his marriage.[69] The allies of Drusus had reacted sharply and effectively to the move to bring Germanicus' backward brother on to the political stage. Claudius learned the lesson and took to dice; what Sejanus did is a matter of controversy.

On 26 October 31,[70] eight days after Sejanus fell, and two days after the execution of his oldest son, his divorced wife Apicata committed suicide. According to Dio, she left a message for Tiberius: Drusus Caesar had been murdered at the orders of his wife Livilla and her lover Sejanus.[71] The story is not easily to be believed. Even with Drusus gone the house of the Caesars was still full. Sejanus in murdering Drusus must have been acting in self-defence: only the life of Tiberius stood between the Praetorian Prefect and political extinction at the hands of his political heir. Even more implausible is the tale of Livilla's complicity. Her husband would guarantee the future of her children, and if ambition was her driving force she would not have turned to Sejanus while Drusus Caesar lived. The accusation of Apicata may be dismissed as the revenge of a woman whose husband had divorced her for one better connected, and whose family was ruined in consequence.[72] It was a stroke of luck for Sejanus when Drusus Caesar died, because at worst he was now free from immediate danger. If he had ever backed Claudius, that horse had to be left out at grass: without a senior running partner he was nowhere, certainly behind young Nero and Drusus in the race. But Sejanus was still not safe if those young men came to power: as the trusted servant of Tiberius he was an obvious object of suspicion to Agrippina; after the Princeps' death there might be a clean sweep of all faithful servants. The gloom that prevailed in the house of Germanicus after his death was transferred now to that of the dead Drusus Caesar, and there lay Sejanus' real chance of permanent power. As the husband of Livilla, Sejanus might hope to take the place of Drusus Caesar in political life as well, and by becoming Tiberius' partner to intervene in the succession as Agrippa had intervened in 18 BC, and Tiberius himself in 6 BC and AD 4. And as the wife of Sejanus the ambitious Livilla might hope to enjoy the dignity of a consort once again, and to advance her children even beyond those of Agrippina; for the difference in age between Nero and the twins was too small to make it likely that they would enjoy power for long, even if Nero put them before any issue of his own.

At the time of Drusus Caesar's death Tiberius had no suspicion that it was anything but natural. The blow was not less cruel for that, and it was only one, if the worst, of the bereavements that Tiberius suffered in the years 20 to 23. Very soon after the suicide of Cn. Piso, Tiberius heard of the death of his former wife, Vipsania. The following year he lost P. Sulpicius Quirinius, like Piso a man he had known and trusted since his youth; and in 23 not only Drusus himself but one of Drusus' twin sons and another close friend, Lucilius Longus, the only senator who had gone with him to Rhodes.[73] Vipsania he had given up for the sake of his own advancement, though he loved her; Piso could be seen as a victim of his own misplaced zeal for the Princeps. There would be regret as well as a sense of loss. The future was bleak, personally and politically, and the Princeps needed a reliable friend and servant. The responsibilities that Tiberius might have hoped to shed – that he had shed during his son's consulship, spending it in Campania 'for his health' – would fall on him again with all their weight. When Tiberius left for Rhodes in 6 BC Augustus had gambled on his own survival. Tiberius, who was eight years older than Augustus had been in 6, though Nero and Drusus were about four years older than their counterparts had been, could not be sure of surviving to ensure the continuity of the regime. In his straits he turned to the Senate.[74] Before the funeral he attended a meeting, excusing himself for his hardihood; he had sought a sterner solace than most: the arms of the state. Nero and Drusus were brought in and commended to the *patres*: it was they who would in some part have to take the place of Germanicus and Drusus Caesar, of the ageing Tiberius himself, to guide the young men. But (he went on) they would have to do more than that; he asked the consuls, indeed other senators, to take on the burden of responsibility for government. The appeal was misunderstood, and heard with scepticism.

In one respect Tiberius departed from the precedent of 6 BC. When Drusus Caesar died he made no attempt to speed up the careers of his grandsons, as Augustus had done in 5. That was only to be expected; but for Agrippina the boys' advancement was agonizingly slow: Nero would not become even quaestor until 5 December 25, and could not expect the consulship until 34.[75] Impatience is detectable. When the pontiffs took their annual vows for the safety of the Princeps at the beginning of 24 Nero and Drusus were mentioned alongside him. Whoever authorized that it was not Tiberius. He noticed the intrusion and summoned the *pontifices* to find out if it was Agrippina who had had their names included. They denied it and got off with a mild lecture. The Senate had to listen to a discourse on the danger of spoiling young boys – but they had not spent seven years on Rhodes.[76] Tiberius was on the lookout for any signs of his former wife in her daughter; she would see his caution in another light: it was due to jealousy.

In the same year Sejanus began systematically to undermine their position. The first attacks were peripheral, aimed at disgracing or at least discrediting Agrippina's friends and relatives, and so frightening off the rest. In 24 C. Silius, an ex-legate of Germanicus and commander on the Rhine, was accused of *maiestas* (treason) on the grounds of complicity in the Gallic revolt of 21, and of extortion after it was over. He committed suicide; Sosia, his wife, a friend of Agrippina, was sent into exile. The prosecutor was the incumbent consul L. Visellius Varro, who had an inherited feud with Silius.[77] The fact that in this case, as in that of Clutorius Priscus three years before, the distinguished and honourable moderate, M. Lepidus, spoke in mitigation of the sentence proposed does not prove that there was a link between them; but he may have been trying to repair the split that was developing between the two branches of the imperial house and in the Senate.[78] In AD 24 he was defeated by C. Asinius Gallus, whose children by Vipsania were kin to Drusus Caesar and whose attitude towards Sejanus was apparently friendly.[79] Another case of the year, scandalous because brought by a son against his father, seems to be a pendant to the Silius affair.[80] Vibius Serenus accused his father of sending agents to the Gallic rebellion from his own province of Baetica. The evidence was not good, and Serenus made inept accusations against two men close to Tiberius, Cn. Lentulus and L. Seius Tubero. But the Princeps' evident hostility to the elder Serenus inspired severe proposals, one of them coming from Asinius Gallus. Some Vibii, the suffect consuls of AD 5 and 8, C. Postumus and A. Habitus, were protégés of Tiberius; Postumus had served in Illyricum. The elder Serenus had appeared as prosecutor at the trial of Libo – one of the things that Tiberius had against him was that like Silius, who boasted that Tiberius owed the Empire to the fidelity of Silius' legions in AD 14, he claimed that the Princeps was in his debt: he had never been rewarded for his part in Libo's conviction. Serenus was loyal to the regime, but his son may have been anxious to detach himself from any dangerous connexions.

One family certainly split by the events of the twenties was that of the Vitellii. P. Vitellius had been one of Germanicus' legates and had distinguished himself as prosecutor of Cn. Piso,[81] and the family had already been under attack from Drusus Caesar's friends. Publius took the hint and, like another member of the prosecuting team, Q. Servaeus, followed Sejanus into the other camp.[82] In 31, when the Prefect fell, he was in charge of the military treasury and ready (it was alleged) to surrender the keys to Sejanus. In 32 he was handed over to the safe custody of his brother Lucius, that friend of Claudius whose glory was only at its beginning when he reached his first consulship in 34.[83]

It may have been to drive the lesson home that another assistant of Germanicus was brought to trial in 24: his quaestor, P. Suillius Rufus.[84] He was accused by an unnamed prosecutor of taking bribes while acting as arbitrator, juryman, or president of a court. He was found guilty; and Tacitus passes no favourable judgment on him and his later career under Claudius as a friend of that Princeps. C. Silius too in Tacitus' view had been guilty of extortion; but that does not mean that the prosecutions were the work of disinterested champions of oppressed provincials and defrauded litigants.

After laying down this creeping barrage, Sejanus felt free to pick off a personal opponent. The immediate political affiliations of the historian A. Cremutius Cordus are not known, although his sentiments were Republican. But he loathed Sejanus and, like Drusus Caesar – they were the only two – dared to make his loathing public. When the theatre of Pompey was burnt down in 22 the Senate had decreed that in recognition of Sejanus' success in containing the fire his statue should be erected in the theatre; which, in Cremutius' words, was its real ruin. Two friends of Sejanus, Satrius Secundus and Pinarius Natta, drew the attention of the senatorial court to aspects of Cremutius' historical works that might be interpreted as treasonable. After making a speech in his own defence the accused man retired to his house and starved himself to death. His works were ordered to be burnt, but his daughter saved copies of them and, like those of Cassius Severus and T. Labienus, they were allowed to circulate again under Caligula.[85]

It was in 25 that Sejanus made his first bid for the hand of Livilla. Tacitus claims to reproduce the content of his letter to Tiberius, and the reply he received. The likelihood of such letters being preserved and made public has been doubted.[86] Yet they were not more embarrassing to the dynasty than the letters that passed between Augustus and his wife on the subject of Claudius' mental and physical capacity;[87] and these reached the light of day in Suetonius' biography. Besides, the second letter encapsulates words and phrases characteristic of Tiberius; either Tacitus so thoroughly understood his subject that consciously or unconsciously he could clothe an invented letter in language suitable to its purported author, or he faithfully preserved expressions actually found by him or his source in original documents. Tiberius prevaricated. He had not made up his mind whether Nero would prove fit to take over from himself directly or whether it would be necessary to introduce a man from an intermediate generation (and that man an *eques*), a step that might tear the dynasty apart. For the moment, Tiberius stuck to his original plan of 23.

If he did not allow Livilla to reinforce her position by marrying, no more in the following year did he grant Agrippina's request for a husband, prevaricating again.[88] The memory of what had happened in 2 BC must have been revived in his mind. Like Julia the elder, her daughter Agrippina hoped to make the succession more secure for her sons by introducing a compliant husband into the dynasty in case the Princeps died prematurely – or in case Tiberius changed his mind about the order of succession. Like his predecessor, though in a less drastic way, the Princeps prevented any interference with the scheme he had laid down.

Adultery with Asinius Gallus was one of the charges eventually to be brought against Agrippina. Tacitus' report of her request names no names, but the widowed Gallus would be an obvious match, and if he was superficially at least on good terms with Sejanus, one that might help to bring together the two halves of Tiberius' house.[89] The story of the adultery may stem from this request, and Tiberius may have believed it precisely because the request had been made. If marriage was in Gallus' mind (and his ambition was to become a byword[90]) it is not surprising that Sejanus developed an implacable enmity towards a man who might set himself up as a potential partner – or a potential rival.

The year 26 saw an attack on a second cousin of Agrippina's who was also a close friend.[91] Cn. Domitius Afer, a talented orator from Narbonensian Gaul, had already reached the praetorship, but aimed higher and undertook the prosecution of Claudia Pulchra, widow of the Quinctilius Varus who had perished in Germany. Adultery was one of the charges against her (the adulterer, Furnius, is obscure); a plan to poison the Princeps; and dealing in magic to bring about his death. Successful against Pulchra, Afer brought a case against her son Quinctilius Varus in the following year, this time in concert with P. Dolabella, who was, shockingly enough, first cousin of the accused.[92] By now the Princeps had left for Campania, and although he had shown marked approval of Afer's virtuosity in 26, calling him 'a master in his own right', the Senate did not venture to settle the case in his absence, and it probably lapsed.[93] Varus was wealthy; Domitius Afer needed money and Dolabella's idea may have been at least to keep some of it in the family (both confident that Varus would be convicted after the destruction of his mother in the previous year). That may explain the prosecution of 27, though Varus was betrothed to Germanicus' daughter Livilla and may have been seen as a threat for that reason.[94] The attack on Pulchra was certainly political, and due to her connexions with Agrippina, who intervened unsuccessfully on her behalf. Pulchra's aunt was that Claudia who had been betrothed to Octavian; her second cousin Ap. Claudius had already paid for his association with the elder Julia; and the son of another cousin, it has been conjectured, was the D. Silanus who went into exile for his adultery with the younger Julia.[95] If these facts were not brought up it is hard to see what plausibility the charge of attempted poisoning would have had; Agrippina does not seem to have been named, but with her eldest sons Tiberius' heirs and her daughter betrothed to Varus the danger was very close.

That form that Agrippina's intervention took well illustrates what was in the minds of the protagonists in the drama of 26. She came upon the Princeps sacrificing to Augustus, and named the trump card that she held – and that all held who were descended from Scribonia. Why did he persecute Augustus' granddaughter, who was more of an image of the deified Princeps than any dumb statue? If the anecdote is to be trusted, Tiberius took Agrippina by the arm and went straight for the ultimate issue between them, quoting a line from tragedy: 'Do you feel wronged, my child, because you do not rule?'[96]

That remark might have been made to her mother, sister, and three brothers. Its irony would have been as lost on them as it was on her. Tiberius knew, or had discovered, what it was to rule. Long ago too he had found out what it was to be envied for his power. The encounter with Agrippina was one incident in a series that determined him to leave Rome permanently. Another, if it is to be believed, was contrived by agents of Sejanus.[97] They convinced Agrippina that Tiberius intended to poison her. When he noticed that she was eating nothing at dinner he took fruit from a dish that had just been brought to the table and offered it to her with a word of commendation. Agrippina handed it straight to her servants. Tiberius said nothing to her, but turned to his mother and remarked that it was not to be wondered at if he took stern measures against someone who alleged that he was trying to poison her. That was the last invitation to dinner that Agrippina received from Tiberius.

This incident too is revealing, if it is genuine. Agrippina was only a nuisance to Tiberius, not a danger. Poisoning he had never seriously been suspected of. If Agrippina believed that Tiberius intended to dispose of her in that way she completely misread her father-in-law's character and over-estimated her own importance. The same episode reveals Tiberius' determination to see how far his daughter-in-law mistrusted him, even to set up situations in which she could display her mistrust.

For they allowed him to see her as a new study in resentment, a second Julia the elder, convinced that he meant ill towards her two sons. Retirement had been honourable and justified in the circumstances of 6 BC; it was so again in AD 26. Besides, he was sixty-seven. Officially he had no partner to share the burdens of empire and the Senate was no more capable now than it had been twelve years before of taking on its proper responsibilities. But he had a helpmeet who could guarantee his security as commander of the Praetorian Guard, relieve him of routine work as an authoritative friend possessed of delegated *imperium*, and give good advice as a man outside and above senatorial politics. So much for Sejanus' part in removing Tiberius from the capital.[98] The astrologers knew better. Ostensibly he left in 26 to dedicate temples of Jupiter and Augustus at Capua and Nola. The astrologers said he would never return: the conjunctions of the stars forbade it. So did the course of Tiberius' past life. There were others who grasped something of the truth: Tiberius was ashamed of his appearance in old age, they said; emaciated, tall and bent, his head bald and his face covered with blotches, some of them patched with plasters.[99] But what Tiberius was trying to hide and patch up was not his complexion but the public disharmony in the dynasty. As for the secret pleasures that he had enjoyed on Rhodes, pleasures that no ordinary, decent Roman shared – the prospect of indulging in them without interruption certainly made Capri more alluring to an elderly amateur of scholarship who enjoyed passing the port.[100]

The prophecies of the astrologers were all but confirmed almost as soon as the Princeps left Rome.[101] He was dining in a cavern at a villa named Speluncae, between the sea at Amyclae and the hills of Fundi, when a fall of rock killed several servants and put the diners to flight. Sejanus threw himself on hands and knees across the Princeps' body and was found in that position by the soldiers who came to the rescue. Probably Tiberius did not consider how precious his life was to the Prefect's career, and gratefully accepted the act as one of selfless courage. Sejanus began to make full use of his credit.[102] His technique was to employ *agents provocateurs* to rouse the suspicions and fears of Agrippina and her son Nero. They have already been seen warning Agrippina against dining with Tiberius; now they concentrated on Nero, who was the greatest threat and now was just holding his quaestorship and so in the public eye. Nero was inclined by nature and encouraged by his freedmen and clients to push himself forward. Cautious men began to avoid him. His blunders and indiscretions were reported to Sejanus by spies who included his wife, Drusus Caesar's daughter Julia. Even his brother Drusus was stupid enough to join Sejanus' side, out of jealousy of Nero's leading position in public life and the greater affection that Agrippina had for him.[103]

During the year 27 Sejanus was able to bring to court a case that had been in preparation since 24, where Tacitus links the victim with C. Silius as one of the powerful friends of Agrippina who had to be destroyed.[104] Titius Sabinus was not in public life as far as we know. There could be no charge of extortion against him as a returning magistrate. Only treason would do. Hence perhaps the delay in bringing the charge: evidence had to be gathered or fabricated. L. Lucanius Latiaris[105] made friends with Sabinus, pretending sympathy for Agrippina and her children. Eventually Sabinus, in the privacy (as he thought) of Latiaris' home, hurled abuse at Sejanus and Tiberius that was overheard by three other senators of praetorian rank concealed in the roof space.[106] Sabinus was arrested at once, and the accusers informed Tiberius by letter of the evidence they had collected. On 1 January 28, Tiberius' reaction was made known to the Senate (the examination of Sabinus' slaves may already have taken place). Tiberius made it clear that some of his freedmen had been bribed and that there had been an attempt on his own life. The execution of Sabinus followed immediately, but no action was taken against Nero, who may have been implicated in the charges. Tiberius contented himself with a letter of thanks to the Senate for punishing an enemy of the state. His own life (he said) was not safe from the plots of his enemies. Everyone knew who were meant. Writing in 30, Velleius Paterculus speaks of a three-year period of anguish for Tiberius, caused by the pent-up fire of grief, indignation, and shame brought upon him by his daughter-in-law and grandson.[107] The starting point for that anguish must be the discovery of Sabinus' hostile activities, real or staged by Sejanus. The trial itself was the point of no return for Agrippina and Nero; their position was now precarious in the extreme, with Tiberius completely alienated from them.

Anguish did its work. It was soon after Livia died in 29 that Tiberius wrote the Senate another letter of accusation. Its terms were savage, but it contained no charge of conspiracy: the worst charge that was ever brought was of contemplating a dash to the German army or an appeal to the people in the Forum at Augustus' statue.[108] Overbearing conduct and an insolent temper were alleged against Agrippina, homosexuality against Nero. That should cause no surprise. As with the two Julias and Agrippa Postumus, a moral took the place of a political charge, and this time no statute at all was invoked (adultery was not a plausible charge to bring against Agrippina). The Princeps followed his predecessor's example in treating Agrippina and Nero like recalcitrant children, while the plain issue – their claim to an immediate share in the power – was kept from Senate and public, which might not react in a way that would be welcome to him. These precautions were not enough. While the Senate debated the letter, a crowd collected outside the Curia carrying placards and portraits of the victims and shouting that the letter did not come from the Princeps but was forged by Sejanus. Even if that had been the case the forgery would not all have been on one side. Pamphlets also circulated purporting to contain denunciations of Sejanus pronounced in the Senate by ex-consuls.[109] Inside, M. Cotta Messallinus – the Princeps' faithful servant – called for the affair to be debated, while Iunius Rusticus, who was in charge of the Senate's records and thought to be in Tiberius' confidence,[110] urged delay. The consuls too were hesitant.[111] The tactics of Agrippina's supporters, which are familiar enough to students of the last two decades of the Augustan principate, were momentarily effective: the Senate did nothing. A second letter arrived, delivering a stinging rebuke for allowing the Princeps' wishes to be slighted; the case was to be remitted to his court. Another communication, in the form of an edict, lashed the populace. The Senate instantly gave way and attested its readiness to vindicate the Princeps in any manner that he would permit. It was probably the angry *paterfamilias* himself who sent Agrippina and Nero into exile, to Pandateria and Pontia respectively, having them hurried off in closed carriages. Nero in addition was declared a public enemy, *hostis*, by the Senate, which may have been taking from

Tiberius' description of Titius Sabinus. The pronouncement was little more than the striking of an attitude by the House when it was dealing, not with a Marius, a Catiline, or an Antonius, but a youth safely incarcerated on an island; the measure (unlike outlawry, *aquae et ignis interdictio*) would take practical effect only if Nero slipped away: he might be killed;[112] but it was one of the few expressions of extreme disapprobation open to the House and peculiarly appropriate if no formal trial had taken place.[113]

For the moment, the other children of Germanicus escaped. Agrippina the younger who, being a girl, presented little danger, had been married to Cn. Domitius Ahenobarbus at the end of the previous year;[114] but Drusus Caesar, whose information had contributed to his brother's downfall, should have been quaestor precisely in 29. There is no evidence that he was,[115] but he would have to be dealt with quickly. Meanwhile, however, he was found a partner: Aemilia Lepida, daughter of the consul of AD 6. But she too, like Livilla, is said to have put up no resistance to Sejanus' charm.[116] Soon every word her husband uttered was being reported to the Prefect. There were other channels – slaves, freedmen, clients, friends – if another seduction does not find credence. Some time in 30, probably in the first half of the year, Drusus too found himself in the Curia facing a bitter attack from Tiberius. Feeling safe with precedents, the Senate declared him too a *hostis*, and he went into confinement in a dungeon under the Palatium.[117]

Tiberius, confronted by indisputable evidence of the depravity and hostility of his second grandson, gave way. The only possible heirs now were Gaius Caligula, who was in his eighteenth year, and Ti. Gemellus, born in AD 19, one each of the children of Germanicus and Drusus Caesar. But they were young and Tiberius was now past seventy. To hope that he would live long enough to secure the peaceful succession of a pair of mature *principes*, well trained in administration and war, would be foolish. Augustus had been younger in AD 4 when he secured the succession for the dynasty by adopting a consular of forty-five and a boy of sixteen. Sejanus was elected to the consulship of 31, with Tiberius as colleague and accession to the proconsular *imperium* (province unknown); the prospect of the tribunician power was clear ahead. To strengthen the tie the betrothal of Sejanus to Livilla was at last announced.[118]

It was not only by destroying the prospects of Agrippina's eldest sons that Sejanus had come to this pitch. He had worked hard for his positive advantages as well. One ingenious gambit was designed

to convert his relatively humble birth into an asset, enhance his popularity at Rome, and emphasize a precedent that would justify his
ambition, however high it rose. Sejanus made himself out to be a second
M. Agrippa, and a latter-day champion of the *plebs*.
The idea was simple but evocative. Agrippa had been the friend and
benefactor of the people, though he showed no sensitivity towards the
Senate and its rights. If Drusus Caesar and his nephews were descendants of Agrippa by blood, Sejanus could be so in politics. That this
was how he wished to be seen is distinctly shown by the comparisons
drawn by Velleius in 30, in those chapters of his history which might
be read as an election manifesto for the Prefect.[119] What Agrippa had
been to Augustus, what the low-born Servius Tullius had been to
Ancus Martius in the far-off days of the kings, which Sejanus also
ransacked for precedents (he set up a statue of Fortune which had once
belonged to Servius Tullius in his own house, a blatant advertisement
of intent[120], these things Sejanus could be to Tiberius, and would be
once he had his consulship.
Election duly took place in the Senate but the pageantry on the
Aventine that followed had a political value.[121] Sejanus appeared as
the champion of the urban *plebs*, a role that had been left vacant by
the Princeps, who had less sympathy for the Gracchi than for their
slayers. The people already had their heroes: the elder Julia and her
family had attempted to take up the interests of the *plebs*, and with
some success. All the more important it became for Sejanus to outbid
her children for urban support; but the appeals to plebeian solidarity,
the discreet demagoguery – it had to be discreet, with Tiberius his
master – were not enough to dim the present popularity of Augustus'
and Germanicus' flesh and blood, to swamp the demonstrations made
in favour of Agrippina and Nero in 29. When Sejanus fell in 31 Macro
was instructed to free young Drusus Caesar and parade him before the
people as an antidote to any movement for Sejanus. There was no
need: jeers and blows accompanied Sejanus to prison.
The composition of Julia's clique had shown that a popular group
need not exclude men of family and distinction. Sejanus was catholic;
he could not afford to be anything else. His access to the Princeps, almost
exclusive as it was, gave him enormous powers of patronage, which
he preferred to use unobtrusively.[122] The accusers of Titius Sabinus
had hoped for the consulship, to be obtained through his favour.
These men were not distinguished. But Sejanus had made friends with
important men like Mam. Scaurus too, and aligned behind himself
those who (like P. Vitellius and Q. Servaeus?) had begun to assess

Agrippina's political acumen as inadequate to her needs; and those who had always been close to Tiberius and who might dread the accession of young men who had learned from their mother to bear a grudge against their grandfather and his friends. Sejanus connected himself with the Cornelii Lentuli by betrothing his son to the daughter of the commander of the Upper Rhine army; another vital area, the Lower Rhine and its legions, was under the command of Lentulus' own father-in-law, L. Apronius.[123] Even the greatest families of the recent past did not shrink from forming an alliance with Sejanus' kinsmen the Blaesi. Perhaps the surviving members of Mark Antony's family thought to restore their fortunes by the alliance. The connexion was to prove unhelpful in the short run, fatal in the long.[124] Sejanus was less successful in securing the sympathy of the absentee governors of Tarraconensis and Syria than he was on the Rhine; but these provinces were far away and could be ignored.[125]

Nevertheless there were senators other than L. Arruntius whose eminence and hostility put them into danger. Asinius Gallus was one. He had been apparently friendly towards the Prefect, and in 28 at the end of the trial of Titius Sabinus he had reacted to Tiberius' letter of thanks by begging him to let the Senate share his fears, so that it might remove them. The enquiry was as ambiguous as Gallus' other interventions in debate, but suggests that he had given up any intention he might once have had of uniting the two branches of the *domus*: Agrippina would not do as a partner and he had better back Sejanus, Livilla, and the young Gemellus, kinsman to his own children. Gallus, as a senior consular, was foremost in proposing most of the important honours conferred on Sejanus, presumably at the moment of his recognition as Tiberius' partner in 30. His anxiety to be one of the envoys sent to Tiberius and Sejanus to inform them of the honours voted them was natural, but Sejanus, who certainly must have considered so eminent and so slippery a backer a menace to his position, may have suspected that something more than a formal message of congratulation was to pass between Gallus and the Princeps. He got in first, and it was on the very day that the legate Gallus was dining with Tiberius on Capri that the imperial missive denouncing him and his jealousy of the Princeps' friendship with Sejanus was read in the Senate.[126] Nor did Sejanus allow any other hostile voices to be heard on the island if he could help it. Curtius Atticus was an equestrian member of Tiberius' court. If Atticus had had anything hostile to say about Sejanus, he went too far and roused the Princeps' anger.[127]

The *dénouement* was not far off. For Sejanus' opponents, the situation looked hopeless. The Princeps was committed, the Prefect all-powerful. But the very violence of Tiberius in defending his protégé betrays uneasiness. He had undertaken to continue the dynasty on lines laid down by Augustus, and he had failed. Now he had to introduce an outsider to power and, however liberal the Claudii towards *novi homines*, they were liberal only because they could afford to be: the position of the Claudii in society and politics was unassailable, that of the dynasty was vulnerable. As for the precedent of M. Agrippa, Tiberius had been his son-in-law; but there is no evidence that he liked the man; and politically they were far apart.[128] Tiberius must have hated what he had had to do. A reaction against Sejanus, if it could be brought about, would be violent indeed. Another point: the very success of Sejanus in ruining the family of Germanicus provided them with a protagonist as cunning as Sejanus himself, who matched his will to power, and whose family connexions made him the ideal leader for a counter-move: Gaius Caligula.

When Tiberius wrote his autobiography, he said that he had punished Sejanus because he had discovered that he was venting his rage against the children of Germanicus.[129] There is an objection to Tiberius' account, one raised by Suetonius himself. By the time Sejanus fell, Nero was dead, but Agrippina and Drusus were not, and they still lingered in prison, and Asinius Gallus in the custody of the magistrates, after 31. That need cause no surprise. Sejanus' technique had been to provoke acts and words of hostility; they were not obliterated by his death. Again, some sources claim or imply that it was a conspiracy against Tiberius himself that brought about Sejanus' downfall.[130] That need give no discomfort. An attack on Tiberius' heirs could and would be construed in the hysteria of the moment as an attack on the Princeps, and the offence so made more monstrous. Tiberius encouraged such constructions by implying in the letter that denounced the Prefect (and we have only this one item from the contents) that he could no longer trust the Guard and that his life was in danger.[131]

The tense of the verb in the sentence from Tiberius' autobiography is worth noting. It implies that Sejanus was still acting against the children at the time of his fall: that is to say, machinations against the youngest son Gaius Caligula were the gravamen of the offence, in Tiberius' own account. In those of Josephus and Dio, the evidence for Sejanus' misdeeds was smuggled to Tiberius on Capri from the house of Antonia, his sister-in-law; and it was in Antonia's house that Gaius was to be found from Livia's death in 29 until he was summoned to Capri, sometime after his eighteenth birthday on 31 August AD 30.[132]

Gaius knew that if Tiberius' place were ever taken by Sejanus, his own life was not worth a farthing. On the positive side his pre-emptive action might give him direct access to the Principate: his elder brothers and the mother who favoured Nero were already disgraced, and as far as they were concerned the way was clear for himself. Gaius, like his brothers, found himself assailed by agents of Sejanus – and duly reported the fact to his grandmother, who passed it on to Capri.

The information may have been genuine: on Capri Gaius was to become notorious for his discretion, and Sejanus' agents could already have been at work: one of them, Sextius Paconianus, was a senator of praetorian rank, and unlikely to have been resident on Capri.[133] But there were others at court who benefited from the downfall of Sejanus. Q. Naevius Cordus Sutorious Macro, formerly Praefectus Vigilum, who executed the coup against Sejanus, benefited through the promotion he won to the post that Sejanus left vacant; his collaborator P. Graecinius Laco, the incumbent Praefectus Vigilum, was also honoured.[134] Ti. Claudius Thrasyllus, the astrologer resident on Capri, benefited: his granddaughter Ennia Thrasylla was married to the new Prefect of the Guard; and she was said to have become Gaius' mistress.[135] Pallas, the slave of Antonia who allegedly carried the letter from Antonia's house to Capri, benefited; at least, he was free and the owner of property in Egypt by the end of Tiberius' principate and soon to embark on a brilliant career as a rationibus (controller of accounts) under Claudius.[136] Claudius too benefited as Gaius' nearest kinsman; but there is nothing to show that he played a part in the movement.

Sejanus' consulship opened to unfavourable omens which, if they are correctly reported, do his opponents great credit for ingenuity.[137] Tiberius remained on the island, detained by ill-health. It was the first time he had entered on the office in absence; distaste for the capital, or fear of the astrologers' predictions that he would never enter Rome alive again, were too strong for convention. There is no reason to believe (with Dio) that he entertained any misgiving about Sejanus yet; the parting was affectionate and tearful. He had been using the term 'socius laborum' again, and the language of the communications from Capri had made it clear how close Sejanus was to his master. When men called the consul Tiberius' collega imperii they were referring to more than collegiality in an office to be held for a few months only, and they had clearly done right to set up statues to the new pair, to have gilded chairs brought into the theatres for both of them, to vote them quinquennial consulships, to sacrifice to the images of Sejanus as they did to those of Tiberius, and to swear by his Fortune.

Then came a doubt, and rumours that grew stronger as the consulships wore on. They were caused by a marked fluctuation in the tone of Tiberius' frequent communications, and by inconsistency in their content. The state of his health and the likelihood of his coming to Rome were variously gauged; he wrote warmly of Sejanus – and coolly. It was all a cunning manoeuvre on the part of a master of deception – or the vacillation of an old man who could not make up his mind. The strands that made up Tiberius' reputation as a dissimulator may have included this one: that often he did not know himself what he thought. This was the man who, in the prime of life, in his element in Germany, did not make a move after the Varian disaster without consulting his *consilium*; and the man who made the word '*dubitatio*' characteristically his own.[138] The consulship came to an end on 8 May, exceptionally in the middle of a month;[139] with Tiberius abdicated, Sejanus could not stay on. Appropriate honours followed to reassure him. Tiberius offered a priesthood, perhaps the augurate, to him and his son. Now, as an ex-consul he would take up the promised *proconsulare imperium*; while the Senate, having voted the priesthood, decreed as an additional gesture, graceful but safe, that all future consuls should be instructed to conduct themselves in emulation of Sejanus.

The discordant note grew more strident. What was happening to Gaius Caligula must have caused Sejanus most unease. Some time after 31 August 30, he was summoned to Capri, not necessarily as a result of the letter that may have reached the island from Antonia's house, though it is tempting to make that inference. The advancement of Sejanus, in Tiberius' eyes, need not mean abandoning Gaius; he and Tiberius Gemellus would be next in line. When the new scheme was firmly adopted, the coming of age of Gaius might now take place. It was long overdue: Gaius, born on the last day of August in AD 12, should have taken the toga of manhood in the twelve months beginning 31 August 26. The fact that nothing was done betrays Tiberius' uncertainty, precisely in the year that he left Rome, about the future of his elder grandsons: Gaius could take the toga neither with ceremony nor without it. He was in the position that Agrippa Postumus had been in after the death of Lucius Caesar, but he was kept in it for much longer. Or was it the death of Nero Caesar that prompted Tiberius to bring Gaius to Capri? Nero was murdered, or forced to suicide, on his island, apparently some time after the expiry of Sejanus' consulship, when Sejanus was already suspect to the Princeps.[140] Indeed it was a letter to the Senate on the subject of Nero's death that raised more doubts about Sejanus' position in the minds of its members: it referred to him as plain 'Sejanus'. Sejanus in danger had an even stronger motive for removing Nero than Sejanus secure; but it may have been this very act (or event) that convinced Tiberius of his guilt. Yet it was not the elevation of Sejanus to partnership with Tiberius or the death of Nero that was the cause of Gaius' removal to Capri. Tiberius' suspicions of Sejanus are a better explanation. Gaius took the toga in a hole and corner style, not after the fashion of a young *princeps*; and on the same day he shaved his beard, a ceremony that usually followed the assumption of the toga at a decent interval.[141] Tiberius was in a hurry.

More followed. When Sejanus and his son were offered their priest-hoods, Gaius was honoured in the same way.[142] The citation spoke well of him and, according to Dio, gave some indication that he was to be Tiberius' successor. Whether he intended the move to test public opinion or not, Tiberius received clear proof of the continued popularity of Germanicus' house, and Sejanus was correspondingly dis-heartened. The next step that Tiberius took was an act of self-denial that involved a set-back to Sejanus: he forbade cult to any living human being and the consideration of any measure in his own honour. The prohibition was no novelty and no doubt had long been neglected. Tiberius' purpose in reiterating it in 31 was clear.[143]

Some time between 1 July and 1 October Sejanus tried to strike back at his enemies, not on the island but in the Senate. For the group had, and needed, members in both places. L. Arruntius was one of its most distinguished partisans and his enmity to Sejanus was of long standing. Aruseius and Sanquinius (if that was his name) brought an indictment against him, perhaps at the very moment that his adopted son, L. Arruntius Camillus Scribonianus, a connexion of the Libones, was canvassing for the consulship of 32. The charge was quashed on the grounds that it was not legal to bring an indictment against an imperial legate in office. The *senatus consultum* enforcing this line was brought forward by a Lentulus, possibly Cossus, the consul of 1 BC who became Praefectus Urbi in 33, a confidant of the Princeps; that perhaps is why Dio says that Tiberius himself was responsible for quashing the indictment, unless the Senate consulted the Princeps on the legal point. The friends of Arruntius now had good grounds for a counter-prosecution for *calumnia* (malicious prosecution). Aruseius and his fellow accuser were convicted.[144]

Even before this, perhaps, the Princeps had not shown himself entirely supine. C. Fufius Geminus, consul *ordinarius* in AD 29, owed his advancement to Livia; but there was no love lost between him and Tiberius, who had suffered from his caustic wit. Fufius' wife too, Mutilia Prisca, was a friend of Livia, and had been instrumental in introducing an ally of Sejanus to the old lady to poison her mind against Agrippina. Yet in 30, at the height of Sejanus' power, the couple were forced to suicide, Fufius being accused of *impietas*, failure of duty and respect, towards Tiberius, which he attempted to disprove by showing Tiberius as equal heir with his children in his will. And in 32, after Sejanus' downfall, Fufius' mother Vitia was destroyed on a charge of mourning her son. It would be good to know who brought the original charges, or if the accusation came from Tiberius himself.[145]

Sejanus was in suspense for more than five months after laying down his consulship. At length, on the night of 17 October, Macro arrived in Rome, where Sejanus had remained at the wish of Tiberius, with a letter from the Princeps and instructions which he communicated to Graecinius Laco and the loyal consul P. Memmius Regulus, who had come into office only on 1 October; his colleague L. Fulcinius Trio had held the post since 1 July, but he was a supporter of Sejanus and it may be that Tiberius waited for Memmius' term to begin before he acted. At dawn Macro met Sejanus on the Palatine, where the Senate was to meet in the temple of Apollo, and told him that he was to be given the tribunician power. When he was safely inside the temple Macro showed the Praetorians on duty his authority from the Princeps, sent them back to barracks and replaced them with the Vigiles (Watchmen) under Laco. He entered the temple, delivered the letter to the consuls and went off to the barracks where he successfully consolidated his authority (the Praetorians were to receive a donative). Tiberius' letter was long-winded and rambling (which gave Macro more time for his manoeuvre by keeping Sejanus away from the barracks)[146] and it seems never to have brought precise charges; but it ended with instructions to imprison Sejanus and punish two of his senatorial friends (Aruseius and Sanquinius?). By the time that point was reached, some senators had actually moved away from Sejanus' place and praetors and tribunes, seeing where their duty lay, surrounded him. Regulus called him out of his seat and, while the whole House joined in the denunciation, put the proposal for imprisonment and handed him over to the waiting Laco. Later on the same day the Senate, encouraged by popular demonstrations against Sejanus and by the absence of the Praetorians, reconvened; not this time in the temple of Apollo but in a building that has appeared before in connexion with conspiracy and its suppression, the temple of Concord. Tiberius had reconstructed

Opimius' temple, which had been the scene of Cicero's attack on the Catilinarians in 63 BC; now it was to witness the condemnation of a latter-day Catiline.[147] The ideology of Sejanus had been turned neatly against him; Regulus knew his history – or he had been instructed by a master. By nightfall Sejanus had been strangled.

The coup could not have been carried out more neatly, but it could easily have failed. The Praetorian Guard accepted Macro's donative, but went on the rampage against the property of Sejanus and his friends;[148] it might well have stayed faithful to its commander of seventeen years. And Regulus, for fear of the relatives and friends of Sejanus who sat in the Senate, was afraid to ask the opinion of more than one consular on the motion for Sejanus' death. According to Suetonius, Tiberius, watching from Capri, had ships ready to carry him away; which overseas province he would have fled to is a matter of speculation, with Egypt or Syria the likeliest. The latter, under the governorship of L. Aelius Lamia and his legates, had been the only province not to display the statue of Sejanus side by side with that of the Princeps. Its governor, after the death of the Praefectus Urbi L. Piso the pontifex in 32, was transferred to that important and prestigious post.[149]

As soon as Sejanus was dead, the hunt began for his relations. His distinguished uncle Q. Blaesus did not long survive. His eldest son, whose full name was probably Aelius Gallus Strabo, was sentenced and executed within a week. In the latter half of November or the first two weeks of December, even his two youngest children, Capito Aelianus and Iunilla, were executed, the girl, who was unmarried, being raped first.[150] Livilla was taken into custody by her mother Antonia, and news of her death became known; complicity in Sejanus' attack on the children of Germanicus earned that, even if the story of Drusus' murder is disregarded, and she suffered 'damnatio memoriae', destruction of her statues and the like, at the beginning of 32.[151] A clean sweep had been made of the immediate family; satellites could bide a while, powerful allies might get off altogether; for it was a dynastic feud, as Tiberius intimated, that came to a bloody end in 31. Nothing can excuse the murder of the two children or exonerate the Senate that authorized it, or Tiberius, if he knew of it. One could say that the vis dominationis, the strains imposed by absolute power, had wrenched the Princeps irrevocably out of the ruck of normal human behaviour;[152] but the act can be explained in political as well as in psychological terms (revenge for the murder of Drusus Caesar): Sejanus had destroyed the dynastic plan that Tiberius had taken over from Augustus and developed, and had tried to introduce himself and probably his children into the scheme. He had risen so high that his family and his children were a danger to the surviving heirs of the Princeps. Therefore they died. The Principate must pass to Tiberius' grandchildren, the great-grandchildren of Augustus.

CHAPTER XI

TIBERIUS AND THE LAW:
THE DEVELOPMENT OF *MAIESTAS*

Tiberius prided himself on his knowledge of Roman law, both sacral and secular, and on his respect for it.[1] The *ius auxilii* inherent in the tribunician power and his *imperium* gave him the right to come to the aid of a citizen who appealed to him against magisterial injustice and to take cognizance of cases from all over the Empire, in Italy, and at Rome.[2] They were already his before AD 14, although he is not likely to have used them when Augustus was available. His return to Rome and his accession to sole power, together with his election to the supreme pontificate on 10 March AD 15,[3] gave full scope to his *auctoritas* (prestige and influence), and at least one senator argued that Senate and *equites* could not carry on their business without his supervision.[4] Tiberius intended to use his influence well, and eight years after his accession could still proclaim the supremacy of law.[5] The Princeps for whom *iustitia* was a cardinal virtue was called '*iustissimus princeps*' by those who sought to do him honour; and he liked to be thought of as '*senator et iudex*', a member of the House, exercising his judicial functions like his peers.[6]

Tiberius' preoccupation with the even-handed administration of justice led him early in his principate to take a place in the praetor's court, at the side of the tribunal or on a seat facing it. His presence (and the lectures he gave on occasion) ensured that the presiding magistrate did his duty, though they detracted, Tacitus believes, from the freedom of action traditionally allowed in the courts (for emotional appeals and the weight of inherited influence).[7] Tiberius may have been prompted to visit the courts by the complaints uttered by L. Piso in the Senate in AD 16,[8] or by the conditions that Piso deplored: *iudices* (arbitrators, jurymen, or the presidents of courts) accepting the bribes that litigants offered to win their cases; hectoring lawyers threatening to deploy their oratorical talents in prosecution.

The Princeps readily gave magistrates his expert advice on points of law and propriety. He advised the consuls of AD 22 not to act as advocates, presumably in private suits, saying that he would not have done so himself.[9] As to criminal proceedings he rightly had no qualms. When C. Silius in 24 asked for his indictment for *res repetundae* (the illegal acquisition of funds or property) and *maiestas* (treason) to be postponed until his accuser laid down his consulship, he quoted the old senatorial injunction to the consuls 'not to allow any harm to come to the Republic' (it formed the substance of the *senatus consultum ultimum* that had been passed against C. Gracchus, Appuleius Saturninus, and Caesar, to name only the most notorious dissidents).[10] The formula was not immediately relevant, but there is no doubt that magistrates were entitled to undertake prosecutions. Tacitus' censure misses the point, which is that the fact that Tiberius was not willing to stretch the law in favour of the defendant and quoted the emergency formula suggested to men's minds that he was ill disposed towards Silius, and so influenced their attitude.

As for the indictment of magistrates, a rescript gave a ruling: it was permissible, but the trial had to be deferred until the defendant had laid down his office.[11] Previously the magistrate had to abdicate before the Senate actually condemned him; that proceeding violated the principles that lay behind the Roman system of magistracies, and it had been distastefully exemplified in the abdications in 87 BC of the optimate consul, Cornelius Merula; in 63 of P. Sura, the Catilinarian praetor; and in 43 of Tiberius' own connexion Q. Gallius who perished for plotting against Octavian; Licinius Murena in 23 BC and M. Libo in AD 16 are other possible victims.[12] The rescript may have been elicited by an incident reported by Dio under the year 22, in which a praetor, probably identical with the Magius Caecilianus mentioned by Tacitus as acquitted in 21, was threatened with prosecution for *maiestas*, went home, took off his robes of office, and returned to the Senate a vulnerable private citizen, to the consternation of the Princeps. The consul Drusus may have referred the case to his father in Campania, and dismissal of the case and the ruling were the result. R. S. Rogers dates the rescript later than 24, when the praetor M. Plautius Silvanus was to have been tried for throwing his wife out of a window, but committed suicide.[13] The praetor's father-in-law summoned Tiberius to the scene of the outrage, and his prompt investigation established Silvanus' guilt (there were signs of a struggle). He could not continue in office, and the Senate decided to make an exception to the rule. Certainly it was not always observed by Tiberius' successors: under Gaius Caligula and Nero aediles and praetors and even a tribune were condemned after losing their offices.[14]

On the modification of statutes Tiberius was equally ready to offer his views. They were usually moderate. Where the law had been allowed to lapse, even if it were a law of Augustus, or when a tightening up of sumptuary restrictions was in prospect, as it was in the debates of 16 and 22, Tiberius expressed himself unwilling to bear the odium for imposing the law in all its rigour.[15] When the law was one that dealt with more than matters of taste and convenience and was of practical value to Italy, as in the case of Caesar's investment law, which was reapplied in AD 33, Tiberius was willing to allow a substantial period of grace to debtors and creditors before requiring conformity.[16] Other legislation was being worked to death. Augustus' last attempt to encourage the upper classes to reproduce, the *lex Papia Poppaea* of AD 9, was giving wide scope to delators because it was being widely evaded. In AD 20 Tiberius gave the task of interpreting the law to a committee of senators.[17] But when it was suggested four years later that the section of the *lex Iulia Maiestatis* that provided rewards for successful prosecutors should be suspended when the accused committed suicide before conviction, he discouraged the proposal in the plainest terms.[18]

In his personal dealings with the law, as elsewhere, Tiberius consciously displayed *civilitas*, the unassuming manner of a private citizen, distinguishing sharply between his official functions and his status as a *privatus*. When he sat in the praetor's court he was acting (potentially at least) as the holder of superior *imperium*; when involved in litigation in any other capacity than as magistrate or *iudex* he was careful not to go beyond his place as a private citizen (of rank). In AD 16 the outspoken L. Piso was seeking to recover a sum of money from Urgulania, a friend of Livia and grandmother of Claudius' wife Urgulanilla.[19] On being cited to appear before the praetor Urgulania had herself conveyed to the Princeps' house, where Piso indomitably pursued her. Tiberius promised his mother to appear as Urgulania's advocate. His journey from the Palatine to the tribunal was studiedly casual and leisurely: the bodyguard was dismissed to a distance and the Princeps found time to converse with anyone who accosted him on his route. Meanwhile, the sum owed Piso had been paid into court by Livia. The episode enhanced Tiberius' reputation (the word *civilis* is twice used in connexion with the case), and, if Tacitus is to be believed, Tiberius' conduct continued admirable in civil cases down to 23 at least: in any dispute with a private person he had recourse to the due processes of law. The men responsible for those processes cannot but have been biased in favour of the Princeps; but his own utterances show his anxiety to be treated, as far as was practicable, as a *privatus*, and that anxiety may have had some compensating effect.

Although Tacitus concedes that the laws were admirably administered during the early years he makes one exception: the *lex Maiestatis*.[20] Tiberius' attitude towards that law is prominent in the ancient sources and is a large component of their (and so of our) judgment of the Princeps. There were changes in existing practice, in the scope of the law and its administration – penalties, rewards to accusers – that made it possible for Seneca to write of a 'frenzy' of accusations which (with exaggeration that serves at least to show how strongly this contemporary witness felt about the scourge) he says led to loss of life greater than that caused by the Civil Wars. It is likely, though Seneca does not say so, that he is referring particularly to the period that followed the death of Sejanus, where Tacitus has a passage very similar in tone.[21] Gaius Caligula found it popular to abolish the charge; the abolition lasted two years during which Tiberius was pilloried for his handling of the law.[22]

The first *maiestas* law, the *lex Appuleia*, aimed at bringing to book those whose conduct 'diminished the majesty of the Roman People', had been brought in by the demagogic tribune L. Appuleius Saturninus at the end of the second century B C.[23] It provided for sedition, incompetence in the field, and unauthorized campaigning. Saturninus' law replaced prosecution before the people by the *perduellio* procedure with a permanent court staffed by *equites*. Proceedings would no longer be dependent on the willingness of a tribune to prosecute, nor would they be subject to tribunician veto; most important, prosecution before the people had laid a double task on the tribune: he had to prove both that the action had been performed and that it merited punishment; the laws that established permanent *quaestiones* defined certain acts as criminal; the prosecution had to prove only that the accused had performed the action for him to be liable to the penalty prescribed.

Maiestas, however, was not straightforward. The nature of the offence made it a peculiarly flexible weapon in the political game. A man might (for instance) take part in a riot and still claim that his action had not diminished the *maiestas* of the Roman people.[24] On the other hand, even the later legislators, such as Sulla, who aimed at being comprehensive and systematic,[25] could not cover every contingency, and it is possible that even the first *maiestas* law included a clause making liable for prosecution anyone who diminished the *maiestas* of the Roman people (by whatever means).[26] If so, the scope of the law, even under the Republic, was or could be very wide indeed, and there was ample opportunities for malicious political prosecution. It is of the vagueness and imprecision of the *crimen* (charge) that Cicero complains in a letter of 50 BC to Ap. Pulcher, who had just escaped the *lex Cornelia*.[27] The passage is corrupt, but Cicero evidently regards it as unsporting to accuse a man of *maiestas* because it is unclear what constitutes the offence: it is 'a mere expression' in contrast with *ambitus* (electoral corruption), where the issue is the straightforward one of whether a man has offered bribes or not. The *crimen maiestatis* was in ill repute a quarter of a century before the foundation of the Principate.

Maiestas minuta, then, had always been a plastic and expandable concept. The majesty of the Roman people, and diminution of it, were interpreted by legislators, advocates, *iudices*, and jurisconsults with particular reference to the *maiestas* of that section of society which exercised, or in their opinion should exercise, real power: for Saturninus the people; after Sulla's time the senatorial oligarchy; under the early Principate the Princeps himself and his family and friends and, by deliberate policy of the Princeps, the Senate whose political supremacy he claimed to guarantee.

It was as part of that policy that there had come about a change of the highest importance in the administration of that law and others, though Tacitus, Suetonius, and Dio do not notice it: the transfer of jurisdiction to a senatorial court, perhaps in 19 or 18 BC, the years of Augustus' final constitutional settlement, as a result of the trials of Primus and Murena. In both these cases the majority verdicts of guilty delivered by the jury of senators and *equites* had not been as overwhelming as Augustus would have wished.[28] Henceforward, as the result of a *lex* or more probably of a simple *senatus consultum*, cases involving the interest, security, or welfare of the Senate as a whole or of individual members were to be tried in the House. Such were *maiestas*, *repetundae*, and adultery in the senatorial order. The exact terms of the resolution are unknown and the difficulty scholars experience in reconstructing the formulation may be due to the fact that the consuls were left discretion as to whether or not they were to take cases in these categories out of the hands of the praetor and his court.[29]

This change was momentous, and in many ways far from beneficial to the ruling class. Looking only to the restoration of their control over provincial governors and their misdemeanours (senators were lenient to their peers), to their victory in an ancient struggle for control of the courts,[30] they might fail to note that they had also become the guardians of the *maiestas* of the Roman people and of its magistrates, and so guardians of the *maiestas* of the Princeps. Deleterious consequences should have become apparent before long. Unlike the *iudices* of the praetorian court, members of the Senate would not be able to keep their vote secret.[31] Speeches had to be made on the penalty to be imposed, if any; it was impossible to remain uncommitted. A senator's views would become known to the Princeps and to lesser faction leaders; his career, even his safety, might be affected. When Gaius Caligula restored the charge he tried to show that each of the victims of Tiberius' principate had been a victim of the Senate, which had supplied accusers, witnesses, and jurymen.[32] Tacitus himself felt that guilt;[33] it made him bitter against the law and against Tiberius; but Augustus should not have escaped without criticism for making the transfer.

Again, although the Senate kept some of the procedural rules laid down in the *leges*, especially for the opening stages of the process, where the language of Tacitus is often technical, and although it had its own procedural rules, it was free to conduct itself much as it wished. Hence irregularity in the course of trials and opportunity for those interventions of the Princeps that will be examined at the end of the chapter. Two extreme examples: Titius Sabinus and Sejanus were hustled away to execution in 28 and 31 in spite of a senatorial decree, made at the instance of Tiberius in 21, forbidding the registration of *senatus consulta* in the Aerarium (and so their coming into force) until ten days after they had been passed.[34] Hence, too, charges under two separate statutes could be brought at the same time instead of being taken successively in separate courts. No case is attested before AD 14, but it was an obvious manoeuvre to tack on to a charge that was likely to end in acquittal, such as *repetundae*, one that the overshadowing interest of the Princeps would incline the Senate to take very seriously indeed,[35] and even to subsume under *maiestas* accusations that would as appropriately have been brought under the *lex Iulia de Adulteriis*. When C. Silius was accused in 24 of *maiestas* and *repetundae*, 'everything was handled on the *maiestas* charge'; an earlier attempt at subsumption was defeated in 17, when Tiberius ruled that the *lex Iulia de Adulteriis* was adequate to deal with the unchastity even of a woman related to the Princeps.[36] In spite of initial setbacks, the technique of tacking continued in use until the end of Tiberius' principate, when *maiestas* was abolished; and Tacitus, with some exaggeration, says that it was a makeweight in every case.[37] Not surprisingly: the *maiestas* charge offered a secondary advantage, making available to the prosecution the evidence of the accused person's slaves, evidence which could then be used to recover information to be used for charges other than *maiestas*.[38]

A 'liberty' akin to this free handling of procedure may lie behind the puzzling charges brought against Clutorius Priscus in the case of 21.[39] Having written verses on the death of Germanicus, and having been rewarded for them, Priscus thought to double his prize by composing a second set, this time on the death of Drusus Caesar. The consul designate proposed the death penalty, and the plea of M. Lepidus for mercy and a sentence of *aquae et ignis interdictio* (outlawry) with confiscation of property received support from only one senator. The penalty proposed by Lepidus was put forward as the one which he would have considered appropriate if Priscus had been charged with *maiestas*; the actual charge, then, was different. It may be that Priscus was charged simply with writing verses upon Drusus' death, and that in 21 we have a reversion to a state of affairs that prevailed before certain acts were defined by statute as illegal. The Senate under the guidance of the consuls took cognizance of the act and dealt with it *ad hoc*. If this view is correct, the dangers of such a procedure are obvious, and it was the plain duty of Tiberius to reproach the Senate not merely with its hasty zeal in having the accused man executed, but with making up the law as it went along. But that duty conflicted with Tiberius' overriding principles of allowing the Senate to be master in its own house. It was a principle that led them, possibly through the 'new and hitherto unheard of charge' of praising M. Brutus and calling Cassius the last of the Romans that was brought against A. Cremutius Cordus in 25, certainly through the hesitant discussion of the offences of Agrippina and Nero in 29 (the handling of Drusus' case in the following year may come into the same category), to the prompt execution of Sejanus in 31 after no trial but the mere hearing of a letter which is said to have contained no outright charge and to the monstrous and illegal killing of two of his children in the Tullianum upon no charge whatsoever, their guilt consisting solely in their paternity.[40] This pernicious development probably did not originate in the principate of Tiberius. If the evidence were better, it might be traceable to the decrees passed by the Senate against Cornelius Gallus and its sanctioning of the exile of Agrippa Postumus to Planasia by *senatus consultum*.[41] Nor did it end in 37. Claudius and Nero conducted trials *intra cubiculum* (in the privacy of their home) and in the praetorian barracks; formal charges and senatorial participation alike went by the board. Under Tiberius senators who cared and had the courage could still appeal to what the law laid down.[42]

Penalties too were subject to variation. Senators might indulge in leniency when it was the provincials who had suffered; but the *maiestas* of the Princeps must be defended with the full rigour of the law, it might even be with measures not strictly laid down in law. By Pliny's time the Senate could be said to have the power to increase or diminish the severity of the laws by altering the prescribed penalties in individual cases.[43] It is orthodoxy to hold that the penalty laid down in Caesar's *lex* was exile in the form *aquae et ignis interdictio*, and that when defendants were executed they were victims of an act that had no sanction in the statute.[44] But the penalty prescribed by Caesar, as by Sulla in his *lex Cornelia*, was execution: Velleius claims that Iullus Antonius, the lover of the elder Julia whose adultery amounted to *maiestas*, was shown clemency in being allowed to choose the manner of his death.[45] Under the Republic men convicted in the courts were not executed but went into exile either before conviction or immediately after it. Against them the tribunes passed an annual *aquae et ignis interdictio* which outlawed them; being unsafe inside the Empire they quitted it for some *civitas libera et foederata*, an independent city which enjoyed treaty relations with Rome, and taking the citizenship of that town they lost that of Rome.[46] Caesar's law did not reduce the penalty but made obligatory the imposition of the interdict. During the Civil Wars and Triumviral period regular trials for *maiestas* seem to have been in abeyance. In 40 BC Q. Salvidienus Rufus was brought before the Senate and forced to suicide: ten years later M. Lepidus was summoned to Actium and executed.[47] By 23 BC cases were being taken in the appropriate court, and men might again expect to avoid execution by going into exile. But Caepio and Murena were killed in flight, and M. Egnatius Rufus in 19 was executed in prison; it is unclear whether the death of L. Paullus, which followed an enquiry instituted by the Senate, was execution or suicide.[48]

The penalty prescribed was not always enough. In aggravated cases the senators might vie with each other in proving the horror they felt at the accused man's guilt. Savage methods of execution,[49] 'damnatio memoriae' in varying forms,[50] exposure of the body on the Gemonian stairs, and denial of burial[51] might all be added. As to these aggravations of the penalty two points should be made. They accrue almost exclusively in four familiar cases: those of Libo Drusus, Cn. Piso, C. Silius, and Aelius Sejanus, and in cases dependent on that of Sejanus; that is to say, in the 'great' *maiestas* cases of Tiberius' principate. Those cases evidently were held to be comparable with the most serious that had occurred under the Republic, and three of them are picked out for mention by the indignant Velleius Paterculus (writing before the fall of Sejanus).[52] Secondly, the additional penalties are well documented under the Republic; their revival or increased use during the principate of Tiberius may in part account for his reputation for the misuse of ancient precedents for his own cruel ends.

Now the death penalty prescribed by the law was being carried out, the Senate had to mean what it said, and it developed a scale of lesser penalties, imposing (in descending order of severity) deportation to an island or oasis with loss of civil rights,[53] *aquae et ignis interdictio*,[54] relegation without loss of civil rights, whether to a specified place or beyond a certain distance from Rome,[55] and *infamia*.[56] The maturing of *aquae et ignis interdictio* as a penalty is indicated by the regulation that Tiberius imposed, probably in AD 23.[57] If a man retired into exile, took the citizenship of another state and thereby extinguished his civil rights, that entailed the loss of his right to dispose of his property under Roman law; the new regulation laid it down that anyone who suffered interdiction (no matter where he was domiciled) should lose the right to make a will.

References to imprisonment grow more and more frequent as Tiberius' principate wears on.[58] It had been used by magistrates as a measure of *coercitio*, a means of securing obedience to the will of a magistrate, under the Republic and in exceptional cases as a means of ensuring that an accused person stood trial or did not evade execution; occasionally it was proposed as punishment, as bv Caesar for the followers of Catiline.[59] Its increasing prominence in the sources is due partly to the introduction of an effective death penalty, which meant that the accused person had to be prevented from escaping both before and after the verdict; when the ten-day rule was introduced in AD 21 condemned persons spent that period in the *carcer* (prison), longer if the wishes of the Princeps were uncertain or if they had been reprieved. Until about AD 30 the only accused persons on whom a guard is known to have been set were (not unexpectedly) Libo Drusus, whose farewell banquet was disturbed by the tread of the soldiers' boots, and Cn. Piso, who had a tribune of the Praetorian Guard assigned to him. From 30 onwards more and more persons were detained in custody of one kind or another, their cases undecided either because the Senate dared not take the final step or because the Princeps had expressly asked to take part in the trial. Its increasing recourse to imprisonment is an index of its confusion and uncertainty.

With death a penalty now enforced it is not surprising that accused persons often anticipated condemnation by suicide, especially as suicides normally preserved their property from confiscation and were allowed burial, presumably on the ground that they died uncondemned.[60] This rule explains the case of Vibulenus Agrippa, who in AD 36 took poison in the Senate-house during his trial, was rushed to the Tullianum, and had the rope put round his neck when he was already dead;[61] but it did not hold when the Senate considered that the guilt of the accused demanded exceptional severity. The trial might be continued and the property confiscated. So it was in the cases of Libo Drusus (AD 16), C. Silius (AD 24), and followers of Sejanus; and confiscation was proposed in that of Cn. Piso (AD 20).[62] Such deaths impinge on the historian's attention in the principate of Tiberius, especially in 32 and after. The increase in numbers cannot be denied, but it is exaggerated for us because we have the conscientious and hostile testimony of Tacitus and Dio and the sensational generalizations of Suetonius. There were deaths in the poorly documented principate of Augustus, but fewer.[63] Under the Republic men had occasionally killed themselves when brought to trial for treason, and even for *repetundae*. Financial ruin and loss of *dignitas* (status) were more than they could face; but the diminishing freedoms of the Principate turned up fewer chances of rehabilitation or survival.[64]

Rewards to successful prosecutors would be in proportion to the seriousness of the offence; they too were varied at the discretion of the Senate, no doubt in the Augustan principate after 18 BC as in that of Tiberius. Provision was made in the *lex Iulia Maiestatis* as in other laws: one-quarter of the defendant's property was the standard material reward, but probably there were others: under some statutes the successful accuser seems to have been entitled to take on the insignia of his victim and his seniority.[65] The case of Libo Drusus may be taken as illustration of the practice. Three of Libo's four accusers received praetorships *extra ordinem* (Libo was praetor either in the year of his trial or in the previous year), and the entire property was divided between them.[66] The rewards guaranteed by the law were thus exceeded; but there is a recognizable relationship to them in the prizes that Libo's accusers carried off. In the case of Cn. Piso the rewards deviated further from the norm. Ex-praetors could hardly be given consulships *extra ordinem*, but they were to be elevated to priesthoods (perhaps in the college or colleges of which Piso had been a member); and L. Fulcinius Trio, who was one of those who had benefited from the death of Libo and who had dealt only with the old charge of *repetundae*, was given a promise of support when he came to stand for office.[67]

'Delators' were hated under the Principate. They were a class of men who acquired the favour of the Princeps, standing, and wealth, through the practice of prosecution. Their first great chance came in the

struggle for supremacy that was fought out in the Senate under
Tiberius, and they were maintained by a series of Principes whose
fears made them tyrannical.[68] The delators hardly looked back until
the reign of Trajan; and Tiberius has been blamed for actively encouraging them, notably by refusing to deprive them of their *praemia*
(rewards) when the defendant committed suicide and by backing individual prosecutions.[69] But in the first place a political explanation
of the phenomenon is not sufficient; in a time of social change new
men fighting against conservative prejudice had (they thought) to
use any means of advancement they could find; and after the economic
expansion of the Augustan principate had come to an end some families
found themselves in financial difficulties.[70] Besides, the notorious practitioners met in the pages of Tacitus and Pliny were only the biggest
fish in a pool that was swarming with greedy lesser fry, who must
already have been hard at work by the time of Tiberius' accession (the
lex Papia Poppaea was a favourite field) if their prosecutions and threats
of prosecutions were enough to make L. Piso think of leaving public
life.[71] Odium attached itself to professional prosecutors (*quadruplatores*)
under the Republic, some of it rubbing off on to serious politicians,
unless they were young men at the beginning of their careers; and when
the prudent Cicero finally embarked on a prosecution (that of Verres)
he claimed good reason for it; even then it was not quite gentlemanly
to accept the extraneous rewards that success brought with it. Nearly
a century later, when the consular Mam. Scaurus joined two professionals in an attack on C. Silanus in 22, he had to go far back into
Republican history for reputable precedents.[72] Nor can it be said that
Tiberius approved of their activities in principle. In defending their
praemia, Tiberius was, as he claimed, defending a system which could
not be replaced. The proposal for abolition apparently dealt only with
maiestas, but the *lex Maiestatis* was not the only statute that offered
rewards; and the innovation would give protection to the property of
guilty as well as innocent defendants; what was required was a harsher
penalty for *calumnia*, malicious prosecution.[73] Tiberius must have been
aware of, perhaps he shared, the old Republican prejudice; and his
own youthful experience as a prosecutor had not been one to remember
with pride.[74] Tiberius hated the delator Vibius Serenus, and when he
promised his political support for L. Fulcinius Trio (who was precisely
the '*accusator*' in the trial of Cn. Piso from whom the avengers of
Germanicus ('*indices, testes*') tried to dissociate themselves), had added
a warning: Trio should not let violence spoil his oratory. Cn. Domitius
Afer, by contrast, won high praise: 'an orator in his own right'.

Rightly or wrongly, Tiberius seems to have adopted a detached attitude towards the delators, judging their performances while he remained at Rome like the connoisseur of oratory that he was.[75]

Encouragement of delators is not the only charge that Tiberius has
to meet. His '*ars*' was responsible for 'bringing back' ('*reduxerat*') the
crimen maiestatis in 15. Tacitus uses a similar phrase of Nero, but that
was in AD 62, after Nero's principate had lasted eight years without a
case being brought.[76] The last known trial for treason under Augustus
took place as late as AD 12,[77] and Tacitus has been taken to task for
his expression. He seems also to imply that the praetor Pompeius Macer
asked Tiberius if charges of *maiestas* were to be entertained at all and
was given an affirmative reply: the laws were there to be enforced.[78]
If he does mean to imply that he is mistaken; the praetor had no business
to ask such a question. He did not preside over the senatorial court;
that was the prerogative of consuls or Princeps. Macer was asking, as
president of the appropriate jury court, if any cases were to be taken
in that court (as well as in the Senate). Tacitus claims that Tiberius,
like Augustus, had been provoked by libels. Yet this issue sinks from
sight, presumably into the praetor's court, where Tacitus does not
choose to follow it (if he has the means); the defendants were probably
persons of no quality. Macer's question and Tiberius' reply are of minor
significance in the history of the *crimen maiestatis*.[79]

Yet Tacitus has some backing for his term. When the first charges
of *maiestas* were brought under Tiberius they imported a new concept,
the *maiestas* of a deified Princeps. This was the first and obvious novelty
of the new principate, and Pliny goes so far in his Panegyric on Trajan
as to claim that Tiberius deified his predecessor *in order that* he might
usher in ('*induceret*') the law.[80]

Offences against the deified Augustus might take two forms:
defamation, and disrespect towards his image. It was Augustus who
had been responsible for bringing defamation within the *maiestas*
category in the first place. There is no reason to believe that libel or
slander was specifically catered for in *leges maiestatis* (though verbal
injury to a magistrate could have been so construed)[81] and Tacitus
says that he extended the law to include defamation of prominent men
and women.[82] The *lex Iulia Maiestatis* in force under the Principate
was a law of Caesar, not of Augustus;[83] he needed a ruling or rulings
that the uttering, writing, and publication of libels in verse or in prose,
whether under one's own name, anonymously, or pseudonymously,
were to be construed as constituting a diminution of *maiestas*. He got
at least one such ruling and deployed it against Cassius Severus, who

was exiled in AD 8, and against other unknown writers in 12.[84] Thus persons of distinction were afforded protection. The Princeps, besides being distinguished, had his official position as a defence; but he took verbal attacks on himself, if they did not threaten something worse, with comparative equanimity; men had uncomfortable moments, none was executed.[85] Tiberius was as anxious as Augustus that senatorial reputations should be protected, and Cassius Severus, who had not learned his lesson, was indicted in 24 for continuing his old practices. Repetition sharpened the Senate's temper; Severus was removed from Crete to Seriphus and suffered *aquae et ignis interdictio* and total loss of property.[86] As far as attacks on himself were concerned Tiberius adopted the Augustan model and proclaimed that there should be free speech in a free state.[87] He put policy into practice. In 15 he intervened in favour of Granius Marcellus, who was accused of slandering him; two years later he refused to allow similar charges against Appuleia Varilla to be entertained at all, and, after consulting her, reported that his mother took the same view of what Varilla had said about her.[88] In 24 he vetoed the conviction of a man who had uttered libellous verse against him[89] and in 32 upheld the appeal of M. Cotta Messallinus, who had accused Gaius Caligula of homosexuality, derided as a funeral feast the banquet in honour of the late Julia Augusta that he was attending, and boasted that he could rely on Tiberius' protection when he went to law.[90] Cotta was right in that; past services outweighed what the Princeps made light of as harmless table talk; but even two years later Mam. Scaurus' *Atreus*, with its admonition to bear the follies of rulers with patience, drew from Tiberius only the remark that he 'would make Scaurus into an Ajax', which does not necessarily mean drive him to suicide; at any rate the play was not included in the indictment that followed, whatever effect it had on the Princeps.[91] These examples of lenity contrast with three other cases, not all so late in the principate that they may be attributed to the tightening hold of tyranny. Libellous verses uttered by Aelius Saturninus brought him before the Senate and then to the Tarpeian rock as early as AD 23, and only two years later the Narbonensian orator Votienus Montanus was relegated to the Balearics. Finally, Sextius Paconianus was executed in 35, three years after narrowly escaping a death sentence and being consigned to prison, where he composed the lampoons on the Princeps that were his final downfall.[92] Tacitus emphasizes his unpopularity with the Senate, and it is not surprising that they took advantage of the second offence of a man already denounced by Tiberius to rid themselves of him once for all. As for the other two cases, the circumstances of Saturninus' death are too obscure to allow profitable speculation, and Tacitus' account suggests that it was the nature of Montanus' slanders that aggravated the penalty: they were sensational enough to put Tiberius right out of countenance, to the embarrassment of the *consilium*; but the witness who repeated them with such conscientious fortitude was a soldier, and Montanus' aim may have been seditious as much as defamatory. The cases are too few and the evidence too poor to show whether this was a criterion consciously and systematically applied.

Immediately after his death the status of the deified Augustus as a possible victim of libel was unclear. Attempts to exploit him under the *maiestas* statute focused themselves on the fact that technically he was now a god, and they concentrated on insults to his image.

The first charges were brought against two Roman knights, Falanius and Rubrius, of whom one was accused of keeping a male prostitute, Cassius, in his domestic college of worshippers of Augustus and of selling a statue of Augustus along with the gardens in which it stood, the other of swearing falsely by the late Princeps; and the charges against Granius Marcellus, the former governor of Bithynia accused of slandering Tiberius, also included that of fitting a head of Tiberius to a statue of Augustus and of setting his own image higher than those of the Caesars.[93] These cases ended in dismissal of the charges or in acquittal. Augustus had not been deified for the destruction of Roman citizens (wrote Tiberius); the actor Cassius, whatever his reputation, had taken part in the ceremonies held by Livia herself in memory of her husband; there was nothing sacrilegious in selling the statue of a god; as for the perjury, Tiberius characteristically brought out a legal maxim to clinch the point: 'Wrongs done the gods are righted by the gods.' Granius' case ran to an acquittal (at least on the charge of *maiestas*) which would never have been granted if the Senate had believed that Tiberius desired conviction. We can take it that he disapproved of the attempt to broaden *maiestas* in this direction.

That is surprising. Even if religious offences had not been catered for in the *leges maiestatis*[94] the deification of Augustus was an act of patent political significance for Tiberius. A slight to the new deity could easily be construed as a slight to the *maiestas* of Tiberius himself.[95] Nor could Pliny's statement be accounted for if the deified Princeps had remained out of account. In AD 17 Tiberius insisted that if Varilla had spoken irreverently of the deified Augustus she was to be convicted (in fact she was acquitted).[96] Ten years after the acquittal of Granius Marcellus came the trial of A. Cremutius Cordus on a charge hitherto unknown: his *Annales* had praised Brutus and described Cassius as the last of the Romans.[97] Tacitus reproduces the gist of his defence. It opens by pointing out that Cordus' guilt lay not in deeds but in words and those not directed against Tiberius or his father, who were protected by the *lex* (that much had been acknowledged, if Tacitus is to be trusted). None the less, the defence passed from precedents for praising the Liberators to precedents for insulting the dynasts, the language of Catullus and Bibaculus. The hostile political implications of the work of Cremutius Cordus may then have been the gravamen of the charge. The author starved himself to death and his writings were sentenced to the bonfire. Tiberius' attitude towards the offenders of 15, 17, and 25 is not inconsistent; there is more to the changes than the sharpening intolerance of an established autocrat. He meant to distinguish words and actions intended ('*hostili animo*') to insult the deified Princeps and to depreciate his achievement from unintentional discourtesies of no political import.[98]

Further, *maiestas* came to adhere to images of the Princeps, as well as of the deified Princeps, in spite of Granius Marcellus' acquittal. No cases of this kind are reported from the principate of Augustus, but the Princeps' artful approach to divinity, even in his lifetime, not to mention his possession for life of the tribunician sacrosanctity, will have made his statues seem to merit different treatment from those of lesser men; by 14 the idea needed only the guarantee of law.

The final stage may be illustrated from the *Digest*, which lists the categories of monument, the melting, selling, or mutilation of which did not incur the *crimen*.[99] Tiberius' chilly reception of the first charge in AD 15 may have discouraged further attempts along these lines until AD 22, when another case, that of a silver statuette of Tiberius melted down for plate, was quashed.[100] Melting down was one thing, insult another. One Pontius would have been brought to trial if a quick-witted slave had not prevented him from relieving himself at a banquet while wearing a portrait ring of Tiberius on his finger.[101] Besides, the case of 22 followed a discussion in the Senate initiated by C. Cestius Gallus,[102] who showed Tiberius and the consul Drusus Caesar the way out of the difficulty of asylum rights abused: the Principes are like gods but, like the gods, they protect only the innocent. Probably a *senatus consultum* was passed which forbade the carrying of the imperial portrait to the detriment of another person.[103] The debate of 21 limited a recognized right; how far back that right went is not known.

The attractions of the *maiestas* charge gives plausibility to what

Seneca says about the mania for bringing prosecutions on that charge and to Tacitus' rhetorical claim that the evil sprang up at the beginning of Tiberius' principate, to be repressed for a while and to break out again with renewed virulence (he means in the twenties and thirties).[104] Tacitus is quite right to imply a stepping up of the number of *maiestas* trials during Tiberius' principate. But he fails to notice an important distinction that should be drawn between the cases of Libo and Piso in the early years of the principate and those that followed the death of Drusus Caesar in AD 23, though he traces the decline of Tiberius' principate in general terms to that year. The guilt of Piso was a hard fact, covered by Republican categories; so, in all probability, was that of Libo.[105] In the twenties, on the other hand, *maiestas* was pitilessly exploited by Sejanus and his allies against Agrippina and her sons and their relatives and friends, in the early thirties by Gaius Caligula and the group that backed him, and finally by Macro, Sejanus' successor in the post of Prefect of the Praetorian Guard, who deployed it against rivals who threatened his ascendancy over Gaius. If the senatorial court was to serve that turn, every charge, plausible and implausible, would be scraped together to form an indictment that would carry weight.

Tacitus' analysis has another failing. He gives full weight to the trials of Libo Drusus, rightly treating it as a paradigm for the principate of Tiberius. But the Princeps takes the blame and the incident is seen in complete isolation. Whatever the legal merits of the case against Libo, the trial may be seen as the final incident in one chapter of a struggle for power that had begun under Augustus (if we demand a single point of departure, it is the death of M. Agrippa in 12 BC); and the struggle had been intensified in the last years of the Princeps, coming to a climax with a series of trials and acts of *coercitio* on the part of Augustus that brought death or exile to half a dozen persons between the years 6 and 8.

On the other hand Tiberius has more to answer for than his absence from Rome from AD 26 onwards and the increasing apathy and cynicism of the ageing Princeps in the face of dangers and abuses of which he was aware.[106] The role of the Princeps in the processes of law was a complex and developing one: his powers were great and the processes fluid. Cases might go before him either for full treatment or for preliminary examination; he might advise on accepting the charges, preside over the trial or attend as an ordinary senator, intervene anywhere in the trial, and quash or modify verdict and sentence.[107]

In earlier cases of his principate, notably in those of Libo and Piso, when presiding over the court, as he seems to have done in cases of prime importance (as *princeps senatus* or in virtue of his consular *imperium?*), he displayed in words and manner a studied impartiality—which those two defendants, probably rightly, since senators could hardly condone diminution of the Princeps' *maiestas* without a strong hint from him, took to be fatal to their cause.[108] Where his own interests were not patently involved the presiding Princeps was less inhibited, and he did not hesitate to embark on a crushing interrogation of C. Silanus, an ex-governor of Asia, whom he took to be guilty of offences comparable with the outrageous crimes of Messalla Volesus.[109]

Judicial impartiality was not his only method of separating the Princeps from the senator. He laid claim to what Augustus lamented he had lost, the right to a private quarrel.[110] Cn. Piso, if he were guilty of exceeding his duty as legate, of insubordination towards his commander, of rejoicing at that commander's death, could expect Tiberius' personal hatred and the vengeance of a private enemy;[111] D. Silanus, returning to Rome from the long sojourn abroad that followed the discovery of his adultery with Julia the younger, was told in the same year, 20, that he could not expect the friendship of Tiberius,[112] and in 32 the Princeps denied his society to Sex. Vistilius for his slanders on Gaius.[113] It was in vain: Piso was overwhelmed by the charges against him; Silanus held no office; and Vistilius killed himself.

Tiberius' interventions in trials over which he was not presiding may be illustrated from the early case of Granius Marcellus.[114] On hearing the charges Tiberius lost his temper and declared that he too would vote, openly and on oath, thus imposing the same obligation on his peers. Then came the famous question of Cn. Piso: at what stage would Tiberius give his verdict? If he voted first Piso would have a lead to follow; if last, he was afraid he might inadvertently be dissenting from the Princeps' view. Piso's Republicanism was blatant; on the other hand he was a trusted friend of Tiberius. It is less likely that he was warning Tiberius against exerting undue influence on the Senate than that he was telling him, if he meant to express disapproval of such charges (and it seems clear from this passage that Tiberius did not intend to make a habit of voting in criminal trials), to make a good job of it and let the Senate know what his views were (certainly they were views of which Piso approved). Tiberius then moved the acquittal of the defendant on the charges of *maiestas*.[115] Very different was the outcome ten years later, when an outburst of indignation seems to have resulted in conviction and a severe sentence.[116]

Sometimes when an unfavourable verdict had been reached an

influence for mercy and moderation may be seen at work, attested equally by Tiberius' own declarations in particular cases (he would have intervened in favour of Libo Drusus in 16 and of Paxaea in 34 if they had not killed themselves), by a number of actions reported by Tacitus, who concedes that his speech was more fluent when he intervened in this sense, and by policy attributed to him in senatorial speeches in the twenties.[117]

Talk was easy when an enemy or an embarrassing ally was dead. That would explain Tiberius' protestations in the case of Libo, and his veto on the deletion of Piso's name from the public records and on confiscation of his property.[118] More probably the Princeps was paying tribute to the eminent family in this case and in that of Appuleia Varilla, who in 17 was spared the penalty prescribed by the *lex Iulia de Adulteriis* and handed over to her family for punishment, an old-fashioned recourse likely to appeal to Tiberius.[119]

His intervention on behalf of an *eques* who had been convicted of lampooning him was well received,[120] but it was not often that his clemency was taken at face value. When in 24 Firmius Catus was condemned for *calumnia* after unsuccessfully prosecuting his sister for *maiestas*, Tiberius vetoed the sentence of deportation and had him expelled from the Senate; that was regarded as the repaying of a debt to one of Libo's accusers, rightly perhaps, but Tiberius may also have felt that the man's abhorrent action in attacking his sister had exacerbated the Senate's hostility towards him – or that he was paying for his attack on Libo.[121] It is not the only example of Tiberius' intervening because he could have feared that perhaps the Senate was neglecting its duty.[122]

The claims of high breeding, friendship, and *fides* (loyalty) inevitably weighed heavily; Tiberius would never have denied that, and he made old services part of his plea for Cotta Messallinus.[123] But the demands of justice or policy doomed Cn. Piso in 20, and the relentless pressure of the succession struggle brought several friends to their death; only two or three of Tiberius' *consilium* survived, claims Suetonius, and even friends of long standing and tried fidelity perished.[124]

It is noteworthy that of the five cases in which Tiberius personally aggravated the penalty imposed by the senatorial court none is earlier than 24. P. Suillius Rufus' later activities fully justified Tiberius' harsh judgment of him (at least in the view of Tacitus); he had been found guilty of accepting bribes while *iudex*, not an offence that Tiberius would take lightly, as his attention to the courts shows; and he would know that many members of the Senate might feel uneasy about penalizing it. Of the later cases, only for that of Iunius Gallio, expelled first from the Senate, then from Italy, and finally returned to Rome and custody when he took up residence in the pleasant island of Lesbos, does any ready explanation offer: he was an associate of Sejanus.[125]

It was not only over the modification of penalties that Tiberius' attitude seems to have changed: he began to initiate charges himself. It was at his instance in 32 that Gallio had been penalized in the first place. The same letter denounced another friend of Sejanus, and in the same year C. Cestius was encouraged by Tiberius, who prejudged the issue by attacking them as 'ringleaders', to undertake the prosecution of Q. Servaeus and Minucius Thermus.[126] The Princeps' ability to look after himself in this way was openly recognized:[127] it was already well established in 31, and its origins go much further back. Two incidents of the year 21 link interference with judicial verdicts and the initiating of prosecution. Two Roman knights, Considius Proculus and Caelius Cursor, had brought a prosecution for *maiestas* against the praetor Magius Caecilianus. It failed and was taken by Tiberius to be malicious. At his instance the two men were punished for *calumnia*.[128] If the Princeps was well informed of the facts his action was in one sense laudable, for it discouraged irresponsible delation of *maiestas*; but it prejudiced the issue and put the weight of Tiberius' *auctoritas* full in the scale of conviction. In the conflict between his own impartiality and the freedom of the Senate on the one hand, and the responsibilities of the Senate and the facts as he saw them on the other, the first pair were failing. The second case of 21 makes this clearer. It concerned a magnate of Macedonia, Antistius Vetus.[129] The praetorian adultery court acquitted Vetus; Tiberius was dissatisfied with this verdict and said so; he accused Vetus of involvement in the rising of Rhescuporis and secured his conviction in the Senate.

Such interventions were the more effective because they were made by letter; the contents had to be accepted or rejected (unthinkable) or the Senate might try to stall. Agrippina's ally Titius Sabinus perished promptly on New Year's Day 28 after a letter arrived from Capri; two were required to make the Senate ready to act against Agrippina herself and Nero Caesar; only one to dispose of Sejanus in 31; probably the same means had procured a sentence of death against Asinius Gallus in 30.

By 37 Sejanus' successor Macro had adapted the technique to his own purposes. It was documents from him that put in motion one of the last prosecutions for *maiestas* of Tiberius' principate, that against Albucilla and some eminent male accomplices (adultery was also alleged).[130] No letter from the Princeps accompanied the claims that the witnesses had given evidence, and slaves had it extracted from them by torture under Macro's supervision. The Senate suspected a put-up job by Macro, who hated L. Arruntius; and acted slowly enough to allow two of the accused to survive.

From the Princeps himself such letters ceased to be effective (to his indignation) only in 37, when it became known that he was dying.[131] And in at least two cases they were effective without being followed by the strict formalities of indictment and trial: the eminence of Agrippina and Nero, the power of Sejanus, both making speed imperative, put those out of the question. The Senate's freedom to adjust its own procedure amounted in the last analysis to freedom to break the fragile restraints imposed by judicial formality. The Senate forgot that it had taken on the responsibilities of a court of law and acted like the political body it really was. But the *senatus consulta* that it produced could be as fatal to the persons arraigned before it as if no legal safeguard had been neglected; and they were carried out at once.

These developments were sanctioned and encouraged by the man who in A D 17 had punctiliously excluded from one indictment charges that properly belonged to another, and who had carefully distinguished one charge from another within the *maiestas* category. The contrast is marked and painful, and it needs explanation.

The letters of Tiberius, from that of 27 onwards, and especially those of the year 32, were concerned with the rights and safety of the Princeps himself. Addressing the Senate before the trial of Piso, Tiberius had insisted on the difference between personal injury and offences against the state; in 25 he had prevented the jurist Ateius Capito from swelling the latter class at the cost of the former.[132] But these injuries were mere affronts. Now he believed that he was in danger and demanded summary and unquestioning punishment. Factional pressures, inner tension, perhaps genuine fear, must be invoked as the source of the misconduct. At the beginning of his principate, for how long Suetonius does not say, Tiberius would enter the House only after dismissing his escort; by 32 he was thought to desire protection precisely amongst his peers.[133]

The inherent faults of the senatorial court are obvious. How far they had developed before Tiberius took over the administration is not clear because the evidence is lacking. The court's essentially political nature and its docility, its ability to accept new charges as well as those on the statute book, its fluid procedure, its freedom to take charges separately or together, to alter penalties and rewards, its uncertain role, doubling court of law and legislative body,[134] all are pernicious failings that emerge to daylight in the pages of Tacitus, Dio, Suetonius, and, for a much later period, Pliny. The Princeps operated with this body, and his own responsibility for its failings is heavy. Beyond making perfunctory gestures of impartiality, he failed to maintain the distinction between his position as senator and *iudex* and his position as Princeps – or failed to recognize that the two roles could not be distinguished. The ambiguity of his position made the status of his remarks ambiguous: advisory or mandatory? In either case, what sanctions might follow? To this ambiguity he added the irresponsible abdication of his departure from Rome and the unleashing of the factions, the imperious impatience of an old man accustomed to rule and to be feared, and finally the vengefulness of one who had been deceived.

Yet there were features of Tiberius' administration of justice that later were looked upon with regret. The senatorial court might fail in its duty but as long as it functioned it knew what was going on; approval is implied in Tacitus' and Dio's accounts of the trial of the equestrian procurator Capito in the Senate in AD 23.[135] The prosecutors of Cn. Piso asked for the case to be taken by the Princeps himself and his *consilium*, which alone shows that function of the Princeps well established by AD 20; yet little is heard of it in Tiberius' principate. That the Princeps should take the case of Livilla in 31 is understandable; as it was in the cases of the Julias and Agrippa Postumus. Cases not involving the *domus* were heard on Capri and deaths followed;[136] but the *intra cubiculum* trial was to grow into a notorious evil only in the time of Claudius, to be renounced by Nero on his accession.[137] Tiberius' use of the Senate, characteristic of his principate and his principles, left that body some say in the administration of justice.

CHAPTER XII

LAST YEARS AND POSTHUMOUS REPUTATION

The fall of Sejanus is marked by Tacitus as a turning point in Tiberius' life and principate.[1] That is correct. In politics the period that followed saw the question of the succession settled and Gaius Caligula, the main contender, consolidating his position with the Princeps, his chief partisan, Macro, eliminating rivals to his own influence through the senatorial court. More striking was the wreaking of vengeance on Sejanus' followers, which created a reign of terror very suitable for Macro's purpose. These developments can be made out from the sources. It is more difficult to imagine the state of mind of Tiberius himself; the initial shock of discovering that his only reliable friend was a murderous schemer who gave no loyalty and no affection to his master must have been intensified almost beyond bearing when Tiberius read the letter from Apicata, whatever he came to believe when he had finished torturing Livilla's alleged accomplices to find out the truth. There is a whining tone of self-pity, a demand for sympathy, common to that part of the denunciation of Sejanus quoted by Suetonius, in which he asks the Senate to send one of the consuls to escort 'an old man all on his own' into their presence, and the inscription in which Tiberius appeals to his fellow tribesmen, the people of Rome, in the aftermath.[2] Sharp though the blow was, the agony of his family's misbehaviour had been going on for more than four years before that, and had forced Tiberius in the end to adopt a plan that cannot have been agreeable to him. Now, one decisive and brilliantly thought out and executed action had rid him of the upstart. There were no more choices to make. By the beginning of 32 Tiberius was in a mood to tease the Senate in his usual manner,[3] and it would be wise to hesitate before taking the famous words of another letter quoted by Tacitus and Suetonius to be what they claim them to be, the utterance of a man in the depth of despair. R. S. Rogers noticed that they came at the beginning of the letter in which he dissuaded the Senate from convicting M. Cotta Messallinus.[4] What Rogers regarded as signs of irritation and impatience I see as a game with words taken for the purpose from the comic poets: 'What I am to write to you, conscript fathers, or how I am to write it, or what I am to refrain from writing at this time, may the gods and goddesses all send me to perdition quicker than I feel I'm going already, if I know.'

The Senate marked the destruction of Sejanus with unseemly celebrations:[5] Sejanus was to suffer '*damnatio memoriae*', a statue of Liberty was to be set up in the Forum, and members of the great priestly colleges were to hold an annual festival in commemoration; oaths were to be taken only in the name of Tiberius, and excessive honours to any man were forbidden for the future, some small exceptions being made for Macro and Laco. Their refusal of rewards was echoed by Tiberius, who declined birthday games and (once more) the title *pater patriae*.

Princeps and Senate now turned their attention to the chastisement of Sejanus' lesser allies. His uncle Q. Blaesus had perished in the first outbursts.[6] Now fell the orator Bruttedius Niger, whose talents had carried him at least to the rank of aedile, and P. Vitellius who, being Prefect of the Aerarium Militare, could conveniently be charged with readiness to open it up for Sejanus' benefit. P. Pomponius Secundus is known only to have offered aid and comfort to his friend Aelius Gallus after Sejanus' execution; he survived in custody, was released by Gaius, and won the suffect consulship and triumphal ornaments under Claudius.[7] There was probably more justice in the charge brought by Tiberius himself early in 32 against the ex-praetor Sextius Paconianus, that he had been used by Sejanus to ensnare Gaius Caligula; at any rate, the downfall of this man was greeted with rejoicing, and he was saved from the death penalty only by turning state's evidence. His choice of victim was equally gratifying to the Senate: it was Lucanius Latiaris, who had struck down Titius Sabinus (his accomplices were to perish later).[8] Soon afterwards C. Cestius undertook the prosecution of another former legate of Germanicus, Q. Servaeus, and the *eques* Minucius Thermus, whose friendship with Sejanus had been, it was thought, completely innocent; but Tiberius insisted on the prosecution and presumably on the conviction of these men. They, however, took a leaf out of Paconianus' book, incriminating the Gaul from the Santones, Julius Africanus, and another obscure person, Seius Quadratus, possibly a dependant of Sejanus' father Seius Strabo or of one of his other relatives of that *gens*.[9] The case of the four consulars, for which Gaius and Macro were probably responsible, is mysterious and differs from others in this series precisely because of the eminence of the accused.[10] It caused consternation in the House: there was hardly a senator who had no tie with these distinguished men. C. Annius Pollio, suffect in an unknown year, C. Appius Silanus, *ordinarius* in 28, Mam. Scaurus, suffect in 21, and C. Calvisius Sabinus, *ordinarius* in 26, were all charged with *maiestas*, along with Annius Vinicianus, Pollio's son. Presumably the accusations linked them with the aspirations of Sejanus. Tampering with the forces stationed in the city was apparently part of the charge, for a man implicated in the case, who turned state's evidence and later committed suicide in prison, was a tribune of the urban cohorts. His evidence freed Appius and Sabinus from suspicion, and the case of the others was postponed so that it might be heard in the presence of Tiberius (it never was).

The year closed with the deaths of three knights, Geminius, Celsus, and Pompeius, on a conspiracy charge; the first certainly had been a friend of Sejanus – he was a man given to the extravagance and luxury that had surrounded Sejanus' early life, though the Prefect himself became a model of self-control – but again, according to Tacitus, there was nothing political about the relationship.[11]

The readiness of the accused to turn state's evidence shows how much afraid they were. What had been going on from the very moments that Sejanus' body had been thrown out on the Gemonian stairs was a witch-hunt; men competed to kick the corpse and show how much they hated him: otherwise their slaves might be able to accuse them of complicity in his crimes.[12] That was one way of clearing oneself. A variant was practised by the consul of 31 who had been one of Sejanus' partisans, L. Fulcinius Trio. It had naturally been Regulus who had been sent to escort Tiberius to Rome (though he had been sent away without being admitted once the need for the charade had passed) and at the end of the year the growing hatred between the two broke out into open discord.[13] Trio tried to rehabilitate himself by hinting that Regulus was being remiss in rounding up Sejanus' supporters (it was better than nothing). That drove Regulus not only to rebut his colleague's allegations, but to make one of his own: Trio was involved in the conspiracy; Regulus demanded an investigation.

They were still quarrelling when they went out of office, and in the following year Haterius Agrippa thought to make capital for himself by reviving an incident which had greatly disturbed the House; so indolent a man as he was had nothing to be afraid of. Haterius accused both consuls of complicity in the 'plot' and of keeping silent for fear of what might be exposed. Q. Sanquinius Maximus checked that move by suggesting that the Princeps would not thank the Senate for adding to his problems.

The same motives, fear, or a senator's desire to ingratiate himself with the Princeps in dangerous times, lay behind two flattering proposals brought before the Senate during the year. As soon as the consuls took office in 32 (one of them was the Princeps' connexion by marriage, Cn. Domitius Ahenobarbus, and he held office all the year; the other was the son of L. Arruntius) the Senate displayed its unwearied zeal by taking its oath to Augustus' and Tiberius' *acta* individually, by passing its measures against Livilla, and by ordering that the property of Sejanus, which had been confiscated to the state treasury, should be transferred to that section of it which was under Tiberius' direct control, the Fiscus.[14] These measures were sponsored by men of rank, Scipios, Silani, Cassii. But the new man Togonius Gallus thought that his loyalty should not go unrecorded, and asked Tiberius to draw up a list of senators from whom twenty would be chosen by lot to act as his armed bodyguard whenever he entered the chamber. Togonius the Gaul was taken in by that part of Tiberius' letter of 18 October which had asked the Senate to send one of the consuls to escort him to Rome. But the House should not have made fun of him. What Togonius was asking Tiberius for was a wholesale grant of certificates of trustworthiness. The reply was not unkind, but pointed out some of the difficulties: one was that Tiberius did not know how to choose. Iunius Gallio's proposal[15] met a different reception. He had moved that veterans of the Praetorian Guard should sit with the *equites* in the fourteen rows reserved for them at the theatre. Tiberius, in a violent and sarcastic onslaught, demanded if he thought he knew better than Augustus; or perhaps, as a satellite of Sejanus, he had the object of stirring up trouble. The Senate took the hint and expelled Gallio from membership. There is no inconsistency between the two cases: Gallio implied that Tiberius owed his survival to the loyalty of the Guard, and Tiberius did not like being reminded of debts of that kind;[16] once he let it be known that he considered Gallio a partisan of Sejanus, that was enough. Gallio perhaps was gambling on the motion securing his position, and lost.

The friendship of Sejanus was not enough to damn everyone who was accused of enjoying it. The accusation was beginning to look like a weapon that was universally effective, but the accusers of the *eques* M. Terentius were disappointed.[17] Terentius pointed out that Caesar too had been a friend of Sejanus, and drew a distinction between plots against the state and the Princeps' life, and friendships renounced at precisely the moment they were renounced by him. Terentius was acquitted and his accusers, who had other crimes to their accounts (perhaps they too were intent on making the first move before they themselves were attacked), were put to death or sent into exile, penalties too severe for mere calumniators.[18]

Many charges were brought at this time simply because it was opportune. As in the case of Terentius, any connexion with Sejanus was sufficient reason to bring a charge against a man who previously had seemed hard to attack. This may be the explanation of the prosecution by the ex-praetor Considius of P. Pomponius Secundus in 31. But such feuds could be carried on by the victim's friends, and often had been in Roman Republican politics. A Considius Proculus was accused of *maiestas* in 33, found guilty, and executed; his sister Sancia suffered *aquae et ignis interdictio*. The fact that Proculus was celebrating his birthday at the moment he was summoned to plead his cause in the Senate did not soften the heart of his accuser; not surprisingly – he was Q. Pomponius, brother of Publius.[19]

Some of these trials may be seen in particular as mopping-up operations instigated by Gaius Caligula and his friends, especially, but not necessarily, if they involved charges of injury or insult to Gaius himself. The trial of Sextius Paconianus is the paradigm of the first class; while M. Cotta Messallinus in 32 was said (amongst other things) to have accused Gaius of homosexuality. But the dominant political characteristic of Cotta was his slavish loyalty to Tiberius; that precisely may have been why the prosecutors wanted him away; but it was worth enough to Tiberius to induce him to intervene on the behalf of the accused.[20]

Someone was operating on the island as well as in the Senate. The charges against Paconianus stemmed from Tiberius himself, and were made in the same letter that attacked Gallio. Sex. Vistilius was another enemy of Gaius, having said much the same of him as Cotta.[21] There was no trial, but Tiberius announced that Vistilius would no longer be welcome company. Vistilius opened his veins, then sent a letter in mitigation. The Princeps was unrelenting, and Vistilius undid the bandages. Other victims, these on Capri itself, were Vescularius Flaccus and Iulius Marinus, both veterans of the Rhodian exile and inseparable from the Princeps. The latter certainly had acted on Sejanus' behalf, and it may have been for that that he died. Yet many may have attached themselves to the minister in the sincere belief that they were acting in the interests of Tiberius and his immediate family, that is to say, in the interests of his grandson Ti. Gemellus. In Upper Germany, in charge of four legions, was a governor who had betrothed his daughter to Sejanus' son. Yet Cn. Lentulus Gaetulicus survived in office. A bold letter to Tiberius saved him, we are to believe, and took his accuser into exile.[22] It is reported by Tacitus, under the year 34, and offers Tiberius the rest of the Empire if he will allow Lentulus his province; recall he will take as a command to die. The threat is clear. The letter reflects credit on its author, but he may not have composed it until some time after its dramatic date. Amongst the Cornelii Lentuli Tiberius had counted some faithful friends.[23] Gaetulicus might have claimed that his motive had been to ensure the smooth succession of Drusus Caesar's son Gemellus. And Tiberius might be convinced by that plea, while he was not one to give in easily to blackmail. But the same argument would not appeal to Gaius, and it was under Gaius that Gaetulicus perished, legions or no legions.[24]

Ti. Gemellus had another friend who held high office late in the principate of Tiberius: A. Avillius Flaccus, appointed to the Prefecture of Egypt after the death of the freedman Hiberus in 32 or 33.[25] He was a close friend of Tiberius and kept his post until the end of the principate and beyond. It was perhaps his devotion to the Princeps that made him attack Agrippina and so incur the anger of her youngest son. He must have feared the coming to power of Gaius Caesar; rightly, for he did not long survive the death of his friend Macro; he was removed from his post, exiled, and finally put to death in 39.

The position of Ti. Gemellus as a potential successor to Tiberius was a very weak one, if his claims are set against those of Gaius. On Gaius focused all the popularity that his lost father, mother, and brothers had once enjoyed (and it was a monopoly, for Agrippina and Drusus remained lost even after the fall of Sejanus). Ti. Gemellus was the child of the much less popular Drusus Caesar, and grandson by blood of the Princeps, no recommendation in the eyes of the populace. Besides, born in December AD 19, he was more than seven years younger than Gaius, who had already taken the toga of manhood, was designated to the augurate and was to become quaestor in 33, at the age of twenty-one.

The year 33 marked an end and a beginning in Tiberius' principate in more ways than one. If it was in 34 that the phoenix made one of its periodic reappearances in Egypt, the bird would have done better to have come a year earlier.[26] Formally 33 was a turning point as 23 (a year of manifest change for the Princeps) had been: they marked the tenth and twentieth anniversaries of the grant of powers that had made Tiberius Augustus' equal in *imperium*, and those powers needed renewal.[27] It was, in the second place, a year of deaths.[28] Successively were announced, or became known, those of Asinius Gallus, young Drusus Caesar, and his mother Agrippina the elder. Gallus died still in custody, of starvation voluntary or enforced. That Drusus was deliberately starved to death in his dungeon on the Palatine is explicitly

stated by Tacitus and Suetonius. He was strong and survived nine days
by gnawing the stuffing of his mattress. That he abused and cursed the
Princeps to the end was known for a fact, because Tiberius had the
record of his exchanges with his gaolers read out in the House. Lastly,
Agrippina, also by starvation, but of her own volition: forced feeding
was attempted. That event too had a powerful effect on the Princeps,
who gave vent to his feelings in a letter to the Senate. She had committed suicide in despair at the death of her lover Gallus. (Tacitus
rightly rejects that suggestion: the woman was a virago, the weaknesses
of her sex destroyed by her ambition.) Tiberius reminded the Senate
that her death and that of Sejanus fell on the same date; that he should
do so is not surprising: it was the conflict between these two rivals
for power, as he realized, that had made his life at Rome intolerable.
He made it a boast that she had not suffered the same fate, strangulation
and exposure on the Gemoniae. He could not have made it clearer that
he put the two offenders in the same category; where indeed they
belonged. The Senate reacted with gross servility. A vote of thanks was
passed for his forbearance (*clementia*) and an annual offering of gold was
voted to Capitoline Jove.

Appropriately the year 33 was also to see the final wiping out of the
conspiracy of Sejanus. A number of persons had been detained in public
custody after condemnation by the Senate, but had not died because
Tiberius had not sanctioned the act. Now he gave the order. The
number executed and exposed on the Gemoniae was very large, up to
twenty, and included women and boys.[29] But the year was also one
of new beginnings, and of marriages. First, the position of Gaius
Caligula was assured; Tiberius had intimated as much before Sejanus
fell. Now he gave him a bride of good family, and a father-in-law
whose loyalty to Tiberius was indisputable.[30] M. Silanus, suffect in 15,
had been able to obtain the recall of his brother Decimus from exile,
and he probably had put forward some of the proposals against Sejanus
that were adopted in 32. That fact puts the proposals in a more favourable light, for his high descent from the Silani and the Claudii Pulchri
and his oratorical talent were matched by his high character; Tiberius'
opinion of his intelligence and probity is shown by his refusal to accept
cases offered him on appeal from Silanus; and he was very often asked
first for his opinion in the Senate.

The year 33 was that of Gaius' quaestorship, which gave him access
to the Senate.[31] The marriage took place on the mainland, and it is
probable that Gaius exercised his functions at Rome. It would be
natural to wonder if the demise of young Drusus Caesar (though not,

of course, that of Agrippina) had any connexion with his presence.
Tiberius cannot be held guilty of the starvation of Drusus. Otherwise
he could not have ordered the recital of the victim's dying words in
the Senate. That was done as an act of self-justification (Tacitus does
not say that the record made clear the manner of Drusus' death).[32]
He probably believed that Drusus killed himself. Perhaps he did, but
his departure left the way clear for Gaius and scotched the rumours
of a reconciliation between Tiberius and his imprisoned grandson that
were beginning to be heard.

But Tiberius did not intend Gemellus, his grandson by blood, to be
passed over. There is more than one indication of that. The first is the
marriages made by Gaius' sisters. Agrippina the younger was the first
to be wed, in Rome at the end of 28.[33] Her bridegroom was Cn.
Domitius Ahenobarbus, who was to hold the consulship in 32. Tacitus
comments on the marriage: what Tiberius was looking for, besides
ancient lineage, was propinquity to the Caesars; and Ahenobarbus'
grandmother was Octavia, making him the great-nephew of Augustus.
At a pinch the young man might be a candidate for the Principate, if
the descendants of Augustus and Tiberius failed. The second and third
daughters of Germanicus were not married until 33,[34] although the
youngest, Livilla, had previously been betrothed to the disgraced connexion of her mother's, Quinctilius Varus. They did not marry as
brilliantly as their sister: Drusilla went to L. Cassius Longinus, the
consul of 30, and her sister to his colleague M. Vinicius. Longinus
was grandson of the Liberator and member of an old plebeian house;
M. Vinicius was grandson of a *novus homo*, one of Augustus' generals;
he was not obvious material for a Princeps, and had no desire to be
considered such; he survived to hold a second consulship in 45, but
fell victim to the intrigues of Messallina. Quite undistinguished was
the husband that Tiberius found for his son Drusus Caesar's daughter
Julia, the sister of Gemellus, in the same year; Tacitus comments on
the disgrace.[35] Not that she deserved better; as the wife of young
Nero Caesar she had spied on her husband and reported his every sigh
to her mother. Now she was quietly married off to C. Rubellius
Blandus, whose grandfather, it was widely recalled, was an *eques* of
Tibur, though Blandus himself had attained the consulship (suffect in
18). But the meaning of this is that there were to be no more inter-
lopers. A single *eques* of exceptional ability might make his way to
the second place in the Empire; a whole gaggle of mediocrities (even
Longinus was nothing in comparison with his talented and impressive
brother Gaius[36]) stood not a chance against the grandsons of the

Princeps, young though they were. For, leaving aside Ahenobarbus, who had been brought in before this scheme was in prospect, they were the only male members of the dynasty who counted. The augurate that had been destined for Gaius was never conferred; instead he was installed in his dead brother's pontificate, and Gemellus took the other priesthood.[37]

The ancient sources differ as to Tiberius' intentions.[38] Some have him preferring the older of his grandsons, because of his age – but his character was suspect; some the younger, because of his descent – but there was the possible taint of bastardy; besides, whatever his preference, could he impose it? Tacitus has the Princeps racked by internal debate, running through the possible candidates, considering even Claudius and rejecting the idea of an outsider because of the humiliation such a choice would impose on the gens Iulia. The reason is valid, but the Princeps' meditation on Claudius destroys faith in the whole paragraph. For twenty years Tiberius had resolutely and consistently opposed the entry of Claudius into public life in any capacity whatsoever above that of priest and leading eques.[39] There need have been no debate. The blueprint had been drawn up years before, and after the appalling results of his adventure with Sejanus the Princeps would be ready to adhere to it religiously. The boys were to be a pair.

An objection will be raised at once. Tiberius was aware of the weakness of his grandson Gemellus in comparison with much older and more popular Gaius. If he intended to raise him to power with his cousin, why did he do nothing to forward his plan? The right solution may be to appeal, not so much to Tiberius' fatalism, marked though it had always been, and probably more marked than ever in his last years on the island, but to his formalism. Gaius, he might reflect (and there would be men to remind him of the fact), had not taken the toga of manhood until he was in his nineteenth year; now, in the year in which he became twenty-two, he was quaestor. If Tiberius followed the rules that had obtained since his own youth for the introduction to public life of young members of the family, he would reach his first consulship at twenty-eight, in this case six years after the quaestorship; and the same treatment precisely should be accorded to Gemellus. He should take the toga in 38; and hold the quaestorship in 41. But Tiberius could not hope to live so long; or could he? Augustus had suffered from weak health all his life, and survived until his seventy-sixth year; when Livia died she had been ten years older; her son Tiberius had always been remarkably robust, and he was taking care of his health in the way he knew best. We do not know what other astrologers told him, only that Gaius' ally Thrasyllus is said in 36 to have made Tiberius believe that he would survive another ten years.[40]

It would be good to be able to offer another indication of Tiberius' intentions: the coinage of the last three years of his principate. H. Gesche's proposal to assign the *clementia* and *moderatio* coins of Tiberius to those years[41] has many seductive features from the numismatic point of view, and the political interpretation that Gesche is able to offer on the basis of her numismatic arguments is even more attractive. The reverses of the coins are inscribed with the virtues which give them their name, and they show each a shield within which is set a small, youthful bust. There are two *virtutes* and so two shields and two persons represented. Examining and rejecting the ideas that Tiberius, Germanicus, or Drusus Caesar is shown, Gesche connects them with the succession. The shields are indeed those set up in memory of Germanicus and Drusus after their deaths (that of Drusus came to its tenth anniversary in 33); the *virtutes* are those of Tiberius himself; his *clementia* towards Agrippina, celebrated in 33; his *moderatio* in allowing her son to succeed him; while the youthful busts represent his grandsons, Gaius and Gemellus, whom he thus indicated as his successors.

Gesche's view deserves the most serious consideration, and if it is not wholly convincing,[42] that does not mean that she is wrong to regard Gaius and Gemellus as joint successors. There is the will, not drawn up, it is true, until 35, when Gemellus was in his sixteenth year, but designating Gaius and Gemellus equal heirs to Tiberius' fortune. The political significance of Caesar's will, of Antony's, and of Augustus' has never been denied; Tiberius' will is not to be denied it either. Its implications are clear: Gaius and Gemellus were seen by Tiberius as prospective partners in power.[43]

It is a matter of wonder to Tacitus that the death of Agrippina was followed by that of her old enemy Munatia Plancina.[44] He believes that she had been protected until then by the friendship of Livia and the enmity of Agrippina; Dio that Tiberius spared her to spite Agrippina. The charges against her are not specified by the sources, but Tacitus calls them 'well known': those of 20, then, brought up again. The accused woman committed suicide. The explanation may be that the charges were brought in retribution for Agrippina's death; probably, that is, at the instigation of Gaius. In 20 Plancina had shown a remarkable will to survive; relying on the patronage of Livia, she had abandoned her husband to his fate (many Roman women thought it right to join their husbands in suicide). Yet now she took her own life. She could look for no protection: Tiberius disliked what she had done in 20, and proffered his mother's defence of her as his mother's and not his own.[45] In 33 Livia was dead and the ultimate accession of a son of Germanicus and Agrippina assured. That Plancina owed her end to the ill-will of Gaius may be a plausible suggestion; but it cannot be demonstrated as true. That is an unsatisfactory feature of the last years of Tiberius' principate, from the historian's point of view. The centre of power and intrigue was with the court on Capri. From there emanated edicts and letters public and private, eye-witness reports and rumours. Sometimes the end result of an intrigue was a prosecution in the Senate, all that can be seen of a political iceberg the shape of nine-tenths of which must be a matter for conjecture.

Not only in purely domestic politics is the evidence fragmentary and baffling. A series of events linking Rome and the Orient took place during the years 31–34. To try to relate any of them with others may be rash; but it would be no less so to ignore the possibility that they may have been connected.

First in chronological order, if Tacitus is to be trusted (Dio has a date three years later), came the epiphany of a false Drusus Caesar in the East.[46] Germanicus' second son appeared on the Cyclades and on the mainland of Asia Minor, and some of Tiberius' freedmen on the spot were claimed to have given him recognition. His goal was said to be the armies of his 'father' Germanicus, Syria or Egypt. The imposter was pursued round Greece from east to west by Poppaeus Sabinus, governor of Moesia, whose pursuit ended at Nicopolis. Sabinus reported the results of his enquiries to Tiberius: the youth now claimed to be a son of M. Silanus; his support had melted away and he had sailed for Italy. Next in order came the attempt of Rubrius Fabatus at the end of 32 to slip away to asylum in Parthia;[47] he was probably a senator, and so debarred from travelling beyond Italy or Sicily without imperial permission, unless he were on official business. Fabatus had reached only the Straits of Messina when he was apprehended. He was brought back to Rome by a centurion but beyond being kept in custody he came to no harm. The affair ends inconclusively, like that of the false Drusus, and seems as inexplicable, except as a case of an uneasy conscience over a connexion with Sejanus. With 33 came the fall of the Euryclids and their affines, the descendants of Theophanes of Mytilene.[48] Pompeia Macrina was sister of the praetor of 15, Pompeius Macer, and daughter of another Macer, the friend of Augustus and Tiberius. The career of the grandfather, Theophanes, who had been the secretary and biographer of Pompey the Great, property on Lesbos, the friendship of the Roman dynasts, and the important equestrian posts held by the knight Macer had brought the family within striking distance of the consulship. Pompeia now was sent into exile, and her brother and father killed themselves to avoid conviction, on charges which included the close friendship between Theophanes and Pompey and the cult offered Theophanes after his death by the Greeks – presumably of Mytilene. This case was consequential upon another. Macrina's husband was C. Iulius Argolicus, son of Laco, of the Euryclid dynasty of Sparta which Tiberius had restored to its position in the Peloponnese soon after his accession. Like his father C. Iulius Eurycles, Laco did not keep his place. Tiberius had punished him and his son by removing them from their position before the trial of Macrina. The offences of Laco are nowhere mentioned, but it is a plausible conjecture of G. W. Bowersock's that the circumstances were similar to those of his father's expulsion: that is that he had tried to extend his power within the Peloponnese and had laid himself open to accusation of sedition and extortion by rival aristocrats in Laconia, like the Brasidas who had accused his father. The trial of Macrina and her kinsmen may be directly connected with the fall of Laco, or it may be the work of separate agents who were taking advantage of the discredit that had attached itself to his relatives.

R. S. Rogers had the courage to offer a theory that links the false Drusus and the Euryclid group.[49] Accepting the date given by Tacitus for the false Drusus (it would be easier to believe that he had escaped from the Palatine dungeon at a time when he had not already been reported dead of starvation), he regards it roundly as the last effort of Agrippina's 'party'. There is much to be said for his view, especially if imperial freedmen really had identified the imposter as Drusus. The story recalls that of Clemens, which may show either that an irresponsible Greek thought he could play the same trick, or that his supporters were not inventive in devising new schemes for their political advancement. But who would support the false Drusus and for what purpose? He had political descendants, the false Neros who troubled the eastern provinces in the principates of Galba and the Flavians.[50] Nothing suggests that they were the puppets of Roman politicians; they were adventurers who arose in the East and perished there, and if they had any support from above it came from Parthia, which hoped to profit from the unpopularity of the new dynasty to stir up trouble in the eastern provinces; and they were followed by the lower classes in the cities of the East. The false Drusus does not quite fit this pattern, for all the support that Dio says he won in the cities:

Parthia could have no hope of unseating the long-established ruler on Capri. Again, the imposter was last heard of *en route* for Italy, strange destination for an Oriental pretender who had come to the end of the road. Then the mention of M. Silanus. That person would not have come into the public eye in the East until his daughter was married to Gaius in 33, and it is tempting to jettison Tacitus' date for the false Drusus; it was not necessary for a man to be alive for him to appear in the East, as the false Neros showed. But the betrothal of Gaius may have taken place some time before 33. Who stood to gain, apart from the imposter, and supposing he was not acting on his own? The attempt came, according to Tacitus, between one month and six weeks after the execution of Sejanus; what is not clear is whether the enterprise was undertaken before or after the disgrace of Sejanus became known in the East. After the disgrace of Sejanus the movement had little point for a politician at Rome, except to ensure the survival of the real Drusus. The imposter's followers would never reach Italy, and if they did the real Drusus had only to be produced for them to be stultified. Before the news arrived there it could be seen as a last attempt of the followers of Agrippina to shake the hold that Sejanus had on Tiberius and the principate; the Syrian legions, after all, were not well disposed towards him and the discontent of the masses in the eastern provinces, topped up by their enthusiasm for the affable and hellenophile Germanicus, might be enough to force Tiberius to drop him (it is the old technique of the popular demonstration writ large); or it might be seen as the same plan executed by the friends of Gaius. The movement was slow to gain impetus; by the time it did, Sejanus was dead, but it could not be stopped. The quiet ending of the affair favours the view that it was a device of Gaius and his friends, readily overlooked by the Princeps; and the involvement of Silanus suggests that he should be added to the list of those who took active steps against Sejanus.

By 34 enquiry into the ramifications of Sejanus' friendships and plans was officially over. Yet some men survived who might safely be disposed of because they were unloved of the Princeps. Mam. Scaurus had already been attacked in 32 with three other consulars as a man certainly well disposed towards the Prefect, and although he had survived because the case was adjourned *sine die*, Tiberius made comments which boded no good. Now in 34 a second attack was made, which Scaurus chose not to survive. His wife, a Sextia of the Sextii Africani, urged him on to suicide and joined him in it.[51] So too (though she did not take the lead) did Paxaea, the wife of Pomponius Labeo, the former governor of Moesia, whom Tiberius deprived of his friendship in the same year. There was a charge of *repetundae* and other offences hanging over him, and Tiberius indignantly accused Labeo of hiding his guilt by bringing odium on himself; as for Paxaea, whatever she had done, she had had nothing to fear.[52] (Tiberius meant either that Paxaea, as a woman, was exempt from the charge of *repetundae*, or that he did not intend to press other charges.) The *renuntiatio amicitiae* (formal severing of a friendship) presumably had nothing to do with the other charges; Tiberius' motives for invoking it are not stated, but he used it in other cases where the honour of Gaius was impugned. As for Scaurus, Tacitus states categorically that his death was due to the enmity of Macro – rather than his friendship with Sejanus. Certainly he had been a supporter of the man Macro had helped to destroy, and one of the charges reeks of that offence: adultery with Livilla. It is worth recalling that the only man who was named as helping plan Gaius' downfall was a Sextius, though his cognomen was Paconianus.[53] M. Paconius happens to be the name of a legate of C. Silanus who joined Mam. Scaurus and two other friends of Sejanus, Bruttedius Niger and Iunius Otho, in accusing him of *repetundae* in 22.[54] Paconius perished at a date unknown, one might suspect in about 33 or 34. He was accused of *maiestas*, but the case apparently was protracted, or the Senate failed to deliver a verdict. Someone was determined to remedy that. The impeccable authority of a consular historian present on the occasion vouches for the truth of the story that a dwarf entertainer asked Tiberius at a dinner party why Paconius was still alive. The Princeps delivered him a rebuke – and wrote to the Senate to ask the same question. It is a nice illustration of the way an aged autocrat might be manipulated at the dinner table. But there are other points to make: first, that Mam. Scaurus had other enemies than Tiberius himself and Macro; and that they probably included M. Silanus, who might have cared as much for his brother Gaius as he did for Decimus, and who was now higher than ever in the councils of state. Secondly, the suicides. The rate seems to increase towards the end of Tiberius' principate. Tacitus and Dio produce an admirable reason for the accused to take that way out[55] – yet Tiberius was indignant that Labeo and Paxaea took it. The truth is stated explicitly only at the end of Tacitus' first hexad, when L. Arruntius proposed suicide and caused surprise to his friends. But Arruntius feared the future. It was not only that Tiberius was becoming hardened to suffering and increasingly careless of the processes of law. He was increasingly malleable in the hands of men who should be his servants; he was not tightening his grip but losing it. Then there would come the inevitable accession of Gaius, the supremacy of Gaius' friends; even if an attack failed in the last years of the old Princeps, it would be renewed in the first years of the new. We have already noticed the example of Plancina.

Other instances may be offered before the last important political trial of the principate is dealt with. First in time, the suicide of L. Fulcinius Trio.[56] Like Mam. Scaurus, he had undergone attack before and survived. More than three years later, in 35, the threat of prosecution came close again. He killed himself, but took a minor revenge on the Princeps who, being mortal, could not protect him. The will contained a lengthy and savage attack on Macro and the leading freedmen of the Princeps, whom he accused of senility and whose continuous absence had made him into little more than an exile. The suicides of two sons of Q. Blaesus, who had died in the first wave of victims in 31, took place the following year;[57] they were not brought to trial, but the priesthoods that they had been promised in the days of their cousin Sejanus' power were allotted to other men, and they took that as a sign that they should die. Next to their death Tacitus notes that of young Drusus Caesar's widow, Aemilia Lepida. While her father M. Lepidus lived his influence with Tiberius was great enough to protect her in spite of her treachery to Drusus. Now she faced a charge of adultery with a slave, unfortunately well founded; Lepida abandoned her defence.

The name of Macro recurs as that of the man responsible for the deaths of Scaurus and Trio at least. It would be hard to gauge how far he and how far Gaius (and others) were behind what happened. It seems at any rate that his influence increased in the last years of Tiberius' life as he tightened his grip on the Praetorian Guard. Not that his hold would prove firm against the will of a child of Germanicus, but he could ensure a speedy and smooth transition of power if, as most of the court must have expected, Gaius came to the Principate without possessing beforehand any of the *imperium* or *potestas*, the official powers, that Tiberius held in 14. Gaius cannot have cared for that situation, and Macro survived only until 38; in a sense the two men were rivals from the start. Yet the enhanced power that he enjoyed as the moment of the transfer drew nearer is attested by the story of Gaius' adultery with his wife Ennia, no matter whose idea the affair was. Tacitus and Dio mention it under the last year of Tiberius' life, 37, but it began earlier, after Gaius lost his wife.[58]

Certainly the last important trial of the principate was the work of Macro. That is shown, not only by the fact, Tacitus notes, that the

evidence was brought to the attention of the Senate by him, without
even an accompanying letter from the Princeps, but by the persons
involved.[59] Laelius Balbus had charged Acutia, formerly the wife of
P. Vitellius, with *maiestas*; she was condemned, but the tribune Iunius
Otho vetoed the grant of *praemia* (rewards) to her accuser. Next the
notorious Albucilla, former wife of Satrius Secundus, was brought to
court on the same charge; her accomplices (and of course lovers) were
Cn. Domitius Ahenobarbus, C. Vibius Marsus, and L. Arruntius, who
was known to be hated by Macro. Arruntius committed suicide, and
Albucilla too dealt herself a wound; it did not prevent the Senate from
ordering her to be carried off to prison. The other two defendants
were less hasty: Ahenobarbus asked time to prepare a defence, and
Marsus hit on a slow method of suicide (by starvation). The lesser fry,
accessories to the protagonists, were dealt with more speedily, the ex-
praetor Carsidius Sacerdos suffering deportation, Pontius Fregellanus
and Laelius Balbus *infamia* (official disgrace). Balbus figures in both
trials, as accuser in the first and defendant in the second, which suggests that the second was a massive retaliation for the first, but which
may mean only that an antagonist of Balbus was prompted to join
or trigger off an attack that was already impending. Tacitus does not
mention the ties of kinship that bound the defendants in the second
trial: D. Laelius Balbus, who was to hold the consulship in 46, had a
sister married to C. Vibius Marsus, the suffect of 17, and his daughter
was married to L. Arruntius Camillus Scribonianus, the son of L.
Arruntius and colleague of Domitius Ahenobarbus in his consulship of
32. A recent enquirer has suggested[60] that Macro's prosecution scotched
a plot to bring Cn. Domitius Ahenobarbus to power in Gaius' place.
Certainly his own birth and his marriage to Agrippina brought him
very close to the Principate – dangerously so. But the solution is a little
melodramatic. Ahenobarbus survived until late in the principate of
Gaius, and died of dropsy.[61] L. Arruntius is another man who was
thought of at one moment or another as a possible candidate – and a
willing one – for the succession to Augustus,[62] and he now killed himself. Perhaps he was the rival. But a consul of AD 6 cannot have been
much less than sixty-four years old in AD 37; Arruntius must have
been beyond such ambitions. A solution in a lower key presents itself.
L. Arruntius, to judge by the attack made on him in 31, had been a
leading figure in the movement against Sejanus. He should have been
high in the councils of the new regime. The same might be conjectured
of Gaius' brother-in-law Ahenobarbus, though he is not known to
have played any part in the downfall of the Prefect, and C. Vibius

Marsus: he had been one of the legates of Germanicus in Germany and Syria. That precisely may have been what Macro feared: he was trying to make away with, or at least discredit, two rivals, not of Gaius, but of himself. As for the prefatory trial, Germanicus is again the clue. The victim was the widow of a legate who had abandoned the family, the prosecutor a kinsman of one who had not; and the tribune who vetoed his rewards, Iunius Otho, was probably a son of the homonymous accuser of C. Silanus, who was known to support Sejanus.[63]

Of the second case Tiberius knew little or nothing. His last four years, after the mopping up of the 'conspirators', were comparatively untroubled. They saw no diminution of his mental powers, nor, perhaps, were they as unhappy as those whom he abandoned may have hoped. Tiberius had his daily reading, from which he would cull items to tease his company of savants (and woe betide anyone who tried to cheat by discovering what book was currently in the Princeps' hands). He had his cucumber frames and his dinner parties, from which, with stiff courtesy, he would dismiss his parting guests standing, a lictor by his side, in the middle of the room; and he had his pet snake.[64] A lonely old man he may have been, but he made the best of it.

Increasing age made the Princeps more and more reluctant to take decisions or even to receive visitors or delegations who might require him to do so. Least of all could he enter Rome, whether because it meant plunging back into affairs of state and subjecting himself to the importunities of its crowds, or because the prophecies of the astrologers acted too powerfully on his mind; perhaps for both reasons. He travelled in Campania and came close to the city more than once.[65] On the first occasion he sailed up the Tiber, which had sentries posted on its banks, as far as the gardens of Caesar; the sight of the city walls was enough to send him downstream again. The second occasion mentioned by Suetonius is more interesting. Tiberius reached the seventh milestone on the Appian Way, when a portent frightened him back. He went to feed his pet snake and found it dead, eaten alive by ants, it was said; and the astrologers told him 'to beware the violence of the multitude'. I have already suggested that it was predictions that he would never return to Rome alive that helped to keep him away; it looks as if astrology was used on this particular occasion for the same purpose. That snake may not have been alive when the ants swarmed over it.

Reports of the last years show Tiberius as sensitive to the failings of other men in positions of responsibility as he was indulgent towards his own; but he had never been slow to remind magistrates of their duties and functions, and that characteristic too could only be expected to develop with age. The Sibylline oracles had been collected and authenticated by Augustus. New items were not readily admitted; they might lead the people astray. In 32 a tribune, Quintilianus, who was presiding over the Senate in the absence of consuls and praetors, put to the house a motion to admit another text to the canon.[66] It was supported by a senior consular and Quindecimvir Caninius Gallus, and it was passed. Tiberius read the minutes of the meeting and delivered the young and inexperienced tribune a mild rebuke; but Caninius was told he ought to have known better than to introduce a writing of dubious authenticity to an ill-attended meeting of the Senate without consulting his fellow priests or allowing the verses to be read and assessed. The Senate went back on its decision and voted that the production be submitted to the scrutiny of the Quindecimviri.

An even more sensitive area was the comportment of the people. A grain shortage in the same year caused the outbreak of demonstrations against the Princeps that went on for several days in the theatre.[67] Tiberius was upset, and held the Senate and magistrates responsible: they should have used the authority vested in them by the state to control the people; in any case his imports of grain exceeded those of Augustus. Thus goaded, the Senate drew up a decree couched in the severe terms of a bygone age, and the consuls issued edicts to match. The silence of the Princeps himself towards the people was taken for haughtiness; but there need be no doubting the truth of Tiberius' claims: he had, as he thought, done all that could be done in the matter.

Where Tiberius' duty was plain and straightforward he continued to do it. To the difficulties of the landed classes in 33 he responded with a generous interest-free three-year loan which came ultimately from his own purse.[68] His response to the problem of Armenia and Parthia, when it arose again in 35, was prompt and rational, and to the disaster that struck Rome in 36, when the Circus Maximus and the Aventine Hill took the main force of a fire, not less generous than it had been in 25, when the Caelian suffered.[69] The victims had the value of their properties assessed by a commission consisting of the men who had married the Princeps' granddaughters, and afforced by P. Petronius on the nomination of the consuls. The losses were met by the Princeps. It was his last act of public munificence, and the senators voted decrees in the Princeps' honour, the last they were to devise.

Tiberius fell ill at Astura in Campania, but rallied enough to reach Cerceii.[70] He was determined not to let his illness be known, remained lucid (neither speech nor expression showed any sign of a mind that was wandering), even displayed a forced gaiety. At Cerceii he attended a tattoo, and hurled javelins at a boar in the arena. He was at once stricken with a pain in the side and caught a chill from becoming overheated and then being in a draught. Still he rallied, and even when he reached his villa at Misenum – it had once been the property of L. Lucullus – he insisted on going on with his normal routine, including the formal dinner parties and other diversions. There he was at pains to prevent the physician Charicles taking his pulse, but failed to deceive him. He planned to return to Capri, but the stormy March weather and his failing health made it impossible. He took to his bed.

There were several accounts of his death, some of them attributing it to Gaius Caligula, who either poisoned or starved him, or to Macro, or to both; in Tacitus' version, when the old man, whom everyone thought to be dead, had come to himself and was demanding food, Macro smothered him with his bedclothes. Those stories have their genesis in Caligula's later unpopularity; they are less convincing than what the elder Seneca wrote less than four years after the event.[71] Tiberius knew that his end was near. He took off the seal ring that was the symbol of his authority, apparently with the idea of giving it to someone; then he put it back on his finger and lay motionless for some time with his left fist clenched. Suddenly he called his servants, but no one came, so he got out of bed. The effort was too much for him. He collapsed just near it, and died. It was 16 March 37.

The day that the news of the 'lion's' death reached Rome (18 March) was a joyful one for the populace, who ran wild, full of ideas for disposing of the body.[72] Macro and Gaius, however, followed the valuable precedent of AD 14. The remains were put in a coffin and a slow and stately cortège carried them to Rome; the pace was exactly the same as that of the funeral procession of Augustus, nearly twenty-three years before;[73] and at Sinuessa the two routes, from Nola and Misenum, joined, and made the parallel closer still. But there were differences. First, the second coffin was carried, not on the shoulders of the councillors of the towns through which the cortège passed, but on those of soldiers.[74] It was appropriate, and perhaps the councillors would not have relished the job. Secondly, the funeral cortège was more of a triumphal progress, with sacrifices being offered up for Gaius and rejoicing all along the route.[75]

The procession entered Bovillae on the morning of 28 March. Gaius now went ahead into Rome; the body was conveyed into the city on the night of 28–29 March, and it was cremated on 3 April at a public funeral at which Gaius delivered the laudation, Augustus and Germanicus receiving much attention. Before that event took place there was a delicate political manoeuvre to be carried out. As soon as Tiberius died Macro had Gaius saluted *imperator* by the armed forces at Misenum and when the news reached Rome the Senate was summoned and likewise accorded Gaius the salutation.[76] But there was a snag. At the next Senate meeting, that which followed the arrival of Gaius and the cortège, and which must have been summoned on 30 March, for the purpose of arranging the funeral, Macro read the will.[77] Tiberius had instituted Gaius and Ti. Gemellus joint heirs. The consuls proposed that the will be declared null and void, on the ground that Tiberius, in making it, had been of unsound mind. The property thus should have fallen to the *liberi*, the descendants under his paternal authority,[78] again Gaius and Gemellus, but with their sisters, so that Gaius should have been worse off financially. But an important political declaration had been made by the Senate, with the support of the mob who had broken into the Curia to help them with their deliberations (this is the last instance of a demonstration organized by one of Scribonia's family that we shall have to notice). They had declared that there was nothing to be said for Tiberius' scheme of sharing power between Gaius and Ti. Gemellus: the boy was too young and did not possess the right even to enter the Senate. In voiding the will on those grounds the Senate presumably did not allow intestate succession, but handed over the property in its entirety to Gaius. Nevertheless, Gaius paid all the legacies. Nobody could complain that they had suffered from Gaius' action (except Gemellus); he even carried out the wishes of Livia's will, which had been neglected for eight years because of a fault that Tiberius had found in the drafting.[79]

But Gaius spelt out his interpretation of his own and Gemellus' positions even more clearly. He adopted Gemellus and made him *princeps iuventutis*.[80] The adoption was a legal nonsense as gross as his *querella de inofficioso testamento*, his complaint that Tiberius' will failed to fulfil his obligations to members of his family. Seven years and four months separated the two young men, not the requisite eighteen years, and there was no reason to believe that Gaius, who was twenty-four, would remain childless: he had lost his wife in childbirth. Like the conferment of the title *princeps iuventutis*, it neatly removed the encumbrance to the next generation and deferred any question of giving him powers: the boy was too young.

The funeral of Augustus had been followed by his apotheosis, an eagle being released from the pyre and the late Princeps being seen to rise therefrom by an independent witness. So far, precedent had been carefully followed; the question was whether it would be followed in this respect also; it seems to have been anticipated at Lugdunum.[81] For Gaius it would be convenient that Tiberius should be given divine status, making him *Divi nepos*, grandson of a deified Princeps. Yet his popularity stemmed from his membership of a family that (in most men's eyes) Tiberius had all but destroyed. Gaius requested the Senate to deify. He was not present at the meeting (he may have been at sea, bringing back the bones of his dead mother and brother[82]), and the Senate was able to prevaricate. It would not be difficult to represent Gaius' request as due to misguided, though admirable, devotion to a grandfather's memory. He let it drop.

Tiberius' reputation stood low in 37. It is misguided to argue that, if the Princeps was not deified, at least he did not suffer '*damnatio memoriae*', for that alternative was not yet in the repertoire;[83] besides, the interests of Gaius counted for something. It would become possible to form a more balanced view only later, when the conduct of Gaius belied his early promise; ironically enough, that Princeps himself came to feel some sympathy for his predecessor,[84] a fact which offers historians some light on the attitudes of Tiberius himself: Gaius had picked up the contempt that Tiberius felt for his subjects and fellow human beings.

Under Claudius and his successor Tiberius could be seen in better perspective. The younger Seneca had been adult for most of his principate, and, writing early in the regime of Nero, he acknowledged that the earlier part of it had been no less good than that of Augustus – that is, it was equal to the model which all Principes professed to adopt and superior to much that had followed under Gaius and Claudius.[85] Tiberian precedents stood alongside Augustan and Claudian in the '*lex de Imperio Vespasiani*' of 70, which empowered Vespasian to perform acts which his predecessors had performed without specific entitlement, and if oaths were not sworn to Tiberius' *acta* as they were to those of Augustus and the other *Divi*, it was only because of the precedent set by Gaius in 38.[86] To Domitian, whose aim was to reduce the Senate's role in politics to a nullity, it was the latter part of the principate that was of interest, and Tiberius' success (as he would see it) in using the *lex Maiestatis* to intimidate his peers. Besides, like Domitian, he had long been kept from power, and brought in only because the favoured heirs were lost. That story, so influential until our own day, will have been put out by the family of the lost heirs, notably by the younger Agrippina, who wrote up her own vicissitudes and those of her family; and it must have been canonical by the time of Domitian's accession to power in 81. Tiberius himself wrote a brief autobiography, but it was his day-books and *acta* that were Domitian's constant study.[87] That did Tiberius no good in senatorial circles. There was another resemblance. It was acknowledged by Seneca that there had been a period of good government under Tiberius. So too with Domitian, until in 83 he had felt strong enough to rid himself of his main rival for power.[88] Then the mask was thrown off. The same explanation would account for the change in Tiberius' principate, though it cannot have been as late as this that Tiberius was first charged with *dissimulatio* (hypocrisy).

Tacitus was writing the *Annals* when Hadrian, not Domitian, was in power, and it is a convincing suggestion that the historian discerned features that Tiberius had in common with the later Princeps, not only with Domitian through whose tyranny he had suffered.[89] The phil-hellenism is one such feature – but Hadrian carried it much farther than Tiberius would have thought proper – and the *consilium coercendi intra terminos imperii*, the view that the Empire should not be extended beyond its existing boundaries. Tacitus saw Tiberius partly in terms of his successors, and with the aid of sources disparate in nature, scope, and veracity. His predecessors' works are now lost. Of these the most important were the cautious, *quasi*-official recital of Aufidius Bassus, and the critical, even hostile, writings of the consul of 35, Servilius Nonianus, an eye-witness to much of what he described.[90] Tacitus used the memoirs of Agrippina too, but the picture he gives of the author's mother can hardly be derived entirely from that work. On the other side, orations of Tiberius had been collected and published.[91] Tacitus incorporates material from those, there is no doubt of it. He may have obtained it not from the collection but from the *acta senatus* themselves, which he claims to have consulted.[92] But it would be impossible to show that the narrative of events in the House was based mainly on that record – an intermediate literary source may always be postulated, and can sometimes be demonstrated. Tacitus was a senator himself and knew men whose fathers and grandfathers had sat in the Senate of Tiberius; he would talk to them of his subject. The personality of the Princeps fascinated him and made the first hexad of the *Annals* his masterpiece. That fascination has proved itself contagious to his followers. Lastly, another kind of oral tradition seems to have made its way to the surface in the *Annals*: the vulgar and hostile tradition about Tiberius' private habits.[93] That Tacitus' portrait is not a convincing whole – more of an expressionist sketch – is a measure of the disparity of the sources and of his honesty in handling them, but also of his impatience of routine detail, of his inability to resist the epigrammatic but misleading punch-line, of his taste for satire (both traits he shared with his subject). For some pedestrian but illuminating items (and for the full blooming of scandal) the student turns to the compilation of archive material and gossip that Suetonius published a few years later under the title *Biographies of the Caesars*.

Both Tacitus and Suetonius (and Dio who wrote a hundred years later) present Tiberius as a man their readers ought to hate. Nineteenth-century scholarship did not avoid the challenge. The Princeps was rehabilitated – at the expense of the historian – on the Continent, in this country, and in the United States. The movement lasted a century and came to its terminal stage with Kornemann's biography, published twelve years after his death, in 1960. 'Étrange coïncidence! La nouvelle force de l'histoire universelle, le Christianisme, reçut à jamais par la crucifixion du Christ et par sa mort une suprême consécration et sa pleine efficacité à l'heure même ou le plus grand martyr de l'État romain touchait, lui aussi, à sa triste fin.'[94] A more recent generation of writers has shown itself less ready to believe in the merits of men in power. (Not surprisingly.) It is the historian writing in a society that was not free who commands sympathy and respect and whose accuracy and insight are to be vindicated. But the antithesis is mistaken. The two men are not to be weighed one against the other. To do that is to forget the origin of the campaign waged on Tiberius' behalf: notoriously, it grew from the material presented by the historian. He had his view of the man; each of his followers and critics has had his own, tempered by that of his predecessors.

It was part of Tiberius' *modestia*, his awareness of his own limitations, to know that individual members of a state, however eminent, were dispensable mortals, while the state went on for ever;[95] and that makes it appropriate that one of the most important events of Tiberius' principate was precisely the death of Augustus and his own accession to sole power; it made the Principate a permanency. Equally appropriate is the fact that the two most striking features of Tiberius' policy as Princeps were, firstly to maintain the form of the new institutions as they had been left by Augustus, to take Augustus' *consilium* as *praeceptum*, holding to be mandatory what his predecessor had regarded as advisable, and secondly, to turn it from a sham into what it purported to be: Tiberius reduced his own role before that of Augustus in the first instance, and before that of the Senate in the second. In his first endeavour, maintaining the form of the Augustan constitution, Tiberius clearly succeeded; and by avoiding innovations he slowed down the pace of social change in Italy and the provinces, allowing them to settle. He failed, partially from the beginning, almost wholly from 26 onwards, to realize senatorial government. Tiberius recognized his failure by retiring to Capri, and so aggravated it and opened the door to the feature of his principate that goes down as paramount in the textbooks: the treason trials. It is significant that this feature too may be attributed to Tiberius making himself scarce – this time in the physical sense of removing himself from the scene.

The man Tiberius is a unified whole, and he is comprehensible.[96] He was shaped by his ancestry (heredity, education, and conscious emulation). The serious-minded boy[97] took to warfare, in which the Nerones had excelled, and embraced the political principles for which his grandfather Claudianus had died in the very month of his birth, and aesthetic tastes to match. There was no escaping the heritage, but one would not wish to escape it; it was a good one. Tiberius became a fatalist, ruled by astrology, a doctrine entirely consistent with the Stoicism which became almost obligatory for conservative Romans active in political life. The ambition natural to a Roman of family, so easily satisfied by a youth who was the Princeps' stepson, forced him to compromise. His responsibilities, to his stepfather and his class, oppressed the young man, and he soon learnt to find release in convivial drinking. Shown a prospect of the whole Empire by Augustus, he would contemplate it only on the understanding that the Principate was to take a form consistent with his own doctrine of senatorial supremacy. Having once compromised, he became sensitive to imputations of dishonesty and devious ambition, and reacted violently to the suspicion and hostility of his wife and his stepsons. Yet there came to be something in the misunderstanding of his peers and the commons in which he almost revelled. Surely it was not only to make manifest the guilt of their authors that the foulest slanders were read out in the Senate without a word omitted? The worse the accusations the more the Princeps could take refuge in his conscious virtue, in the sense of superiority that set him apart even from the men he chose to regard as his equals (it earned him a simultaneous reputation for arrogance and hypocrisy). When the calumnies of Julia were repeated by Agrippina, it was only natural for him to withdraw once again, this time to Capri, with the cronies whose interests he shared. Becoming more and more himself as he got older, he may even have come to relish the degradation and fear of the senators; impatience fell into cruelty. The man became harder and harder to reach, withdrawn on the island and into himself. Tiberius' dealings with his humbler and remoter subjects were of a piece with his conduct towards his social peers. He was aware of obligations towards them, but they were the obligations of a noble towards his clients, raised to a high degree by the position in which he found himself. First came the Roman people and Italy, and his sense of duty towards them was enough to make him interrupt the solitude he sought. The provinces came far behind, though pecuniary help was forthcoming when a disaster was massive. It is futile to pass judgment, favourable or unfavourable, on his 'administration' of the provinces. He met what he saw as his obligations punctiliously, if not always with dispatch. To blame him for failing to advance the juridical status or economic prosperity of his subjects is misplaced. He had no idea that there was such a goal to be reached. Men looked after their own material welfare (provided that they were not overwhelmed by catastrophe); as for advancement in status, that was available (as it always had been) to men of substance who had earned it. In the end, Tiberius would not even deny himself the last resort of the disgusted politician: retirement. Tiberius had known near exile, and on Rhodes he must have felt the righteous indignation of a Rutilius Rufus. The withdrawal to Capri was the nearest a Princeps could approach to a complete retirement on the lines of a Lucullus (fishponds or cucumber-frames, it is all one). He was not to know, of course, that the first Princeps to abdicate was to be Diocletian, two and a half centuries in the future. In his ignorance Tiberius nearly achieved it, and he believed that he had earned his rest.

LIST OF ABBREVIATIONS

Works are not included in this list if they appear in the Bibliography and are cited in a form that is easily recognized.

AE	L'Année épigraphique	CW	Classical Weekly
A e R	Atene e Roma	EJ²	V. Ehrenberg and
AHR	American Historical Review		A. H. M. Jones, eds., Documents illustrating the
AJA	American Journal of Archaeology		Reigns of Augustus and Tiberius, 2nd ed.,
AJP	American Journal of Philology		Oxford, 1955
Ant. class.	L'Antiquité classique	Epigr.	Epigraphica
Ath.	Athenaeum	G and R	Greece and Rome
Ath. Mitt.	Mitteilungen des deutschen archäologischen Instituts (in Athen)	GRBS	Greek, Roman, and Byzantine Studies
		Herm.	Hermes
		Hist.	Historia
BCH	Bulletin de correspondance hellénique	HSCP	Harvard Studies in Classical Philology
BGU	Ägyptische Urkunden aus den Staatlichen Museen zu Berlin, Griechische Urkunden	IG	Inscriptiones Graecae
		IGR	Inscriptiones Graecae ad Res Romanas Pertinentes
BJ	Bonner Jahrbücher	ILS	H. Dessau, Inscriptiones Latinae Selectae
CAH	Cambridge Ancient History	IRT	J. M. Reynolds and J. B. Ward Perkins eds.,
CIG	Corpus Inscriptionum Graecarum		Inscriptions of Roman Tripolitania, Rome, 1952
CIL	Corpus Inscriptionum Latinarum	JHS	Journal of Hellenic Studies
CJ	Classical Journal		
CP	Classical Philology	JRS	Journal of Roman Studies
CQ	Classical Quarterly		
CR	Classical Review	Lat.	Latomus
CREBM	H. Mattingly et alii, Coins of the Roman Empire in the British Museum, London, 1923–	MAAR	Memoirs of the American Academy in Rome
		MH	Museum Helveticum
		Mnem.	Mnemosyne
Sutherland, CRIP	C. H. V. Sutherland, Coinage in Roman Imperial Policy, London, 1951	Broughton, MRR	T. R. S. Broughton, Magistrates of the Roman Republic, 2 vols. and supplement, New York, 1952

NC	Numismatic Chronicle	RIC	H. Mattingly, E. A.
NNM	Numismatic Notes and		Sydenham, et alii, The
	Monographs		Roman Imperial Coinage,
NRS	Nuova Rivista storica		5 vols., London, 1923–38
OCD²	Oxford Classical Dic-	RM	Rheinisches Museum für
	tionary, 2nd ed., Oxford,		Philologie
	1970	Röm. Mitt.	Mitteilungen des deutschen
PBA	Proceedings of the British		archäologischen Instituts,
	Academy		Römische Abteilung
PBSR	Papers of the British School	Syme, RR	R. Syme, The Roman
	at Rome		Revolution, Oxford, 1939
PCPS	Papers of the Cambridge	Cichorius,	C. Cichorius, Römische
	Philological Society	RS	Studien, Leipzig and
Phil.	Philologus		Berlin, 1922
Phil. Woch.	Philologische Wochen-	SEG	Supplementum Epigraphi-
	schrift		cum Graecum
Phoen.	Phoenix	SIG	W. Dittenberger,
PIR	Prosopographia Imperii		Sylloge Inscriptionum
	Romani		Graecarum
Grant,	M. Grant, Roman	Jones,	A. H. M. Jones, Studies
RAI	Anniversary Issues,	Studies	in Roman Government and
	Cambridge, 1950		Law, Oxford, 1960
RE	Paulys Real-Encyclopädie	TAPA	Transactions and Proceed-
	der classischen Altertums-		ings of the American
	wissenschaft		Philological Association
REA	Revue des Etudes anciennes	WS	Wiener Studien
REL	Revue des Etudes latines	YCS	Yale Classical Studies
RG	Res Gestae Divi Augusti	ZfPE	Zeitschrift für Papyrologie
			und Epigrafik

NOTES

CHAPTER I

1* The main source is Suet., *Tib.*, 1–6. For individuals see *RE* and *MRR*. For education, see H. I. Marrou, *Histoire de l'Éducation dans l'Antiquité*, 6th ed., Paris, 1965 (*History of Education in Antiquity*, tr. of 3rd ed. by G. Lamb, New York, 1964), and M. L. Clarke, *Higher Education in the Ancient World*, London, 1971. For Tiberius' education see J. C. Tarver, *Tib. the Tyrant*, 143 ff.

1 Tac., *Ann.*, IV, 38, 1; Suet., *Tib.*, 19; Claudius: Tac., *Ann.*, XI, 24, 1, with N. P. Miller, *RM*, 1956, 312.

2 F. Münzer, *RE*, XIII, 1927, 882, suggests that Livia's father was a Nero, but his reason for rejecting the clear statement of Suetonius is not convincing. Note the reference to Claudia Quinta in Tac., *Ann.*, IV, 64, 4; she must have been a member of the Pulcher family, if the mention of her by Cic., *pro Cael.*, 14, 34, is to be relevant.

3 See R. M. Ogilvie, *A Commentary on Livy Books 1–5*, Oxford, 1965, 273 f., for story and sources. The Claudii were 'one of many nomadic shepherding clans who settled at Rome with the rise of agricultural prosperity'.

4 For attempts to reconstruct a 'Claudian' policy see Th. Mommsen, *Röm. Forsch.*, I, Berlin, 1864, 285 ff.; G. C. Fiske, *HSCP*, 1902, 1 ff.; P. Lejay, *Rev. de Phil.*, 1920, 92 ff.; A. Garzetti, *Ath.*, 1947, 175 ff.; E. S. Staveley, *Hist.*, 1959, 410 ff.; F. Cassola, *I Gruppi politici Romani nel III secolo A.C.*, Trieste, 1962, 128 ff.

5 For Valerius Antias as the creator of Livy's Claudii, see Ogilvie, *op. cit.*, 300; 376.

6 Tac., *Ann.*, I, 4, 3, appeals to 'vetere atque insita Claudiae familiae superbia', with the approval of Koestermann, *ad loc*. It is an inherited characteristic for Tiberius, but not for Tiberius' nephew Germanicus.

7 Livy, II, 58, 6 ff., with Ogilvie, *op. cit.*, 383.

8 For Clodius as a true *popularis* in contrast to the pretended *populares* Pompey, Caesar, and Crassus, see E. Gruen, *Phoen.*, 1966, 120 ff.

9 He is speaking in the person of the Censor, *pro Cael.*, 14, 34.

10 M. H. Prévost, *Les Adoptions politiques à Rome sous la République et le Principat*, Paris, 1949. Whether Claudianus was adopted in due form, or whether he was simply named chief heir in Livius Drusus' will, on condition that he took Drusus' *nomen*, is not clear (on the legal distinctions see E. J. Weinrib, *HSCP*, 1967, 252 ff.). Slightly in favour of adoption in due form is the fact that Claudianus used the *praenomen* Marcus, which a patrician Claudius is unlikely to have borne before his adoption. For his natural father, see F. Münzer, *RE*, XIII, 1927, 882 (who opts for 'testamentary adoption').

11 For *testimonia* on the Drusi see A. H. M. Greenidge and A. M. Clay, *Sources for Roman History 133–70 B.C.*, 2nd ed. by E. W. Gray, Oxford, 1960, 46; 128 ff.

12 Claudianus' support of the Triumvirs: Cic., *ad Att.*, II, 7, 3, where Cicero calls him 'Pisaurensis' (perhaps his mother came from Pisaurum: see F. Münzer, *RE*, XIII, 1927, 854 f.); his post in 50 BC: *ad Fam.*, VIII, 14, 4. Livia was born on 30 January 58 BC: *Acta Frat. Arv.*, ed. E. Pasoli, Bologna, 1950, fr. 5e, p. 108 f.; fr. 9bc, p. 111. For her mother, see Suet., *Cal.*, 23, 2, with T. P. Wiseman, *Hist.*, 1965, 333 f., who claims that she was an Alfidia from Marruvium of the Marsi. That is not convincing, and many ties connect the Claudii with Campania: E. Rawson, *Hist.*, 1973, 220 ff. For such marriages, see Wiseman, *New Men in the Roman Senate, 139 B.C.-A.D. 14*, Oxford, 1971, 53 ff. Following Syme, *RR*, 424, n. 4, and *Hist.*, 1964, 156 f., he mentions (277 f.) that of a daughter or sister of Ti. Nero to Q. Volusius (of Cingulum?). For Claudianus at Philippi, see Vell. Pat., II, 71, 3.

13 Hor., *Odes*, IV, 4, 37 ff. Neronian inferiority: Syme, *RR*, 19; Tarver, *Tib. the Tyrant*, 87, implausibly suggests that it was due to want of ambition.

14 Legateship: App., *Mith.*, 95; Florus, I, 41, 9; speech: Sall., *Cat.*, 50, 4; App., *BC*, II, 1, 5.

15 Cic., *ad Q. Fratr.*, III, 1, 15, *cf.* 2, 1. In a letter of recommendation, *ad Fam.*, XIII, 64, Cicero describes him as 'adulescentis nobilis, ingeniosi, abstinentis'.

16 *Ad Att.*, VI, 6, 1.

17 For his career, see [Caes.,] *Bell. Alex.*, 25, 3; Suet., *Tib.*, 4, 1 f.; Dio, XLII, 40, 6; Vell. Pat., II, 75.

18 For Nero's part in this episode, see Suet., *Tib.*, 4, 2 f.; Vell. Pat., II, 75 ff.; Dio, XLVIII, 15, 3 f. Suetonius' story (6, 1) tells how the infant Tiberius almost betrayed the fugitives with his crying.

19 Suet., *Tib.*, 5, arguing against rival views; *ILS*, 108; other evidence is collected in *PIR²* C 941.

20 For the wedding of Octavian and Livia (dated in *Fasti Verul., Inscr. Ital.*, XIII, ii, 160 f.) and Drusus' birth, see Suet., *Div. Claud.*, 1, 1; Dio, XLVIII, 44; with *PIR²* C 857, and G. V. Sumner, *Lat.*, 1967, 424, n. 1 (arguing for March or April 38 BC as the month of Drusus' birth). J. Carcopino, *Rev. Hist.*, 1929, 225 ff., suggested a political motive for Nero's action; for the marriage with Scribonia it is stated by App., *BC*, V, 53.

21 Tiberius' age: Suet., *Tib.*, 6, 4. Octavian's tutorship: Dio, XLVIII, 44, 5.

22 *Cf.* Tac., *Agr.*, 28, 4 ff.

23 *Cf.* Suet., *Gram.*, 17, 1.

24 Suet., *Gram.*, 16, 2.

25 See Syme, *Tac.*, II, 700 ff.; N. P. Miller, *AJP*, 1968, 1 ff., and especially 14 ff. In Suet., *Tib.*, 25, 1, he quotes the saying found in Terence, *Phorm.*, 506; Augustus, in 21, 5, adapts a famous phrase of Ennius in compliment to him. The phraseology of 67, 1 (= Tac., *Ann.*, VI, 6, 1), is comic; see above, pp. 201-2. For the diet, Hor., *Ep.*, II, 1, 50 ff.

26 Suet., *Tib.*, 56; 70, 3. Tiberius was not alone in enjoying the game; see M. L. Clarke, *op. cit.*, 24.

27 For the *Conquestio de morte L. Caesaris* and Tiberius' models in Greek verse and Latin prose, see Suet., *Tib.*, 70. Of his Greek models, the third-century poet Euphorion wrote *epyllia* and epic poems known to Catullus and Gallus; he used

material from the Trojan cycle and Attic legend, was interested in aetiology and geography, and was proverbially obscure; Cicero mocks the Alexandrian poets of Rome by calling them 'cantores Euphorionis' (*Tusc.*, III, 45). Rhianus, also of the third century, was a Homeric scholar, and wrote epigrams and, like Euphorion, epics on local legends (Thessaly, Achaea, Elis, Messene); they were replete with mythological, historical, and geographical lore; but his language was simpler. Parthenius, who worked at Rome in the mid first century BC, wrote elegy and was himself influenced by Euphorion; he was regarded as comparable with Callimachus himself (see W. V. Clausen, *GRBS*, 1964, 187 ff., and notices in *OCD*²). As patron and dedicatee Tiberius received not only commentaries on his three favourite poets and the learned and improving *Memorabilia* of Valerius Maximus, but Apollonides' commentary on the *Silli* (*Lampoons*) of Timon (Diog. Laert., IX, 109), which suggests that he was interested in that form; Germanicus' translation of the *Phaenomena* of Aratus (*PIR*² I 221, p.184); and Manilius' *Astronomica*. These last dedications clearly suit Tiberius' preoccupation with astrology and a Stoic outlook; see below, n. 36.

28 *Fasti Praen.*, *Inscr. Ital.*, XIII, ii, 131, *cf.* 448.

29 Nestor: [Luc.] *Macr.*, 21, *cf.* Strabo, XIV, p. 675; with Cichorius, *RS*, 278, n. 2. For Athenaeus and Marcellus, *RS*, 271 ff. Tiberius' legal and historical expertise: Tac., *Ann.*, III, 64, 4; IV, 38, 3.

30 Tiberius' precocity: Suet., *Tib.*, 8, shows him conducting his first cases at the age of seventeen or eighteen; his talent: Tac., *Ann.*, XIII, 3, 2; high education: Vell. Pat., II, 94, 2 f., *cf.* Macr., *Sat.*, II, 5, 2. Sir R. Syme made the point about Augustus' education in a paper delivered at Balliol College in 1970.

31 The retinue in the East: Hor., *Ep.*, I, 3, 15; 8, 2; II, 2; Porph. *ad* Hor., *Ep.*, I, 3, 1. It is discussed by Tarver, *Tib. the Tyrant*, 154 ff. The company on Capri: Tac., *Ann.*, IV, 58, 1; Suet., *Tib.*, 56, *cf.* 70; Plut., *de Def. Orac.*, 17. See Cichorius, *RS*, 348.

32 The trip to Rhodes, made as a youth: Damascius, *Vit. Isid.*, 64 (p. 94, Zintzen), quoting Plutarch, *cf.* Quint., III, 1, 17, who puts the tuition during the exile. For Theodore, see *Suda s.v.*; Suet., *Tib.*, 57; G. M. A. Grube, *AJP*, 1959, 337 ff. Theodore knew Tiberius as a child and must have taught him in Rome *c.* 30 BC (V. Stegemann, *RE*, VA, 1934, 1847 f.). For education as the pretext for Tiberius' visit of 6 BC, see Dio, LV, 9, 5; 8. Theodore on clarity: Quint., IV, 2, 32. Tiberius was 'Theodoreus' and disliked the style of the 'hot' and 'inspired' Nicetes (Sen., *Suas.*, III, 7).

33 Messalla Tiberius' master: Suet., *Tib.*, 70, 1. His vocabulary: N. P. Miller, *art. cit.*; Syme, *Tac.*, I, 284; archaism: Suet., *Div. Aug.*, 86, 2, and perhaps Tac., *Ann.*, IV, 19, 3; and see above, n. 25; purism: Dio, LVII, 17, 1 ff.; obscurity: Suet., *loc. cit.*; Tac., *Ann.*, I, 11, 4; 33, 2, and *cf.* *ILS*, 6688; wordiness: Tac., *Ann.*, III, 51, 2, and *cf.* the 'verbosa et grandis epistola' from Capri (Juv., X., 71); style improved on pleasant occasions: Tac., *Ann.*, IV, 31, 4; or when he

NOTES

spoke impromptu: Suet., *Tib.*, *loc. cit.*; the ambiguity deliberate: Tac., *Ann.*, XIII, 3, 5; irony: VI, 2, 5, *cf.* Syme, *Tac.*, I, 284; 319; 428 f. I am inclined to accept the suggestion of Seager, *Tib.*, 32, following Thiel, *Tib.*, 31 f., that Tiberius was not quick-witted in debate: hence silence and slowness; deliberate reticence would also be calculated to allow freedom to other speakers, and obscurity might be intended for tact.
34 Rhodes: Suet., *Tib.*, 11, 1 f.; 13, 1; the philhellene friends of Tiberius are noted by G. W. Bowersock, *Augustus and the Greek World*, Oxford, 1965, 133 f. Olympia: *SIG*³ 782 (= *EJ*² 78); Thespiae: *AE*, 1960, 307.
35 Sculpture: Suet., *Tib.*, 74; Pliny, *NH*, XXXIV, 62; Dio, LV, 9, 61. Painting: Suet., *Tib.*, 44, 2. Scientific interests: 11, 2.
36 Fortitude: Sen., *Cons. ad Pol.*, 15, 5 (Nero Drusus: 'exercitum . . . ad morem Romani luctus redegit'); *Cons. ad Marc.*, 15, 3 (Drusus and Germanicus Caesar); Tac., *Ann.*, III, 3 ff. (Germanicus); Tac., *Ann.*, IV, 12 (Drusus Caesar, with Roman precedents cited in his edict). The theme is treated by Val. Max., V, 10. Many of his other 'virtues' (below, Ch. VI) were Stoic: E. V. Arnold, *Roman Stoicism*, Cambridge, 1911, 305, n. 30. Sense of fitness (according to Professor P. A. Brunt, in his inaugural lecture, Oxford, 1971, a mark of the Stoic): Tac., *Ann.*, II, 59, 3; III, 6, 2; 12, 7; 53, 3 f.; 54, 9; 64, 4 f.; IV, 38, 1; Suet., *Tib.*, 29. Cf. P. Grenade, *Essai sur les Origines du Principat*, Paris, 1961, 452: 'L'austerité de son caractère était renforcée par l'influence du Portique.' For Rhodes as the home of Panaetius and the school of Posi-

donius perhaps inherited from him, see F. H. Cramer, *Astrology in Roman Law and Politics*, Philadelphia, 1954, 61.
37 Tiberius as astrologer and intimate of Thrasyllus: Tac., *Ann.*, VI, 20, 3 (study on Rhodes); Suet., *Tib.*, 14, 4; Dio, LV, 11 (on Rhodes); Suet., *Div. Aug.*, 98, 4 (*c.* AD 14); Dio, LVII, 15, 7 f. (early in the principate of Tiberius?); Suet., *Tib.*, 62, 3, and Dio, LVIII, 27, 1 ff. (death of Thrasyllus in AD 36; his influence at that time); Cramer, *op. cit.*, 90 ff.; A. H. Krappe, *AJP*, 1927, 359 ff.; Cichorius, *RS*, 390 ff.; W. Gundel, *RE*, VIA, 1937, 581 ff.; Syme, *Tac.*, II, 525. Citizenship: *CIL*, III, 7107. Note the dedication to Tiberius (see Cramer, *op. cit.*, 96 f.) of Manilius' *Astronomica*, with its Stoic outlook (I, 111; 476 ff.; II, 60 ff.). R. M. Ogilvie, *The Romans and Their Gods*, London, 1969, 54, draws attention to Suet., *Tib.*, 69, where neglect of religion is blamed on Tiberius' astrological beliefs; Tiberius' references to religion are conventional (e.g., Tac., *Ann.*, IV, 38; and note also the prime position of *religio* in Valerius Maximus' work). We cannot expect perfect consistency but Stoicism may be relevant here (not that the Stoics themselves were consistent throughout their history: Arnold, *op. cit.*, 217). They acknowledged the existence of gods, including deified human beings, but did not approve of conventional forms of worship (*op. cit.*, 223; 233 ff.). Tiberius' philosophical convictions were in conflict with his duty as Pontifex Maximus and with his concern for Roman tradition (hence alike his preoccupation with *ius divinum* (see below, Ch. VI, n. 3)

and his distaste for foreign novelties),
giving rise to such divergent views
as those of W. Warde Fowler, *The
Religious Experience of the Roman
People*, London, 1911, 447, n. 2, and
Thiel, *Kaiser Tib.*, 16, n. 2.

CHAPTER II

II* For Tiberius' early career the
main sources are Suet., *Tib.*, 5–9; Vell.
Pat., II, 94 f.; Dio, LIII f.
1 N. P. Miller, *AJP*, 1968, 5.
2 M. Gallius of the will: Suet., *Tib.*,
6, 3; for M. Gallius Q.f., serving
under Caesar in 47: Cic., *ad Att.*, XI,
20, 2; as *praetorius* under Antony at
Mutina: *Phil.*, XIII, 26. App., *BC*,
III, 95, mentions his brother Quintus' fate, *cf.* Suet., *Div. Aug.*, 27, 4.
The will was probably drawn up
after the birth of Nero Drusus in 38.
It may have been because of this will
that D. Claudius Nero Drusus took the
name Nero Claudius Drusus (Suet.,
Div. Claud., 1, 1).
3 Nep., *Att.*, 19, 4, *cf.* Sen., *Ep.*, 21,
4. The betrothal took place in Atticus'
lifetime; he died on 31 March 32 BC
(Nep., *Att.*, 22, 3). Agrippa's gain:
Vell. Pat., II, 96, 1.
4 Suet., *Tib.*, 6, 4; for the date of
the *Lusus*, see Dio, LI, 22, 4.
5 *Fasti. Praen.*, *Inscr. Ital.*, XIII, ii,
130 f. (= *ILS*, 8744a), *cf.* Suet., *Tib.*,
7, 1.
6 Dio, LIII, 26, 1; evidently Tiberius
made an impression on the civilian
population as well: *ILS*, 144 (Carthago Nova); 146 (Tarraco, 16–14
BC, with mention of a pontificate,
conferred at an unknown date, perhaps in immediate succession to Ti.

Nero); *CIL*, II, 1113 (Italica: 'patron');
1529 (Ulia: 'patron'); 476? (Emerita:
possibly Claudian).
7 The marriage: Dio, LIII, 27, 5.,
Marcellus' prospects: Vell. Pat., II,
93, 1, and other sources cited in
PIR² C 925.
8 Dio, LIII, 28, 3 f.; Tac., *Ann.*, III,
29, 1 f.
9 Suet., *Tib.*, 8, with *CQ*, 1971,
478 ff., and *CR*, 1974, 186, for chronology and connexions; a different
chronology is proposed by G. W.
Bowersock, *Augustus and the Greek
World*, Oxford, 1965, 157 ff. For
Claudian influence in the East see E.
Rawson, *Hist.*, 1973, 219 ff.
10 See E. Badian, *Mnem.*, 1974,
160 ff., arguing that Tiberius, holding the prestigious quaestorship attached to the consul (Augustus), would
yet carry out the duties mentioned
by Velleius and by Suet., *Tib.*, 8.
11 Dio, LIV, 1, 3 f., *cf.* RG, 5, 2.
12 RG, 34, 1, *cf.* Vell. Pat., II, 89,
4, and *ILS*, 8393, Ch. II, 35.
13 Dio, LIII, 12, *cf.* Tac., *Ann.*,
XIII, 4, 3.
14 Dio, LX, 23, 6, seems decisive.
For other evidence see K. M. T.
Atkinson, *Hist.*, 1960, 453 ff.
15 Ethiopia and Arabia: RG, 26, 5;
Britain: Dio, LIII, 22, 5; see C. E.
Stevens, 'Britain between the in-
vasions (BC 54–AD 43): a Study in
Ancient Diplomacy', in *Aspects of
Archeology in Britain and Beyond:
Essays presented to O. G. S. Crawford*,
ed. W. F. Grimes, London, 1951,
332 ff.
16 See T. R. S. Broughton, *TAPA*,
1935, 18 ff.; Levick, *CQ*, 1971, 478.
For other issues see H. H. Scullard,
From the Gracchi to Nero, 3rd ed., Lon-
don, 1970, 443 f.

17 For the trial of Primus the only source is Dio, LIV, 3, 1 ff. For the date, see S. A. Jameson, *Hist.*, 1969, 204 ff.

18 For the identity of counsel, consul, and conspirator see D. L. Stockton, *Hist.*, 1965, 32 ff.; Jameson, *art. cit.*; *contra*, Atkinson, *art. cit.*; R. A. Bauman, *Hist.*, 1966, 420 ff.; M. Swan, *HSCP*, 1967, 235 ff.; E. J. Weinrib, *Phoen.*, 1968, 49 ff. First and last are identified by Dio, LIV, 3, 4; for the conspirator's closeness to Augustus see Dio, LIV, 3, 5, and Vell. Pat., II, 91, 2.

19 Vell. Pat., II, 91, 2 ('ante erat pessimus'). See also *PIR²* F 117. Fannii had been staunch supporters of senatorial government since the consulship of C. Gracchus' opponent C. Fannius in 122. For these men, see *MRR* with *Additions and Corrections*, 24. The conspirator's *cognomen* belonged to the Servilii; when their last male representative died in 67 BC his *cognomen* was taken by his nephew M. Iunius Brutus, the assassin of Caesar. Fannius Caepio should be a connexion of Brutus or of the Servilii.

20 Suet., *Div. Aug.*, 66, 3.

21 Dio, LIV, 3, 3 f., differently interpreted by E. Cary in his Loeb translation. Before he could be prosecuted a consul would have to abdicate his office. Murena did not do so, *cf.* Obseq., 70 (130): 'constat neminem, qui magistratum collegae abstulerat, annum vixisse'; Augustus lived. See Weinrib, *art. cit.*, 32 ff. A. H. M. Jones, *The Criminal Courts of the Roman Republic and Principate*, ed. J. A. Crook, Oxford, 1972, 65, admits that contumacious absence from *nominis delatio* could lead to conviction, *cf.* A. J. H. Greenidge,

The Legal Procedure of Cicero's Time, Oxford, 1901, 462 f.

22 Caepio: Macr., *Sat.*, I, 11, 21; Murena: Strabo, XIV, p. 670; Vell. Pat., II, 91, 2: 'quod vi facere voluerant, iure passi sunt', suggesting that they were killed without trial.

23 Suet., *Tib.*, 8; significantly, Velleius is silent. For distaste for prosecution (even of a Verres), see Cic., *Div. in Q. Caec.*, 1 ff., and Levick, *CQ*, 1971, 175 f. A mitigating factor: relations between the Servilii Caepiones and the Livii Drusi had been destroyed in a celebrated trial of the mid-nineties: see E. Badian, *Hist.*, 1957, 318 ff. (= *Studies in Greek and Roman History*, Oxford, 1964, 34 ff.).

24 Votes for acquittal: Dio, LIV, 3, 6; Athenaeus: Strabo, XIV, p. 670 (for this man, see Cichorius, *RS*, 271 ff.).

25 For these events see *PIR²* I 215, p. 162.

26 M. Reinhold, *M. Agrippa*, Geneva and New York, 1933, 167 ff., thinks of *proconsulare imperium* over imperial provinces, with Syria as his special province, *maius imperium* over the senatorial provinces east of the Ionian Sea from 18 onwards, extended to western provinces in 13; but *cf.* E. W. Gray, *ZfPE*, VI, 1970, 227 ff., who argues that Agrippa began in 23 with overall *imperium aequum*, renewed for five years in 18 and made *maius* in 13. I agree with L. Koenen, *ZfPE*, V, 1970, 217 ff., that the *imperium* referred to in the papyrus is *maius* (μηθενὸς including Augustus). I take it to refer to the grant of 13 BC. In 23 Agrippa perhaps received *imperium aequum* in the eastern provinces, with Syria as his special province, in 18 *imperium aequum* throughout the Empire.

234

27 So Syme, *RR*, 338.

28 Tac., *Ann.*, II, 43, 3 (Piso); Dio, LIII, 32, 4 (Sestius). Tacitus and Dio say that the posts were offered by Augustus. That view may be influenced by later imperial control over the office; or the offer may have taken the form of a challenge.

29 Dio, LIV, 1, 3, *cf. RG*, 5, 1; Augustus celebrated the end of the conspiracy at the end of October; Jameson, *art. cit.*, 226 f.

30 Dio, LIV, 6, 1 ff.; 10, 1 f.

31 Dio, LIV, 10, 5. See A. H. M. Jones, *JRS*, 1951, 112 ff. (= *Studies in Roman Government and Law*, Oxford, 1960, 1 ff.).

32 Vell. Pat., II, 93, 1; Dio, LIII, 30, 4 f.; 33, 4.

33 Suet., *Tib.*, 8. For the relationship of these two functions, the 'duplex cura', see Levick, *art. cit.*, 280 f.; but note Badian, *art. cit.*, 164 ff.

34 Dio, LIV, 6, 5; 12, 5, *cf. RG*, 6, 2.

35 The 'vocabulum': Tac., *Ann.*, III, 56, 2. Agrippa: see above, n. 26; Dio, LIV, 28, 1, *cf. CREBM*, I, 21 ff., nos. 103, 107, 110 ff., 121 ff. (*EJ*² 70): note Gray's reservation, *art. cit.*, 238 (not coextensive with Augustus'); he emphasizes Josephus' phrase διάδοχος Καίσαρι (*AJ*, XV, 350).

36 On Parthia, see J. G. C. Anderson, *CAH*, X, 239 ff.; N. C. Debevoise, *A Political History of Parthia*, Chicago, 1938; K. H. Ziegler, *Die Beziehungen zwischen Rom und dem Partherreich*, Wiesbaden, 1964 (with bibliography); B. Levick, *Roman Colonies in Southern Asia Minor*, Oxford, 1967, 165 ff.

37 Suet., *Tib.*, 9, 1 ('exercitus'; Suetonius thinks that Tiberius went to Syria, but he also believes that he received the *signa*); 14, 3; Hor., *Ep.*,

I, 3, 3; Vell. Pat., II, 4, 4 ('exercitus', 'legiones'); Dio, LIV, 9, 5. For these and other sources for the mission, see *PIR*² C 941, p. 220. M. Parker, *The Roman Legions*, Oxford, 1928, 91, thinks of 'The Illyrian and Macedonian legions with possible detachments from Syria'; Kornemann, *Tib.*, 18, of 'six légions'.

38 *RG*, 29, 2; Vell. Pat., II, 91, 1; Suet., *Div. Aug.*, 21, 3; Justin, XLII, 5, 11 f.; Dio, LIV, 8, 1 ff. Suetonius' view (*Tib.*, 9, 1) that Tiberius received the *signa* is followed, e.g., by Kornemann, *Tib.*, 18, by Ziegler, *op. cit.*, 47, and by Polacco, *Il Volto di Tiberio*, 159 ff., who identifies as Tiberius the figure receiving the standard in the centre of the corselet of the Prima Porta statue of Augustus; J. M. C. Toynbee, *JRS*, 1956, 161, concurs. Seager, *Tib.*, 18, is undecided. But the silence of Velleius is decisive; and why did Augustus go all the way to Syria only to concede the moment of glory to Tiberius? For the date, see Ovid, *Fasti*, V, 595 ff.; *Fer. Cum.*, *ILS*, 108; *Fasti Maff.*, *Inscr. Ital.*, XIII, ii, 76; *Philocalus, ibid.*, 247 (*EJ*² p. 48), with Degrassi, *ibid.*, 456 f.

39 Jos., *AJ*, XV, 105, *cf. RG*, 27, 2; Tac., *Ann.*, II, 3, 4; Dio, LIV, 9, 4 f.; Vell. Pat., II, 94, 4; 122, 1. On the claim, P. A. Brunt, *JRS*, 1963, 174 f.

40 LIV, 9, 5.

41 See above, n. 38; for coins: Sutherland, *CRIP*, 37 f.; 44 ff.; *CREBM*, I, 3 f., nos. 10 ff., 73 f., 427 ff. (*EJ*² 26 ff.). Literature: Propertius, IV, 6, 79 ff.; Hor., *Odes*, IV, 15; *Ep.*, I, 12, 27 f.; Ovid, *Fasti*, V, 567 ff.

42 Dio, LIV, 10, 3 f., *cf. CREBM*, I, 1 f., nos. 2 ff., *cf.* 63 f., nos. 358 ff. (*EJ*² 29).

43 Dio, LIV, 9, 5; 10, 4 (19 BC), *cf.* Hor., *Ep.*, I, 12, 26 f.; Diodorus of Sardis, *AP*, IX, 219; and Crinagoras, *AP*, XVI, 61, with Cichorius, *RS*, 298 ff., 313 f., interpreting Diodorus' σοφίη in terms of diplomacy. Is there a reference to the sojourn on Rhodes (*cf.* W. R. Paton's translation 'in the schools')? In Velleius' view (II, 122, 1) he deserved an ovation.

44 Suet., *Tib.*, 14, 3; Dio, LIV, 9, 6. See P. Collart, *Philippes, Ville de Macédoine*, Paris, 1935, 223 ff., and F. Vittinghoff, *Römische Kolonisation und Bürgerrechtspolitik unter Caesar und Augustus*, Mainz, 1951, 23 and 128 f., for the population of Philippi. Other supernatural signs: Suet., *Tib.*, 14, 2 ff. Possibly the story comes from Tiberius' autobiography.

45 Vell. Pat., II, 94, 4: 'ad visendas ordinandasque, quae sub Oriente sunt, provincias, praecipuis omnium virtutum experimentis . . . editis'; 122, 1: 'ordinatis rebus Orientis'. Velleius is anticipating Tiberius' later position in the East.

46 Dio, LIV, 10, 4. For the success of Tiberius' marriage, see Suet., *Tib.*, 7, 2.

47 Bowersock's suggestion, *op. cit.*, 160 f., that the defence of the Thessalians belongs to this period has little to be said for it. The brief belongs to 26–25 and was owed to hereditary ties with the area (Professor E. Badian has kindly drawn my attention to the activities of Ap. Nero there in the early second century BC: see *CR*, 1974, 186, and 'Titus Quinctius Flamininus: Philhellenism and *Realpolitik*', Cincinnati, 1970, 44 f.). For a governorship in Gaul, 19–18, see Syme, *JRS*, 1933, 15 ff., following E. Ritterling, *BJ*, 1906, 174 f.; *RE*,

XII, 1925, 1223. It would be the occasion for his reconstitution of *legio* I (Tac., *Ann.*, I, 42, 3). It is passed over in E. Ritterling's *Fasti des röm. Deutschland unter dem Prinzipat*, ed. E. Groag, Wien, 1932.

48 For sources and date, see *PIR²* L 311; for the slightness of the reverse, see Syme, *JRS*, 1933, 17 f.; other German incursions: Dio, LIV, II, 2 (19 BC); 32, 1 (12 BC).

49 Dio, LIV, 19, 6. For Britain, see Stevens, *art. cit.*, 337 f. Tiberius' legateship: Ritterling, *Fasti*, 6 f. He did not leave Rome until after 29 June, on which he and Nero Drusus gave games to celebrate the dedication of the temple of Quirinus: Dio, LIV, 19, 5; *Fasti Ven., Inscr. Ital.*, XIII, ii, 59.

50 Suet., *Tib.*, 12, 2; Tac., *Ann.*, III, 48, 3, *cf.* Vell. Pat., II, 102, 1; see Syme, *RR*, 429.

51 For these campaigns, see Syme, *CAH*, X, 347 ff.; K. Christ, *Hist.*, 1957, 416 ff.; C. M. Wells, *The German Policy of Augustus*, Oxford, 1972, 59 ff., rightly emphasizing the importance of the operations of Nerva (who yet remained on good terms with his successor: Vell. Pat., II, 116, 4 f.). See also Syme, *RR*, 329; 390. Syme, also in *JRS*, 1933, 23, n. 62, remarks on the difficulty of defining the commands of generals operating in northern Italy; Nerva had been proconsul of Illyricum: *ILS*, 899. The view of A. von Premerstein, *Jahresheft*, I, 1898, Beiblatt, 158 ff., still held by A. Mócsy, *Pannonia and Upper Moesia*, London, 1974, 24, that Tiberius operated in Thrace late in 15, has little to be said for it: Syme, *art. cit.*, 117 f., with addendum in *Danubian Papers*, Bucharest, 1971, 66.

52 Syme, *CAH*, X, 351 ff. For different views, see W. A. Oldfather and H. V. Canter, *The Defeat of Varus and the German frontier policy of Augustus*, Urbana, 1915; P. A. Brunt, *JRS*, 1963, 175 ff.; Wells, *op. cit.*

53 Sources: *PIR*² C 857, p. 196.

54 Dio, LIV, 33, 1 and 5; 34, 1.

55 *Cf.* Tac., *Ann.*, I, 3, 1: 'Tiberium Neronem et Claudium Drusum priuignos imperatoriis nominibus auxit, integra etiam tum domo sua.'

56 For sources, see *PIR*² I 316, p. 166, and 222, p. 186.

57 The theory was first propounded by Kornemann, *Doppelprinzipat und Reichsteilung*, but in a rigid and schematic form; C. H. V. Sutherland used it discreetly in *CRIP*; it was expounded to me many years ago by Mr C. E. Stevens, and restated in *Lat.*, 1966, 229 ff.; 1972, 782 ff.

58 For Agrippa's date of birth see M. Reinhold, *op. cit.*, 4.

59 For parallelism between the early careers of Tiberius and Nero Drusus, see Levick, *Lat.*, 1966, 231: it can be seen in quaestorship, *ornamenta praetoria* (Dio, LIV, 10, 4; 22, 3), praetorship, and consulship. Tiberius was pontifex, perhaps in direct succession to his father, certainly by 13; Nero Drusus was augur (*ILS*, 146 f.).

60 See P. Colon, inv. no. 4701, published by Koenen, *art. cit.*

61 Dio, LIV, 27, 1, *cf.* Suet., *Div. Aug.*, 56, 2, with *Lat.*, 1972, 786, n. 3.

62 For Drusus' birth date, see *Fer. Cum.*, *ILS*, 108. For the year, see Mommsen, *Ges. Schrift.*, IV, 262; Rogers, *Studies*, 92; Levick, *art. cit.*, 236 ff.; G. V. Sumner, *Lat.*, 1967, 427 ff., argues for 14, followed by Seager, *Tib.*, 25, n. 2.

CHAPTER III

III* The main sources are Suet., *Tib.*, 9–14; Vell. Pat., II, 94–103; Dio, LIV, 28–LV, 13. Modern works: Syme, *RR*, 349 ff.; E. Groag, *WS*, 1918, 150 ff.; 1919, 74 ff.; M. L. Paladini, *NRS*, 1957, 1 ff.; P. Sattler, 'Julia und Tiberius'; E. Meise, *Untersuchungen*, 3 ff. (fully documented); Levick, *Lat.*, 1972, 779 ff.

1 For sources and date, see M. Reinhold, *Agrippa*, 125 f.

2 Sources in *PIR*² C 941, p. 221; C. M. Wells, *The German Policy of Augustus*, 155, with Tiberius 'completing the conquest of the Sava Valley and Bosnia begun by M. Vinicius (14) and Agrippa (13)'.

3 Geryon: Suet., *Tib.*, 14, 3, *cf.* Plut., *Vit. Caes.*, 47.

4 For the law, see P. Corbett, *The Roman Law of Marriage*, Oxford, 1931, 250 f. Tiberius' divorce and remarriage: Suet., *Tib.*, 7, 2 f.; *Div. Aug.*, 63, 2; Vell. Pat., II, 96, 1; Tac., *Ann.*, I, 12, 6; 53, 2; IV, 40, 9; Dio, LIV, 31, 2; 35, 4.

5 Dio, LIV, 31, 1. The 'concept of the guardian or regent' is still used by Seager, *Tib.*, 22.

6 Military honours: for the sources, see *PIR*² C 857, p. 197, and 941, p. 221; Tiberius received *ornamenta triumphalia* in 12 BC and an ovation in 10; Drusus the same honours in 11 and 9: see a paper called 'Military Titles and Honours of some junior Members of Augustus' Family', to be offered to CQ, *cf.* A. E. Gordon, *Quintus Veranius, consul A.D. 49*, Berkeley and Los Angeles, 1952, 312; Seager, *Tib.*, 26 f., believes that Tiberius was awarded two ovations; but this is impossible: see Vell. Pat.,

II, 122; Mommsen, *Res Gestae Divi Aug.*, 2, 13 ff. The will: Suet., *Div. Claud.*, 1, 5. Drusus a prop and future *princeps*: Sen., *ad Marc.*, 4, 2. The funerals: Agrippa: Dio, LIV, 28, 3 ff.; Drusus: LV, 2, 2 f.; *Epit. Liv.*, CXLII; *Cons. Liv.*, 67 ff.; 161 ff; 217 ff.; Tac., *Ann.*, III, 5; Suet., *Div. Claud.*, 1, 3; Augustus: Suet., *Div. Aug.*, 100, 2 ff.; Dio, LVI, 31 ff. The model was Sulla's: Appian, *BC*, I, 492 ff., Plut., *Sulla*, 38.

7 Tac., *Ann.*, IV, 39, 5, and 40, 8, with Suet., *Div. Aug.*, 63, 2, for the date.

8 Suet., *Tib.*, 60, 1 (perhaps ultimately from the memoirs of the younger Agrippina); Dio, LIV, 36, 2 ff.

9 See Wells, *op. cit.*, 156, 267.

10 The dash into Germany: Val. Max., V, 5, 3; Pliny, *NH*, VII, 84; the slow march: Suet., *Tib.*, 7, 3; *Cons. Liv.*, 89 ff.; 171 ff. Neither this nor the later journey with the body of Augustus is mentioned by Velleius; perhaps because of the contrast between piety towards deceased members of the house and severity towards the living: Tac., *Ann.*, IV, 52, 4.

11 Suet., *Div. Claud.*, 1, 4 f., rejects the story, *cf.* Tac., *Ann.*, II, 82, 3. Personality of Drusus: see *PIR*ⁱ C 857, p. 198.

12 Dio, LIV, 15, 1 ff.

13 Dio, LV, 6, 1.

14 Tiberius' theory: Suet., *Tib.*, 29: 'dixi et nunc et saepe alias, p.c., bonum et salutarem principem, quem vos tanta et tam libera potestate instruxistis, senatui servire debere et universis civibus saepe et plerumque etiam singulis; neque id dixisse me paenitet, et bonos et aequos et

faventes vos habui dominos et adhuc habeo'. *Cf.* Tac., *Ann.*, XIII, 4 (Nero's similar programme, a comparison which I owe to Mr C. E. Stevens). Practice is dealt with above, Chs. VII and VIII.

15 Suet., *Div. Aug.*, 94, 8, *cf.* Tac., *Ann.*, I, 12, 1: 'quaecumque pars sibi mandaretur, eius tutelam susceptaturum', and Vell. Pat., II, 124, 2: 'cum quidquid tuendum non suscepisset, periturum videret'. For *tutela*, see J. Béranger, *Recherches sur l'Aspect idéologique du Principat*, Basel, 1953, 257 ff., 266 ff.

16 Suet., *Div. Claud.*, 1, 4; Tac., *Ann.*, I, 33, 3; II, 82, 3.

17 Dio, LIV, 35, 2; Cic., *de Lege Agr.*, I, 23; and other passages cited by V. Fadinger, *Die Begründung des Prinzipats*, Berlin, 1969, 323, n. 2.

18 Dio, LV, 3; 4, 3.

19 For Crassus, see *PIR*² L 186, and Syme, *RR*, 308; Drusus: Suet., *Div. Claud.*, 1, 4.

20 Agrippa's refusals: Dio, XLVIII, 49, 3 f. (37 BC); LIV, 11, 6 (19); 24, 7 (14). Balbus: *Inscr. Ital.*, XIII, i, 633 ff. For the honours of Tiberius and Drusus, see above, n. 6. Tiberius as legate: *RG*, 31, 1. For the pretext, and its inadequacy, see Gordon, *op. cit.*, 308 f.; Sattler, 'Julia', 497. Piso: Dio, LIV, 34, 7.

21 Sources for Tiberius' campaigns in Germany, 8-7 BC: *PIR*² C 941, p. 221 f. See Wells, *op. cit.*, 156 ff.

22 Drusus' funeral like a triumph: Sen., *ad Marc.*, 3, 2. For the date of his death, see Levick, *art. cit.* (n. III*), 783, n. 5.

23 Vell. Pat., II, 99, 1: 'tribuniciae potestatis consortione aequatus Augusto'.

24 Tribunician power: Suet., *Tib.*,

9, 3; Vell. Pat., II, 99, 1; Tac., *Ann.*,
III, 56, 3. *Imperium maius*: Suet., *Tib.*,
11, 3 (lictors, *vocatio*, and tribunal on
Rhodes); Dio, LV, 9; 4 (Armenia),
cf. 9, 6 (Paros). See Levick, *art. cit.*,
781 f.

25 For the reasons offered see Sattler, 'Julia', 492, n. 15; 494, n. 19. For
the work of the Princeps, see F. G. B.
Millar, *JRS*, 1967, 9 ff.

26 For the date of the assumption of
Augustus' tribunician power, on or
soon after 26 June 23, see *PIR²* I 215,
p. 162; it was the date of Tiberius'
adoption in AD 4: *Fasti Amit.*, *Inscr.
Ital.*, XIII, ii, 187, *cf.* Vell. Pat., II,
103, 3 (27 June), and perhaps of his
second grant of tribunician power.

27 Dio, LV, 8, 1 f.

28 For the significance of the temple
of Concord, see Levick, *art. cit.*, 803 ff.

29 Original success of the marriage:
Suet., *Tib.*, 7, 3; Julia and Tiberius'
celebrations: Dio, LV, 2, 4; 8, 2.

30 For Julia, see Meise, *Untersuchungen*, 19 ff.; Levick, *art. cit.*, 795 ff.; her
father's daughter: Macrob., *Sat.*, II, 5,
8.

31 Tiberius on women in politics:
Tac., *Ann.*, I, 14, 3, and below, Ch. X,
n. 32; not Julia's equal: 53, 2.

32 For the events of 6 BC, see Dio,
LV, 9, and Suet., *Tib.*, 10 f., with
Levick, *art. cit.*, 786 ff.

33 Levick, *art. cit.*, 788 f., and works
cited there.

34 *CREBM*, I, 85 f., no. 498 f.; see
Sutherland, *CRIP*, 68 f.

35 See, e.g., Tac., *Ann.*, IV, 37 f.:
'validus alioqui spernendis honoribus
. . . quae saxo struunter . . . pro
sepulchris spernuntur'; Vell. Pat., II,
124, 2: '. . . ut potius aequalem civem
quam eminentem liceret agere principem'.

36 For honours to C. Caesar, and
three years later to L. Caesar, see
PIR² I 216, p. 166 f., and 222, p. 186.

37 Tac., *Ann.*, I, 53, 5.

38 Suet., *Tib.*, 10, 2: 'matri sup-
pliciter precanti'.

39 For this episode (Dio, LV, 9, 6),
see Levick, *art. cit.*, 792 f., 805.

40 See *PIR²* I 216, p. 167; and
Akveld, *Germanicus*, 77 f., who dis-
tinguishes various grades of *imperium
maius*.

41 A. Gell., *NA*, XV, 7, 3: 'ἀνδρ-
αγαθούντων ὑμῶν καὶ διαδεχομέν-
ων stationem meam'. Note number
and tense.

42 Sources: *PIR²* I 222, p. 186 f.

43 Full documentation on these men
in Meise, *Untersuchungen*, 21 ff.

44 Vell. Pat., II, 100, 4, with Levick,
art. cit., 796.

45 The tribune: Dio, LV, 10, 15;
Gracchus: Tac., *Ann.*, I, 53, 6; not
identical: E. Groag, *RE*, IIA, 1923,
1372.

46 Vell. Pat., II, 100, 5; for connexions between Quinctii and Sempronii, see Levick, *art. cit.*, 798, n. 2.

47 Vell. Pat., *loc. cit.* For Ap.
Claudius' descent, see T. P. Wiseman, *HSCP*, 1968, 207 ff.; he was
connected with the Quinctii (Levick,
loc. cit.) and was first cousin once removed to Octavian's first bride
Claudia, who was returned to her
mother Fulvia a virgin (Dio, XLVIII,
5, 3). For Scipio's descent, see Groag,
PIR² C 1345.

48 Scribonia in exile: Vell. Pat., II,
100, 5; Dio, LV, 10, 15. Her character:
Sen., *Ep.*, 70, 10: 'gravis femina';
Suet., *Div. Aug.*, 62, 2.

49 See Levick, *art. cit.*, 798, n. 7.

50 Marsyas: Sen., *de Ben.*, VI, 32, 1;
Pliny, *NH*, XXI, 9, with Sattler,

'Julia', 520 f., and Levick, *art. cit.*, 799 ff. Tribunician agitation: Dio, LV, 9, 10; 10, 1. Meise, *Untersuchungen*, 8, n. 39, is sceptical.

51 Tac., *Ann.*, III, 48. L. Volusius Saturninus was suffect, probably Tiberius' first cousin; see above, Ch. I, n. 12.

52 *PIR²* A 771; Vell. Pat., II, 43, 4, praises him, but the Veteres were eminent at the time of writing.

53 *PIR²* C 287. His loyalty: Tac., *Ann.*, III, 16, 5.

54 Censorinus: *RE*, XIV, 1930, 1551; Vell. Pat., II, 102, 1; Corvinus: *RE*, VIIA, 1955, 159; Vell. Pat., II, 112, 1; he was the son of Tiberius' oratorical model (Suet., *Tib.*, 70, 1).

55 *PIR²* A 1229.

56 Macrob., *Sat.*, II, 6, 3. Livia's favour: Suet., *Galba*, 5, 2.

57 *RE*, IA, 1920, 2034. Livia's favour and the gossip: Suet., *Otho*, 1, 3. For his mastership of the mint, see Levick, *art. cit.*, 806.

58 Dio, LV, 10, 10.

59 *RE*, XVIII, 1942, 1671.

60 Ahenobarbus: Vell. Pat., II, 104, 2; Suet., *Nero*, 4; Syme, *JRS*, 1934, 128; *RR*, 400; Wells, *op. cit.*, 158 f.; Saturninus: Vell. Pat., II, 105, 1 f.; *RE*, IIA, 1923, 1511 f.; Syme, *RR*, 401, n. 1; 435, n. 4.

61 See Syme, *RR*, 401, n. 3. The marriage connexion: above, Ch. II, n. 60.

62 For the date of his legateship of Galatia, see Levick, *Roman Colonies in Southern Asia Minor*, 203 ff.; a trimmer: Syme, *RR*, 425; his marriages: Tac., *Ann.*, III, 22, 1 ff., with Wiseman, *art. cit.*, 220.

63 Gallus: D. Magie, *Roman Rule in Asia Minor*, Princeton, 1950, II, 1342, n. 38. Turranius: *RE*, VIIA, 1948,

1441; he was superseded in Egypt by 2–1 (*BGU*, IV, 1200); *praefectura annonae*: Tac., *Ann.*, I, 7, 3; Syme, *RR*, 437.

64 The elder Lucilius: Plut., *Vit. Brut.*, 50; *Vit. Ant.*, 69; Appian, *BC*, IV, 129. The younger: Tac., *Ann*, IV, 15, 3, with Syme, *RR*, 363, n. 1; 434 f. He was suffect consul in 7.

65 Suet., *Tib.*, 42, 1, *cf.* 59, 1; Dio, LVIII, fr. 3; Pliny, *NH*, XIV, 16; 64; 145.

66 Suet., *Tib.*, 12, 2, *cf.* Vell. Pat., II, 99, 4.

67 Suet., *Tib.*, 11, 4. For the legal issues see Levick, *art. cit.*, 810, n. 2. For the details of Tiberius' life on Rhodes, see Suet., *Tib.*, 11 ff.

68 See Levick, *art. cit.*, 811, n. 2.

69 Visit to Gaius: Suet., *Tib.*, 12, 3 (Samos); Dio, LV, 10, 19 (Chios), *cf.* Vell. Pat., II, 101, 1 (a very different version).

70 Syme, *RR*, 428, n. 4, recalls the activities of Ti. Nero; for Agrippa, see *CIL*, XII, 3153 f.; *AE*, 1920, 43 (= *EJ²* 75: Maison Carrée, *cf. CIL*, XII, 3156). Gaius as patron gives a *xystus*: 3155.

71 Tac., *Ann.*, III, 48, 3; Suet., *Tib.*, 13, 2; Vell. Pat., II, 102, 1, *cf.* 97, 1; Pliny, *NH*, IX, 118.

72 Suet., *Tib.*, 15, 1; young Drusus was probably being educated by Antonia: Jos., *AJ*, XVIII, 14, 3. For the 'Pompeiana domus' in Antony's hands, in 44 and in 39, see Vell. Pat., II, 77, 1; App., *BC*, II, 525. Maecenas left his property to Augustus to dispose of as he wished (Dio, LV, 7, 5).

73 See *PIR²* I 222, p. 187, for the date.

74 Fortitude of Augustus: Suet., *Div. Aug.*, 65, 2. Death of Gaius: see *PIR²* I 216, p. 168.

CHAPTER IV

IV* The main sources: Suet., *Tib.*, 15–22; Dio, LV, 10a, 6–LVI, 30, 5; Vell. Pat., II, 102–23; Tac., *Ann.*, I, 3–7. The period has been treated by Syme, *RR*, 419 ff.; J. Schwartz, *Rev. Phil.*, 1945, 21 ff. (I do not accept the chronological framework set up in that paper); A. E. Pappano, *CP*, 1941, 30 ff.; F. Norwood, *CP*, 1963, 150 ff.; E. Meise, *Untersuchungen*, 35 ff.; A. Ferrill, *Hist.*, 1971, 718 ff. (oversimplified); B. Levick, *Lat.*, 1976. For Tiberius' legal position, see H. Dieckmann, *Klio*, 1918, 339 ff.; L. Dupraz, *MH*, 1963, 172 ff.; M. L. Paladini, *Hommages M. Renard*, II, 573 ff.

1 Tac., *Ann.*, IV, 1, 3, *cf.* H. Bird, *Lat.*, XXVIII, 1969, 61, n. 3; Vell. Pat., II, 101, 2 f., with G. V. Sumner, *HSCP*, LXXIV, 1968, 265 ff.

2 For L. Paullus, see *PIR²* A 391.

3 Dio, LV, 13, 1; Suet., *Div. Aug.*, 65, 3. For speculation on the reason for the change, see Meise, *Untersuchungen*, 28 f.

4 Agrippa Postumus was born after his father's death in March of 12; Agrippa was campaigning in the Balkans during the autumn of 13. I do not accept the arguments of V. Gardthausen, *Aug. und seine Zeit*, II, 844, n. 1. Gaius' death: *Fasti Gabin., Inscr. Ital.*, XIII, i, 257 f.; the news: *ILS*, 140.

5 *Fasti Cupr., Inscr. Ital.*, XIII, i, 245. His mind affected: Dio, LV, 10a, 8; Vell. Pat., II, 102, 2 f.

6 See Levick, *Lat.*, 1966, 227 ff.; for a different interpretation, Instinsky, *Herm.*, 1966, 332 ff. Tiberius' German command: Vell. Pat., II, 104, 2; Suet., *Tib.*, 16, 1: 'delegatus pacandae Germaniae status, Parthorum legati mandatis Augusto Romae redditis eum quoque adire in provincia iussi', suggesting *imperium maius* over all the provinces, with Gaul and the German frontier as his special province, *cf.* Dio, LV, 13, 2. The tribunician power: *locc. citt.*, and Tac., *Ann.*, I, 3, 3. For the ten-year grant, see Mommsen, *Res Gestae Divi Aug.²*, 31 (Dio correct against Suetonius).

7 See Levick, *art. cit.* The objections raised by Sumner, *Lat.*, 1967, 413 ff., will be met below. Note the numismatic evidence cited by M. Grant, *From Imperium to Auctoritas*, Cambridge, 1946, 268 f. For the inferences drawn from Suetonius' statement (*Tib.*, 15, 2) that Tiberius was 'forced' to adopt Germanicus before his own adoption (*cf.* Tac., *Ann.*, I, 3, 5), see Seager, *Tib.*, 37 f. Tiberius was legally debarred from adopting anyone *after* his own adoption: Levick, *CR*, 1972, 309 ff. The view of Timpe, *Kontinuität*, 29, and Seager, *Tib.*, 37, that the adoption of Germanicus was intended to give additional security to Tiberius is not supported by Tac., *Ann.*, I, 3, 5, which they cite.

8 Germanicus' marriage: Mommsen, *Ges. Schrift.*, IV, 272. Claudius' betrothal: Suet., *Div. Claud.*, 26, 1.

9 Favour felt to Germanicus; his swearing in of provincials and troops: Tac., *Ann.*, I, 34 ff.; Suet., *Cal.*, 1 ff. Political views: 33, 3; relations with Drusus: II, 43, 6, *cf.* Dio, LVII, 18, 7; replaces Agrippa Postumus in the Balkans: Dio, LV, 32, 1.

10 Similarly, Meise, *Untersuchungen*, 32, 44. See above, p. 153 f.

11 Dio, LV, 13, 3, where the purge is connected with the arrangements made in AD 4. See Jones, *Studies*, 21 ff.

12 For recent discussion of the *lex Valeria Cornelia* and of the *Tabula Hebana*, to which we owe our knowledge of it, see R. Frei-Stolba, *Untersuchungen zu den Wahlen in der röm. Kaiserzeit*, 120 ff.; E. S. Staveley, *Greek and Roman Voting and Elections*, London, 1972, 218 ff.; Levick, *art. cit.* (n. IV*).

13 Tac., *Ann.*, I, 15, 1; Vell. Pat., II, 124, 3, interpreted by Jones, *JRS*, 1955, 18 f. = *Studies*, 46 f.

14 For the Sentii Saturnini, see Vell. Pat., II, 92, 1 ff.; 105, 1 f. For the Aelii Tuberones, *cf.* the consul of 11 B C and Seius Tubero, a close friend of Tiberius, Tac., *Ann.*, IV, 29, 1.

15 For this family, see Syme, *RR*, 424 f., and E. J. Weinrib, *HSCP*, 1968, 247 ff. Medullina: Suet., *Div. Claud.*, 26, 1.

16 See Syme, *RR*, 424, 434. Dolabella: Vell. Pat., II, 125, 5.

17 For L. Volusius Saturninus, P. Quinctilius Varus, the Nonii, and Piso, see Syme, *RR*, 424, with connexions in n. 2. The legateship of Volusius in Syria: *BMC Galatia*, etc., 159, no. 60 f.; of Nonius under Varus in Germany: Vell. Pat., II, 120, 3. For Piso, see *PIR²* C 289, p. 64 f., with Suet., *Tib.*, 42, 1, for the merrymaking.

18 For the old collaboration, see F. Münzer, *Röm. Adelsparteien*, 41, *cf.* Syme, *RR*, 422, n. 3; eastern posts: 435. Vell. Pat., II, 112, 4, is critical, *cf.* E. Koestermann, *Herm.*, 1953, 377, n. 2. Claudius' marriage: Suet., *Div. Claud.*, 26, 2.

19 Syme, *RR*, 424; 437; for Africa, see E. Birley, *JRS*, 1962, 221. Cossus eventually went on to the prefecture of the city; for Tiberius' trust, see

Sen., *Ep.*, 83, 15, and *cf.* Vell. Pat., II, 116, 2, and Dio, LVII, 24, 8.

20 Vell. Pat., II, 116, 3; he became governor of Syria and finally succeeded L. Piso as *praefectus urbi*: *PIR²* A 200.

21 Jos., *AJ*, XVIII, 1 ff.

22 Syme, *RR*, 363, n. 1. Apronius and Postumus in Illyricum: Vell. Pat., II, 116, 2. Apronius' connexions: Tac., *Ann.*, IV, 22, 1 ff.; VI, 30, 3. Origin of Postumus: Syme, *RR*, 362, n. 7. Governor of Asia in 13: *BCH*, 1884, 467; *Ath. Mitt.*, 1900, 207.

23 See Vell. Pat., II, 16, 2, for his ancestry. Syme, *RR*, 434, includes him in the list of Tiberius' protégés; attack on Libo: Tac., *Ann.*, II, 32, 4.

24 See Syme, *RR*, 362, 434; Moesia: Tac., *Ann.*, I, 80, 1; VI, 39, 3 (death in 35 after twenty-four years as governor).

25 Blaesus in Pannonia: Tac., *Ann.*, I, 16, 2; his origin: Syme, *RR*, 363, n. 1; 434. For the connexions of Sejanus, see Sumner, *Phoen.*, 1965, 134 ff.; Hennig, *Seianus*, 5 ff.; stemma below. Prefecture of the Guard: Tac., *Ann.*, I, 7, 3; 24, 3.

26 Tac., *Ann.*, III, 48, 3.

27 Cassius son of the Liberator? See *PIR²* C 502. Cinna: Sen., *ed Clem.*, I, 9; Dio, LV, 14 ff. (under A D 4); an adherent of Tiberius: Syme, *RR*, 425.

28 Syme, *RR*, 512 (the orator); 423, n. 3 (his family). M. Valerius Messalla Messallinus, *cos.* 3 B C, was legate in Illyricum in A D 6, winning triumphal ornaments (Vell. Pat., II, 112, 1 f., with high praise), *cf.* Tac., *Ann.*, I, 8, 5; III, 18, 3. M. Aurelius Cotta Maximus Messallinus, *cos.* A D 20: II, 32, 2; III, 17, 8; V, 3, 4; VI, 5: 'Tiberiolus meus'. He sent the exiled Ovid the pleasing gift of silver

reliefs of Augustus, Tiberius, and
Livia (*ex Ponto*, II, 8, 1 ff.).
29 Cornelia: *PIR*² C 1475. Julia
reached marriageable age in about
7–6 BC: Mommsen, *Ges. Schrift.*,
VIII, 192. In *PIR*² I 635, her marriage is dated *c.* 4 BC. Scipio the adulterer, his father, and grandfather:
*PIR*² C 1435; 1438; 1437; with 1395.
30 C. Silanus: Tac., *Ann.*, III, 24,
1 ff. Manius' sister: III, 22 f.; Suet.,
Tib., 49, 1; Syme, *JRS*, 1955, 22 ff.
Claudius' engagement: Suet., *Div.
Claud.*, 26, 1. M. Torquatus: Pliny,
NH, VII, 58; *CIL*, VI, 27034; X,
8041, 21; Mommsen, *op. cit.*, 197.
31 Tertulla (or Tertia): *PIR*² I
865; Tac., *Ann.*, III, 76, 2. The Triumvir's wife: *PIR*² I 850. Connexions
of the consul of 25 BC: *IG*, VII, 1851
f.; *BCH*, 1926, 440, no. 76. For D.
Silanus' mother, see T. P. Wiseman,
HSCP, 1970, 219 ff.
32 See Syme, *art. cit.* Praise from
Vell. Pat.: II, 114, 5; 125, 5.
33 The influence of M. Silanus: Tac.,
Ann., III, 21, 5. Creticus Silanus: *PIR*²
C 64; Syme, *JRS*, 1966, 57.
34 Agrippa takes the *toga virilis*:
Dio, LV, 22, 4. The request of AD 20:
Tac., *Ann.*, III, 29, 1 f.
35 For the military situation in AD 4
and Tiberius' campaigns, see Wells,
The German Policy of Augustus, 159 ff.
Vell. Pat., II, 104, 2, and 105, 1, has
Tiberius departing for Germany 'pro-
tinus'; the doubts of Schwartz, *art.
cit.* (n. IV*), 48 are groundless. For
his return, see Vell. Pat., II, 105, 3
(December AD 4: 'pietas'); 107, 3
(AD 5: 'eadem . . . festinatione'); Dio,
LV, 27, 5 (under AD 6). He was
probably unable to return at the end
of 6 and 7: see Levick, *art. cit.* (n.
IV*), n. 102.

36 Natural disasters in 5: Dio, LV,
22, 3; in 6: 26, 1 ff. for the cumulative
effects, 27, 1 ff., *cf.* Pliny, *NH*, VII,
129. Other sources and chronology
are discussed by Schwartz, *art. cit.* (n.
IV*), 50 ff. Demands for discharge
and bounty: Dio, LV, 23, 1; 24, 9–25,
6. Maroboduus: J. Dobiáš, *Klio*, 1960,
155 ff. Tiberius received his third
salutation as *imperator* in AD 6 (Dio,
LV, 28, 6 f., on conclusion of a truce
with the Germans, *cf. ILS*, 107 =
*EJ*², 61); the fourth presumably belongs to his victory over the Pannonians in 8. Sources for the rebel
lion: *PIR*² C 941, p. 223. Tiberius
probably was assigned Illyricum as his
special province in addition to or
instead of Gaul and Germany; the
phrase used by Vell. Pat., II, 111, 1
('respublica ab Augusto ducem in
bellum poposcit Tiberium'), recalls
previous occasions when public agitation was intended to lead to the appointment of a general: Cic., *de imp.
Cn. Pomp.*, 44; *RG*, 25, 2. Seriousness
of the revolt: Vell. Pat., II, 110, 6 (ten
days' march from Rome, *cf.* Dio, LV,
30, 1); Suet., *Tib.*, 16, 1. Sources for
the course of the rebellion: *PIR*² C
941, p. 223, with Syme, *CAH*, X,
369 ff.; E. Koestermann, *Herm.*, 1953,
345 ff.; Wells, *op. cit.*, 237 f.; Seager,
Tib., 38 ff. Tiberius' conduct under
criticism: Dio, LV, 31, 1, where
Augustus' discontent is inferred (by
sources hostile to Tiberius?) from the
sending of reinforcements, *cf.* Suet.,
Tib., 21, 5, for later praise of his
handling of affairs. But anxiety is
shown by the excessive numbers of
legions arriving in the area in 7: Vell.
Pat., II, 113, 1 f. Tiberius is 'optimus
eorum quae agebat iudex et utilia
speciosis praeferens quodque semper

eum facientem vidi in omnibus bellis, quae probanda essent, non quae utique probarentur sequens'.
37 Vell. Pat., II, 112, 7; so interpreted by F. W. Shipley in his Loeb translation; contra, E. Hohl, Herm., 1935, 360, n. 1; Pappano, art. cit. (n. IV*), 36, n. 41; A. Degrassi, Inscr. Ital., XIII, i, 214. Syme, CAH, X, 372, dates the battle.
38 Fasti. Ost., Inscr. Ital., XIII, i, 183: 'Agrippa Caesar [abdicatus est?]', Degrassi. Meise, Untersuchungen, 29 f., dates the relegation to late 5 or early 6 (two years after the adoption). There is no reason to believe that Agrippa Postumus is the commander referred to in AE, 1964, 107 (so J. Reynolds, JRS, 1966, 119).
39 Suet., Div. Aug., 65, 1 and 4; Dio, LV, 32, 2.
40 Vell. Pat., II, 111, 3 f.
41 Dio, LV, 31, 1; substitute for Agrippa: 32, 1. For Germanicus' achievements in the war, see PIR² I 221, p. 180. Sumner, Lat., 1967, 426, argues for 6 as the year of Germanicus' quaestorship; but cf. Levick, art. cit., (n. IV*).
42 See Levick, Hist., 1972, 673 ff. In that paper I regrettably overlooked J. Crook, CQ, 1954, 153 f., who made many of the same points. S. A. Jameson, Hist., 1975, 287 ff., argues for a different interpretation.
43 See Hohl, art. cit., 350, n. 3; Pappano, art. cit. (n. IV*), 33, n. 21; Norwood, art. cit. (n. IV*), 162, n. 18. I described him as 'not a promising youth' (Lat., 1966, 228, n. 2), Seager as 'a young man of low intelligence and uncouth disposition' (Tib., 46); it would be dangerous to go beyond that. Treating political opponents as if they were insane is a technique still in use.

44 Dio, LV, 27, 1 ff. (translated by E. Cary in the Loeb edition); Suet., Div. Aug., 19, 1.
45 For Drusus' birth date, see above, Ch. I, n. 20. But the year of these games is not 6 but 7. The year 6 is that usually given, but it does not allow enough time for the period of the famine. Did the famine, the tax, the fire, and the conspiracy, all pass by March of 6? As for the dedication of the temple of Castor and Pollux, which took place on 27 January (Fasti Praen., Inscr. Ital., XIII, ii, 117), that a fortiori belongs to a later year (pace J. G. Frazer, The Fasti of Ovid, II, 262 ff.; EJ², 46; and Seager, Tib., 39); perhaps the misunderstanding alleged to have arisen between Augustus and Tiberius in 7, and the sending out of Velleius and Germanicus, suggest that Tiberius stayed the winter in the Balkans. He was at Rome in the winter of 7–8: cf. Vell. Pat., II, 114, 5. For Suetonius' dating of the dedication (Tib., 20), apparently after the triumph of 12, see F. W. Shipley, MAAR, 1931, 39, n. 6.
46 Suet., Div. Aug., 51, 1.
47 Dio, LV, 32, 1. For the significance of the appellation Neptune, see E. Pappano, art. cit. (n. IV*), 35. For Sex. Pompeius, M. Agrippa, and Neptune, see S. Weinstock, RE, XVI, 1935, 2528 ff.
48 Dio, LV, 34, 3.
49 Julia died in AD 28 after twenty years of exile (Tac., Ann., IV, 71, 6 f.). She may have suffered temporary relegation at the time of her husband's death; the Scholiast on Juvenal, VI, 157 f., has her once recalled. Syme, Ammianus and the Historia Augusta, Oxford, 1968, 86, and Meise, Untersuchungen, 88, dismiss his evidence.

Meise argues for the simultaneous disgrace of Julia and Paullus in A D 8, with D. Silanus as a mere adulterer used as scapegoat (40, n. 26); the Scholiast made two exiles out of two reasons for one exile (40 ff.). For the Scholiast's sources, see G. B. Townend, *CQ*, 1972, 380. Professor Townend thinks the Scholiast unlikely to have derived all his material from Suetonius. Ovid: W. Kraus, *RE*, XVIII, 1942, 1916 ff.; the arguments of Schwartz, *art. cit.* (n. IV*), 27 ff., for 9 are not convincing. On Ovid's exile see most recently J. C. Thibault, *The Mystery of Ovid's Exile*, Berkeley and Los Angeles, 1964, reviewing theories to date; Meise, *op. cit.*, 223 ff.; R. Verdière, *Ant. Class.*, 1971, 623 ff. For Ovid's own statements, see S. G. Owen, *P. Ovidii Nasonis Tristium Liber secundus*, Oxford, 1924, 1 ff.

50 See Syme, *RR*, 468; so H. Dessau, *Gesch. der röm. Kaiserzeit*, I, 469.

51 Suet., *Div. Aug.*, 19, 1 f. For the implications of the name Asinius Epicadus, see Levick, *art. cit.* (n. IV*). For the problem of the islands, see Meise, *Untersuchungen*, 29 f.

52 Julia's alleged marriage: Περὶ τοῦ Καισαρείου γένους, ed. Sp. Lampros, Νέος Ἑλληνομνήμων, 1904, 149. What Ovid saw: *Trist.*, II, 103 ff.; III, 5, 49 f.; 6, 27 ff. His timidity: IV, 4, 39; *ex Ponto*, II, 2, 17. The value of advice: *Trist.*, III, 6, 13 f. S. Reinach, *Rev. Phil.*, 1910, 347, draws attention to the word 'funestus', which Ovid uses in connexion with his 'error': *Trist.*, III, 6, 28. It makes a nice oxymoron in the context of marriage and Ovid uses it thus in *Ep.*, XII, 140 (Medea), and *Fasti*, I, 521 (Evander). Julia's child: Suet., *Div. Aug.*, 65, 4,

53 This may be the victory of 3 August '[in] Inlyrico' (*Fasti Ant.*, *Inscr. Ital.*, XIII, i, 328). Dio, LVI, 1, l, says that Tiberius returned to Rome 'after the winter'. An entry took place on 16 January (*Fasti Praen.*, *CIL* I², 231) and may be attributed to 9 (as by D. M. Pippidi, *REL*, 1933, 435, and Schwartz, *art. cit.* (n. IV*), 55) or to 10 (*cf.* Suet., *Tib.*, 17, 2), with G. Wissowa, *Herm.*, 1923, 377; A. Stein, *PIR²* C 941; Hohl, *Die Siegesfeiern des Tiberius*, tabulating other proposals (24); and Seager, *Tib.*, 44, n. 5. *EJ²* p. 45, following L. R. Taylor, *AJP*, 1937, 185 ff., refer the document to the ovation of 9 B C, probably rightly. Dio's account is circumstantial.

54 Suet., *Tib.*, 17, 2, *cf.* P. Kniessl, *Die Siegestitulatur der röm. Kaiser*, Göttingen, 1969, 29 f. The award of a triumph went with Tiberius' fifth salutation as *imperator* (Dio, LVI, 17, 1; *RIC*, I, 82, no. 220; *CREBM*, I, 50, no. 271 ff.).

55 Arrival of the news: Vell. Pat., II, 117, 1, *cf.* Dio, LVI, 18, 2; Tiberius' reaction: Vell. Pat., II, 120, 1; Suet., *Tib.*, 17, 2. Hohl, *art. cit.*, 23, n. 67, makes Tiberius approach Germany in too leisurely a way (not until 10). The celebration of Augustus' birthday in Germany (Dio, LVI, 25, 3) indicates the objective of these expeditions. It was in Germany that Tiberius won his sixth acclamation (Mommsen, *Res Gestae Divi Aug.²*, 16 f.).

56 Dio, LVI, 25, 1; *Fasti Praen.*, *CIL* I² 231; Verul., *AE*, 1937, 5 = *EJ²* p. 45; Ovid, *Fasti*, I, 639 f. For discussion of this temple and its significance to Tiberius, see T. Pekáry, *RM*, 1966–67, 105 ff.; Levick, *art. cit.* (n. IV*), 803 ff.

57 Dio, LVI, 17, 1 ff.

58 See Sumner, *Lat.*, 1967, 413 ff. He accepts Suetonius' statement (*Cal.*, 1, 1) that Germanicus held the quaestorship a *quinquennium* before the normal age, and does not recognize the irregularity of Germanicus' advancement, which was caused by the extraordinary political situation.

59 Suet., *Tib.*, 20, 1; Vell. Pat., II, 121; Ovid, *ex Ponto*, II, 1; II, 2; III, 3, 85 ff. For the day, see *Fasti Praen.*, *Inscr. Ital.*, XIII, ii, 135 = *EJ²* p. 54; for the year (12 rather than 11), see Sumner, *HSCP*, 1968, 274, n. 107. For the previous scope of Tiberius' *imperium*, see P. A. Brunt, *ZfPE*, XIII, 1974, 171 ff.; but I do not believe that he could use his *imperium* within the city until 13.

60 Suet., *Tib.*, 21, 1, *cf. Div. Aug.*, 27, 5; Vell. Pat., II, 121, 1 (apparently implying that the law preceded the triumph, but see Brunt, *loc. cit.*); *RG*, 8, 4; Dio, LVI, 28, 6. There can be no doubt that Tiberius possessed *imperium domi* in AD 14: he gave the watchword to the Praetorian Guard and appointed a new *praefectus*: Tac., *Ann.*, I, 7, 7; 24, 3.

61 Dio, LVI, 28, 1; Tac., *Ann.*, I, 10, 7; *RG*, 6, 2.

62 Tac., *Ann*, I, 7, 4 f.; Suet., *Tib.*, 23, 1.

63 *CREBM*, I, 87, no. 506 ff. = *EJ²* 81 (Tiberius); 23, no. 110 ff., (= *EJ²* 70), *cf.* nos. 103, 107, 121 ff. (Agrippa).

64 See above, p. 38. For the first coins, see *CREBM*, I, 50, nos. 217 ff., 94 f., nos. 570 ff., with Sutherland, *CRIP*, 73 ff.; for a warning against interpreting acts of Augustus as showing hostility to his son and heir; see Levick, *CR*, 1972, 309 ff.

65 Augustus' question: Suet., *Div. Aug.*, 99, 1. Tiberius used a bodyguard at Rome in September 14: Tac., *Ann.*, I, 7, 7. At the funeral precautions were taken that Tacitus mocks: *Ann.*, I, 8, 7; a second prefect appointed: 24, 3. Piso: see *PIR²* C 289, p. 64 f.

66 Tac., *Ann.*, I, 5, 1 f.; Dio, LVI, 30, 1. Modern treatments; M. P. Charlesworth, *AJP*, 1923, 145 ff.; E. Hohl, *Herm.*, 1935, 350 ff.; Pappano, *art. cit.* (n. IV*), 42 ff.: W. Allen, jr., *TAPA*, 1947, 131 ff.; M. L. Paladini, *Acme*, 1954, 313 ff.; J. D. Lewis, *Auckland Classical Studies presented to E. M. Blaiklock*, 172 ff.; R. Detweiler, *CJ*, 1970, 289 ff.

67 Suet., *Div. Aug.*, 101, 1. On the language of the will see Levick, *art. cit.* (n. 64).

68 For the death of Fabius, see *PIR²* F 47. It would be risky to make too much of his patronage of Ovid, and of Ovid's third wife's connexion with his house (*PIR²*, *loc. cit.*).

69 I cannot accept Seager's interpretation (*Tib.*, 50) of Tac., *Ann.*, I, 6, 2: 'nihil de ea re Tiberius apud senatum disseruit: patris iussa simulabat', *cf.* XIII, 21, 9. For the murder, see also I, 53, 2.

70 So Seager, *Tib.*, 49 f., and Jameson, *art. cit.* (above, n. 42), 313 f.

71 For Clemens, see Tac., *Ann.*, II, 39 f.; Suet., *Tib.*, 25, 1; Dio, LVII, 16, 3 f. Not all Agrippa's slaves seem to have passed to Augustus: note Sex. Vipsanius M. f. Clemens, *CIL*, V, 3257.

72 This theory, which is adumbrated by Suet., *Tib.*, 22, does not square with Tiberius' statement that Augustus had simply given orders that Agrippa was not to survive him

(Tac., *Ann.*, I, 6, 2). But Tiberius' concern was to preserve quiet and prevent the development of crisis. The lie he told was a small and salutary one.

73 See Syme, *Tac.*, I, 271 ff., discussing Aufidius Bassus' laudatory *Bellum Germanicum* and his *Histories*, the much more influential senatorial writer Servilius Nonianus (on whom see also *Herm.*, 1964, 408 ff.), and Agrippina, eschewing the enthusiasm of B. R. Motzo, *Studi Cagliaritani*, 1927, 19 ff.; and allowing due place for the development of oral tradition.

74 Note that in 8 Augustus made a journey to Ariminum to meet him and discuss (it was said) affairs in Illyricum—as if Tiberius did not know perfectly well how to handle them (Dio, LV, 34, 3).

CHAPTER V

V* The main sources are Tac., *Ann.*, I, 7–52; Vell. Pat., II, 123–25; Dio, LVI, 31–47; Suet., *Div. Aug.*, 97–101; *Tib.*, 22–26. Modern studies: Ph. Fabia, *Rev. Phil.*, 1909, 28 ff.; A. Lang, *Beiträge zur Geschichte des Kaisers Tiberius*, 55 ff.; Marsh, *Reign*, 45 ff.; E. Hohl, *Herm.*, 1933, 106 ff.; J. Béranger, *MH*, 1948, 178 ff.; *Recherches sur l'aspect idéologique du principat*, Basel, 1953, 3 ff.; F. Klingner, *Tacitus über Augustus und Tiberius*; H. H. Schmitt, *Hist.*, 1958, 378 ff.; D. Timpe, *Untersuchungen zur Kontinuität des frühen Prinzipats*, 27 ff.; K. Wellesley, *JRS*, 1967, 23 ff. (proposing an impossibly rapid chronology); D. Flach, *Hist.*, 1973, 552 ff.

1 Vell. Pat., II, 123, 3, and Suet., *Tib.*, 21, 1, for the meeting; Dio, LVI, 31, 1, against; Tac., *Ann.*, I, 5, 5 f., undecided. Dio, LVI, 30, 5, claims to know the day of death, Suet., *Div. Aug.*, 100, 1, the hour, with details of the death scene; and 19 August is also the official date: *Fasti Ostiens.*, *Amit.*, *Antiat. minist.*, *Inscr. Ital.*, XIII, i, 185; ii, 191 and 208 = *EJ*² pp. 40; 50. This implies that it was only after a delay of a few hours that Livia issued the correct time. Yet Suetonius gives Augustus and Tiberius a whole day together, and the time of Tiberius' arrival must have been known. Suetonius' and Velleius' versions could not have survived if the discrepancy had been very great; they were unlikely to survive any discrepancy. That there was a delay in announcing the death is stated also by Suetonius, but he gives a different reason. We can admit the delay without denying that Tiberius found Augustus alive. See Timpe, *Kontinuität*, 29 ff. For the literary origin of the story of Livia's deceit, see M. P. Charlesworth, *CR*, 1927, 55 ff., and R. H. Martin, *CQ*, 1955, 123 ff.; for a different account, see D. C. A. Shotter, *Mnem.*, 1965, 359 ff.

2 Augustus' plan: Dio, LVI, 33, 1. For the Sullan precedent, see J. Carcopino, *Sylla ou la monarchie manquée*, Paris, 1928, 222 ff. The procession through the *coloniae* and *municipia*: Suet., *Div. Aug.*, 100, 2 f.; Dio, LVI, 31, 2. The edict and first meeting of the Senate: Tac., *Ann.*, I, 7, 5 f.; 8; Suet., *Tib.*, 23, 1; Dio, LVI, 31, 2 ff.

3 Consecration of Augustus: *Fasti Amit.*, *CIL*² 1, 244; *Inscr. Ital.*, XIII, ii, 510 = *EJ*² 52; 13 October: Jos., *AJ*, XVIII, 6, 10; 3 September: K. Wellesley, *art. cit.* (n. V*), 27.

4 The slowness of the procession

was rightly emphasized by J. C. Tarver, *Tib. the Tyrant*, 81, and the figure of about fifteen days given by M. P. Charlesworth, *CAH*, X, 610, is in accord with the account given here; *cf.* also A. Lang, *op. cit.* (n. V*), 8 f. The timetable also fits that of the obsequies of Tiberius himself, for which Gaius used the Augustan precedent. Tiberius died at Misenum on 16 March 37; his body entered Rome on the 29th, preceded by Gaius, who entered on the 28th: *Fasti Ostiens., Inscr. Ital.*, XIII, i, 191 = *EJ*² 43; *Acta Fratr. Arv.*, ed. W. Henzen, xliii. The two routes to Rome converged at Sinuessa; before that the *cortège* of Tiberius passed through Cumae, Liternum, and Volturnum, two stages fewer than that of Augustus. Tiberius' body entered Rome thirteen days after his death; Augustus' should have taken two days longer to arrive.

5 Tiberius was cremated on 3 April: *Fasti Ostiens., loc. cit.* Marciana, who died at Rome on 29 August 112, was accorded a censor's funeral, probably on 3 September: *Fasti Ostiens., op. cit.*, 201 = E. M. Smallwood, *Documents illustrating the Principates of Nerva, Trajan and Hadrian*, Cambridge, 1966, 22 (I owe this point to the kindness of Mr F. A. Lepper).

6 See E. Liechtenhan, *MH*, 1947, 52 ff.; J. J. Wilkes, *CQ*, 1963, 268 ff.; Seager, *Tib.*, 58 ff. The attempt to proclaim Germanicus was not seriously meant; but the influence of soldiers recently recruited at Rome is emphasized by Tacitus, *Ann.*, I, 16, 4; 31, 4; the 'vernacula multitudo' would have no love for Tiberius.

7 Tac., *Ann.*, I, 46, 1, *cf.* Timpe, *Kontinuität*, 50 f.

8 This is the solution of P. A. Brunt, *JRS*, 1961, 238; the objections of Wellesley, *art. cit.* (n. V*), 25 f., are not conclusive. Another, better, explanation is that Drusus Caesar, in spite of Tacitus' words (*Ann.*, I, 14, 5) '... quod designatus consul praesensue erat', which seem to imply his presence at the debate, was already on his way to Pannonia. Tacitus by 'praesens' (a future participle would be preferable, but 'praefuturus' has a different sense) would mean 'domiciled at Rome'. Drusus' presence in the House would be no bar to a consular bill conferring *imperium proconsulare*. This solution is suggested in Gerber-Greef, *Lexicon Taciteum, s.v. praesens* (*cf. Ann.*, II, 26, 4), *cf.* also Flach, *art. cit.* (n. V*), 556 ff.

9 Tac., *Ann.*, I, 46, 1, *cf.* Lang, *op. cit.* (n. V*), 24 f.; Flach, *art. cit.*, 558.

10 Jos., *AJ*, XVIII, 224, *cf. BJ*, II, 190; *cf.* Béranger, *L'Aspect idéologique*, 24.

11 The claim of Suet., *Tib.*, 26, 2, *cf.* Dio, LVII, 2, 1, and 8, 1 f., that Tiberius refused to accept the title Augustus and used it only in his dealings with foreign potentates, is false: see *PIR*² C 941, p. 225, and M. Grant, *Aspects*, 41 f. (going beyond the evidence). No doubt Augustus asked for it to be taken (see Timpe, *Kontinuität*, 55, against Mommsen, *Staatsrecht*, II, ii³, 773), but Tiberius prevented the Senate from confirming the title. The view of Timpe, *loc. cit.*, that it was voted to him at the second meeting (on 17 September) contradicts Dio, who says that he never allowed it to be voted him. Tiberius' right to it continued to depend on Augustus' wishes, expressed in the will, and he had to permit its use for the sake of his own heirs; i.e., he

took it as Augustus' heir, not on his own merits. The title *pater patriae* was steadfastly refused: Suet., *Tib.*, 26, 2; 67, 2; Tac., *Ann.*, I, 72, 2 (AD 15); II, 87, 2 (19); Dio, LVII, 8, 1; LVIII, 12, 8 (31). It is ascribed to him by error in the Gytheion inscription of AD 15 (*AE*, 1929, 99 = *EJ²* 102); perhaps the offer of 15 was known, and the refusal not credited. For other occurrences see M. Grant, *Aspects*, 44. So with *imperator*. Tiberius' claim to the uncivil *praenomen* was greater in virtue of his military successes than that of the young Octavian; that perhaps was why he was offered it: he declined but it sometimes appears before or instead of Ti. in inscriptions: Suet., *Tib.*, 26, 2; Dio, LVII, 2, 1; 8, 1 f., *cf. ILS*, III, i, p. 262. In the oath of Palaipaphos space is twice left for the later insertion of the title (T. B. Mitford, *JRS*, 1960, 75 ff.).

12 *ILS*, 154; *Fasti Praen.*, *CIL* I², p. 233; *Fasti Vat.*, ibid., p. 242 = *EJ²* p. 47.

13 See Timpe, *Kontinuität*, 35 ff. Seager, *Tib.*, 53 f., believes that Tiberius' powers were defined in terms of those of Augustus; when Augustus died, they required redefinition: it was not powers that Tiberius lacked but a province. It was careless of Augustus to have Tiberius' powers defined in such a way that they would have to be conferred again when he died, especially as it was the purpose of his succession policy to avoid such an hiatus; and it would be a constitutional solecism for one man's power to require redefinition because another had died.

14 Fabia, *art. cit.* (n. V*), 53 ff.; Marsh, *loc. cit.* (n. V*); Hohl, *art. cit.* (n. V*); similarly Syme, *RR*, 438 f.;

Tac., I, 410 ff. (rightly suggesting that the debate petered out).

15 Béranger, *loc. cit.* (n. V*).

16 Suet., *Tib.*, 24, 1.

17 Tac., *Ann.*, XIII, 4, 3, an important passage drawn to my attention by Mr C. E. Stevens.

18 G. Kampff, *Phoen.*, 1963, 25 ff., with the bald statement that the consuls put forward a motion proposing Tiberius as Princeps for life.

19 Tac., *Ann.*, I, 6, 6, 'neve Tiberius vim principatus resolveret cuncta ad senatum vocando'.

20 Tac., *Ann.*, I, 11, 2.

21 The *libellus*; Tac., *Ann.*, I, 11, 5 ff.; Dio, LVI, 33, 2, brings it out at the meeting of 4 September: see Fabia, *art. cit.* (n. V*), 34 f. Tiberius' promise: Tac., *Ann.*, I, 12, 1 ff.: 'quaecumque pars sibi *mandaretur*, eius tutelam suscepturum', *cf.* Vell. Pat., II, 124, 2: 'quicquid *tuendum* non suscepisset, periturum videret'. Dio, LVII, 2, 4, speaks of a geographical distribution (Rome and Italy, armies, provinces); it is surely his own.

22 Asinius' ambitions: Tac., *Ann.*, I, 13, 2; on his remark: Fabia, *art. cit.* (n. V*), 37 ff.; Lang, *op. cit.* (n. V*), 18 ff.; on the man, Syme, *Tac.*, I, 381 f. He may have been one of the friends who, between sessions of the Senate, gave Tiberius private encouragement: Suet., *Tib.*, 24, 1.

23 For Q. Haterius' remark, see Fabia, *art. cit.* (n. V*), 44 f. For his connexions, see Tac., *Ann.*, II, 51, 1, with *PIR²* H 24 f. Tiberius' apology: Suet., *Tib.*, 29.

24 Tac., *Ann.*, I, 13, 6. Suet., *Tib.*, 24, 2 ('recepit imperium'), and Dio, LVII, 7, 1 (τὴν ἀρχὴν οὐδὲν ἔτι εἰρωνευόμενος ὑπεδέξατο), are misleadingly positive, perhaps because they knew that Tiberius, after all, was Princeps. Suetonius quotes Tiberius: 'dum veniam ad id tempus quo vobis aequum possit videri dare vos aliquam senectuti meae requiem'. It is regrettable that he did not tell us what Tiberius undertook to do until that time. Fabia, *art. cit.* (n. V*), 47, prefers the version of Suetonius.

25 Vell. Pat., II, 124, 2.

26 Tac., *Ann.*, I, 13, 4.

27 Vell. Pat., *loc. cit.*, *cf.* E. Koestermann, 'Statio Principis', *Phil.*, 1932, 358 ff.; 430 ff.; Béranger, *MH*, 1948, 194, n. 109.

28 'Suspicax animus': Tac., *Ann.*, I, 13, 4. Tiberius the scholar and philosopher quibbled over words (I, 46, 3). He particularly disliked being called 'auctor' (Suet., *Tib.*, 27). For another metaphor, see Ovid, *ex Ponto*, IV, 13, 27 f.: 'qui frena coactus saepe recusati ceperit imperii'.

29 Lang, *op. cit.* (n. V*), 10 f., claims categorically that Tacitus describes the events of one session, but rightly continues the discussion into October (22). Seager, *Tib.*, 55, denies that proconsular power could be conferred on Germanicus while Tiberius' own position remained unsettled, and claims that Velleius' account shows that the election arrangements of 14, 'the first of Tiberius' tasks as princeps', preceded the mutinies; he dates the accession to 17 September. But the constitutional powers of Tiberius were not in question, and if Velleius intends us to believe that mutinies followed accession it is only to protect Tiberius from such strictures as those of Tac., *Ann.*, I, 46.

30 See D. M. Pippidi, *Autour de Tibère*, 125 ff.

31 The oath: Tac., *Ann.*, I, 7, 1 ff.: 'Ruere in servitium consules, patres, eques . . .' On 4 September there was already a proposal that it should be renewed every year (8, 5). For its significance, see A. von Premerstein, *Vom Werden und Wesen des Prinzipats*, Munich, 1937, 57 ff.; Timpe, *Kontinuität*, 38 f.; P. Herrmann, *Der römische Kaisereid*, Göttingen, 1969, reviewed by J. Briscoe, *CR*, 1971, 260 ff. Danger: Vell., Pat., II, 124, 1, *cf.* above, Ch. IV, n. 65. The dispatch of Drusus to Pannonia might be a means of avoiding it.

32 'Maius aliquid et excelsius a principe postulatur' (Tac., *Ann.*, III, 54, 3). For *princeps* and Princeps see Timpe, *Kontinuität*, 33 ff.

CHAPTER VI

VI* For the coinage of Tiberius, see *CREBM*, I, 120 ff.; *RIC*, I, 98 ff.; Grant, *Aspects*, 1 ff. For the interpretation of Tiberian 'virtues', see M. P. Charlesworth, *Harvard Theological Review*, 1936, 107 ff.; *PBA*, 1937, 105 ff.; C. H. V. Sutherland, *JRS*, 1938, 129 ff.; Rogers, *Studies*, 3 ff.; Grant, *RAI*, 3 ff.; Sutherland, *CRIP*, 79 ff.; Béranger, *L'aspect idéologique*; Syme, *Tac.*, II, 754 ff.; H. Gesche, *Jahrb. f. Numismatik u. Geldgesch.*, 1971, 37 ff.; Levick, *The Ancient Historian and his Materials*, London, 1975, 123 ff.

1 See W. S. Ferguson, *AHR*, 1913, 32 f.

2 Oath to Augustus' *acta*: Dio, LI, 20, 1; LIII, 28, 1; by Tiberius: LVII, 8, 5. Apidius Merula lost his seat in 25: Tac., *Ann.*, IV, 42, 3.

3 Strabo, VI, p. 288: κανόνα τῆς

διοικήσεως καὶ τῶν προσταγμάτων
ποιούμενος ἐκεῖνον; Tac., Ann., I,
77, 4: 'neque fas Tiberio infringere
dicta eius' (on corporal punishment
for actors); IV, 37, 4: 'qui omnia
facta dictaque eius vice legis observem'
(on the building of temples to him in
the provinces); Agr., 13, 2: 'consilium id divus Augustus vocabat,
Tiberius praeceptum' (failure to invade Britain); cf. Ann., I, 14, 6; III,
24, 7: 'integras parentis sui offen-
siones'; VI, 3, 2: 'repperisse prorsus
quod divus Augustus non providerit'.
Cf. also II, 50, 2; 59, 3; III, 68, 1;
VI, 46, 3 (attributed by Tacitus).
4 CREBM, I, 124, no. 28 f.; 130, no.
74 f.; RIC, I, 95, no. 1 ff.; Sutherland, NC, 1941, 97 ff.; CRIP, 84 ff.;
Grant, RAI, 33 ff.; Aspects, 103 ff.;
C. M. Kraay, Die Münzfunde von Vindonissa, bis Trajan, Basel, 1962, 34 f.;
Th. Pékary, Schweiz. Münzbl., 1965,
128 f. The issues continue after 37.
Views are summarized by A. S.
Robertson, Roman Imperial Coins in
the Hunter Coin Cabinet, University of
Glasgow, I, 1962, liv f.
5 E. V. Arnold, Roman Stoicism,
Cambridge, 1911, 233.
6 Affection: Suet., Tib., 21, 4 ff.,
cf. Div. Aug., 51, 3; D. C. A. Shotter,
G and R, 1966, 207 ff., is puzzled by it
because he believes that Augustus'
dynastic policies 'contained little to
conciliate Tiberius'.
7 The temple to Augustus: Tac.,
Ann., VI, 45, 2; Suet., Tib., 47, 4, cf.
Dio, LVII, 10, 1. A shrine to the gens
Iulia and a statue were dedicated at
Bovillae in AD 17: Tac., Ann., II, 41, 1
(for numismatic references to the gens,
see Grant, Aspects, 92 ff.); a temple of
Augustus at Nola in 26: Suet., Tib.,
40. The sacrifice: Tac., Ann., IV, 52,

3, made, according to Furneaux and
Koestermann, ad loc., in his capacity
as Sodalis Augustalis (cf. I, 54, 2), but
evidently at home.
8 The documents: Tac., Ann., I, 11,
5 ff.; Suet., Div. Aug., 101, 4; Dio,
LVI, 33; Vell. Pat., II, 124, 3. The
view that Tiberius helped to draw up
the breviarium was put forward by
G. P. Baker, Tib., 144 f.
9 See above, Ch. I, n. 36.
10 Compare the views of A. H. M.
Jones, Essays in Roman Coinage Presented to H. Mattingly, Oxford, 1956,
13 ff., with those of C. H. V. Sutherland, JRS, 1959, 46 ff. For the
limitation of 'virtues' as evidence, see
F. W. Walbank, G and R, 1944, 30;
for their history, S. Weinstock, Divus
Julius, Oxford, 1971, 228 ff.
11 See D. C. Earl, The Moral and
Political Tradition of Rome, London,
1967, 1 ff. Tiberius himself adhered to
tradition in advancing politicians: see
Tac., Ann., I, 80, 3; 81, 2.
12 Tac., Ann., I, 72, 2: 'cuncta mor-
talium incerta'; II, 36, 3, on pride and
instability; III, 54 (cf. II, 33, 6), on
luxury, with the medical metaphor
favoured by conservative moralists
(see R. M. Ogilvie ad Livy, II, 32,
8 ff.). Tiberius' seeming misgivings
about his own character and mental
poise (Suet., Tib., 67, 2 ff.) should not
be taken seriously; they are arguments adduced ad hoc.
13 The laws to be enforced: Tac.,
Ann., I, 72, 5; II, 36, 5; better re-
pealed than ineffective: IV, 30, 4;
dire consequences of their neglect:
III, 54, 3 f.; law versus imperium: III,
69, 7: 'ne verterent sapienter reperta
et semper placita; satis onerum principibus, satis etiam potentiae. Minui
iura, quotiens gliscat potestas, nec

utendum imperio, ubi legibus agi possit.'
14 Position and responsibility of the Princeps: Tac., *Ann.*, I, 47, 2 ff.: '...
maiestate salva, cui maior e longinquo reverentia ... Quod aliud subsidium, si imperatorem sprevissent?' (a view imputed to Tiberius), *cf.* III, 47, 2 f.; 'neque decorum principibus ... omissa urbe, unde in omnia regimen'; III, 3, 1: 'inferius maiestate sua' (imputed view); 6, 2: 'non enim eadem decora principibus viris ... quae modicis domibus'; 53, 4: 'maius aliquid et excelsius a principe postulatur'; 54, 8: 'hanc ... curam [the corn supply] sustinet princeps'; IV, 8, 8: 'ita nati estis [Nero and Drusus Caesar] ut bona malaque vestra ad rem publicam pertineant'; 40, 1: 'principum diversam esse sortem'.
15 See above, p. 76, Ch. I, n. 36, and n. 14, for Tiberius' remarks on the subject, and add Tac., *Ann.*, II, 87, 2; III, 35, 1; 47, 5; 59, 2; IV, 38, 1 ff.; Suet., *Tib.*, 26 ff. Note especially the remark about *auctoritas* (I owe this observation to Mr C. E. Stevens). The historians' verdict: Tac., *Ann.*, IV, 6, 2; Suet., *Tib.*, 26 ff.; Dio, LVII, 7, 2 ff.
16 For Concordia on coins, see *CREBM*, I, 91, no. 544 f.; 124 ff., no. 30 ff., with K. Kraft, *Zur Münzprägung des Augustus*, Wiesbaden, 1969, 248 f.; the figure has been taken for Pax (H. Mattingly, *CREBM*, I, *ad loc.*) and Salus (J. Liegle, *Herm.*, 1942, 304). Concord, according to Sallust, belongs to the years before Carthage fell in 146: see D. C. Earl, *Political Thought of Sallust*, Cambridge, 1961, 33. Rebuilding of the temple: see above, Ch. III, pp. 36–37, with n. 27 f., Ch. IV, p. 62, with

n. 56. Feriae: Fasti Verul., Inscr. Ital., XIII, ii, 161. Libo Drusus: Tac., *Ann.*, II, 32, 3. The dedications: *CIL*, VI, 91 ff., 904, 3674 (3075 = 30856); *ILS*, 3783; *EJ*² 215); discussed by Th. Pekáry, *Röm. Mitt.*, 1966–67, 105 ff., who argues for dating them to the period immediately before Sejanus' fall in 31. I see them rather as voluntary offerings made after the precedent had been set in 16 by the official dedications. The interpretation given in the text does not preclude an allusion to the *concordia* of the brothers Tiberius and Nero Drusus, Drusus and Germanicus Caesar; for the cousins Ti. Gemellus and Caligula see Gesche, *art. cit.*, 62 f.
17 The statues: Dio, LIV, 35, 2, *cf.* Ovid, *Fasti*, III, 881 f. (Salus, Concordia, Pax); see Grant, *Aspects*, 81. Marius: Val. Max., VIII, 6, 2. Connotations of Salus: above, Ch. III, p. 34; and sources cited in *Lat.*, 1972, 802, n. 2; 803, n. 3. Augustus 'cum sciret quis volenti omnia post se salva remanere accersendus foret ... revocavit filium': Vell. Pat., II, 123, 1. Salus on the coins: *CREBM*, I, 131, no. 81 ff.; *RIC*, I, 106, no. 23; n. 16 above. Interamna: *ILS*, 157 (= *EJ*² 51); 'salutaris princeps': Suet., *Tib.*, 29; Val. Max., II, 9, 6; VIII, 13 pr., *cf.* I pr.
18 For *pax*, see Grant, *Aspects*, 77 ff. Philo, *Leg.*, 141 (*cf.* 8), is eloquent, *cf.* Vell. Pat., II, 126, 3; 131, 1. Tiberius' concern for peace abroad is mentioned by Tac., *Ann.*, II, 64, 2 (perhaps it was expressed to the Senate); 65, 1; IV, 6, 7; VI, 32, 1. His preoccupation with order in the Senate is orally expressed in I, 80, 2: 'ne ambitu comitia turbarent'. Hopes raised by the adoption: Vell. Pat., II,

104, 5. Tiberius' actions do show concern for *quies* and *pax*; they are dealt
with in Chs. VIII and IX. *Tranquillitas* was a word Tiberius favoured (IV,
40, 8; N. P. Miller, *AJP*, 1968, 15);
he cared for his own peace by retreating to Capri; an edict enjoined 'ne
quis quietem eius inrumperet' (IV, 67,
1, *cf.* the language of his letter to
Sejanus, 40, 7: 'qui te invitum per-
rumpunt'), *cf.* III, 15, 4; unexpected
callers had a rough welcome: Suet.,
Tib., 60. Concern for his peace of
mind: Tac., *Ann.*, IV, 38, 3: 'quietam
. . . mentem duint'. It is not for the
historian to speculate on causal connexions between Tiberius' desire for
quies in the state and for himself: but
for the 'strain of violence in Tiberius'
see Syme, *Tac.*, II, 701.
19 Tac., *Ann.*, IV, 71, 4: 'nullam
aeque . . . ex virtutibus suis . . . dili-
gebat'; *cf.* I, 75, 4, and Vell. Pat., II,
126, 4; 'oderint dum probent': Suet.,
Tib., 59, 2. Care for his reputation:
Tac., *Ann.*, VI, 46, 4, with Furneaux, *ad
loc.*, and IV, 38, 1 (*cf.* III, 54, 1; IV, 40,
1). Virtue as the hypocrite's mask: W.
Süss, *Ethos*, Leipzig, etc., 1910, 251 ff.
20 Tiberius claims, or is ascribed,
clementia: Tac., *Ann.*, II, 31, 4; III,
50, 3 (by implication); 68, 2; VI, 25,
4 (by implication), *cf.* III, 22, 4; IV,
31, 2 (he is aware of the reputation it
gives); 42, 3 ('inclementiam'); VI, 1,
4 (sarcastic); 14, 4 (denied); 25, 5,
cf. Suet., *Tib.*, 53, 2. *Clementia* is
assigned a chapter by Val. Max., V,
1. The virtue is treated by Weinstock,
op. cit., 233 ff.; a word to be avoided:
236; and Charlesworth, *art. cit.*, 1937,
112 f.; Grant, *RAI*, 48 f.; Syme, *Tac.*,
II, 703. For the Clupeus, see *RG*, 34,
2; for *virtus* in general, Earl, *op. cit.*,
18 ff.

21 Suet., *Tib.*, 17, 2.
22 For *pietas*, see Weinstock, *op. cit.*,
248 ff., and Syme, *Tac.*, I, 415. On
the coinage: *CREBM*, I, 133, no. 98,
discussed by Grant, *RAI*, 35 ff., and
see Weinstock, *op. cit.*, 255, n. 8.
Note the Ara Pietatis Augustae
vowed in 22 during Livia's illness but
dedicated only by Claudius: *ILS*, 202;
Tac., *Ann.*, III, 64, 3, *cf. ILS*, 3785.
Vell. Pat., II, 99, 2, ascribes Tiberius'
departure in 6 BC to 'mira quaedam et
incredibilis atque inenarrabilis pietas',
cf. 105, 3; 130, 1 ('pia munificentia').
Tiberius' *pietas* towards his brother
Drusus is a theme of Val. Max., V, 5, 3;
but the section on 'pietas erga parentes'
(V, 4) is silent on the Princeps. For implied changes in the Principate, see
Vell. Pat., II, 126, 2.
23 Vell. Pat., II, 129, 3, attributes the
defeat of Florus and Sacrovir to
Tiberius' *virtus*. Marius: Weinstock,
op. cit., 231 f.
24 The coins: *CREBM*, I, 132, no.
85 ff., n. *; *RIC*, I, 107, no. 30 f. The
altar: Tac., *Ann.*, IV, 74, 3. For the
date of the *dupondii*, see Sutherland,
CRIP, 191 ff. (22–23), Grant, *RAI*,
47 ff., and Gesche, *art. cit.* (n. VI*)
(34–37). For their interpretation, see
Sutherland, *art. cit.* (n. VI*); and
CRIP, 97 f.; Rogers, *Studies*, 35 ff.;
Gesche, *art. cit.*, 48 ff.; and Levick,
art. cit. (n. VI*). The view that shields
were presented to Tiberius was
originated by R. Mowat, *RN*, 1911,
335 f.
25 Clutorius' death: Tac., *Ann.*, III,
51, 2 f.; Antistius Vetus tried for
maiestas: 38, 2.
26 Bato: Suet., *Tib.*, 20 (an example of *fides* rather than of *clementia*).
Rogers, *Studies*, 42 ff., cites favourable
responses made to Maroboduus and

Catualda in 19: Tac., *Ann.*, II, 63, 1 f.; 6.

27 Tiberius' forbearance: Tac., *Ann.*, VI, 25, 4 f.

28 Libo Drusus: Levick, *art. cit.* (n. VI*). Nero: Tac., *Ann.*, XIV, 12, 5 f. ('lenitas'); Vitellius: *CREBM*, I, 384, no. 78 ff.; and Tac., *Hist.*, I, 75: 'Vitellius victor clementiae gloriam tulit.'

29 *Moderatio* (or what gives rise to it, *modestia*) claimed by Tiberius: Tac., *Ann.*, II, 36, 2: 'grave moderationi suae tot eligere, tot differre'; III, 12, 11: 'cetera pari modestia tractentur'. Practised by him: I, 7, 6: 'verba edicti fuere pauca et sensu permodesto'; 14, 3: 'moderandos feminarum honores dictitans eademque se temperantia usurum in iis quae sibi tribuerentur' (*cf.* V, 2, 1); III, 12, 1: 'orationem habuit meditato temperamento'; 69, 8: 'prudens moderandi'; *cf.* II, 29, 2; V, 2, 1; VI, 2, 6; 45, 2. Ascribed to him by others: III, 50, 2: 'principis moderatio'; 56, 1: 'fama moderationis parta'; 4: 'modestiae Neronis' (Augustus' view); IV, 38, 4 (one view of Tiberius' refusal of the temple in Baetica); I, 8, 6 ('adroganti moderatione'), is a jibe at Tiberius' cardinal virtue; it is implausibly taken in an active sense (= Tiberius restrained the senators) by D. C. Shotter, *Mnem.*, 1965, 364. *Moderatio* is ascribed to Tiberius by Vell. Pat., II, 122, 1, and by Suet., *Tib.*, 32, 2, *cf.* 57, 1: 'moderationis simulatione'; it is celebrated by Valerius Maximus, IV, 1, with C. Claudius Nero as one prize specimen, and the 'cunctatio' of Camillus in taking up his powers another (I, 2; 9). An exhaustive collection of material has been made by Rogers,

Studies, 60 ff.; not all relevant to the present purpose; *cf.* Béranger, *L'Aspect idéologique*, 159.

30 *Cf.* Sen., *de Clem.*, II, 3, 1 f., with Gesche, *art. cit.*, 74, n. 143.

31 Tac., *Ann.*, III, 54, 5.

32 *Iustitia:* see Weinstock, *op. cit.*, 243 ff. Coins: *CREBM*, I, 131, no. 79 f., with Sutherland, *CRIP*, 97 f. Inscriptions: *ILS*, 159 (AD 32–33) and 3783 (one of the dedications to Concordia, see above, n. 16). Val. Max., VI, 5, is devoted to *iustitia* and Vell. Pat., II, 126, 2, considers it one of the benefits of the regime.

33 '. . . mihi . . . intellegentem humani divinique iuris mentem duint', Tac., *Ann.*, IV, 38, 3. Instances of expertise: I, 62, 3 (*cf.* Koestermann, *ad loc.*, and E. Badian, *Arethusa*, I, 1968, 45, n. 57); 73, 4; 76, 2; III, 64, 4 f.; 71, 3 f.; VI, 12, 1 (all 'divini iuris'; for the importance that Tiberius attached to the supreme pontificate, see Grant, *Aspects*, 45); III, 21, 4; IV, 19, 2 f. (rights of consuls and proconsuls), *cf.* II, 30, 3. See also above, n. 11. Cocceius Nerva: IV, 58, 1; VI, 26, 1; *Dig.*, I, 2, 2, 48.

34 So F. W. Walbank, *G and R*, 1944, 30. *Liberalitas* is not mentioned on coins until the principate of Hadrian; Val. Max. assigns it a chapter (IV, 8), but Tiberius did not like it celebrated: Dio, LVII, 17, 8.

35 Tac., *Ann.*, I, 75, 4 (compensation to Aurelius Pius and subvention to Propertius Celer and possibly to others): 'virtutem diu retinuit' (*cf.* Dio, LVII, 17, 8); II, 48, 1: 'grata liberalitate, quod bona . . . locupletis intestatae . . . Aemilio Lepido . . . et . . . divitis equitis Romani hereditatem . . . tradidit M. Servilio . . . nobilitatem utriusque pecunia iuvandam praefatus'; III, 8, 2: 'sucta erga filios familiarum nobiles liberalitate'; VI, 45, 1: 'damnum [of the fire on the Aventine in 36] ad gloriam vertit'; *cf.* Suet., *Tib.*, 48; *Div. Claud.*, 6, 2. Other examples are plentiful, and lack any suggestion of self-consciousness, but Velleius harps on *munificentia* and *liberalitas*: II, 126, 4; 130, 1 f.

36 The Gallic revolt: Tac., *Ann.*, III, 47, 1: 'se consiliis superfuisse'. *Prudentia* in war is ascribed to Tiberius by Vell. Pat., II, 111, 4, *cf.* 129, 1 ff. ('astu' in Tac., *Ann.*, II, 64, 2), and Suet., *Tib.*, 18, 1, 'caelestis providentia' in general by Val. Max., I, pr; the 'consilium' and 'providentia' displayed by Nero and Salinator in the Hannibalic War (*id.*, VII, 4, 4), may be noted. Philo, *Leg.*, 33, speaks of Tiberius as φρονήσει βαθείᾳ χρώμενος, *cf.* 142: καὶ ἔτι νέος ὢν ὁ πρεσβύτης ἐλέγετο δι᾽ αἰδῶ τὴν περὶ τὴν ἀγχίνοιαν. Tac., *Ann.*, VI, 46, 5, has him 'providus futurorum' in the sense that men might connect with his astrological skill. PROVIDENTIA occurs on *aes* commemorating Augustus: *CREBM*, I, 143, n. *; *RIC*, I, 95, no. 6; it is discussed by Grant, *RAI*, 63 f.; for the date, see Gesche, *art. cit.*, 64 f., connecting it with the securing of the succession. For *providentia* in general see Charlesworth, *art. cit.* (n. VI*); Rogers, *Studies*, 20 ff.; Béranger, *L'Aspect idéologique*, 210 ff.

37 See Rogers, *Studies*, 26 ff.; Syme, *Tac.*, I, 416; *ILS*, 157 f., *cf.* A. B. West, *Corinth*, VIII, ii, Cambridge, Mass., 1931, 90, no. 5, and 110 (a cult of *Providentia Aug.* and *Salus Publica*). Val. Max., IX, 11, ext. 4, also refers to *providentia* in the context of Sejanus' conspiracy. *Cf.* Cic., *in Cat.*, III, 6, 14.

38 Tac., *Ann.*, I, 13, 4: 'suspicax animus'; II, 30, 3: 'callidus'; XI, 3, 2: 'calliditas'.

39 Tac., *Ann.*, IV, 38, 1: 'rerum vestrarum [the Senate] providum'; III, 54, 8 (Rome and Italy).

40 Strabo, XIII, p. 627 (πρόνοια); Jos., *AJ*, XVIII, 172 (προμήθεια), *cf.* Tac., *Ann.*, IV, 6, 7: 'ne provinciae … turbarentur providebat'.

41 Tac., *Ann.*, IV, 38, 1, *cf.* 37, 3. *Constantia* a Stoic virtue (εὐπάθεια): Cic., *Tusc.*, IV, 5, 10; 6, 14; 21, 47; see Grant, *NC*, 1950, 23 ff.; Syme, *Tac.*, II, 544. For Tiberius and his troops, see Vell. Pat., II, 114, 3.

42 Suet., *Div. Iul.*, 75, 1.

43 Val. Max., IV, 1, 1 ff.; 11; 15. See Weinstock, *op. cit.*, 229.

CHAPTER VII

VII* See Tac., *Ann.*, I ff.; Suet., *Tib.*, 26 ff.; Dio, LVII f. H. Furneaux, *The Annals of Tacitus*, I, 89 ff.; J. C. Tarver, *Tib. the Tyrant*, 353 ff.; E. Ciaceri, *Tib. successore di Aug.*, 246 ff.; and Seager, *Tib.*, 123 ff., have treated the topic.

1 *Maiestas* of the Senate: Vell. Pat., II, 126, 2. The Augustan *consilium*: Dio, LIII, 21, 4 (27 BC); LVI, 28, 2 (AD 13); Suet., *Div. Aug.*, 35, 2; *SEG*, IX, 8 (= *EJ*² 311), line 87; Tiberius: Suet., *Tib.*, 55; Dio, LVII, 7, 3; LX, 4, 3; see J. A. Crook, *Consilium Principis*, Cambridge, 1955, 8 ff.; Syme, *RR*, 408, n. 3.

2 Tac., *Ann.*, IV, 6, 2; 15, 3, *cf.* Suet., *Tib.*, 30: 'neque tam parvum quicquam neque tam magnum publici privatique negotii fuit, de quo non ad patres conscriptos referretur'; Dio, LVII, 7, 2.

3 E.g., Tiberius requests privileges for Nero Caesar in AD 20: Tac., *Ann.*, III, 29, 1; informs the Senate of Tacfarinas' rising in 21 and tells them that they must choose a competent governor (cf. II, 86, 1, on recruiting a Vestal; IV, 16, 1, on the Flamen Dialis); initiates a *senatus consultum* in response to 'preces sociorum' in 23: IV, 13, 1; draws the Senate's attention to the need to deal with 'immodestia histrionum' in the same year: IV, 14, 1, cf. III, 37, 1. For other punitive measures, see III, 37, 1; Suet., *Vit.*, 2, 2.

4 Tiberius' intervention was not always decisive: Suet., *Tib.*, 31, 3 f.; Dio, LVII, 7, 3. Its form: Tac., *Ann.*, III, 53, 2; Dio, *loc. cit.*, 4; 21, 1.

5 See Vell. Pat., II, 126, 4: 'facere recte cives suo . . . faciendo docet; cumque sit imperio maximus, exemplo maior est'. Training the Senate: Tac., *Ann.*, III, 35, 11; 47, 5; 51, 2 (AD 21); 59, 2 (22); IV, 6, 2 (down to 23); VI, 13, 2 (32); Suet., *Tib.*, 26 ff. Aware of being a cynosure: Tac., *Ann.*, III, 53, 1.

6 Tac., *Ann.*, I, 75, 3; III, 31, 4 ff.

7 Tac., *Ann.*, I, 8, 4 ff. (Augustus); II, 83; IV, 9, 2 f. (honours to Germanicus and Drusus); III, 48, 1 (Sulpicius Quirinius); IV, 15, 3 (Lucilius Longus); VI, II, 6 (L. Piso the pontifex); 27, 2 (L. Lamia).

8 Tac., *Ann.*, III, 24.

9 Tiberius refers appeals to the Senate: Tac., *Ann.*, I, 75, 6 f., confirmed by Vell. Pat., II, 129, 3. Hortalus: Tac., *Ann.*, II, 37 f. Generosity to 'nobilitas': 48, 1 ff.

10 Tac., *Ann.*, II, 48, 3, with Suet., *Vit.*, 2, 2, for the procedure.

11 Appianus: T. P. Wiseman, *HSCP*, 1968, 220; Marius Nepos:

Sen., *de Ben.*, II, 7, 2 ff.; for Q. Vitellius, his brother's success, and an attack on them by Cassius Severus, see Suet., *Vit.*, 2.

12 Tac., *Ann.*, II, 33; III, 52 ff. For senatorial fears, see D. Daube, *Roman Law, Linguistic, Social, and Philosophical Aspects*, Edinburgh, 1969, 117 ff. Augustus' legislation is mentioned by A. Gell, *NA*, II, 24, 14; Suet., *Div. Aug.*, 34, 1; Dio, LIV, 2, 3 (22 BC). Augustus or Tiberius is credited with an edict raising the sum allowed for banquets (A. Gell, *loc. cit.*); for other Tiberian measures, see Suet., *Tib.*, 34; Pliny, *NH*, XXXIII, 32 f.

13 Tac., *Ann.*, I, 15, 1; Vell. Pat., II, 124, 3. See Jones, *Studies*, 46 f.; Syme, *Tac.*, II, 756 ff.; R. Frei-Stolba, *Untersuchungen zu den Wahlen in der römischen Kaiserzeit*, 136 ff. I cannot accept the interpretation of E. S. Staveley, *Greek and Roman Voting and Elections*, London, 1972, 220. See also Dio, LVIII, 20, 3 (electoral manoeuvres); Tac., *Ann.*, XIV, 28, 1 (competition), with Jones, *Studies*, 47 f.

14 Tac., *Ann.*, II, 51. Koestermann, *ad loc.*, argues from the *lex Malacitana* (*ILS*, 6089), LVI, that the candidates had obtained the same number of votes. More probably candidates with fewer children were disqualified.

15 Pliny, *Ep.*, III, 20, 2.

16 Tac., *Ann.*, I, 81, 3. D. C. Shotter discusses this passage, in *CQ*, NS XVI, 1966, 321 ff.; I can accept only some details of his interpretation.

17 Dio, LIX, 20, 4.

18 Dio, LIII, 21, 6 f. (Augustus).

19 On the *Fasti* between AD 5 and 31, see G. Tibiletti, *Principe e Magistrati Repubblicani*, 239 ff. *Nobiles* favoured: Marsh, *Reign*, 116; *Novi* *homines*: R. Sealey, *Phoen.*, 1961, 111. The view of Grant, *Aspects*, 55, n. 20, commends itself.

20 Tac., *Ann.*, IV, 6, 2.

21 Tac., *Ann.*, XI, 21, 3.

22 See, e.g., Orth, *Provinzialpolitik*, 100 f. Dio, LIX, 9, 5, attests neglect late in the principate.

23 *ILS*, 212.

24 See T. P. Wiseman, *New Men in the Roman Senate 139 B.C.–A.D. 14*, Oxford, 1971, nos. 415 (C. Stertinius Maximus of Hasta), 336 (C. Pontius Paelignus of Brixia), 442 (T. Trebellenus Rufus of Concordia), 304 (Sex. Palpellius Hister of Pola), 88 (C. Caetronius of ?Atria); note also nos. 517 f., senators of uncertain date from Aquileia and Pola. Tiberius was familiar with Cisalpina at least from 11 BC (see above, pp. 31 ff.); his child by Julia had been born at Aquileia (Suet., *Tib.*, 7, 3).

25 *Contra*, Jones, *Studies*, 30 ff., neglecting Suet., *Div. Vesp.*, 2, 2.

26 Vell. Pat., II, 124, 4.

27 *ILS*, 946.

28 Wiseman, *op. cit.*, no. 330, with references.

29 Wiseman, *op. cit.*, nos. 5, 149.

30 See *PIR*² I 756 (Gallio); A 617 (Seneca); S. J. de Laet, *Samenstelling*, no. 719 (Pedanius Secundus); 852 (Umbonius Silo); *PIR*² I 344 f. (L. and M. Iulius Graecinus); de Laet, *op. cit.*, no. 812; *ILS*, 212 (Valerius Asiaticus and his brother); *PIR*² D 126 (Domitius Afer); de Laet, *op. cit.*, no. 804 (Togonius Gallus); Levick, *Roman Colonies in Southern Asia Minor*, 107 f. (M. Calpurnius Rufus).

31 Tac., *Ann.*, VI, 2, 2 ff. (Togonius and Gallio); Dio, LX, 24, 5 f. (Silo).

32 The principle: Tac., *Ann.*, III, 53, 3 (AD 22). Practice: I, 7, 4: 'nam Tiberius cuncta per consules incipiebat . . . ne edictum quidem . . . nisi tribuniciae potestatis praescriptione posuit' (AD 14); IV, 6, 3: 'sua consulibus, sua praetoribus species; minorum quoque magistratuum exercita potestas' (up to 23). *Cf.* Vell. Pat., II, 126, 2; Suet., *Tib.*, 30, 1; 31, 2 f.; Dio, LVII, 11, 2 (up to 19); note his absenting himself from Rome on 1 January, partly to avoid obscuring the glory of the consuls on their first day of office (Dio, LVII, 8, 5), and his communications with the consuls as late as 33 (LVIII, 21, 3).

33 Tac., *Ann.*, I, 77.

34 Tac., *Ann.*, XIII, 28.

35 Tac., *Ann.*, III, 33 f.; IV, 20, 4, *cf. Dig.*, I, 16, 4, 2, with Orth, *op. cit.*, 65 ff.

36 Polyb., VI, 13, 1.

37 The generals: E. Badian, *Roman Imperialism in the late Republic*, 2nd ed., Oxford, 1968, 76 ff. Wealth of the Principes: Lucan, III, 168 (a reference which I owe to Mr C. E. Stevens). Subsidies: *RG*, 17. Working of the imperial system: Jones, *Studies*, 99 ff.; P. A. Brunt, *JRS*, 1966, 75 ff.

38 *RG*, 17; Dio, LV, 24, 9 ff.; 32, 2; Tac., *Ann.*, I, 78, 2; II, 42, 6.

39 Tac., *Ann.*, I, 75, 6 f.; II, 38, 8; Vell. Pat., II, 129, 3 ('senatu auctore'), *cf.* Dio, LVII, 10, 3.

40 Tac., *Ann.*, I, 75, 4.

41 Tac., *Ann.*, II, 47, 3. See Brunt, *art. cit.*, 86, n. 74. For consultation of the Senate 'de vectigalibus et monopoliis' as normal Tiberian practice, see Suet., *Tib.*, 30. It is not clear if reference was made to the Senate in 17 about the reduction of the 'centesima rerum venalium': Tac., *Ann.*, II, 42, 6, *cf.* I, 78, 2, and Dio, LVIII, 16, 2.

42 Tac., *Ann.*, IV, 13, 1 (three years' remission).

43 Tac., *Ann.*, IV, 20, 1 f.: 'ea prima Tiberio erga pecuniam alienam diligentia fuit'; VI, 2, 1 (Sejanus); 19, 1 (property of Sex. Marius).

44 Tac., *Ann.*, VI, 16 ff., and see above, pp. 104-5, 133.

45 The Vestal: Tac., *Ann.*, II, 86; the Senate's role, taken over from the people: A. Gell, *NA*, I, 12, 12; Dio, LV, 22, 6. Maluginensis: Tac., *Ann.*, III, 58 f.; 71. His son: IV, 16. Authority of Pontifex Maximus: A. H. M. Jones, *Criminal Courts*, 10. Priestly elections: A. N. Sherwin-White *ad* Pliny. *Ep.*, IV, 8, 3. Sibylline Books: Tac., *Ann.*, VI, 12, 1 ff.; see above, p. 218. Augustus' interest in the maintenance of traditional religion: Suet., *Div. Aug.*, 31, 2 f.; Dio, LIV, 36, 1.

46 *SEG*, IX, 8 (= *EJ*², 311), lines 72 ff.

47 *Dig.*, XL, 1, 24, *cf.* XLVIII, 8, 11, 2 (*lex Iunia Petronia* of 19); Tac., *Ann.*, IV, 16, 4 f. (23); *Cod. Iust.*, IX, 21; 31, 1 (*lex Visellia* of 24 (?); see Mommsen, *St.*, III, i, 424, n. 3); Gaius, *Inst.*, II, 134; *Dig.*, XXVIII, 2, 29; *Inst. Iust.*, II, 13, 2 (*lex Iunia Vellaea* (?) of 28). In general see Mommsen, *St.*, III, i, 346, and H. Jolowicz, *Historical Introduction to Roman Law*, 2nd ed., Cambridge, 1954, 365 ff.; 372 ff. *Leges* were employed by Claudius.

48 Tac., *Ann.*, III, 25 ff.; differently interpreted by R. Bauman, *Impietas in Principem*, 54.

49 Tac., *Ann.*, III, 36; see above, p. 194.

50 Tac., *Ann.*, III, 60 ff., especially 63, 1.

51 Tac., *Ann.*, IV, 30, 3 ff.

52 Tac., *Ann.*, VI, 16 ff.; Suet., *Tib.*, 48, 1, where the loan is treated as an act of public munificence; Dio, LVIII, 21, 4 ff., showing that Tiberius himself made the sum over to the Aerarium for the purpose of the loan.

53 See below, Ch. XI, n. 29.

54 Jones, *Studies*, 69 ff.; J. Bleicken, *Senatsgericht und Kaisergericht*, Göttingen, 1962, 53 ff.; P. Garnsey, *Social Status and Legal Privilege in the Roman Empire*, Oxford, 1970, 17 ff. Murder: Tac., *Ann.*, III, 12, 10.

55 Tac., *Ann.*, XIII, 4, 3 (Italy and the 'public' provinces), *cf.* Polyb., VI, 13, 4 f. (Italy), *cf.* 7 (foreign affairs). Furneaux and Koestermann *ad loc.* give examples of senatorial activity in Italy (Nero and early Vespasian) and the 'public' provinces (Claudius and Nero).

56 The flood of AD 15: Tac., *Ann.*, I, 76, *cf.* 79; the delimitation of 8-7 BC: *ILS*, 5923 a-d (Gallus), 5924 a-d (Augustus). The permanent board: Dio, LVII, 14, 8. Suet., *Div. Aug.*, 37, 2, includes the *Curatores* among the boards devised by Augustus: 'curam operum publicorum, viarum, aquarum, alvei Tiberis, frumenti populo dividundi, praefecturam urbis, triumviratum legendi senatus et alterum recognoscendi turmas equitum'. This testimony is rejected by Mommsen, *St.*, II, ii², 1046, n. 2; but according to Koestermann, *ad loc.*, the two commissioners were acting as heads of the *Curatores . . . Tiberis* and of the *Curatores Aquarum*; Capito headed the latter from 13 to 22 (Front., *de Aquis*, II, 102). The record commission: Dio, LVII, 16, 2, *cf.* *ILS*, 972; for another example, see above, p. 105, and another Augustan precedent, a three-man economy commission, chosen by lot: Dio, LV, 25, 6 (AD 6).

57 The Senate's involvement in public works under Tiberius: Suet., *Tib.*, 30; M. Lepidus: Tac., *Ann.*, III, 72, 3; the theatre of Pompey: 72, 4, *cf.* VI, 45, 2.

58 Tac., *Ann.*, II, 85, *cf.* Jos., *AJ*, XVIII, 65 ff.

59 Actors: Tac., *Ann.*, IV, 14, 4 (on the motion of Tiberius), *cf.* Suet., *Tib.*, 37, 2; Dio, LVII, 21, 3. For the appeal of Florentia and the other towns, and other Italian business dealt with by the Senate, see Tac., *Ann.*, I, 79; II, 35, 3 (AD 16); Suet., *Tib.*, 31, 1 (Trebia, no date). The catastrophe at Fidena: IV, 63, 3 f.

60 Tac., *Ann.*, III, 60 ff., *cf.* IV, 14 (AD 23). Tiberius referred embassies from the senatorial province of Africa to the consuls: Suet., *Tib.*, 31, 2, *cf.* Tac., *Ann.*, IV, 37, 1 (Baetica). For the intertwining roles of Senate and Princeps in the provinces see F. Millar, *JRS*, 1966, 156 ff.

61 Earthquake relief: Tac., *Ann.*, II, 47, 4 f. Achaea and Macedonia: Tac., *Ann.*, I, 76, 4; the Senate decided (at whose suggestion?) to transfer the provinces to imperial control; *cf.* 80, 1. Syria and Judaea: II, 42, 7; mentioned in the Senate: 43, 1.

62 See above, p. 21; Pollio: *Cat. of Coins of the Roman Empire in the Ashmolean Museum*, I, Oxford, 1975, 1363.

63 Tac., *Ann.*, IV, 15, 4 ff.; 37, 4; 55 f.

64 Tac., *Ann.*, IV, 43.

65 Achaea and Macedonia: Tac., *Ann.*, I, 80, 1. Sparta free: A. H. M. Jones, *The Greek City*, Oxford, 1940, 129. Aegium: Tac., *Ann.*, IV, 13, 1.

66 Tac., *Ann.*, III, 12, 2, *cf.* II, 43, 3: 'praefecerat Pisonem [sc. Tiberius]'.

67 'Militis commoda': Tac., *Ann.*, I, 26, 5 f.; Report to the Senate: Tac., *Ann.*, I, 52, 2 (*cf.* Suet., *Tib.*, 30); IV, 4, 4 ff. For the legal position, see P. A. Brunt, *ZfPE*, 1974, 162 ff. The edict: 78, 2 f., with 79, 1: 'Actum *deinde* in senatu . . .'

68 Tac., *Ann.*, VI, 3, 1 f.

69 Imperial auspices: *AE*, 1940, 68 (= *EJ*² 43). Tiberius referred envoys from Africa to the consuls: Suet., *Tib.*, 31, 2. The choice of Blaesus: Tac., *Ann.*, III, 32; 35. For Lepidus, see Syme, *JRS*, 1955, 22 ff.

70 The Augustan system: Suet., *Div. Aug.*, 47; Dio, LIII, 13 f.; Mommsen, *St.*, II, i³, 243 ff. Five-year interval: *lex Pompeia* of 52 BC: Dio, XL, 56, 1. Debate is implied by Caes., *BC*, I, 5, 9, *cf.* the prorogation of imperial favourites such as Eprius Marcellus, *PIR*² E 84. Blaesus was prorogued by the Senate in 22: Tac., *Ann.*, III, 58, 1, *cf.* Syme, *Tac.*, I, 441. Debate on the merits of candidates: Tac., *Ann.*, III, 32, 2; Suet., *Tib.*, 30, 2: 'denique quibus imperium prorogari aut extraordinaria bella mandari' (a generalization from the discussion of 21, according to Orth, *Provinzialpolitik*, 41).

71 Dolabella's proposal: Tac., *Ann.*, III, 69, 1 ff. (Val. Max., VI, 9, takes up Tiberius' theme of 'mutatio morum'). C. Galba: VI, 40, 3; Suet., *Galba*, 3, 4. Galba was impoverished and killed himself not at the dishonour but because he had lost his chance of restoring his fortunes: see Orth, *Provinzialpolitik*, 70, n. 3. It would be worth knowing to whom Tiberius' grim letter was addressed. When he declared against the candidature of Maluginensis (see above, p. 102) he was motivated by regard for the law

or for Augustan precedent (so Orth, *op. cit.*, 48).

72 Tiberius' complaint: Tac., *Ann.*, VI, 27, 3. Dio, LVIII, 23, 5, attributes the shortage to Tiberius' executions. The regulation of AD 15: LVII, 14, 5. Absentee governors: Tac., *Ann.*, I, 80, 4; VI, 27, 2; Suet., Tib., 63, 2, *cf.* 41; Dio, LVIII, 8, 3; 19, 5 f., with Orth, *Provinzialpolitik*, 82 ff., and Syme, *Tac.*, I, 442 f.

73 Capito: Tac., *Ann.*, IV, 15, 3; Dio, LVII, 23, 5. Claudius: Tac., *Ann.*, XII, 60.

74 The following paragraphs are heavily indebted to Orth, *Provinzialpolitik*, 57 ff.

75 For the coinage, see Grant, *Aspects*, 8 ff.; *IX Hispana:* Tac., *Ann.*, III, 91; IV, 5, 4; 23, 2; *CIL*, V, 4329, line 5; the move was made in consultation with the Senate: Suet., *Tib.*, 30, with Rietra, *ad loc.* Deployment: Tac., *Ann.*, IV, 24, 3. Recruitment: *CIL*, VIII, 14603 (AD 36–39), with Brunt, *art. cit.*, 164 ff. Decorations: Tac., *Ann.*, III, 21, 3 f. (L. Apronius in 20); Suet., *Tib.*, 31, 2 (generalization). Reports to Senate: Suet., *loc. cit.*

76 Gaul: Tac., *Ann.*, III, 41, 4. Vitellius in the East: VI, 32, 3: 'cunctis . . . praefecit'; he received instructions on dealing with Artabanus: Jos., *AJ*, XVIII, 96, and 101, *cf.* 124. His replacement of Pilate: 88 ff. For his powers, see D. Magie, *Roman Rule in Asia Minor*, II, 1364, Orth, *Provinzialpolitik*, 58 f.

77 Vell. Pat., II, 129, 4; 'Dat negotium Blaeso [sc. Tiberius]': Tac., *Ann.*, III, 73, 4.

78 Tac., *Ann.*, IV, 23, 2.

79 The execution of Gracchus by L. Asprenas in AD 14, perhaps on

Tiberius' orders (Tac., *Ann.*, I, 53, 9), was an affair of state and nothing to do with routine administration.

80 Road works of Lamia: *IRT*, 930 (= *EJ²*, 291: 'imp. Ti. Caesaris Aug. iussu'); by Rubellius Blandus in 35–36: *IRT*, 330 f.; limitation by C. Marsus in 29–36: *CIL*, VIII, 22786a, f, k.

81 *ILS*, 5829; 5829a; *CIL*, III, 3199.

82 The theory, Polyb., VI, 12, 2; 13, 7, *cf.* Livy, XXIX, 16, 6 ff., and (for client kings) Caes., *BC*, III, 107, 2, with access through the consuls; for Augustus, *cf.* Dio, LIII, 21, 6; 25, 1; LV, 33, 5 (a consular committee); LVI, 25, 7 (Augustus). Tiberius and client kings: Suet., *Tib.*, 30.

83 Tac., *Ann.*, II, 42, 2 ff.; Dio, LVII, 17, 3 ff. *Cf.* Suet., *Tib.*, 8.

84 Tac., *Ann.*, II, 63, 1 ff.

85 Tac., *Ann.*, II, 88, 1 f.

86 Tac., *Ann.*, II, 64 ff. The anecdote about Pyrrhus is recorded by Val. Max., VI, 5, 1.

87 Tac., *Ann.*, IV, 26, 4.

88 Instances of opposition: Suet., *Tib.*, 31, 1. Messalla: Tac., *Ann.*, I, 8, 5, *cf.* III, 70, 3 (Ateius Capito).

89 Tac., *Ann.*, II, 40, 6.

90 Gaul: Tac., *Ann.*, III, 47, 1; Vell. Pat., II, 129, 3. Apronius: Tac., *Ann.*, IV, 74, 1.

91 Tac., *Ann.*, VI, 31 ff.; 41, 2 ff.

92 Aufidius Bassus: Ph. Fabia, *Les Sources de Tacite dans les Histoires et les Annales*, Paris, 1893, 392 ff.; contra, Syme, *Tac.*, I, 276 ff.; taken up by Pliny's *Histories*: Pliny, *Ep.*, III, 5, 6; terminal date 31. Mommsen, *Ges. Schr.*, VII, 677 ff., *cf.* Syme, *Tac.*, II, 698 f. Syme advocates Servilius Nonianus as a source: *Ten Studies in Tacitus*, Oxford, 1970, 104 f. G. B. Townend, *Herm.*, 1961, 115 ff., Balb-

edition, I, 13. The *acta*: *Ann.*, XV,
74, 3.
93 Tac., *Ann.*, IV, 74, 2; Vell. Pat.,
II, 130, 4.
94 Tac., *Ann.*, III, 53, 1 (apology for
communicating by letter in AD 22);
see Crook, *op. cit.*, 131 f. (above, n. 1).
Until 26 Tiberius seems to have spent
most of the business year at Rome
except for a projected absence in 16,
Tac., *Ann.*, II, 35, 2 – implicitly
denied by Suet., *Tib.*, 38, who says
he failed to put a foot out of doors for
two years after he took power – and
an absence during 21–22 (Tac., *Ann.*,
III, 31, 2–64, 1), during which he went
no farther than Antium (Suet., *loc.
cit.*). Note the complaint of M.
Terentius in 32: 'abditos principis
sensus': Tac., *Ann.*, VI, 8, 9.
95 Tac., *Ann.*, II, 35 (AD 16).
96 Dio, LVIII, 21, 2.
97 Timing and tone of interventions: Tac., *Ann.*, I, 74, 5 f.; Suet.,
Tib., 30 f.; Dio, LVII, 7, 3 ff. (or
does this refer to the *consilium*?).
Written advice: Tac., *Ann.*, I, 73, 3,
with Furneaux *ad* III, 31, 4, for letters written during his absence in
AD 21–22. Veto: see below, Ch. XI,
n. 107.
98 Tac., *Ann.*, III, 65, 3 (recorded
under AD 22). For the Gauls see *Ann.*,
XI, 23.
99 Vell. Pat., II, 124, 2; Tac., *Ann.*,
III, 47, 2; III, 53, 3; IV, 40, 1 (AD 25),
cf. I, 47, 3 (thoughts attributed to
Tiberius); V, 5, 1 (AD 29).

CHAPTER VIII

VIII* See Seager, *Tib.*, 136 ff.; Z.
Yavetz, *Plebs and Princeps*, Oxford,

1969; R. Syme, *Herm.*, 1956, 257 ff.;
R. F. Newbold, *Athen.*, 1974, 110 ff.
1 *Concordia ordinum*: see above, pp.
51 f.
2 Privileges to knights: see above,
p. 52; *novi homines*: p. 98; antecedents: pp. 13, 19; friends: *Hor.*,
Ep., I, 3; 8; Pompeius Macer, Strabo,
XIII, p. 618; A. Avillius Flaccus,
Philo, *in Flacc.*, 2; 158, etc. T;. Caesonius Priscus, Suet., *Tib.*, 42; Curtius
Atticus, Tac., *Ann.*, IV, 58, 1. Massurius Sabinus the jurist, 'made an
eques late in life, perhaps in order to
qualify him for the *amicitia principis*':
Crook, *Consilium principis*, 36; C.
Sallustius Crispus, Tac., *Ann.*, III, 30;
Seius Strabo, Vell. Pat., II, 127, 3; C.
Turranius can hardly be denied the
title of friend; see Syme, *RR*, 437;
Vescularius Flaccus, Tac., *Ann.*, II,
28, 1 and VI, 10, 2, a friend from the
days of the Rhodian exile; the status
of Iulius Marinus (VI, 10, 2) was
probably not lower.
3 Gold ring: Pliny, *NH*, XXXIII,
32, with Jones, *Studies*, 40 ff., and
M. I. Henderson, *JRS*, 1963, 65 ff. =
Seager, ed., *Crisis of the Roman Republic*, Cambridge, 1969, 73 ff., *cf.*
T. P. Wiseman, *Hist.*, 1970, 81 f.; *New
Men in the Roman Senate*, Oxford,
1971, 69. *Lex*: *Cod. Iust.*, IX, 21, 1; 31,
1; Gaius, *Inst.*, I, 33; Ulpian, Fr. 3, 5;
Rogers, *Trials*, 85. Dio, LIX, 9, 5, attests neglect in the last years.
4 Suet., *Tib.*, 35, 2, *cf.* Tac., *Ann.*, II,
85, 2 (*senatus consultum* of 19 provoked by one case).
5 Tac., *Ann.*, IV, 40, 5 ff.
6 Procuratorial encroachment: Tac.,
Ann., IV, 15, 3, *cf.* 6, 7; Dio, LVII,
23, 4 f. Herennius: Jos., *AJ*, XVIII,
158, with *PIR²* H 103, and P. A.
Brunt, *Lat.*, 1966, 464 f., who re-

marks that Tac., *Ann.*, IV, 6, implies a decline. Domitian: *ILS*, 1374.

7 Freedmen controlled: Tac., *Ann.*, IV, 6, 7. Hiberus: Dio, LVIII, 19, 6; Philo, *in Flacc.*, 2; see Brunt, *loc. cit.*, who regards this as analogous to the encroachment of equestrian officials. Bribery: Tac., *Ann.*, IV, 70, 1; Jos., *AJ.*, XVIII, 145 (cited by Brunt). Trio: Tac., *Ann.*, VI, 38, 2.

8 Vell. Pat., II, 103, 1 and 3 ff.; 104, 3 f.; 111, 2, *cf.* Suet., *Tib.*, 59. Other lampoons: Tac., *Ann.*, I, 72, 5 (AD 15); Suet., *Tib.*, 66 (late in the principate). For his reaction, see above, pp. 192 f.

9 Drusus honoured: see above, pp. 58 f. Concord: Dio, LVI, 25, 1. Ceres and Ops: *Fasti Val.*, *Amit.*, and *Ant. Min.*; see *Inscr. Ital.*, XIII, ii, 493 = *EJ²*, p. 50.

10 'Agrippa's' followers: Tac., *Ann.*, II, 40, 1; Suet., *Tib.*, 25, 1; Dio, LVII, 16, 3. Demonstration for Agrippina and Nero: Tac., *Ann.*, V, 4, 3 f.

11 Gaius Caligula: Dio, LVIII, 8, 2. Drusus Caesar: Tac., *Ann.*, VI, 23, 5; Suet., *Tib.*, 65, 2; Dio, LVIII, 13, 1. Sejanus and the plebs: Syme, *art. cit.* (n. VIII*); S. A. Jameson, *NC*, 1966, 120 f. Granaries: *CIL*, VI, 238; 9471. The fire: Tac., *Ann.*, III, 72, 4 ff. Note delegations to Princeps and Sejanus by all three orders, that of the *plebs* led by tribunes and plebeian aediles (AD 29): Dio, LVIII, 2, 8. The Aventine: Syme, *art. cit.*, and A. Merlin, *L'Aventin dans l'Antiquité*, Paris, 1906, 254 ff. Revulsion of feeling: Juv., X, 71 ff.; Dio, LVIII, 11, 3.

12 *ILS* 6044 = *EJ²* 53 (I am much indebted to Mr M. W. Frederiksen for giving me a fresh tracing of the stone).

13 In line 4 Dessau in *ILS* prints '[q]uae', but there is no trace of the 'V'; *cf.* Mommsen, *CIL*, VI, 10213. 'Sixty years' goes back to 30 BC and the end of the Civil Wars; hence the supplement; or perhaps the gap conceals a reference to the Aventine fire of that year. Syme suggests '[efflag]itatio', but, as he suspects, there is insufficient room; his '[flag]itatio' is very attractive.

14 'Supplex' is used in an electoral context by Horace, *Ep.*, II, 2, 102. Tiberius' pedantry: see above, Ch. I, n. 33. For the disturbances that followed Sejanus' fall, see Dio, LVIII, 12, 1 ff.; and Pliny, *NH*, VIII, 194, with Syme, *art. cit.*, 261.

15 'Agrippa': Dio, LVII, 16, 3, with mention of 'Gaul'; 'Drusus': Tac., *Ann.*, VI, 5.

16 Concern for order: Suet., *Tib.*, 37, 1 ff. Populus delighted at his death: 75, 3, with A. Piganiol, *Recherches sur les Jeux romains*, Paris, 1923, 112 ff.

17 *Op. cit.* (n. VIII*), 108 ff.

18 Tac., *Ann.*, IV, 2, 1; Suet., *Tib.*, 37, 1, *cf. Div. Aug.*, 49, 1; Dio, LVII, 19, 6; 24, 5.

19 Agents active: Tac., *Ann.*, II, 40, 3 (AD 16). Awareness of public opinion: III, 6, 1 (20); 54, 11 (22); IV, 38, 1 (25); VI, 13, 2 (32); 15, 5 (33). Discontent and quietude: I, 15, 2; II, 82; III, 11, 3. Corn: III, 87, 1; VI, 13, 1. See Yavetz, *op. cit.* (n. VIII*), 4 and 14.

20 Pliny, *NH*, XXXIV, 62.

21 Suet., *Tib.*, 37; Tac., *Ann.*, IV, 27, 3 (incipient slave revolt in 24); edicts: I, 7, 6 (AD 14); V, 5, 1 (29); VI, 13, 2 (32, with an account of his efforts to keep up the corn supply; see above, p. 218). Efforts acknowledged by Tacitus: II, 87, 1 (subsidy of 19); IV, 6, 6 (in general), *cf.* Vell. Pat., II, 126, 3. The debate of 22: III, 54, 7.

22 *Congiaria* of 300 sesterces in 17

for Germanicus' triumph: Tac., *Ann.*, II, 42, 1, with Furneaux, *ad loc.*, *cf.* Suet., *Tib.*, 20; of 375 in 20 and 23 for the *tirocinia* of Nero and Drusus: *Fasti Ost.*, *CIL*, XIV, 244 = 4534; Tac., *Ann.*, III, 29, 3; IV, 4; Suet., *Tib.*, 54, *cf.* RG, 15; Dio, LV, 10. See D. van Berchem, *Les Distributions de Blé et d'Argent à la Plèbe romaine sous l'Empire*, Geneva, 1939, 144 ff. Vell. Pat., II, 129, has 'quotiens'. Augustus' bequest: Suet., *Div. Aug.*, 101, 2 f.; *Tib.*, 57, 2; Dio, LVII, 14, 1 ff.

23 Floods: see above, pp. 105 f. Fires in 16: Dio, LVII, 14, 8; in 27: Tac., *Ann.*, IV, 6, 1 ff., where it is noted that Tiberius' departure would have been blamed for the disasters of the year by the 'vulgus' but for his generosity; Vell. Pat., II, 130, 2; Suet., *Tib.*, 48; in 36: Tac., *Ann.*, VI, 45, 1 f.; see above, p. 218.

24 Vell. Pat., II, 114 (officers); Rhodes: Suet., *Tib.*, 11, 2.

25 Tiberius' tone: Yavetz, *op. cit.*, 105 ff. Shows restricted: Suet., *Tib.*, 34, 1, *cf.* 47 (he gave no *spectacula* and rarely attended); Tac., *Ann.*, I, 54, 4; 76, 6 (absence in 15); Dio, LVII, 11, 4 ff., calls Tiberius a frequent though unenthusiastic attender; but that is in the period before Germanicus' death; and he mentions an occasion on which Tiberius was forced to free an actor, which was exactly what Suetonius says deterred him from attending. Actors: Tac., *Ann.*, I, 77, 1 ff., *cf.* Dio, LVII, 14, 2. Restored: LIX, 2, 5. The Oscan farces: Tac., *Ann.*, IV, 14, 4, *cf.* Suet., *Tib.*, 37, 2, and Dio, LVII, 21, 3. Fidena: IV, 62, 3. Triumphus: Sen., *de Prov.*, 4, 4. Demonstration of 32: *Ann.*, VI, 13, 1.

26 New buildings: Tac., *Ann.*, II, 41,

1 (for the associations of Fors Fortuna, see Syme, *art. cit.*, 265, *cf.* Hennig, *Seianus*, 76); VI, 45, 1: 'modicis privatis aedificationibus ne publice quidem nisi duo opera struxit, templum Augusti et scaenam Pompeiani theatri; eaque perfecta, contemptu ambitionis an per senectutem, haud dedicavit'; Suet., *Tib.*, 47, and *Cal.*, 21, claims them unfinished, but *cf.* RIC, I, 109, no. 38; II, 49, 1: a list of temples which Augustus had begun to repair, completed by Tiberius; *cf.* Dio, LVII, 10, 1 ff., and Vell. Pat., II, 130, 1. Whether Tiberius was responsible for the construction of the temples at Capua and Nola which he dedicated in 26 (Tac., *Ann.*, IV, 57, 1; Suet., *Tib.*, 40; Dio, LVI, 46, 3) is uncertain.

27 Tac., *Ann.*, IV, 38, 2. Augustus: RG, 19 ff.; Suet., *Div. Aug.*, 28, 3–29.

28 Popularity of Germanicus and Agrippina: Tac., *Ann.*, I, 33, 4; II, 13, 1; 41, 4; 43, 7; 59, 1, *cf.* EJ² 320 (b); 72, 3, *cf.* III, 29, 3; IV, 12, 2; 15, 5; VI, 46, 1; Suet., *Cal.*, 4, with Yavetz, *op. cit.*, 109 ff. Public grief at his death and funeral: II, 71 f.; III, 1 ff.; Dio, LVII, 18, 6 ff.; trial of Piso: Tac., *Ann.*, III, 12 ff., and see above, pp. 196 f. Portraits of Germanicus: see PIR² I 221, p. 185.

29 The edict: Tac., *Ann.*, IV, 67, 1; see Yavetz, *op. cit.*, 112. Mr Stevens drew my attention to a nice parallel: the unpopularity of Queen Victoria during the seclusion of her widowhood. The verse: Suet., *Tib.*, 45.

30 Tac., *Ann.*, VI, 46, 1.

31 So J. P. V. D. Balsdon, *The Emperor Gaius (Caligula)*, Oxford, 1937, 182, citing Suet., *Div. Aug.*, 101; Dio, LVI, 32, 2; LIX, 2, 1 ff. There is an advance of five million sesterces to the *populus*.

CHAPTER IX

IX* See Marsh, *Reign*, 134 ff.; C. E.
Smith, *Tib. and the Rom. Emp.*, 182 ff.;
P. A. Brunt, *Hist.*, 1961, 189 ff.; G.
Alföldy, *Lat.*, 1965, 824 ff.; Orth,
Provinzialpolitik; Seager, *Tib.*, 162 ff.
For separate areas, see notes to each.
1 Messalla: Sen., *de Ira*, II, 5, 5 (*cf.*
above, pp. 109 ff.); Tac., *Ann.*, III,
68, 1. On the *communis opinio*, see
Brunt, *art. cit.* (n. IX*), 189 ff.; Orth,
Provinzialpolitik, 126. The *senatus consultum Calvisianum*: F. de Visscher,
Les Édits d'Auguste découverts a Cyrène,
Brussels, 1940; *EJ*² 311 V. For foreign
clientelae, see E. Badian's work under
that title, Oxford, 1958, and Syme,
RR.
2 Orth, *op. cit.*, 131 f. To his list of
prorogations add J. Morris, *BJ*, 1965,
88 ff.: Munatius Plancus Paulinus, *cos.*
13, legate of Pannonia for seventeen
years (after Q. Blaesus). That the
distinction between the positions of
the two kinds of governor is of name
only is argued by F. Millar, *JRS*, 1966,
156 ff.
3 Orth, *op. cit.*, 82 ff.; see above,
Ch. VII, n. 72. For the 'centralized
monarchy', see S. J. de Laet, *Samenstelling*, 298.
4 Pilate: see P. L. Hedley, *Journ.
Theol. Stud.*, 1934, 56 f.; E. M. Smallwood, *Journ. Jewish Stud.*, 1954,
12 ff.; Orth, *op. cit.*, 132. The Jewish
complaint: Jos., *BJ*, II, 352.
5 'Principem longa experientia',
Tac., *Ann.*, I, 46, 2, *cf.* 4, 3, and (in
other areas) VI, 48, 4. See Orth, *op.
cit.*, 13; 15. For the journeys, see Ch.
II. 'Virtutes': Vell. Pat., II, 94, 4. For
a possible connexion with Pisidian
Antioch, see Levick, *Roman Colonies
in Southern Asia Minor*, 81, n. 6.

Rhodes: Suet., *Tib.*, 11 f. A priest of
Ti. Claudius Nero at Pergamum:
Ath. Mitt., 1907, 321 f., n. 50.
Spanish connexions: see above, Ch.
II, n. 6.
6 Rhodians: Suet., *Tib.*, 32, 2, and
Dio, LVII, 11, 2, in each case as an
example of *moderatio* (could a common source have transferred this
item from the exile to the principate?).
Sparta and Messene: Tac., *Ann.*, IV,
43, 1 ff. Patronage: Suet., *Tib.*, 6,
2.
7 Tac., *Ann.*, I, 46 f.; 21: III, 47, 2;
23: IV, 4, 2; often down to 26:
Suet., *Tib.*, 38, with Rietra, *ad loc.*,
cf. Dio, LVII, 3, 2 (illness as the pretext). It was Professor P. A. Brunt
who kindly drew my attention to
Augustus' keeping to Italy in his later
years.
8 Germany: Tac., *Ann.*, II, 26, 3 ff.,
cf. I, 62, 3. Cn. Piso: II, 43, 4 f.; III,
16, 1 f. Egypt: II, 60, 3 f.; Suet., *Tib.*,
52, 2.
9 The Empire a 'belua': Suet., *Tib.*,
24, 1, *cf.* Tac., *Ann.*, I, 11, 1 ff. Careful
generalship: 18. Literary tastes: see
above, p. 16. Avoidance of public
contacts: see below, n. 49.
10 Prorogations: Tac., *Ann.*, I, 80,
2 ff.; Dio, LVIII, 23, 5. Flies: Jos.,
AJ, XVIII, 171 ff. The complaint:
Tac., *Ann.*, VI, 27, 3.
11 Orth, *op. cit.*, 80 f., relies heavily
on this as an explanation; Brunt, *art.
cit.*, 210, n. 59, favours a preference
for mediocrity. For Tiberius' *cunctatio*,
real and alleged, see, besides passages
cited in preceding nn., descriptions of
his 'accession', above, pp. 71 ff.; his
conduct of affairs from 27 onwards:
Suet., *Tib.*, 41; Jos., *AJ*, XVIII, 169 ff.
(embassies and trials): μελλετὴς εἰ
καί τις ἕτερος βασιλέων ἢ τυράννων

γενόμενος (implying a change); *cf.*
Philo, *In Flacc.*, 128 f.; over the
succession: Tac., *Ann.*, VI, 46, 1.
12 Tac., *Ann.*, I, 80, 4; *Hist.*, II, 65,
2; Suet., *Tib.*, 63, 2, *cf.* 41, 1; Dio,
LVIII, 19, 5. For the real explanation,
see E. J. Weinrib, *HSCP*, 1968, 276 f.
For Piso, see Tac., *Ann.*, IV, 45;
Pacuvius in Syria, Sen., *Ep.*, 12, 8:
'ein äusserst ungünstiges Bild' (Orth,
op. cit., 90). The view adopted in the
text is diametrically opposed to that of
Marsh, *Reign*, 159.
13 See above, n. 7. Recruitment
without fear is one of Velleius'
themes: II, 130, 2; see P. A. Brunt,
Italian·Manpower, Oxford, 1971, 241
f.; 414. For the effect abroad, see
Tac., *Ann.*, IV, 46, 2 (Thrace).
14 'Sheep': Dio, LVII, 10, 5, *cf.* Suet.,
Tib., 32, 2. Supplies: Tac., *Ann.*, III,
54, 6 ff. Gracchan attitude: E. Badian,
Roman Imperialism, 2nd ed., Oxford,
1968, 44 ff. 'Caput rerum': Tac., *Ann.*,
I, 47, 1, *cf.* III, 44, 2; 47, 3.
15 Dress: above n. 8. Equality: Jos.,
AJ, XVIII, 207 f. Exposure: Tac., *Ann.*,
III, 12, 7. While in Egypt Germanicus
relieved a famine by opening the
granaries, II, 59, 2, *cf.* Jos., *Contra Ap.*,
2, 5; but Tacitus makes it clear that
this was not the object of the visit (so
Suet., *Tib.*, 52, 1). Tiberius might well
have objected to that measure above
all, given the attitude ascribed him in
the text, especially if there were any
connexion between that and the
famine at Rome of 19 (*Ann.*, II, 87,
1); there is no reason to believe there
was. Germanicus in Egypt: *P. Oxyrh.*,
2435; *P. Germ.* (Hunt and Edgar,
Select Papyri, II, 211 (= *EJ*² 320)). See
U. Wilcken, *Herm.*, 1928, 48 ff.; =
Koestermann, *Hist.*, 1958, 348 ff.;
Akveld, *Germanicus*, 94 ff.; D. G.

Weingärtner, *Die Ägyptenreise des
Germanicus*.
16 Tac., *Ann.*, I, 76, 4; 80, 1.
17 Syme, *JRS*, 1934, 113 ff., repr.
with Addendum in *Danubian Papers*,
Bucharest, 1971, 40 ff.; A. Stein, *Die
Legaten von Moesien, Diss. Pann.*, I, 11,
Budapest, 1940, 9 ff., arguing that the
province was created by Tiberius (*cf.*
App., *Illyr.*, 30); A. Mócsy, *Pannonia
and Upper Moesia*, London, 1974, 33
ff.; P. A. Brunt, *Lat.*, 1960, 499, n. 1,
suggests that Tiberius imposed the
first census.
18 Drusus' command: Tac., *Ann.*,
II, 44 ff.; III, 7, 1; *imperium* and
ovatio: 20, 4; see Orth, *op. cit.*, 36,
n. 7. Activities: Mócsy, *loc. cit.*; J. J.
Wilkes, *Dalmatia*, London, 1969, 229;
A. and J. Šašel, *Inscriptiones Latinae,
quae in Iugoslavia inter Annos MCMXL
et MCMLX repertae et editae sunt*,
Ljublana, 1963, 257; G. Alföldy, *art.
cit.* (n. IX*), 838 (grants of citizenship); *CIG*, II, 3612 = *IGR*, IV, 219
(= *EJ*² 227), *cf.* 3630 (clearance of
pirates from the Propontis); honoured
at Athens as Ares: *IG* II/III², 3257
(= *EJ*² 136).
19 Fall of Maroboduus: Tac., *Ann.*,
II, 62 f.
20 Roads and fleet: Wilkes, *op. cit.*,
452 ff.; Mócsy, *op. cit.*, 44 f. See
above, Ch. VII, n. 81. Distance from
Rome: Vell. Pat., II, 111, 1, *cf.* Dio,
LV, 30, 1.
21 For roads of 32–34, see C. H. V.
Sutherland, *The Romans in Spain*,
London, 1939, 171; C. E. van Sickle,
CP, 1929, 77 ff.; Orth, *op. cit.*, 102.
22 Grain: Jos., *BJ*, II, 383, with
R. M. Haywood, *Econ. Surv. of Anc.
Rome*, IV, 42 ff.
23 Asprenas: *ILS*, 151 = *EJ*² 290;
Lamia: *IRT*, 930 = *EJ*² 291.

24 The war: Tac., *Ann.*, II, 52 (Camillus); III, 20 f. (Apronius); 32, 73 f. (Blaesus); IV, 23 ff. (Dolabella); Aur. Vict., *Ep.*, 2, 3 ('lactrocinia'); with L. Cantarelli, *A e R*, 1901, 3 ff.; T. R. S. Broughton, *The Romanization of Africa Proconsularis*, Baltimore and London, 1929, 88 ff. Syme, *Stud. in Rom. Econ. and Soc. Hist. in Honor of A. C. Johnson*, 113 ff.; P. Romanelli, *Storia delle Provincie Romane dell' Africa*, Rome, 1959, 228 ff. Landhunger: M. Rostovtzeff, *Soc. Econ. Hist. Rom. Emp.*², I, 319, *cf.* Broughton, *op. cit.*, 91, and Syme, *art. cit.*, 121, n. 30.

25 Alföldy, *art. cit.* (n. IX*), 837, citing Tac., *Ann.*, II, 52, 3, and III, 73, 3. *Cf.* Syme, *art. cit.*, 129 f.

26 Syme, *art. cit.*, 118 ff.; *JRS*, 1933, 25 ff.

27 Fabatus: *ILS*, 2721. Galba: Suet., *Galba*, 7 f.; Aur. Vict., *Ep.*, 4, 2. Marsus: *CIL*, VIII, 22, 786 a, f, k, with Orth, *op. cit.*, 60, n. 3. Madauros: Syme, *art. cit.*, 122.

28 The revolt: Tac., *Ann.*, III, 40 ff., with A. Grenier, *REL*, 1936, 373 ff.; A. J. Christopherson, *Hist.*, 1968, 354 ff.; 365 f.

29 Gallic money-making: Strabo, IV, p. 195; Exports: Jos., *BJ*, II, 372 f. See Grenier, *Econ. Surv. of Anc. Rome*, III, 465 ff. (Augustus' gifts, 490 f.).

30 Tac., *Ann.*, II, 33 (*cf.* Dio, LVII, 15, 2), with reference to the fate of Libo Drusus; see D. Daube, *Roman Law. Linguistic, Social, and Philosophical Aspects*, Edinburgh, 1969, 117 ff.; III, 52 ff., especially 53, 5; R. M. Wheeler, *Rome beyond the Imperial Frontiers*, London, 1954, 137 ff., shows where the money went.

31 Tac., *Ann.*, VI, 16 ff.; Suet., *Tib.*, 48, 1, *cf.* 49, 2; Dio, LVIII, 21, 5; see

above, p. 104. See M. Crawford, *JRS*, 1970, 46 f.: 'to preserve social status'. For the offerings, see Th. Pekáry, *Röm. Mitt.*, 1966–67, 105 ff., and for the date, Tac., *Ann.*, II, 32, 3.

32 Frugality: Tac., *Ann.*, III, 52, 2: ('antiquae parsimoniae', *cf.* VI, 45, 1: 'modicus privatis aedificationibus'); Suet., *Tib.*, 46 ('parcus et tenax'), *cf.* 34, 1 (half-boars served at dinner). Old-fashioned economics: I am indebted for this point to Miss N. G. Watts. According to Suet., *Cal.*, 37, 3, Tiberius left 2,700 million sesterces, which Caligula spent in a year; *cf.* Dio, LIX, 3, 4: 2,300 or 3,300, with Caligula in need during his second year; Augustus had left his heirs only 150 millions. But see J. P. V. D. Balsdon, *The Emperor Gaius*, 182. The question might be obscure to contemporaries: Tiberius gave up publishing *rationes imperii* (Suet., *Cal.*, 16, 1). Indifference? Or knowledge that the Aerarium and Fiscus could not balance their accounts without his aid?

33 The charges in Suet., *Tib.*, 49, are dealt with by G. B. Townend, *Lat.*, XXI, 1962, 484 ff., and by Rogers, *Trials*, 176 f. See also Tac., *Ann.*, IV, 20, 1 f. (Silius, with note that it was the first example of 'diligentia'). In 32 'bona Seiani ablata aerario ut in fiscum cogentur': VI, 2, 1 (presumably on the same grounds that part of the property had been Caesar's gift). Marius, 'Hispaniarum ditissimus', accused of incest and thrown from the Tarpeian rock; his mines (gold and copper) 'quamquam publicarentur, sibimet . . . seposuit' (presumably to the Fiscus): VI, 19, 1 f.; Dio, LVIII, 22, 2, says that it was Tiberius' favour that made Marius

rich. When Fufius Geminus read his will out in the Senate it was not because he knew Tiberius wanted the property but to prove his goodwill towards the Princeps: Dio, LVIII, 4, 5. For Tiberius' abstention from private property (AD 17), see Tac., *Ann.*, II, 48, 1 ff. For the Fiscus as opposed to the private purse as the destination of the confiscated property, see P. A. Brunt, *JRS*, 1966, 81 f. Domitian: Suet., *Dom.*, 12.

34 Grenier, *art. cit.*; see above, n. 28. For the Treviri, see G. W. Clarke, *Hist.*, 1965, 335 ff.; *contra*, Christopherson, *loc. cit.*

35 Census: Tac., *Ann.*, I, 31, 3; II, 6, 1. No new burdens: IV, 6, 7. Horses: II, 5, 3, *cf.* I, 71, 3, where Gaul, Spain, and Italy vie with each other in making up the losses of 15 ('arma equos aurum'). *Auxiliares*: II, 16, 3. Immunities: Suet., *Tib.*, 49, 2. Cyzicus: 37, 3; Tac., *Ann.*, IV, 36, 2; Dio, LVII, 24, 6 (no mention of immunity, but there may be cases that have escaped the attention of the sources).

36 Administration: Acilius Aviola was legate of Lugdunensis in 21 (Tac., *Ann.*, III, 41, 2). Finance continued centralized: *ILS*, 1514 (= *EJ*² 158). Druids: Pliny, *NH*, XXX, 13; Suet., *Div. Claud.*, 25, 5, credits Claudius with complete abolition.

37 Tac., *Ann.*, IV, 6, 7; Strabo, XIII, p. 627; Jos., *AJ*, XVIII, 172; Vell. Pat., II, 126, 4.

38 Prorogations undesirable: Brunt, *art. cit.*, 206 ff.; Orth, *op. cit.*, 77 f. Number of cases: Brunt, *art. cit.*, 224 ff., with Orth, *op. cit.*, 64, n. 2.

39 The trials of Silanus and Capito: Tac., *Ann.*, III, 66 ff.; IV, 15, 3; and Dio, LVII, 23, 4 f., contrasting the

Tiberian position with that in his own day. Action by the *koinon*: Brunt, *art. cit.*, 212 f.

40 Procuratorial encroachment: see previous n. and Brunt, *Lat.*, 1966, 463 ff. Emperor's appointees formidable: Brunt, *art. cit.* (IX*), 208 ff. Capito was not charged with *repetundae*; he may have been exempt as an *eques* (see below, Ch. XI, n. 135), but there is no mention of monies extorted.

41 Tac., *Ann.*, IV, 45.

42 Tac., *Ann.*, IV, 72 ff. (AD 28); XI, 19, 1 f. (47); but *cf.* XIII, 54, 1 ff. (58). For the Frisii, see E. A. Thompson, *The Early Germans*, Oxford, 1965, 104 ff. Apronius: VI, 30, 3 (AD 35); dedication to Tiberius on Mount Eryx by him and his son: *CIL*, X, 7257.

43 On Pilate, see Smallwood, *Lat.*, 1956, 314 ff., and Hennig, *Seianus*, 160 ff. The military standards and the aqueduct: Jos., *BJ*, II, 169 ff.; *AJ*, XVIII, 55 ff., with Kraeling, *Harv. Theol. Rev.*, 1942, 263 ff., and L. H. Feldman *ad loc.*; Eus., *Dem. Evang.*, VIII, 2, 123. Shields: Philo, *Leg. ad Gaium*, 299 ff., with Smallwood *ad loc.* Smallwood accepts the view of Pilate as a creature of Sejanus, like E. Bammel, *Theol. Literaturzeitung*, 1952, 207 ff., *cf.* P. L. Maier, *Church History*, 1968, 8 ff.; *contra*, Orth, *op. cit.*, 36, and Hennig, *loc. cit.* A. H. M. Jones, *The Herods of Judaea*, Oxford, 1938, 172, is relatively favourable.

44 Philo, *Leg.*, 159 ff., with Smallwood, *ad loc.*; *In Flacc.*, 1; Eus., *Hist. Eccl.*, II, 5, 7; *Chron.*, p. 176 Helm. Smallwood dissociates the attack mentioned by Philo, which comes at the end of Sejanus' career, from the expulsion of 19, so dated by Tac., *Ann.*, II, 85, 5, and Dio, LVII, 18, 5a, *cf.* Suet., *Tib.*, 36, 1; Sen., *Ep.*, 108, 22; Jos., *AJ*, XVIII, 65 ff. (AD 30, attracted there, according to Smallwood, *art. cit.* (see above, n. 43), 326, by the peril mentioned by Philo). Philo needed the expulsion later than 19 if Sejanus were to take the blame; Josephus may have followed him. See also Feldman, *ad loc.*, E. T. Merrill, *CP*, 1919, 365, and W. A. Heidel, *AJP*, 1920, 38 ff.; R. S. Rogers, *AJP*, 1932, 252 ff., and Hennig, *op. cit.*, 171 ff. The Jews and followers of Isis were expelled to avoid future scandal and criminality.

45 See above, Ch. VI, n. 18.

46 *AE*, 1963, 104. Note also the Jewish threat in *John*, 19, 12: 'If thou let this man go, thou art not Caesar's friend', with Bammel and Maier, *artt. citt.*, *cf.* Hennig, *op. cit.*, 178, n. 54.

47 *Imp.* VIII: Tac., *Ann.*, II, 18, 2, with H. Gesche, *Chiron*, 1972, 339 ff.; *contra*, P. A. Brunt, *ZfPE*, 1972, 179 f. For the salutations of Germanicus, see D. Timpe, *Der Triumph*, 36, n. 34. *Ornamenta*: A. E. Gordon, *Q. Veranius, Consul A.D. 49*, 312, with comment, 309, on Dio, LVIII, 4, 8.

48 Alföldy, *art. cit.*, 837 ff. Dio, LVI, 33, 3, has this as one of Augustus' injunctions, implausibly. He was 'very sparing' of the citizenship (Suet., *Div. Aug.*, 40, 3), but that was in comparison with Caesar.

49 See F. Millar, *JRS*, 1967, 9 ff. Tiberius dilatory: see above, n. 11; 'sacras occupationes': Tac., *Ann.*, II, 87, 2; Suet., *Tib.*, 27. His desire to be alone (*cf.* Tac., *Ann.*, IV, 67, 1, with the characteristic word 'inrumperet'; Suet., *Tib.*, 40) was ingrained (*cf.*

Suet., *Tib.*, 68, 3: 'incedebat cervice rigida et obstipa, adducto fere vultu, plerumque tacitus, nullo aut rarissimo etiam cum proximis sermone eoque tardissimo') and may have become pathological.

50 *ILS*, 206 = Smallwood, *Docs. illustr. the Princ. of Gaius, Claudius and Nero*, Cambridge, 1967, 368.

51 Tiberias, see Jos., *BJ*, II, 168; *AJ*, XVIII, 36 ff., with Orth, *op. cit.*, 111. Tiberia: Malalas, X, 236, 1 f., *cf.* Orth, *loc. cit.* Tiberiopolis in Phrygia and in Pisidia: D. Magie, *Roman Rule in Asia Minor*, I, 500; II, 1359 f. For Germanicopolis in Cilicia Tracheia, see M. Pani, *I re D'Oriente*, 201.

52 Vell. Pat., II, 7, 6 ff. Augustus: Dio, LIV, 25, 6. For colonies late in his principate, see Levick, *Rom. Colonies*, 33 ff., and, *contra*, E. L. Bowie, *JRS*, 1970, 204. Emona: Orth, *op. cit.*, 100, n. 2; Mócsy, *op. cit.* (see above, n. 17), 74.

53 The month: Suet., *Tib.*, 26, 2, with Rietra, *ad loc.*, *cf.* Dio, LVII, 18, 2. The eye: *Div. Aug.*, 79, 2.

54 Asia: Tac., *Ann.*, IV, 15, 4 f. Baetica: 37 f.

55 Dio, LVII, 9, 1 f.; see list in Orth, *op. cit.*, 111 ff.

56 *SEG*, XI, 922 f. = *EJ*² 102; S. B. Kougéas, 'Ελληνικά, 1928, 16 ff.; E. Kornemann, *Neue Dok. zum lakon. Kaiserkult, Abh. der Schles. Gesellsch. f. Vaterländ. Cultur*, I, Breslau, 1929, 6 ff.; M. Rostovtzeff, *Rev. Hist.*, CLXIII, 1930, 2 ff.

57 Tac., *Ann.*, I, 74, 4.

58 Aezani: *ILS*, 9463 = *EJ*² 319.

59 Orth, *op. cit.*, 111 ff.; Tiberius: Tac., *Ann.*, IV, 38, 2, with misgivings at 5 f.: 'melius Augustus, qui speraverit . . . contemptu famae contemni virtutes', *cf.* Suet., *Tib.*, 67, 2 ff. A

general prohibition: Suet., *Tib.*, 26, 1.
60 Earthquake relief in 17: Tac., *Ann.*, II, 47 (twelve cities of Asia destroyed), *cf.* Pliny, *NH*, II, 200; Dio, LVII, 17, 7; Eus., *Chron.*, p. 172 Helm., dating to 18 and adding Ephesus; Strabo, XII, p. 576. The gratitude of the cities: *BCH*, 1887, 89 f., no. 9 (AD 31). Cibyra and Ephesus contributed to the Naples basis: *CIL*, X, 1624 = *EJ*² 50 (AD 30); Cibyra was helped, with Aegium in Achaea, in 23: Tac., *Ann.*, IV, 13, 1. Nysa: *SIG*³ 781 = *EJ*² 316.
61 Tac., *Ann.*, III, 48, 3, gives prime examples of both; *cf.* I, 12, 6 ff.; IV, 21, 2; Suet., *Tib.*, 57, 1 ('saeva ac lenta natura'); 21 ('lentis maxillis').
62 Nemausus: Suet., *Tib.*, 13, 1. Archelaus: Tac., *Ann.*, II, 42, 2 ff.; Suet., *Tib.*, 37, 4; Dio, LVII, 17, 3 ff.; Philostr., *Vit. Apoll.*, I, 12. See Magie, *Roman Rule*, II, 1349 (Tigranes IV); E. Bammel, *Hist.*, 1958, 497 ff.; Bowersock, *Augustus and the Greek World*, 54; 158 ff.; *contra*, Levick, *CQ*, 1971, 478 ff. Zeno: Pani, *I re d'Oriente*, 173 ff. For the fate of Archelaus, *cf.* that of the Euryclids of Sparta, also protégés of Tiberius: Bowersock, *JRS*, 1961, 112 ff.
63 For Livia in domestic politics, see above, p. 153. Intervening for a Gaul under Augustus: Suet., *Div. Aug.*, 40, 3. As educator of Germanicus' children: Tac., *Ann.*, IV, 8, 5. Antonia and the children of Cotys: Mommsen, *Eph. Epigr.*, II, 257. Agrippa I: Jos., *AJ*, XVIII, 143; 156; 164 ff.; 183 ff.; 202; 236. It was only natural that Mark Antony's daughter should be a protector of Eastern dynasts; for the origins of the ties, see Bowersock, *Augustus and the Greek World*, 42 ff. Mr E. W. Gray has

kindly pointed out to me the relevance of the Claudian patronage of Sparta (Suet., *Tib.*, 6, 2) to the establishment of C. Iulius Eurycles as dynast there; he lost the position, but his son C. Iulius Laco was installed in it early under Tiberius (Bowersock, *JRS*, 1961, 117). For the value of provincial notables, see Dio, LII, 19, 2 f.
64 The annexation of Cappadocia and Commagene and the death of Philopator: Tac., *Ann.*, II, 42, 6 f.; 56, 4 f.; Strabo, XVI, p. 749. Nature of conflict in Commagene: Jos., *AJ*, XVIII, 53. Philopator's principality annexed, according to most writers, but *cf.* Bammel, *art. cit.*, 497, n. 14. Possessions of Archelaus II: Tac., *Ann.*, VI, 41, 1; XII, 55, *cf.* Jos., *AJ*. XVIII, 140, with Feldman, *ad loc.* Condition of Cappadocia: Jones, *op. cit.*, 174 ff.; W. E. Gwatkin, *Cappadocia as a Roman Procuratorial Province*, Columbia, Miss., 1930. Equestrian governor: Dio, LVII, 17, 7, with Magie, *Roman Rule*, II, 1355. Revenues: Tac., *Ann.*, II, 42, 6, *cf.* I, 78, 2. Caesarea Mazaca: Orth, *op. cit.*, 95, n. 4. The mint: *BMC Galatia*, etc., 46, no. 11 ff.
65 C. Caesar: Vell. Pat., II, 101, 1 ff. Vespasian's reorganization: Magie, *op. cit.*, I, 572 ff.
66 Jos., *BJ*, I, 668; *AJ*, XVII, 189; XVIII, 106 ff.; 137; XX, 138; *Vit.*, 187. See Jones, *The Herods of Judaea*, 174 f.
67 For these events, see Tac., *Ann.*, II, 64, 2 ff.; 67 (AD 19); III, 38, 2 ff. (21); IV, 5, 5 (23); 46 ff. (26). See Jones, *Cities of the East. Rom. Prov.*², 8 ff.
68 Annexation and fighting: Eus., *Chron.*, p. 180 Helm, *cf.* Tac., *Ann.*, XII, 63, 3; *CIL*, II, 3272; *RE*, XII,

1925, 1250 f.; VIA, 1937, 452. Trajan: ILS, 1052.

69 See C. E. Stevens, *Aspects of Archaeology in Britain and Beyond, Essays presented to O. G. S. Crawford*, ed. W. F. Grimes, London, 1951, 332 ff., and S. S. Frere, *Britannia*, London, 1967, 44 f. Official policy: Strabo, IV, p. 200.

70 Tac., *Ann.*, I, 11, 7, *cf. Agr.*, 13, with *Ann.*, IV, 32, 4; Dio, LVI, 33, 5. Alföldy, *art. cit.*, 828, cites Val. Max., II, 9, intr., and Curtius Rufus, IX, 2, 9 ff., and 3, 7 ff., as exponents of the doctrine.

71 Jos., *AJ*, XVIII, 109 ff.; 120 ff. See Alföldy, *art. cit.*, 828.

72 The main ancient source for Germanicus' campaigns is Tac., *Ann.*, I, 50 ff. (AD 14); 55 ff. (15); II, 5 ff. (16). See E. Koestermann, *Hist.*, 1957, 429 ff.; better, Timpe, *Der Triumph*, with bibliography, 1, n. 2; reviewed by E. W. Gray, *CR*, 1970, 347 ff.; Wells, *The German Policy of Augustus*, 240 ff. (forts).

73 Tac., *Ann.*, II, 41, 1 ff., for triumph and arch. SIGNIS RE-CEPT(is) DEVICTIS GERM(anis) appears on undated *dupondii* of Germanicus: *CREBM*, I, 160 f., nos. 49 ff.; 93 ff.; *RIC*, I, 108, no. 36, *cf.* 119 f. The arch: Timpe, *op. cit.*, 51 ff.

74 Tac., *Ann.*, II, 26, 3, *cf.* 64, 2; VI, 32, 1; see above, Ch. VI, n. 36. *Vis* and *consilium* combined: see Timpe, *op. cit.*, 60 ff.; Gray, *art. cit.*, 349.

75 Tac., *Ann.*, II, 62 f. See Thompson, *The Early Germans*, 72 ff.

76 Alföldy, *art. cit.*, 829, n. 1, and, for the creation of the province of Raetia, n. 3.

77 Above, pp. 24 ff. For Gaius, see

CAH, X, 273 ff., and K. Ziegler, *Die Beziehungen zwischen Rom und dem Partherreich*, Wiesbaden, 1964, 53 ff.

78 Suet., *Tib.*, 16, 1.

79 Vonones: Tac., *Ann.*, II, 1, 1; 2, 1; 3, 1; 4, 4; 58, 3; (death) 68, 3; Suet., *Tib.*, 49, 2; Jos., *AJ*, XVIII, 46 ff. See Pani, *I Re d'Oriente*, 173 ff.

80 Germanicus' mission in Armenia: Tac., *Ann.*, II, 43, 1 ff.; 56 ff.; Suet., *Cal.*, 1, 2. Complaints about taxation: 42, 7. See *CAH*, X, 743 ff.; Ziegler, *op. cit.*, 57 ff.

81 Tac., *Ann.*, VI, 31 ff.; 42 ff.; Jos., *AJ*, XVIII, 96 ff.; Dio, LVIII, 26, 1. See *CAH*, X, 747 ff.; Ziegler, *op. cit.*, 60 ff.

82 Suet., *Cal.*, 14, 3; *Vit.*, 2, 4; Dio, LIX, 27, 3. See A. Garzetti, *Stud. in Onore di A. Calderini e R. Paribeni*, I, Milan, 1956, 211 ff.

83 *Cf.* Levick, *Rom. Cols.*, 165 f.

CHAPTER X

X* Marsh, *Reign*, 160 ff.; Seager, *Tib.*, 58 ff.; 178 ff.; Akveld, *Germanicus*; Koestermann, *Hist.*, 1957, 429 ff.; Timpe, *Der Triumph des Germanicus*; D. G. Weingärtner, *Der Ägyptenreise des Germanicus*; K. Scott, *CP*, 1930, 155 ff.; Rogers, *Studies*, 89 ff.; *TAPA*, 1931, 141 ff.; W. Allen, *TAPA*, 1941, 1 ff.; Meise, *Untersuchungen*, 49 ff. (with full documentation); Koestermann, *Ath.*, 1965, 167 ff.; Meissner, *Sejan, Tiberius, und die Nachfolge im Prinzipat*; Cichorius, *Herm.*, 1904, 461 ff.; G. V. Sumner, *Phoen.*, 1965, 134 ff.; H. E. Bird, *Lat.*, 1969, 85 ff.; Syme, *Herm.*, 1956, 525 ff.; Koestermann, *Herm.*, 1955, 350 ff.; A. Boddington, *AJP*, 1963,

1 ff.; J. Nicols, *Hist.*, 1975, 48 ff.; D. Hennig, *L. Aelius Seianus.*

1 Tac., *Ann.*, I, 14, 4. For his previous status see *PIR²* I 221, p. 180, and Akveld, *Germanicus*, 36, n. 2 (the subject is still unclear). The command presumably covered the same ground as had Tiberius' ten years before; see above, Ch. IV, n. 6.

2 Possibility of Germanicus' attempting a coup: Tac., *Ann.*, I, 31, 1. Offered the Principate by soldiers; loyalty to Tiberius: 34, 1; 35, 4 ff.; Vell. Pat., II, 125, 2; Suet., *Tib.*, 25, 2; *Cal.*, 1, 1; Dio, LVII, 5, 1 ff.; 6, 2; 18, 8; Hunt and Edgar, *Sel. Papyri*, II, 211 = *EJ²* 320 (b). Tiberius' impartiality: Tac., *Ann.*, III, 56, 5, *cf.* Strabo, VII, p. 288; Ovid, *ex Ponto*, IV, 13, 31. See Levick, *Lat.*, 1966, 244, n. 4.

3 Tac., *Ann.*, II, 44, 1, *cf.* III, 19, 4. See Levick, *art. cit.*, 240, n. 3, and note the epigram of Honestus, *BCH*, 1902, 153 ff., discussed by Nicols, *art. cit.* (n. X*).

4 Tac., *Ann.*, II, 43, 6, *cf.* 53, 1, and Dio, LVII, 18, 7.

5 Drusus' interview with Piso: Tac., *Ann.*, III, 8, 3 f.; his tears: 12, 11. Concord of the brothers: see above, Ch. VI, n. 16.

6 The official charge: *Fasti Amit.*, *CIL* I², 244 = *EJ²* 52; the literary sources are less precise (see Rogers, *Trials*, 12). The main accounts are those of Tac., *Ann.*, II, 27 ff., and Dio, LVII, 15, 4 f. The contemptuous tone of Tacitus makes it impossible to accept Marsh's claim, *CP*, 1926, 291 ff.; *Reign*, 59, n. 1, that his account derives from the Scribonii. Tacitus used several sources, some hostile: 29, 2. Libo's praetorship: see below, n. 14.

7 Tac., *Ann.*, II, 27, 2; 29; 30, 2

('miseranda'); 31, 1 f.; Sen., *Ep.*, 70, 10 ('stolidus'; but he had hopes). Defences of Tacitus' account: A. Passerini, *Studi giuridici in Memoria di P. Ciapessoni*, 219 ff.; Syme, *Tac.*, I, 399 f.; Sumner, *Phoen.*, 1966, 81, is judicious.

8 Tac., *Ann.*, II, 32, 5; 33; Dio, LVII, 15, 1 f.; 8 ff.

9 Tac., *Ann.*, II, 32, *cf.* Dio, LVII, 15, 5. For the offerings, see Levick, *The Ancient Historian and his Materials*, 132 f. For the penalties and the rewards, see above, pp. 187, 189.

10 For these men, see Syme, *JRS*, 1956, 18 f., and *Tac.*, II, 749 f. For the friendship of Cotta, Lentulus, and Flaccus with Tiberius, see Tac., *Ann.*, VI, 5, 1; IV, 29, 1, *cf.* Dio, LVII, 24, 8; Suet., *Tib.*, 42. For the advancement of Apronius and Mutilus, see Syme, *RR*, 363, 434. For Gallus' position, see above, Ch. V, n. 22.

11 Elucidated by E. J. Weinrib in *HSCP*, 1967, 247 ff.

12 Tac., *Ann.*, II, 29, 1.

13 Sen., *Ep.*, 70, 10; for Scribonia and Julia, see Vell. Pat., II, 100, 5 ('permansit').

14 Tac., *Ann.*, II, 28, 3, *cf.* Vell. Pat., II, 129, 2 ('ingratum'). Usually 16 is taken to be Libo's year of office; and the legal objections are removed by Weinrib, *Phoen.*, 1968, 32 ff. But it is surprising that Tacitus does not make more of his being charged while in office. Libo could have been praetor in 15, elected alongside Velleius, and that may be why Velleius, speaking of his colleagues, refers to them only as 'nobilissimis ac sacerdotalibus viris' (124, 4); Libo, not surprisingly, was a pontifex: Suet., *Tib.*, 25, 3. Weinrib also tries to dispose of 17 as a possibility, but his arguments work

only if the praetorian elections followed the trial (*cf.* Tac., *Ann.*, II, 36,
a disagreement between Gallus and
Tiberius over the election of praetors). But the episodes may not be
in chronological order, and Syme's
suggestion that Cotta owed his
prominence in the list of senators responsible for the adulation of 14 September (see above, n. 10) to the fact
that he was praetor designate (*cf. Inscr.
Ital.*, XIII, i, 297) is attractive. In a
normal year the praetorian elections
were over by mid-September.
15 Suet., *Tib.*, 25, 1.
16 *Trials*, 22. Rogers deals at length
with both cases.
17 Tac., *Ann.*, II, 39; the other
sources are Suet., *Tib.*, 25, which
twice sets the attempts of Libo and
Clemens side by side, and Dio, LVII,
16, 3 f. For a sceptical view of the
earlier attempt, see Mogenet, *Ant.
Class.*, 1954, 321 ff.
18 See above, Ch. IV, n. 65; Ch. V,
n. 31.
19 Tac., *Ann.*, I, 53.
20 For the idea of an assassination of
all three *principes*, see Marsh, *Reign*,
59. Tiberius more than once requested Germanicus to return: Tac.,
Ann., II, 26, 3: 'crebris epistulis',
when the soldiers were already in
winter quarters. Tiberius' eighth
salutation as *imperator* had already
been won for him during the summer (18, 2, *cf.* H. Gesche, *Chiron*,
1972, 339 ff., against P. A. Blunt,
ZfPE, 1972, 179 f.). The triumph was
not celebrated until 26 May 17 (41,
2), but the return of Germanicus
must have been expected during the
autumn or winter of 16–17.
21 C. Silius: Tac., *Ann.*, IV, 18, 1;
he was a friend of Germanicus. M.

Lepidus: G. Alföldy, *Fasti His-
panienses*, Wiesbaden, 1969, 13; but
cf. A. J. Woodman, *CQ*, 1975, 295,
n. 5. P. Dolabella: Orth, *Provinzialpolitik*, 36, n. 7; his views: above, p. 52.
Q. Silanus: Tac., *Ann.*, II, 43, 3, showing ties with Germanicus.
22 Tac., *Ann.*, I, 16, 4: 'Percennius
. . . dux olim theatralium operarum,
dein gregarius miles' (in Pannonia);
31, 4: 'vernacula multitudo, nuper
acto in urbe dilectu' (on the Rhine).
Their recruitment: Dio, LV, 31, 1
(for the Pannonian revolt); LVI, 23,
3 (after the disaster to Varus).
23 Dio, LVII, 16, 3. The name of L.
Audasius, who meant to carry off
Agrippa to the armies (Suet., *Div.
Aug.*, 19, 1), is found in Cisalpine
Gaul; *CIL*, V, 3503 ff.; 5759; 8879.
Sympathizers may have had estates
there.
24 Dio, LVII, 15, 3.
25 *Cf.* Rogers, *Trials*, 21, on L.
Pituanius and P. Marcius, executed
for practising astrology.
26 Vell. Pat., II, 112, 4.
27 Sympathizers in high places:
Tac., *Ann.*, II, 40, 6. Clementia: 31,
4, with Levick, *art. cit.*, 130 ff. Concordia: 32, 4; and see above, p. 62.
28 Tac., *Ann.*, I, 4, 5. For the dual
succession, see E. Kornemann, *Doppelprinzipat*, 40 ff.; Levick, *Lat.*, 1966,
239 ff. Relations between the
brothers: see above, Ch. IV, n. 9.
29 See Mommsen, *Herm.*, 1878,
245 ff. (= *Ges. Schr.*, IV, 271 ff.).
30 *PIR*[2] I 636.
31 Tac., *Ann.*, IV, 4, 2.
32 Livia's political 'achievements'
are documented in *PIR*[2] I 301. They
include the murders of Marcellus and
C. and L. Caesar, the return and adoption of Tiberius, the exile and murder

of Agrippà Postumus, the murder of Augustus, and the concealment of Augustus' death. Most items may be credited to the imagination of Scribonia and her supporters, and other detractors of Tiberius: Livia needed only to exist to incur hatred. Help for her son and other politicians: Tac., *Ann.*, V, 2, 1; Suet., *Tib.*, 51, 1; *Div. Claud.*, 4, 1 ff.; Vell. Pat., II, 130, 5: 'accessione dignitatis'; L. R. Taylor, *MAAR*, 1956, 7 ff. See also above, Ch. IX, n. 63. Honours curtailed: Tac., *Ann.*, I, 14, 1 ff.; IV, 37 f.; Dio, LVII, 12; Suet., *Tib.*, 26, 2; 50, 2 (during her lifetime); Tac., *Ann.*, V, 1, 4; 2, 1; Dio, LVIII, 2, 1 ff.; Suet., *Tib.*, 51, 2; *Cal.*, 16, 3; *Galba*, 5, 2 (after death). Bad relations with Tiberius: see above and Tac., *Ann.*, I, 72, 5; IV, 57, 4; Suet., *Tib.*, 59, 1. Chastity, etc.: V, 1, 5 f.; Val. Max., VI, 1, 1; Vell. Pat., II, 75, 3. Ulysses: Suet., *Cal.*, 23, 2. The sketch by J. P. V. D. Balsdon, *Roman Women*, London, 1962, 90 ff., is just.

33 For Agrippina's character, see Tac., *Ann.*, I, 33, 5; II, 72, 1; III, 1, 1; see above, p. 51. Heroism at the bridge and its effect on Tiberius: I, 69.

34 For Germanicus' powers, see Tac., *Ann.*, II, 43, 2, and Akveld, *Germanicus*, 74 ff. For political motives for the grant, Tac., *Ann.*, II, 5, 2. For the mission, 53 ff., 69 ff., and other sources in *PIR²* I 221, p. 181 ff. Birth of Julia Livilla: Tac., *Ann.*, II, 54, 1.

35 Cn. Piso, appointment and temperament: Tac., *Ann.*, II, 43, 3 ff. See also *PIR²* C 287 and D. C. Shotter, *Hist.*, 1974, 230 ff.

36 See above, Ch. IX, n. 15.

37 C. Caesar: *cf.* Oros., VII, 3, 4

f., 'ad ordinandas Aegypti Syriaeque provincias missus', *cf.* Pliny, *NH*, II, 168; VI, 160; XII, 55; Suet., *Div. Aug.*, 93.

38 For the effect of Germanicus' visit on Tiberius, see Tac., *Ann.*, II, 59, and Suet., *Tib.*, 52. Tacitus' 'acerrime increpuit' probably refers to the contents of a private letter; the rebuke in the Senate may have been mild.

39 For the vicissitudes of Vonones, see above, Ch. IX, n. 79.

40 For the date, see *Fasti Ant.*, *Inscr. Ital.*, XIII, ii, 209.

41 Tac., *Ann.*, III, 1 ff.; see above, Ch. VIII, n. 28.

42 Tac., *Ann.*, II, 83, and *EJ²* 94a, adding five centuries of Germanicus to those of C. and L. Caesar. See S. Weinstock, *JRS*, 1957, 144 ff.; R. P. Fink, A. S. Hoey, W. F. Snyder, *YCS*, 1940, 136 ff. For Drusus, see Tac., *Ann.*, IV, 9; 2; and *EJ²* 94b (five more centuries).

43 Tac., *Ann.*, III, 8 f., *cf.* Suet., *Cal.*, 2.

44 For the trial, see Tac., *Ann.*, III, 12 ff., and Rogers, *Trials*, 36 ff.; and above, Ch. XI.

45 Tac., *Ann.*, II, 84, 1 f.; see *PIR²* I 224; 226, where the date of the twins' birth is taken, with O. Hirschfeld, *Herm.*, 1890, 366 ff. (= *Kl. Schr.* 857 ff.), and Degrassi, *Inscr. Ital.*, XIII, i, 216, to be 20 rather than 19; but see Furneaux and Koestermann, *ad loc.*, and Meise, *Untersuchungen*, 66, n. 116. The coins: *CREBM*, I, 113, no. 95 ff.; *RIC*, I, 107, no. 28.

46 Tac., *Ann.*, III, 29, 1 ff.; Suet., *Tib.*, 54, 1. Meise, *Untersuchungen*, 64 f., thinks that they were eclipsed by the twins, *cf.* D. Hennig, *Seianus*, 44, n. 17.

47 See above, pp. 62 f.

48 Tac., *Ann.*, III, 29, 4; IV, 60, 4; VI, 27, 1; Dio, LX, 18, 4.

49 Tac., *Ann.*, IV, 4, 1, Suet., *loc. cit.*

50 Tac., *Ann.*, III, 56, with other evidence cited in *PIR*² I 219, p. 176. For the date see Rogers, *AJP*, 1940, 457 ff.

51 The trip to Pannonia: Tac., *Ann.*, I, 24 ff. No part in the Pannonian Revolt: Dio, LVI, 17, 3. Ovid credits him with 'vigor' in *ex Ponto*, II, 2, 72. Illness of 21: Tac., *Ann.*, III, 49, 1.

52 Ovation (28 May 20, three years and two days after Germanicus' triumph): Tac., *Ann.*, III, 11, 3; 19, 3, *cf.* 56, 4; *Fasti Ost.*, *Inscr. Ital.*, XIII, i, 186 f.; 216 (= *EJ*² p. 41). Tiberius on ovations: Tac., *Ann.*, III, 47, 5 (but Drusus needed military distinction, Tiberius no longer did so).

53 Drusus 'rudis dicendi' as consul designate in AD 14: Tac., *Ann.*, I, 29, 1. For Drusus' popularity, Rogers, *Studies*, 152 f., cites Tac., *Ann.*, III, 37, 2 f. (contrast with Tiberius' unpopularity); M. Stuart, *CP*, 1940, 64 ff., counts the numbers of extant portraits.

54 Dissoluteness and cruelty: Tac., *Ann.*, I, 29, 4; 76, 5; II, 44, 1; III, 37, 3; IV, 10, 2; Plut., *Mor.*, 624 C; Pliny, *NH*, XIV, 144 f. (like Tiberius, on whom see Suet., *Tib.*, 42, *cf.* Dio, LVIII, fr. 3; but Tiberius was a connoisseur: Pliny, *NH*, XIV, 16; 64). Drusus was exempted by Tiberius from speaking first at the trial of Aemilia Lepida, Tac., *Ann.*, III, 24, 6; but that does not mean (*pace* Rogers, *Trials*, 55) that Drusus had a taste for convictions. He is wrongly said to have

presided over the trial of Clutorius Priscus (so Rogers, *Trials*, 63; *Studies*, 129; followed by Levick, *The Ancient Historian and his Materials*, 123). Drusus had been succeeded by a suffect by the time of the trial ('fine anni': Tac., *Ann.*, III, 49, 1). He caused offence by taking up the *tribunicia potestas* in absence: III, 59, 3; he may have been convalescent (so Seager, *Tib.*, 122).

55 *Fasti Ant.*; *Viae dei Serpenti*, *Inscr. Ital.*, XIII, i, 329; ii, 214 f. = *EJ*² P. 52. Other references in *PIR*² I 219, p. 176.

56 See e.g. R. Syme, *Tac.*, I, 402 f.; Th. Pekáry, *Röm. Mitt.*, 1966–67, 115 ff.; Boddington, *art. cit.* (n. X*).

57 'Plena Caesarum domus': Tac., *Ann.*, IV, 3, 1. Origins: 1, 3; *Vell. Pat.*, II, 127, 3. Modern accounts (n. X*, most recently D. Hennig, *Seianus*, 5 ff.) neglect the language of Velleius, which suggests that Sejanus' consular brothers and cousins were (like the uncle) on his mother's side.

58 Caecilia: Tac., *Ann.*, II, 43, 7.

59 Tac., *Ann.*, IV, 1, 3; see above, p. 47.

60 Seius, Strabo had been succeeded, if he was Prefect of Egypt, by AD 16: A. Stein, *Die Präfekten von Ägypten in der römischen Kaiserzeit*, Bern, 1950, 24, *cf.* Hennig, *Seianus*, 7 f.

61 See above, p. 121.

62 Tac., *Ann.*, IV, 3, 2 (under 23: 'recenti ira': Drusus had hit Sejanus); Dio, LVII, 22, 1 (under AD 23: Sejanus struck Drusus "ποτε"), *cf.* 14, 9 (AD 15: Drusus struck a distinguished *eques*). See Scott, *art. cit.* (n. X*), with Hennig, *Seianus*, 32, n. 1. Drusus and Sejanus seem to have moved in the same circle: Gavius Apicius the gourmet was a link: Tac.,

Ann., IV, 1, 3; Dio, LVII, 19, 5; Pliny, *NH*, XIX, 137.

63 Tac., *Ann.*, IV, 2, 4, *cf.* Dio, LVIII, 4, 3 (AD 30), Vell. Pat., II, 127, 3: 'principalium onerum adiutorem', *cf.* 128, 4. Tacitus might be taking the title back too far, but *cf.* Dio, LVII, 19, 7. Tacitus is insistent at IV, 7, 2 ('incolumi filio adiutorem imperii alium vocari'), and Tiberius had already praised Sejanus' 'labor vigilantiaque' in checking the fire that burnt down Pompey's theatre in 22 (III, 72, 4 f.); perhaps there was an implied criticism of Drusus' conduct at a fire: Dio, LVII, 14, 10. Strained relations between Tiberius and Drusus: 13, 1 f.; 22, 3; Tac., *Ann.*, I, 76, 3 f., Suet., *Tib.*, 52, 1 f. Story that Tiberius poisoned Drusus: Dio, LVIII, 22, 3; Tac., *Ann.*, IV, 10, 1 ff. For *socii laborum*, see P. Grenade, *Essai sur les Origines du Principat*, Paris, 1961, 444 ff. Strabo applied it to Germanicus and Drusus: VI, p. 240. It fits the official picture of Sejanus (Vell. Pat., II, 127, 3; Tac., *Ann.*, IV, 39, 3), brought out by Seager, *Tib.*, 196.

64 Dio, LVII, 19, 7; see Mommsen, *St.*, I³, 456 ff.

65 Tac., *Ann.*, III, 29, 5 f., *cf.* Suet., *Div. Claud.*, 27, 1. See Furneaux, *ad loc.*

66 See Suet., *Div. Claud.*, 5 f. (attempts at promotion); Tac., *Ann.*, III, 2, 4; 3, 2 (interment of Germanicus); 18, 4 ff. (L. Asprenas' query).

67 Tac., *Ann.*, III, 49 ff. See Rogers, *Trials*, 62 ff.; see above, 185 f. The consul who admitted the charge was Mam. Aemilius Scaurus or Cn. Tremellius. But Scaurus seems later to have been a friend of Sejanus (Tac.,

Ann., VI, 29, 5 f.; Dio, LVIII, 24, 5), and in 22 he joined other supporters of the prefect in prosecuting C. Silanus (III, 66, 1).

68 See *PIR*² H 25. Haterius was half cousin to Drusus, half nephew to Agrippina, and half cousin once removed to Germanicus; the connexion with Agrippina explains why Tac., *Ann.*, II, 51, 2, should say that Germanicus and Drusus favoured him as 'propinquum Germanici'.

69 For the Vitellian group, see Syme, *Tac.*, I, 386. Petronius and Claudius: Sen., *Apoc.*, 14, 2. Claudius' wife Plautia Urgulanilla: Suet., *Div. Claud.*, 26, 2. For the Plautii, see L. R. Taylor, *MAAR*, 1956, 7 ff. Nicols, *art. cit.* (n. X*), denies Claudius' divorce of Plautia Urgulanilla and his marriage to Aelia Paetina (Suet., *Div. Claud.*, 26, 2), a connexion of Sejanus, any political significance.

70 *Fasti Ost.*, *Inscr. Ital.*, XIII, i, 186 f. = *EJ*² p. 42.

71 Dio, LVIII, 11, 6, *cf.* Tac., *Ann.*, IV, 8, 1 f.; 10 f.; Suet., *Tib.*, 62, 1; Eus., *Chron.*, s.a. 22, p. 172 Helm. Jos. *AJ*, XVIII, 206, has a natural death. Foul play is denied by W. Eisenhut, *MH*, 1950, 123 ff.; J. P. V. D. Balsdon, *CR*, 1951, 75; Syme, *Tac.*, I, 401 f., Seager, *Tib.*, 181 ff. Dio is wrong in one respect at least: Apicata can have seen only one of her children dead on the Gemoniae: the others survived until November or December (*Fasti Ost.*, *loc. cit.*).

72 Tac., *Ann.*, IV, 3, 5, seems to put the divorce under AD 23, before the death of Drusus; 23 is accepted by *PIR*² A 913, but the date is not firm.

73 Vipsania: Tac., *Ann.*, III, 19, 4. Quirinius: III, 48; Longus and the twin (Germanicus); IV, 15, 1 f.

74 Tac., *Ann.*, IV, 8, 2 ff.

75 Tiberius and Nero Drusus had entered their consulships at twenty-eight; Germanicus and Drusus Caesar at twenty-six (see Levick, *Lat.*, 1966, 227 ff.); the careers of the latter were irregular departures from the 'norm', caused by special political circumstances: above, pp. 62–63, and see Levick, *Lat.*, 1976. The precedent cited (Tac., *Ann.*, III, 29, 2) was Tiberius' own and Nero Drusus'; no mention of Germanicus and Drusus Caesar.

76 Tac., *Ann.*, IV, 17, 1 ff., *cf.* Suet., *Tib.*, 54, 1.

77 Tac., *Ann.*, IV, 18 ff. For the view that Sejanus' part in the trials of 24–27 was smaller than has been supposed, see Hennig, *Seianus*, 41 ff.

78 M. Lepidus' proposals: Tac., *Ann.*, III, 50, IV, 20, 3, with character sketch.

79 *PIR²* A 1229. Cultivates Sejanus: Dio, LVIII, 3, 1 f., *cf.* Tac., *Ann.*, IV, 71, 3 ff.

80 Tac., *Ann.*, IV, 28 ff.; Dio, LVII, 23, 2, with Bauman, *Impietas*, 114 f. Another intended victim of the younger Serenus in the following year was C. Fonteius Capito, proconsul of Asia and Germanicus' colleague in the consulship of AD 12: 36, 4 f. The attempt to dispose of two close friends of Tiberius is interesting. For the Vibii, see above, p. 53.

81 Pliny, *NH*, XI, 187; Tac., *Ann.*, III, 13, 3.

82 Tac., *Ann.*, II, 56, 5; III, 13, 3; 19, 1; VI, 7, 2 ff., with Syme, *Tac.*, I, 325.

83 Tac., *Ann.*, V, 8, 1 ff.

84 Tac., *Ann.*, IV, 31, 5 f.

85 The statue: Tac., *Ann.*, III, 72, 5, *cf.* IV, 7, 3; Sen., *ad Marc.*, 22, 4.

The trial: Tac., *Ann.*, IV, 34 f.; Sen., *loc. cit.*, and 1, 2 ff.; Dio, LVII, 24, 2 ff., *cf.* Suet., *Tib.*, 61, 3. The books: Suet., *Cal.*, 16, 1. Satrius Secundus became 'coniurationis index': Tac., *Ann.*, VI, 47, 2. For legal aspects of the trial, see above, pp. 193 f.

86 Tac., *Ann.*, IV, 39 ff., sceptically handled by Syme, *Tac.*, I, 404, and II, 702; he notes a careful choice of words. These are 'perrumpo' (40, 7), 'tranquillitas' (8), 'dubitatio' (9), 'excelsus' (of things) (12); see N. P. Miller, *AJP*, 1968, 14 ff. Seager, *Tib.*, 195 ff. accepts the correspondence and treats it in detail; his interpretation of 39, 6 (*Livia's* 'domus', with Koestermann against Furneaux), is unacceptable.

87 Suet., *Div. Claud.*, 4, 1 ff.

88 Tac., *Ann.*, IV, 53, 2 f.

89 Adultery alleged by Tiberius: Tac., *Ann.*, VI, 25, 2, with Furneaux sceptical.

90 Tac., *Ann.*, I, 13, 2, with Syme, *Tac.*, I, 381 f.

91 Tac., *Ann.*, IV, 52. For speculation as to her descent, see Wiseman, *HSCP*, 1968, 215 ff.; either a daughter of Marcella (Minor) by M. Valerius Barbatus Appianus, *cos.* 12 BC (so Syme, *RR*, stemma III), or of Marcella (Major) by Pulcher Claudius (so Wiseman, followed here). Furnius may be a connexion of the consul of 17 BC, formerly a follower of Antonius (*PIR²* F 591).

92 Tac., *Ann.*, IV, 66. For the relationship, see Syme, *RR*, 424, 434, and *stemma* VII.

93 *Contra*, Seager, *Tib.*, 205, because of the absence of Varus' family from subsequent history. Seager thinks (201) that the charge of *maiestas* against Pulchra had been allowed to drop.

94 Betrothal: Sen., *Contr.*, I, 3, 10, *cf. PIR*² I 674.

95 See Wiseman, *art. cit.*, 220 (*stemma*); 221, n. 65.

96 Tac., *Ann.*, IV, 52, 3 ff.; Suet., *Tib.*, 53, 1. Greek was the language of the extorted confession.

97 Tac., *Ann.*, IV, 54; Suet., *loc. cit.* ('simulans veneni se crimine accersi').

98 For the causes of Tiberius' leaving Rome, see Tac., *Ann.*, IV, 57 (Sejanus, the cause cited by most historians, *cf.* 41, 2; desire to hide cruelty and vices; shame at appearance; secret pleasures; Livia). Suet., *Tib.*, 51, 2, and Dio, LVII, 12, 6, both offer Livia. The astrologers: Tac., *Ann.*, IV, 58, 2 ff.

99 Tac., *Ann.*, IV, 57, 3, *cf.* Suet., *Tib.*, 68, 1 ff. Tiberius was addicted to cucumbers; he may as well as eating them have used them to soothe his skin (Pliny, *NH*, XIX, 64).

100 His companions on Capri were the consular jurisconsult M. Cocceius Nerva, Sejanus, another *eques illustris*, and a number of savants, mainly Greeks, whose conversation entertained him: Tac., *Ann.*, IV, 58, 1, and see above, p. 16. Juvenal thinks of them as astrologers: X, 94. For drink, see above, n. 54. No doubt there were other pleasures (for sources, see below, Ch. XII, n. 93): Tiberius had been free since his divorce at forty. It is only on Rhodes and Capri, where no one knew what was going on, that scandal arises; on campaign and at Rome Tiberius seems to have been more discreet than the Duke of Wellington.

101 Tac., *Ann.*, IV, 59, 1 f.

102 Tac., *Ann.*, IV, 59, 5; 60.

103 Tac., *Ann.*, IV, 60, 5 f., under the year of 26.

104 Tac., *Ann.*, IV, 18, 1; 19, 1; 68 ff.; Dio, LVIII, 1, 1 ff.; Pliny, *NH*, VIII, 145, mentioning the slaves and implicating Nero: 'ex causa Neronis', a chronological slip.

105 For the name, see Syme, *JRS*, 1949, 13, and *Tac.*, I, 277, n. 7.

106 Tac., *Ann.*, IV, 68, 2: Porcius Cato, suffect in 36 and *curator aquarum* for a month before perishing in 38: *cf.* 71, 1 ff., and see Koestermann and Furneaux, *ad loc.*; Petilius Rufus, on whom see A. Birley, *Britannia*, 1973, 180 f.; M. Opsius: see *IG*, XIV, 719 (Naples).

107 Vell. Pat., II, 130, 4.

108 Tac., *Ann.*, V, 1 ff., unequivocal on the order of events and supported by Syme, *Tac.*, I, 405, n. 2. The date of Livia's death is put towards the end of 29 by Rogers, *Trials*, 98, who follows N. Cortellini, *Riv. di stor. ant.*, 1898, 19; but Tacitus says that her death was followed by a rebuke to a 'consul'—who left office in June (V, 2, 3). Agrippina and Nero urged to take refuge: IV, 67, 6; Suet., *Tib.*, 53, 2. For a careful account of these events see now Hennig, *Seianus*, 91 ff.

109 Tac., *Ann.*, IV, 5, 5, correctly interpreted by Bauman, *Impietas*, 122.

110 For his connexions, see *PIR*² I 813, *cf.* 730, and Syme, *Tac.*, II, 559.

111 Tac., *Ann.*, V, 2, 3, *cf.* 3, 5: 'aliis a primoribus maximeque a magistratibus trepidabatur'. The consuls *ordinarii* were C. Fufius Geminus and L. Rubellius Geminus, the former a protégé of Livia and his wife, if she is the Mutilia Prisca of IV, 12, 6 f., a friend of Livia's who was the means of damaging relations between her and Agrippina. In the second half of the year the consuls were A. Plautius and L. Asprenas; the former was to win an ovation as Claudius' commander in Britain; the latter was son of the suffect of 6 who had spoken up for Claudius in 20, and legate of Dolabella in Africa (*CIL*, II, 4129). Neither was likely to be a partisan of Sejanus.

112 Punishment: Suet., *Tib.*, 53, 2; 54, 64; *Cal.*, 7; 15, 1. For the declaration of men as *hostes*, see A. W. Lintott, *Violence in Republican Rome*, Oxford, 1968, 155 ff., a political move devised only in 88 B C. Sabinus: Tac., *Ann.*, IV, 70, 4. For the consequences of *aquae et ignis interdictio*, see above, pp. 187 f.

113 Rogers, *Trials*, 101 (so Bauman, *Impietas*, 90), believes that 'judicial proceedings against Nero and Agrippina followed, because of Pliny's reference to the 'causa Neronis' and 'the statement of Philo [*in Flacc.*, 3, 9] that the principal prosecutor of Agrippina was Avillius Flaccus'. Philo's expression is καὶ τῶν συνεπιθεμένων τῇ Γαΐου μητρί, καθ' ὃν χρόνον εἶχε τὰς αἰτίας ἐφ' αἷς ἀνῃρέθη, γεγονώς. Neither this nor Pliny's 'causa' nor Suetonius' 'damnationem' (*Tib.*, 64) implies a formal trial.

114 Tac., *Ann.*, IV, 75, and for other sources see *PIR*² D 127; this marriage was to produce the Princeps Nero.

115 Dio, LVIII, 3, 8: he was simply sent to Rome by Tiberius (perhaps for that purpose?).

116 Tac., *Ann.*, VI, 40, 4; Dio, LVIII, 3, 8; *ILS*, 1848.

117 Dio, *loc. cit.*; Suet., *Tib.*, 54, 2; 64; *Cal.*, 7; Tac., *Ann.*, VI, 23, 4 ff. The disgrace of Drusus should come before the elections of 30, if it is causally connected with Sejanus'

elevation. A Cassius was involved in the attack (Dio) and it has been assumed that one of the consuls of the year, L. or C. Cassius Longinus, is meant. The objections of Rogers, *Trials*, 106, n. 327, have some force: the *ordinarius*, L. Longinus, married Drusus' sister three years later. Perhaps the consul played a purely official part in the attack, reading out the Princeps' letter; or an obscure Cassius is meant.

118 Consulship: *ILS*, 6044 = *EJ*² 53; Tac., *Ann.*, VI, 8, 6; Suet., *Tib.*, 65; 1; Dio, LVII, 20, 2; LVIII, 4, 3; 6, 2; 8, 3. (He was to hold the post again five years ahead with the same colleague: 4, 4.) *Proconsulare imperium*: 7, 4 f. Priesthoods for Sejanus and his son: 7, 4 f. (perhaps the augurate: *PIR*² I 217, p. 170). Tribunician power: Suet., *Tib.*, 65, 1; Dio, LVIII, 9, 2; 4; 10, 3. The betrothal: 3, 9, *cf.* 7, 5; Tac., *Ann.*, VI, 27, 1, *cf.* V, 6, 2 ('generum'), *cf.* Suet., *loc. cit.* Tacitus' word suggests that Livilla was the woman Sejanus was to marry; but Zonaras calls her τῇ τοῦ Δρούσου θυγατρί. See Seager, *Tib.*, 213, n. 6, and Meise, *Untersuchungen*, 57 ff. Tiberius called Sejanus παῖδα καὶ διάδοχον; John of Ant., fr. 79, 8 (Müller, *FGH*, IV, 570).

119 Vell. Pat., II, 127 f. See Syme, *art. cit.* (n. X*).

120 Dio, LVIII, 7, 2, *cf.* Pliny, *NH*, VIII, 197; XXXVI, 163.

121 For what follows see above, p. 119.

122 Tac., *Ann.*, IV, 41, 3, *cf.* VI, 8, 4; Dio, LVIII, 5, 1; 10, 8; Jos., *AJ*, XVIII, 181.

123 The political connexions of Sejanus are elucidated by Bird, *art.*

cit. (n. X*). For the success of his friends and kinsmen, see Tac., *Ann.*, VI, 8, 4; Dio, LVIII, 10, 8. Cn. Lentulus Gaetulicus and L. Apronius: Tac., *Ann.*, VI, 30, 2 ff.
124 The link is shown by Tac., *Hist.*, III, 38, 3, and emphasized by Sumner, *art. cit.* (n. X*), 144 f.
125 For absentee governorships of these provinces by L. Arruntius and L. Lamia, see above, p. 128 f., with the enmity of Sejanus rejected as a reason. But Arruntius was hostile (see above, p. 176), and so probably Lamia (see above, p. 178).
126 The embassy and its consequences: Dio, LVIII, 3, 1 ff. For legal aspects, see below, Ch. XI, n. 51. Tiberius complained of Gallus' jealousy, when he was friendly with Vallius Syriacus, a Theodorean forensic orator who fell with him (Dio, *loc. cit.*, 7). It is a guess to suggest that what was objected to in each friend was a propensity to bring accusations (*cf.* Sen., *Contr.*, IX, 4, 18).
127 Tac., *Ann.*, IV, 58, 1; VI, 10, 2.
128 The views of Sealey, *Phoen.*. 1961, 97 ff., esp. 105 ff., are untenable.
129 Suet., *Tib.*, 61, *cf.* Tac., *Ann.*, VI, 3, 4. Seager, *Tib.*, 214, writes 'had plotted'.
130 Parricide, etc.: Val. Max., IX, 11, ext. 4. Tac., *Ann.*, VI, 8, 11, makes a defendant ask that 'insidiae in rem publicam, consilia caedis adversum imperatorem puniantur: de amicitia et officiis idem finis et te, Caesar, et nos absolverit'. But that is general. *Cf.* Jos., *AJ*, XVIII, 181; Juv., X, 86. The sources are listed by Rogers, *Trials*, 110, n. 345, who holds that there was a plot against Tiberius, against Marsh, *Reign*, 304 ff. Seager, *Tib.*, 216, thinks the plot, if not pure

fiction, undertaken as a last hope of survival when Sejanus found out that Tiberius had turned against him. For the Guard, see Suet., *Tib.*, 65, 1. Nicols, *art. cit.*, explains the story of the attack on Tiberius as stemming from a source later than the assassination of Gaius Caligula; Meise, *op. cit.*, 77 ff., as the official charge.
131 Suet., *Tib.*, 65, 1.
132 The message: Jos., *AJ*, XVIII, 181 ff.; Dio, LXV, 14, 1 f. The important role ascribed to Antonia herself in exposing Sejanus (accepted by Seager, *Tib.*, 216 f.) is accounted for by Nicols, *art. cit.* (n. X*). Gaius' moves: Suet., *Cal.*, 10, 1 (the birthday) 8, 1, confirmed by the *Fasti Val.*, and Pigh., *Inscr. Ital.*, XIII, i, 317; ii, 218 = *EJ*² p. 51.
133 Gaius on Capri: Suet., *Cal.*, 10, 2; Paconianus: Tac., *Ann.*, VI, 3, 4 f.
134 Dio, LVIII, 9, 2, with 12, 7 for additional honours proposed for Macro and Laco. For Macro's full and correct name and offices, see *Rend. d. Acc. Naz. Lincei*, Cl. di Sci. mor., stor. e filol., 1957, 39 ff. = Smallwood, *Documents illustrating the Principates of Gaius, Claudius and Nero*, 254. For Laco see *PIR*² G 202: he became *procurator Galliarum* and in 44 was awarded consular *ornamenta* by Claudius: *ILS*, 1336; Dio, LX, 23, 3.
135 For Ennia Thrasylla, see *PIR*² E 65. If Cichorius, *RS*, 391 ff., is correct, Thrasyllus married his daughter to an Ennius (perhaps the *eques* saved from prosecution for *maiestas* by Tiberius in 22: Tac., *Ann.*, III, 70). The sexual intrigue, if genuine, dates to the period after the death of Gaius' first wife Iunia Claudilla or Claudia, whom he married in 33 (Tac., *Ann.*, VI, 20, 1; Dio, LVIII, 25, 2, wrongly

has 35) and who died in childbirth (Suet., *Cal.*, 12, 2).

136 See *PIR*² A 858, with *Rylands Papyrus*, II, 255, no. 192 (a), for the property. Note also (M. Antonius?) Hiberus, Prefect of Egypt in 32: see *PIR*² A 837. Probably he was there supervising Antonia's property when the death of Sejanus ended Galerius' term, and was a quick and safe replacement. When Antonia Caenis was freed is not known.

137 What follows is derived from Dio, LVIII, 3 ff., and 4, 9 ff. The chronology is uncertain.

138 Suet., *Tib.*, 19, 1; Miller, *AJP*, 1968, 14.

139 *ILS*, 6124; 15 May according to Suet., *Tib.*, 26, 2 (a corruption in the text). The *Ludi Martiales* opened on 12 May, and should be given by the consuls; Tiberius was on Capri; *cf.* Dio, LVI, 46, 4.

140 Suet., *Tib.*, 54, 2, *cf.* 61, 1 ('suspecto Seiano'); note the position of the event in Dio's narrative: LVIII, 8, 4.

141 Suet., *Cal.*, 10, 1. *Cf.*, e.g., *Nero*, 12, 4, for the date of Nero's ceremony (61, at the age of twenty-three or twenty-four).

142 Dio, LVIII, 8, 1, *cf.* 7, 4; Suet., *Cal.*, 12, 1, with *PIR*² I 217, p. 170. Seager, *Tib.*, 217, dates the grant early in the year.

143 Dio, LVIII, 8, 4, *cf.* Suet., *Tib.*, 26, 1; Tac., *Ann.*, IV, 38, 1 ff.

144 Dio, LVIII, 8, 3 (before the letter about Nero); *senatus consultum* and date: *Dig.*, XLVIII, 2, 12 pr. For the possible charge, see Weinrib, *Phoen.*, 1968, 52 ff. Seager, *Tib.*, 218, n. 6, denies that the passage proves that a Lentulus defended Arruntius. For Cossus as the Lentulus, see Rogers,

Trials, 109, and *CP*, 1931, 37 ff. Conviction for *calumnia*: Tac., *Ann.*, VI, 7, 1; *cf.* Dio, LVIII, 10, 1? For the names of the accusers, Syme, *JRS*, 1949, 9 and 15.

145 Fufius: Tac., *Ann.*, V, 2, 2 f. His wife: IV, 12, 6. Their fall: Dio, LVIII, 4, 5 ff. His mother: Tac., *Ann.*, VI, 10, 1. This case is probably the basis of Suet., *Tib.*, 51, 2.

146 Juv., X, 71; part of contents: Suet., *Tib.*, 65, 2.

147 See above, p. 37. Sejanus as *hostis*: *ILS*, 157; Juv., X, 85. Regulus' loyalty: Dio, LVIII, 13, 3.

148 Pliny, *NH*, VIII, 197; Dio, LVIII, 12, 2. Sejanus' hold over the Guard is clearly brought out by Dio (8, 2) and by Jos., *AJ*, XVIII, 181.

149 Suet., *Tib.*, 48, 2, *cf.* Tac., *Ann.*, IV, 2, 4. Lamia: VI, 27, 2, and Dio, LVIII, 19, 5, with *PIR*² A 200.

150 Val. Max., IX, 11, ext. 4: 'omni cum stirpe sua populi Romani viribus obtritus'. Blaesus: Tac., *Ann.*, V, 7, 2. Strabo and the children: *Fasti Ost.*, *Inscr. Ital.*, XIII, i, 186 ff. = *EJ*² p. 42; Tac., *Ann.*, V, 9; Dio, LVIII, 11, 5. *Cf.* Hennig, *Seianus*, 14, n. 40.

151 Dio, LVIII, 11, 6 f., attributing responsibility for her death to Tiberius, Suet., *Tib.*, 62, 1, but reporting a story that he spared her and she was starved by Antonia. Probably he conducted a family enquiry (*cf.* Suet., *Tib.*, 62, 1) and handed her over for punishment (*cf.* Tac., *Ann.*, II, 50, 4). 'Damnatio memoriae': VI, 2, 1. Adultery with Drusus' poisoner Eudemus was an easy frill: Pliny, *NH*, XXIX, 20. Hennig, *Seianus*, 38, posits death from natural causes.

152 Tac., *Ann.*, VI, 48, 4 (L. Arruntius).

CHAPTER XI

XI* A. H. M. Jones, *Hist.*, 1955, 464 ff. = *Studies*, 67 ff.; *The criminal Courts of the Roman Republic and early Principate*, ed. J. Crook, Oxford, 1972; J. Bleicken, *Senatsgericht und Kaisergericht*, Göttingen, 1962; Marsh, *Reign*, 106 ff.; 289 ff.; Rogers, *Trials*; *JRS*, 1959, 90 ff.; E. Koestermann, *Hist.*, 1955, 72 ff. (bibliography: 75, n. 5); C. W. Chilton, *JRS*, 1955, 73 ff.; J. E. Allison and J. D. Cloud, *Lat.*, 1962, 711 ff.; Bauman, *Maiestas* and *Impietas* (bibliographies).

1 See above, p. 89, with Ch. VI, nn. 32, 33, and below, Ch. XII, n. 79.

2 Dio, LI, 19, 6; Suet., *Div. Aug.*, 33, 3. Jones, *Studies*, 51 ff., discusses the origin of these rights, *cf.* D. Flach, *Hist.*, 1973, 569. For Tiberius, see Dio, LVII, 7, 2; LXI, 8, 4 (refused cases on appeal from M. Silanus, suff. AD 15); Tac., *Ann.*, II, 48, 1 f. ('bona'); Suet., *Tib.*, 57, 2 (summary execution; Mr G. E. M. de Ste Croix kindly drew my attention to this passage).

3 *Fasti Praen.*, and *Vat.*, *Inscr. Ital.*, XIII, ii, 120 f.; 172 f.; *ILS*, 154 = *EJ*[2] p. 47.

4 Tac., *Ann.*, II, 35, 2 (Asinius Gallus).

5 Tac., *Ann.*, III, 69, 6: 'minui iura quotiens gliscat potestas, nec utendum imperio, ubi legibus agi possit'.

6 Vell. Pat., II, 129, 2.

7 Tac., *Ann.*, I, 75, 1 f. (under AD 15); Suet., *Tib.*, 33; Dio, LVII, 7, 6 (under AD 14).

8 Tac., *Ann.*, II, 34, 1 f.; IV, 21, 1. *Cf.* (for improvement) Vell. Pat., II, 126, 2: 'sepultae . . . iustitia, aequitas . . . civitati redditae; accessit . . . iudiciis gravitas'.

9 Dio, LVII, 21, 1.

10 Tac., *Ann.*, IV, 19, 2 f. For the participation of magistrates in criminal proceedings, denied by Bauman, *Hist.*, 1966, 420 ff., see S. A. Jameson, *Hist.*, 1969, 206 ff., and E. J. Weinrib, *Phoen.*, 1968, 32 ff.

11 *Dig.*, XLVIII, 5, 39 (38), 10.

12 For the Republican cases, see Broughton, *MRR*, and the full discussion of Weinrib, *art. cit.*, 46 ff., excluding Murena as tried in a *quaestio* and distinct from the consul of 23; see above, Ch. X, n. 14.

13 The praetor: Dio, LVII, 21, 2 (AD 22), identified by Weinrib, *art. cit.*, 48, with the praetor Magius Caecilianus: Tac., *Ann.*, III, 37, 1 (AD 21). Rescript: Rogers, *Trials*, 178. Silvanus: Tac., *Ann.*, IV, 22, discussed by Weinrib, *art. cit.*, 48, n. 65, *cf.* Jones, *Criminal Courts*, 112, with different interpretations of 'datis iudicibus'.

14 Caligula: Dio, LIX, 23, 8. Nero: Tac., *Ann.*, XIV, 48, 2 (political case); XIII, 44 (*crime passionel* committed by a tribune).

15 Tac., *Ann.*, II, 33; III, 52 ff. For minor regulations (some affecting *plebs* rather than senators), see Suet., *Tib.*, 34, 1, and A. Gell., *NA*, II, 24, 14.

16 Tac., *Ann.*, VI, 16 f.

17 Tac., *Ann.*, III, 25, 1 ff.; 28, 4 ff., *cf.* Suet., *Div. Claud.*, 23, 1.

18 Tac., *Ann.*, IV, 30, 3 ff.; see above, p. 190.

19 Tac., *Ann.*, II, 34, 3 ff.; IV, 21, 1.

20 Tac., *Ann.*, IV, 6, 7.

21 Sen., *de Ben.*, III, 26, 1, *cf.* Dio, LVIII, 23, 4 (AD 33), and Tac., *Ann.*, VI, 7, 4, with medical metaphor.

22 Dio, LIX, 4, 3; 16, 1 f., *cf.* Suet., *Cal.*, 15, 4. For the interpretation of such abolitions, see Bauman, *Impietas*, 191 ff. They may help to explain why Tacitus thought that Tiberius 'brought back' the charge (*Ann.*, I, 72, 3).

23 Date: Broughton, *MRR*, I, 565, n. 4; interpretation: Bauman, *Maiestas*, 34 ff. For procedure and changes before the *lex Appuleia*, *id. ibid.*, 16 ff.; M. I. Henderson, *JRS*, 1951, 78; Jones, *Criminal Courts*, Ch. I, esp. 15 ff.

24 Cic., *de Or.*, II, 25, 107. *Cf.* Cicero's defence of C. Cornelius in 65: Asc., 61C.

25 Sources: Broughton, *MRR*, II, 75. Interpretation: Bauman, *Maiestas*, 68 ff., underestimating the comprehensiveness of Sulla's law: see K. M. T. Atkinson, *Iura*, 1967, 305 f.

26 *Cf. Auct. ad Her.*, II, 12, 17. The sixth surviving clause of the '*lex de Imperio Vespasiani*' (*ILS*, 244 = *EJ*² 364) serves a comparable purpose.

27 Cic., *ad Fam.*, III, 11, 3, where I suggest 'verbum tamen est maiestas'. For other remedies and interpretations, see Bauman, *Maiestas*, 247 ff. For the judgment, *cf.* Pliny, *Pan.*, 42, 1.

28 Dio, LIV, 3, 4 ff.

29 The view that the high court of the Senate was Tiberius' creation (W. Kunkel, *Roman legal and constitutional History*, tr. J. Kelly, Oxford, 1970, 67) is unwarranted. The change is attested by AD 8 (Ovid, *Trist.*, II, 131 f., *cf. SEG*, IX, 8 = *EJ*² 311, of 4 BC). It is discussed by Jones, *art. cit.* (n. XI*), who favours a *lex*; *contra*, Weinrib, *Phoen.*, 1968, 46 (consular *coercitio* with the Senate as *consilium*); by Bleicken, *op. cit.* (n. XI*), 17 ff.; by P. Garnsey, *Social Status and legal Privilege in the Roman Empire*, 17 ff. Murder seems not to have been included: Tac., *Ann.*, III, 12, 10 (con-

venience demanded that the murder of Germanicus should be taken with the other charges); IV, 22, 3 ('datis iudicibus').

30 Tac., *Ann.*, XII, 60.

31 See Mommsen, *St.*, III, ii, 992 f.; Jones, *Criminal Courts*, 111. After the Murena affair Augustus had demanded open voting in cases that went by default: Dio, LIV, 3, 6. Procedure in the Senate is illustrated by Pliny, *Ep.*, VIII, 14, 13; that voting was normally secret is not shown by Tac., *Ann.*, I, 74, 5.

32 Dio, LIX, 16, 2, *cf.* LVIII, 16, 3.

33 Tac., *Agr.*, 45, 1.

34 Dio, LVIII, 10 ff.; Tac., *Ann.*, III, 51, 2 ff.

35 *Cf.* Tac., *Ann.*, III, 67, 5: 'ne quis . . . iuvaret periclitantem, maiestatis crimina subdebantur'. Tiberius (68, 1) treated Volesus Messalla's offences as precedents for those of Silanus; was he too accused of *maiestas*? But see Seager, *Tib.*, 160.

36 Silius: Tac., *Ann.*, IV, 19, 5, with Henderson, *JRS*, 1951, 77 f., for overlapping charges. Varilla: II, 50.

37 Tac., *Ann.*, III, 38, 1: 'omnium accusationum complementum'; *cf.* Rogers, *Trials*, 193. Sixteen cases of tacking (if husbands, wives, and partners in adultery are taken separately) are recorded for the principate of Tiberius, *id. ibid.*, 206 ff.

38 Bauman, *Impietas*, 21, 54 ff., makes this valuable point.

39 Tac., *Ann.*, III, 49 ff.; Dio, LVII, 20, 3 f. For magic as the charge see Ciaceri, *Processi politici e Relazioni internazionali*, 160 f.; M. P. Charlesworth, *CAH*, X, 630; Bauman, *Impietas*, 62 ff.; Koestermann, *art. cit.*, 99, n. 64, approves.

40 Cordus: Tac., *Ann.*, IV, 34, 1.

The charge here might be *maiestas* with a new content (so Bauman, *Impietas*, 99 ff.); it depends on the meaning of 'neque haec in principem aut principis parentem, quos lex maiestatis amplectitur' (3). Tiberius' letter: Dio, LVIII, 10, 1, *cf.* Juv., X, 69 ff. Sejanus' children: Tac., *Ann.*, V, 9; illegality: *Dig.*, XLVIII, 19, 20, 25. See Bauman, *Impietas*, 177 ff., for cases of 'manifest guilt' and the *'nullo crimine'* technique (but beginning under Claudius).

41 Dio, LIII, 23, 7; Tac., *Ann.*, I, 6, 2; Suet., *Div. Aug.*, 65, 4.

42 See Bauman, *locc. citt.*, and (approving of Tiberius' attitude) 227. Tiberian appeals to law: Tac., *Ann.*, III, 50, 6; IV, 20, 3; 34, 3. *Cf.* II, 51. Such an appeal was still possible in 62: XIV, 48, 6.

43 Pliny, *Ep.*, IV, 9, 17, with Bleicken, *Senatsgericht*, 37 ff., and A. N. Sherwin-White, *ad loc.*

44 So, e.g., E. Levy, *Die röm. Kapitalstrafe, Sitzungsb. d. Heidelberger Akad. d. Wiss.*, phil-hist. Kl., V Abh., 1930–31, 42 ff.; C. W. Chilton, *art. cit.* (n. XI*), 74 f.; Allison and Cloud, *art. cit.* (n. XI*), 723 ff.; Koestermann, *art. cit.* (n. XI*), 100, n. 66; Bauman, *Impietas*, 11; *contra*, Jones, *Studies*, 191, n. 65, and *Criminal Courts*, 74. The evidence is Cic., *Phil.*, I, 23; Tac., *Ann.*, III, 38, 3; 50, 6; [Paul] *Sent.*, V, 29, 1.

45 Vell. Pat., II, 100, 4. I hope to return to this point elsewhere.

46 See A. H. J. Greenidge, *The Legal Procedure of Cicero's Time*, 510 ff.

47 Rufus: Dio, XLVIII, 33, 3; *Epit. Liv.*, 127. Lepidus: see *PIR²* A 368, *cf.* Cornelius Gallus in 27: the Senate voted that he should be convicted in he courts (Dio, LIII, 23, 7).

48 Caepio and Murena: Dio, LIV, 3, 5; Egnatius: Vell. Pat., II, 91, 4; Paullus: *PIR²* A 391.

49 'More maiorum' (scourging) proposed for Vibius Serenus in AD 24 (Tac., *Ann.*, IV, 30, 1; he was already in exile – and was hated by Tiberius); some followers of Sejanus in 31 and Sex. Marius in 33 were thrown from the Tarpeian rock (VI, 19, 1; Dio, LVIII, 15, 3; 22, 2 ff.: the charge against Marius was incest with his daughter, where tried is not clear). Another example: LVII, 22, 5 (AD 23: libel). Mere *mathematici* were always liable to such penalties: Tac., *Ann.*, II, 32, 5.

50 See F. Vittinghoff, *Der Staatsfeind in der röm. Kaiserzeit*, Berlin, 1936, esp. 64 ff. Mourning: Caepio's father had got away with provocative behaviour: Dio, LIV, 3, 7; Fufius' mother was executed for mourning him in 32: Tac., *Ann.*, VI, 10, 1, *cf.* Suet., *Tib.*, 61, 2, generalizing, but *cf. Ann.*, VI, 19, 4; later rule: *Dig.*, III, 2, 11, 3; XI, 7, 35; for Republican precedents, see Mommsen, *St.*, III, ii, 1190, n. 1. Erasure from the *Fasti* was an Augustan novelty: L. Paullus, *PIR²* A 391. The name and other inscriptions of Antony had suffered; they were later restored, those of his son Iullus not touched: Tac., *Ann.*, III, 17, 8; 18, 1, a reason for Tiberius' refusing erasure of Cn. Piso's name (but it was removed from some monuments: Rogers, *Trials*, 50). Asinius Gallus suffered: *PIR²* A 1229, p. 248; Sejanus: 255, p. 42; Livilla: L 303. The banning of a convicted man's *cognomen* (Libo Drusus': Tac., *Ann.*, II, 32, 2) or *praenomen* (Cn. Piso's: III, 17, 8) goes back to M. Antonius (Dio, LI, 19, 3) and early Republican precedents, including an act of the Claudii (Mommsen, *St.*, III, i, 18, n. 1; Suet., *Tib.*, 1, 2). The total banning of a man's *imago* was Republican: Cic., *pro. Rab. Perd. Reo*, 9, 24; those of Brutus, Cassius, and Cato were not shown in public under the Principate (see Furneaux, *ad* Tac., *Ann.*, III, 76, 6) but kept privately (Dio, LIII, 32, 4). In 16 that of Libo Drusus was forbidden in the same sense (Tac., *Ann.*, II, 32, 2), in 24 that of C. Silius banned altogether (XI, 35, 2). The fate of Sejanus' statues (Dio, LVIII, 11, 3; Juv., X, 58), like those of Piso (next note), was probably not due to any sentence of the Senate; that came later (Tac., *Ann.*, VI, 2, 1, including Livilla). The holding of a man's birthday accursed goes back to M. Antonius, (Dio LI, 19, 3); the converse celebration of death was voted in the case of Libo Drusus (Tac., *Ann.*, II, 32), Sejanus, and Agrippina (VI, 25, 5).

51 The first instance known in Tiberius' principate is that of Sabinus in 28 (Dio, LVIII, 1, 3; Pliny, *NH*, VIII, 145); then came Sejanus and his children (11, 5 f.; *Fasti Ost., Inscr. Ital.*, XIII, i, 188 f. = *EJ*² p. 42) and an 'immensa strages' of his followers in 33 (Tac., *Ann.*, VI, 19, 3; twenty according to Suet., *Tib.*, 61, 4; 'complures' in *Fasti Ost., loc. cit.* = *EJ*² p. 43). The view that exposure on the Gemoniae was a device thought up by Tiberius and mentioned by his admirer Val. Max., VI, 3, 3, as employed in 236 BC ('semel laesa maiestate') to give it respectability will not do: note the melancholy name of the Scalae and the people's attempt in 20 to drag Cn. Piso's statues down them (Tac., *Ann.*, III, 14, 6); the hook and

other features are mentioned by Ovid, *Ibis.*, 163 ff., in AD 8 (so Seager, *Tib.*, 228). Refusal of burial is known under the Republic: Mommsen, *St.*, II, ii², 1190, n. 1; the bodies of the Gracchi were thrown into the Tiber: Plut., *Ti. Gracchus*, 20, 2; *C. Gracchus*, 17, 4. Under the Principate it is an optional extra (Mommsen, *loc. cit.*, n. 1), adopted in cases of *maiestas* (*Dig.*, XLVIII, 24, 1). Tiberius gave permission for the burial of Asinius Gallus, who starved to death in 33, though still *reus*: Tac., *Ann.*, VI, 33, 2; either Dio, LVIII, 3, 3, is mistaken in saying that he had been condemned in the Senate or (better) Tiberius had disallowed the verdict, raising doubts as to Gallus' status.

52 Vell. Pat., II, 130, 3.

53 For *deportatio* and other forms of exile, see *Dig.*, LXVIII, 22; *RE*, V, 1905, 231 ff., *s.v.* It was a device of the Principate, combining *aquae et ignis interdictio* (and loss of civil rights) with confinement to one place: Dio, LVI, 27, 3 (implied for AD 12); Tac., *Ann.*, III, 38, 3 (AD 21); 68, 2 (22); IV, 13, 2 (23); VI, 48, 6 (36: the technical term is used in the last two instances).

54 For the origin of interdiction, see above, pp. 187 f. Early in the Principate it might be inflicted alone or aggravated by specification of an island exile as it was for C. Silanus in 22, presumably after the model of Volesus Messalla in 12: Tac., *Ann.*, III, 68, 2. The year 12 was that in which the conditions of life of those who had suffered it were made more severe: Dio, LVI, 27, 3; and see below, n. 57. The simple gave way to the aggravated form: *Dig.*, XLVIII, 19, 2, 1.

55 Relegation had been practised as a measure of *coercitio*, against noncitizens; it was used against a citizen in 58. As a legal penalty it began with Cicero's *lex de Ambitu*: Greenidge, *op. cit.*, 334; 425.

56 For Republican *infamia* in varying degrees, see Greenidge, *op. cit.*, 508.

57 Dio, LVII, 22, 5. See Ciaceri, *Stud. stor.*, II, 1108, 396; J. L. Strachan-Davidson, *Problems in the Roman Criminal Law*, Oxford, 1911, II, 55 ff.

58 *Coercitio*: Tac., *Ann.*, III, 36, 4 (AD 21). Custody: Asinius Gallus, in the charge of magistrates *c.* 30–33: Dio, LVIII, 3, 5; 25, 6. The Senate sent a quaestor to Fufius Geminus to see that he died: 4, 6. Sejanus, in prison a few hours: 10, 8; P. Vitellius and P. Pomponius Secundus, entrusted to their brothers in 31: Tac., *Ann.*, V, 8, 2, *cf.* Dio, LIX, 6, 2; Asellius Sabinus 'in carcere ... indemnatus' with 'Seianianos locupletes ... parricidas', *c.* 31: Sen., *Contr.*, IX, 4, 19 ff., *cf.* Dio, LVIII, 15, 2. Rubrius Fabatus, who tried to slip off to Parthia in 33, had 'custodes additi': Tac., *Ann.*, VI, 14, 3 f. Eutychus and Agrippa I, in chains, 36–37: Jos., *AJ*, XVIII, 169 ff., Lampon; Philo, *in Flacc.*, 128. Punitive: Drusus Caesar, in Palatium *c.* 30–33 (presumably comparable with exile on an island): Tac., *Ann.*, VI, 23, 2; 24, 2 f.; Suet., *Tib.*, 54, 2; 61, 1; Dio, LVIII, 22, 4. Gallio, in custody of magistrates, 32: Tac., *Ann.*, VI, 3, 3; Sextius Paconianus was in the *carcer* 32–36: VI, 3, 5, *cf.* 39, 1; in 33 others 'accusati societatis cum Seiano' who were being kept in the *carcer* were executed on Tiberius' orders: VI, 19, 2. Iulius Celsus committed suicide 'in vinclis' in 33: VI, 14, 2; Rogers, *Trials*, 141,

suggests that, like Paconianus, he had escaped execution by turning state's evidence. Albucilla in 37 'iussu senatus in carcerem fertur': VI, 48, 6. She died there: Dio, LVIII, 27, 4.

59 See Greenidge, *op. cit.*, 333 f.; 513 ff.; Jones, *Criminal Courts*, 13 f.

60 Tac., *Ann.*, VI, 29, 2; Dio, LVIII, 15, 2; 4 ff. Rogers' rejection of these statements, *TAPA*, 1933, 18 ff., *Trials*, 182 ff., is unconvincing: see Chilton, *art. cit.* (X*), 78 ff.

61 Tac., *Ann.*, VI, 40, 1; Dio, LVIII, 21, 2 ('Vibullius'), *cf.* Suet., *Tib.*, 61, 4 (generalization).

62 Libo Drusus: Tac., *Ann.*, II, 32, 1; Piso: III, 17, 8; Silius: IV, 20, 1; 30, 3; Sejanus' followers: Dio, LVIII, 15, 41. For continuation of the trial, attested in the cases of Caepio and Murena (Dio, LIV, 3, 5), Libo (Tac., *Ann.*, II, 31, 4), and Piso (III, 16 f., especially 17, 6), see *Dig.*, XLVIII, 4, 11 (aggravated cases). For an early Republican precedent, see Livy, III, 58, and below, n. 64.

63 Tac., *Ann.*, I, 10, 3.

64 E. S. Gruen, *Roman Politics and the Criminal Courts 149–7 B.C.*, Cambridge, Mass., 1968, 304 ff., records six suicides in his period; two belong to the Marian 'terror' of 87. Note also the suicide of Licinius Macer, prosecuted for *repetundae* before Cicero in 66, 'ne sua bona hastae posset subici' (Val. Max., IX, 12, 7; *ad Att.*, I, 4, 2). Cicero was 'aequus' because 'de eo nihil pronuntiavit'. For the anxiety of defendants, see Tac., *Ann.*, II, 29, 2; IV, 28, 2; VI, 3, 3; Suet., *Tib.*, 61, 4.

65 Tac., *Ann.*, IV, 20, 3. See L. R. Taylor, *Party Politics in the Age of Caesar*, Berkeley and Los Angeles, 1949, 112 ff.

66 Tac., *Ann.*, II, 32, 1. Vibius Serenus was passed over (IV, 29, 4), Bauman, *Impietas*, 60, suggests because he had prosecuted for astrology, not *maiestas*, and failed. Bauman's objection, *loc. cit.*, n. 46, that the generosity of dividing the entire property amongst the accusers was unparalleled, is not weighty.

67 Tac., *Ann.*, III, 19, 1. The property was not confiscated (18, 2); presumably the accusers got their quarter from the state: Dio, LVIII, 4, 8.

68 Vicissitudes of delators: Tac., *Ann.*, I, 74, 1 f. (Caepio Crispinus as *exemplum*); II, 28, 4, *cf.* VI, 38, 2, with Dio, LVIII, 25, 2 (L. Fulcinius Trio); III, 66, 5 f., *cf.* Juv., X, 83 (Bruttedius Niger); IV, 29, 4 (C. Vibius Serenus); 68, 2, *cf.* 71, 1, and VI, 4, 1 (accusers of Titius Sabinus); Dio, LVIII, 14, 4 f. (Sejanus' friends). For Tiberian delators, see Marsh, *Reign*, 107 ff.; Syme, *Tac.*, I, 326 ff., and for later developments Sherwin-White *ad* Pliny., *Ep.*, I, 5, 1; V, 13, 6.

69 *Praemia*: Tac., *Ann.*, IV, 28, 4 f.; see above, p. 104. Prosecutions: I, 74, 2 ('occultis libellis saevitiae principis adrepit'; this is Caepio Crispinus, see Syme, *Tac.*, II, 693 f., yet the prosecution failed); VI, 18, 2 (an excuse). For Tiberius encouraging delation, see Furneaux, *The Annals of Tacitus*, I, 143 f., and Koestermann, *art. cit.* (n. XI*), 83 ff.

70 Tac., *Ann.*, I, 74, 2: 'egens, ignotus, inquies'; III, 66, 4: 'obscura initia'; IV, 52, 2: 'modicus dignationis'; see previous note.

71 L. Piso and *accusatores*; see above, n. 8. The *lex Papia Poppaea*: 'omnis domus delatorum interpretationibus subverteretur' (Tac., *Ann.*, III, 25, 2).

72 Cicero on prosecution: *pro Rosc. Am.*, 56; *Div. in Q. Caec.*, 1; on *praemia*: *pro Balbo*, 57, *cf.* Asc., 54 C; on 'boys' and *quadruplatores*: *Div. in Q. Caec.*, 24; 68. See Jones, *Criminal Courts*, 62. Scaurus: Tac., *Ann.*, III, 66, 2 ff.

73 Tac., *Ann.*, IV, 30, 4 f. Tiberius is defended along these lines by Marsh, *Reign*, 171, but Koestermann, *art. cit.*, 85, n. 31, objects that all *maiestas* cases were carried on after the suicide of the accused; hence the delators were to lose their *praemia* only if the accused were acquitted; but *cf. Dig.*, XLVIII, 4, 11. The penalty for *calumnia* was exclusion from senatorial or municipal orders and disqualification from bringing further accusations, but exile or relegation were sometimes imposed *extra ordinem* (*Dig.*, XLVII, 10, 43; XLVIII, 2, 4; *ILS*, 6085, line 120). Firmius Catus, convicted of *calumnia* in 24, was sentenced to deportation to an island; Tiberius reduced the sentence to removal from the Senate; Tac., *Ann.*, IV, 31, 7 f. In 32 he approved sentences of death and exile imposed on the accusers of M. Terentius (*calumnia* was not the only charge): VI, 9, 1; Dio, LVIII, 19, 5.

74 See above, p. 22. *Cf.* Suet., *Tib.*, 28.

75 Tac., *Ann.*, III, 10, 2; 19, 1 (Trio); IV, 29, 4 f. (Serenus); 52, 7 (Afer). In 22 Tiberius refused to sharpen the teeth of the sumptuary laws, and Tacitus credits him with 'fama moderationis parta, quod ingruentis accusatores represserat' (III, 56, 1); but what he represents Tiberius as avoiding is the outcry against delation: 54, 1.

76 Tac., *Ann.*, I, 72, 3: 'legem

maiestatis reduxerat'; XIV, 48, 3: 're-
vocata ea lex'. See Koestermann, *art.
cit.* (n. XI*), 76, n. 7: Tiberius might
have abolished the law like Caligula
and Claudius; *contra*, Bauman, *Impietas*, 221.

77 Dio, LVI, 27, 1.

78 Tac., *Ann.*, I, 72, 3 ff., *cf.* Suet.,
Tib., 58.

79 So, clearly, P. Garnsey, *Social
Status and legal Privilege*, 19; Furneaux,
ad loc., and *cf.* Bauman, *Impietas*,
222; Seager, *Tib.*, 152, makes the
suggestion in a footnote. *Contra*,
Marsh, *Reign*, 61; Koestermann, *art.
cit.* (n. XI*), 78 ff., overestimates the
importance of the reply, and the contrast he draws between Tiberius'
encouragement of this law and his restriction of the *lex Papia Poppaea* (84,
n. 30) fails. He thinks (85) that the
theme of libel is picked up again in
74, 3. But that was not the first trial
in the series (74, 1), and Marcellus
was acquitted.

80 Pliny, *Pan.*, 11, 1.

81 Tac., *Ann.*, I, 72, 4. For Republican remedies, see R. E. Smith,
CQ, 1951, 169 ff.; Bauman, *Maiestas*,
246 ff. For magistrates, Jones, *Criminal
Courts*, 107.

82 Tac., *Ann.*, I, 73, *cf.* Dio, LVII,
24, 7?

83 That the *lex Iulia Maiestatis* of
Dig., XLVIII, 11, was Augustus'
work has been argued by K. M. T.
Atkinson, *Hist.*, 1960, 446 ff., and by
Bauman, *Maiestas*, 266 ff. The view
cannot hold against the objections of
Allison and Cloud, *art. cit.* (X*).

84 Tac., *Ann.*, I, 72, 3 f.; Suet., *Div.
Aug.*, 55, perhaps referring to the
placards of Dio, LV, 27, 1 (AD 6).
Iunius Novatus was fined for his
'asperrima epistula' (Suet., *Div. Aug.*,

51, 1), probably after Agrippa's
abdication in AD 6; Eus., *Chron.*, p.
176b Helm, gives 8–9 as the year of
Severus' exile; there is no call to remove it to 12 on the basis of Dio,
LVI, 27, 1 (so Koestermann, *art. cit.*
(n. XI*), 80). Further references and
full discussion are given by Bauman,
Maiestas, 246 ff.

85 Suet., *Div. Aug.*, 51, 1; 3 (advice
to Tiberius). The remarks of Rufus
(Sen., *de Ben.*, III, 27) were threatening, not slanderous, and could have
proved troublesome to him; a Cassius got 'leve exilium' for something
similar (Suet., *Div. Aug.*, 51, 1).

86 Tac., *Ann.*, IV, 21, 5.

87 Suet., *Tib.*, 28, *cf.* Dio, LVII, 19, .
1. The charge in 61, 3, is grossly
exaggerated, though it takes account
of the Cremutius Cordus case. See
also Dio, LVII, 9, 2 f.

88 Marcellus: Tac., *Ann.*, I, 74, 3 ff.
The item that caused Tiberius' indignation (if it was not the whole
indictment) was probably the slander
alleged by Crispinus rather than the
mutilation of the statues claimed by
Romanus Hispo; both mentions of
Hispo (for the *nomen* see E. Badian,
Riv. Stor. dell' Ant., 1973, 77 ff.) seem
to be afterthoughts. Varilla: II, 50,
2 f. The prosecution of women for
maiestas was a novelty of Tiberius'
principate, but it is unlikely that
Caesar's law limited the person who
might be prosecuted to magistrates or
even men. Cassius Severus (above,
n. 86) was not a senator, Athenaeus of
Seleucia (Strabo, XIV, p. 670) not
even a citizen. Tac., *Ann.*, VI, 10, 1,
'quia occupandae rei publicae argui
non poterat', means that certain
crimina in the *maiestas* category were
unlikely to stick. In 24 Sosia was

exiled and lost part of her property (IV, 20, 2 f.). Her husband had been charged with *maiestas* and *repetundae*: 'conscientia belli Sacrovir diu dissimulatus, victoria per avaritiam foedata et uxor socia [*v.l.* Sosia] arguebantur' (19, 4). The *lex Iulia Repetundarum* specified persons liable to prosecution (see M. Gelzer, *Caesar, Politician and Statesman*, tr. P. Needham, Oxford, 1968, 94. Women were not included, and after Silius' trial Cotta Messallinus promoted a *senatus consultum* making governors responsible for their wives' misconduct (20, 6, *cf. Dig.*, I, 16, 4, 2, dated to 20; see Orth, *Provinzialpolitik*, 66 f.); the activities of Plancina had provoked an ineffectual debate three years before (III, 33 f.). By Trajan's time the woman herself might be put on trial (Pliny, *Ep.*, III, 9, 19 ff.). See Brunt, *Hist.*, 1961, 198; for a different view, Sherwin-White *ad* Pliny, *loc. cit.*

89 Tac., *Ann.*, IV, 31, 1.

90 Tac., *Ann.*, VI, 5 ff., with Rogers, *Trials*, 131 ff., and Bauman, *Impietas*, 103.

91 The poetical works were burnt, according to Suet., *Tib.*, 61, 3 (anonymous poet of an *Agamemnon*), like those of T. Labienus, Cassius Severus, and others in the later years of Augustus. But *cf.* Tac., *Ann.*, VI, 29, 5 f., and Dio, LVIII, 24, 5 (the *charges* were adultery with Livilla and consulting astrologers). Macro, not the accusers, 'detulerat' the tragedy. For Tiberius' language, *cf.* Suet., *Tib.*, 57, 2; the most favourable interpretation is that Tiberius was threatening to write a tragedy of an *Ajax* maddened and suicidal with envy, in which Scaurus would recognize himself (*cf.*

Suet., *Tib.*, 28); or, with Bauman, *Impietas*, 127, that it constituted *renuntiatio amicitiae*; but Bauman thinks that Scaurus killed himself because of the *renuntiatio*.

92 Saturninus: Dio, LVII, 22, 5, *cf.* Rogers, *Trials*, 72 f. If Saturninus was of servile origin (*cf. ILS*, 1568), it is surprising that he was brought before the Senate. Montanus: Tac., *Ann.*, IV, 42, 1 ff. For Montanus as a corruptor of soldiers, see Marsh, *Reign*, 61, 115, n. 1; 173. Paconianus: Tac., *Ann.*, VI, 3, 4; 39, 1.

93 Tac., *Ann.*, I, 73 f., *cf.* Dio, LVII, 9, 3. For the name Falanius or Faianius, see Syme, *JRS*, 1949, 12 f.

94 *Cf.* Bauman, *Impietas*, 3 ff.

95 See above, pp. 82 f. Bauman, *Impietas*, 80, overestimates the significance of Tiberius' 'vice legis observem' for the development of *maiestas*.

96 Tac., *Ann.*, III, 70, 2 ff.

97 Tac., *Ann.*, IV, 34 f.; Dio, LVII, 24, 2 ff., *cf.* Suet., *Tib.*, 61, 3, and Sen., *Cons. ad Marc.* Seager, *Tib.*, 195, n. 3, thinks Cordus' speech an invention of Tacitus; so Syme, *Tac.*, I, 337, n. 10. As to whether the history was the main charge, opinions differ: see M. Columba, *A e R*, 1901, 361 ff.; Marsh, *Reign*, 290 ff.; Rogers, *Trials*, 86 ff.; Syme, *loc. cit.* Tacitus gives the report of a preliminary hearing; we know of no other charges.

98 *Cf. Dig.*, XLVIII, 4, 11.

99 *Dig.*, XLVIII, 4, 5 f.

100 Tac., *Ann.*, III, 70, 2.

101 Sen., *de Ben.*, III, 26, 1 f., *cf.* Dio, LVIII, fr. 2.

102 Tac., *Ann.*, III, 36, *cf.* Philostr., *Vit. Ap.*, I, 15. See above, p. 103.

Koestermann, *art. cit.* (n. XI*), 95 ff., exaggerates the terror that was created but rightly says that cases must have arisen from the abuse.
103 *Dig.*, XLVII, 10, 38. Bauman, *Impietas*, 85 ff., argues for a total ban on seeking refuge at statues or images, dating from the trial of Agrippina in 29.
104 Tac., *Ann.*, I, 73, 1, with Koestermann, *art. cit.*, 82, n. 23; for other interpretations see Furneaux, *ad loc.*
105 Tac., *Ann.*, III, 12, 6 (Piso); *Fasti Amit.*, *CIL*, I, 243 = *EJ*² p. 52 (Libo), *cf.* Cic., *in Pis.*, 50 ('exire provinciam'); *Dig.*, XLVIII, 4, 1 ('... quo quis magistratus ... quive imperium potestatemve habet occidatur; quove quis contra rem publicam arma ferat ... quive milites sollicitaverit concitaveritve ...'). Koestermann's interpretation of Libo's trial, *art. cit.*, 88 ff., is unduly sympathetic to the defendant. The view of Marsh, *op. cit.*, 291 ff., that more serious charges against Libo, Piso, and Cremutius Cordus are omitted from the record presented by Tacitus because they killed themselves when their trials were still in the preliminary stages, is dealt with by Koestermann, *art. cit.*, 89, n. 41. It is not trivial *charges* that Tacitus offers, but flimsy *evidence*.
106 Suet., *Tib.*, 28: 'omnium inimicitiae ... ad nos deferentur'.
107 As Koestermann argues (*art. cit.*, 93, n. 50) against Marsh, *Reign*, 123 f., a hearing before Tiberius was planned in the Piso case (Tac., *Ann.*, III, 10, 3), but he held only a preliminary hearing with an informal *consilium* (10, 6). Tiberius inspected the scene of a murder at the request of the victim's

father: IV, 22, 1 ff., *cf.* Jos., *AJ*, XVIII, 83 (embezzlement). Depositions were secured by Macro: Dio, LVIII, 21, 3; 24, 2. For Albucilla in 37 (Tiberius' role uncertain), see Tac., *Ann.*, VI, 47, 4. For acceptance of charges, see Tac., *Ann.*, I, 73, 3 ff.; II, 50, 2 f.; III, 22, 4; 70, 2 ff. (a veto: 'vetuit'; 'perstititque intercedere'); IV, 15, 3: 'audirent socios'. For Tiberius presiding, see Tac., *Ann.*, II, 29, 2 (Libo); III, 17, 8 (Piso); 22, 4 (Lepida); 68, 1 (Silanus). Modification of the sentence: Tac., *Ann.*, III, 18, 1; IV, 30, 2; Libo (II, 30, 4) and Silanus (III, 67, 4) address 'preces' to Tiberius. His veto on sentence or admission of charges was probably a technical use of his right of *intercessio*, regarded as part of his *ius auxilii* (a Sullan view) and usually reserved for such occasions (but *cf.* Suet., *Tib.*, 26, 2). Nero wanted to use it for the same purpose: XIII, 43, 7; XIV, 48, 3; XVI, 11, 6. See IV, 30, 1: 'intercessit'. Tiberius' right to act was implicitly recognized in 21, when the ten-day rule was introduced, enabling him to intervene from a distance (III, 51, 3 f.); it was neglected in cases brought at the instigation of the Princeps or involving danger if execution were delayed, such as that of Sejanus and perhaps of Titius Sabinus, IV, 70, 1 and 5.
108 Tac., *Ann.*, II, 29, 2 (Libo); III, 12, 1 ff.; 15, 4 (Piso); 22, 4 (Lepida, and 'miscuit irae et clementiae signa').
109 Tac., *Ann.*, III, 67, 2. There was a charge of *maiestas*, on which Silanus may have been acquitted: see Seager, *Tib.*, 160.
110 Suet., *Div. Aug.*, 66, 2. For *renuntiatio amicitiae* as a substitute for

the *crimen maiestatis*, see Bauman, *Impietas*, 109 ff.

111 Tac., *Ann.*, III, 12, 4.

112 Tac., *Ann.*, III, 24, 7.

113 Tac., *Ann.*, VI, 9, 2 ff.

114 Tac., *Ann.*, I, 74, well discussed by Seager, *Tib.*, 153 f.

115 'Tulit absolvi': see Gerber-Greef, *Lexicon Taciteum*, *s.v.*, and Koestermann, *art. cit.*, 87, n. 35. *Cf.* 'laturum' above; *contra*, Sumner, *Phoen.*, 1966, 80. The oath does not prove that Tiberius' vote was to be unfavourable to Marcellus: *cf.* Suet., *Div. Claud.*, 22. Dio, LVII, 24, 7, combining features of the trials of Falanius and Granius Marcellus, has the Princeps called upon to vote first and opting for acquittal. See also Marsh, *Reign*, 110; *contra*, Koestermann, *art. cit.*, 86.

116 Tac., *Ann.*, IV, 42, 2.

117 Tac., *Ann.*, II, 31, 4 (Libo); VI, 29, 3 (Paxaea). Eloquence in asking for mercy: IV, 31, 4; *clementia* praised: III, 50, 3; 68, 2.

118 Tac., *Ann.*, III, 18, 1 f.; for 'nobilitas domus', 17, 1.

119 Tac., *Ann.*, II, 50, 4, with Furneaux, *ad loc.*

120 Tac., *Ann.*, IV, 31, 1 ff.

121 Tac., *Ann.*, IV, 31, 7 f.

122 Tac., *Ann.*, III, 68, 1 (22, against C. Silanus); IV, 31, 5 (24, against P. Suillius, with an oath that it was *e republica*); and see above, p. 180.

123 Tac., *Ann.*, VI, 5, 2; *cf.* his swift intervention for Cn. Lentulus in 24: IV, 29, 1; Dio, LVII, 24, 8.

124 Suet., *Tib.*, 55; Tac., *Ann.*, VI, 9, 2 ff. (Vistilius); 10, 2 (Vescularius Flaccus, Julius Marinus).

125 Suillius: see above, n. 122;

Gallio: Tac., *Ann.*, VI, 3, 1 ff., *cf.* Dio, LVIII, 18, 3 f. For the five cases, see Rogers, *Trials*, 203 f.

126 Tac., *Ann.*, VI, 7, 2 f. Q. Pomponius Secundus attacked Considius Proculus in 33 (18, 1 f.), at the Princeps' instigation, according to Rogers, *Trials*, 145.

127 Tac., *Ann.*, VI, 4, 4.

128 Tac., *Ann.*, III, 37, 1. Compare the case of Cotta Messallinus, acquitted in 32 after appeal to Tiberius: 'tum facta patribus potestas statuendi de C. Caeciliano . . . qui plurima adversum Cottam prompserat' (VI, 7, 1).

129 Tac., *Ann.*, III, 38, 2 ff. See Seager, *Tib.*, 158.

130 Tac., *Ann.*, VI, 47, 2 ff. For the earlier cases, see above, Ch. X, and note that of M. Paconius, where the Senate was prompted to pass sentence (Suet., *Tib.*, 61, 6).

131 Suet., *Tib.*, 73, possibly an inaccurate echo of the trial of Albucilla, of which Tacitus thought Tiberius knew nothing; *cf.* Dio, LVIII, 27, 3.

132 Tac., *Ann.*, III, 12, 4; 70.

133 Suet., *Tib.*, 30; Tac., *Ann.*, VI, 2, 3.

134 F. Millar, *JRS*, 1968, 222.

135 Tac., *Ann.*, IV, 15. 3 f.; Dio, LVII, 23, 4, *cf.* Suet., *Tib.*, 30. *Equites* had been exempted from the *lex Iulia*: Cic., *pro Rab. Post.*, 12. Brunt, *Hist.*, 1961, 193, n. 15a, sees Capito charged with *vis publica*.

136 Tac., *Ann.*, VI, 10, 2; Suet., *Tib.*, 62, 2 (Capri). The accusation of Votienus Montanus 'apud Caesarem' by Narbo in Sen., *Contr.*, VII, 5 (20), 12, may be Augustan.

137 Tac., *Ann.*, XIII, 4, 2.

CHAPTER XII

XII* The main sources are Tac., *Ann.*, VI; Dio, LVIII; 12 ff.; Suet., *Tib.*, 41 ff.; Jos., *AJ*, XVIII, 161 ff. See Marsh, *Reign*, 200 ff.; Z. Stewart, *AJP*, 1953, 70 ff.; D. Timpe, *Kontinuität*, 57 ff.; P. Y. Forsyth, *Phoen.*, 1969, 204 ff.; Seager, *Tib.*, 224 ff.

1 Tac., *Ann.*, VI, 51, 6.

2 *ILS*, 6044 = *EJ*² 53; and Suet., *Tib.*, 65, 2.

3 Tac., *Ann.*, VI, 2, 5 f.: 'ludibria seriis permiscere solitus'.

4 Tac., *Ann.*, VI, 6; Suet., *Tib.*, 67, 1, with Rogers, *Trials*, 134. 'Quid scribam vobis, patres conscripti, aut quo modo scribam aut quid omnino non scribam hoc tempore, di me deaeque peius perdant quam perire me cotidie sentio, si scio' ('quam cotidie perire sentio', Suetonius). See Lewis and Short, *s.v. perdo*, citing 'Di (deaeque omnes) te perduint.'

5 Dio, LVIII, 12, 4 ff. Previous refusal of title *pater patriae*: LVII, 8, 1 (AD 14); Tac., *Ann.*, I, 72, 2 (15: 'a populo saepius ingestum'); II, 87, 2 (19).

6 Tac., *Ann.*, V, 7, 2.

7 Niger: Juv., X, 82; P. Vitellius and P. Pomponius Secundus: Tac., *Ann.*, V, 8. Release: Dio, LIX, 6, 2 (confusing him with his brother). Suff. 44, *ornamenta triumphalia* 50: Tac., *Ann.*, XII, 28, 2.

8 Tac., *Ann.*, VI, 3, 4 ff.

9 Tac., *Ann.*, VI, 7, 2 ff.

10 Tac., *Ann.*, VI, 9, 5 ff.; death of the tribune: 14, 2. Silanus seems to have been the son of C. Silanus, *cos.* 10 (see *PIR*² I 822). He is strange bedfellow for Scaurus, who had prosecuted his father in 22 (III, 66, 2). To C. Annius Pollio Scaurus proposed that he

should become just that (Sen., *de Ben.*, IV, 31, 4), which argues some intimacy. Scaurus had been friendly towards Sejanus (see above, pp. 213 f.) and Calvisius Sabinus, who was probably the brother-in-law of his colleague in the consulship, Cn. Gaetulicus (see *PIR*² C 354), may have given his name to P. Pomponius Secundus, who appears during his consulship as '. . . isius Sabinus P. Pomponius Secundus'. Secundus' mother was Vistilia (Pliny, *NH*, VII, 39), and his uncle probably the Sex. Vistilius who had just lost the friendship of Tiberius for attacking Gaius as unchaste (VI, 9, 2 f.); these ties are elucidated by Syme, *JRS*, 1970, 27 ff. Domitius Corbulo was another son of Vistilia. He married a daughter to an Annius Vinicianus (*PIR*² A 700), who would be a son of the L. Annius Vinicianus charged in 32. Syme connects Corbulo with L. Vitellius, P. Petronius, and the partisans of Germanicus. Perhaps two of the consulars, Silanus and Pollio, were too sympathetic to the cause of Drusus Caesar to be acceptable to Gaius and Macro. This view is supported by the antecedents of Vistilius: he had been a member of Nero Drusus' entourage. The others might be unacceptable for a different reason: devotion to Gemellus (shown by their former allegiance to Sejanus).

11 Tac., *Ann.*, VI, 14, 1. For Geminius, *cf. CIL*, VI, 904, a dedication by C. Geminius Atticus in a series to which L. Fulcinius Trio contributed: Th. Pekáry, *Röm. Mitt.*, 1966–67, 105 ff. Sejanus' habits: Tac., *Ann.*, IV, 1, 3 f.; Vell. Pat., II, 127, 4.

12 Juv., X, 85 ff.

13 Tac., *Ann.*, V, 11; VI, 4, 2 ff.

Regulus' mission: Dio, LVIII, 10, 2, *cf.* 13, 3; Suet., *Tib.*, 65, 1.

14 Tac., *Ann.*, VI, 2. Oaths: Dio, LVIII, 17, 2 f.: Tiberius had refused to allow the oath 'for many years', *cf.* LVII, 8, 4 f.; Tac., *Ann.*, I, 72, 2; Suet., *Tib.*, 26, 2 (veto); 67 ('quia aliquo casu mutari posset').

15 Tac., *Ann.*, VI, 3, 1 ff.

16 Tac., *Ann.*, IV, 18, 5.

17 Tac., *Ann.*, VI, 8; Dio, LVIII, 19, 1 ff., adding L. Caesianus, a praetor who had poked fun at the bald.

18 For the penalty for *calumnia*, see above, Ch. XI, n. 73.

19 Tac., *Ann.*, VI, 18, 1 f.

20 Tac., *Ann.*, VI, 5 ff.

21 Tac., *Ann.*, VI, 3, 4 f.

22 Tac., *Ann.*, VI, 30, 2 ff. It is surprising that the accusation came so late in the day. It must mark the developing power of Gaius and Macro.

23 Syme, *RR*, 424, 436.

24 Dio, LIX, 22, 5; Sen., *QN, IVA*, pr. 15; *Acta Arv.*, ed. Henzen, xlix.

25 See *PIR²* A 1414, modified by A. N. Sherwin-White, *Lat.*, 1972, 820 ff.

26 Tac., *Ann.*, VI, 28 (34); Pliny, *NH*, X, 5 (36); Dio, LVIII, 27, 1 (36). Probably 36 is correct; see below, n. 46.

27 Dio, LVIII, 24, 1 (*celebration* by the consuls of 34), *cf.* LVII, 24, 2: he did not ask for renewal (23 or 24?); the consuls celebrated the decennial festival. Perhaps they did not venture to mention that the power was coming to an end. Celebration was tactful prorogation.

28 Tac., *Ann.*, VI, 23 ff. (Gallus, Drusus, and Agrippina), *cf.* Suet., *Tib.*, 54, 2 (Drusus); 53, 2 (Agrippina); Dio, LVIII, 22, 4 f.; 25, 4 (Agrippina and Drusus).

29 Tac., VI, 19, 2 ff.: 'Immensa strages'; Suet., *Tib.*, 61, 4: twenty on one day; *Fasti Ost.*, *Inscr. Ital.*, XIII, i, 188 f.: 'complures'. At least two survived: Sextius Paconianus to be executed on another day: Tac., *Ann.*, VI, 3, 4, *cf.* 39, 1; Pomponius lingered on: V, 8, 4.

30 The marriage: Tac., *Ann.*, VI, 20, 1; Suet., *Cal.*, 12, 1; Dio, LVIII, 25, 2 (AD 35). For the bride's father see *PIR²* I 832.

31 Dio, LVIII, 23, 1; Dio does not say that the quaestorship was 'not in the first rank' (so E. Cary, Loeb edition) but that he was not designated for the following year; i.e., he was designated late in 31 for 33.

32 So Seager, *Tib.*, 234.

33 Tac., *Ann.*, IV, 75; for Ahenobarbus' family, see Suet., *Nero*, 1 f. It was Mrs A.-M. Dabrowski who drew my attention to the mediocre matches of Gaius' sisters and cousin.

34 Tac., *Ann.*, VI, 15, 1; Dio, LVIII, 21, 1; Suet., *Cal.*, 24, 3; Jos., *AJ*, XIX, 251; Schol. Juv., I, 155. Quinctilius Varus: Sen., *Contr.*, I, 3, 10. Origins of Vinicius: Syme, *RR*, 192; 362; his fate: Dio, LX, 27, 4.

35 Tac., *Ann.*, VI, 27, 1; Dio, LVIII, 21, 1.

36 *Cf. PIR²* C 501; 503.

37 Espérandieu, *Inscr. lat. de Gaule*, 618. For the arrangement, see Levick, *Lat.*, 1966, 234.

38 Philo, *Leg.*, 24 f. (he favoured Gemellus); Jos., *AJ*, XVIII, 188; 211 f.; 214 f.; 219 (Gemellus, but Agrippa I backed Gaius); Tac., *Ann.*, VI, 46, 1 ff. (he was undecided); Suet., *Tib.*, 62, 3 (he meant to kill them both); *Cal.*, 19, 3 (he preferred Gemellus); Dio, LVIII, 23, 1 ff. (Gaius). Admirable tabulation by Meise, *Untersuchungen*, 53. Allowance must be made for the ill repute acquired by Gaius, especially among the Jews.

39 Suet., *Div. Claud.*, 4 f.

40 Health: Suet., *Tib.*, 68. Astrological predictions: 62, 3, *cf.* Dio, LVIII, 27, 1 ff.

41 H. Gesche, *Zeitschr. f. Num. u. Geldgesch.*, 1971, 37 ff.

42 Another interpretation is offered in *The Ancient Historian and his Materials*, 123 ff.

43 The will: Suet., *Tib.*, 76 (with date); *Cal.*, 14, 1; Dio, LIX, 1, 1 ff.; Philo, *Leg.*, 23. Timpe's attempt (*Untersuchungen*, 71 f.) to represent the will as a private document is rebutted by Gesche, *art. cit.*, 72 f.

44 Tac., *Ann.*, VI, 26, 4 f. ('criminibus haud ignotis'); Dio, LVIII, 22, 5 (execution). Her brother may just have been coming to the end of his seventeen-year governorship of Pannonia: see above, Ch. IX, n. 2.

45 Tac., *Ann.*, III, 15, 1 ff.; 17, 2. Tiberius used this technique more than once: Suet., *Tib.*, 51, 1.

46 Tac., *Ann.*, V, 10, dating the appearance to the same time as the execution of Sejanus' younger children (end of 31); *cf.* Dio, LVIII, 25, 1: after the deaths of Labeo, Scaurus, and others (34). It cannot be said that the peregrinations of 'Drusus' went on long enough for Tacitus to be speaking of the beginning of the affair and Dio of the end: it was 'acri magis quam diuturno rumore'. Tacitus could have put the affair after the exposure of the children in 31, rather than that of the conspirators in 33, on the Gemoniae; or Dio may have confused the two attacks on Scaurus (32 and 34). There are other discrepancies: the marriage of Gaius and the phoenix are both dated two years later by Dio than they are by Tacitus (35 and 36 instead of 33 and 34). Dio's date for the phoenix is confirmed by Pliny, *NH*, X, 5. In the view of G. B. Townend, *Herm.*, 1961, 118 ff., Tacitus inserted an item from Balbillus at the first convenient point.

47 Tac., *Ann.*, VI, 14, 3 f.

48 Tac., *Ann.*, VI, 18, 3 ff. For the family of Theophanes, see Syme, *Tac.*, II, 748 f., and above, p. 98. For the Euryclids, see G. W. Bowersock, *JRS*, 1961, 112 ff. (*stemma*, 118).

49 Rogers, *Trials*, 126 f., 145 f.

50 See Levick, *Rom. Cols. in South. Asia Minor*, 167 f.

51 Tac., *Ann.*, VI, 29, 4 ff. Sextia: see Syme, *JRS*, 1949, 12. For the charges, see above, Ch. XI, n. 91. The same accusers attacked Varius Ligus, but were bribed by him to desist (Tac., *Ann.*, VI, 30, 1). A 'P. Varius P. f. Aem. Ligus filius' honoured Gemellus in an inscription of Alba Pompeia (*ILS*, 171).

52 Tac., *loc. cit.*, 1 ff. *Renuntiatio* used against Vistilius; see above, p. 205.

53 Tac., *Ann.*, VI, 3, 4.

54 Tac., *Ann.*, III, 66 f. The dwarf: Suet., *Tib.*, 61, 6. The historian was probably Servilius Nonianus, the consular historian, no friend to the Princeps: See Syme, *Tac.*, I, 277. Tac., *Ann.*, XVI, 29, 3, speaks of Paconius as an innocent victim (*cf.* 28, 2).

55 See above, p. 188.

56 Tac., *Ann.*, VI, 38, 2 ff.

57 For the Blaesi and Lepida, see Tac., *Ann.*, VI, 40, 3 f.

58 Tac., *Ann.*, VI, 45, 5; Dio,

LVIII, 28, 4. See *PIR*² E 65 for other references, and above, Ch. X, n. 135. For Claudilla's death, see Tac., *Ann.*, VI, 45, 4; Philo, *Leg.*, 9; Suet., *Cal.*, 12, 2 (in childbirth), cf. Dio, LIX, 8, 7 (divorced).

59 Tac., *Ann.*, VI, 47, 2 ff.

60 Forsyth, *art. cit.* (n. XII*).

61 Suet., *Nero*, 5, 2.

62 Tac., *Ann.*, I, 13, 2.

63 For P. Vitellius, see above, p. 202. C. Vibius Marsus: Tac., *Ann.*, II, 74, 1; IV, 56, 3. Bird thinks, *Lat.*, 1969, 75, that he must have defected: he was proconsul of Africa in the late twenties. But the Vibii had been protégés of Tiberius first; and in Claudius' principate he was legate of Syria: XI, 10, 1. Otho: III, 66, 2; the son died for his veto, presumably under Gaius.

64 Intellect: Tac., *Ann.*, VI, 50, 1. Reading and quizzes: Suet., *Tib.*, 56; 70, 3. Cucumbers: see above, Ch. X, n. 99. Parties: Suet., *Tib.*, 72, 3. 'Serpens draco': 72, 2.

65 Suet., *Tib.*, 72, 1 f.; AD 32: Tac., *Ann.*, VI, 1, 1 f.; AD 35: 45, 1 ff. Cf. Dio, LVIII, 21, 1: AD 33, during the marriages of his granddaughters, a distance of four miles.

66 Tac., *Ann.*, VI, 12.

67 Tac., *Ann.*, VI, 13; see above, p. 121.

68 Tac., *Ann.*, VI, 16 f.; see above, p. 133.

69 Parthia: see above, pp. 145 ff. Fire of 36: Tac., *Ann.*, VI, 45, 1 ff.; Dio, LVIII, 26, 5; of 27: IV, 64.

70 Last days: Suet., *Tib.*, 72, 2 ff.; *Cal.*, 12, 2 f.; Tac., *Ann.*, VI, 50; Jos., *AJ*, XVIII, 205 ff.; Dio, LVIII, 28. For Tiberius and doctors, see Tac., *Ann.*, VI, 46, 9; Suet., *Tib.*, 68, 4.

71 *Apud* Suet., *Tib.*, 73, 2. The elder Seneca died before his son's exile in 41. The accounts of Tiberius' death are well discussed by Seager, *Tib.*, 244 f.

72 See above, p. 124. For the date, cf. *Acta Arv.*, ed. Henzen, xliii = Smallwood, *Docs. Illustrating the Principates of Gaius, Claudius and Nero*, Cambridge, 1967, p. 10. The lion: Jos., *AJ*, XVIII, 228, with Feldman, *ad loc.*

73 For the timetable, see above, Ch. V, n. 4.

74 Suet., *Tib.*, 75, 3; *Fasti Ost.*, *Inscr. Ital.*, XIII, i, 190 f. = *EJ*² p. 43, cf. Suet., *Div. Aug.*, 100, 2.

75 Suet., *Cal.*, 13.

76 Misenum: see Balsdon, *The Emperor Gaius*, 25. Balsdon's whole discussion of the accession of Gaius is very lucid. Senate: *Acta Arv.*, ed. Henzen, *loc. cit.*

77 Dio, LIX, 1, 2 ff.; Suet., *Cal.*, 14, 1.

78 For the *querella de inofficioso testamento*, see *Inst. Iust.*, II, 18. Before Justinian the situation was that 'si parum, quam ei debebatur, fuerit consecutus, movere de inofficioso testamento querellam concedatur': *Nov. Theod.*, I, 22. It led to intestate succession: *Dig.*, V, 2; 8; 13; 16. By law Gaius was receiving exactly what he was entitled to, and the Senate acted explicitly on political grounds, accepting the implications of the will for the succession. Seager, *Tib.*, 246, calls Dio's suggestion that Tiberius bequeathed the Principate jointly to Gaius and Gemellus 'absurd'. But that was the inference drawn by the Senate.

79 Dio, LIX, 2, 4; Suet., *Cal.*, 16, 3, cf. Tac., *Ann.*, V, 1, 6; Suet., *Tib.*, 51, 2.

80 Philo, *Leg.*, 26 ff.; Suet., *Cal.*, 15, 2; Dio, LIX, 8, 1.

81 Augustus: Suet., *Div. Aug.*, 100, 4; Tac., *Ann.*, I, 10, 8; Dio, LVI, 46, 1 ff. Tiberius: Dio, LIX, 3, 7. Lugdunum: *CREBM*, I, cxliv; 146, no. 1 ff.; *RIC*, I, 116, no. 9 f., with Sutherland, *CRIP*, 107, *cf.* Vittinghoff, *Der Staatsfeind in der röm. Kaiserzeit*, 87, n. 382.

82 Dio, LIX, 3, 5, *cf.* Suet., *Cal.*, 14, 2; 15, 1.

83 See Vittinghoff, *op. cit.*, 84 ff.

84 Dio, LIX, 16, 1 ff. Sacrifice was offered 'ob memoriam' in May and on Tiberius' birthday even in 38 (*Acta Arv.*, ed. Henzen, xliv; xlvii = Smallwood, *Documents*, p. 11 ff.).

85 Sen., *De Clem.*, I, 1, 6, *cf. Apocol.*, 1, 2; Stewart, *AJP*, 1953, 70 ff., connects Seneca with the circle of Sejanus (not altogether convincingly). A balanced view is not to be expected from Philo, the Jew of Alexandria whose co-religionists had suffered there from the pogroms that Gaius did nothing to stop and in Judaea from his attempt to have his statue set up in the Temple: Tiberius gains by the contrast.

86 The *lex*: *ILS*, 244 = *EJ*[2] 364 A. The *acta*: Dio, LIX, 9, 1 f.

87 Autobiography (*commentarius*): Suet., *Tib.*, 61, 1; daybooks (*commentarii*): *Dom.*, 20. For *commentarii* see E. M. Wightman, *The Ancient Historian and his Materials*, 98 f.

88 Suet., *Dom.*, 10, 1; *PIR*[2] F 355; for Tiberius, *cf.* Tac., *Ann.*, VI, 51, 5.

For the tradition about Tiberius established by Tacitus' day, see Harrer, *AJP*, 1920, 57 ff.

89 Syme, *Hist.*, 1974, 491.

90 See Syme, *Herm.*, 1964, 408 ff., and Townend, *Lat.*, 1962, 489 ff.

91 For the *Memoirs*, see Tac., *Ann.*, IV, 53, 3, with Syme, *Tac.*, I, 278, n. 2. Orations: II, 63, 4 (cited from the *Acta*, according to Furneaux, *ad loc.*).

92 The speeches used: Syme, *Tac.*, I, 283; Miller, *AJP*, 1968, 1 ff. *Acta* consulted: *Ann.*, XV, 74, 3, *cf.* III, 3, 2. Syme, *Tac.*, I, 281 ff.; *art. cit.*, 489 f., makes much of this. But e.g., 'Perculsus . . . paulum reticuit; dein collecto animo respondit' (*Ann.*, I, 12, 3), owes something to a literary intermediary, though Tacitus may have read the debate in the *Acta* too.

93 The anecdote in Suet., *Tib.*, 44, 2, of an erotic picture of Atalanta and Meleager bequeathed to him with the alternative of ten thousand sesterces if he did not care for the subject suggests that he struck high society as a prude (wrongly if so: he hung the picture in his bedroom). In the first section of 44 ('pueros . . . institueret, ut *natanti sibi* inter femina . . .') the invention (of the lower classes?) is similarly limited by prudery. (I owe this point to a friend.)

94 Kornemann, *Tibère*, 234.

95 Tac., *Ann.*, III, 6, 5.

96 Syme, *art. cit.*, 481 ff.

97 Philo, *Leg.*, 142, *cf.* Suet., *Tib.*, 57, 1, and Dio, LVIII, fr. 1 (he was 'mud mixed with blood').

SELECT BIBLIOGRAPHY

For further references see the opening notes to chapters.

BIOGRAPHIES AND COLLECTIONS OF ESSAYS

Baker, G. P., *Tiberius Caesar*, London, 1929.
Balsdon, J. P. V. D., Review of Pippidi, D.M., *Autour de Tibère, JRS*, 1946, 168 ff.
Ciaceri, E., *Tiberio Successore di Augusto*, Milan, 1934.
Cichorius, C., *Römische Studien*, Berlin and Leipzig, 1922.
Gelzer, M., 'Iulius (Tiberius)', *RE*, X, 1919, 478 ff.
Kornemann, E., *Tiberius*, Stuttgart, 1960; tr. into French by F. Delaloue, Paris, 1962.
Lang, A., *Beiträge zur Geschichte des Kaisers Tiberius*, Jena, 1911.
Marañon, G., *Tiberius, a Study in Resentment*, tr. G. B. Welles, London, 1956.
Marsh, F. B., *The Reign of Tiberius*, Oxford, 1931.
Passerini, A., 'Per la Storia dell'Imperatore Tiberio', *Studi guiridici in Memoria di P. Ciapessoni*, Pavia, 1948.
Pippidi, D. M., *Autour de Tibère*, Bucharest, 1944.
Rogers, R. S., *Studies in the Reign of Tiberius*, Baltimore, 1943.
Seager, R., *Tiberius*, London, 1972.
Smith, C. E., *Tiberius and the Roman Empire*, Baton Rouge, 1942.
Tarver, J. C., *Tiberius the Tyrant*, London, 1902.
Thiel, J. H., 'Kaiser Tiberius. Ein Beitrag zum Verständnis seiner Persönlichkeit', *Mnem.*, 1935, 245 ff.; 1935–36, 177 ff.; 1936–37, 7 ff.; repr., Darmstadt, 1970.

ANTECEDENTS

Fiske, G. C., 'The Politics of the Patrician Claudii', *HSCP*, 1902, 1 ff.
Linderski, J., 'The Mother of Livia Augusta and the Aufidii Lurcones of the Republic', *Hist.*, 1974, 463 ff.
Mommsen, Th., 'Die patricischen Claudier', *Röm. Forsch.*, I, Berlin, 1864, 287 ff.
Münzer, F., 'Claudii Nerones', *RE*, III, 1899, 2773 ff.
Rawson, E., 'The eastern Clientelae of Clodius and the Claudii', *Hist.*, 1973, 219 ff.
Wiseman, T. P., 'The Mother of Livia Augusta', *Hist.*, 1965, 333 ff.

EARLY LIFE AND SUCCESSION TO THE PRINCIPATE OF AUGUSTUS

Allen, W., jr., 'The Death of Agrippa Postumus', *TAPA*, LXXVIII, 1947, 131 ff.

Badian, E., 'The Quaestorship of Tiberius Nero', *Mnem.*, 1974, 160 ff.
'The Thessalian Clients of Tiberius Nero', *CR*, 1974, 186.

Béranger, J., 'L'Hérédité du Principat', *REL*, 1939, 171 ff.
'Le Refus du Pouvoir', *MH*, 1948, 178 ff.

Charlesworth, M. P., 'Tiberius and the Death of Augustus', *AJP*, 1923, 145 ff.

Detweiler, R., 'Historical Perspectives on the Death of Agrippa Postumus', *CJ*, 1970, 289 ff.

Dieckmann, H., 'Die effective Mitregentschaft des Tiberius', *Klio*, 1918, 339 ff.

Dupraz, L., 'Autour de l'Association de Tibère au Principat', *MH*, 1963, 172 ff.

Fabia, Ph., 'L'Avènement officiel de Tibère', *Rev. Phil.*, 1909, 28 ff.

Ferrill, A., 'Prosopography and the last years of Augustus', *Hist.*, 1971, 718 ff.

Flach, D., 'Der Regierungsanfang des Tiberius', *Hist.*, 1973, 552 ff.

Groag, E., 'Studien zur Kaisergeschichte III. Der Sturz der Julia', *WS*, 1918, 150 ff.; 1919, 74 ff.

Hohl, E., 'Wann hat Tiberius das Prinzipat übernommen?', *Herm.*, 1933, 106 ff.
'Primum facinus novi Principatus', *Herm.*, 1935, 350 ff.
'Zu den Testamentum des Augustus', *Klio*, 1937, 323 ff.
Die Siegesfeiern des Tiberius und das Datum der Schlacht im Teutoburgerwald. Sitzungsb. der deutschen Akad. der Wiss. zu Berl., Kl. f. Gesellsch. Wiss., no. 1, 1952.

Instinsky, H. V., 'Augustus und die Adoption des Tiberius', *Herm.*, 1966, 332 ff.

Jameson, S. A., 'Augustus and Agrippa Postumus', *Hist.*, 1975, 287 ff.

Kornemann, E., *Doppelprinzipat und Reichsteilung im Imperium Romanum*, Leipzig and Berlin, 1930.

Levick, B. M., 'Drusus Caesar and the Adoptions of A.D. 4', *Lat.*, 1966, 227 ff.
'The Beginning of Tiberius' Career', *CQ*, 1971, 478 ff.
'Atrox Fortuna', *CR*, 1972, 309 ff.
'Tiberius' Retirement to Rhodes in 6 B.C.', *Lat.*, 1972, 779 ff.
'Abdication and Agrippa Postumus', *Hist.*, 1972, 674 ff.
' "Julians and Claudians" ', *G and R*, 1975, 29 ff.
'The Fall of the younger Julia', *Lat.*, 1976, forthcoming.

Lewis, J. D., 'Primum facinus novi Principatus?', *Auckland Classical Essays presented to E. M. Blaiklock*, ed. B. F. Harris, Auckland and Oxford, 1971, 165 ff.

Martin, R. H., 'Tacitus and the Death of Augustus', *CQ*, 1955, 123 ff.

Meise, E., *Untersuchungen zur Geschichte des Julisch-Claudischen Dynastie*, *Vestigia*, X, Munich, 1969.

Nesselhauf, H., 'Die Adoption des römischen Kaisers', *Herm.*, 1955, 477 ff.

Norwood, F., 'The Riddle of Ovid's Relegatio', *CP*, 1963, 150 ff.

Paladini, M. L., 'La Morte di Agrippa Postumo e la Congiurra di Clemente',
  Acme, 1954, 313 ff.
'I Poteri di Tiberio Cesare dal 4 al 14 d.C.', *Hommages M. Renard*,
  Brussels, 1969, 573 ff.
'A proposito del Retiro di Tiberio a Rodi e della sua Posizione prima
  dell'Accessione all'Imperio', *NRS*, 1957, 1 ff.
Pappano, A. E., 'Agrippa Postumus', *CP*, 1941, 30 ff.
Pekáry, Th., 'Tiberius und der Tempel der Concordia in Rom', *Röm. Mitt.*,
  1966-67, 105 ff.
Questa, C., 'La Morte di Augusto secondo Cassio Dione', *Parola del Passato*,
  1959, 41 ff.
Rogers, R. S., 'The Deaths of Julia and Gracchus', *TAPA*, 1967, 383 ff.
Sattler, P., 'Julia und Tiberius. Beiträge zur römischen Innenpolitik zwischen
  den Jahren 12 v. und 2 n. Chr.', in *Studien aus dem Gebiet der
  Altengeschichte*, Wiesbaden, 1962, 1 ff. = *Augustus*, ed. W.
  Schmitthenner, Darmstadt, 1969, 486 ff.
Schmitt, H. H., 'Der Pannonische Aufstand des Jahres 14 N. Chr. und der
  Regierungsantritt des Tiberius', *Hist.*, 1958, 378 ff.
Schwartz, J., 'Recherches sur les dernières Années du Règne d'Auguste
  (4-14 apr. J.-C.)', *Rev. Phil.*, 1945, 21 ff.
Shotter, D. C. A., 'Julians, Claudians and the Accession of Tiberius', *Lat.*,
  1971, 1117 ff.
Sumner, G. V., 'Germanicus and Drusus Caesar', Lat., 1967, 413 ff.
Syme, R., *The Roman Revolution*, Oxford, 1939, repr. 1954.
Taylor, L. R., 'Tiberius' *ovatio* and the *Ara numinis Augusti*', *AJP*, 1937, 185 ff.
Timpe, D., *Untersuchungen zur Kontinuität des frühen Prinzipats. Historia*,
  Einzelschriften, Heft 5, Wiesbaden, 1962.
Villers, R., 'La Dévolution du Principat dans la Famille d'Auguste', *REL*,
  1950, 235 ff.
Weller, J. A., 'Tacitus and Tiberius' Rhodian Exile', *Phoen.*, 1958, 31 ff.
Wellesley, K., 'The *Dies Imperii* of Tiberius', *JRS*, 1967, 23 ff.
Wiseman, T. P., 'Pulcher Clodius', *HSCP*, 1970, 207 ff.

THE PRINCEPS AND HIS FAMILY

Akveld, W. F., *Germanicus*, Groningen, 1961.
Charlesworth, M. P., 'The Banishment of the Elder Agrippina', *CP*, 1922,
  260 f.
Christ, K., *Drusus und Germanicus*, Paderborn, 1956.
Eisenhut, W., 'Der Tod des Tiberius – Sohnes Drusus', *MH*, 1950, 123 ff.
Grant, M., 'An Asian Coin of Drusus Junior', *NC*, 1950, 140 ff.
Koestermann, E., 'Die Feldzüge des Germanicus', *Hist.*, 1957, 429 ff.
'Die Mission des Germanicus im Orient', *Hist.*, 1958, 331 ff.
Meise, E., 'Der Sesterz des Drusus mit den Zwillingen und die
  Nachfolgepläne des Tiberius', *Jahrb. f. Num.*, 1966, 7 ff.

Mommsen, Th., 'Die Familie des Germanicus', *Herm.*, 1878, 245 ff. = *Ges. Schr.*, IV, 271.
Rogers, R. S., 'The Conspiracy of Agrippina', *TAPA*, 1931, 141 ff.
    'Drusus Caesar's Tribunician Power', *AJP*, 1940, 457 ff.
Scott., K., 'Drusus, nicknamed Castor', *CP*, 1930, 155 ff.
Timpe, D., *Der Triumph des Germanicus. Untersuchungen zu den Feldzügen der Jahre 14-16 n. Chr. in Germanien*, Bonn, 1968.
Weinstock, S., 'The Image and the Chair of Germanicus', *JRS*, 1957, 144 ff.

POLITICIANS AND THEIR FATES

Adams, F., 'The Consular Brothers of Sejanus', *AJP*, 1955, 70 ff.
Allen, W., 'The Political Atmosphere of the Reign of Tiberius', *TAPA*, 1941, 1 ff.
    'A minor Type of Opposition to Tiberius', *CJ*, 1948, 203 ff.
Bird, H. E., 'Aelius Sejanus and his Political Significance', *Lat.*, 1969, 85 ff.
Boddington, A., 'Sejanus. Whose Conspiracy?', *AJP*, 1963, 1 ff.
Ciaceri, E., 'L'Imperatore Tiberio e i Processi di lesa maestà', *Processi politici e Relazioni internazionali*, 1918, 249 ff.; reprint.
    'La Responsabilità di Tiberio nell'Applicazione della Lex Julia Maiestatis', *Stud. Stor. per l'Ant. Class*, 1909, 377 ff.; 1910, 19 ff.
Cichorius, C., 'Zur Familiengeschichte Seians', *Herm.*, 1904, 461 ff.
Columba, G. M., 'Il Processo di Cremuzio Cordo', *A e R*, 1901, 361 ff.
Forsyth, P. I., 'A Treason Case of A.D. 37', *Phoen.*, 1969, 204 ff.
Hennig, D., *L. Aelius Seianus. Untersuchungen zur Regierung des Tiberius*, Vestigia, XXI, Munich, 1975.
Jülg, J., *Vita L. Aeli Seiani Tiberio Imperante*, Oeniponti, 1882.
Katzoff, R., 'Tacitus, *Annales*, I, 74; the Case of Granius Marcellus', *AJP*, 1971, 68 ff.
Kierdorf, W., 'Die Einleitung des Piso-Prozesses', *Herm.*, 1969, 246 ff.
Koestermann, E., 'Der Sturz Sejans.', *Herm.*, 1955, 350 ff.
Krapper, A. H., 'Tiberius and Thrasyllus', *AJP*, 1927, 339 ff.
Marsh, F. B., 'A Modern Historical Myth. A Defense of Tacitus', *CW*, 1925-26, 135 ff.
    'Roman Parties in the reign of Tiberius', *AHR*, 1925-26, 233 ff.
Meissner, E., *Sejan, Tiberius und die Nachfolge im Prinzipat*, diss., Erlangen, 1968.
Mogenet, J., 'La Conjuration de Clemens', *Ant. Class.*, 1954, 321 ff.
Nicols, J., 'Antonia and Sejanus', *Hist.*, 1975, 48 ff.
Rogers, R. S., 'Lucius Arruntus', *CP*, 1931, 31 ff.
    'The Date of the banishment of the Astrologers', *CP*, 1931, 203 ff.
    'Two criminal cases tried before Drusus Caesar', *CP*, 1932, 75 ff.
    'An incident of the opposition to Tiberius', *CJ*, 1951, 114 ff.
Scott, K., 'Ein Aspruch des Tiberius an Galba', *Herm.*, 1932, 471 ff.
Sealey, R., 'The Political Attachments of Aelius Sejanus', *Phoen.*, 1961, 97 ff.

Shotter, D. C. A., 'Tiberius' part in the Trial of Aemilia Lepida', *Hist.*, 1966, 312 ff.

'The Trial of Gaius Silius (A.D. 24)', *Lat.*, 1967, 712 ff.

'The Case of Pomponius Labeo', *Lat.*, 1969, 154 ff.

'The Trial of Clutorius Priscus', *G and R*, 1969, 14 ff.

'Tiberius and Asinius Gallus', *Hist.*, 1971, 443 ff.

'Cnaeus Calpurnius Piso, Legate of Syria', *Hist.*, 1974, 230 ff.

Stewart, Z., 'Sejanus, Gaetulicus, and Seneca', *AJP*, 1953, 70 ff.

Sumner, G. V., 'The Family Connections of L. Aelius Seianus', *Phoen.*, 1965, 134 ff.

Syme, R., 'Personal Names in *Annals*, I–VI', *JRS*, 1949, 6 ff.

'Marcus Lepidus, *Capax Imperii*', *JRS*, 1955, 22 ff.

'Sejanus on the Aventine', *Herm.*, 1956, 527 ff.

'Some Pisones in Tacitus', *JRS*, 1956, 17 ff.

Townend, G. B., 'The Trial of Aemilia Lepida in A.D. 20', *Lat.*, 1962, 484 ff.

Weinrib, E. J., 'The Family Connexions of M. Livius Drusus Libo', *HSCP*, 1967, 247 ff.

THE PRINCEPS IN ROME AND ITALY

Allison, J. E., and Cloud, J. D., 'The Lex Julia Maiestatis', *Lat.*, 1962, 711 ff.

Astin, A. L., 'Nominare in Accounts of Elections in the early Principate', *Lat.*, 1969, 863 ff.

Bauman, R. A., *Impietas in Principem, a Study of Treason against the Roman Emperor with special reference to the first century A.D.*, Münch, Beitr. zur Papyrusforsch. und ant. Rechtsgesch. 67 Heft, Munich, 1974.

Charlesworth, M. P., 'The Virtues of a Roman Emperor', *PBA*, 1937, 105 ff.

'The Refusal of divine Honours, an Augustan Formula', *PBSR*, 1939, 1 ff.

Chilton, C. W., 'The Roman Law of Treason under the early Principate', *JRS*, 1955, 73 ff.

Crook, J., *Consilium Principis. Imperial Councils and Counsellors from Augustus to Diocletian*, Cambridge, 1955.

Frank, Tenney, 'The Financial Crisis of 33 A.D.', *AJP*, LVI, 1935, 336 ff.

Frei-Stolba, R., *Untersuchungen zu den Wahlen in der röm. Kaiserzeit*, Zurich, 1967.

Gagé, J., 'La Victoria Augusti et les Auspices de Tibère', *Rev. Arch.*, 1930, 1 ff.

Gesche, H., 'Die Datierung der 8. imperatorischen Akklamation des Tiberius', *Chiron*, 1972, 339 ff.

Grant, M., *Aspects of the Principate of Tiberius*, NNM, no. 116, New York, 1950.

Heidel, W. A., 'Why were the Jews banished from Italy in 19 A.D.?', *AJP*, 1920, 38 ff.

Kampff, G., 'Three Senate meetings in the early Principate', *Phoen.*, 1963, 25 ff.

Koestermann, E., 'Die Maiestätsprozesse unter Tiberius', *Hist.*, 1955, 72 ff.

Kornemann, G., 'Der Prinzipat des Tiberius und der Genius Senatus', *Sitz. Ber. Akad. H. 1.*, Munich, 1947.

Lacey, W. K., 'Nominatio and the Elections under Tiberius', *Hist.*, 1966, 167 ff.

de Laet, S. J., *De Samenstelling van den romeinschen Senaat gedurende de eerste Eeuw van het Principaat*, Antwerp, 1941.

Levick, B. M., 'Imperial Control of the Elections under the early Principate: Commendatio, Suffragatio, and Nominatio', *Hist.*, 1967, 207 ff.

'Mercy and Moderation on the Coinage of Tiberius', *The Ancient Historian and his Materials*, ed. B. Levick, London, 1975, 123 ff.

Merrill, E. T., 'The Expulsion of the Jews from Rome under Tiberius', *CP*, 1919, 365 ff.

Newbold, R. F., 'Social Tension at Rome in the Early Years of Tiberius' Reign', *Ath.*, 1974, 110 ff.

Pani, M., *Comitia e Senato. Sulla Trasformazione della Procedura elettorale a Roma nell'età di Tiberio*, Bari, 1974.

Pekáry, Th., 'Zur Datierung der Divus Augustus Pater/Providentia-Prägungen', *Schweiz. Münzbl.*, 1965, 128 ff.

'Tiberius und der Tempel der Concordia in Rom', *Röm. Mitt.*, 1966-67, 105 ff.

Rogers, R. S., *Criminal Trials and Criminal Legislation under Tiberius*, Middletown, Conn., 1935.

'Tiberius' Reversal of an Augustan Policy', *TAPA*, 1940, 532 ff.

'Tiberius' Travels, A.D. 26-27', *CW*, 1945-46, 26 ff.; 42 ff.

'Treason in the Early Empire', *JRS*, 1959, 70 ff.

Scott, K., 'Tiberius' Refusal of the title "Augustus" ', *CP*, 1932, 43 ff.

'The Diritas of Tiberius', *AJP*, 1932, 139 ff.

Seibert, J., 'Der Huldigungseid auf Kaiser Tiberius', *Hist.*, 1970, 224 ff.

Shotter, D. C. A., 'Elections under Tiberius', *CQ*, 1966, 321 ff.

'Tiberius and the Spirit of Augustus', *G and R*, 1966, 207 ff.

'Tiberius and the Senate', *Mnem.*, 1968, 359 ff.

Sutherland, C. H. V., 'The "Virtues" of Tiberius: a Numismatic Contribution to the History of his Reign', *JRS*, 1938, 129 ff.

'Divus Augustus Pater. A Study in the Aes coinage of Tiberius', *NC*, 1941, 97 ff.

Coinage in Roman Imperial Policy, London, 1951.

Taylor, L. R., 'Tiberius' Refusals of Divine Honours', *TAPA*, 1929, 87 ff.

Tibiletti, G., *Principe e Magistrati repubblicani*, Rome, 1953.

Yavetz, Z., *Plebs and Princeps*, Oxford, 1969.

PROVINCIAL AND FOREIGN AFFAIRS

Alföldy, G., 'La Politique provinciale de Tibère', *Lat.*, 1965, 824 ff.

Bammel, E., 'Die Schatzung des Archelaos', *Hist.*, 1958, 497 ff.

Dobiáš, J., 'King Maroboduus as Politician', *Klio*, 1960, 155 ff.

Grant, M., 'The official coinage of Tiberius in Galatia', *NC*, 1950, 47 ff.

'The Coinage of Tiberius in Cyprus', Melbourne, 1957.

Grenier, A., 'Tibère et la Gaule', *REL*, 1936, 373 ff.

Kraeling, C. H., 'The Episode of the Roman Standards at Jerusalem', *Harv. Theol. Rev.*, 1942, 263 ff.

de Laet, S. J., *Aspects de la Vie sociale et économique sous Auguste et Tibère*, Brussels, 1944.

Liechtenhan, E., 'Das Ziel des Aufstandes der Rheinarmee', *MH*, 1947, 52 ff.

Mitford, T. B., 'A Cypriot Oath of Allegiance to Tiberius', *JRS*, 1960, 75 ff.

Orth, W., *Die Provinzialpolitik des Tiberius*, diss., Munich, 1970.

Pani, M., *Roma e i Re d'Oriente da Augusto a Tiberio (Cappadocia, Armenia, Media Atropatene)*, Bari, 1974.

Rostovtzeff, M., 'L'Empereur Tibère et le Culte Impériale', *Rev. Hist.*, 1930, 2 ff.

Šašel, J., 'Drusus Ti. f. in Emona', *Hist.*, 1970, 122 ff.

Smallwood, E. M., 'The Date of the Dismissal of Pontius Pilate from Judaea', *Journ. Jewish Stud.*, 1954, 12 ff.

'Some notes on the Jews under Tiberius', *Lat.*, 1956, 314 ff.

Syme, R., 'Tacfarinas, the Musulamii and Thubursicu', *Stud. in Rom. Econ. and Soc. Hist. in Honor of A. C. Johnson*, Princeton, 1951, 113 ff.

Vanderpool, E., 'Athens honors the Emperor Tiberius', *Hesperia*, 1959, 86 ff.

Weingärtner, D. G., *Die Ägyptenreise des Germanicus*, Bonn, 1969.

von Wilamowitz-Moellendorff, U., and Zucker, F., 'Zwei Edikte des Germanicus auf einem Papyrus des Berliner Museums', *Sitzungsb. d. Berl. Akad.*, 1911, 794 ff.

Wilcken, U., 'Zum Germanicus-Papyrus', *Herm.*, 1928, 48 ff.

Wilkes, J. J., 'A note on the Mutiny of the Pannonian Legions in A.D. 14', *CQ*, 1963, 268 ff.

ICONOGRAPHY AND THE LITERARY SOURCES

Bergmans, J., *Die Quellen der vita Tiberii in B.57 des Cassius Dio*, Amsterdam, 1903.

Borzsák, St., 'Das Germanicusbild des Tacitus', *Lat.*, 1969, 558 ff.

Bringmann, K., 'Zur Tiberius biographie Suetons', *RM*, 1971, 268 ff.

Daitz, S. G., 'Tacitus' Technique of Character Portrayal', *AJP*, 1960, 30 ff.

Ehrenberg, V., and Jones, A. H. M., edd., *Documents illustrating the Reigns of Augustus and Tiberius*, ed. 2, Oxford, 1955.

Furneaux, H., ed., *The Annals of Tacitus*, 2 vols.; 2nd ed. (Vol. II, rev. H. F. Pelham and C. D. Fisher), Oxford, 1896–1907.

Garzetti, A., 'Sul Problema di Tacito e Tiberio', *Riv. stor. it.*, 1955, 70 ff.

Harrer, G. A., 'Tacitus and Tiberius', *AJP*, 1920, 57 ff.

Jaeger, H., *De Cassii Dionis Liberum 57 et 58 Fontibus*, Berlin, 1910.
Jerome, T. S., 'The Tacitean Tiberius: A Study in Historiographic Method', *CP*, 1912, 283 ff.
Aspects of the Study of Roman History, New York and London, 1923.
Kessler, G., *Die Tradition über Germanicus*, Berlin, 1905.
Kiss, Z., *L'Iconographie des Princes Julio-Claudiens au Temps d'Auguste et de Tibère*, Warsaw, 1975.
Klingner, F., 'Tacitus über Augustus und Tiberius', *Sitzungsb. d. Bayer. Akad. d. Wiss.*, *Phil. hist. Kl.*, 1953, H.7.
Koestermann, E., *Cornelius Tacitus Annalen erläutert und mit einer Einleitung*, 4 vols., Heidelberg, 1963–68.
Marsh, F. B., 'Tacitus and Aristocratic Tradition', *CP*, 1926, 289 ff.
Mendell, C. W., *Tacitus, the Man and his Work*, Yale, 1957.
Miller, N. P., 'Tiberius Speaks', *AJP*, 1968, 1 ff.
Motzo, B. R., 'I commentari di Agrippina Madre di Nerone', *Studi Cagliaritani*, 1927, 19 ff.
Pani, M., 'Osservazioni intorno alla Tradizione su Germanico', *Ann. d. Tac. di Mag. Univ. Bari*, 1966, 107 ff.
Pippidi, D. M., 'Tacite et Tibère', *Ephemeris Dacoromana*, 1938, 233 ff. = *Aut. de Tibère*, 11 ff.
Polacco, L., *Il Volto di Tiberio: Saggio di Critica iconografica*, Rome, 1955.
Rietra, J. R., *C. Suetoni Tranquilli Vita Tiberii — C.24 – C. 40 neu Kommentiert*, Amsterdam, 1928.
Rogers, R. S., 'Ignorance of the Law in Tacitus and Dio', *TAPA*, 1933, 18 ff.
'A Tacitean Pattern in Narrating Treason Trials', *TAPA*, 1952, 279 ff.
Ryberg, I. S., 'Tacitus' Art of Innuendo', *TAPA*, 1942, 385 ff.
Shotter, D. C. A., 'Three Problems in Tacitus' *Annals* I', *Mnem.*, 1965, 359 ff.
'Three Notes on Tacitus, Annales 1 and 2', *CP*, 1967, 116 ff.
'Tacitus, Tiberius and Germanicus', *Hist.*, 1968, 194 ff.
Stuart, M., 'Tacitus and the Portraits of Germanicus and Drusus', *CP*, 1940, 64 ff.
Sumner, G. V., 'The Truth about Velleius Paterculus: Prolegomena', *HSCP*, 1968, 257 ff.
Syme, R., *Tacitus*, 2 vols., Oxford, 1958.
'The Historian Servilius Nonianus', *Herm.*, 1964, 458 ff.
'History or Biography. The Case of Tiberius Caesar', *Hist.*, 1974, 481 ff.
Townend, G. B., 'The Sources of the Greek in Suetonius', *Herm.*, 1961, 98 ff.
Toynbee, J. M. C., Review of L. Polacco, *Il Volto di Tiberio*, *JRS*, 1956, 157 ff.
Walker, B., *The Annals of Tacitus. A Study in the Writing of History*, Manchester, 1951.
Woodman, A. J., 'Questions of Date, Genre, and Style in Velleius: some Literary Answers', *CQ*, 1975, 272 ff.

1 Italy in Tiberius' time, showing places named in the text

2 The eastern Roman Empire

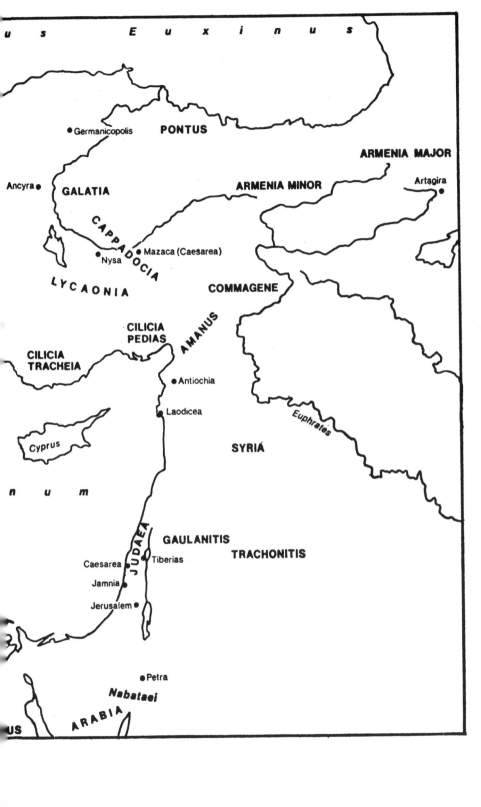

3　Western areas of the Roman Empire

A The connexions of Tiberius

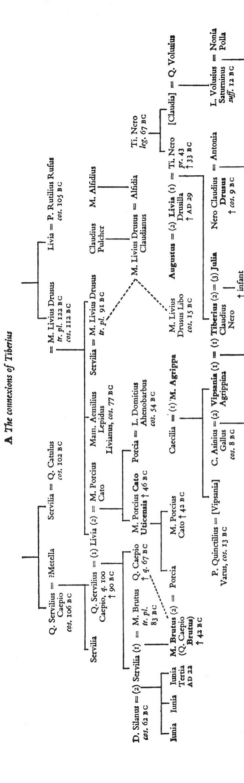

Names given in bold type are in each case the form by which their owner is most commonly known.

------- = Adoption

B The family of Augustus

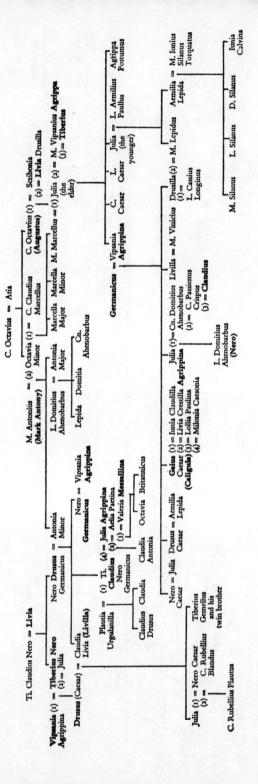

Names given in bold type are in each case the form by which their owner is most commonly known.

C *The descendants of Scribonia*

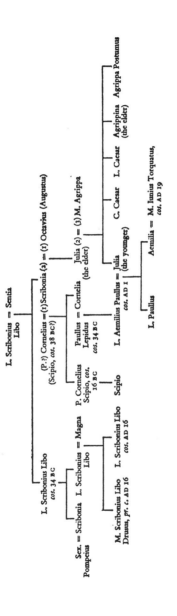

D *Stemma of Sejanus (conjectural)*

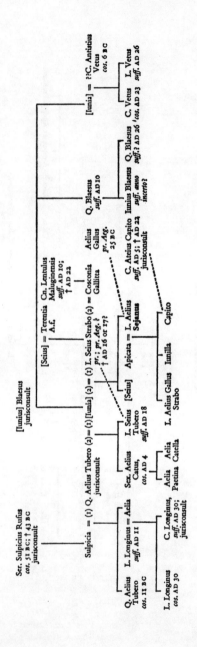

Names given in **bold type** are in each case the form by which their owner is most
commonly known.

.... = Adoption

INDEX

Most classical sites indexed may be found on the maps. Towns and districts are indexed by their classical names; rivers and other geographical features by their modern names. An italic *A, B, C,* or *D* signalizes persons to be found in the *stemma* so indicated. Celebrated figures (Principes and families, literary men, etc.) are indexed by the names most familiar to English readers, in each case followed in parentheses by their name(s) in full. Parts of names are given in parentheses when the word in question can only be inferred rather than attested. Reference is made to the notes only when the material in question is not accessible through the text. Abbreviations: Tib. for Tiberius; *sen.* for senator(s); *cos.* for consul (*ordinarius*); *cos. des.* for designated consul; *pr.* for praetor; *tr. pl.* for *tribunus plebis; eq.* for *eques; aed.* for aedile; 'II', etc., for 'for the second time', etc.

abdicatio, 57 f., 64
'accession' of Tib., 69, 76, 79 f.; according to ancient authors, 74 f., 79 f.
Achaea, 107, 125, 129 f., 146
Acilius Aviola, *sen.*, 266, n. 36
acta senatus, 113, 222
actors, 100, 105 f., 122, 193,

255, n. 3; see also theatre; *claqueurs*
Acutia, 216
adlection, 98
adoption: importance of, 12, 29, 49; 'testamentary', 19, 228, n. 10
adrogantia, 11, 121, 224
adultery, dealt with in Senate, 105, 184
aediles, 181, 261, n. 11
Aedui, 132, 134
Aegium, 101, 107, 268, n. 60
Aelia Paetina, *B, D,* 274, n. 69
Aelius Catus, Sex., *cos.* AD 4, *D,* 52
Aelius Gallus, Prefect of Egypt, 159
(? Aelius Gallus) Strabo, son of Sejanus, *D,* 175 f., 178, 202
Aelius Lamia, L., *cos.* AD 3; 53, 111, 125, 128 f., 131, 172, 178, 255, n. 7
(Aelius) Marullinus, *sen.,* 98 f.
Aelius Saturninus, 192 f.
Aelius Sejanus, L., Praetorian Prefect, *cos.* AD 31, *D:* origin, 158 f.; early career, 47, 159; influence with Tib., 53 f., 116 f., 175 f.; prefect, 73; in Pannonia, 71; relations with Drusus Caesar, 159 ff.; alleged murder of Drusus, 161; concentrates Guard, 121; detains governors? 128; political plans, 161 f.; asks for Livilla, 164 f.; manoeuvres Tib. out of Rome? 167; saves Tib.'s life, 168; allies, 164,

171 f., 211; advancement, 170; betrothal, 170; honoured by Senate, 164, 172, 175; courts *plebs*, 118 f., 171; *collega imperii,* 174; priesthood, 118; attack on, 213; fall, 86, 171, 172–3, 177, 199 f.; in custody, 284, n. 58; executed, 178, 186, 288, n. 107; on Gemoniae, 203, 283, n. 51; '*damnatio memoriae*', 283, n. 50; fate of property, 101, 133; attacks on friends, 202 ff.; fall celebrated, 202; importance of case, 187, 201; philhellene, 17; alleged anti-Semite, 136; counterweight to Agrippina, 207
Aemilia, Basilica, 106
(Aemilia) Lepida, sister of *cos.* of AD 11; 47, 55, 273, n. 54, 288, n. 107
Aemilia Lepida, daughter of *cos.* of AD 6, *B,* 55, 174, 215
Aemilia Lepida, daughter of L. Aemilius Paullus, *B, C,* 55, 59
Aemilii Lepidi, 55
Aemilius Lepidus, M., *cos.* II 42 BC, Triumvir, 55
(Aemilius) Lepidus, M., son of Triumvir, 187
Aemilius Lepidus, M., *cos.* AD 6; 55, 106, 109, 113, 151, 186; protects daughter, 215
Aemilius Lepidus, M'., *cos.* AD 11; 47, 55
Aemilius Lepidus, Paullus, *suff.* 34 BC, *C,* 47
Aemilius Paullus, L., *cos.*

Aemilius Paullus—cont.
AD 1; *B, C*, 47 f., 50, 54
f., 58 f., 151, 187, 282,
n. 50
Aemilius Paullus, L., son of
Julia the younger, 50
Aemilius Rectus, Prefect of
Egypt, 129
Aemilius Scaurus, Mam.,
suff. AD 21; 78, 171, 190,
192, 213 f., 274, n. 67
Aerarium Militare, 101,
202
Aerarium Saturni, 100 f.,
133, 185, 265, n. 32
Aezani, 140
Africa, province of, 108 ff.,
110, 121, 126, 131 f.,
138, 258, nn. 60, 69
Agricola, see Iulius Agricola, Cn.
Agrippa I (M. Julius
Agrippa) of Judaea, 117,
141 f., 284, n. 58
Agrippa II (M. Julius
Agrippa) of Judaea, 142
Agrippa, Marcus (M. (Vip-
sanius) Agrippa), *cos.*
III 27 BC, *A, B, C*:
origin, 159; name, 29;
marriage to Caecilia, 19;
marriage to Julia the
elder, 24, 29; children,
29 f.; official powers, 23
f., 29, 49, 154; policies,
171; head on coins, 63;
in East, 23 f.; in Bal-
kans, 236, n. 2, 240, n. 4;
triumphs refused, 35;
gifts to Nemausus, 45;
founds naval base, 60;
Baths, 121; and Nep-
tune, 60; relations with
Tib., 19, 29 f., 173;
death, 31; consequences
for Tib., 31 f.; funeral,
69, 156; Sejanus' model,
171; descendants, 19,
161, 171
Agrippa Postumus (M.
Vipsanius Agrippa Pos-
tumus, Agrippa Julius
Caesar), *B, C*; birth, 31,
48; takes *toga virilis*, 48,
56, 175; adopted, 49;

name, 58; prospects, 50;
advancement, 56, 158,
243, n. 38; supporters,
54, 57, 59; disgrace, 50,
57 f., 169, 186, 200;
exiled to Surrentum, 59,
to Planasia, 60; 'schizo-
phrenia', 58; attacks
Augustus, 60; solicits
navy, 60; attempted res-
cue of him, 61, 65 f.,
150 f.; death, 61, 65,
112; death as murder by
Livia, 271–2, n. 32; fate
of property, 59 f., 101;
impersonated, 118, 120
Agrippina the elder ((Vipsania) Agrippina), *B, C*;
marriage, 50; political
activities, 51, 150, 165;
ineptitude, 171 f.; rela-
tions with Tib., 50 f.,
157 f., 163, 166 f.; relations with Julia the
younger, 51; supporters,
168; popularity: on the
Rhine, 74, 144, 153 f.,
in the East, 154 f., 165;
not allowed to remarry,
165; under attack, 165,
177, 195; 'adultery', 207;
disgrace, 88, 118, 124,
169 f., 186, 198 f.;
behind false Drusus? 213;
confined after Sejanus'
death, 124, 206 f.; '*damnatio memoriae*', 283, n.
50; '*clementia*' of Tib.
towards, 207, 210; Taci-
tus on, 222; counter-
weight to Sejanus, 207
Agrippina the younger
(Julia Agrippina), *B*:
marriage to Cn. Aheno-
barbus, 170, 208;
memoirs, 66, 221 f.,
237, n. 8, 246, n. 73
Albucilla, 199 f., 216, 284,
n. 131, 288, n. 107,
289, n. 58
Alexandria: Germanicus
in, 129, 155; grain shor-
tage, 264, n. 15; pog-
roms, 294, n. 85
Alexandrianism of Tib., 16

Alfidia, mother of Livia, *A*,
13, 116
Alps, conquest of, 27 f.,
126
Amanus, principality of,
141
Ammaedara, 131
Anauni, 138
Ancus Martius, 171
Andecavi, 132, 134
Angrivarii, 144
Annius Pollio, C., *suff.* ?
AD 21, 22; 202 f.
Annius Vinicianus, 290,
n. 10
Annius Vinicianus, L., *suff.*
before AD 41; 203
Antioch, in Syria, 129
Antioch, towards Pisidia,
263, n. 3
Antiochus III of Comma-
gene, 141
Antiochus III, the Great,
111, 130
Antipas, Tetrarch, 138, 143
anti-Semitism, 136; see
also Aelius Sejanus;
Alexandria; Gaius; Pon-
tius Pilate
Antistius Labeo, M., *sen.*,
89
Antistius Vetus of Mace-
donia, 198
Antistius Vetus, C., *cos.*
6 BC, *D*, 42
Antonia Minor, *A, B*, 141
f., 156, 173 f., 178, 239,
n. 72
Antonius, Iullus, *cos.* 10 BC,
41, 187
Antonius, L., *cos.* 41 BC,
14 f.
Antonius Pallas, freedman,
174
Antony, Mark (M. An-
tonius), *cos.* II 34 BC, *B*:
Triumvir, 14 f.; con-
nexions with Tib., 42,
44; Parthian campaign,
24; *hostis*, 170; '*dam-
natio memoriae*', 282, n.
50; will, 210; house
passes to Tib., 46; de-
scendants and supporters,
154, 160, 172, 275, n. 91

Apicata, *D*, 161, 201, 274, n. 72
Apidius Merula, *sen.*, 249, n. 2
Apollo, temple of, 177
Apollonides, critic, 230, n. 27
Apoxyomenos of Lysippus, 121
Appia Claudia, wife of C. Silanus, 55
Appius Appianus, *sen.*, 95
Appius Iunius Silanus, C., *cos.* AD 28; 202 f.
Appuleia Varilla, 192 f., 197
Appuleius Saturninus, L., *tr. pl.* II 100 BC, 86, 138, 181, 183 f.
Appuleius, Sex., *cos.* AD 14; *relatio* of, 78 ff.
Apronius, L., *suff.* AD 8; 53, 149 f., 172, 265, n. 24
Apronius Caesianus, L., *cos.* AD 39; 291, n. 17
aquae et ignis interdictio, 186 ff., 192, 205
Aquileia, *sen.* from, 255, n. 24
Aquincum, 145
Aquitania, 134
Arabia, 21, 154
Archelaus I of Cappadocia, Tib.'s client, 20, 26, 111, 140 f., 145
Archelaus II of Cappadocia, 141
Aretas IV of Nabataei, 143, 155
Argentoracum, 145
Ariobarzanes of Media Atropatene, 143
Ariovistus of the Suebi, 112
Armenia Major: Roman claim to, 25; Tib. in, 24, 26, 126; seized by Tigranes III, 145; fighting in, 48; troops ordered to, 155; Tib.'s dealings with, 145 ff., 218
Armenia Minor, 25
armies: cost, 122, 133; recruitment, 127, 129, 152, 264, n. 13; of Africa, 131; Balkans, 26, 40 f.,

44, 152; East, 145; Rhine, 40; Spain, 41, 55; demands of, 51, 71; political affiliations, 44 f., 56, 151 f., 169
Arminius of the Cherusci, 111, 143 f.
Arruntius, L., *cos.* AD 6; 52, 105 f., 125, 128 f., 172, 176, 199, 214, 216
Arruntius (Furius) Camillus Scribonianus, L., *cos.* AD 32; 176, 204, 216
art, Tib.'s taste in, 18, 40, 121 f., 294, n. 93
Artabanus III of Parthia, 145 f.
Artavasdes, claimant to Armenia Major, 145
Artavasdes of Media Atropatene, 25
Artaxes I of Armenia, 25 f.
Artaxes III of Armenia, also known as Zeno of Pontus, 140, 146
Aruseius, 176 f.
Asellius Sabinus, 284, n. 58
Asia, province of: false Drusus in, 211 f.; earthquake relief, 101, 107; selection of governor, 108; governor's powers, 109 f., 125; embassies from, 106; Ti. Iulii in, 138
Asia Minor: Augustus in, 26; Tib. in, 126
Asinius Epicadus, freedman, 61
Asinius Gallus, C., *cos.* 8 BC, *A*: in Asia, 44; in Senate, 114, 280, n. 4; on Tiber flood, 105; view of empire, 77 f.; relations with Tib., 43, 114, 149 f.; relations with Sejanus, 163, 172; denounced by Tib., 712, 198; and Agrippina, 165; in custody, 173, 284, n. 58; death, 206;, as *reus*, 283, n. 51; '*damnatio memoriae*', 282, n. 50
Asprenas, L., see Nonius Asprenas, L.

astrology: influence on Tib., 18, 167, 210, 217, 224; practitioners punished, 149; consultation forbidden, 287, n. 91
asylum, right of, 103 f., 106, 194
Ateius Capito, C., *suff.* AD 5, *D*, 105 f., 199, 259, n. 88
Atella: farce of, 122 f., 124; festival of, 120 f.
Athenaeus of Seleucia, philosopher, 16, 22 f., 286, n. 88
Athens, 154, 264, n. 18
Atrebates, 145
Atria, *sen.* from, 98
Attaleia in Pamphylia, *sen.* from, 99
Atticus (T. Pomponius Atticus), *eq.*, descendants, 159
auctoritas, 29, 96; of Tib., 36, 75, 79; his view of it, 85, 89
Audasius, L., 61, 271, n. 23
Aufidius Bassus, 113, 246, n. 73
Augusta Praetoria, 28
Augusta Taurinorum, 28
Augustus, *cognomen*, 62, 75
Augustus Caesar (C. Octavius, *Imp. Caesar Divi filius*), *cos.* XIII 2 BC, *A*, *B*, *C*: training, 126; early career, 14 f., 38, 85; marriages, 15; father of Nero Drusus? 15, 33; relations with Tib., 45, 56; on Claudius, 165; autobiography, 33; 're-stores Republic', 21, 33 f.; powers, 21, 23, 29, 125; and crisis of 23 BC, 21 ff.; purges Senate, 95; campaigns: 20, in Egypt, 155, in East, 24 f.; policy: in Africa, 131 f., in East, 24 ff., see also Arabia; Britain; Ethiopia; grants of citizenship, 138; colonies, 139; admission of provincials to Senate, 98; gifts

Augustus Caesar—cont.
to Gauls, 133; wealth,
100 f.; heir of Maecenas,
239, n. 72; buildings,
123; health, 151, 209;
succession plans, 20, 24,
29, 31 f., 35 f., 37, 40 f.,
47 ff., 56, 63 f.; stays in
Italy, 127, 170; visits
Agrippa Postumus, 64 f.;
orders Postumus' death?
65 f.; death, 65, 68;
death as murder by
Livia, 272, n. 32; funeral,
68 ff., 156, 219 f.; will,
64, 121 f., 210; political
advice, 83; cult, 70, 75,
81 f., 166, 193, 220 f.;
temple at Nola, 167,
250, n. 7, 262, n. 26;
temple at Caesarea, 136;
altar at Lugdunum, 281,
n. 32; statue in Forum,
169; Prima Porta, 234,
n. 38; Bovillae, 123,
250, n. 7; Gytheum,
139 f.; later repute, 220;
maiestas, 191 ff.; oath to
acta, 82; example fol-
lowed by Tib., 56, 82,
100, 121 f., 223 f., 258 f.,
n. 71
Aurelius Cotta Maximus
Messallinus, M., cos. AD
20: in Senate, 100, 169,
287, n. 88; prominent
in AD 16; 271, n. 14;
gift to Ovid, 241 f., n.
28; attack on Gaius, 205;
friend of Tib., 149;
accused, 192; saved by
Tib., 197, 201, 289, n.
128
Aurelius Pius, sen., 94
autobiography: of Augus-
tus, 33; of Tib., 173,
222; see also Agrippina
the younger
Aventine Hill: associations
of, 119 f.; election of
Sejanus, 171; fire on,
218, 254, n. 35, 261, n. 13
Avillius Flaccus, A., Prefect of Egypt, 206, 260,
n. 2, 277, n. 113

Baetica: sen. from, 98 f.;
Vibius Serenus in, 163;
embassy to Senate, 258,
n. 60; request for temple
refused, 89, 129
Balbillus, see Claudius Bal-
billus, Ti.
Balkans: Agrippa in, 31;
Tib. in, 31 f., 35, 57, 61
f., 110, 126; changes
under Tib., 129 f.; see
also armies; Dalmatia;
Illyricum; Thrace
Barcino, sen. from, 99
Bastarnae, 35
Bato of Pannonia, 88
Belgae, 73
Belgica, 134
Berenice, mother of
Agrippa I, 141
Bibaculus (M. Furius Bi-
baculus), 194
Bibulus, M., see Cal-
purnius Bibulus, M.
Blaesi, see Iunii Blaesi
Bononia (Gesoriacum),
Tib. at, 140
Bovillae, 123, 250, n. 7
Brasidas, dynast, 212
brigandage: in Sardinia,
106, 136; rebellion of
Tacfarinas as, 132
Britain: invasion planned,
21; upheavals in, 27; Tib.
and, 142 f., 250, n. 3
Brixia, sen. from, 98
Bructeri, 28
Bruttedius Niger, sen., 202,
214, 285, n. 68
Brutus, M. (M. Iunius
Brutus, Q. Caepio
Brutus), cos. des. 41 BC,
A, 44, 55, 186, 194, 233,
n. 19
buildings: erected by
Augustus and Tib., 123;
in Gaul, 132 f.
burden of Principate, 36,
76 f., 138
burial, refusal of, 187

C. Caesar, see Gaius Caesar
Caecilia Attica, A, 116

Caecilianus, C., 289, n. 128
Caecilius Epirota, Q.,
freedman, 16
Caecilius Metellus Creti-
cus Silanus, Q., cos. AD
7; 55, 56, 145 f., 151 f.,
154 f.
Caecina Severus, A., suff.
I BC, 71, 74, 144
Caelian Hill, 218
Caelius Cursor, eq., 198
Caepio Crispinus, 285, n.
68 f.
Caesarea, in Judaea, 137;
temple of Augustus at,
136
Caesianus, L., see Apronius
Caesianus, L.
Caesonius Priscus, T., eq.,
260, n. 2
Caetranius, C., sen., 256,
n. 24
Caligula, see Gaius (also
known as Caligula)
Callipides, 127
Calpurnius Bibulus, M.,
cos. 59 BC, 91
Calpurnius Fabatus, L.,
eq., 132
Calpurnius Piso, Cn., cos.
23 BC, 23
Calpurnius Piso, Cn., cos.
7 BC: friend of Tib.,
42 f., 190, 195; in
Senate, 114, 196; with
Germanicus in Syria,
107, 113, 127, 154 f.;
'murder' of Germanicus,
124; trial and death,
107 f., 156 f., 162, 164,
190, 195, 197, 199 f.;
fate of statues, 283, n. 51;
praenomen forbidden,
282, n. 50; penalty miti-
gated, 197; accusers re-
warded, 189; importance
of case, 187 ff., 195
Calpurnius Piso the pontifex, L., cos. 15 BC, 17,
35, 53, 64, 178, 255, n. 7
Calpurnius Piso, L., sen.,
180, 182, 190
Calpurnius Piso, L., sen.
(son of cos. of 15 BC?),
128, 135

Calpurnius Piso, M., 90, 157
Calpurnius Rufus, M., sen., 99
calumnia, 176, 190, 197 f.
Calvisius Sabinus, C., cos. AD 26; 202 f.
Caninius Gallus, L., suff. 2 BC, 218
Capito Aelianus, D, 178, 186
Cappadocia, client kingdom of, 25 f., 141
Capri: Augustus on, 68; reason for Tib.'s withdrawal to, 167, 224; life on, 17, 124, 167, 217; Tib.'s entourage on, 17, 89; Gaius on, 173 f.
Capsa, 131
Capua, 262, n. 26
Carnuntum, 145
Carsidius Sacerdos, sen., 216
Carthago Nova, 232, n. 6
Cassii, in Senate, 203
Cassius, 'actor', 193
Cassius: attacks Drusus Caesar, 277, n. 117, cf. L. Cassius Longinus, cos. AD 30
Cassius, threatens Augustus, 286, n. 85
Cassius Longinus, C., cos. des. 41 BC, 186, 194, 208, 283, n. 50
Cassius Longinus, C. suff. AD 30; 208, 277, n. 117
Cassius Longinus, L., suff. AD 11; 54
Cassius Longinus, L., cos. AD 30; 208
Cassius Severus, 164, 191 f., 286, n. 88, 287, n. 91
Castor and Pollux, temple of, 58, 118
Catiline (L. Sergius Catilina), pr. 68 BC: hostis, 170; and Sejanus, 170
Cato (M. Porcius Cato (Uticensis)), tr. pl. 62 BC, A, 283, n. 50
Cato the elder (M. Porcius Cato), cos. 195 BC, in school curriculum, 16

Catualda, Goth, 130, 144 f.
Catullus (C. Valerius Catullus), 194, 229, n. 27
Catulus, Q., see Lutatius Catulus, Q.
Catuvellauni, 143
Celsus, eq., 203
census, AD 13-14; 68
Ceres, cult on Aventine, 119
Ceres Mater, altar to, 118
Cestius Gallus, C., cos. AD 35; 103, 194, 198, 202
Charicles, physician, 219
Chatti, 143 f.
Chauci, 28
Cherusci, 130, 144
Chios, 21, 44
Cibyra, 101, 268, n. 60
Cicero (M. Tullius Cicero), cos. 63 BC: novus, 159; prosecutor, 190; judge, 284, n. 64; and Catilinarians, 37, 178; reluctant governor, 128; on maiestas, 281, n. 24; and Ti. Nero, 13 f.; political philosophy, 33 f., 52; in school curriculum, 16
Cilicia Tracheia, 141, 156
Cinithii, 131
circus, seating in, 52
Circus Maximus, burnt, 218
Cirta, 132
Cisalpina, 98, 256, n. 24
citizenship: Augustus and, 138; Tib. and, 98, 138; Claudius and, 138; Drusus Caesar grants, 264, n. 18
civilitas, of Tib., 89, 182
claqueurs, theatrical, 152, 159; conscription of, 247, n. 6
Claudia, daughter of Clodius and Fulvia, her relations, 41 f., 166, 238, n. 47
(Claudia) Livia Julia, see Livilla
Claudia Pulchra, wife of P. Varus, 165 f., 275, n. 91
Claudia Quinta, 228, n. 2

Claudii, 11, 173, 224; clients, 268, n. 63
Claudius, Princeps (Ti. Claudius Nero Germanicus, Ti. Claudius Caesar Augustus Germanicus), A, B: mental capacity, 165; prospects, 209; promotion, 202; holds games, 58; engagement: to Lepida, 50, broken, 59, to Livia Medullina, 52, 59; marriage to Urgulanilla, 53; supporters, 160 f., 164, 277, n. 111; at Germanicus' funeral, 156; and Sejanus, 160; benefits from Sejanus' fall, 174; acclaimed by Guard, 81; administration, 138; abolishes maiestas, 285 f., n. 76; intra cubiculum trials, 186, 200; and 'public' provinces, 257, n. 55; and procurators, 110, 137; and Gallic chiefs, 115; abolishes Druids, 266, n. 36; grant to Agrippa II, 142; annexes Thrace, 142; invades Britain, 142 f.; on Tib., 98; dedicates Ara Pietatis, 252, n. 22; deification, 70
Claudius, Ap., 41, 55, 166
Claudius Balbillus, Ti., 259, n. 92, 292, n. 46
Claudius Caecus, Ap., censor 312 BC, 11, 53
Claudius (Crassus Inregillensis Sabinus), Ap., Decemvir 451-449 BC, 11
Claudius Drusus Germanicus, Nero, see Nero Drusus
Claudius Marcellus, M., aed. 23 BC: education, 16; advancement, 19 f., 157; marriage, 20; prospects, 20, 38; death, 24; as murder by Livia, 271, n. 32
Claudius Nero, Ap., pr. 195 BC, 235, n. 47

Claudius Nero, C., cos. 207 BC: victory, 13; moderatio, 253, n. 29; 'consilium', 254, n. 36

Claudius Nero, Ti., cos. 202 BC, 13

Claudius Nero, Ti., sen., 13

Claudius Nero, Ti., pr. 42 BC, A, B: father of Tib., 11; career, 13 ff., 19; follower of Caesar, 14; founds colonies, 14, 45; ally of Antony, 14 f., 19, 26 f.; Republicanism, 14; pontifex, 236, n. 59; divorce, 15; death, 15, 19

Claudius Pulcher, Ap., cos. 143 BC, 12

Claudius Pulcher, Ap., cos. 79 BC, 12

Claudius Pulcher, Ap., cos. 54 BC, 184 f.

Claudius Thrasyllus, Ti., 18, 174, 210

Clemens, slave of Agrippa Postumus, 61, 66, 112, 118, 120, 150 ff., 212; in Gaul, 152, 261, n. 15

clementia: of Tib., 87 f., 91, 152, 197, 207; altar of, 88; Valerius Maximus on, 252, n. 20

client kings: Roman use of, 25, 142; Senate and, 111 f.; education of, 141

clients: Tib.'s, 20, 27; attitude to, 140 f., 225

Clodius Pulcher, P., tr. pl. 58 BC, 12, 41

Clupeus Virtutis, 87

Clutorius Priscus, eq., 88, 160, 163, 186

Cn. the augur, see Cornelius Lentulus, Cn.

Coccius Nerva, M., suff. AD 21 or 22; 89, 276, n. 100

Coelaletae, 142

coercitio, 188, 195

cohort of Lusitanians, seventh, 132

coins: as advertisement, 38, 63, 84 f., 87 f., 89, 157; commemorating Tib.'s

victories, 43; Augustus, 82; gens Iulia, 250, n. 7; deification of Tib., 221; moderatio and clementia, 88 f., 210; naming governors, 110; see also currency

colonies: few founded by Tib., 139; see also Appuleius Saturninus; Augustus; Ti. Claudius Nero

Comata, Gallia: Tib. governor of, 27, 126; restive, 27 f.; revolt in, 90, 110, 112, 115, 126, 132 f., 163

Commagene: client kingdom of, 25; annexed, 141

Concord, see concordia

Concordia, sen. from, 98

concordia (concord), 34, 62, 84, 86, 91; of imperial family, 152 f.; dedications to goddess, 86, 149; temple of goddess, 36 f., 52, 62, 118, 177 f.; on coins, 86; ordinum, 52, 116

Considius Proculus, eq., 198, 205, 289, n. 126

consilium principis, 92 f., 260, n. 97

constantia, of Tib., 83, 89 ff.

consular power, 23, 63, 105; Tib.'s distaste for, 63, 69, 99 f.

consuls: election of, 96 f.; in AD 30, 119; suffects, 96 f.; prerogatives and functions, 104, 184, 218, 220, 284, n. 58; respected by Tib., 39, 63, 99 f., 253, n. 33, 279, n. 139; and 'public' provinces, 106; Tib. as consul, 180 f., abdication, 233, n. 21

Corbonas, treasure, 136

Corbulo, Cn., see Domitius Corbulo, Cn., sen.

Corduba, sen. from, 99

Cornelia, C, 54

Cornelii Lentuli, 53 f., 206

(Cornelii) Scipiones, 204

Cornelius Balbus, L., the younger, sen., 35

Cornelius Cinna Magnus, Cn., cos. AD 5; 54

Cornelius Dolabella, P., cos. AD 10; 52, 109 ff., 130 ff., 151, 277, n. 111

Cornelius Gallus, C., eq., Prefect of Egypt, 186, 229, n. 27, 282, n. 47

Cornelius Lentulus the augur, Cn., cos. 14 BC, 53, 149, 163, 289, n. 123

Cornelius Lentulus, Cossus, cos. 1 BC, 53, 176

Cornelius Lentulus Gaetulicus, Cn., cos. AD 26; 54 f., 172, 205 f.

Cornelius Lentulus, Cn., cos. 3 BC, 53

Cornelius Lentulus Maluginensis, Ser., cos. AD 10, D, 53, 102, 258, n. 71

Cornelius Lentulus Sura, P., pr. 63 BC, 181

Cornelius Merula, L., suff. 87 BC, 181

(Cornelius) Scipio (P.?), C, 41

Cornelius Sulla, Dictator 81 BC: booty, 100; politics, 184; constitution, 33; and courts, 105; lex Maiestatis, 183; funeral, 69

(Cornelius) Sulla, L., 94

Coruncanius, Ti., cos. 280 BC, 159

Cotta Messallinus, see Aurelius Cotta Maximus Messallinus, M.

Cotys, son of Rhoemetalces, of Thrace, 112, 142

courts, abuses of, 180, 197 f.

Crassus, see Licinius Crassus Dives, M.

Cremutius Cordus, A., 164, 193 f.

Crete, 106, 192

Cromwell, Thomas, 158

Ctesiphon, 146

cubiculum, trials intra, 186 200

cucumbers, cultivated by Tib., 217, 225, 260, n. 99
Cunobelin of the Catuvellauni, 143
Curatores Alvei Tiberis, 105 f.
Curatores Aquarum, 257, n. 56
currency, shortage of, 102, 104, 123, 133
Curtius Atticus, *eq.*, 172, 260, n. 2
Curtius Rufus, *sen.*, 97
Curvius Silvinus, Sex., *sen.*, 99
Cyprus, 106
Cyzicus, 130, 134

Daci, 53
Dacia, province of, 145
Dalmatia: district of, 57, 62, 130; province of (Upper Illyricum), 151
'*damnatio memoriae*', 178, 187, 202, 204, 221, 283, n. 50
Danube, 43, 53, 131, 145; see also Balkans
Darius, son of Artabanus III, 147
debt: problem of, 104 f., 133; of Libo Drusus, 149
Decidius Saxa, L., *tr. pl.* 44 BC, 24 f.
deification: consequences of Augustus' for Tib., 75, 81 f., 193; consequences for *maiestas*, 191 ff.; of Tib. discouraged, 176; cult at Nysa, 140; cult at Pergamum, 263, n. 5; mooted after Tib.'s death, 221 f.; see also personality, cult of; Augustus; Claudius; Julius Caesar; Theophanes; temple
delatores, 103 f.; rewards, 104, 182, 189 f., 216; Tib. and, 190; hated, 189 f.; Trajan and, 189
deportation, 188
Diana, cult of, on Aventine, 119

Diana Limnatis, temple of, 107
dies imperii, see 'accession'
Dii, 142
dilatoriness: of Tib., 75 f., 128, 138, 175, 217; of Furius Camillus, 253, n. 29
Dio Cassius, on Tib., 223
Diocletian, Princeps, abdicates, 225
diplomacy, Tib.'s preference for, 144 f.
dissimulatio, of Tib., 17, 175, 222
doctors, Tib. and, 293, n. 70
Dolabella, P., see Cornelius Dolabella, P.
Domitian, Princeps, 117, 133, 221 f.
Domitius Afer, Cn., *suff.* AD 39; 99, 165 f., 190
Domitius Ahenobarbus, Cn., *cos.* AD 32; 170, 209, 216
Domitius Ahenobarbus, L., *cos.* 16 BC, 43
Domitius Corbulo, Cn., *sen.*, 94
Domitius Corbulo, Cn., *suff.* ?AD 39; 136, 290, n. 10
Druidism, 134
Drusilla (Julia Drusilla), daughter of Germanicus, B, 208
Drusus Caesar (Nero Claudius Drusus, Drusus Julius Caesar), *cos.* II AD 21, A, B: ancestry, 159; birth, 30; prospects, 37; education, 141; takes toga, 46; position in AD 4, 49 f.; advancement, 62 f.; relations with Germanicus, 50, 148 f., 152 f.; at Augustus' funeral, 70, 72 f.; in Pannonia, 71 ff., 158; honoured at Gytheum, 139 f.; at Athens, 264, n. 18; command in Balkans, 145; powers, 130, 148; grants citi-

zenship, 264, n. 18; ovation, 130, 158; at Germanicus' funeral, 156; in Senate, 96, 115; as consul, 100, 103 f., 181, 194, 273, n. 54; tribunician power, 158, 273, n. 54; personality, 158; popularity, 158, 206; poem on death of, 160 f., 186; death, 158, 161 f.; death as murder, 161, 178, 274, n. 63; honours, 156, 210; centuries of, 116, 274, n. 63; children's prospects, 162 f.
Drusus Caesar (Drusus Julius Caesar), son of Germanicus, A, B: prospects, 161 ff.; marries Aemilia Lepida, 55, 170; advancement, 158, 163; attacks Nero Caesar, 168; disgraced, 170, 186; imprisoned, 118, 173, 284, n. 58; impersonated, 120, 211 f.; supporters, 290, n. 10; death, 124, 206 ff.
dual principate, 29 f., 48, 63 f.

economy: of Italy under Augustus, 190; to be protected, 95, 129; of Gaul, 132 ff.; economy commission, 257, n. 56
Egnatius Rufus, M., *pr.* 19 BC, 187
Egypt: booty from, 133; Roman attitude to, 155; provincials 'flayed', 129; C. Caesar in, 154 f.; Seius Strabo in, 159; Germanicus in, 127, 129, 154 f.; 'Drusus Caesar' makes for, 211; property of Pallas in, 174; governor loyal in AD 31, 178; phoenix in, 206
elections: Tib.'s influence on, 42 f., 52, 96 f.; modi-

elections—cont.
  fied in AD 5: 51, 116; in
    AD 14: 52, 83, 95 f.,
    120 f.; held by Gaius, 97;
    consular, of 6 BC, 37 ff.;
    of AD 7, 60; of AD 30,
    119, 171; of Vestals and
    pontiffs, 102; praetorian,
    96, 270, n. 14
emancipation, 58
Emerita, 232, n. 6
Emona, 72, 139
Empire, policy of checking
  growth, 83, 142 f., 222
Ennia Thrasylla, 174, 215,
  278, n. 135
Ennius, Q., 16, 229, n. 25
Epaticcus, 143
Ephesus, 268, n. 60
Eprius Marcellus, T.
  Clodius, suff. AD 62, II
  74; 258, n. 70
equites: privileges and
  status, 51 f., 70, 108,
  116 f., 159, 204; property
  qualification, 103, 106,
  118; granddaughters forbidden prostitution, 106,
  117; as iudices, 183 f.; as
  procurators, 135; as
  governors, 141; at Ger-
  manicus' funeral, 156; in
  politics, 153, 208 f.; support for Clemens, 152;
  and Claudius, 160
Eryx, Mount, 266, n. 42
Ethiopia, 21
Eudemus, 279, n. 151
Euphorion, 229, n. 27
Euphrates, 146 f.; see also
  Parthia; Armenia
Euryclids of Sparta, 211,
  268, n. 61
Eutychus, 284, n. 58
execution, aggravated
  forms of, 187
exile, forms of, 187 f.
extravagance: measures
  against, 95, 114, 122,
  133, 149, 182; of Gaius,
  133, 265, n. 32

Fabius Maximus, Paullus,
  cos. 11 BC, 64

Falanius, eq., 193
Fannius, C., cos. 122 BC,
  233, n. 19
Fannius Caepio, 22, 32, 105,
  187
Fidena, disaster at, 106, 123
financial policy, 100 ff.,
  133; see also Aerarium;
  Fiscus
fires, at Rome, 56, 118 f.,
  122 f., 218
Firmius Catus, sen., 197,
  285, n. 73
Fiscus, 101, 132 f., 204
Flamen Dialis, 102, 255,
  n. 3
floods, Tiber, 56, 105 f.,
  118, 122
Florentia, 106
Florus, see Julius Florus
Fonteius Capito, C., cos.
  AD 12; 275, n. 80
foreign affairs, Senate and,
  111
Fors Fortuna, temple of,
  123
Fortune, Sejanus' statue of,
  171
Forum Iulii, 99, 145
freedmen: encroachments
  of, 116 f.; in politics,
  153, 211; Tib.'s, bribed,
  168; attacked, 215
Frisii, 28, 112, 126, 136
frugality, of Tib., 133
Fufius, Geminus, C., cos.
  AD 29; 176 f., 266, n. 33,
  276, n. 111, 282, n. 50
Fulcinius Trio, L., suff. AD
  31; 117, 156 f., 177, 189
  f., 203, 215, 285, n. 68,
  290, n. 11
Fulvia, wife of Mark
  Antony, 14, 41, 238,
  n. 47
funeral: ceremonial of, 32,
  35, 70, 89; political significance, 69, 156; censor's, 247, n. 5; public,
  94; of Tib., 94
Furius Camillus, M., Dic-
  tator V 367 BC, 36 f., 52,
  91, 253, n. 29
Furius Camillus, M., cos.
  AD 8; 52, 59 f., 265, n. 24

Furnius, 165, 275, n. 91

Gaetuli, 132
Gaius Caesar, also known
  as Caligula, see Gaius
  (also known as Caligula)
Gaius Caesar (C. Julius
  Caesar), cos. AD 1, B, C:
  birth and adoption, 29;
  popularity, 30; advancement, 44, 48, 49, 79,
  157; elected to consul-
  ship, 37 f., 40, 51; attitude to Tib., 45 f., 71;
  Tib.'s heir, 39; marriage,
  47, 153; supporters, 45,
  54, 159; in East, 44 f.,
  141, 145, 154 f.; powers,
  154; fatal wound, 46,
  48 f.; death as murder by
  Livia, 271, n. 32; funeral,
  156; centuries of, 116
Gaius (also known as
  Caligula), Princeps (C.
  Caesar Augustus Ger-
  manicus), B: supporters,
  141; on Capri, 175 f.;
  priesthood, 118; at-
  tacked, 174, 202; pros-
  pects, 170; takes toga,
  175 f.; advancement,
  175 f., 201, 209, 215;
  behind fall of Sejanus,
  173 f.; on coins? 210;
  initiates prosecutions,
  202, 205, 210 f., 215;
  betrothal, 214; married,
  207; widowed, 215, 220;
  lover of Ennia, 174;
  accused of homo-
  sexuality, 192, 196, 205;
  popular, 124, 158, 219;
  and death of Tib., 219;
  accession, 81, 220; pays
  Tib.'s legacies, 124; attitude to Tib., 221; adopts
  Ti. Gemellus, 220; re-
  verses Tib.'s policies, 97,
  122, 133, 164, 181, 183,
  195, 216, 285 f., n. 76;
  credited with Parthian
  settlement, 147; grants
  tetrarchy to Agrippa I,

Gaius—cont.
   142; disappointment as
   Princeps, 66
Galba, Princeps (L. Livius
   Ocella Ser. Sulpicius
   Galba, Imp. Caesar
   Augustus), 43, 132
Galba, C., see Sulpicius
   Galba, C., cos.
Galerius, C., Prefect of
   Egypt, 155, 279, n. 136
Gallius, M., ?pr. 44 BC, 19
Gallius, Q., pr. 42 BC, 19,
   181
games (ludi): to be given by
   substantial persons, 106;
   restricted, 122 f.; Mar-
   tiales, date of, 279, n.
   139; Megalensian, 156;
   Augustales, 79, 156;
   secular, 29; in honour of
   Nero Drusus, 118; of
   Augustus at Naples, 68
Garamantes, 131
Gaul: Augustus in, 127;
   Tib. in, 27, 32, 242, n.
   36; economy of, 132 f.;
   roads built in, 133; Ti.
   Iulii in, 138; Clemens
   in, 152; see also Aquitania; Belgica; Cisalpina;
   Comata; Narbonensis
Gaulanitis, 142
Gavius Apicius, M., 273,
   n. 62
Gemellus, see Tiberius
   Gemellus
Geminius, eq., 203
Gemonian steps, 88, 157,
   187, 203, 207
Germanicus, twin son of
   Drusus Caesar (Germani-
   cus Julius Caesar), B, 157,
   162
Germanicus Caesar (Nero
   Claudius Drusus Ger-
   manicus, Germanicus
   Julius Caesar), cos. II AD
   18, A, B, C: adopted, 50;
   married, 50; relations
   with Tib., 50 f., 127,
   148, 152 f.; relations
   with Drusus Caesar, 50,
   148 f.; kin, 50; sup-
   porters, 95, 190, 217;

advancement, 62 f., 245,
   n. 58; in Balkans, 57;
   holds games, 58;
   honoured at Gytheum,
   139 f.; in Germany, 143,
   151; powers, 74, 127,
   148, 249, n. 29; and
   mutiny, 73 ff.; popu-
   larity, 50, 71, 124, 134,
   148, 158; triumph, 148;
   in East, 127, 141, 146,
   148, 154 f.; death, 124,
   160; honours, 156, 210,
   255, n. 7; poem on
   death, 186; centuries of,
   116; praised at Tib.'s
   funeral, 220; literary
   work, 230, n. 27
Germany: invaded by
   Nero Drusus, 28, 35;
   Tib.'s command in, 35
   f., 49, 56; Tib.'s campaigns in, 35 f., 62, 126
   f., 175; policy, 144;
   Germanicus' campaigns
   in, 143 f.; disturbances
   in, 49, 62; standards lost
   in, 123; forts in, 144
Geryon, 31
governors: appointment
   of, 109; reluctant to
   serve, 128; prorogued,
   125, 127 f., 253, n. 33;
   absentee, 109, 125 f.,
   128 f.; freedom, 109 f.;
   prerogatives, 117, 125,
   135; controlled by Tib.,
   135 f.
Gracchus, C., see Sem-
   pronius Gracchus, C.
Gracchus, Ti., see Sem-
   pronius Gracchus, Ti.,
   tr. pl.
Graecinius Laco, P., 174,
   177, 202, 278, n. 134
grain, supply of: to Rome,
   12, 20 f., 23, 118 f., 121
   f., 129, 131, 218; at
   Alexandria, 264, n. 15
Granius Marcellus, M.,
   sen., 140, 192, 194, 196
Greek dress, 45, 129, 155
guardian of the state, see
   tutor reipublicae
Gytheum, 139, 248, n. 11

Habitus, see Vibius Habi-
   tus, A.
Hadrian, Princeps, 222
Hasta, sen. from, 98
Haterius Agrippa, D., cos.
   AD 22; 96, 161, 203
Haterius, Q., suff. 5 BC, 77
   f., 161
Herennius Capito, C.,
   procurator, 117
Herod Agrippa, Antipas,
   see Agrippa I, Antipas
Hiberus, freedman, Pre-
   fect of Egypt, 117, 206,
   279, n. 136
Hispanus Pompeius Mar-
   cellus Umbonius Silo,
   see Umbonius Silo, Marcellus, L. Hispanus Pompeius
Hispania, see Baetica; Tarraconensis
Hortalus, M., see (Hortensius) Hortalus, M.
(Hortensius) Hortalus, M.,
   sen., 94
hostis, declarations of, 169
   f.
hypocrisy, see dissimulatio

Iader, 130
Iberi, 146
Idistaviso, battle of, 144
Ilium, 130
Illyricum, province of:
   235, n. 51; Tib. in, 126
   f., 130, 242, n. 36; under
   Drusus Caesar, 130; see
   also Balkans; Dalmatia;
   Pannonia
imperator: title, 137, 143;
   declined, 35; as prae-
   nomen, declined, 247 f.,
   n. 11; Tib. saluted, III,
   IV, 242, n. 36, V, 244,
   n. 54, VI, 244, n. 55,
   VIII, 267, n. 47, 271, n.
   20; Gaius saluted, 220
imperium: use of, 31, 76; of
   Tib., 49, 63, 75, 79 f.,
   180, 182, 245, n. 59 f.,
   270, n. 1; Tib.'s view of
   it, 85

imprisonment, as penalty, 188

infamia, as penalty, 188

informers, see *delatores*

insanity, alleged to discredit politicians, 58

inscriptions: wording of, 85; use of, 85, 119 f.; showing citizenship, 138

insignia: praetorian, see *ornamenta praetoria*; of a triumph, see *ornamenta triumphalia*

Interamna, in Umbria, 106

Isis, devotees punished, 106, 136

Italica, 98 f., 232, n. 6

Italy, senatorial province of, 105; Tib. cleaves to, 126 f.; primacy for Tib., 129, 137, 225; investment in, 104; economy supported, 95, 129; *sen.* from, 53, 98; 'Drusus Caesar' sails for, 211, 213

Iulia, gens: temple of, 123; 250, n. 7

Iulius Agricola, Cn., *suff.* AD 77; 99

Iulius Argolicus, C., 212

Iulius Celsus, 284, n. 58

Iulius Eurycles, C., 212, 268, n. 63

Iulius Graecinus, L., *sen.*, and M., 99

Iulius Laco, C., 212, 268, n. 63

Iulius Marinus, *eq.*, 205, 260, n. 2

Iunia Claudilla (or Claudia), *B*, 278 f., n. 135

Iunia Tertulla (or Tertia), *A*, 55

Iunii Blaesi, 172

(Iunii) Silani, 55, 204

Iunilla (Aelia Iunilla), *D*, killed, 178, 186

Iunius Blaesus, *sen.*, *D*, 215

Iunius Blaesus, Q., *suff.* AD 10, *D*, 71 f., 109 f., 132, 159, 178, 202, 264, n. 24

Iunius Blaesus, Q., *suff.* ? AD 26, *D*, 72 f., 215

Iunius Brutus, M. (Q. Caepio Brutus), see Brutus, M.

Iunius Gallio, *sen.*, 99, 113 f., 198, 204 f., 284, n. 58

Iunius Novatus, 59 f., 294, n. 84

Iunius Otho, *sen.*, 214

Iunius Otho, *tr. pl.* AD 37; 216 f.

Iunius Rusticus, *sen.*, 169

Iunius Silanus, C., *cos.* AD 10; 55 f., 135, 152, 190, 196, 214, 217, 274, n. 67, 283, n. 54, 288, n. 107; his son, 290, n. 10

Iunius Silanus, D., *cos.* 62 BC, *A*, 55

Iunius Silanus, D., *sen.*, 55, 60 f., 94, 152, 166, 196, 207

Iunius Silanus, M., *cos.* 25 BC, 55

Iunius Silanus, M., *suff.* AD 15; 56, 94, 207, 211, 213 f., 279, n. 2

Iunius Silanus Torquatus, M., *cos.* AD 19, *B*, *C*, 55

ius auxilii, 180

iustitia, 89; see also law

iustitium, of AD 14; 70, 72

Jamnia, 117

Jerusalem, 136

Jews, 106, 136; see also anti-Semitism

Judaea, 107, 136 f., 146

Jugurtha of Numidia, 142

Julia the elder, daughter of Augustus, *A*, *B*, *C*: married to Marcellus, 20; married to M. Agrippa, 24, 29; married to Tib., 31, 37, 39; children, 29, 37, 50; personality, 37; supporters, 41 f.; politics, 153, 165, 167; attack on Tib., 37, 41; downfall, 41 f., 166, 169, 200; Tib. pleads for, 88; divorce, 44; exile, 48; and Agrippa Postumus, 61, 151; death, 151

Julia the younger ((Vipsania) Julia), daughter of M. Agrippa, *B*, *C*; marriage, 47, 54; politics, 48 ff., 54, 60 f., 153; relations with Agrippina, 51; 'adultery' and disgrace, 55, 59 f., 106, 169, 196, 200; marriage to D. Silanus? 61; exile, 61; and Agrippa Postumus, 61; death, 88, 150 f.

Julia, daughter of Drusus Caesar, *B*, 153, 157 f., 168, 208

(Julia) Drusilla, see Drusilla

Julius Caesar, C., Dictator in perpetuity 44 BC: and Catilinarians, 188; politics, 228, n. 2; *senatus consultum* against, 181; booty, 100; regulates investment, 182; enactment neglected, 104 f.; and provincials, 125; and colonies, 139; and citizenship, 138; on coins, 63; will, 210; gardens, 217; deified, 82

Julius Africanus, 202

Julius Florus, 126, 132 f.

Julius Sacrovir, 126, 132 f.

Junian Latins, in the Vigiles, 116

Jupiter: offerings to, 149, 207; temple at Capua, 167, 262, n. 26

knights, see *equites*

L. Caesar, see Lucius Caesar

Labeo, see Antistius Labeo, M.

Labienus, T., 164, 286, n. 91

Laco, see Iulius Laco, C.

Laelia, 216

Laelius Balbus, D., *cos.* AD 46; 216

Lamia, L., see Aelius Lamia, L.

Lampon of Alexandria, 284, n. 58

Laodicea, on Lycus, 21

Larinum, 53

law: Tib.'s interest in, 27, 85, 89, 102 f., 180 f., 258, n. 71; rule of in Tib.'s principate, 184; see also *iustitia*; *lex*

legio, legiones: *I*, 235, n. 47; *III Augusta*, 110; *IX Hispana*, 73, 110 f., 137

Lentulus the augur, see Cornelius Lentulus the augur, Cn.

Lentulus, Cossus, see Cornelius Lentulus, Cossus

Lentulus Maluginensis, Ser., see Cornelius Lentulus Maluginensis, Ser.

Lepcis Magna, 131 f.

Lepidi, see Aemilii Lepidi

Lepidus the Triumvir, see Aemilius Lepidus, M., *cos.* II 42 BC

Lepidus, M., see (Aemilius) Lepidus, M., son of Triumvir

Lepidus, M., *cos.* AD 6, see Aemilius Lepidus, M.

Lepidus, M'., see Aemilius Lepidus, M'.

Lesbos, 98, 198

lex, leges: and *senatus consulta*, 102 f., see also law; *Appuleia Maiestatis*, 183; *Cornelia Maiestatis*, 184, penalty, 187; '*de Imperio Vespasiani*', Tib. as precedent in, 221, sixth clause of, 281, n. 26; *Iulia de Adulteriis*, 185, 197, penalty evaded, 117; *Iulia Maiestatis*, Caesar's, 103 f., 182 ff., 187, scope, 286 f., n. 88, penalty, 187, rewards, 189, 'brought back' by Tib., 191, Tib.'s use of it, 221, see also *maiestas*; *Iulia Repetundarum*, 103, scope, 286 f., n. 88, 289, n. 135; *Iunia Petronia*,

257, n. 47; *Iunia Vellaea*, 257, n. 47; *Malacitana*, 255, n. 14; *Papia Poppaea*, abused, 182, 190, 285, n. 79, set aside, 96, clarified, 103; *Pompeia de Provinciis*, 258, n. 70; *Valeria Cornelia*, 51, 116; *Visellia*, 116, 257, n. 47

libel (seditious): and Princeps, 58 f., 124; as *maiestas*, 191 f.; Tib.'s attitude to, 192 f.

Liber Pater, cult of, 119

liberalitas (munificence), of Tib., 89 f., 91, 101, 106 f., 124, 218

Liberty, statue of, in Forum, 202

Libones, see Scribonii Libones

Licinius Crassus, M., *cos.* 30 BC, 34

Licinius Crassus Dives, M., *cos.* II 55 BC: Triumvir, 228, n. 8; defeat, 24, 34, 228, n. 8

Licinius Lucullus, L., *cos.* 74 BC, 219, 225

Licinius Macer, C., *tr. pl.* 75 BC, 285, n. 69

Licinius Murena A. Terentius Varro, L., *cos.* 23 BC, 21 f., 105, 184, 187

Livia Drusilla (Julia Augusta, Diva Augusta), *A, B*: ancestry, 11 ff.; connexions, 150; character, 12; marriages, 14 f., 39, 42; political role and protégés of, 37, 40, 42, 45, 53 f., 64, 68, 124, 141, 151, 153, 157, 176 f., 182, 192, 210, 271, n. 32, 276, n. 111; and Claudius, 165; relations with Tib., 153, 275, n. 98; 'murders', 64, 271 f., n. 32; at funeral of Augustus, 70; absent from Germanicus' funeral, 156; and cult of Augustus, 193; associated in Augustus' cult, 107, 135, 139; in charge of

Gaius, 173; long-lived, 209; death, 169; honours, 167, 192; will executed by Gaius, 200

Livia Medullina, 52, 59

Livilla ((Claudia) Livia Julia), daughter of Nero Drusus, *A, B, C*: wife of C. Caesar, 47; wife of Drusus Caesar, 153; children, 153, 157; 'adultery', 161; 'murder' of Drusus Caesar, 161; accomplices, 201; aims, 162; sought by Sejanus, 164; punishment, 200; death, 178; '*damnatio memoriae*', 203, 282 f., n. 50

Livilla (Julia Livilla), *B*, 166, 208

Livii Drusi, 233, n. 23

Livius Andronicus, L., 16

Livius Drusus, M., *cos.* 112 BC, *A*, 12, 15

Livius Drusus, M., *tr. pl.* 91 BC, *A*, 11 f., 15

(Livius) Drusus (Claudianus), M., *sen.*, 12 f., 14 f., 224

Lollius, M., *cos.* 21 BC, 27, 43, 145 f.

Lucanius Latiaris, L., *sen.*, 168, 202

Lucilius Capito, Cn., procurator, 110, 117, 135, 200

Lucilius Longus, *suff.* AD 7; 44, 154, 255, n. 7

Lucius Caesar (L. Julius Caesar), *B, C*: birth and adoption, 29; in politics, 38; supporters, 54; Tib.'s heir, 39; advancement, 40 f., 44, 48 f., 78; betrothed, 47; death, 46; death as murder by Livia, 271, n. 32; commemorated by Tib., 16, 46 f.; funeral, 156; centuries of, 51, 116

Lucullus, L., see Licinius Lucullus, L.

ludi, see games

Lugdunensis, 134

Lugdunum: altar near, 28, 32; mint at, 63; Tib. on coins of, 221

Lusitani, seventh cohort of, 132

Lutatius Catulus, Q., *cos.* 78 BC, 33 f.

Lycaonia, 141

Macedonia, 107, 125, 129 f., 146, 198

Macrinus, Princeps, 159

Macro, see Naevius Cordus Sutorius Macro, Q.

Madauros, 132

Maecenas, C., *eq.*, 22, 239, n. 72

magistrates: role of, 99 f., 218; prosecution of, 181

Magius Caecilianus, *pr. c.* AD 21; 181

magnates, provincial: cultivated by Augustus, 125; cultivated by Tib., 126; of Asia, 138; of Macedonia, 198

maiestas: of Tib., 193 f.; of the Senate, 92; cases of, 183 ff.; as a political weapon, 195; taken in Senate, 184; role of Princeps, 195 f.; see also *lex Iulia Maiestatis*

Manilius, M., poet, 230, n. 27, 231, n. 37

Marcella Major (Claudia Marcella), *B*, 159, 161, 275, n. 91

Marcella Minor (Claudia Marcella), *B*, 275, n. 91

Marcia, 64

Marciana, Augusta, 247, n. 5

Marcius, P., 271, n. 25

Marcius Censorinus, C., *cos.* 8 BC, 42

Marcius Rutilus Censorinus, C., *cos.* 310 BC, 91

Marcomanni, 56, 130

Marius, C., *cos.* VII 86 BC, 86 f., 125, 159, 170

Marius, Sex., 101, 133, 282, n. 49

Marius Nepos, Q., *sen.*, 95

Maroboduus of Marcomanni, 56, 111 f., 130, 144 f.

Mars, offerings to, 149

Marsi, 143 f.

Marsyas, 42

Massilia, 46, 107

Massurius Sabinus, *eq.*, 260, n. 2

Mazaca (Caesarea), 141

Memmius Regulus, P., *suff.* AD 31; 177 f., 203

Messallina (Valeria Messallina), wife of Claudius, *B*, 298

Messene, 107, 126

military men, favoured by Tib., 44, 52 f., 97

mines: of Spain, 133; of Cappadocia, 141

Minucius Thermus, *sen.*, 198, 202

Misenum: naval base at, 60; Tib. dies at, 219

Mithridates, brother of Pharasmenes of Iberi, 146

moderatio: of Tib., 87, 89, 91; celebrated by Valerius Maximus, 253, n. 29

modestia, of Tib., 223, 253, n. 29

Moesia, 53, 125, 129 f., 138

Moguntiacum, 73 f.

mourning, forbidden, 282, n. 50

Mucius Scaevola, Q., the pontifex, *cos.* 95 BC: *moderatio* of, 91

Munatia Plancina, 157; suicide, 210, 215, 287, n. 88

Munatius Plancus Paulinus, L., *cos.* AD 13; 263, n. 2

murder, cases taken in Senate, 105, 281, n. 29

Musulamii, 131 f.

Mutilia Prisca, 177, 276, n. 111

Mytilene, magnates from, 98, 211 f.

Naevius Cordus Sutorius Macro, Q., *eq.*: name, 278, n. 134; and fall of Sejanus, 174, 177; honoured, 202; and Gaius, 201, 215; initiates prosecutions, 198 f., 202, 214 ff., 288, n. 107; use of *maiestas*, 195; attacked, 215; and death of Tib., 219; fall, 206

Narbo, 289, n. 136

Narbonensis, 14, 45, 99, 133

navy: Claudii and, 13 ff.; Tib. and, 15; Germanicus and, 15; base at Misenum, 60; fleet on Danube, 131

Nemausus, 45, 99, 133

Neptune, 60

Nero, Princeps (Nero Claudius Caesar Augustus Germanicus), *B*: parentage, 277, n. 114; accession speech, 76, 82, 106; on Italy and senatorial provinces, 257, n. 55; and Seneca, 99; cuts beard, 279, n. 146; use of veto, 288, n. 107; and magistrates, 100, 181; brings back *maiestas*, 191; *intra cubiculum* trials, 186, 200; impersonated, 212 f.

Nero, Ap., see Claudius Nero, Ap.

Nero Caesar (Nero Julius Caesar), son of Germanicus, *B*: prospects, 161 f., 165; marriage, 157 f., 168; advancement, 56, 157, 163, 255, n. 3; attacked by Sejanus, 168; disgraced, 88, 118, 169, 186, 199 f.; death, 124, 173, 175 f.; bones collected, 221

Nero Drusus (Nero Claudius Drusus Germanicus) *cos.* 9 BC, *A, B*: birth and paternity, 15; *praenomen*, 232, n. 2; early career, 27; gives

Nero Drusus—cont.
games, 235, n. 49; campaign in Alps, 28; in Germany, 28, 35, 143; use of fleet, 15; prospects, 27 f., 32; allies, 32 ff., 85; personality, 33; popularity, 34; relations with Tib., 32 ff., 39; ovation, 35; augurate, 236, n. 59; death, 33, 35, 160; commemorated, 36, 58 f., 62, 118; descendants, 160; career as precedent, 158
Nestor, philosopher, 16
Nicetes, rhetorician, 230, n. 32
nobiles, Tib. and, 97 f.
Nola, temple of Augustus at, 167, 262, n. 26, 250, n. 7
Nonii, 53
Nonius Asprenas, L., suff. AD 6; 52, 131, 259, n. 79, 276, n. 111
Nonius Asprenas, L. suff. AD 29; 276, n. 111
Nonius Quinctilianus, Sex., cos. AD 8; 52, 60
Noricum, 130, 138
novi homines: rise of, 159; and Tib., 44, 53, 97 ff.; access to consulship, 99
Numidia, Gaetuli in, 132
Nysa, 20, 140

oath of loyalty: to Tib. in provinces, 73; of Palaipaphos, 248, n. 11; by legions, 73 f.; at Rome, 80, 112; to acta, 82, 204, 221
Octavia (Minor), B, 41, 208
Octavian, see Augustus Caesar
Odrysae, 21, 142
Olennius, ex-centurion, 136
omens: of Tib.'s rise, 26 f., 31; of his destruction, 217; of Sejanus' fall, 174

Opimius, L., cos. 121 BC, 37, 177
Ops Augusta, altar to, 118
Opsius, sen., 276, n. 106
ornamenta praetoria: of Tib., 26; Germanicus, 63; Sejanus, 160
ornamenta triumphalia, introduction of, 35; L. Piso, 35; Tib. and Nero Drusus, 236 f., n. 6; M. Messalla, 241, n. 28, Germanicus, 63; Galba, 132; granted by Tib., 137
Orodes III of Parthia, 145
Ostorius Scapula, Q., Praetorian Prefect, Prefect of Egypt, 43
ovation: earned by Tib., 235, n. 43; of Tib. and Nero Drusus, 236, n. 1; of Tib., 32, 35, 244, n. 53; see also Drusus Caesar
Ovid (P. Ovidius Naso); disgrace, 60 f., 105; exile, 128; gift from Cotta Maximus, 241 f., n. 28; and Fabius Maximus, 245, n. 68

Paconius, M., sen., 214, 289, n. 130
Pacuvius, 129
Pallas, see Antonius Pallas
Palpellius Hister, Sex., suff. AD 43; 98
Pannonia: district of, rebels, 57, 61 f., 98, end of rebellion, 61, 130; province of (Lower Illyricum), mutiny among soldiers, 64, 69, 71 ff., 108, 126 f., 150; end of, 73, 130, under Drusus Caesar, 130, Ti. Iulii in, 138
Papius Mutilus, M., suff. AD 9; 53, 149 f.
Pappa Tiberiopolis, in Pisidia, 138
Parthenius, 230, n. 27
Parthia: Rome and, 24 ff.,

36, 141, 218; standards lost in, 24 f.; settlement of 20 BC, 26, 144; Tib. and, 113, 145 ff.; encourages imposters, 212 f.
pater patriae, title refused by Tib., 75, 202
patricians, favoured by Tib., 52 f., 97
Paullus, L., see Aemilius Paullus, L., son of Julia the younger
Pax, statue of, 34, 86
Paxaea, 197, 213 f.
Pedanius Secundus, L., suff. AD 43; of Barcino, 99
penalties, legal, varied, 187 ff., 197 f.
Percennius, 271, n. 22
perduellio, 183
Pergamum, priest of Tib. at, 263, n. 5
personality, cult of the, 38, 63, 85, 139 f., 202; see also deification
Perusia, 14
Petilius Rufus, sen., 276, n. 106
Petronii, 161
Petronius, P., suff. AD 19; 161, 218, 290, n. 10
philhellenism, of Tib., 17, 45, 55, 222
Philip, son of Herod, tetrarchy of, 142
Philippi, omens for Tib. at, 27
Philippopolis, 138, 142
Philo Judaeus, 136
phoenix, return of, 206
Phraataces (Phraates V) of Parthia, 145
Phraates IV of Parthia, 25, 145; his son at Rome, 25, 146
pietas: of Tib., 62, 87, Valerius Maximus on, 252, n. 22; Ara Pietatis, 252, n. 22
Pinarius Natta, 164
pirates, 130
Pituanius, L., astrologer, executed, 271, n. 25

Planasia, Agrippa Postumus exiled to, 60; rescue attempts, 61, 65 f.; Agrippa Postumus visited by Augustus, 64, 68

Plancina, see Munatia Plancina

Plautii, connexions of, 161, 274, n. 69

Plautius, A., *suff.* AD 29; 276 f., n. 111

(Plautius?) Rufus, P., *sen.*, 58; see also Rufus

Plautius Silvanus, *pr.* AD 24; 181

Plautius Silvanus, M., *cos.* 2 BC, 53

Plautius Venox, C., censor 312 BC, 53

plebs: in politics, 23, 37 ff., 58, 64, 118, 129; stimulated by politicians, 42, 48, 52, 56, 118, 169, 220; *congiaria*, 90, 121 f., 124; courted by Sejanus, 170; see also elections

Pliny the elder (C. Plinius Secundus), *eq.*, 113

Pola, *sen.* from, 98

Pompeia Macrina, 211 f.

Pompeius, *eq.*, 203

Pompeius, Sex., *cos.* AD 14, *relatio* of, 78 ff.

Pompeius Macer, procurator of Asia, 98, 211 f., 260, n. 2

Pompeius Macer, Q., *pr.* AD 15; 98, 191, 211 f.

Pompeius Magnus Pius, Sex., *cos. des.* 35 BC, 14 f., 42, 60

Pompeius Theophanes, Cn., 98

Pompey the Great (Cn. Pompeius Magnus), *cos.* III 52 BC: supported by Ti. Nero, 13; politics, 228, n. 8; and provincials, 125; booty, 100; house passes to Tib., 46; theatre of, burnt, 119, 164, 274, n. 63; theatre of, restored, 106, 123

Pomponius Flaccus, L., *cos.* AD 17; 142, 149

Pomponius Labeo, *sen.*, 213 f.

Pomponius Secundus, *suff.* AD 41; 205, 289, n. 126

Pomponius Secundus, P., *suff.* AD 44; 284, n. 58, 290, n. 10, 291, n. 29

Pontifex Maximus, 75, 102, 253, n. 33

pontifices, 102, 163, 236, n. 59

Pontius, 194

Pontius Fregellanus, *sen.*, 216

Pontius Paelignus, C., 256, n. 24

Pontius Pilatus, *eq.*, Prefect of Judaea, 126, 136

Poppaeus Sabinus, C., *cos.* AD 9; 53, 125, 130, 142, 211

popularity: of Julia the elder and her kin, 30, 38, 51, 118; of Germanicus, 119, 124; of Agrippa Postumus,118; of Agrippina and her sons, 171

Porcius Cato, M., *suff.* AD 36; 276 n. 106

Porsena, Lars, 112

portraits, and *maiestas*, 193 f.

Posidonius, 18

Postumus, see Agrippa Postumus

Praetorian Guard: importance, 43, 64, 81; functions, 156, 186, 188; privileges, 108, 204; bequests to, 124; in Pannonia, 71 f.; concentrated, 121, 123, 159; untrustworthy in AD 31, 173; won over by Macro, 177 f., 215

praetors, 34, 89, 100, 104, 181, 191

Primus, M., *sen.*, 21 f., 105, 184

princeps and Princeps, 80

princeps iuventutis, title of, 38, 220

Proculian school, 89

procurators, powers of, 110, 117

Propertius Celer, *sen.*, 253, n. 35

prostitution, measures against, 106, 116

providentia, 89 ff.

provinces: Tib.'s care for, 90, 125 ff., 225, 255, n. 3; *sen.* from, 98, 107, 137; Senate and, 105 ff., 129

Ptolemy of Mauretania, 112

Pulcher, Ap., *cos.* 54 BC, see Claudius Pulcher, Ap.

Pulcher Claudius, P. *sen.*, 275, n. 91

Pyrrhus of Epirus, 111 f., 130

quaestiones perpetuae, 183 f.

quaestors, 100, 284, n. 58

querella de inofficioso testamento, 220

quies, 86

Quinctii, connexions, 55, 238, n. 46 f.

Quinctilii, connexions, 53

Quinctilius Varus, son of P., 166, 208

Quinctilius Varus, P., *cos.* 13 BC, *A*, 30, 43 f., 52, 143, 165 f.

Quinctius Cincinnatus, L., Dictator 458 BC, 91

Quinctius Crispinus Sulpicianus, T., *cos.* 9 BC, 41

Quinctius Crispinus Valerianus, T., *suff.* AD 2; 47

Quinctius Flamininus, T., *cos.* 198 BC, 139 f.

Quintilianus, *tr. pl.* AD 32; 218

Quirinus, temple of, 235, n. 49

Raetia, 28, 130, 138

Reate, 106

'regency', 31

relegation, 188

religion in politics, 102

renuntiatio amicitiae, 196, 214, 287, n. 91

repetundae, res, 105, 135, 184 f.
Republicanism, 14, 21 f., 32 ff., 37, 42, 44, 54
Rhescuporis of Thrace, 112, 142, 198
Rhianus, 230, n. 27
Rhine: armies of, 40, 50, importance of, 151, 172, Agrippa Postumus to be taken to, 66, 152, mutiny of, 69, 71, 73 ff., 126 ff., 150; frontier, declining importance of, 145
Rhodes: centre of learning, 17 f.; Tib. on, 17, 39 f., 44 ff., 122, 126, 167; snubbed by Tib., 126
Rhoemetalces II of Thrace, 138, 142
roads: Tib.'s interest in, 111; see also Africa; Illyricum; Spain
Romanus Hispo, 286, n. 88
Rubellius Blandus, C., *suff.* AD 18; 208, 259, n. 80
Rubellius Geminus, L., *cos.* AD 29; 276, n. 111
Rubrius, *eq.,* 193
Rubrius Fabatus, *sen.?,* 211, 284, n. 58
Rufus, 286, n. 85; see P. (Plautius?) Rufus
Rutilius Rufus, P., *cos.* 105 BC, *A,* 225

Sacrovir, see Julius Sacrovir
Saguntum, *sen.* from, 99
Sallustius Crispus, C., *eq.,* 65 f., 151, 260, n. 2
Salonae, 130
Salus, 34, 86, 90
Salvidienus Rufus Salvius, Q., *cos. des.* 39 BC, 187
Salvius Aper, Praetorian Prefect, 43
Salvius Otho, L., *suff.* AD 33; 43
Salvius Otho, M., *sen.,* 43
Sancia, 205
Sanquinius, 176 f.
Sanquinius Maximus, Q., *suff.* II AD 39; 203

Sardinia, 106, 136
Satrius Secundus, 164
Scaevola, Q., see Mucius Scaevola, Q.
science, interest of Tib. in, 122
Scipio, see (Cornelius) Scipio (P.?)
Scipios, see (Cornelii) Scipiones
Scribonia, *B, C*: marriage with Octavian, 15; in politics, 41 f., 150; descendants, 54, 66, 150, 166, 220; exile, 54
Scribonii Libones, 176
Scribonius Libo, L., father of Scribonia, *C,* 150
Scribonius Libo Drusus, L., *cos.* AD 16, *C,* 149
Scribonius Libo Drusus, M., *pr.* ?AD 16, *C*: connexions, 150; date of praetorship, 270 f., n. 14; abdication? 181; conspirator, 86, 88, 95, 149 f., 197; trial, 163 f., 288, n. 107; accusers rewarded, 189, 197; *cognomen* forbidden, 282, n. 50; importance of case, 187 ff., 193
Segesta, 107
Segestes of the Cherusci, 143
Seius Quadratus, 202
Seius Strabo, L., Praetorian Prefect, *D,* 17, 54, 64, 80, 159, 202, 260, n. 2
Seius Tubero, L., *suff.* AD 18, *D,* 163
Sejanus, see Aelius Sejanus, L.
Sempronii, 55, 237, n. 46
Sempronius Gracchus, poet, 41 f., 151, 259, n. 79
Sempronius Gracchus, C., *tr. pl.* 123–122 BC, 12, 37, 105, 129, 138, 171, 181, 283, n. 51
Sempronius Gracchus, Ti., *tr. pl.* 133 BC, 12, 103, 171, 283, n. 51
Sempronius Gracchus, Ti., *sen.,* 47

Senate: regular meetings established, 34; agenda, 92 ff., 192; debates, 113; proceedings, 185; freedom, 199; disorders, 93; committees, 103, 105 f., 182, 218; role, 218, 223 f.; in elections, 52, 95 ff.; as court, 105, 184 ff., 199 f.; subsidizes members, 94 f.; grants state funerals, 94; and taxation, 256, n. 41; and provinces, 108; foreign affairs, 111 ff.; responsibilities, 162, 186; privileges, 52, 115 f.; *maiestas* 92, 184; army and, 81; Augustus and, 21; temple in Asia, 107, 135, 139; self-interest, 103 f., 114; attitude to Tib., 81; servility, 114 f., 160, 207; honours Sejanus, 164, 172, 179; Agrippa and Nero in, 169; deserts Sejanus, 177 ff., 202; Tib.'s policy towards, 76 ff., 83, 89, 163; avoids deifying him, 221; recognizes Gaius, 220; see also adlection; magistrates; *senatus consultum*
senators: property qualification, 103; *maiestas,* 191 f.; supported by Tib., 90; appeals to Senate, 94, 103; resignation, 95; from northern Italy and provinces, 98 f., 115 f.; travel restricted, 211; support Clemens, 152
senatus consultum, consulta, 92, 95, 100, 105, 110, 116, 125, 134, 146, 184, 186, 191, 194, 255, n. 3, 260, n. 4; status, 102 f.; registration, 185; *ultimum,* 181; *Calvisianum,* 103
Seneca the younger (L. Annaeus Seneca), *suff.* AD 56; 99, 106, 150, 183, 221, 294, n. 85

Sentius Saturninus, C., *cos.* 19 BC, 43

Sentius Saturninus, C., *cos.* AD 4; 43, 52

Sentius Saturninus, Cn., *suff.* AD 4; 43, 52, 156

Sequani, 73

Servaeus, Q., *sen.*, 141, 156 f., 164, 172, 198, 202

Servilia, mother of M. Brutus, *A*, 55, 153

Servilii Caepiones, 232, n. 3, 233, n. 19

Servilius Nonianus, M., *suff.* AD 35; 222, 246, n. 73, 259, n. 92, 292, n. 54

Servius Tullius, 171

Sestius Quirinalis Albinianus, L., *suff.* 23 BC, 23

Sextia, 213

Sextii Africani, 213

Sextius Paconianus, *sen.*, 174, 192, 202, 205, 214, 284, n. 58, 291, n. 29

Sibylline Books, 102, 105, 113, 218

Silani, see (Iunii) Silani

Silanus, C., see Iunius Silanus, C.

Silanus, D., see Iunius Silanus, D., *cos.*

Silanus, M., *cos.*, see Iunius Silanus, M., *cos.*

Silanus, M., *suff.*, see Iunius Silanus, M., *suff.*

Silius, C., *cos.* AD 13; 101, 133, 163, 168, 181, 185, 187 ff., 283, n. 50

slave(s): in politics, 153; evidence of, 185; as accusers, 203; of Agrippa Postumus, 245, n. 71; see also Clemens

Smyrna, 107

Sodalis Augustalis, Tib. as, 250, n. 7

Sosia, 163, 286 f., n. 88

Spain: Tib. in, 19 ff.; L. Caesar sent to, 41; Ti. Iulii in, 138; see also Baetica; Lusitania; Tarraconensis

Sparta, 107, 111, 126

Spartacus, revolt of, 132

Speluncae, 167 f.

spolia opima, 34 f.

statio, meaning of, 78 f.

Stertinius Maximus, C., *suff.* AD 23; 256, n. 24

Stoicism: cardinal virtues of, 87; Tib. and, 18, 82 f., 91, 124

Suebi, 130, 145

Suetonius Tranquillus, C., *eq.*, on Tib., 223

Sugambri, 27

suicide, 188 f., 214 f.

Suillius Rufus, P., *suff.* AD 41–45; 164, 197

Sulla, see Cornelius Sulla

Sulla, L., see (Cornelius) Sulla, L.

Sulpicius Galba, C., *suff.* 5 BC, 43

Sulpicius Galba, C., *cos.* AD 22; 109

Sulpicius Quirinius, P., *cos.* 12 BC, 42, 46 f., 53, 55, 149, 162, 255, n. 7

Sura, P., see Cornelius Lentulus Sura, P.

Syria, 25 f., 106, 125, 127 f., 146, 152 f., 178, 213

Tabula Hebana, 241, n. 12

Tacape, 131 f.

Tacfarinas, 110, 126, 131 f., 255, n. 3

Tacitus (Cornelius Tacitus), *suff.* AD 97: on Tib., 165, 222 f.; on *maiestas*, 185; on Agrippina the elder, 222; sources, 92, 113, 222

Tarpeian rock, 192, 282, n. 49

Tarraco, 232, n. 6

Tarraconensis, 55, 125, 128 f., 131, 135

taxation, 107, 129, 132 ff., 141, 143, 146, 256, n. 41

temple(s), of Tib.: in provinces, 250, n. 3; in Asia, 107, 135; in Baetica, 89, 139; see also Apollo; Augustus Caesar; Castor and Pollux; Concord; Fors Fortuna; *Iulia, gens*; Jupiter;   Quirinus;

Venus; deification; personality, cult of the

Terentius, M., *eq.*, 205, 260, n. 94, 285, n. 73

Termestini, 135

theatre, 121 f., 218; see also actors; Pompey

Theodore of Gadara, 17

Theophanes of Mytilene (Cn. Pompeius Theophanes), 211 f.

Thessalians, 20 f., 235, n. 47

Thrace, 35, 130, 142, 235, n. 51, 264, n. 13; see also Odrysae

Thrasyllus of Alexandria, see Claudius Thrasyllus

Thyatira, in Lydia, 21

Tiberia, in Thrace, 138

Tiberias, in Galilee, 138

Tiberieum, in Caesarea, 137

Tiberiopolis, in Phrygia, 138 f.

Tiberius Gemellus (Ti. Julius Caesar Nero), *B*: birth, 157; prospects, 170, 175, 206, 208, 220; on coins, 207; supporters, 205 f., 290, n. 10, 292, n. 51; adopted by Gaius, 220

Tigranes II, of Armenia, crowned by Tib., 25 f.

Tigranes III, anti-Roman claimant, 145

Tigranes IV, supported by Augustus, 145

Tiridates, supported by Tib., 146 f.

Tiridates of Parthia, supported by Augustus, 25

Titius Sabinus, *eq.*, 117, 168 f., 185, 283, n. 51 285, n. 68, 288, n. 107

toga virilis, significance of taking, 175

Togonius Gallus, *sen.*, 99, 204

Torquatus, see Iunius Silanus Torquatus, M.

Trachonitis, 142

Trajan, Princeps, 123, 126, 145, 190

Tralles, 20 f., 107
tranquillitas, 86, 137, 252, n. 18
Trebellenus Rufus, T., *sen.*, 142, 256, n. 24
Trebia, 258, n. 59
Tremellius, Cn., *suff.* AD 21; 274, n. 67
Treviri, 132
tribunes of the *plebs*, 41 f., 100, 181, 183, 216, 261, n. 11
tribunician power: intended for C. Caesar, 48; intended for Sejanus, 170; significance, 24, 36, 49, 158 f.; use by Tib., 63, 78, 114, 195, 197; veto used by Tib., 288, n. 107, 291, n. 14
Tridentum, 138
triumph(s): disallowed, 35, 89; of Tib., 35, 43, 244, n. 54; of Tib., postponed, 62; celebrated, 63, 68; of Germanicus, 137, 144, 154
Triumphus, gladiator, 123
Turoni, 132, 134
Turranius, C., Prefect of Egypt, 44, 54, 80, 260, n. 2
tutor reipublicae, 33 f., 237, n. 15

Ubii, 71, 74
Ulia, 232, n. 6
Umbonius Silo, Marcellus, L. Hispanus Pompeius, *sen.*, 99
unpopularity, of Tib.: 54, 64, 66, 86 f., 91, 117 ff., 182, 218 f.; in Senate, 81; see also libel; *plebs*
Urban Cohorts, 124
urbanization, 131 f., 138 f.
Urgulania, 182
Urgulanilla (Plautia Urgulanilla), wife of Claudius, B, 53, 182, 274, n. 69
Usipetes, 28

Valerius Antias, 228, n. 5
Valerius Asiaticus, D., *cos.* II AD 46; 99
Valerius Maximus, 84, 230, n. 27; on virtues, 91, 252, nn. 20, 22, 253, nn. 20, 29, 32
Valerius Messalla Barbatus Appianus, M., *cos.* 12 BC, 275, n. 91
Valerius Messalla Corvinus, M., *cos.* 31 BC, 17, 54
Valerius Messalla Messallinus, M., *cos.* 3 BC, 42, 112, 241, n. 28
Valerius Messalla Volesus, L., *cos.* AD 5; 54, 125, 196, 281, n. 35, 283, n. 54
Valerius Poplicola, P., *cos.* V? 504 BC, 91
Vallius Syriacus, 278, n. 126
Vannius of the Quadi, 144 f.
Varius Ligus, 292, n. 51
Varro Murena, see Licinius A. Terentius Varro Murena, L.
Vedius Pollio, P., *eq.*, 107
Velleius Paterculus, *sen.*: career, 13, 47 f., 57, 98, 270, n. 14; and Tib., 84; on Tib.'s supporters, 43, 52 f.; and relations, 168 f.; on C. Caesar, 48; on Sejanus, 159, 171
Venus, temple of on Mount Eryx, 107
Veranius, Q., *sen.*, 141, 156
Verica, 143
Verres, C., *sen.*, 190
Vescularius Flaccus, *eq.*, 205, 260, n. 2
Vespasian, Princeps, 81, 126, 141, 159, 221, 257, n. 55
Vesta, statue of, 40
Vestals, 102, 255, n. 3
Vetera, 74 f.
Via Appia, 149
Via Egnatia, 26
Vibia, 216
Vibius Habitus, A., *suff.* AD 8; 53, 163

Vibius Marsus, C., *suff.* AD 17; 132, 21 f., 259, n. 80
Vibius Postumus, C., *suff.* AD 5; 53, 163, 241, n. 22
Vibius Serenus, *sen.*, son of C., 163, 275, n. 80
Vibius Serenus, C., *sen.*, 163, 190, 282, n. 49, 285, nn. 66, 68
Vibulenus Agrippa, *eq.*, 188 f.
'vices': of Tib., 43, 124, 167, 222 f.; of Nero Caesar, 169; of Gaius, 205, 214
Victoria, Queen, 262, n. 29
Vienna (Vienne), 99
Vigiles, 116, 124
Vindelicii, 28
Vindonissa, 74, 145
Vinicius, M., *suff.* 19 BC, 208, 236, n. 2
Vinicius, M., *cos.* II AD 45; 208
Vipsania Agrippina, A, B, 19, 27, 31, 37, 43, 162, 163
Vipsanii, 159
Vipsanius Clemens, Sex., 245, n. 71
Virgil (P. Virgilius Maro), 16
Viriasius Naso, P., 90
virtus, virtutes, 87, 210
Visellius Varro, C., *suff.* AD 12; 53
Visellius Varro, L., *cos.* AD 24; 163
Vistilia, 290, n. 10
Vistilius, Sex., 196, 205, 290, n. 10
Vitellia, 161
Vitellii, 95, 160, 164
Vitellius, L., *cos.* III AD 47; 143, 146, 161, 164, 290, n. 10
Vitellius, P., *sen.* 156 f., 164, 171, 202, 216,
Vitellius, Q., *sen.*, 95
Vitia, 177
Volusius, Q., *sen.*, A, 229, n. 12
Volusius Saturninus, L. *cos.* 12 BC, A, 52 f.

Volusius Saturninus, L., cos. AD 3, *A*, 53
Vonones I of Parthia and Armenia, 145 f., 155
Votienus Montanus, 289, n. 136

Walsingham, Sir Francis, 66

Wellington, Duke of, 276, n. 100
wills, 39, 55, 64, 188, 210; of Livius Drusus, 228, n. 10; of Julius Caesar and Mark Antony, 210; of M. Gallius, 19; of Augustus, 121 f., 124, 210; of Livia, 220; of Tib., 124, 210, 220
wine: Tib.'s taste for, 44, 158, 167, 224; Drusus

Caesar's taste for, 158
women: in politics, 61, 141, 153; Tib. on, 37; in provinces, 100; liability to prosecution, 214, 286 f., n. 88

Zeno of Pontus, see Artaxes III